KV-638-336

Giant Book of
KNOWLEDGE

Contributors: John Bailie Neil Grant
Derek Hall Nathaniel Harris
Judy Maxwell Louise Pritchard
Janet Slingsby Caroline White
Colin Wilson

Acknowledgements

Photographs
Robin Bernard 233; British Museum, London 87 top left, 87 right; Bruce Coleman – Eric Crichton 52; Bruce Coleman – Dieter and Mary Plage 43; David Gavine, Edinburgh 48; Photographic Giraudon 59; Hamlyn Group Picture Library 142, 168, 185; Hans Hinz, Allschwil 305 right; Hirmer Verlag, Munich 305 left, 321; Keystone Press Agency, London 442, 463; Paolo Koch, Zollikon 417; Meteor Crater Enterprises Inc., Winslow Arizona 301; Museo del Prado, Madrid 383; N.A.S.A., Washington D.C. 32, 201, 294, 299, 319, 400, 437, 477, 484; National Museum of Wales, Cardiff 87 bottom left; Natural History Photographic Agency – K. Preston Mafham 189; Novosti Press Agency, London 199; Photri, Alexandria, Virginia 445; The Post Office, London 444; Judy Todd, London 325, 326; University of York 150; Reg Wilson, London 190; ZEFA (UK) – Hoffmann Burchardi 42; ZEFA (UK) – D. Baglin 49; ZEFA (UK) – Photri 124; United Nations 468

Published 1984 by
The Hamlyn Publishing Group Limited
London · New York · Sydney · Toronto
Astronaut House, Feltham, Middlesex, England

ISBN 0 600 38856 5
Printed in Czechoslovakia
52077

Giant Book of KNOWLEDGE

HAMLYN

London · New York · Sydney · Toronto

Introduction

The Giant Book of Knowledge is a family encyclopedia containing over two thousand entries arranged alphabetically for easy reference. Five hundred colour pictures amplify and illustrate the text.

Subjects covered include science, history, the world around us, famous people, botany, zoology, the arts, space and transport. From aardvark to Zulu, from dinosaur to laser, this book is packed with facts which will amaze and inform both adults and children.

How to use this book

Looking up a specific person or topic is very easy as the entries are arranged in alphabetical order with no subject divisions. This also means that the book can be delved into at random to reveal a fascinating range of valuable, general knowledge information.

Every major country in the world is included in the alphabetical listings. At the very end of the book you will find a relief map of the world showing the continents, plus a list of countries and their capitals divided by continent. The flags of some of the world's major nations are also pictured.

If your want to find a particular country on a map, look at the tables of the end of the book to see which continent it is in, then turn to the alphabetical entry on the relevant continent. For example, if you want to find Malawi on a map, look at the list of continents and you will see that Malawi is in Africa. Turn to the entry on Africa in the book, and you will be able to find Malawi on the map of Africa.

Aardvark is a mammal which grows to a length of 2 m (6 ft), and has a long, narrow head with a pig-like snout and long ears. Its four feet have strong digging claws. The aardvark's name means 'earth pig', and this is a good description of it. It is found in Africa, where it feeds by ripping open termites' nests and licking up the insects with its long tongue. It spends the day living in large burrows, which it can excavate extremely quickly, coming out at night to feed.

Abacus is a calculating device, which takes the form of rows of beads strung on wires and set in a frame. When counting in decimals, the top row stands for units, the next row for tens, the next for hundreds, and so on. By moving the beads from side to side, it is possible to add and subtract with surprising speed.

The abacus was invented several thousand years ago, and was very widely used until recent centuries. In parts of the East it is still used for reckoning by traders.

Abalone is a type of mollusc belonging to the class Gastropoda. Abalones, or ormers as they are also called, have a large, one-piece shell perforated with small holes. The inner surface of the shell is marked with a beautiful mother-of-pearl pattern. Abalones live on or under rocks to which they can cling tightly to avoid being washed away.

Abbeys: *see* Cathedrals and Abbeys.

Aborigine is a term which comes from the Latin *ab origine* meaning 'from the beginning', and the word aborigines is still sometimes used to describe the earliest inhabitants of any land. However, Aborigines is usually used to refer to the inhabitants of Australia before the arrival of Europeans in the late 18th century, and to their descendants down to the present.

The Aborigines are thought to have arrived in Australia in two waves, probably about 20000 years ago. The first group were eventually driven south-east into Tasmania; the second – and racially quite different – group occupied the rest of Australia.

The Aborigines developed a complex culture and a religion. These gave rise to an interesting art which included paintings on their bodies, on rocks, in caves and on bark; and chants, and music played on a kind of trumpet, the didgeridoo. However, their material life remained at a Stone-Age level. They lived in a semi-nomadic fashion, hunting with wood and stone spears, and boomerangs, and gathering (but not cultivating) edible plants, grubs and so on.

On this level they were superbly skilful

John King was the only survivor of Burke and Wills' expedition to cross Australia in 1860. He was found by a rescue party, living with some Aborigines.

and well-adapted to the Australian environment – until the arrival of Europeans. This was a disaster for the Aborigines. They are believed to have numbered about 300 000 in the late 18th century, while now there are only a few tens of thousands. The Tasmanians were soon completely wiped out, and the Aborigine way of life was destroyed. As in the case of the American Indian, although conditions have improved for many people in the 20th century, the Aborigines remain poor and deprived, and uncertain what their place should be in modern Australia.

Absolute zero is the lowest possible temperature that there can be. All substances are made up of atoms and molecules, and at high temperatures these move very fast. As the temperature is lowered, the molecules move less and less, and at absolute zero it is thought that they would not move at all. Absolute zero is just over 273 degrees Centigrade below zero. In laboratories, temperatures very close to this have been reached, but absolute zero has never been reached.

Absolute zero is the lowest starting point for a scale of temperature often used in science. This is known as the absolute or Kelvin scale of temperature. Each degree on this scale is known as a kelvin, and is the same as each degree Centigrade. To change from the Centigrade to the Kelvin scale 273 is added. So, 27 degrees Centigrade is 300 kelvin.

Abstract art is painting or sculpture which does not represent things in the way the eye sees them, but instead concentrates on arrangements of shapes and colours for their own sake. All good painting is concerned with arrangements of that kind to some extent and, in reality, abstract art differs from representational art only in concentrating on this aspect to the exclusion of others.

In the West, abstract art is a recent development, no older than this century, though there are several quite different kinds. It is sometimes difficult to decide what is truly art and what is simply pattern making.

Much Islamic art is abstract because Muhammad condemned the maker of images, who tries to imitate God by creating living beings. This did not mean that Islamic artists should never make pictures of people, only of idols. Nevertheless, no pictures of people are to be found in Islamic religious art.

Acacia is an evergreen shrub or tree that is native to Australia, and is now widely found in tropical and subtropical regions. There are 600 species of acacia, which have small leaves and yellow or white flowers. The blossom of one species, called the Wattle, is on Australia's coat-of-arms.

Acceleration is an increase in the speed or velocity of an object. It is caused by a force. If, for instance, a pen is dropped it falls to the ground, pulled by the force of gravity. As it falls, it moves with an acceleration due to gravity of 9.8 m per second per second (32 ft per second per second.) This means that after one second it is moving at 9.8 m per second (32 ft per second). After two seconds it is moving twice as fast. If it was dropped from a great height, it would be moving very fast when it hit the Earth.

If a car is travelling at a steady 50 km/h (31 mph), it has no acceleration. It is moving, but the rate at which it is moving – its velocity – is not changing. If it slows down it *loses* acceleration. This is known as deceleration.

Accipiter, see Hawk.

Acetylene whose chemical formula is C_2H_2, is a colourless, poisonous gas with a sweet smell. It is also called ethyne, and can be made from natural gas. Mixtures of acetylene and air or oxygen can explode. Acetylene burns in air with a bright flame, and used to be widely used for lighting.

Acetylene burns in oxygen with a very hot flame. The oxy-acetylene torch mixes and burns acetylene and oxygen. It is used to cut through iron and steel and to weld, or join together, metals.

Achilles, in Greek legend, was the greatest warrior among the Greeks at the siege of Troy. At the beginning of Homer's *Iliad*, Achilles quarrels with Agamemnom, the Greek leader, and retires to his tent, refusing to fight. But when his friend Patroclus is killed by the Trojan hero Hector, Achilles storms into battle and kills Hector.

Achilles was supposed to be invulnerable to weapons because his mother, Thetis, dipped him in the River Styx as a baby. She held him by his heel – the only part of him that could be injured. From this comes the phrase 'Achilles heel', a person's weak point.

Acid is a substance which, when dissolved in water, gives a solution containing hydrogen ions as the only positive ions. If it is dissolved in a lot of water, it is called a dilute acid. If it is in only a little water, it is a concentrated acid.

Fruits such as lemons taste sour. This is

Acorns and leaves of a durmast oak. Unlike in the common oak, the acorns are not stalked, but are attached directly to the twigs.

because they contain citric acid. All acids taste sour. Vinegar is sour because it contains acetic acid. Milk which tastes sour does so because some of the milk has turned to lactic acid.

Acids also burn. The poisons which are injected into the skin by bees and ants are also acids. Our stomachs contain hydrochloric acid to digest food. The stomach lining protects us from the acid. If the lining breaks, the acid can burn and cause an ulcer.

Acids react with bases to form salts. Large amounts of nitric, hydrochloric and sulphuric acids are made, much of which are used to make salts.

Acids change the colour of some substances, known as indicators. Litmus paper is an example of an indicator. Acids turn litmus paper red. *See also* Base; Salt.

Acorn is the fruit of the oak tree. It is produced in late summer, and in most species looks like a yellow-brown, barrel-shaped structure sitting in a protective cup. When an acorn lands in a suitable place, it germinates to produce a new tree. Many acorns never germinate, however, for huge numbers are eaten by birds, pigs and other animals.

Acropolis was a small, walled hill where the citadel was built in the cities of ancient Greece, but it especially refers to the citadel at Athens. There stands the remains of the most famous group of buildings in the world, of which the largest is the temple to the goddess Athena known as the Parthenon. These buildings are from the time of Pericles in the 5th century BC. Earlier buildings on the Acropolis had been destroyed in the Persian Wars, and they represent a peak of Classical Greek architecture. Because of air pollution and wear by tourists' feet, these buildings are now deteriorating faster than at any time in the past 2400 years.

Acupuncture is a type of medicine. It has been used in China for thousands of years, though there are now acupuncturists (people who treat others using acupuncture) in many

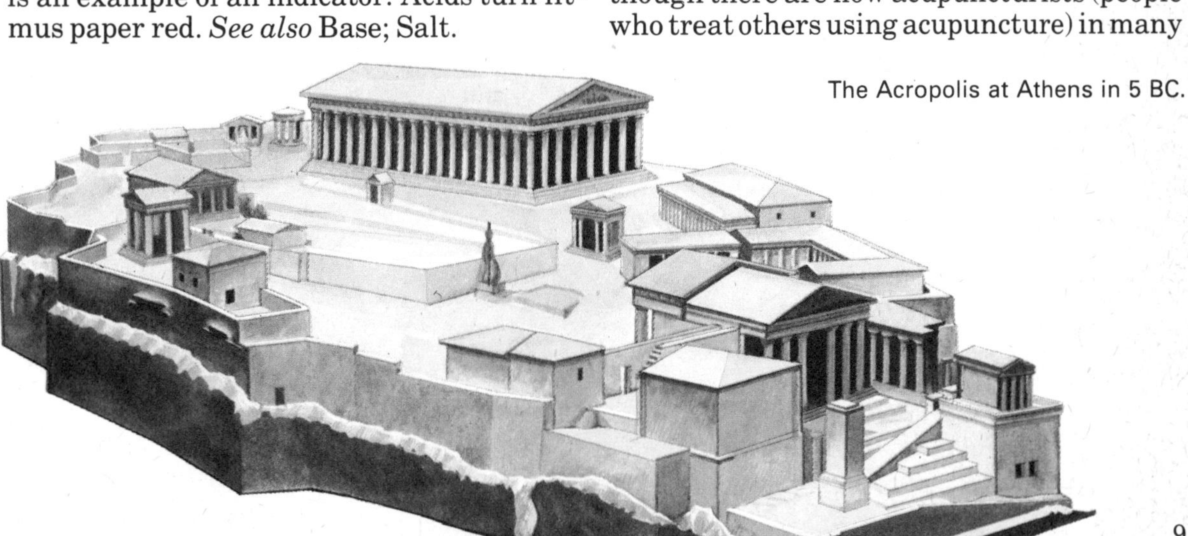

The Acropolis at Athens in 5 BC.

other countries. Even today no one really understands how it works.

In acupuncture, fine needles are put into the patient's skin and carefully twisted. They are inserted in particular places around the body, depending on the illness to be treated. Acupuncture is used to cure illness and to stop the pain of, for example, headaches and arthritis. Patients can even be operated on using acupuncture to stop the pain.

Adam and Eve, according to the account of the Creation in the Bible, were the first man and woman made by God. Adam, says the Book of *Genesis*, was made from the dust and given life by God's breath. Eve was made from one of Adam's ribs. They lived in the Garden of Eden in a state of perfect innocence, but were forbidden to eat the fruit of the 'tree of knowledge of good and evil'. Tempted by a serpent, Eve ate the fruit and gave some to Adam. For their disobedience they were expelled from the Garden, and the troubles of the human race date from that time.

In Christian belief, the story justifies the doctrine of Original Sin – that men and women are born in a state of sin.

Adam, Robert (1728–1792), was a Scottish architect. He was the most famous member of a family of architects who introduced a style in buildings and decoration which is known after them. The Adam style, based on Classical Greece and Rome, is light, elegant and misleadingly simple. The Adam brothers designed, built or decorated many great mansions, and also one of the first rows of town houses with a single, unified front.

Adder is a venomous snake found in parts of Europe. It can be distinguished by the dark zig-zag pattern along its back, and the V or X marking just behind the head. Males are yellow, brown or silvery in colour, and are about 60 cm (24 in) long. The reddish brown to yellow females are about 45 cm (18 in) long.

The adder prefers sandy heathland, where it hunts for lizards, mice and voles. Mating takes place during late spring, and the young are born alive in September, hatching from eggs which remain in the mother's body. The myth that the mothers ate their young arose from the fact that unborn baby adders were often found inside mothers that had been killed and cut open. When cornered by an enemy, the adder may feign death. The body goes limp, and the tongue hangs from the side of the mouth.

Adder

Aden is a seaport on the south-west coast of Arabia, national capital of the People's Democratic Republic of Yemen (the former British colony of Aden). The port of Aden has been an important centre for trade since ancient times. From the 16th to the 19th century, Europeans and Turks battled for control; the British held it from 1839 to 1963. The people are mainly Arabic-speaking Muslims, and the traditional occupations are fishing and farming. Products include grain, dates, tobacco, coffee and soap.

Adenauer, Konrad (1876–1967), was a German statesman, Chancellor of West Germany from 1949 to 1963. Under his leadership his country recovered from defeat in the Second World War and became prosperous. He strongly supported Western European unity and friendship with France.

Adonis, in Greek myth, was a beautiful young man who was loved by Aphrodite (Venus), the goddess of love. He died from wounds when hunting a wild boar, and Aphrodite asked Zeus to restore him to life. Zeus granted her request in part. He said that for six months every year Adonis should live in the world, and for six months he should return to Hades, the world of the dead.

Other societies in the ancient world told similar stories, which perhaps began as a way of explaining the changing seasons of the year.

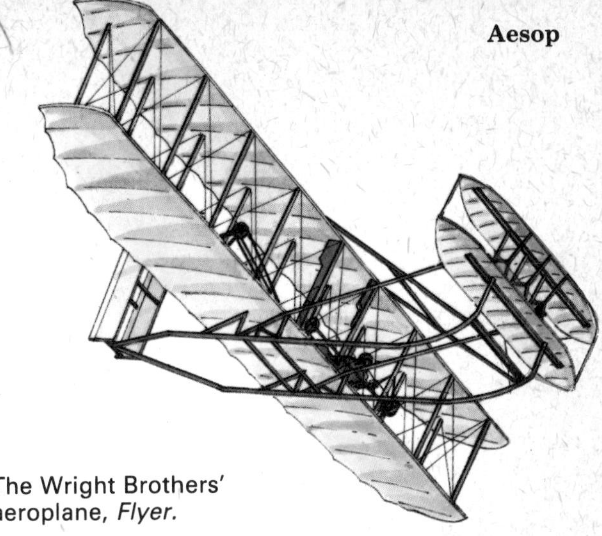

The Wright Brothers' aeroplane, *Flyer.*

Aeroplane is a heavier-than-air machine with wings. It can fly, and be controlled in flight. The aeroplane uses one or more engines to give it forward speed, which causes air to flow rapidly over the wings. Each wing is specially shaped so that its top surface is raised: air has to travel quicker over the top of the wing than it does underneath, and this creates a low pressure area above the wing, so 'sucking' the aircraft into the sky. Early attempts by human beings to fly by strapping wings to themselves, or turning propellers by pedal, failed because people were not powerful enough to lift the weight of their aircraft.

The first true aeroplane to carry a person was built by the Wright brothers in the USA in 1903, but most early development was carried out in Europe, especially in France, where Louis Blériot made the first air crossing of the English Channel in a single-wing monoplane of his own design on 25 July 1909. Progress was very swift, and by the First World War both sides had fleets of aircraft for reconnaissance. As the war dragged on, fighters and bombers were built, as was the first all-metal aircraft. In 1919 the Atlantic was flown non-stop in a converted bomber.

All these aircraft were powered by internal combustion engines, which continued to dominate both military and civil aviation until well after the Second World War. During that war, however, the jet engine was invented in both Germany and England and this offered far more power with less weight, both very desirable in an aeroplane. Once fitted to the first passenger aeroplanes – the British Comet and the American Boeing 707 – jets halved the time taken by propellor-driven aircraft.

Since that time (circa 1952) passenger aircraft have become larger (the latest Boeing 747 jumbo jet carries over 530 people) and fly higher (circa 15 000 m/9.32 miles) where the air is thinner and so causes less drag. Because of the high price of petrol, however, modern jets do not fly much faster than those first jets, apart from the very expensive Concorde, the world's only faster-than-sound passenger aeroplane. *See also* Blériot, Louis; Comet; Concorde; Engine, internal combustion/jet; Flying boat; Glider; Man-powered flight; Wright brothers.

Aesop (died 564 BC), was the supposed author of *Aesop's Fables*, though the stories were first written down much later. The fables are tales about animals which contain a lesson about human behaviour. For

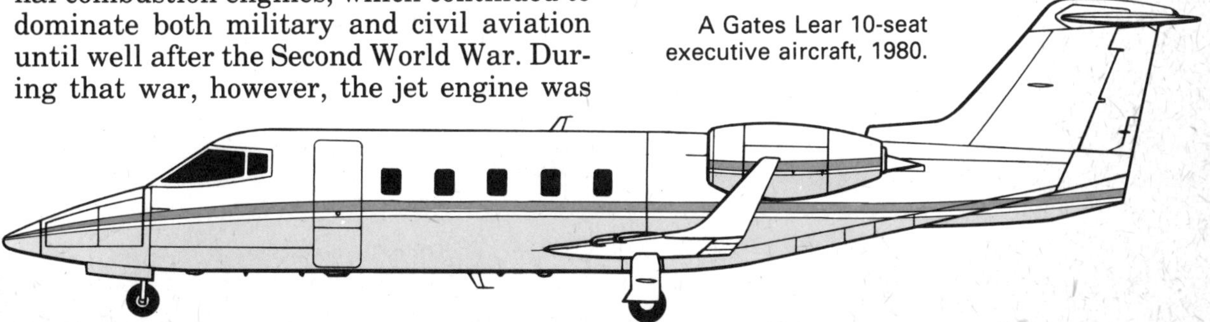

A Gates Lear 10-seat executive aircraft, 1980.

instance, the story of the race in which the tortoise beats the hare teaches that slow and steady progress is better than a few bursts of speed between spells of idleness. The fables, whether invented by Aesop or not, were probably first used to make points in debates, not as entertainment.

Afghanistan is a republic in south-central Asia. Capital, Kabul; area about 636 000 sq km (245 500 sq miles). The country is very mountainous, especially in the north, where the peaks of the Hindu Kush rise to about 8000 m (23 000 ft).

Throughout history Afghanistan has been troubled by powerful neighbours. In the 18th century an independent Afghan empire was created by Ahmad Shah Durrani, but it became the prey of rival European powers, Britain and Russia, though keeping some independence under local rulers. The monarchy was overthrown in 1973 and a republic was set up. In 1981 Soviet troops went into the country, to maintain Soviet influence, but became involved in a guerilla war.

The Afghans are a racially mixed people, speaking several languages; nearly all are Muslims. Economic resources such as hydroelectric power and mining, have not yet been fully developed. There are few roads and fewer railways. Major products are grain, fruit, cotton and wool textiles; also, the beautiful stone, lapis lazuli.

Africa is the second largest continent, area about 30 250 000 sq km (11 679 600 sq miles). It stretches from the Mediterranean, in the north, to the South Atlantic. In the northwest, Africa is only 14 km (8.7 miles) from Europe across the Strait of Gibraltar. In the north-east, it is joined to Asia by the Isthmus of Suez. The equator crosses the centre of Africa, and three-quarters of the continent's area is in the Tropics.

History Africa may have been the first continent to be inhabited by human beings. Fossils discovered in eastern Africa show that man-like creatures lived there millions of years ago. The continent also had one of the world's earliest civilizations – the great culture of ancient Egypt. At later periods, several other African civilizations developed. But to people in other parts of the world, Africa seemed dark and mysterious.

In the 1700s and 1800s, European governments seized vast areas of the continent, turning them into European colonies. By the early 1900s, only two African countries – Abyssinia (Ethiopia) and Liberia – were independent. Even as late as 1950, only four countries had control of their own affairs. Today, colonization has come to an end and Africa's countries take an important part in world affairs. African governments are working to develop the continent's rich natural resources, to modernize agriculture, and to build new industries.

Land The greater part of Africa consists of vast plateaux (high plains). In most places, the edges of the plateaux rise sharply from narrow coastal plains. In the south, the plateau is tilted upwards from west to east, and its south-eastern edge – called the Drakensberg range – rises to more than 3350 m (11 000 ft). In the east, the plateaux are split by a series of faults in the Earth's crust called the Great Rift Valley.

Africa is the hottest continent. Nearly two-fifths of it is parched desert land, dried out by the trade winds blowing towards the equator. The Sahara, the world's largest desert, extends across the widest part of Africa. Southern Africa has its deserts, too, but they are small compared with the Sahara.

The Atlas Mountains in the north-west are fold mountains that form a wall between the arid Sahara and the rich Mediterranean coastal areas of Morocco, Algeria, and Tunisia. The Cape Ranges in the south-west are also fold mountains.

Four of the world's greatest rivers flow through Africa. The Nile – the source of irrigation for all the farms of Egypt and Sudan – is the longest river in the world. The Zaïre, in central Africa, drains more than one-eighth of the entire continent. The Niger is the principal river in the western bulge of Africa – both the Zaïre and the Niger drain to the Atlantic. The Zambezi, in southern Africa, follows an S-shaped course to the Indian Ocean.

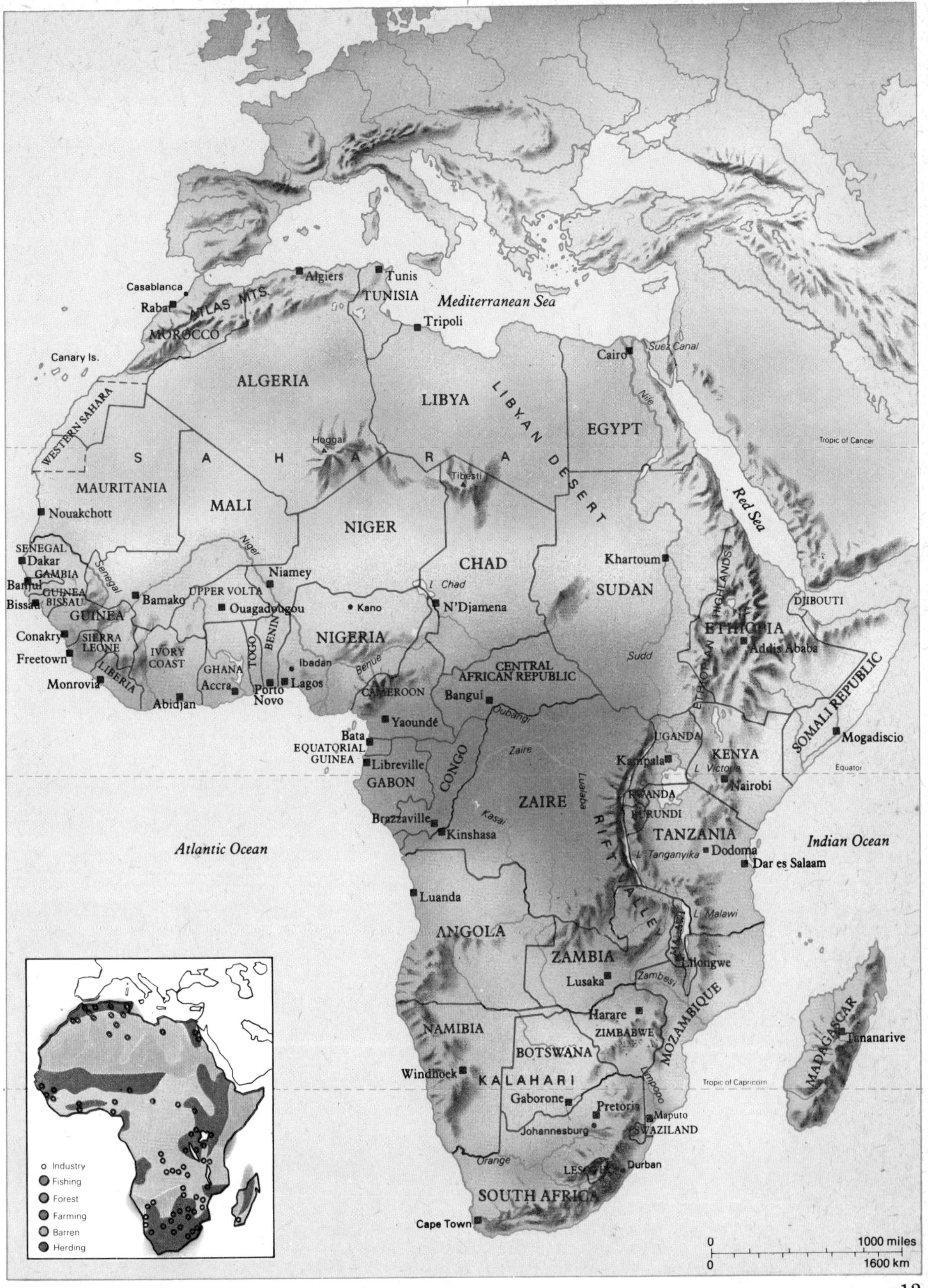
Casablanca
Rabat
ATLAS MTS.
MOROCCO
Algiers
Tunis
TUNISIA
Mediterranean Sea
Tripoli
Canary Is.
ALGERIA
LIBYA
LIBYAN DESERT
Cairo
Suez Canal
Nile
EGYPT
WESTERN SAHARA
Hoggar
S A H A R A
Tibesti
Tropic of Cancer
Red Sea
MAURITANIA
MALI
NIGER
Nouakchott
CHAD
Khartoum
SUDAN
SENEGAL
Dakar
GAMBIA
Banjul
GUINEA BISSAU
Bissau
Senegal
Niger
Niamey
L. Chad
UPPER VOLTA
Bamako
Ouagadougou
Kano
N'Djamena
DJIBOUTI
GUINEA
Conakry
SIERRA LEONE
Freetown
LIBERIA
Monrovia
IVORY COAST
Abidjan
GHANA
Accra
TOGO
BENIN
Porto Novo
NIGERIA
Ibadan
Lagos
Benue
CAMEROON
Yaoundé
CENTRAL AFRICAN REPUBLIC
Bangui
Oubangui
Sudd
ETHIOPIA
ETHIOPIAN HIGHLANDS
Addis Ababa
SOMALI REPUBLIC
Mogadiscio
Bata
EQUATORIAL GUINEA
Libreville
GABON
CONGO
Zaire
UGANDA
Kampala
KENYA
L. Victoria
Nairobi
Equator
ZAIRE
Lualaba
Kasai
RWANDA
BURUNDI
RIFT VALLEY
Brazzaville
Kinshasa
TANZANIA
Dodoma
Dar es Salaam
L. Tanganyika
Atlantic Ocean
Indian Ocean
Luanda
ANGOLA
L. Malawi
MALAWI
Lilongwe
ZAMBIA
Lusaka
Zambesi
MOZAMBIQUE
Harare
ZIMBABWE
NAMIBIA
BOTSWANA
Windhoek
KALAHARI
Gaborone
Pretoria
Maputo
Johannesburg
SWAZILAND
Limpopo
Tropic of Capricorn
MADAGASCAR
Tananarive
Orange
LESOTHO
Durban
SOUTH AFRICA
Cape Town
Industry
Fishing
Forest
Farming
Barren
Herding
0
1000 miles
0
1600 km

Zulu warriors who fought against the British in the Zulu war in southern Africa in 1879.

Most parts of Africa are hot throughout the year. With the exception of regions near the equator, there are distinct wet and dry seasons, the bulk of the rain being generally in the hottest months. The equatorial lowlands have rain all the year round. Parts of the south are temperate for all or most of the year. The north-western coast, the coast of eastern Libya, and the Cape coast in the extreme south-east have a Mediterranean climate, with cool humid winters and hot, dry summers.

Plants and animals Dense tropical rain forest covers parts of western and central Africa, occupying about one-ninth of the total area of the continent. In places, it is fringed by coastal mangrove swamps.

The forest gradually merges, north and south, into belts of savannah (tropical grassland). Savannah, the most typical vegetation of Africa, covers two-fifths of the total area. Near the rain forest, the grassland has patches of trees that gradually give way to sparse and dry vegetation. The savannah eventually merges into semi-desert where only widely-spaced shrubs grow. This, in turn, gives way to desert.

The mountainous regions of the east have rich grasslands and forests of bamboo. Southern Africa has wide areas of temperate grasslands called the *grassveld*, as well as areas of low succulent plants, many with beautiful flowers. Cork oaks and maquis (*macchia* or *fynbos* in the Cape) are characteristic of the regions with a Mediterranean climate.

Only South America can rival Africa in the richness of its wildlife. Even the desert has its animals, such as the fennec, the desert fox. In the forests, monkeys, chimpanzees, and gorillas inhabit the forest canopies and the clearings. Hippopotamuses and crocodiles live in the rivers and pools. But the greatest variety and numbers of animals live on the savannah. They include antelopes, zebras, elephants, giraffes, buffaloes, and other grazing animals, as well as the fierce carnivores – lions, leopards, cheetahs, and hyenas. Birds include ostriches and flamingoes.

People The greater part of Africa is sparsely populated. In the desert and semi-desert regions, scarcely anybody lives, except for the small populations at the oases, the nomads who herd their sheep and goats from place to place, and (in the Kalahari) the hardy tribesmen who live by hunting and digging up roots.

Africa has more than 1000 different languages and dialects. However, only a few of them are of more than local importance: Hausa (spoken in western Africa), Swahili (a Bantu dialect used in eastern Africa), Amharic (the principal language of Ethiopia), and Arabic. Three languages of European origin are also of importance – Afrikaans, English, and French.

The great barrier of the Sahara divides the peoples of Africa into two broad types, the Negroids and the Caucasoids. The Negroid peoples, who live south of the Sahara, are divided into several groups, based on history, language, and physical characteristics.

Apart from the Negroids and the northern Caucasoids, Africa also has other groups of peoples. Millions of people in southern Africa are descended from European settlers. They include the Afrikaners of South Africa. Many people of Asian origin also live in Africa.

Economy – Minerals are among Africa's leading exports. Nigeria, Libya, and Algeria are major exporters of petroleum. Zambia and Zaïre have important copper mines, uranium is found in Zaïre, and iron in Liberia and Mauritania. South Africa's minerals include coal, gold, and diamonds.

Less than 8 per cent of Africa's land is under cultivation, but three-quarters of the people depend on farming for a living. In many areas, farming is at subsistence level: the people can grow just enough food to live on. In many savannah regions, where rainfall is sparse and unreliable, the people keep livestock instead of growing crops. But the quality of their cattle is nearly always low, and the pasture lands are spoilt by overgrazing.

In many parts of Africa, manufacturing is confined chiefly to craft goods, and factory industries are concerned mainly with the processing of agricultural and mineral products. But in some countries, other industries are being developed, often with government participation. Industries tend, however, to be localized in the major cities, and chiefly in ports. Countries of industrial importance include Egypt, Nigeria, Zambia, Zimbabwe, South Africa, Zaïre, and Ghana.

For further information, see under individual countries.

Afrikaner, or Boer, is a white South African, mainly of Dutch descent, whose language is Afrikaans. In 1652 the Cape of Good Hope became a Dutch colony. As it grew, settlers moved far inland and became farmers, their language developing from Dutch into Afrikaans. British rule was established in South Africa in 1806. Discontented under this, thousands of Cape Afrikaners made the Great Trek, a mass migration into southern Natal. Afrikaner republics were successfully established in the Transvaal and Orange Free State.

Discoveries of gold and diamonds led to friction between Afrikaners and British, culminating in the South African War of 1899 to 1902. The defeated Afrikaner republics were incorporated into the Union of South Africa.

However, the Afrikaner sense of separateness remained strong. Since 1948 the Nationalist Party, a mainly Afrikaner body, has controlled the government and enforced the Afrikaner doctrine of apartheid, or racial separation.

Agincourt, Battle of, took place in north-western France on 25 October 1415. It was part of the long struggle between England and France known as the Hundred Years' War. An English army, led by King Henry V, soundly defeated a much larger French one. The victory was mainly due to the skill with which the English soldiers used their longbows against the heavily armoured French knights.

Agriculture is the cultivation of crops for food, and the term also includes animal husbandry and other aspects of farming.

Despite industrialism, farming is still the main occupation of the majority of the human race. For most of their history, men and women have been hunters and food gatherers. By 7000 BC a few had become farmers, in the Middle East and possibly elsewhere, having already begun the domestication of animals.

It took several thousand years for agriculture to spread over most of the Earth's cultivatable land, and differences in culture and climate led to the development of different systems. Over an even longer period, improvements in farming techniques (for example, in the design of ploughs) were relatively small and slow, though often of considerable importance.

An 'Agricultural Revolution' began in the 18th century, in Britain, with a new system of sowing, new crops, improved animal husbandry and new fertilizers. The growing size of farms and increasing mechanization eventually transformed advanced industrial countries, such as the USA and Australia, where a small percentage of the population produces enough food for the whole country.

Air is the mixture of gases in our atmosphere. It is mainly nitrogen (78 per cent) and oxygen (21 per cent). The rest is chiefly argon. There are also tiny amounts of carbon dioxide, neon, helium, hydrogen, ozone, krypton, methane and xenon. The air also contains water. It is this which forms rain clouds.

Factories and houses produce smoke and dust which goes into the air. These can be harmful and are known as air pollution.

Almost all the living things on Earth need air. Animals breathe in air to obtain the

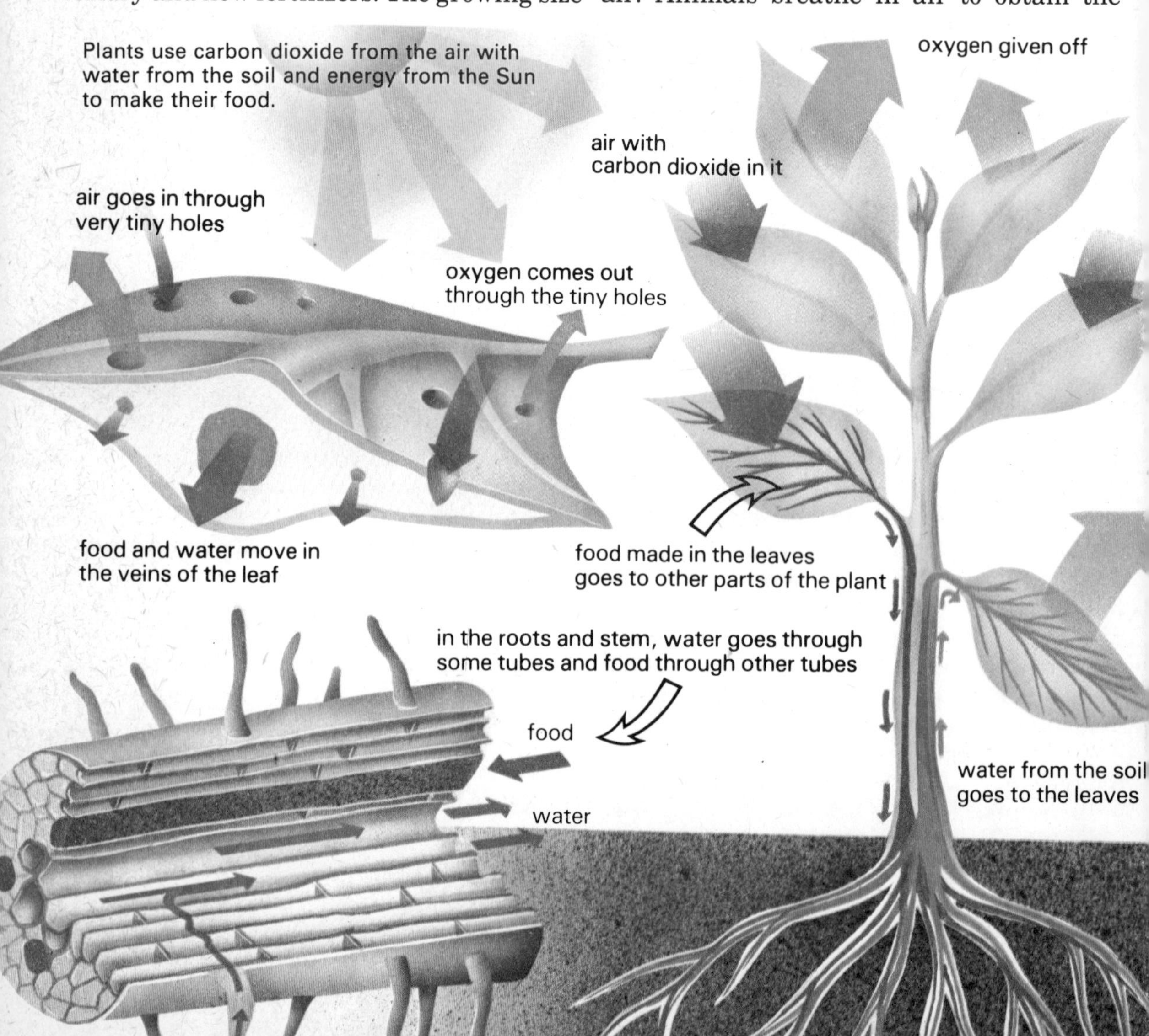
Plants use carbon dioxide from the air with water from the soil and energy from the Sun to make their food.
oxygen given off
air with carbon dioxide in it
air goes in through very tiny holes
oxygen comes out through the tiny holes
food and water move in the veins of the leaf
food made in the leaves goes to other parts of the plant
in the roots and stem, water goes through some tubes and food through other tubes
food
water
water from the soil goes to the leaves

oxygen they need to stay alive. Plants take carbon dioxide out of the air for photosynthesis.

Airline is a company which operates aeroplanes in commercial service, carrying passengers or freight. Some airlines are very large, such as British Airways or Qantas; others may be very small, with only one aircraft.

Airship is a lighter-than-air flying machine which flies because it contains gas bags full of very light gas (hydrogen or helium). Passengers or freight are contained in 'gondolas' suspended under the ship, and forward motion is achieved by engines, also hung beneath the airship. The first airship flew in 1852, driven by a small steam engine, but it was only with the development of lightweight internal combustion engines that airships became really practical.

One of the pioneers was the German, Count Ferdinand von Zeppelin, whose airships ran the first commercial services (in 1910) and carried out the first-ever bombing raids (on London in the First World War). During the 1930s airships were the only practical means of long-distance air travel, and craft built by America, Germany and Britain cruised the skies, crossing all the major oceans. Some of these were very large, over 240 m (787 ft) long.

The end of the airship era came with a few highly-publicized crashes, notably the British R101 in 1930 and the German *Hindenburg* in 1937. Both craft were burnt out because the hydrogen used to supply their lift was highly inflammable. The production of helium, which was far safer and offered much the same amount of lift, came too late to save the airship, because the public lost faith in the idea and turned their attention instead to heavier-than-air aeroplanes. A few enthusiasts still believe in a great future for the airship, since it is cheap to run, and a number of modern helium-filled designs are under development for freight-carrying. *See also* Airline; Engine, internal combustion; Zeppelin.

Akbar the Great (1542–1605), Mogul Emperor of India, ascended the throne of Delhi in 1556 and set out to unite the whole country under his rule. He conquered northern India and later the Deccan in the south, and eventually created a vast empire. He was an able and just ruler, who reformed the tax system and encouraged the development of trade with other countries. Although he was a Muslim, he showed tolerance towards the many people in India who held different religious beliefs.

Akhenaten (reigned 1379–1362 BC), was King of Egypt of the 18th Dynasty. He was the son of Amenhotep III, who built the famous monuments at Karnak and Luxor. Akhenaten tried to replace the traditional Egyptian religion (in which there was a supreme god, Amon, and several lesser gods) with the worship of the sun-god, Aken, alone. He also changed the capital of Egypt from Thebes to Tell-el-Amarna. After his death his religious reforms were abolished and his new temples destroyed.

Alamein, Battle of, was one of the decisive battles of the Second World War. A force of German and Italian troops led by General Erwin Rommel, which had been advancing rapidly through Libya and into Egyptian territory, was halted at Alamein. On 23 October 1942 the British Eighth Army, commanded by General Bernard Montgomery, and assisted by Australian, New Zealand and Indian soldiers, began a devastating counter-attack. This compelled the Germans and Italians to retreat and eventually led to their expulsion from North Africa.

Alaska is a state of the USA, forming the north-west peninsula of the North American continent. Capital, Juneau; area 1519000 sq km (586400 sq miles). The Arctic Circle runs through the middle of Alaska and it is therefore very cold. It was first discovered by Russian explorers, but bought from Russia by the USA in 1867 for $7000000 – a bargain! Then, it was inhabited by only a few Eskimo and fur traders. In recent years oil (discovered 1968) has made it economically valuable, but despite pipelines, oil rigs and airfields, it is still very thinly populated.

Albania is a republic in south-east Europe, bordering Yugoslavia and Greece. Capital, Tirana; area 29000 sq km (11000 sq miles). It is a very mountainous, rather poor country, the home of two ancient peoples, the Ghegs in the north and the Tosks in the south. For centuries it was under foreign rule, falling to the Turks in the 15th century despite the resistance of the Albanian hero, Scanderbeg. It became independent after the First World War, and since 1946 it has been a communist republic.

The many rivers provide hydro-electric power, and products include chemicals and chrome. The majority of the people are, however, Muslim peasants, living much as they have done for centuries.

Albatross looks a little like an enormous gull. It has a long, hooked beak with which it catches squid and other sea creatures. Albatrosses pair for life and, because it takes nearly a year for the single egg to hatch and the chick to grow, they only breed every other year.

These huge birds of the southern oceans keep airborne for hours because of their skilful use of the wind and air currents. They glide effortlessly on their long, narrow wings, with very few wing beats.

The wandering albatross is the largest albatross, and has the longest wing span of any bird. From tip to tip the wings can measure 3.5 m (11 ft).

Albert, Prince Consort (1819–1861), was the second son of the Duke of Saxe-Coburg Gotha. He married Queen Victoria of England, his first cousin, in 1840. He was a serious-minded and hard-working man and a patron of the arts and sciences. He also played a notable part in the organization of the Great Exhibition of 1851. His death in 1861, which was in part due to overwork, was a tragic loss to the Queen and affected her deeply.

Albino is an animal whose skin pigments (the substances that give the skin its colour) have failed to develop. The condition is called albinism, and the lack of pigmentation can affect not only the skin, but also structures associated with the skin such as hair, feathers, scales and eyes. A complete albino human has milky-white skin and hair, and pink irises. Sometimes albino plants are discovered. These are the result of a lack of development of the pigment known as chlorophyll.

Alchemy was an early form of chemistry. There were Greek alchemists in Egypt as early as AD 100. One of the main goals of alchemists was to change one element into another. This is known as transmutation. Gold has always been a highly valued metal. Therefore, alchemists wanted to find a way to change other metals into gold. They searched for something called the Philosopher's Stone, an imaginary substance which they believed would turn other substances into gold and cure all 'ills'. Alchemy was popular until the early 17th century when the modern science of chemistry began. Today transmutation takes place in nuclear reactors as plutonium is formed from uranium.

Alcock and Brown – John Alcock (1892–1919) and Arthur Whitten-Brown (1886–1948) converted a First World War Vickers Vimy bomber, a twin-engined 5600 kg (12 348 lb) biplane, and in 1919 flew the Atlantic Ocean from Newfoundland to Ireland, a distance of 3116 km (1936 miles), in 16 hours 27 mins. It was the first non-stop air crossing of the Atlantic, and the flight was complicated by instrument failure and bitterly cold weather – Brown had to climb out on to the wings to chip off ice. *See also* Biplane.

Alcohol is an organic compound containing one or more hydroxyl (—OH) groups replacing hydrogen atoms. The term generally refers to ethyl or grain alcohol derived from fruits or grains, which has stimulating and intoxicating effects. It is usually made from certain sugars, especially glucose, by fermentation. This process involves treating grain with malt and adding yeast. Alcohol is widely used in medicine and industry. Industrial alcohol is always made unfit for human consumption.

Alder trees occur mainly in Europe, North Africa, Asia Minor and North and South America. They are related to birches, and there are about 30 wild species of these deciduous trees, often occurring in damp places. Alders bear flowers in catkins, and produce rounded, toothed leaves. Alder timber was once used for making charcoal in the manufacture of gunpowder, and for the soles of shoes. It is still used today in the manufacture of plywood.

Aldrin, Edwin, see Apollo project.

Alexander III, the Great (356–323 BC), was King of Macedonia and conqueror of the Persian Empire. A pupil of the philosopher Aristotle, he came to the throne in 336 BC after the assassination of his father, Philip II, who had already brought Greece under Macedonian control. Alexander inherited his father's ambition to destroy the Persian Empire. Having defeated the Persians at Issus, he went on to conquer Syria, the Phoenician cities and Egypt, where he founded Alexandria. In 331 BC he routed a huge Persian army at Arbela and proclaimed himself King of Persia. He moved eastwards, capturing Persian cities and marrying a Persian princess. After a pause he marched on to India, crossed the River Indus and brought most of the Punjab under his control. Forced to turn back by his soldiers, who refused to go any further, he died at Babylon in 323 BC, leaving his empire to be divided up among his generals.

Alexander the Great.

Alexander Nevsky (1220–1263), Russian hero and military leader, succeeded his father as Prince of Novgorod in 1236. He won a great victory against the Swedes in 1240 at the mouth of the Neva River. Two years later he defeated the Teutonic (German) knights in a battle fought on the frozen surface of

Lake Peipus. Although he successfully dealt with the threats against Russia from the west, he was not strong enough to fight the Mongols who had invaded his country from the east, and followed a policy of co-operation with them.

Alfred the Great (849–899), became King of Wessex in 871 after the death of his brother Ethelred I. He was almost constantly at war with the Danes during his reign. He defeated them at Edington in Wiltshire in 878, and it was largely due to his efforts that they were prevented from conquering the whole of England. He managed to confine them to a certain part of the country, known as the Danelaw, and built a fleet to prevent further Danish invasions. Alfred captured London in 886 and after that was generally recognized as the leader of the English people. He did much to revive learning, translated important Latin works into English and codified his country's laws.

Algae are a large group of primitive non-flowering plants. They are among the most abundant of the plants, occurring wherever there is water or, in the case of a few tiny single-celled species, wherever there is just moisture.

Some of the simplest single-celled algae give the trunks of old trees their characteristic green colour. Other single-celled algae called diatoms form beautiful silica cell walls. *Spirogyra* is a common thread-like alga often found in ponds, and each thread consists of many cells.

The largest and the most important algae are the seaweeds. Although they make their own food by photosynthesis just as all algae do, the colours of some seaweeds are masked by other pigments. The wracks, so common on many rocky sea shores, are one of the brown algae. The red algae occur on the seashore and in deeper water, and are among the most beautiful of plants, some species resembling autumn leaves, for example.

Some single-celled algae form a close association with certain fungi, and live together as the group of plants known as lichens.

Algeria is a republic of North Africa. Capital, Algiers; area about 2382000 sq km (919700 sq miles).

History The coast of North Africa, including Algeria, was colonized by the Phoenicians and then the whole region came under the control of the Romans. After the Muslims had established dynasties in the 7th century AD, most of North Africa was taken over by Ottoman Turks. Algeria came under French control in the 19th century and suffered a disastrous civil war in the 1960s before the French withdrew. Connections with France are still quite close.

Land and People Algeria is an Arab, Muslim nation though many of the people, including the desert dwellers, are of Berber descent. Arabic is the national language.

Though large, 80 per cent of Algeria is desert, and most people live in the coastal belt, north of the Atlas Mountains, which is very fertile.

Economy Cereals, fruits, especially grapes for wine, cork and cotton are important products; oil is the most valuable export. There are also factories making plastics, chemicals and other goods. Outside the towns, most people raise sheep, goats and crops such as maize and dates.

Alhambra is the citadel of Granada, Spain, built by the Muslim rulers of Granada in the 13th and 14th centuries. It is one of the finest buildings in the architecture of Islam. From afar, it looks like a powerful fortress, but inside the walls it is more like a rambling fairy palace, with charming courtyards, fountains and slim colonnades, delicate decoration of walls and ceilings, and trees and flowers. Much of the original palace has disappeared (eight of the thirteen original towers, for instance), but the most famous features, like the Court of Lions, are not greatly different from the original design of the Muslim builders.

Alkali is a base dissolved in water. Alkalis react with acids to give salts. This reaction is called neutralization. Strong alkalis remove oil and grease. Many household cleaning fluids, bleaches and soap contain them. Common alkalis are sodium hydroxide (known as caustic soda) and potassium hydroxide (known as caustic potash). They are called caustic because they burn. All strong alkalis can give serious burns, and have to be handled carefully. They are also poisonous.

Indigestion pills are often weak alkalis. They neutralize the acids in the stomach.

Alkalis change the colour of substances known as indicators. They turn litmus paper blue. *See also* Acid; Base; Salt.

Allah is the God of Islam. His followers, called Muslims, believe there is no god but Allah, who is seen as the omnipresent and merciful rewarder. *See also* Islam; Koran.

Allegory is a story which has a deeper meaning than appears on the surface. As a rule, the story and the characters are simple but stand as symbols for something else. The most famous example in English literature is John Bunyan's *Pilgrim's Progress* (1678). The hero, Christian, travels through places with names like the Valley of the Shadow of Death to reach the Celestial City, meeting characters like Giant Despair. George Orwell's *Animal Farm* (1945), about a farm taken over by the pigs, one of which becomes a dictator, is a political allegory about democracy and totalitarianism.

Alligators are reptiles, and have changed little from their ancestors which ruled the Earth millions of years ago. They have long, scaly, armoured bodies and tails, and pointed teeth. Although ungainly on land, they are powerful swimmers, and are capable of catching and eating quite large prey – sometimes even pulling animals into the water from the bank.

Alligators live in the USA and China. They can be distinguished from the similar-looking crocodile by the fact that a crocodile's teeth meet but do not overlap, whereas an alligator's top teeth overlap the bottom teeth. The fourth lower tooth of a crocodile is visible when it closes its mouth, but when an alligator closes its mouth, this tooth is hidden in a recess in the upper jaw. Alligators can be up to 5.8 m (19 ft) long.

Allotropy is the name given when substances can be found in different forms. The different forms are known as allotropes. Diamond is the hardest natural substance known. Graphite is soft and flaky. Both are allotropes of carbon. Therefore, allotropes can look and feel very different from each other.

Phosphorus has two allotropes. White phosphorus is a soft yellowish solid and is very poisonous. Red phosphorus is a reddish brown powder and is not poisonous.

Elements and compounds may show allotropy. Calcium carbonate has allotropes known as calcite and aragonite. Marble, stalactites and stalagmites are calcite. Shells and pearls are aragonite.

Alloy is usually a substance made up of a mixture of two or more metals. It may be made by heating the metals, by electrolysis or by some other process. Alloys are often more useful than the metals they are made of. Combining copper and tin gives the alloy bronze. This was the first alloy made and it was used for thousands of years, during what is known as the Bronze Age. Brass is a mixture of copper and zinc. Bronze and brass are much stronger and harder than the individual metals of which they are made. Pewter is

The head of a crocodile (top) and an alligator, showing their teeth.

a combination of tin and lead.

Non-metals can also be added to metals to give an alloy. Iron mixed with a little carbon gives the much stronger alloy, steel.

Alloys also occur naturally. Electrum is a natural alloy of gold and silver. It is used in jewellery.

Almond tree is a relative of the peach tree. It is grown in many temperate parts of the world, and is much admired for its pink or white flowers which are produced each spring. The fruit of the almond tree is a tasty nut which is eaten straight from the shell or used to flavour foods. There is another almond nut which is not edible, from which almond oil is extracted.

Alphabet is a set of characters or letters used in a system of writing. The word comes from *alpha* and *beta*, the first two letters of the Greek alphabet. Each letter of an alphabet stands for a single sound.

The ancient Egyptians had a different picture-character for every word, and other peoples used a different character for every syllable. Alphabetic systems – easily the most simple and convenient – developed last of all, some time before 1000 BC, and spread fairly quickly over the Middle East and to Greece. Britain, most other European nations and many other countries use the Latin alphabet which originated with the ancient Romans.

Early writing used signs developed from pictures.

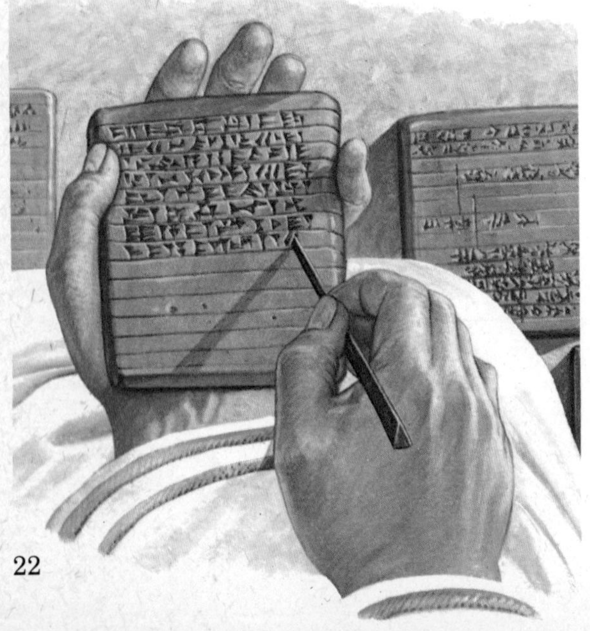

Alpha Centauri is one of the brightest stars in the sky, and is the second closest to our own Sun. It is a binary, or double star, consisting of two stars revolving round each other roughly every 80 years. It is nearly 4.4 light years from the Sun, one-tenth of a light year further away than the much fainter Proxima Centauri.

Alpha (α) ray is a stream of particles. Each particle contains two protons and two neutrons. An alpha particle is the same as the nucleus of a helium atom. It has a positive charge, because protons are positively charged. Alpha rays can travel a long way through the air, but they cannot pass through solids such as metals.

Alpha rays were discovered by Lord Rutherford in 1899. The atoms of radium and other radioactive elements give off alpha rays. As they do this they change into the atoms of another element. This is known as transmutation. Alpha rays cause many substances to shine. Luminous dials in watches contain small amounts of a radioactive element. The alpha rays given off make the dial shine.

Alps are the greatest range of mountains in Europe, running for 1100 km (683 miles) from north Italy, through Switzerland, into Austria. Mont Blanc (4810 m, 15750 ft) is the highest point. There are a number of passes and tunnels for traffic, and many areas are devoted to winter sports.

Aluminium is the commonest metal in the Earth's crust. This blue-white metal has the chemical symbol Al. It is very light – only one-third as heavy as iron – and is a good conductor of electricity and heat. It can easily be made into different shapes, such as long, thin wire and flat sheets of foil. All these things make aluminium the most useful metal after iron.

Food is often wrapped or cooked in aluminium foil, cans, pots and pans. Electricity is often carried in aluminium cables with steel cores. Aluminium alloys are strong as well as being very light. They are used to make aircraft and other vehicles.

Most of the aluminium used today comes from Australia, the West Indies and South America.

Amalgam is the name given to any alloy formed by combining mercury with other metals. If part of a tooth is bad, a dentist will drill it away and fill it. The filling is an amalgam. Amalgams are used for many other things including 'silvering' glass to make a mirror.

An amalgam may be liquid or solid, depending on the amount of mercury in it. Silver, tin, zinc and gold are often made into amalgams with mercury. *See also* Alloy.

Amazon, is a river in South America. It is the largest river in the world measured by volume of water. It flows from the Andes through a huge tropical rainforest in Brazil, containing areas still almost unexplored, for over 6500 km (4040 miles), taking in many tributaries. Ocean-going vessels can sail up it for half its length, as it follows a gentle slope down to the sea. A Spanish explorer, Orellana, sailed down the Amazon (more by luck than by plan) in 1541, but the river was almost unknown to Europeans until the middle of the 19th century.

Amazon scene, with a manatee, or sea cow, which is found in some tropical rivers.

Amazons, in Greek mythology, were a warlike race of women. They appear in a number of myths and were believed to have taken part in the Trojan War. Many Greek vase-paintings show the warrior Achilles slaying the Amazon queen Penthesilea.

America, see United States of America

American Ballet Theatre is a ballet company founded in New York in 1940. Its original aim was to produce both the best historical works as well as new American ballets. Its early history was troubled, but it has become one of the foremost ballet companies in the world, offering a wide range of different personalities and productions.

American Civil War (1861–1865), was fought between the 11 southern states of the USA and the northern states. There were a number of reasons for the war, but the chief one was disagreement over whether slavery could be introduced into the new states which were being settled in the western USA. In 1860, Abraham Lincoln, who wanted to prevent the extension of slavery, was elected President. The 11 southern states then separated to form a new country, which they called the Confederate States of America, but Lincoln refused to recognize their right to do this and fighting began in April 1861. At first the southern states won a number of victories, but the north, which was richer and had a larger population, gradually got the upper hand. The northern army won a notable victory at Gettysburg in 1863, and the northern navy blockaded southern ports. The south finally surrendered in April 1865, thus ending a war which had cost 600 000 lives.

American War of Independence (1775–1783), was the struggle in which the 13 colonies of North America won their independence from Britain. The Americans strongly disliked being taxed in order to pay for the army which Britain kept in North America, especially since the Americans were not represented in Parliament in London. Protests at taxation and other controls led to acts of rebellion, including the Boston Tea Party (1773).

War began in 1775 when British troops and colonists opened fire on each other at Lexington and Concord. The following year, on 4 July, the American Congress issued the Declaration of Independence. At first the British forces won a number of victories, notably at Bunker Hill and New York, but under the leadership of George Washington the American army became an effective fighting force. The war on land ended when the British general Cornwallis surrendered at Yorktown in 1781. In 1783 Britain acknowledged the independence of the USA.

Ammonia is a colourless gas with the chemical formula NH_3. It has a strong, unpleasant smell and makes people's eyes water. It is one of the most useful chemicals, and large amounts of it are made. Many ammonium salts are then made from it. Most ammonia is used to make fertilizers. These are added to soil to help plants to grow. It is also used to make nitric acid and other chemicals.

Many household cleaners contain ammonia. Its unpleasant smell is used in smelling salts to shock people back to consciousness after they have fainted. Smelling salts contain ammonium carbonate. Ammonium chloride is used in batteries.

Ammonites are cephalopod molluscs that lived in the waters of the late Paleozoic and Mesozoic eras (between about 400 and 65 million years ago). Their coiled and sculptured shells left distinctive fossils. This and their rapid evolutionary change make ammonites extremely useful in geological dating. *See also* Prehistoric animal.

An ammonite from the Mesozoic Era.

Amoeba is a single-celled animal which lives in water. It has an almost colourless, granular body which flows along by pushing out finger-like projections called pseudopodia. The rest of the animal then flows into the pseudopodia. It feeds by flowing round tiny particles and engulfing them. Amoeba reproduce by splitting into two.

A close relative of amoeba, called entamoeba, is a parasite which causes the disease known as amoebic dysentery. *See also* Protozoan.

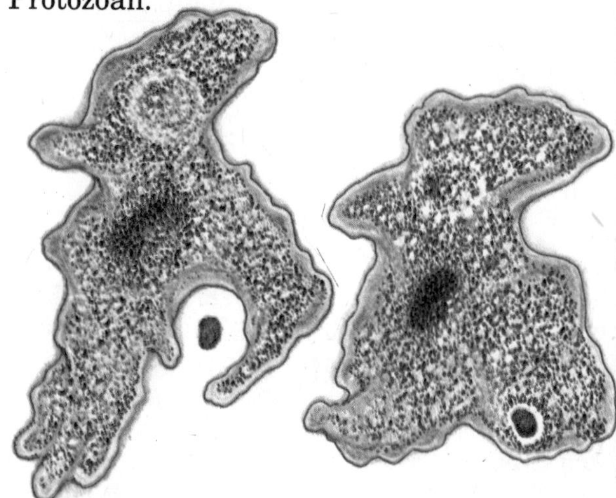

An amoeba (greatly enlarged) engulfing food.

Amon, or Amun, was one of the gods of ancient Egypt. His name means 'hidden', which probably indicates that he was a spirit, not a physical creature. However, the Egyptians pictured him in several ways; for example, as a ram with powerful horns, or as a bearded man wearing feathers.

Amon was identified with various other gods. As Amon-Ra he was linked with the Sun god Ra (or Re). He was especially important at Thebes, and the Thebans built him a great temple at Karnak.

Amphibian is a term which comes from the Greek word meaning 'double life'. Most amphibians do, indeed, have a two-stage life: they begin as aquatic tadpoles, and later turn into land-living creatures, returning to the water to breed.

Amphibians are the most primitive of the land-living vertebrates. They include the salamanders, newts, frogs, toads and the

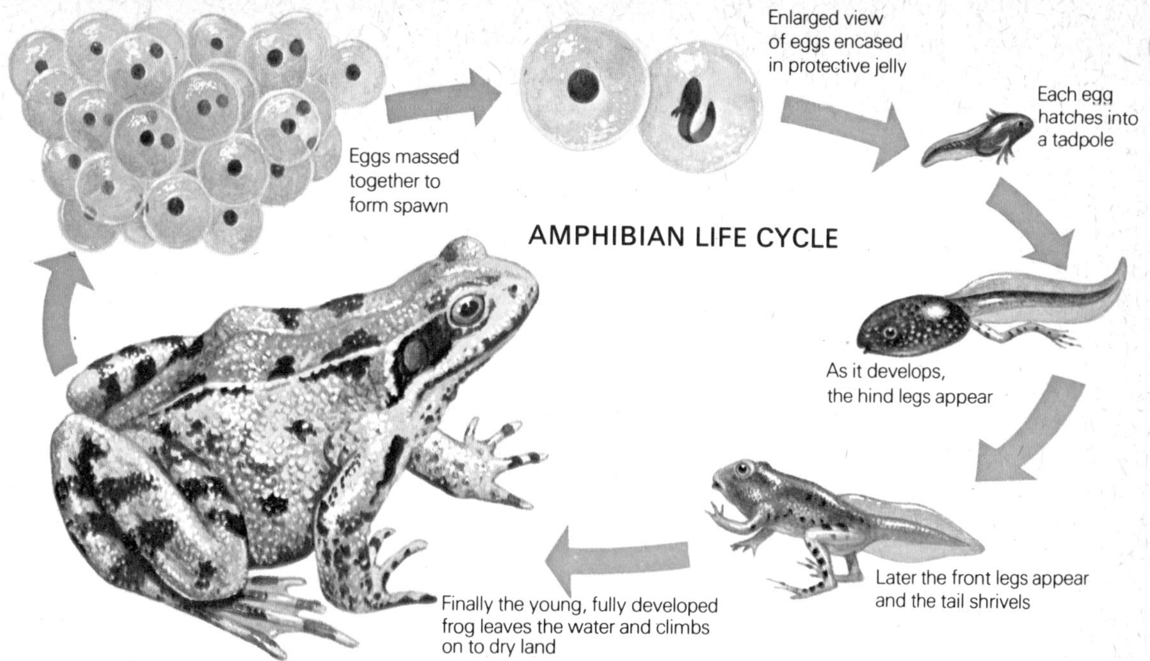
Enlarged view
of eggs encased
in protective jelly
Each egg
hatches into
a tadpole
Eggs massed
together to
form spawn
AMPHIBIAN LIFE CYCLE
As it develops,
the hind legs appear
Later the front legs appear
and the tail shrivels
Finally the young, fully developed
frog leaves the water and climbs
on to dry land

little-known caecilians – blind, burrowing worm-like creatures. The skin of amphibians is usually used for breathing, and may be as important as the lungs for this purpose in some species. The skin can also secrete poisons; natives of South America place the skin secretions of arrow-poison frogs on the ends of their darts and arrows to kill their victims more quickly. Many amphibians have brightly coloured skins which warn other animals that they are poisonous.

Although they are still dependent on water to complete their life cycle, amphibians have been able to colonize many types of habitat. There are even some species which can live in deserts. Amphibians were most numerous during the Carboniferous period between 345 to 280 million years ago, when giant 4.5 m- (14 ft-)long amphibians such as *Eogyrinus* roamed the Earth.

Amundsen, Roald (1872–1928), a Norwegian explorer, was the first man to reach the South Pole. He took part in both Arctic and Antarctic exploration, then in 1910 he sailed from Norway in a race with a British expedition led by Robert Falcon Scott to get to the South Pole. He arrived there on 14 December 1911, beating Scott by one month. He died in 1928 while attempting to rescue an Italian explorer in the Arctic.

Anaconda is a large snake which lives in tropical South America. Like pythons, anacondas kill their prey by constriction – squeezing the victim until it suffocates. This process breaks many of the prey's bones, making it easier to swallow. Anacondas hunt among the trees as well as in water, and many grow to a length of 10 m (33 ft).

Anaesthetic is a substance in medicine given to a patient to reduce the feeling of pain. It may be injected into a part of the body to deaden the nerves there. This is known as a local anaesthetic. Dentists often use a local anaesthetic to stop the pain from a tooth being drilled or taken out.

Another sort of anaesthetic is called a general anaesthetic. This may be given by injection or by breathing an anaesthetic gas. General anaesthetics stop all parts of the body feeling pain by causing the brain to 'go to sleep'. They are used during many surgical operations. Nitrous oxide, ether and chloroform were the first general anaesthetics to be used. Nitrous oxide and ether are still often used. Nitrous oxide is also known as laughing gas because small amounts of it make people laugh hysterically.

Anatomy is the scientific study of the structure of plants and animals. It is also the term used to describe the arrangement of the various parts of the body of a plant or animal in relation to each other.

From a study of the anatomy of an animal such as a starfish, for instance, we learn that it is an echinoderm, or spiny-skinned animal, related to the sea-urchins. In addition, we see how it eats, moves, breathes and reproduces. The study of anatomy also helps to give us information about the evolution of an animal or plant.

Andersen, Hans Christian (1805–1875), was a Danish writer. Lonely and backward as a boy, he became world-famous through the publication of his collection of fairy stories, the first of which appeared in 1835. Stories like *The Ugly Duckling* or *The Snow Queen* were not invented by him, but the poetic way Andersen retold them made him one of the greatest figures in children's literature. He always thought his adult plays and novels were more imporant than his fairy stories, but no one else agreed.

Andes are a mountain range in South America, running the whole length of the continent near the Pacific coast, sometimes splitting into several parallel ranges. There are several peaks over 6500 m (21 300 ft) and some volcanoes that are still active. Parts of the Andes are rich in valuable minerals such as gold, silver, mercury and copper.

Andorra is a tiny state in spectacular mountain country between France and Spain. Capital, Andorra-la-Vielle; area 465 sq km (180 sq miles). The people speak Catalan, and they have enjoyed a reasonably independent existence under the joint overlordship of France and Spain since the Middle Ages. Andorra has good pastures and orchards, though tourism is the main industry. (Once it was smuggling!)

Angiosperms are flowering plants. They include the grasses, shrubs and broadleaved trees, as well as all the popular flowers of woodland, garden and meadow. Angiosperms produce ovules enclosed within the ovary. After fertilization the ovary becomes a fruit.

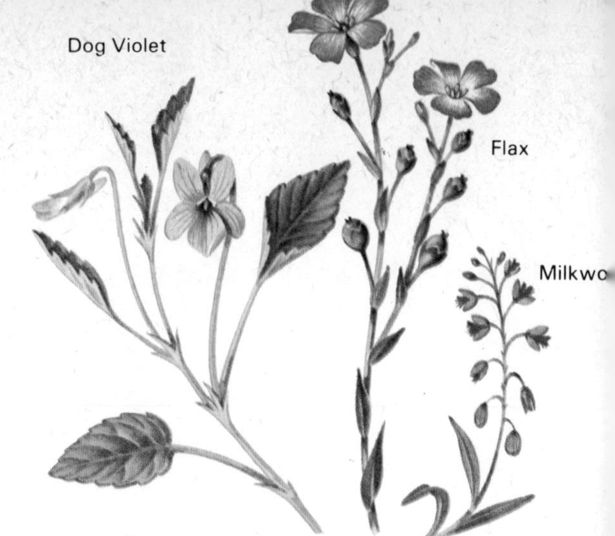

Some examples of angiosperms.

The angiosperms can be divided into two groups, the monocotyledons and the dicotyledons.

Angler fish is a very cunning creature. Rather than swim around looking for food, it attracts tiny fish and other creatures towards it by means of a lure. This is produced from part of the dorsal fin, which hangs over the head in front of the mouth. It can be waggled about or, in deep-sea angler fish, it has a luminous bulb on the end. When a curious fish comes to investigate – perhaps thinking that the lure is food – it is immediately gulped into the angler fish's huge, gaping mouth.

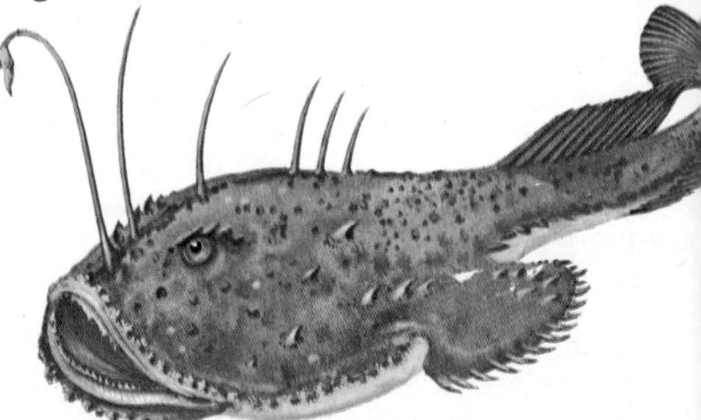

Anglo-Saxons were the Germanic tribes who began to invade England in the second half of the 5th century. These people – the Angles, Saxons and Jutes – came from Denmark and Germany. They drove the Celtic Britons westwards into Wales and Cornwall, and gradually established a number of sep-

The Anglo-Saxon King of Kent welcomes St Augustine to Canterbury.

arate kingdoms in England (which means 'the land of the Angles'). Converted to Christianity by St Augustine, they became united in the 9th century and lived in the kingdom of Wessex.

Angola is a republic in south-west Africa. Capital, Luanda; area 1 247 000 sq km (481 350 sq miles). Much of the south is desert or dry savannah, which accounts for the small population.

Angola gained independence from Portugal in 1975 after nearly 400 years of colonial rule and several rebellions. During the 18th century, parts of the country were almost stripped of people, due to the slave trade to the Brazilian plantations. A lack of unity, growing partly from old tribal differences, has caused political problems since 1975. Cuban troops have assisted the government against guerillas, and the railway system, a good one, has often been put out of action.

Angola is mainly agricultural. Coffee, sugar and cotton are exported, but most people grow only enough food for themselves. Mining is of growing importance, and many diamonds of the quality used in industry are exported. There is also an oil refinery and hydro-electric stations where the plateau, which forms most of the interior, dips towards the coast.

Anguilla is an island in the Leeward Islands, West Indies. Area about 91 sq km (35 sq miles). Formerly a British colony, it separated from the Associated State of St Christopher-Nevis in 1969, but this only formally came into effect in 1980 after the Anguilla Act was passed in the UK Parliament. It is now a separate dependency.

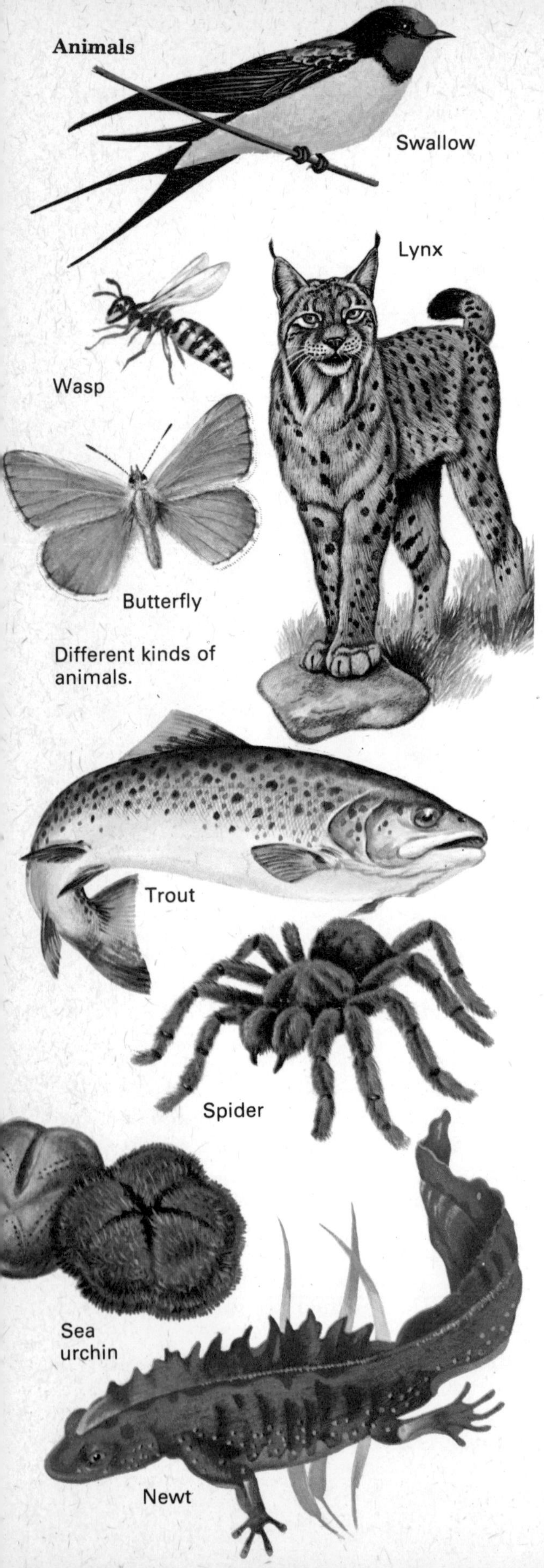

Different kinds of animals.

Animals, together with plants, make up the living world. Animals usually feed upon organic matter, can normally move rapidly in response to a stimulus, have cells which are enclosed by flexible cell membranes and whose growth is limited. Throughout the world, there are many different kinds of animals, ranging from tiny creatures only seen with a microscope, to creatures as large as the blue whale – the largest animal ever known to have lived. Among the more common animals to be found throughout the world are sponges, worms, jellyfish, snails, oysters, octopuses, insects, crabs, spiders, starfish, fish, frogs, toads, newts, salamanders, birds and mammals. The mammals include such well-known animals as lions, tigers, bats, rabbits, dogs, elephants – even ourselves, humans. The most numerous animals in the world are the insects – indeed, there are more insects than all the other animals put together. It is very difficult to decide whether some microscopic organisms are plants or animals, for many tiny creatures show features of both plants and animals. For instance, the protozoan *Euglena* has a green chloroplast, just as most plants do; but it also moves along by means of a long whip-like hair known as a flagellum, and movement of this kind is normally thought of as an animal characteristic.

Anne (1665–1714), Queen of Great Britain and Ireland, was the last Stuart monarch. The daughter of the Roman Catholic James II, she was brought up as a Protestant and came to the throne on the death of her brother-in-law William III in 1702. During her reign, which saw the Act of Union between England and Scotland and the War of the Spanish Succession, she was strongly influenced by the Duchess of Marlborough. None of her children survived childhood, and when she died in 1714 the succession passed to George I of Hanover.

Annual rings are a series of almost concentric rings on trees of a temperate region, seen when they are cut down. These rings show where the new year's growth has added cells to the tree. The age of a tree can be calculated by counting these rings (each ring represents one year). They can also show, for example, whether the tree lived partly in the shade, or if it was damaged at some point in its life.

Ant is an insect belonging to the order Hymenoptera. Ants usually live underground socially in nests consisting of many tunnels and chambers. Except during times of mating, ants do not have wings. They are extremely tough creatures, able to lift and carry eggs and items of food, such as other insects, many times their own weight. They are also extremely aggressive in defence of their nests and in their general behaviour towards other insects. Some species have frequent raiding parties to attack other nests. There are species of ants which make slaves of other insects, and some which farm aphids for their 'milk'. The nomadic soldier and driver ants of South America and Africa march in their millions, eating anything in their path. *See also* Social insect.

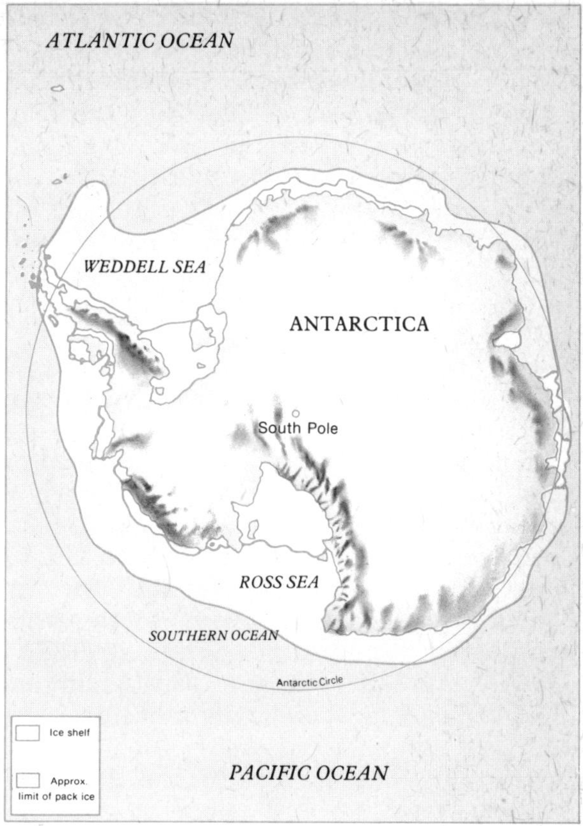

Antarctica is a continent, with the South Pole near its centre. Land area 13 200 000 sq km (5 100 000 sq miles). It is covered by an ice cap 1.5 km (nearly 1 mile) thick, which breaks off at the edges to form icebergs in the ocean. It is extremely cold and windy, even in mid-summer. Very few plants or animals can live there, though some penguins breed, and the seas around are full of whales and seals.

Many countries have scientific bases in Antarctica. Parts of the continent, divided like slices of a cake, are claimed by various countries, but these claims are not enforced. Antarctica remains, like the oceans, an international area. It has great mineral resources, but they are too hard to get at to make mining worthwhile – yet.

Anteaters are insect-eating mammals which live in South America. They have long, slender muzzles and tiny mouths with a long, sticky tongue. They are so adapted to licking up and swallowing insects that they have no teeth in their jaws. Giant anteaters, which can be up to 2.4 m (8 ft) long, walk on their knuckles, which helps to keep the long claws sharp for ripping open ants' and termites' nests. The insects are then licked up with the tongue. Lesser anteaters live mostly in trees where they feed on ants. The dwarf anteater also lives in trees, where it feeds on bees.

Antelopes are herbivorous, hoofed mammals which live in Africa and Asia. Antelopes range in size from the royal antelope, only 30 cm (1 ft) tall, to the giant eland, which stand 2 m (6 ft) tall. Some species of antelope live on the open plains in huge herds, and others live alone or in pairs in forests. Duiker, kudu, gazelle, springbok, gnu, oryx, impala, blackbuck, nilgai and saiga are among the most familiar species of antelope.

Antenna (plural antennae) is one of a pair of structures found on the heads of animals such as insects, lobsters, crabs and centipedes. Antennae are used for several purposes, but most often to sense the surroundings. They may be used to touch insects or other objects, to detect prey or warn of danger, and some kinds – for instance, those found on moths – can pick up tiny traces of chemicals and so inform the insect about food sources or females ready for mating. The tiny water flea, *Daphnia*, uses its antennae for swimming. By flicking them, it can 'row' itself along in the water. Some parasitic creatues use their antennae to attach themselves to their hosts.

Antibiotic is a substance produced by one living organism which kills other living organisms. Antibiotics can often be used to cure diseases in plants or animals, for they only kill certain harmful organisms already in the body of a victim and not the victim itself. One of the best-known antibiotics is penicillin. This was discovered by the British scientist Sir Alexander Fleming (1881–1955). It is produced naturally by the fungus *Penicillium*, and is used to fight bacteria.

Antigua is the largest of the Leeward Islands, West Indies. It is part of Antigua and Barbuda which comprises three islands: Antigua (area 280 sq km/108 sq miles), Barbuda 40 km/25 miles to the north (area 161 sq km/62 sq miles) and uninhabited Redonda, 40 km/25 miles to the southwest (area 1 sq km/0.4 sq miles). Capital, St John's; total area 442 sq km (171 sq miles). Antigua is beautiful and hilly, with shores fringed by coral. It was colonized by the English in the 17th century, and most of the people living there now are descendants of the African slaves who worked the sugar plantations. Growing sugar cane and making sugar are still the main occupations. Though small, Antigua and Barbuda is self-governing, but keeps a close association with Britain.

Antimatter is a form of matter which has been made during nuclear reactions. The matter around us is composed of atoms. Each atom has positively charged particles called protons in the middle with negatively charged particles called electrons orbiting around it.

An atom of antimatter would have negatively charged antiprotons in the middle, and positively charged positrons orbiting it. Antiprotons and positrons are known as antiparticles.

On the Earth, antimatter lasts for an incredibly short time. When an antiproton collides with a proton, they are both destroyed. All antiparticles are quickly destroyed by collisions with the many ordinary particles around them.

Antiseptic is the name given to a substance which lessens or stops the growth of the micro-organisms that cause disease. The first antiseptic to be used was carbolic acid. Joseph Lister (1827–1912) used carbolic acid in surgery to clean his hands and tools and his patient's skin. This stopped his patients' wounds becoming infected. Before this, some patients died from infected wounds after surgery.

Today, sterilizers and disinfectants are used during surgery. These are much more powerful than ordinary antiseptics, and kill all the micro-organisms. Antiseptics are still used in homes and hospitals, for example, to clean cuts and grazes.

Antony, Mark (83–30 BC), Roman soldier and statesman, served under Julius Caesar in Gaul and, after Caesar's murder, joined in the Second Triumvirate (government headed by three people) with Lepidus and Octavian. He defeated Brutus and Cassius, two of the conspirators against Caesar, at the Battle of Philippi in 42 BC. He fell in love with Cleopatra, Queen of Egypt, and broke off his alliance with Octavian. When Rome declared war on Egypt, Antony was defeated at the naval battle of Actium (31 BC) and subsequently committed suicide.

Apennines are a mountain range in Italy, running the length of the country, north to south. Monte Corno (2912 m; 9354 ft) is the highest point. The lower slopes are fertile, with pastures, olive trees and vines. There are few minerals, but valuable marble is quarried.

Apes are hairy mammals which, with the

monkeys and animals such as lemurs and lorises, make up the order known as the primates. Apes can be distinguished from monkeys by the fact that monkeys have tails, and apes do not. Apes also have longer arms and larger brains.

Apes live in the tropical forests of Africa and Asia, often in large family groups. The largest ape is the gorilla, which with the orang-utan and chimpanzee are known as the 'great apes'. The other apes include the six species of gibbon.

Aphids are most familiar as the greenfly or blackfly which are garden pests, but there are many hundreds of different species of aphid. They are all soft-bodied insects known as bugs, and they have a remarkable reproduction rate. If all the descendants of one aphid survived they would, in one year, themselves produce a weight of aphids equal to 600 million people! Fortunately, this does not happen, for these sap-sucking insects fall prey to ladybirds, birds and other animals. Ants sometimes 'farm' them for the sticky, sweet honeydew they secrete.

Aphids are unusual in that during the summer unfertilized females can produce female offspring. These offspring can also produce new females without being fertilized. Male aphids are only produced in the autumn.

Aphrodite, in Greek myth, was the goddess of love, and is better known by her Roman name, Venus. She was born from the sea (though she is also called the daughter of Zeus), and is the goddess of sailors as well as of love, beauty and marriage. Her husband was Hephaestus, though she was also linked with Ares, among others, and her son was Eros (Cupid).

Aphrodite was very widely worshipped, and appears in a great number of myths, such as the heavenly beauty competition which she won from Hera and Athena by the Judgement of Paris. As the ideal of female beauty, she was often represented in art. Perhaps the most famous example is a sculpture, the Venus de Milo, made about 100 BC and now in the Louvre, Paris.

Apollo, one of the gods of ancient Greece, was the most widely worshipped after his father, Zeus. He was worshipped in many aspects: as the god of punishment, sending death by his arrows; as the god of deliverance in times of danger; as the god of prophecy, especially at Delphi where his oracle was; as the god of sheep and cattle; and as the god of the Sun (his chariot). In Roman myth, he was mainly a god of healing.

Figures of Apollo, always represented as a very handsome young man, were the commonest subjects of early Greek sculptors.

Bronze statue of Apollo from 5th century BC.

Apollo project was the final stage of the American programme to place a man on the Moon and get him back safely to Earth. The Apollo package consisted of three ingenious spacecraft, each with their own job to do. The Command Module was a three-man capsule similar in principle to those which had been used by the Mercury and Gemini projects (only much bigger). This was where the three astronauts sat for take-off; it was also the only part of the massive spaceship to return to Earth. The Service Module was attached to the Command Module and contained the fuel and supplies for the mission. This was thrown away just before the Command Module re-entered Earth's atmosphere. The Lunar Module was the small, self-contained spaceship in which two of the astronauts travelled from the Command Module down to the Moon's surface. When their stay on the lunar surface was over, the astronauts flew the Lunar Module back to the Command and Service Modules, docked with them, climbed back into the three-man capsule and the whole Lunar Module was then abandoned. This method was very expensive, because almost every item of equipment was left in space, but it was safe and it worked.

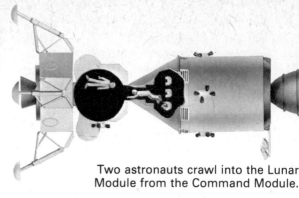

Two astronauts crawl into the Lunar Module from the Command Module.

After a number of test flights, first around the Earth and then around the Moon without landing, a giant Saturn V rocket lifted Apollo 11 from Cape Kennedy in Florida on 16 July 1969. On board were astronauts Neil Armstrong, Edwin Aldrin and Michael

Apollo Flight Plan
The Apollo flight plan required a spacecraft made up of three sections, or modules. The three-man crew were housed in the command module (CM), linked to the main equipment section, the service module (SM). For the outward flight the CM was mated to the lunar module (LM) as shown below. When the craft reached lunar orbit, two of the astronauts transferred to the LM, separated from the CM, and descended to the lunar surface. After their 'moonwalk' they returned to dock with the CM orbiting above. The LM was then discarded before the flight home

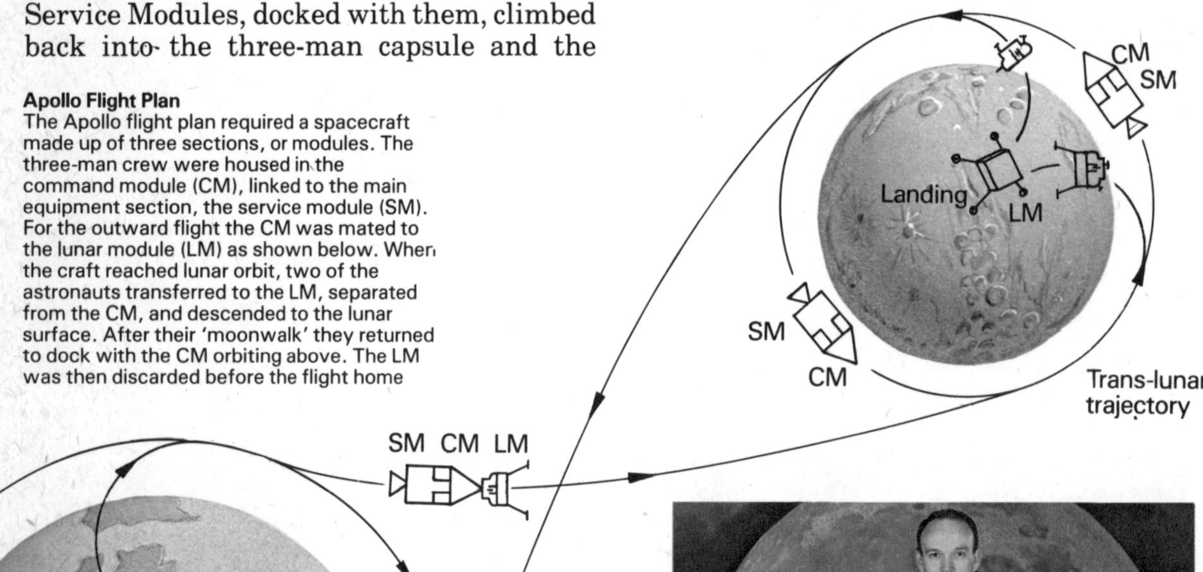

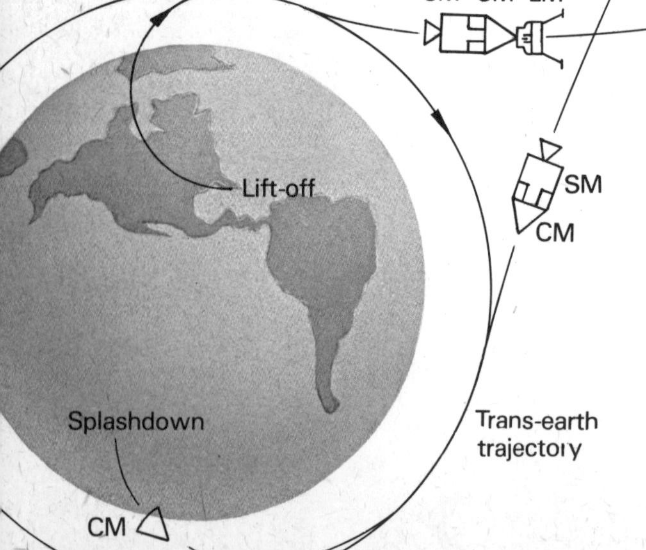

The Apollo 11 crew: Neil Armstrong, Michael Collins and Edwin Aldrin.

Collins. Four days later, the Lunar Module landed Armstrong and Aldrin on the Moon, and Armstrong stepped on to the surface on 21 July. Five later Apollo missions to the Moon were much more ambitious, the final ones including a lunar 'buggy' – an electric car which the astronauts assembled on the Moon and drove about on the surface, complete with a colour TV camera mounted on it. The Apollo project was estimated to have cost approximately $24 000 000 000.

Appalachians are a mountain range in North America running roughly parallel with the Atlantic coast, from Canada to Alabama in the USA. It includes the White Mountains (New Hampshire), the Allegheníes (Pennsylvania) and the Blue Ridge (Virginia). The early colonies of North America were confined to Appalachia, i.e. east of the mountains. Their chief importance today is as a holiday area.

Apple trees are members of the rose family and they occur as natives in temperate Europe, North America and Asia. Today apple farming is an important industry, and many new and vigorous hybrids have been developed from the 25 or so naturally occurring species. They have been introduced into New Zealand, Australia and southern Africa. The apple, the fruit of the tree, is highly nutritious. Apart from being eaten cooked or raw, it is also used for making apple juice, cider and apple jelly.

April is the fourth month of the year in the modern calendar, and lasts for 30 days. Its name comes from the ancient Roman month *Aprilis*. The first of the month is April Fools' Day, when people play tricks on each other.

Arachnids form a class, or division, of the phylum Arthropoda. Spiders, scorpions, mites and ticks are all arachnids. They have a body which is divided into two parts – a head region called the cephalothorax, and an abdomen. Arachnids all have four pairs of legs, unlike insects which have three pairs. They do not have antennae.

Right: A whip scorpion – an arachnid.

Arboretum is a special collection of living trees. Usually an arboretum contains many exotic species. These are introduced into a particular country to see how they grow under different conditions, and to try to produce hardy hybrids from them. Arboreta provide a pleasant place for visitors to come and look round.

Archaeology is an area of research and study that is closely related to history. The archaeologist specializes in finding and examining objects, or fragments of objects, that have survived from the past. These may include the remains of buildings and graves, household goods, food, tools and weapons. They have usually become buried over the centuries, and must be carefully excavated or dug out. Techniques for recovering even underwater objects are highly developed, and in 1982 British archaeologists succeeded in raising an entire Tudor battleship, the *Mary Rose*, from the sea-bed.

Although archaeologists may study any place or time, many of their most valuable discoveries concern people of whom there are no written records – including the whole of prehistory (prehistoric times), which is known only through archaeological evidence – or peoples whose everyday lives may be rarely mentioned in such records. The triumphs of archaeology include the discovery of ancient Pompeii and Troy, and the unearthing of the Egyptian king Tutankhamen's tomb and its fabulous treasures.

Many early archaeologists were actually more interested in treasure or sensational facts than finding out about the everyday past. Only in the late 19th century did the

modern scholarly approach begin to be adopted. Nowadays, archaeologists keep painstaking records of every site and its humblest contents, and their skills are supplemented by carbon dating and other advanced scientific techniques.

Archaeopteryx was the earliest known bird. About 120 years ago, scientists in Germany found a fossil which looked like that of a reptile, with solid bones, a long tail and jaws with teeth. However, something about the fossil was very unlike a reptile, for this creature had had wings and feathers, just like those of a bird. Scientists named it *Archaeopteryx*. This creature lived between 140 and 170 million years ago. Because it still had so many features of reptiles (from which modern birds evolved), it is unlikely that *Archaeopteryx* was able to fly as gracefully as present-day birds can. It is more likely that it struggled to the tops of trees by climbing, and then flapped and glided back to Earth again.

Archer fish, which lives in the freshwater rivers of Asia, has a very unusual method of catching food. It swims along until it sees an insect or spider on a branch or leaf overhanging the water. A jet of water squirted from its mouth knocks the creature into the water, and it is then seized by the waiting fish. Unlikely as it seems, the archer fish hardly ever misses, even if its prey is several metres away.

Archimedes (circa 287–212 BC) was one of the greatest Greek scientists and mathematicians. He lived in Syracuse, in Sicily. He showed that objects float because they displace a weight of liquid equal to their own weight. He is said to have made this discovery while in the bath.

He explained how a lever works and invented the pulley. Other machines said to have been invented by him include the water pump called the Archimedean screw. This is still used for irrigation in some parts of the world. He also invented war machines for the defence of his city. Archimedes was killed when the Romans invaded Syracuse.

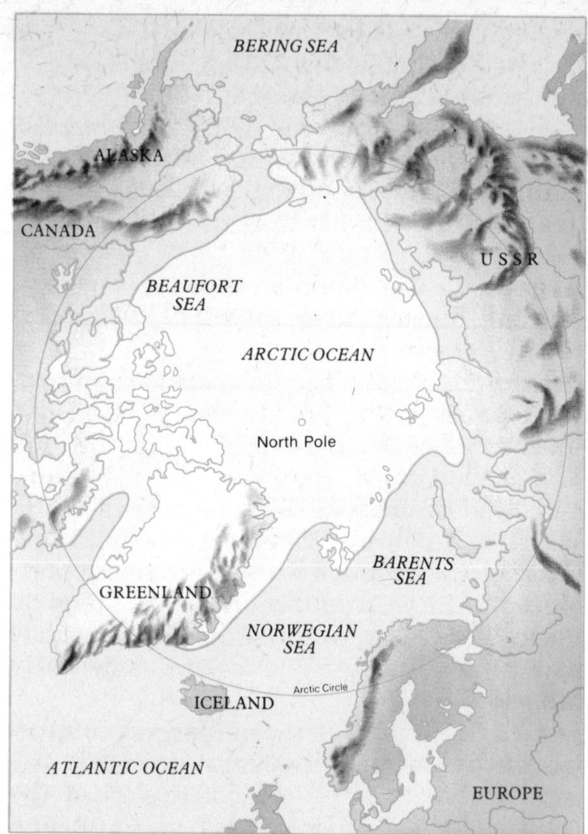

Arctic is the northernmost region of the world, within the Arctic Circle. Northern parts of Europe, Asia and North America are in the Arctic, but most of the region consists of the Arctic Ocean, covered with shifting ice. It has rich wild life, including polar bears, reindeers, musk oxen, many birds and even flowers during the short summer. Eskimos have managed to live successfully in some parts since long before European explorers ventured so far north. The Lapps, who live in the northern forests of Scandinavia, herd their reindeer into the Arctic regions in summer.

It is possible, though very difficult, for modern ships to sail through parts of the Arctic Ocean, e.g. along the coast of Siberia. The Arctic lands produce coal and oil, among other products.

Ares was the Greek god of war, who became identified with the Roman Mars. He was the son of Zeus (Jupiter) and Hera (Juno), and the lover of Aphrodite. In spite of his distinguished birth, Ares was regarded as a rather second-rate god by the Greeks. The Greek playwright Sophocles called him 'the god unhonoured among the gods'.

The Roman Mars was much more impressive – the most important god after Jupiter – mainly because the Romans valued military qualities more highly than the Greeks.

Argentina is a republic in South America. Capital, Buenos Aires; area 2 777 800 sq km (1 072 500 sq miles).

History The region became part of the Spanish empire in the 16th century. It gained independence in 1816 under José de San Martín, but there were frequent rebellions and other disorders. After the Second World War, Juan Peron established a popular dictatorship, with much working-class support. More recently, Argentina has been ruled by the military. Despite its rich resources, it has had many economic problems, especially inflation.

Land and People The second largest country in South America, it occupies roughly the southern half of the continent east of the Andes. Much of Argentina is level plain, and the vast, fertile pampas form the most productive and most thickly populated region. Cereals, especially wheat and maize, and cattle, herded by *gauchos* (cowboys), are

A gaucho herding cattle in Argentina.

raised in huge quantities, making Argentina one of the world's chief food exporters. Its main industries, meat-packing and food-processing, result from this cattle raising.

Juan Peron, who ruled Argentina from 1940–1955, addressing the people.

Farther south, in Patagonia, where the climate is more severe, sheep are raised in stony pastures. Heavy industry and mining are less developed, one problem being a lack of energy sources such as coal or oil.

The Argentinians are of mixed origin. There are few people of pure Indian descent left, and there has been heavy immigration of Europeans, especially Spaniards and Italians. The language is Spanish and the chief religion Roman Catholicism.

Argon is a gas which forms nearly one per cent of the air. The chemical symbol for argon is Ar. It has no colour or smell, and is an inert gas, which means that it does not react with any other substances.

There are a number of inert gases, which together are known as noble gases. Argon was discovered in 1894 by Lord Rayleigh and Sir William Ramsay. It was the first noble gas to be discovered.

Large amounts of argon are obtained from the air. It is used in lamps, fluorescent tubes and electric light bulbs. It is also used in the welding of many metals.

Aristotle (384–322 BC) was a Greek philosopher and doctor. A pupil of Plato, he was the teacher of Alexander the Great. His work included the study of science, logic and politics.

He believed that the Earth was the centre of the universe and that the other planets and the Sun moved in circles around it. This idea was believed by many people until after the Middle Ages, even though it was wrong and held up progress in science.

He watched animals closely and grouped similar animals together. In this way, he started the system of classification of animals and plants still used today.

Armada, Spanish, was a large fleet of ships sent by Philip II of Spain in 1588 in an attempt to invade England. When the Armada anchored off Calais, it was broken up by English fireships (vessels loaded with explosives and set adrift to destroy the enemy's ships). The Spanish and English fleets fought a battle off Gravelines, in which the Armada suffered heavily. Storms caused further Spanish losses, and out of a total of 130 ships only about half returned to Spain.

The Spanish called their Armada invincible, but the British beat them in battle, in the English Channel.

Armadillos are mammals which live in most regions of Central and South America. Their skin is covered with bony plates, and only their tail and pointed head can be seen as they trundle along looking for food. They eat insects and other small animals, which they dig out of the ground with powerful claws. The claws can also help them to burrow into the ground to escape predators, although sometimes they just roll up into a ball instead. There are about 20 species of armadillo; the giant armadillo is about 1 m (3 ft) long, and the fairy armadillo – the smallest – is only 15 cm (6 in) long.

Giant armadillo

Armstrong, Louis (1900–1971), was a US jazz musician, known as Satchmo ('Satchel Mouth'). He learned to read music in an orphanage. After playing trumpet with various bands around his home town of New Orleans, he joined the band of King Oliver, a pioneer of New Orleans jazz in the North, in 1922. He formed his own band in 1925 and soon built up a reputation as the finest jazz trumpeter alive. A master of improvisation, he also had a remarkable, gravelly singing voice. He recorded over 1000 numbers and appeared in many films.

Armstrong, Neil (1930–), was the first man to walk on the Moon, when he stepped from the Lunar Module of Apollo 11 on 21 July 1969. As he stepped off the last rung of the ladder, he spoke the famous words: 'That's one small step for man, one giant leap for mankind'. Before undergoing astronaut training, Armstrong was a test pilot. *See also* Apollo project.

Arnhem Land is a large Aboriginal reserve in the north of the Northern Territory, Australia. It is largely composed of dense jungle, mangrove swamps and rugged tableland. Many sacred sites and paintings can be found there. *See also* Aborigine.

Arsenic is a grey solid which has the chemical symbol As. It looks rather like a metal, although it is not.

Arsenic and its compounds are poisonous. They are used in rat poison, insecticides, sheep dips and so on. They are also sometimes used to treat skin diseases and in dyes. Arsenic oxide is a deadly poison. It is the 'arsenic' used by poisoners.

Art Deco was an international style of decoration in the 1920s and 1930s. It followed Art Nouveau, which it resembled in some ways. The most striking difference is that the flowing curves of Art Nouveau design were abandoned in favour of straight lines and hard angles in Art Deco, which was influenced by abstract painting as well as the streamlined modern design of the Bauhaus school. *See also* Bauhaus.

Artemis was a Greek goddess who became identified with the Roman Diana. A daughter of Zeus, she was worshipped in many aspects; for instance, as the goddess of childbirth. But she was chiefly the goddess of wild life and the countryside, and therefore of hunting. She is also an opponent of Aphrodite, the goddess of love, for Artemis had no lover nor husband.

One story tells how she turned the hunter Actaeon into a stag because he caught sight of her bathing. As a result Actaeon was torn to pieces by his own hounds.

Artery is a large blood vessel which takes blood from the heart to the body organs and the limbs. To withstand the powerful pumping action of the heart, an artery wall is made up of strong layers of fibres and muscles. The arteries eventually become branched, and these smaller branches are called arterioles.

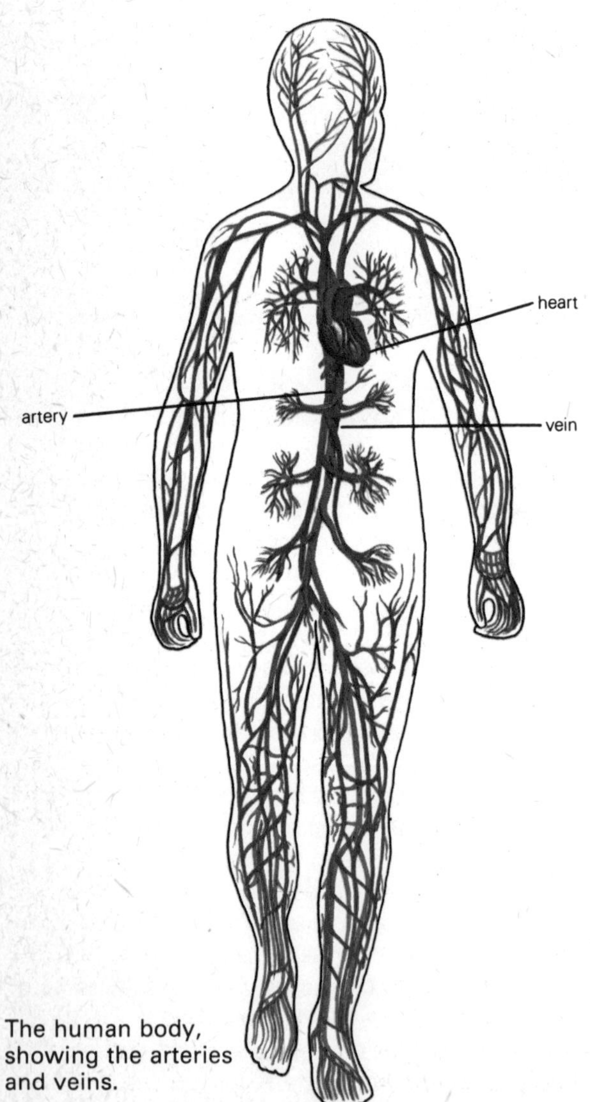

The human body, showing the arteries and veins.

Arthropod is the name given to any animal which is a member of the phylum Arthropoda. The phylum Arthropoda contains the onychophorans, king crabs, centipedes, millipedes, arachnids (spiders, scorpions, mites and ticks), crustaceans (crabs, shrimps, lobsters and barnacles) and the insects. Over 800 000 species of arthropod are known; they make up 80 per cent of all animals. They are by far the most successful group of animals, and have managed to make a home in every sort of environment on land and in fresh or sea water, often in huge numbers.

Arthropod means 'joint-limbed' in Greek, and almost all arthropods have jointed limbs which, together with their tough body shell are called an exoskeleton. All the muscles and body organs of an arthropod are protected inside the exoskeleton.

Arthur, is a legendary British hero whose story has been told by many writers. The most famous version is the *Morte d'Arthur* by Sir Thomas Malory (1485). Arthur was a king with a court of gallant knights including Sir Lancelot and Sir Gawain. They were known as the Knights of the Round Table, and were engaged in a search for the Holy Grail, the cup supposed to have been used by Jesus at the Last Supper. Other stories of Arthurian legend tell of the love affair between Arthur's queen, Guinevere, and Sir Lancelot; how Arthur came to the throne at Camelot because he was the only man who could pull the sword Excalibur out of a rock; and how he was instructed by the magician Merlin. There are many similar stories throughout Europe.

There may have been a real King Arthur, a leader of the ancient Britons about AD 500 who fought against the invading Saxons and had his court in Somerset. *See also* Camelot.

Art Nouveau was the distinctive decorative style of the period 1890–1910. Its chief characteristic was a flowing line, based on plant forms and it was influenced by Japanese prints. Art Nouveau is an element in the painting of the period, notably in Vienna, but it is primarily associated with the design of useful objects like jewellery, cutlery and

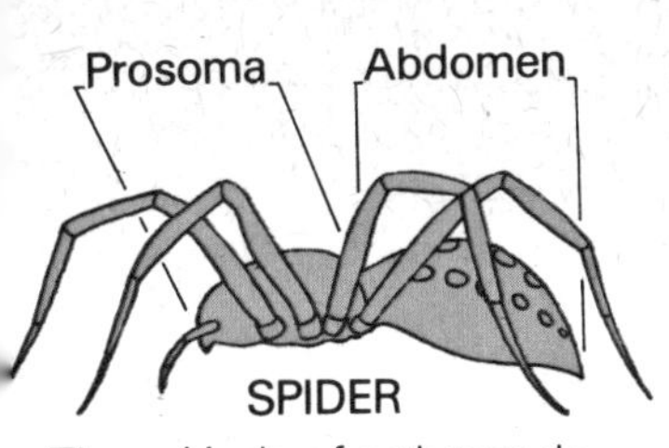

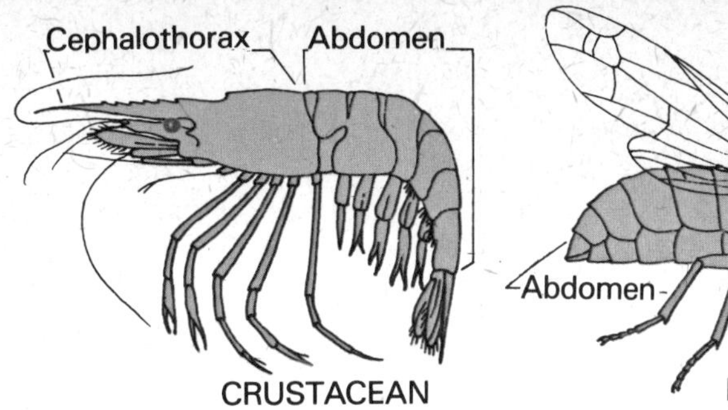

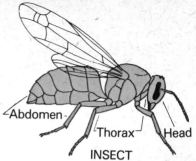

Three kinds of arthropods.

china, the coloured glass lamps of Tiffany in New York, or the furniture of the Scottish architect Charles Rennie Mackintosh.

Asbestos is the name for a number of minerals. They are fibrous, which means that they are made up of long strands known as fibres. Chrysotile is the most commonly used asbestos. It is mined in Canada, southern Africa and USSR. An asbestos mine in Quebec, Canada, is over 1.6 km (1 mile) across and nearly as deep.

Asbestos does not burn. It is also a good insulator, which means that heat and electricity cannot pass through it very easily. For these reasons it is used in houses, factories and clothes to insulate and protect them from fire, heat and electricity. It can be dangerous to breathe in asbestos dust, and people who work with it wear masks.

Ascension Island is a small volcanic island in the South Atlantic. Area 90 sq km (35 sq miles). It is ruled by Britain as part of the colony of St Helena, and there is one tiny settlement, in Georgetown, with a refuelling base for ships and aircraft. Some vegetables grow and a few sheep graze among the rocks.

Asgard, in Norse (Scandinavian) myth, is the home of the gods. People lived in Midgard, the Earth, surrounded by the ocean. Asgard was reached from Midgard by a rainbow bridge, Bifröst. Asgard, a gloomy, solemn place, was doomed to destruction, for the Giants, the forces of evil, would triumph over it in the end. Valhalla, the 'heaven' to which brave heroes went after their death, was a hall in Asgard.

Ash trees and shrubs are a group of 70 or so deciduous species found mainly in Europe, Asia, Java and North America. Clusters of small flowers appear in spring, and these develop into fruits which have the appearance of dangling keys. Some familiar species are the common ash of Europe, North Africa and western Asia, the white ash of North America and the desert ash of Australia.

Leaves, buds, flowers and fruits of the ash tree.

Ashton, Sir Frederick (1904–), is a British dancer and choreographer, composer of the steps and dances in a ballet. He became chief choreographer of Sadler's Wells (later the Royal Ballet) in 1935. From 1963 to 1970 he was director of the company. Ashton was among those responsible for the high reputation of British ballet in recent years. Witty, elegant and versatile, he was a classicist at heart even in such thoroughly modern works as *Enigma Variations* (music by Elgar; 1968). As a dancer he had great success in character parts, for example, in the film *Tales of Beatrix Potter* (1971), which he also choreographed.

Ashurbanipal (died circa 630 BC), was the last great king of Assyria. He came to the throne in 668 BC, and during his reign the Assyrian empire reached its highest level in art, architecture, literature and science. He is best known as the builder of the palace and library at Nineveh.

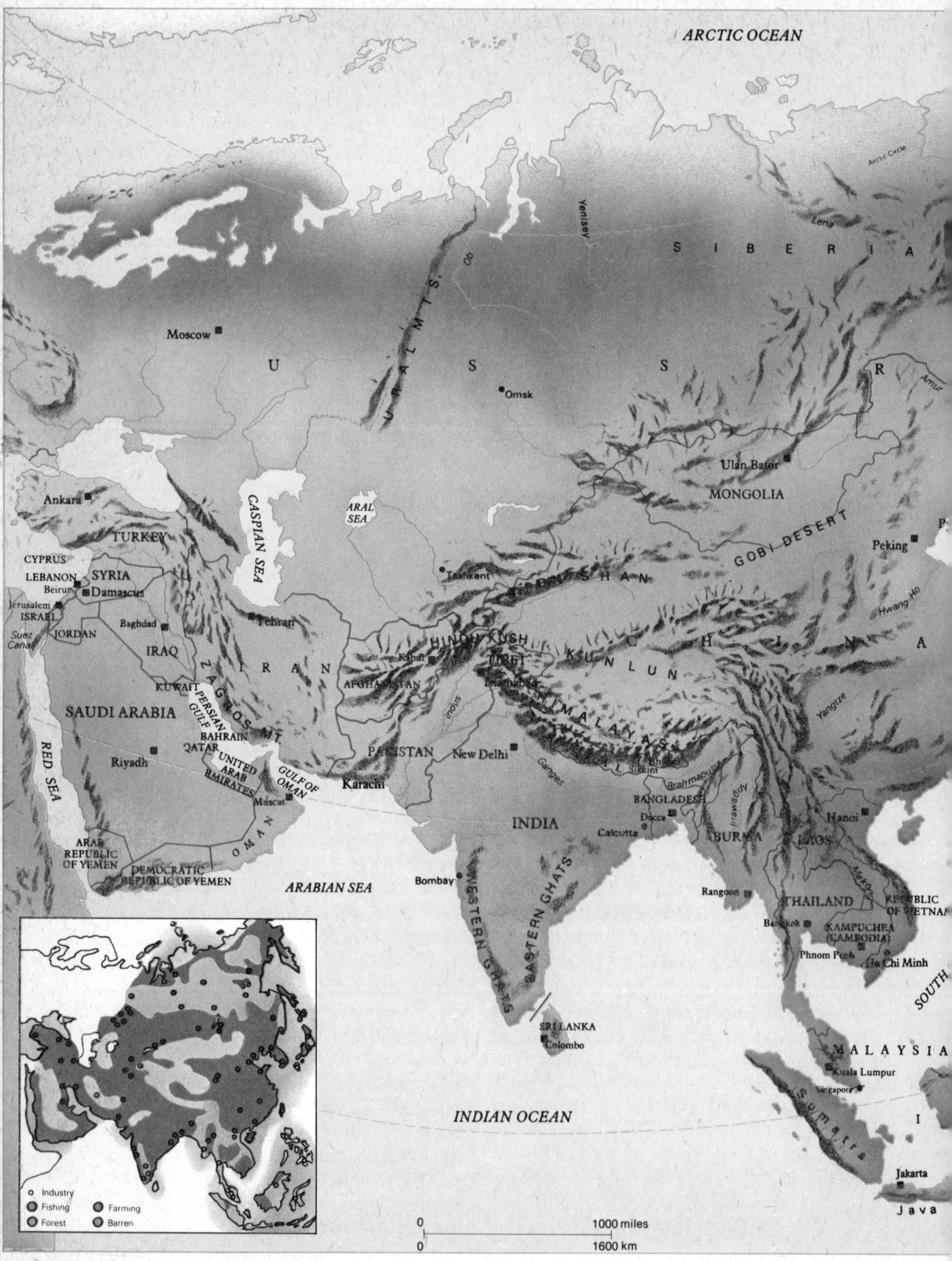
ARCTIC OCEAN
Arctic Circle
Lena
Yenisey
Ob
S I B E R I A
URAL MTS.
Moscow
U S S R
Omsk
Amur
Ulan Bator
MONGOLIA
GOBI DESERT
Peking
Hwang Ho
Ankara
CASPIAN SEA
ARAL SEA
TURKEY
CYPRUS
LEBANON
SYRIA
Beirut
Damascus
Jerusalem
ISRAEL
JORDAN
Suez Canal
Baghdad
IRAQ
Tehran
Tashkent
I R A N
KUWAIT
ZAGROS MT.
PERSIAN GULF
BAHRAIN
QATAR
SAUDI ARABIA
Riyadh
UNITED ARAB EMIRATES
GULF OF OMAN
Muscat
OMAN
RED SEA
ARAB REPUBLIC OF YEMEN
DEMOCRATIC REPUBLIC OF YEMEN
ARABIAN SEA
Kabul
AFGHANISTAN
HINDU KUSH
Islamabad
Indus
PAKISTAN
Karachi
New Delhi
Ganges
TIBET
K U N L U N
C H I N A
Yangtze
HIMALAYAS
Sikkim
Bhutan
Brahmaputra
BANGLADESH
Dacca
Calcutta
INDIA
Bombay
WESTERN GHATS
EASTERN GHATS
SRI LANKA
Colombo
Irrawaddy
BURMA
Rangoon
Hanoi
LAOS
Mekong
THAILAND
Bangkok
KAMPUCHEA (CAMBODIA)
Phnom Penh
Ho Chi Minh
MALAYSIA
Kuala Lumpur
Singapore
Sumatra
Jakarta
Java
INDIAN OCEAN
Industry
Fishing
Forest
Farming
Barren
0
1000 miles
0
1600 km

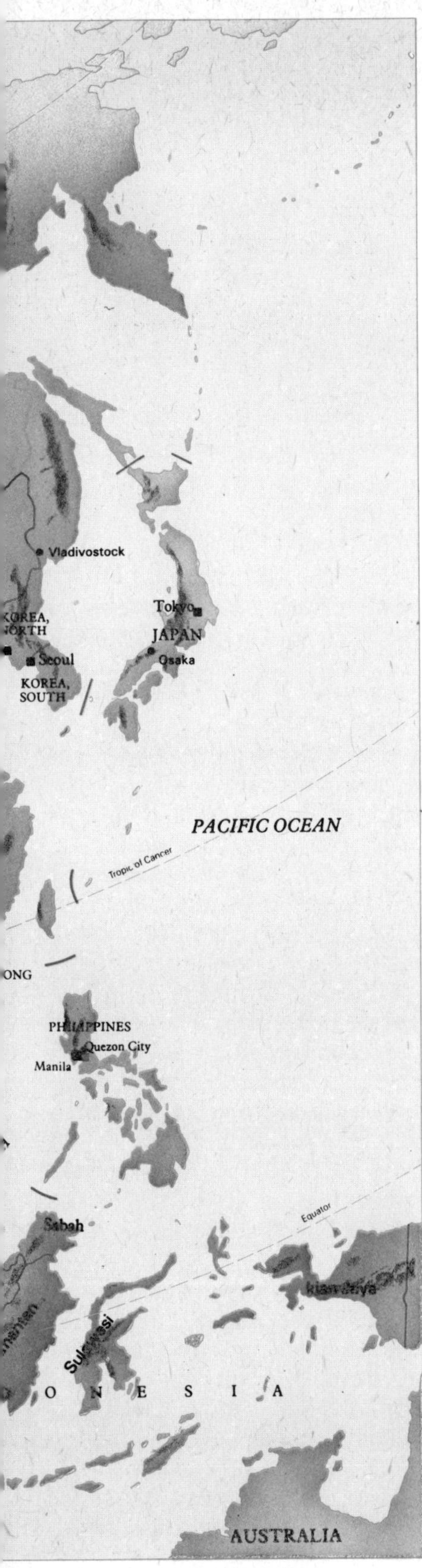

Asia is the world's largest continent, forming nearly one-third of the Earth's total land surface: area about 44 000 000 sq km (16 000 000 sq miles). It is divided from Europe by the Ural Mountains and from Africa by the Red Sea and Suez Canal.

History Some of mankind's earliest civilizations developed in Asia, in the south-western region known as Mesopotamia. Eastern Asia has one of the oldest continuous civilizations, that of China, which has existed for 3500 years. All of the great religions had their origins in Asia – Hinduism, Buddhism, Judaism, Christianity, Islam—as well as Shinto and the great ethical systems of Taoism and Confucianism.

Asia's history and peoples are described in more detail under individual countries as the regions do not have a common past – they are united by little except the mass of the continent itself.

Land The geographical make-up of Asia is also very complex, but the continent can be divided into six major regions, marked off by mountain ranges: northern, central, eastern, south-western, southern, and south-eastern Asia.

Northern Asia, the region called Siberia, extends across the north of the continent from the Ural Mountains in the west to the Pacific Ocean in the east. Its most northerly belt lies within the Arctic Circle. The Arctic's treeless plains, the tundra, are ice-bound except during the short summer period. South of the tundra are broad belts of steppes (steep grassland) and woodland. They are bounded by the Tien Shan and other mountain ranges.

Central Asia is a wild plateau region bounded on the north by the Tien Shan mountains, and on the south by the Himalayas. Much of it consists of grassland, generally sparse, but it also has deserts: the largest are the Takla Makan and the Gobi.

Eastern Asia, a region of plateaux and lowland plains, has a long coastline on the Pacific Ocean. A chain of islands stretching southwards from the Kamcharka Peninsula include the islands that make up Japan and the island of Taiwan.

South-western Asia includes the Caucasus Mountains and the lowlands bordering the Caspian Sea, as well as Afghanistan and the Middle East. The Middle East, the region where Asia, Europe and Africa meet, consists largely of two peninsulas – Anatolia and Arabia.

Southern Asia, a huge triangular peninsula, is sometimes called the Indian sub-continent. Its northern boundary is marked by the Hindu Kush and Karakoram mountain ranges and the Himalayas. Between the Hindu Kush and Karakoram are the Pamir Mountains; their central peaks are known as the Pamir Knot.

To the south of the great mountains are two major geographical regions: a wide belt of plains crossed by rivers that have their sources in the mountains, and the Deccan plateau, occupying the greater part of central and southern India.

South-eastern Asia comprises Burma, the Indo-China Peninsula and its extension the Malay Peninsula, and the large number of islands that were once known to navigators as the East Indies. The islands belong mainly to Indonesia, the Philippines and Malaysia; they also include the tiny but rich island-country of Singapore.

Asia is so large that its various regions have almost every type of climate. The dominating influences, apart from latitude, are the oceans on the east and the south, and the vast distances separating the seas of the interior regions. Central Asia, removed from moisture-laden ocean winds and moderating influences of ocean currents, is dry and has extreme variations of temperature seasonally.

Eastern, south-eastern, and southern Asia are subject to the monsoons, winds that change direction with the seasons. Most of these regions have hot, wet summers, and cool, dry winters. In south-western Asia, in contrast, summers are hot and dry. Winters are sometimes very cold, and have rain and snow.

A stilt house in Thailand.

Tin mining in Malaysia. The tin is being dredged up from the river bed.

In Siberia, the weather is seldom warm, and the winters are cold and icy. The higher regions of central Asia are also cold; because they are dry, they have little vegetation.

Plants and animals The continent has extremely varied vegetation, much of it lying in distinct belts. The northernmost belt, in the Arctic coastal region, is tundra; further south is the taiga, the immense coniferous forests of Siberia, and further south again are the grass covered steppes and the deserts – hot in the west (with scattered oases where palms, citrus fruits, and cereals grow), often cold in the east. The monsoon lands are fertile in the river valleys, and have tropical rain forests, where palms, rubber trees, and such valuable hardwood trees as teak are found.

Polar bears and sea-living animals such as seals and walruses are among the sparse wildlife of the Arctic regions. Reindeer, foxes, and a diminishing number of wolves live seasonally on the tundra; the best-known animal is the moss-eating lemming. Wolves live also in the taiga, as do brown bears, lynxes, and elks. Central and south-western Asia are relatively poor in animals;

one of the best-known and most useful animals in these regions is the camel, and central Asia is the home of the wild horse, Przewalski's horse. The south and southeast has rich wildlife, including monkeys, apes, elephants, leopards, cheetahs, jackals, and many kinds of snakes. Tigers and yaks were once common, but now few of them are seen. The giant panda, which lives in the Chinese uplands, has always been a rare animal.

Economy The continent is rich in natural resources. Only a few countries – Bangladesh, Nepal, Bhutan, Laos – are without major mineral deposits, though in many places resources have yet to be fully exploited.

Asia has most of the world's petroleum – in the countries around the Persian Gulf, and in the USSR, China, Indonesia, and elsewhere. Siberia is believed to have about half of the world's coal, and is also rich in natural gas. Uranium, another source of energy, is found in many countries. India, Pakistan, China, and the USSR are among the countries whose rivers have vast hydro-electric potential.

Almost all the major industrial metals are found in Asia. The largest deposits include iron, tin, antimony, manganese, chromium, lead, and tungsten.

Only relatively few Asian countries are able to grow enough food for their people. Partly, this results from the climate – the continent suffers from both drought and floods – and partly from outmoded farming methods and shortage of land suitable for cultivation. But India and some other countries have greatly increased food production by co-operative work, mechanization, and the use of improved seeds.

Exports from Asia to other parts of the world still consist mainly of primary products – raw materials and agricultural goods. But manufacturing industry is increasing in some parts of the continent. The most highly-developed industrial countries are the USSR, which has its own raw materials as well as its own sources of energy, and Japan, which has to import most of the industrial materials it needs. Taiwan, Singapore, North and South Korea, and Hong Kong have gained a recognized place in light industry. India has made major technological

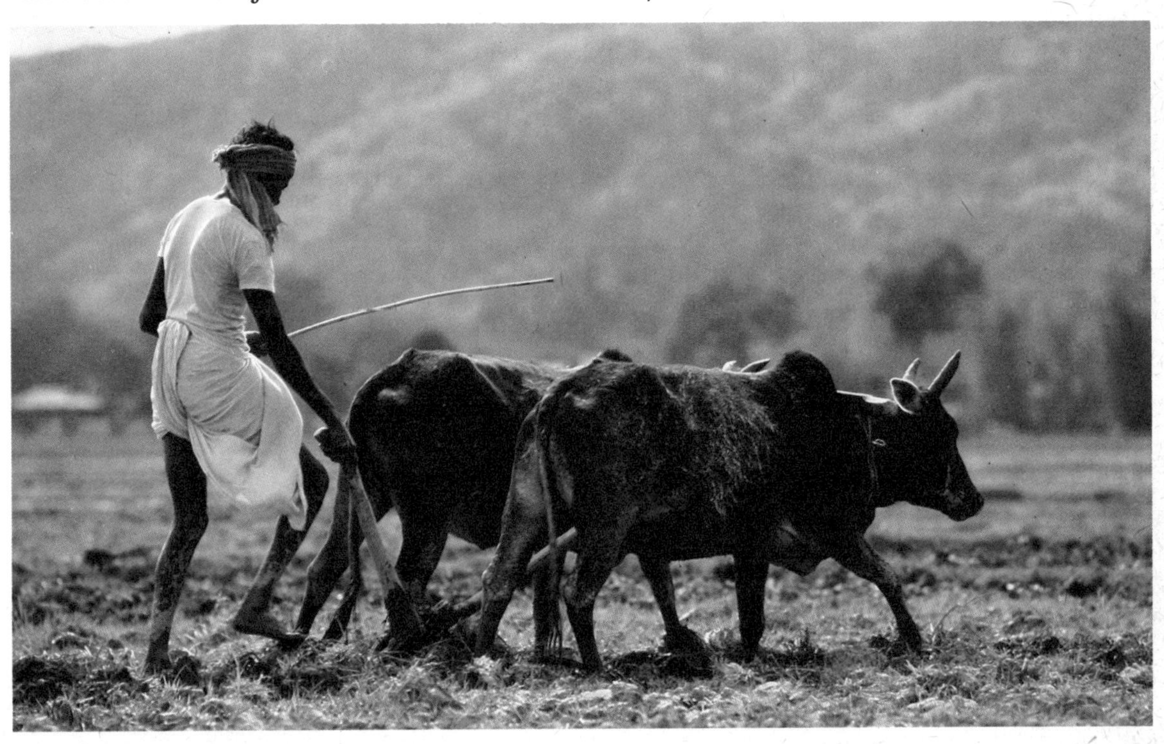

A farmer ploughing in the Brahmaputra River valley.

and industrial advances; its metallurgical, engineering, and chemical industries rival such long-standing industries as the manufacture of textiles. China, too, has developed its manufacturing capacity, heavy industry being based on the mineral wealth of the north-east. More detail is given under individual countries.

Asoka (died 232 BC), Emperor of India, was the grandson of Chandragupta, who founded the Maurya dynasty. He came to the throne about 272 BC. His empire covered all northern and central India and also included Afghanistan. Horrified at the cruelties of war, he became a Buddhist and attempted to rule his empire in accordance with Buddhist principles. He had the edicts of the new religion carved on rocks and pillars in many parts of India. *See also* Buddhism.

Assembly line is a system used for putting together, or assembling, goods such as cars. At one time, a car would be assembled by a small group of workers. They would move around, fitting all the pieces of a car together. This method is still used for some expensive cars.

Most cars are now assembled whilst they are moved along a line of workers. Each worker stays in the same place and fits a particular piece on to each car. At the end of the assembly line, the finished car is tested and then sent out of the factory.

Assyrian empire was an ancient kingdom in northern Mesopotamia, centred on the Upper Tigris river. The Assyrians arrived in the region towards the end of the 3rd millennium BC. Between about 1900 and 1700 BC the kingdom expanded, but then declined in importance. It grew powerful again under Tiglathpileser I who conquered Babylon. His successors brought Syria, Palestine, Babylonia and Persia under Assyrian control. By the end of the 7th century BC, however, the Medes and Babylonians had destroyed the Assyrian empire. Modern archaeology has revealed the splendours of the civilization created by this warlike race.

Asteroids are heavenly bodies thought to be pieces of the original material from which the planets were formed. They are also called planetoids. Thousands have been recorded, although it is thought that there are hundreds of thousands of asteroids. Most of them have orbits which lie in a belt between Mars and Jupiter. The largest asteroid is Ceres, which is over 1000 km (620 miles) in diameter. Some are only a few hundred metres in diameter. Some are made of carbon compounds and others are made of silicon compounds.

The British astronomer Sir William Herschel gave asteroids their name because they look star-like (aster meaning 'star').

Astrology is the story of how the stars and planets are supposed to affect people on Earth.

An astrologer divides up an area of the sky, known as the zodiac, into twelve parts. These parts of the sky are known as signs of the zodiac and are named after groups of stars within them. They are: Aries (the ram), Taurus (bull), Gemini (twins), Cancer (crab), Leo (lion), Virgo (virgin), Libra (scales), Scorpio (scorpion), Sagittarius (archer), Capricorn (goat), Aquarius (watercarrier), and Pisces (fish).

A chart known as a horoscope is drawn up which shows the positions of the Sun, Moon and planets in the zodiac at the moment of a person's birth. From this, the astrologer attempts to predict that person's character and future. Most scientists consider this to be of little or no value, unlike the true science of astronomy, in which knowledge is gained through observation, measurement and so on. The distinction between the two studies is quite a recent one and famous astronomers, such as Kepler, also worked as court astrologers.

Astronaut is somebody who travels in space. The first astronaut was the Russian, Yuri Gagarin. His spacecraft orbited the Earth in 1961. Since then there have been many astronauts. For example, the American Apollo programme had 33 astronauts. These included Neil Armstrong and Edwin Aldrin, the first people to walk on the Moon, on 21 July 1969. The first female astronaut was the Russian, Valentina Tereshkova. Astronauts can now work in space for months.

Astronauts have to go on extensive training programmes before they can travel in space. They must become used to different conditions, such as weightlessness. Away from the Earth, there is no gravity to hold anything down or give it weight. Astronauts must practise eating, drinking and walking while they are floating around, weightless.

Astronomical unit is the unit used for measuring distances in the Solar System. An astronomical unit (au) is just under 150 million km (93 million miles). This is the average distance of the Earth from the Sun.

The average distances of the planets from the Sun are: Mercury 0.4 au, Venus 0.7 au, Earth 1 au, Mars 1.5 au, Jupiter 5.2 au, Saturn 9.5 au, Uranus 19 au, Neptune 30 au, and Pluto 39 au.

Other units, light years and parsecs, are used to measure distances outside the Solar System.

Astronomy is the study of the sky or heavens. It is the oldest science. For thousands of years people have looked at the stars and planets. Many ancient astronomers recorded their positions in the sky and the ways in which they moved. These star charts showed the stars arranged in groups known as constellations. From these observations they tried to find answers to their questions about their universe.

Astronomers today have the same aims. With modern telescopes and other equipment they can probe the depths of space. They can send telescopes up above the Earth's atmosphere for a clearer view of parts of the universe. They can even send spacecraft to land on or pass close to other planets.

These instruments have shown space objects unknown to ancient astronomers, such as nebulae, galaxies, pulsars and quasars. They have transformed our ideas about the universe.

Atahualpa (1500–1533), the last Inca king of Peru, came to the throne after defeating his half-brother, who also claimed the kingdom. In 1532 at a meeting with Pizarro, the Spanish conquistador, Atahualpa was arrested and imprisoned for refusing to be converted to Christianity, and his followers were massacred. Atahualpa himself was killed on Pizarro's orders in the following year.

Athena, or Athene, was one of the greatest goddesses of ancient Greece and the protector of Athens. She is said to have emerged, fully armed, from the head of her father Zeus, and she is a powerful, serious figure, combining strength and wisdom. Apart from city life and politics, she was connected with farming and crafts such as spinning and weaving.

The Solar System, showing the positions of the nine planets. Astronomers estimate that our Sun is just one of millions of stars in the galaxy, and that there may be 10 000 million galaxies in the Universe.

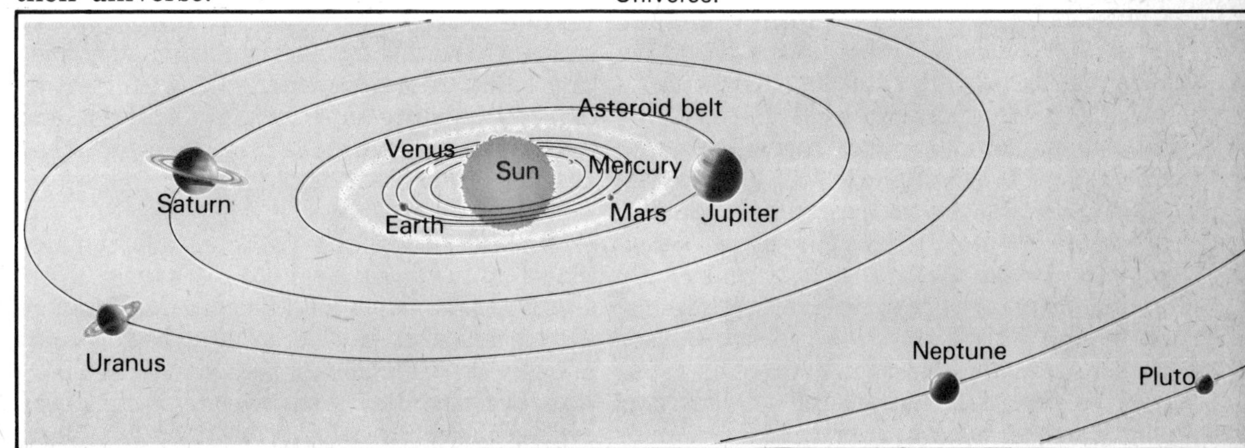

Artists pictured her as a solemn figure in a long robe, often with helmet and shield.

The Romans identified Athena with Minerva, goddess of wisdom, but Minerva is a much less important figure.

Athens is the capital of Greece. Modern Athens is a bustling place with a bad traffic problem. Over 2000 years ago, it was the birthplace of European civilization, when it was the leading state in Greece and home of the first Western philosophers, writers and artists. The ruins of their ancient buildings are still one of Athens' greatest attractions.

Atlantic Ocean is the second largest ocean, lying between Europe and Africa on the east, and North and South America on the west. Area 86 500 000 sq km (33 400 000 sq miles). In places it is nearly 10 000 m (132 800 ft) deep; elsewhere mountain ridges rise to the surface to create islands, like the Azores. The Atlantic was first crossed by the Vikings, travelling via Iceland, but the most important, direct crossing was made by Christopher Columbus in 1492.

Atlas, in ancient Greek myth, was one of the Titans, a race of supernatural creatures who were overthrown by Zeus and the gods of Olympus. For his part in this war Atlas was condemned by Zeus to stand at the edge of the world and carry the sky on his shoulders.

Early European map-makers used to put a picture of Atlas on their works, and that was how his name came to mean a book of maps.

Atlas Mountains are a mountain range in North Africa, stretching about 2500 km (1550 miles) through Morocco, Algeria and Tunisia. They run roughly parallel with the coast, and cover a very broad area, including high plateaus. The highest peaks are in the central, High Atlas, where they rise over 4000 m (13 000 ft) and have permanent snowcaps. Coastal parts of the Tell Atlas are very fertile, and elsewhere there are rich mineral deposits.

Atmosphere is the gas around a planet. It is held there by gravity. The atmosphere near the surface of the Earth is composed of air. Air contains oxygen, nitrogen and small amounts of other gases. The Earth is the only planet in the Solar System which has a lot of oxygen in its atmosphere. Farther away from the Earth the atmosphere is no longer air. The Earth's atmosphere is roughly 700 km (435 miles) high. It has different layers. Most of the air is in the first layer, the troposphere. This is 10 km (6.2 miles) high.

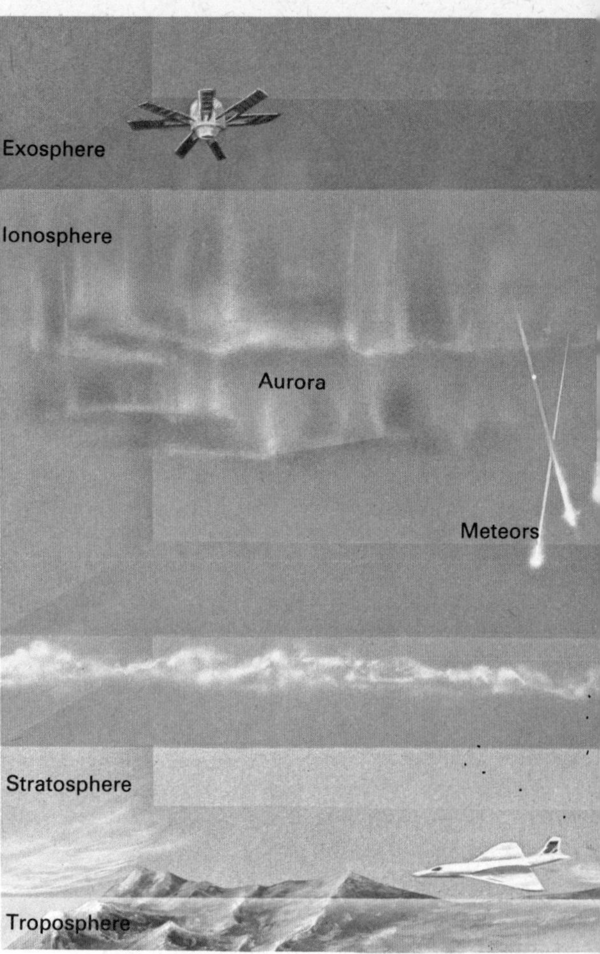

Diagram of the Earth's atmosphere showing the different layers. Each layer has its own characteristics.

Atoll is a type of coral reef – that is, a reef built up from the skeletons of small marine creatures. The atoll is a coral reef shaped like a ring or horseshoe, enclosing a lagoon, and is found in the tropical waters of the western and central Pacific Ocean. It is often fertile, thanks to the wind and tides depositing soil and carrying seeds.

Various theories have been put forward to explain the shape of atolls. The great naturalist Charles Darwin first suggested the commonly held theory that each atoll developed as a reef surrounding an island which later submerged. However, no explanation seems to fit all cases.

Atom is the smallest part of an element. An atom is so small that 100 million of them side by side would only measure 1 cm (0.4 in). Everything is made of atoms. The centre of an atom is called the nucleus. This contains particles called protons and neutrons. Other particles called electrons move around the nucleus in orbits. Protons have a positive charge, neutrons have no charge and electrons have a negative charge. Usually, an atom always has an equal number of protons and electrons. This means that it has no charge, for the positive and negative electrons cancel each other out.

Neutrons and protons are very much heavier than electrons. So, the mass of an atom is measured by the mass of its nucleus.

Each element has a different atom with a different mass. The simplest and lightest atom is that of hydrogen. Its nucleus consists of a proton, and one electron orbits it. Most of an atom is empty space. If the nucleus of a hydrogen atom were as big as a marble, the electron would be 200 m (656 ft) away.

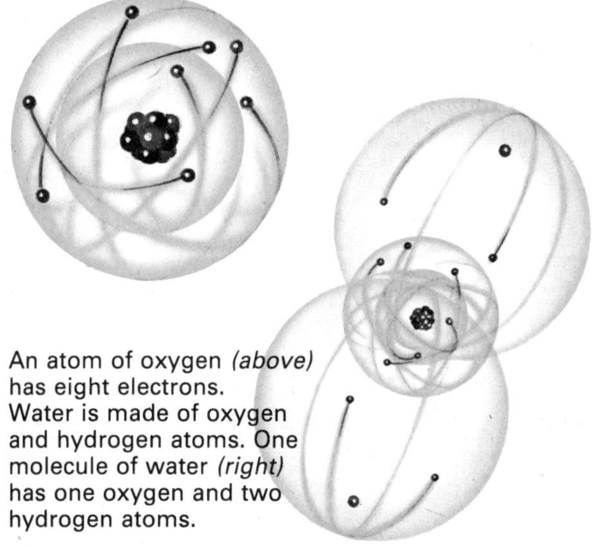

An atom of oxygen *(above)* has eight electrons. Water is made of oxygen and hydrogen atoms. One molecule of water *(right)* has one oxygen and two hydrogen atoms.

Atom bomb is a very powerful weapon made from either of the radioactive substances uranium or plutonium. The bomb's force, or energy, comes from the breaking, or fission, of the uranium or plutonium nuclei.

The atom bombs were exploded in 1945 by the Allied Forces. They were dropped on the cities of Hiroshima and Nagasaki in Japan. Many more have been exploded in deserted places for tests.

The explosion of an atom bomb looks like a huge, mushroom-shaped ball of fire. The explosion, fires, and radiation destroy a large area and can kill huge numbers of people. Dangerous radioactive dust from atom bombs can spread over a wide area and may fall to the ground even years after the explosion. This is called fallout. *See also* Nuclear fission.

Atomic number is the number of protons in the atomic nucleus of a particular element. Each element has a different atomic number from every other element. The simplest element, hydrogen, has an atomic number of 1. This means it has one proton in its nucleus. The number of protons and electrons in an atom are the same. So, a hydrogen atom also has one electron. Helium has an atomic number of 2. This means that it has two protons and two electrons.

Changing the number of protons in a nucleus changes the atomic number of the atom. This makes it an atom of a different element. It is known as transmutation and can be done in nuclear reactors.

Elements are grouped by their atomic number in a table known as the periodic table.

Attila (circa 406–453), king of the Huns, overran much of central Europe with his armies and threatened both the Eastern and Western Roman Empires. In 451 he turned westwards and invaded Gaul, reaching Orléans. He was, however, decisively beaten by a combined Roman and Visigothic army at Châlons-sur-Marne. In 452 he devastated northern Italy and was planning another invasion of that country when he died suddenly. After his death his empire collapsed.

Attlee, Clement Richard, 1st Earl (1883–1967), British statesman, was Prime Minister of the first Labour government to have a majority in Parliament. During the Second World War he was Deputy Prime Minister in Winston Churchill's coalition government, becoming Prime Minister in 1945 after the Labour Party's victory in the general election. His government nationalized the major industries and introduced a sweeping programme of social reform, including the creation of the National Health Service. During his term of office India, Pakistan and Sri Lanka were granted independence.

Auden, Wystan Hugh (1907–1973), was an English poet. He was the leading member of a group of gifted young writers with strong socialist sympathies in the 1930s. In 1939 he moved to the United States and became a US citizen, though he returned to England shortly before his death. His political sympathies changed, and he returned to Christianity in the 1940s.

His first book, *Poems*, was published in 1930, and many more followed, including drama in co-operation with Christopher Isherwood, criticism, libretti (texts) for operas, etc. He was the master of many forms of poetry and is renowned for his extraordinary technical ability.

Colourful aurora seen in the southern hemisphere.

August is the eighth month of the year in the modern calendar, and lasts for 31 days. It is named in honour of the Roman Emperor Augustus.

Augustine, Saint (354–430), was one of the greatest of the early fathers of the Christian Church. He was born in North Africa, showed great ability as a child, and was educated to be a teacher. He became a Christian at 37, was ordained priest and in 395 became bishop of Hippo.

Augustine was a philosopher and a great writer as well as a theologian. His most famous works are *The City of God*, one of the first and greatest works of Christian theology, and *Confessions*, a frank and searching autobiography.

Augustus, Gaius Julius Caesar Octavianus (63 BC–AD 14), was the first Roman Emperor. After the death of Julius Caesar, who had adopted him as his son, Augustus ruled Rome in a triumvirate (government headed by three people) with Mark Antony and Lepidus. He and Antony defeated Brutus and Cassius, who had plotted Caesar's death, at Philippi. However, the two men subsequently came into conflict, and Augustus defeated Antony at Actium in 31 BC, thus becoming master of the Roman world. He received the title of 'Augustus' and was given wide powers of government. His reign was notable for administrative reforms, and he brought stability and prosperity to his country.

Aurora is a beautiful pattern of light that can sometimes be seen in the sky. It looks like brilliantly coloured streamers or bands. Particles from the Sun hitting the Earth's atmosphere cause the aurora. These particles are attracted by the Earth's magnetic field. Therefore, an aurora usually occurs near the Earth's magnetic poles. An aurora near the north magnetic pole is called aurora borealis, or the northern lights. An aurora near the south magnetic pole is known as aurora australis or the southern lights.

Because of their strong magnetic properties, auroras affect radio and television signals.

Austen, Jane (1775–1817), was an English novelist. The quiet daughter of a country parson, she was still almost unknown when she died at 41. She is now recognized as one of the greatest English novelists. She knew little of the world and never met another author. Her novels were limited in range – concerning the domestic affairs of people of her own class and background. But besides her sharp wit, she had an extraordinary insight into human nature, and the characters in her fiction seem completely 'real'. Her completed novels are *Sense and Sensibility* (1811), *Pride and Prejudice* (1813), *Mansfield Park* (1814), *Emma* (1815), *Northanger Abbey* (1818; the manuscript lay in a publisher's desk for several years) and *Persuasion* (1818).

Australasia is a term used to describe the region in the South Pacific including Australia, New Zealand and certain other islands.

Australia is an island country, often regarded as a continent in itself, in the South Pacific. It includes the small island of Tasmania off the south coast. Capital, Canberra; area about 7686000 sq km (2775600 sq miles).

History The country was first inhabited by the Aborigines who reached Australia from southern Asia over 20000 years ago. Abel Tasman, a Dutch navigator, sailed around the southern coast of Australia in 1642; the island of Tasmania and the Tasman Sea are named after him. In 1768 Captain James Cook sailed from England and eventually landed at Botany Bay near Sydney after sailing around New Zealand. He claimed the eastern coastal region for Britain in 1770 and the British government soon established a penal settlement there, where convicts were sent to serve their sentences in very harsh conditions. Free settlers, however, soon began to arrive and exploration gradually opened up the whole continent. The discovery of gold in 1851 in New South Wales attracted many more immigrants but by the late 1850s opportunities for individual prospectors had declined and people turned to the land for employment. The enormous sheep farms and wheatfields of Australia were to become a source of wealth equalling, for some, the riches of the goldfields.

Derelict hulks were used as prisons for convicts deported from England.

Early settlers measuring out a sheep enclosure.

Australia

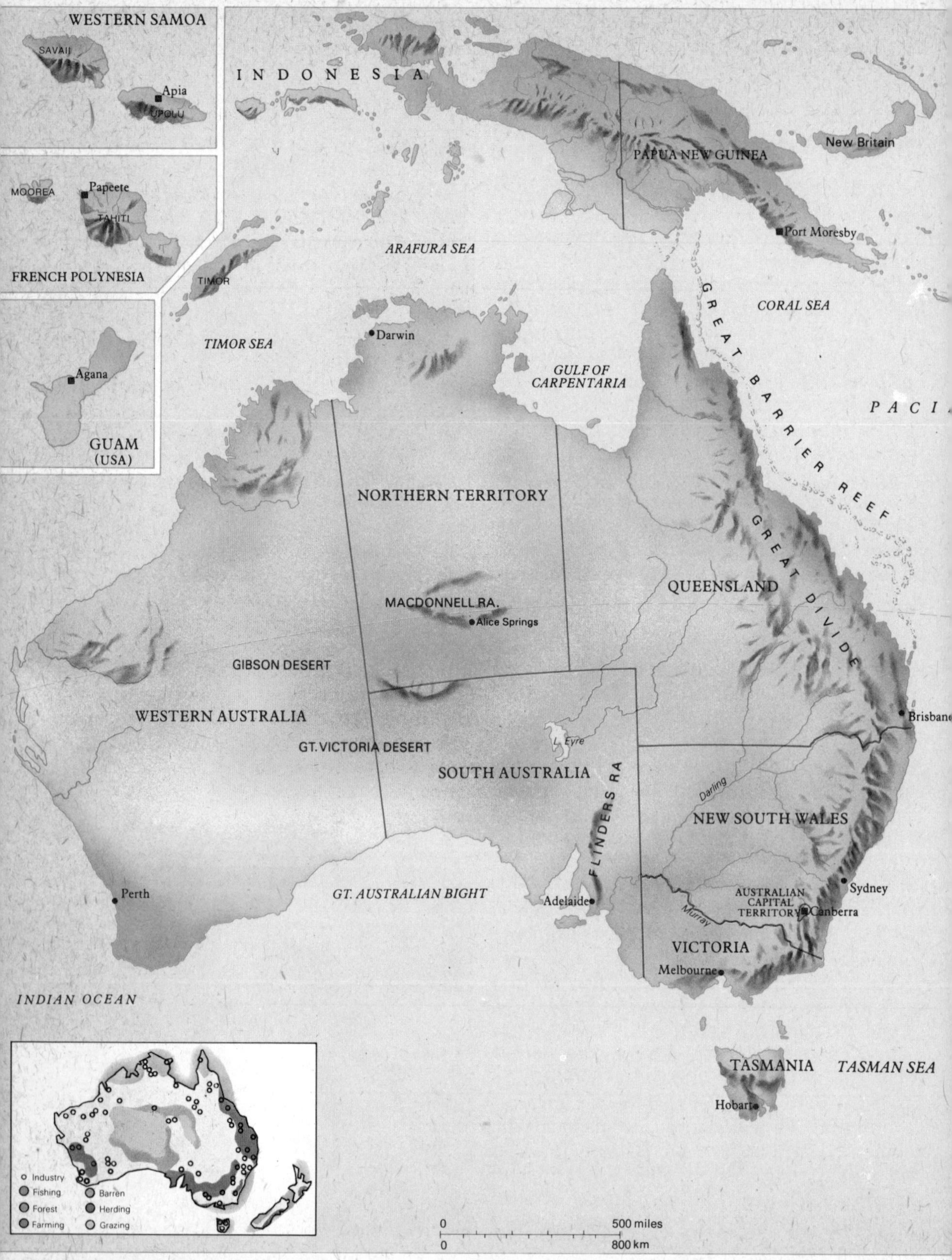
WESTERN SAMOA
SAVAII
Apia
UPOLU
MOOREA
Papeete
TAHITI
FRENCH POLYNESIA
Agana
GUAM
(USA)
INDONESIA
TIMOR
ARAFURA SEA
TIMOR SEA
PAPUA NEW GUINEA
New Britain
Port Moresby
CORAL SEA
GREAT BARRIER REEF
Darwin
GULF OF CARPENTARIA
PACI
NORTHERN TERRITORY
QUEENSLAND
GREAT DIVIDE
MACDONNELL RA.
Alice Springs
GIBSON DESERT
WESTERN AUSTRALIA
GT. VICTORIA DESERT
L. Eyre
SOUTH AUSTRALIA
FLINDERS RA
Brisbane
Darling
NEW SOUTH WALES
Sydney
AUSTRALIAN CAPITAL TERRITORY
Canberra
Murray
Perth
GT. AUSTRALIAN BIGHT
Adelaide
VICTORIA
Melbourne
INDIAN OCEAN
TASMANIA
TASMAN SEA
Hobart
Industry
Fishing
Forest
Farming
Barren
Herding
Grazing
0
500 miles
0
800 km

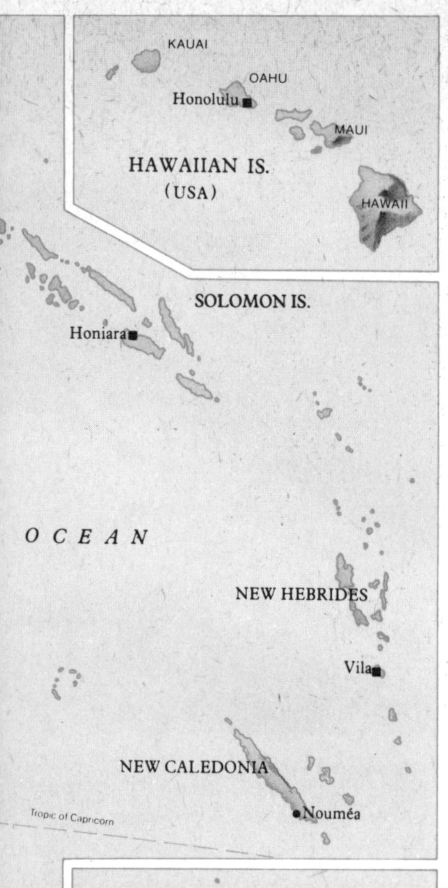

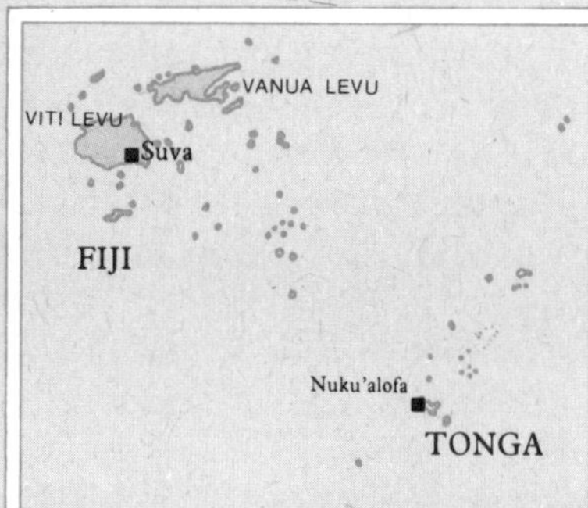

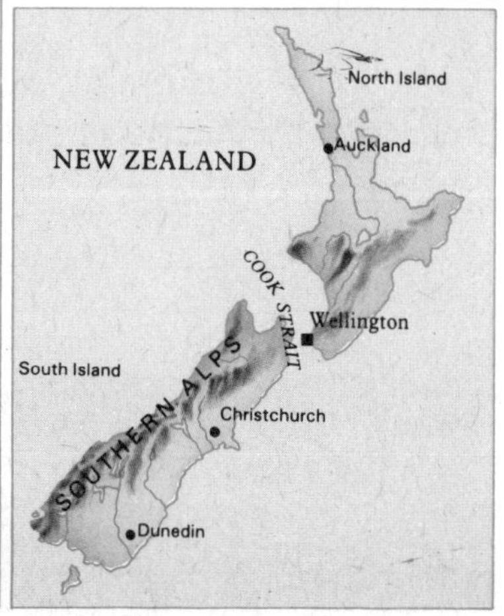

Throughout this period Australia was divided into separate British colonies but it was clear the colonies wished to move towards self-government. During the second half of the 19th century they discussed whether they should join a federation or be independent regions. By 1901 it was agreed that the people of New South Wales, Queensland, South Australia, Tasmania, Victoria and Western Australia would be united in a federal Commonwealth. The new states would run their own internal affairs but would have a federal government based at Canberra, in charge of such things as trade and defence.

Australia played an important part in the First World War, supporting Britain in what was, to Australians, a very distant fight. In 1931 Britain gave Australia the right to decide its own foreign policy; in the Second World War Australia again supported Britain. This time the war affected Australia more closely with 15 000 Australians captured by the Japanese at Singapore. The Japanese also attacked Darwin in 1942.

After the war Australia prospered, developing closer relations with Asian countries and trading with Japan and America.

Land and People The western two-thirds of Australia consist of a huge plain, the West-

Australian and New Zealand troops spearheading the attack on Achi Baba, Gallipoli, in 1915, during the First World War.

ern Plateau. The only high mountains are in the east, and much of the interior is desert or semi-desert. Over 60 per cent of Australia is too dry for farming of any kind, but as Australia is such a huge country this still leaves room for over 130 million sheep and 30 million cattle!

The population of Australia is small – if it was spread out all over the country there would be less than two people per square kilometre (about five per square mile) but in fact huge areas are uninhabited and over 50 per cent of the population live in the five major coastal cities – Adelaide, Brisbane, Melbourne, Perth and Sydney. Australians are mainly of European descent, especially British. The original inhabitants, the Aborigines, form a minority. In the 1870s there were about 300 000 Aborigines in Australia. Now there is only one-third of that number.

In the dry, dusty interior of Australia, known as the 'outback', there are huge sheep and cattle stations wherever there is a source of water. Many of these farms cover several thousand square kilometres. Wool and meat are major exports. Crops like wheat, sugar beet, oats and fruit are grown in the wetter coastal regions and in the south-east corner of Australia. Elsewhere the rainfall is too unreliable.

There are few forests, but Australia is well supplied with minerals including gold, silver, iron, aluminium, copper, lead and zinc. These form a valuable source of raw materials for Australian industries and are also valuable exports. Fuels are in rather short supply apart from coal; however natural gas and oil have been developed in recent years.

States and Territories The Commonwealth of Australia is made up of six states, two mainland territories and several external territories.

Western Australia is the largest of the states with an area of 2 525 500 sq km (975 920 sq miles). The state capital is Perth; nearby Fremantle acts as its port. The population is concentrated in the south-west which has a Mediterranean-type climate and where dairying, fruit growing, timber and tobacco are important. Large areas inland are desert and semi-desert but these barren lands do yield rich mineral wealth.

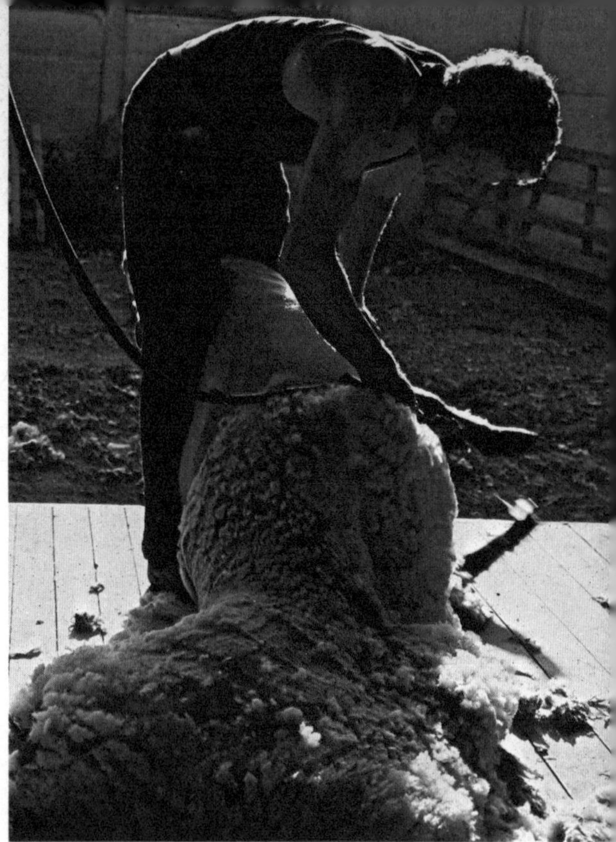

A merino sheep being sheared. The merino is famous for its wool. It carries five times more wool fibres per square centimetre, than any other related breed of sheep.

South Australia's capital is Adelaide. The area of the state is 984 375 sq km (380 070 sq miles). The dry desert land in the north gives way to more fertile regions near the coast where most of the population live. The main products are wheat and wool and wine is also produced.

Queensland has an area of 1 727 200 sq km (786 550 sq miles). The state capital is Brisbane. Queensland's east coast plain has the highest rainfall in Australia. Sheep, sugar and beef are important products of this state which also has copper and coal deposits.

New South Wales has an area of 801 600 sq km (309 433 sq miles). The state capital is Sydney. Sydney is the largest city in Australia and has a fine natural harbour. It is an administrative, commercial and financial centre as well as an important manufacturing city. The coastal belt of New South Wales has dairy farms and banana plantations. Further inland sheep farms and wheat growing are important. Extensive irrigation schemes have greatly increased the amount of fertile land.

Victoria is the smallest mainland state – 227 600 sq km (87 884 sq miles). The capital is Melbourne. The fertile lowlands in the south rise steeply to the Central Highlands and Australian Alps, dropping again to the Murray river basin in the north. Exports include fruit, wool and wheat.

Tasmania (originally called Van Dieman's Land, after Anthony Van Dieman, the Governor-General of the Dutch East Indies), is the island state of Australia, separated from mainland Victoria by Bass Strait. It has an area of 7800 sq km (26 383 sq miles). The capital is Hobart. Launceston is a major town and port in the north, on the river Tamar estuary. Fruit growing, especially apples, is a major industry and the island is also rich in minerals.

Northern Territory became a territory in its own right in 1911, having previously been annexed first to New South Wales and then to South Australia. Its area is 1 346 200 sq km (519 800 sq miles) and the capital and port is Darwin. Desert covers vast areas but there are valuable mineral resources and cattle are reared in the less arid regions. Alice Springs, which is right in the centre of Australia, was the capital of the former state of Central Australia. Now in Northern Territory, it is a small mining town and tourist destination.

Australian Capital Territory is an area within the state of New South Wales containing the capital of Australia, Canberra.

Animals and Plants Australia has many plants, such as the giant eucalyptus and the bottle tree, and many animals, such as the kangaroo, koala, platypus and emu, which are only found in that region. It is generally believed that millions of years ago, all the land masses on earth were joined together and have only gradually drifted apart. The land mass of which Australia was part broke away before the rest, thus preventing later forms of animal and plant life, which evolved in other parts of the world, from reaching Australia. This left Australia's unique animals and plants to flourish undisturbed.

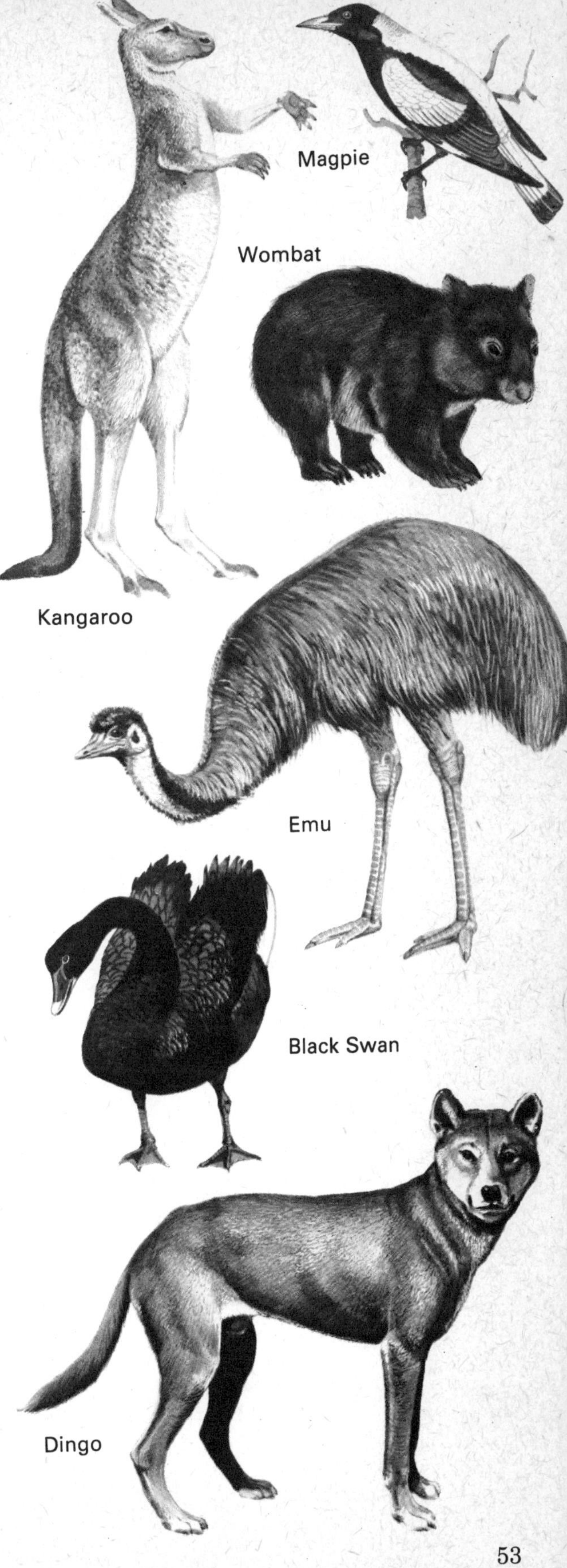

The Australian flag.

Prime Ministers of Australia

Edmund Barton	1901–1903
Alfred Deakin	1903–1904
John Watson	1904
George Reid	1904–1905
Alfred Deakin	1905–1908
Andrew Fisher	1908–1909
Alfred Deakin	1909–1910
Andrew Fisher	1910–1913
Joseph Cook	1913–1914
Andrew Fisher	1914–1915
William Hughes	1915–1923
Stanley Bruce	1923–1929
James Scullin	1929–1931
Joseph Lyons	1931–1939
Sir Earle Grafton Page	1939
Robert Menzies	1939–1941
Arthur Fadden	1941
John Curtin	1941–1945
Francis Forde	1945
Joseph Chifley	1945–1949
Robert Menzies	1949–1965
Harold Holt	1965–1967
John McEwen	1967–1968
John Gorton	1968–1971
William McMahon	1971–1972
Gough Whitlam	1972–1975
Malcolm Fraser	1975–1983
Bob Hawke	1983–

Governors-General of Australia

John Louis, Earl of Hopetoun	1901–1902
Hallam, Baron Tennyson	1902–1904
Henry Stafford, Baron Northcote	1904–1908
William Humble, Earl of Dudley	1908–1911
Thomas, Baron Denman	1911–1914
Sir Ronald Munro-Ferguson	1914–1920
Henry William, Baron Forster of Lepe	1920–1925
John Lawrence, Baron Stonehaven	1925–1931
Sir Isaac Isaacs	1931–1936
Alexander Gore Arkwright, Baron Gowrie	1936–1945
HRH Prince Henry, Duke of Gloucester	1945–1947
Sir William McKell	1947–1953
Sir William Slim	1953–1960
William Shepherd, Viscount Dunrossil	1960–1961
William Philip, Viscount De Lisle	1961–1965
Richard Gardiner, Baron Casey	1965–1969
Sir Paul Hasluck	1969–1974
Sir John Kerr	1974–1977
Sir Zelman Cowen	1977–1982
Sir Ninian Stephen	1982–

Austria is a republic in central Europe. Capital, Vienna; area about 83 800 sq km (32 300 sq miles). Today Austria is a rather small state, though its glorious past, when it was the heart of the Hapsburg empire, can still be sensed, especially in Vienna, with its grand palaces.

History The country was inhabited by Celtic peoples when in 15 BC it became part of the Roman Empire. It remained under Roman rule for 400 years. It was then occupied by Germanic tribes, then Slavs and then Magyars. In 955 the Holy Roman Emperor, Otto I, drove out the Magyars. Austria became part of the Hapsburg Empire in the 13th century and was later increased in size to include Bohemia and Hungary. It began to decline as a great power in the 19th century and, when it became a federal republic in 1919, it had lost most of its territories. Germany took possession of it in 1938, but it became an independent country again in 1955.

Land and People It is a very mountainous, forested country, famous for its splendid scenery. The main river is the Danube, which runs across northern Austria, and there are many lakes, especially in the west and south. Though it has no sea coast, Austria is a popular country for holidays.

The population is mainly Roman Catholic

and German-speaking, but there are many smaller groups such as Slovenes and Croatians.
Economy The Austrian economy is mainly dependent on manufacturing industries as good farming land and minerals, especially fuels, are in short supply. However, hydroelectric stations provide nearly all the power required.

Avocado is an edible fruit, which is pear-shaped and green or black in colour. It grows on avocado trees, which are evergreens found in tropical areas. They grow 7 to 9 m (22 to 30 ft) high, though can reach 18 m (60 ft). The fruit's single large seed is surrounded by soft green flesh.

Axolotl is the larval stage of an amphibian known as the American salamander. The axolotl is remarkable because it never changes into an adult, but reproduces whilst in this larval state. Breeding axolotls only occur in certain places; in other places where American salamanders are found the axolotl turns into an adult salamander before it breeds.

Ayers Rock is the largest single rock in the world, 348 m (1140 ft) high, 6 km (3.7 miles) long and 2.5 km (1.5 miles) wide. It is situated in the Northern Territory of Australia. The Aborigines regarded it as a sacred place, and it is now also a great tourist attraction, famous for the way it changes colour as the Sun's rays strike it from different angles.

Azores are an island group in the Atlantic Ocean. Area about 2300 sq km (890 sq miles). The Azores are a province of Portugal, having first been discovered in the 15th century. They are a popular holiday resort, especially during the European winter when the climate is mild. They produce wine, fruit, especially pineapples, and vegetables, and also some attractive pottery. The people are mainly of Portuguese descent.

Aztecs were a race of American Indian people speaking the Nahuatl language who settled in central Mexico in the 13th century. They eventually created an empire which stretched right across the country. Aztec civilization was notable for its art, the splendid architecture of its vast palaces and temples, and an elaborate religion which demanded human sacrifice. The empire, weakened by internal warfare, was overthrown in the early 16th century by the Spaniards led by Hernan Cortez.

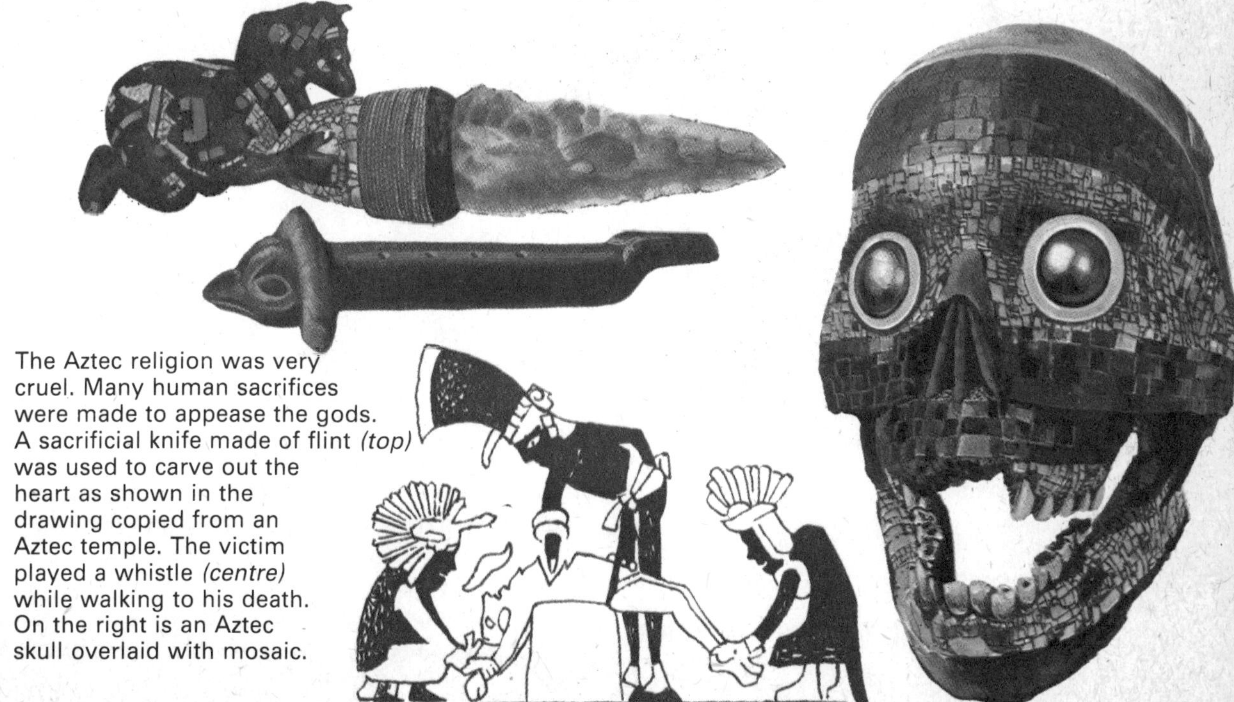

The Aztec religion was very cruel. Many human sacrifices were made to appease the gods. A sacrificial knife made of flint *(top)* was used to carve out the heart as shown in the drawing copied from an Aztec temple. The victim played a whistle *(centre)* while walking to his death. On the right is an Aztec skull overlaid with mosaic.

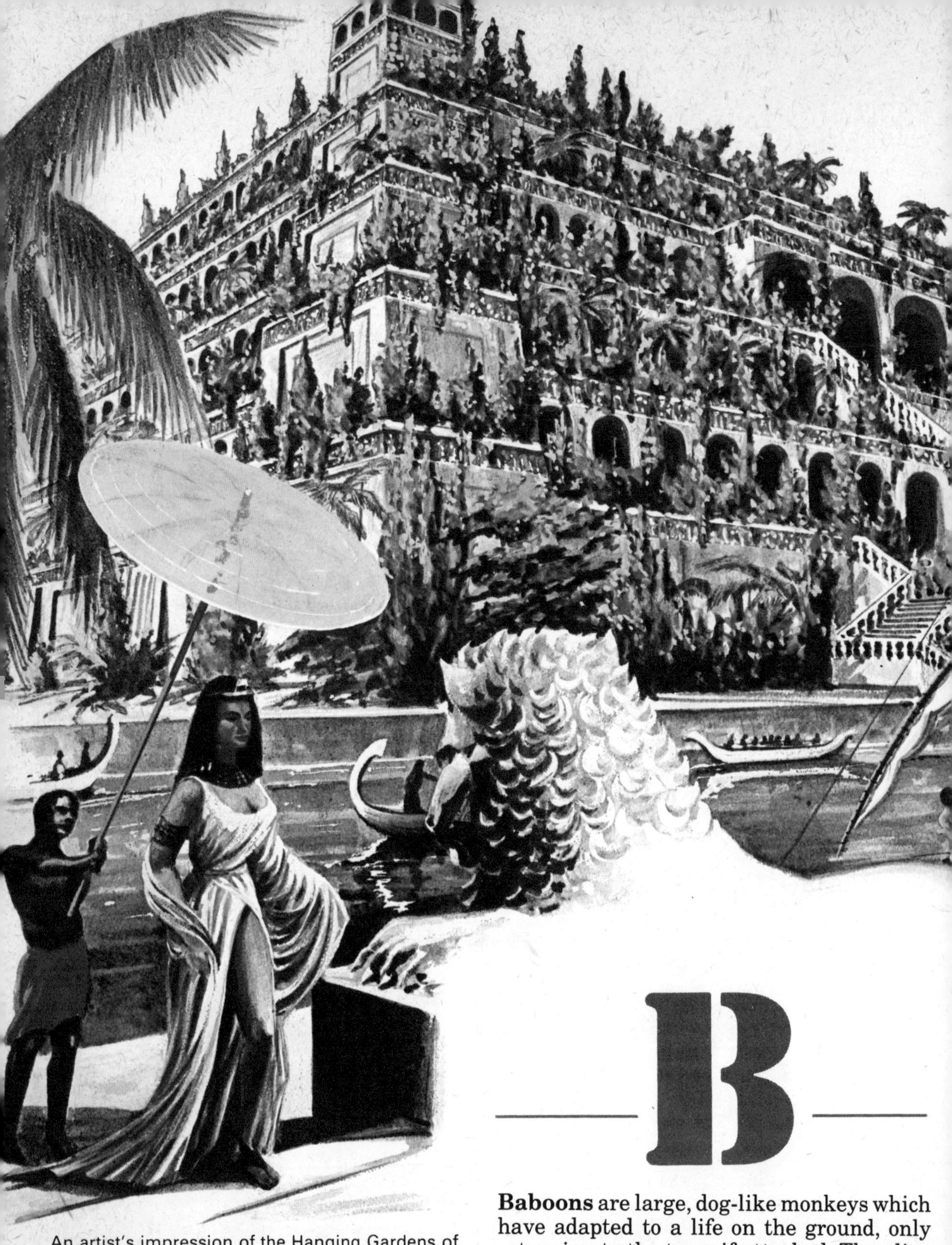

An artist's impression of the Hanging Gardens of Babylon, one of the seven Wonders of the World. Nebuchadnezzar had the gardens built in terraces for his wife who disliked the flatness of Babylon.

B

Baboons are large, dog-like monkeys which have adapted to a life on the ground, only returning to the trees if attacked. They live in open grassland in family groups called troops, ruled by a big male. They are fierce

fighters, and have long canine teeth.

Living in the forests of west Africa are relatives of the baboon, the drill and mandrill. The nose, cheeks and hind regions of the mandrill are brightly coloured red and blue to attract females.

Babylonia was an ancient kingdom in southern Mesopotamia on the lower reaches of the Tigris and Euphrates rivers. Named after its capital city, Babylon, it first became prominent about 2100 BC under the Amorite dynasty, whose most famous king was Hammurabi. It laster came under Assyrian domination, but achieved independence again under Nebuchadnezzar I in the 12th century BC. Babylonia achieved a brief period of splendour during the reign of Nebuchadnezzar II before being absorbed in the Persian Empire.

Bach, Johann Sebastian (1685–1750), was a German composer. The son of an organist, he studied the same instrument and held the post of court musician in Anhalt-Cöthen in 1717, moving to St Thomas' Church, Leipzig, in 1723. He remained there for the rest of his life, and most of his work is sacred music.

Today Bach is regarded as the greatest composer of the Baroque age, though in his own time he had a higher reputation as an organist. Few of his compositions were even printed until after his death. People thought his music old-fashioned – Bach was not attracted to such new forms as the sonata and he thought opera was not for serious musicians. But genius outlives fashion. Bach's reputation began to rise rapidly in the early 19th century as more of his work became widely known. The decisive event was, perhaps, a performance of his St Mathew's Passion conducted by Mendelssohn in Berlin, 1829.

Bach is famous both for his secular music, such as the Brandenburg Concertos, mostly composed at Cöthen, and for religious music, like the Mass in B Minor. The imagination and passion of his music, his versatility and intelligence – and his enormous output – explain Wagner's verdict on Bach: 'the most stupendous miracle in all music.'

Four of Bach's sons also composed music: Wilhelm Friedemann, Carl Philip Emanuel, Johann Cristoph Friedrich and Johann Christian.

Bacteria are minute organisms which are found everywhere – in the air, in the soil, and on and in plants and animals. Bacteria consist of just one cell, although sometimes groups of cells join together to form chains or other shapes. There are many different types of bacteria, but even the largest is still too small to see without the aid of a microscope. Some bacteria are spherical, some are oblong and others are long and wavy. Bacteria are usually considered to be plants, although they do not possess the pigment chlorophyll, and normally obtain their energy by breaking down plant or animal tissues.

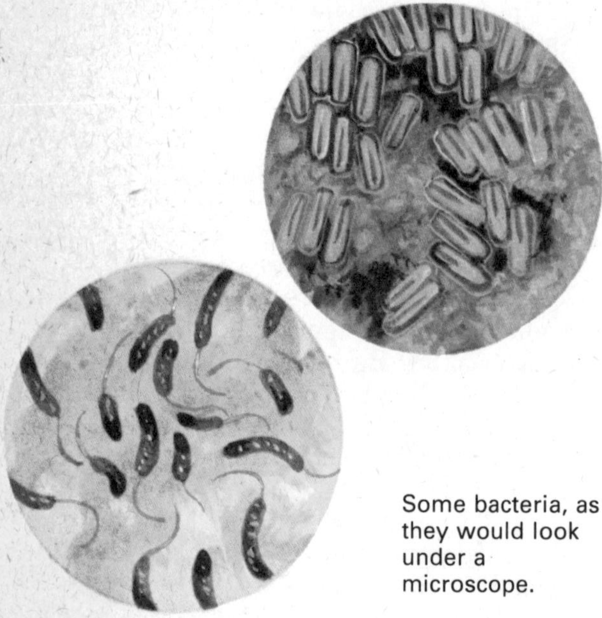

Some bacteria, as they would look under a microscope.

Most bacteria reproduce by splitting into small fragments. This can occur as often as once every 20 minutes. Although many bacteria are harmful, causing disease and even death, they perform a vital role in the cycle of nature. Without bacteria, dead plants and animals would not be broken down into valuable minerals for future generations, and all life on Earth would soon cease.

Bactrian, see Camel.

Baden-Powell, Robert Stephenson Smyth, 1st Baron (1857–1941), was a British soldier and founder of the Boy Scout movement. He served in the army in India and Africa, taking part in the Matabele campaign (1896–1897). His defence of Mafeking during the Boer War made him a national hero. He organized the Boy Scout movement in 1908 and with his sister founded the Girl Guides two years later. Both movements rapidly acquired world-wide popularity.

Badger is a burrowing mammal. It sleeps during the day in its underground home called a sett, coming out at night to search for food. The Eurasian badger is about 1 m (3 ft) long and weighs 13 kg (29 lb). The American badger is slightly smaller. Both have a black and white striped face.

Bahamas, Commonwealth of, is an island group, and the northernmost of the West Indies. Capital, Nassau; area about 14 000 sq km (5400 sq miles). The smaller islands (cays) are uninhabited. The Bahamas, which are mainly formed of coral, are a popular holiday resort, with a mild winter climate. They were a British colony from the 17th century until 1973, when they became independent. The people are mainly of African descent but some are of mainly British origin. The islands produce fruit and tomatoes for export, timber from the pinewoods, and fish.

Bahrain is a state consisting of a number of islands in the Persian Gulf. Capital, Bahrain; area about 660 sq km (255 sq miles). The islands are low-lying and the climate very hot in summer. Bahrain was a British protectorate until it declared its independence in 1971. The most important economic factor by far is the existence of rich oil fields, first discovered in 1932, which made tiny Bahrain one of the world's chief oil suppliers. Most of the people are Muslim Arabs.

Baird, John Logie (1888–1946), was the first person to transmit moving pictures. He was born in Scotland and studied electronic engineering at the Royal Technical College, Glasgow, then worked as an engineer, but had to stop because of illness. Later he started to do research into television.

In 1929 he invented the first television

system; this could transmit pictures from one place to another. The pictures were scanned on a screen made up of 240 horizontal lines, and the system was first used by the British Broadcasting Corporation. In Britain, it was replaced in 1936 by a system which scanned across 405 lines. Now, a 625-line system is usually used.

He also experimented with stereophonic sound, colour television and three-dimensional images. *See also* Television.

Balanchine, George (1904–1983), was a Russian-born choreographer, the most influential figure in international ballet since Fokine and Nijinsky. His unorthodox work caused arguments as early as 1922. He was chief choreographer for Diaghilev's company, 1925–1929, when he began his long association with the composer Stravinsky. In 1934 he went to the United States and founded what eventually became the New York City Ballet. For this company he created the most choreography by one person in the history of ballet.

Balearic Islands are islands forming a province of Spain, in the western Mediterranean. The largest are Majorca, Minorca and Ibiza. Capital, Palma de Mallorca (Majorca); area about 5000 sq km (1930 sq miles). The islands have an ancient history, and Majorca was a centre of learning in the Middle Ages. Minorca was held by Britain in the 18th century.

The islands produce wine, fruit and fish, but they are known chiefly as a holiday area, having a mild climate and beautiful scenery.

Bali is an island, part of Indonesia and separated from Java by a narrow strait. Area about 5620 sq km (2170 sq miles). Though small and mountainous, this tropical island has extremely fertile soil, from volcanic ash, which produces heavy crops of rice, coffee, sugar cane, maize, etc. The arts of the people of Bali, especially their complicated dance, are world-famous. Though Indonesia is mostly Muslim, a form of Hinduism survives from the time when Java was the centre of a Hindu empire.

Balkan states are a group of countries in south-western Europe comprising Albania, Bulgaria, Greece, Romania and Yugoslavia. From the 3rd century BC they were under Roman domination and in the 5th century AD became part of the Byzantine Empire. The region was ruled by the Ottoman Turks from the 15th century onwards. During the 19th century the Balkan states gradually won their independence from Turkey. However, there was much political unrest and the general instability of the area helped to bring about the First World War. After the Second World War all Balkan countries except Greece were governed by communist regimes. More detail is given under individual countries.

Ballet is a theatrical form of dance. Traditional or 'classical' ballet is based on a strict technique which goes back to the 17th century or earlier. Nowadays, however, 'ballet'

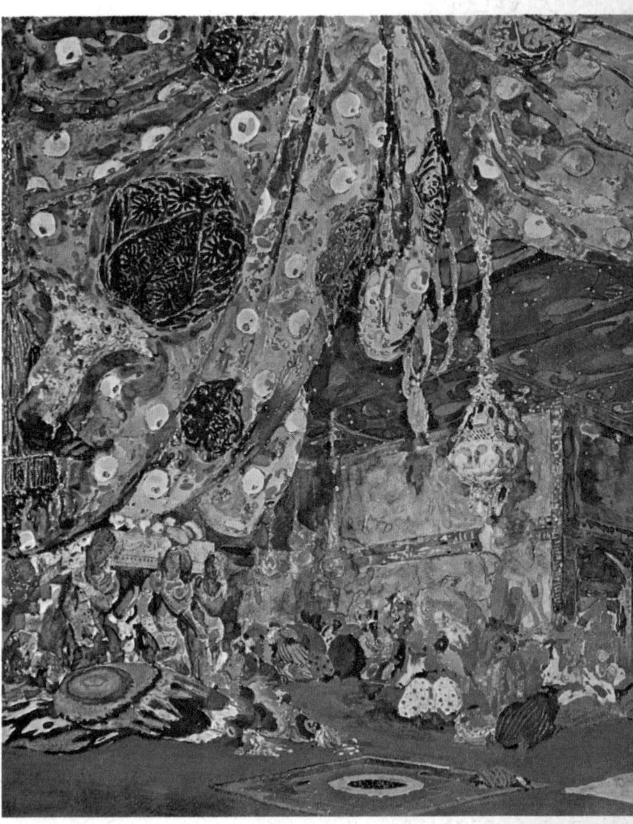

A design for a set in Diaghilev's ballet, *Schéhérazade*, painted by Bakst.

sometimes means any kind of dance which is an arranged performance on stage (or film).

In Renaissance Italy, theatrical spectacles were organized in which dancing, as well as singing, poetry and other arts, played some part. But the real origin of ballet dates from the court of Louis XIV in 17th-century France. It was at first performed by courtiers, but it developed into a professional occupation, with approved movements for the dancers, before 1700. During the 18th century it became an entirely independent form of entertainment. Technique was organized according to a code which dancers had to learn.

Very popular in the early 19th century, ballet went into a decline later – except in Russia, where it flourished. During the 1920s Diaghilev revived its popularity in Western Europe with his Russian Ballet (Ballet Russe). In the past 50 years, national schools of ballet have been created in many countries and the popularity of ballet has increased enormously.

Balsa is a tree which is found in tropical America. It grows very fast – a height of 18 m (60 ft) may be reached in about six years. Balsa leaves are similar in appearance to those of a maple, being large and trilobate. The flowers develop into seed pods which burst open when ripe, scattering the large seeds. The wood of a balsa tree is extremely light, and is used to make model aeroplanes, for packing delicate items, and in some lifebelts.

Baltic Sea is an area of water in northern Europe, bordered by the Scandinavian countries, the Soviet Union, Poland and Germany. Area about 386 000 sq km (150 000 sq miles). Though linked to the North Sea, it is amost entirely enclosed by land, and in history has been very important to rival nations in northern Europe, especially Russia, as a shipping route and fishing grounds. It is not very salty (you can catch freshwater fish in it) and most of it is frozen in winter.

Balzac, Honoré de (1799–1850), was a French novelist. He gave up law studies to become a writer and produced much hack work under false names before he established his reputation with *Scenes of Private Life* (1830). Soon afterwards he began his great project, the *Comédie Humaine* ('Human Comedy'), in which he aimed to picture the whole history of French society, in every aspect, as it was in his lifetime. By 1847 about 90 titles had been published – novels, novelettes and short stories – though he remained deep in debt, largely due to extravagance. (A concern with money is a major theme of the *Comédie Humaine*.) This terrific work rate, together with his hectic social life, ruined his health.

Bamboos are tall, woody stemmed perennial grasses. There are over 700 species, most of which are tropical, although a few grow in colder climates. The stems of bamboos are marked with prominent joints, and the leaves grow from twigs arising from these joints, or nodes. Bamboos can grow extremely fast – 5 cm (2 in) an hour has been recorded! Some can also grow extremely tall, reaching a height of 30 m (98 ft) or more. Bamboo can be eaten when the stems are young and soft. When older, they are used in the manufacture of furniture and fishing rods. Other uses include clothing, paper, blinds, utensils, and pipes for irrigation.

Banana is the edible fruit of the banana plant. Many different species of banana are cultivated for their fruit, which is long, curved, with yellow or red skin and soft creamy flesh. Banana trees grow in tropical areas, such as Australia, Asia, Africa and America.

Bandicoot is an Australian marsupial mammal which looks rather like a large shrew. Its name is a corruption of an Indian word meaning 'pig-rat'. The 19 species inhabit open plains, thick grass along the banks of swamps and rivers, thick scrub and forests.

Although bandicoots are protected in Australia by the Fauna Preservation Act, several species are in danger of extinction, mainly because the Australian Aborigines hunt them for food.

Bangladesh is a republic in southern Asia, between India and Burma. Capital, Dacca; area about 144 000 sq km (55 600 sq miles).
History From 1947, when British rule in the Indian sub-continent ended, the country formed the eastern province of Pakistan. The Bengalis had little in common with their fellow-Pakistanis in the western province and in 1971 civil war broke out between them. Bangladesh, helped by India, gained independence.
Land and People It is mainly a flat, wet country (average yearly rainfall is over 1500 mm/59 in) crossed by the great rivers, Ganges and Brahmaputra (Jamuna). It therefore has very fertile soil, but severe flooding has sometimes caused many deaths. The people of Bangladesh are Bengalis and mainly Muslim.
Economy Floods and cyclones (severe storms), together with high population, poor fuel and industrial resources, and the lack of high-earning exports make Bangladesh a very poor country. Products include rice, tea, timber and fish.

Bank of England is the central bank of Britain, situated in Threadneedle Street in the City of London. It does not deal with the general public but acts as a banker to other large British banks and to the Government. Bank of England notes and coins are the main form of currency in Britain.

The Bank of England was founded in 1694 and was privately owned until 1946, when it was nationalized.

Banking is a business that handles people's money. There were bankers of a sort in ancient times, offering safe places to deposit valuables. Banking became a great convenience, as well as a source of security, when cheques came into use, making it possible to pay or receive sums of money by a simple paper transaction.

A bank earns most of the money it makes by lending or investing a proportion of the deposits left with it. It is able to do so because only a minority of depositors will be taking out much of their money at any given time.

As well as commercial banks, there are savings banks and merchant banks, which mainly finance trade and guarantee loans.

Banyan is a strange-looking tree which grows in the tropical regions of India and southern Asia. The huge crown of leaves is supported by not only one trunk, but many. As the tree grows, it produces more and more trunks until the tree may take over an area

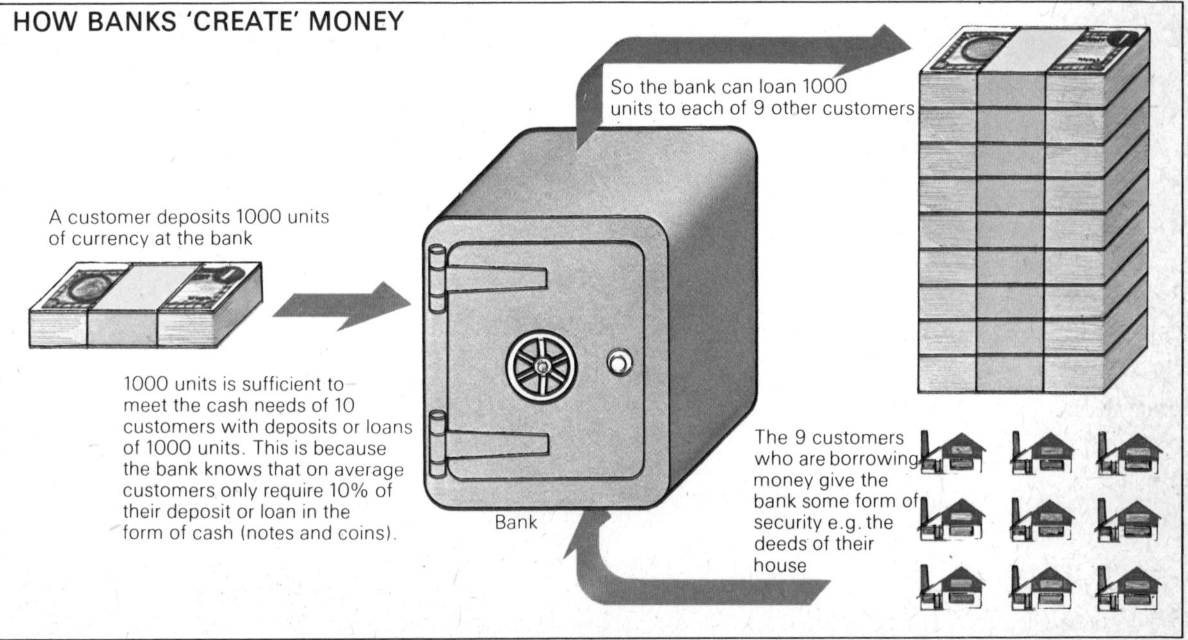
HOW BANKS 'CREATE' MONEY
A customer deposits 1000 units of currency at the bank
1000 units is sufficient to meet the cash needs of 10 customers with deposits or loans of 1000 units. This is because the bank knows that on average customers only require 10% of their deposit or loan in the form of cash (notes and coins).
Bank
So the bank can loan 1000 units to each of 9 other customers
The 9 customers who are borrowing money give the bank some form of security e.g. the deeds of their house

of several hectares. The additional trunks are, in fact, aerial roots produced by the branches, and they take root in the soil. Alexander the Great is believed to have camped his complete army under a banyan tree. Whether or not this is true, Indian merchants (called banyans) certainly used the shady banyan tree as a market place for selling their goods.

Baobab is a curious looking tree which grows in the dry parts of Australia and central Africa. A baobab only 15 m (50 ft) high may have a huge trunk, almost 9 m (30 ft) in diameter. The trunk tapers to a crown of stout, horizontal branches. The tissues within the tree act as a water reservoir to see it through the dry season.

Baptists are a branch of the Christian religion. Baptists are so named because of the importance they put on the ritual of baptism. Instead of sprinkling a few drops of holy water, they believe in immersing the whole body, as practised by St John the Baptist in the Bible.

There are many Baptist Churches, and beliefs sometimes differ because of the Baptist belief in religious liberty and spiritual freedom – the right of each person to make his or her own interpretation.

Barbados is an island republic east of the Windward Islands in the West Indies. Capital, Bridgetown; area about 430 sq km (166 sq miles). One of the first British colonies in the Americas, it became a rich sugar-growing colony, and many of the people are descended from the African slaves who were brought to work the sugar plantations. It became independent in 1966.

The island is mainly coral rock, with fertile volcanic soil on top, producing heavy crops, chiefly sugar. With its byproducts, molasses and rum, sugar is the main export. Barbados has no streams or rivers. The climate is mild and changes little through the year, attracting the tourists who provide a major part of the island's income.

Barge is a special craft for carrying freight on inland waterways (canals and rivers), with a flat bottom to allow passage in shallow water. Early barges were towed by horses or used sails; modern barges are fitted with internal combustion engines. Because they sail narrow waterways, barges are usually very long and narrow.

Bark is the protective outer layer of trees. It is composed of dead, corky cells produced by a layer of cells called the cork cambium. The bark also covers part of the root system. Throughout the plant it helps prevent harmful insects from entering the tree, and also helps to insulate the tree from extremes of weather.

Barges on the River Danube. They are an important means of transport and a great variety of goods are carried.

Acorn barnacles

Barnacles are probably familiar to anyone who has visited the seashore, for these small crustaceans, safely enclosed in a cone-shaped limy shell, encrust shells, rocks, piers and jetties in huge numbers. When the tide comes in, barnacles feed by extending their legs and driving sea water laden with tiny creatures into their mouths. In addition to the more familiar cone-like barnacles, there is another type called the goose barnacle. The shell of this barnacle consists of two flat plates, and is attached to a fleshy stalk.

Barnard, Dr Christiaan Neethling (1922–), is a well-known surgeon, who performed the first human-to-human heart transplant on 3 December 1967.

This was done on Louis Waskansky, who died on 20 December 1967. In 1974 Barnard was the first to implant a second heart in a patient and to link the circulations of the two hearts so that they worked together as one.

He holds numerous honorary doctorates, foreign orders and awards for his outstanding contributions to the field of medical science, and is professor of surgical science at the University of Cape Town in South Africa.

Barometer is an instrument used for measuring the pressure of the air. Air presses down on the Earth, pulled by the Earth's gravity. Evangelista Torricelli showed this in 1643. He put a tube in a dish of mercury. The mercury always rose to a height of roughly 76 cm (nearly 30 in) in the tube. (The height varies slightly according to the temperature and air pressure.) The air was pushing down on the mercury in the dish and forcing it up the tube. This was the first barometer, known as a mercury barometer. It measures air pressure in centimetres of mercury. Another barometer often used is the aneroid barometer in which air pressure is indicated by a pointer on a dial.

The air pressure changes slightly as the weather changes. For example, a drop in air pressure signifies worse weather. Barometers are thus used in weather forecasting.

Baroque was the style in European art and architecture from the end of the 16th to the early 18th century. It developed out of the style of the Renaissance period, which in turn was based on the Classical 'orders' of ancient Greece and Rome. The Baroque, however, abandoned the discipline and order of Classicism for the sake of greater vigour, movement, colour and flamboyance.

The Baroque, more characteristic of Catholic than Protestant countries, was not really a single style at all. Italian Baroque architecture, for example, is most striking for the brilliant imagination and flair of those like Bernini. But in France, Baroque buildings could be rather heavy and solemn, though certainly grand – as at the royal palace of Versailles. In England the Baroque style was more restrained; in North America it hardly existed but in South America it was an influence until the 19th century.

Bartók, Béla (1881–1945), was a Hungarian composer. A brilliant pianist, he developed an interest in Hungarian folk music, which he collected and published. This had a strong influence on most of his own compositions, features of which were lively rhythm and strong melody. Forced into exile to the United States in 1940, his last years were sad: his work was not performed very often and his health was failing. His music, which includes orchestral and piano works, a remarkable series of string quartets, two ballets and an opera, remains popular today.

Basalt is a dark rock, relatively rich in iron and magnesium, which originated as volcanic lava. The famous 'Giant's Causeway' in Northern Ireland consists of about 40 000 columns of basalt that has cracked in cooling and weathered to produce a curious effect.

Base, in chemistry, is a substance which reacts with an acid to give a salt. Most bases are metal oxides and hydroxides. A metal oxide is a metal combined with oxygen. An example is magnesium oxide. A metal hydroxide is a metal combined with hydrogen and oxygen. An example is sodium hydroxide. Some other substances, such as ammonia, are also bases.

Bases which dissolve in water are called alkalis.

Bats are the only truly flying mammals. There are about 1000 species throughout the world. They range in size from tiny species such as the pipistrelle, with a body length of only 5 cm (2 in), to the tropical fruit bats, such as the kalong, the largest bat, with a body 30 cm (12 in) long and a wingspan of 1.5 m (5 ft). Bats' wings are made of thin skin which is stretched between their very elongated finger bones. This skin is also connected to the legs.

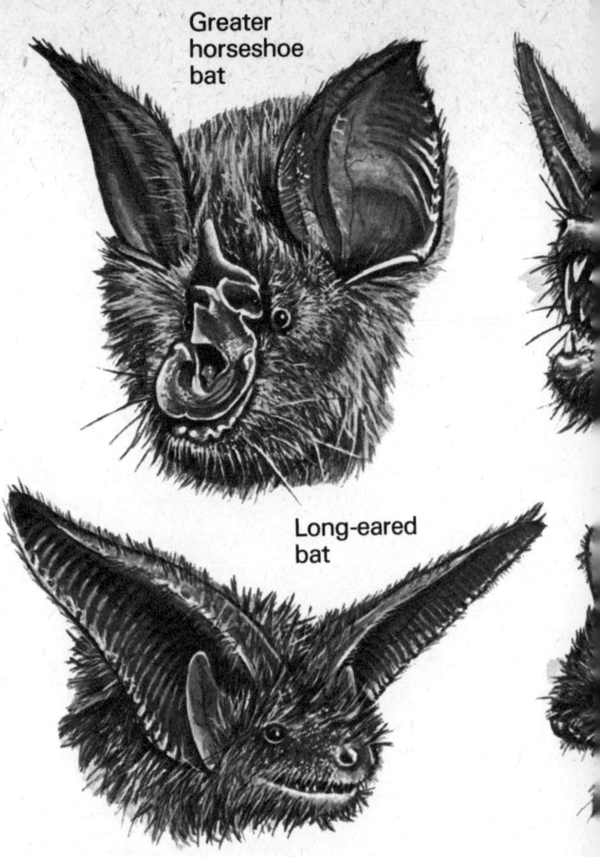

Bats are divided into two groups, the microchiropterans and the megachiropterans. The microchiropterans are mainly small, insect-eating bats, although some catch fish and the vampire bat sucks blood. Microchiropterans find their way about by echo-location. They emit very high-pitched sounds which bounce back from objects

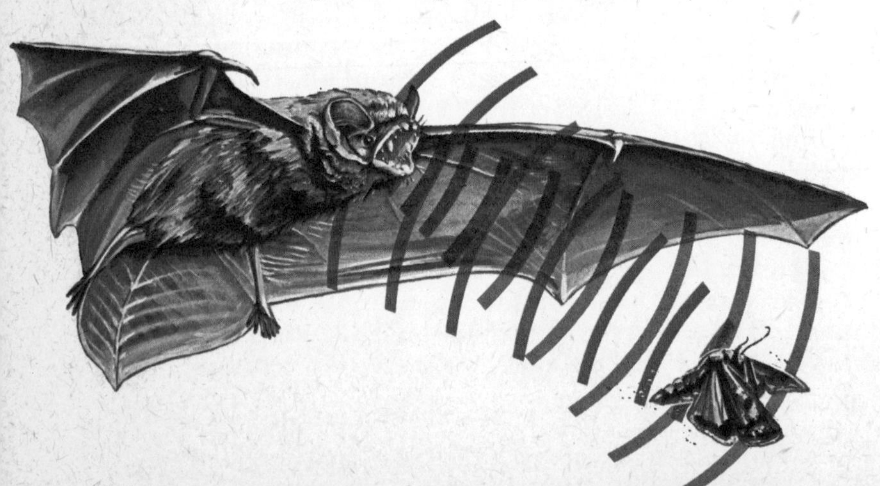

Bats use echo-location to find food as well as to find their way about. They listen for echoes of their squeaks which bounce off the prey.

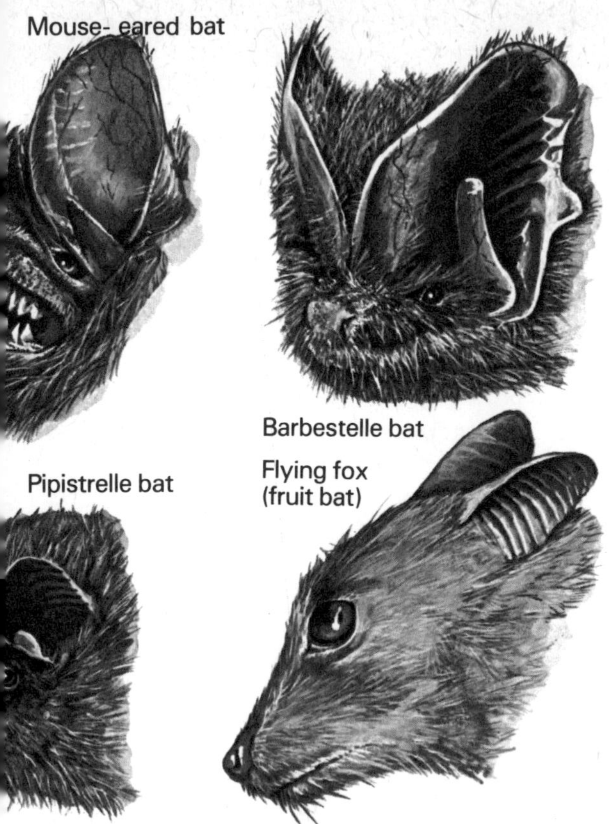

informing them of obstacles – or food – in their path. Despite popular belief, bats are not blind, but in the darkness echo-location is a much more satisfactory way of getting about. Due to the scarcity of insect food, bats in cold climates hibernate during the winter. They find a safe place like a cave, or beneath a bridge or the loft of a building, and sleep until spring.

The megachiropterans are known as fruit bats and flying foxes. They look like small, winged foxes and, because they hunt at dusk or even during the day, they have larger eyes, which they use to find their way about and their food – mainly figs, bananas and dates.

Battery is a device which produces electricity from chemicals. It contains many electrical cells joined together. Batteries are used in, for example, torches and portable radios. These contain cells known as dry cells. When the dry cells stop producing electricity, the battery is useless and must be thrown away.

A car battery contains different sorts of cells. These are known as lead-acid cells or lead accumulators. When this battery stops producing electricity it can be recharged. An electric current from another battery or a mains power source is passed through it. This recharging makes it as good as new. *See also* Cell.

Right: A simple dry cell battery, as used, for example, in a hand torch. When the torch is switched on, the top of the carbon rod in the battery is connected, through the bulb, to the zinc case. This makes the chemicals surrounding the rod produce electrons. A current flows through the bulb and the filament lights up.

+
Brass cap
Carbon rod
Ammonium chloride paste
Manganese dioxide
Muslin bag
Zinc case
–

Battles		
Marathon	490 BC	Athenians and allies defeated Persians.
Salamis	480 BC	Greek fleet destroyed Persian fleet.
Syracuse	413 BC	Athenian besiegers of Syracuse decisively beaten.
Aegospotami	405 BC	Athenian fleet defeated by Spartan fleet, ending Peloponnesian War.
Allia	390 BC	Gauls defeated Romans and then sacked Rome.
Arbela	331 BC	Alexander the Great routed Persian army.
Metaurus	207 BC	Romans defeated Carthaginians under Hasdrubal.

Zama	202 BC	Roman victory over Carthage ended Second Punic War.
Carrhae	53 BC	Roman army routed by Parthians.
Actium	31 BC	Roman fleet under Octavian defeated combined fleet of Antony and Cleopatra.
Teutoburg Forest	AD 9	Roman army destroyed by Germanic tribesmen.
Adrianople	378	Visigoths defeated and killed Roman emperor Valens.
Châlons-sur-Marne	451	Romans and Visigoths defeated Huns under Attila.
Yarmuk	636	Decisive Arab victory over Byzantines.
Tours	732	Franks under Charles Martel defeated Muslims, so keeping western Europe Christian.
Edington	878	Alfred the Great routed Danes.
Brunanburh	937	Athelstan defeated combined force of Danes and Scots.
Hastings	1066	Norman victory over the Saxons, leading to Norman rule in England.
Manzikert	1071	Seljuk Turks defeated the Byzantines.
Las Navas de Tolasa	1212	Spanish victory over the Muslims.
Bouvines	1214	French victory over the English.
Bannockburn	1314	English invaders of Scotland defeated by Robert Bruce.
Crécy	1346	English under Edward III defeated French and allies.
Poitiers	1356	English defeated French and captured king of France.
Kulikovo	1380	Russian victory over the Tartars.
Kossovo	1389	Balkan army defeated by Turks.
Agincourt	1415	Henry V defeated the French.
Orléans	1429	Joan of Arc defeated English besieging force.
Bosworth	1485	Henry Tudor defeated and killed Richard III in final battle of the Wars of the Roses.
Mohács	1526	Turkish victory over the Hungarians.
Lepanto	1571	Christian fleet defeated the Turks.
Armada	1588	Spanish invasion fleet routed by English.
White Mountain	1620	Protestant army of Frederick of Bohemia defeated by Catholic forces.
Rocroi	1643	French victory over the Spanish.
Naseby	1645	Decisive defeat of Charles I in Civil War.
Boyne	1690	William III defeated James II.
Blenheim	1704	British and allies under Marlborough defeated the French.
Poltava	1709	Russians routed Swedish invasion force.
Plassey	1757	Robert Clive defeated Nawab of Bengal's army.
Quebec	1759	British forces led by James Wolfe captured Quebec from the French.

Saratoga	1777	British troops surrended to American colonial forces.
Valmy	1792	French Revolutionary forces defeated the Prussians.
Nile	1798	British fleet under Nelson destroyed French fleet.
Trafalgar	1805	British fleet under Nelson destroyed Franco-Spanish fleet.
Austerlitz	1805	Napoleon I defeated combined Austro-Russian army.
Leipzig	1813	French forces under Napoleon defeated by Austrian, Prussian and Russian armies.
Waterloo	1815	French defeated by British and Prussians.
Gettysburg	1863	Union victory over the Confederates in the American Civil War.
Sadowa	1866	Prussians defeated Austrians and won Seven Weeks' War.
Sedan	1870	Prussians defeated French.
Tsushima	1905	Japanese fleet destroyed Russian fleet.
Tannenberg	1914	German victory over the Russians.
Marne	1914	British and French forces halted German invasion of France.
Verdun	1916	French held Verdun for ten months against German offensive.
Somme	1916	British and French pushed back Germans with huge losses on both sides.
Jutland	1916	Inconclusive battle between British and German fleets.
Taranto	1940	British fleet defeated Italian fleet.
Coral Sea	1942	American fleet repelled Japanese invasion fleet.
Midway	1942	American fleet defeated Japanese fleet.
Alamein	1942	British forces drove German and Italian armies out of Egypt.
Stalingrad	1942–1943	German army surrendered to Russians.
Kursk	1943	Russians defeated Germans in tank battle.
Normandy	1944	Allied forces invaded north-western France.
Ardennes	1944–1945	German counter-attack against Americans and British failed.
Dieu Bien Phu	1944	Besieged French surrendered to Vietminh forces.
Vietnam	1972	'Tet' offensive by Vietcong against American and South Vietnamese forces.

Bauhaus was a German school for architects and artists, founded in 1919. Under Walter Gropius and such varied talents as those of Marcel Breuer, Paul Klee, Wassily Kandinsky, Lazlo Moholy-Nagy and Ludwig Mies van der Rohe, it produced a highly distinctive modern approach to design. Bauhaus architecture in particular was severely functional. When it was closed down by the Nazis in 1933 it moved to the United States, where it eventually became part of the Illinois Institute of Technology.

Bauxite is a variably coloured kind of clay, which has been important since the 19th century as the main source of aluminium. It is also used to make fire-bricks and other fire resistant items. Large deposits occur in France, Hungary, the USA, Guyana, Jamaica, Suriname, Italy, Greece, the USSR and Australia.

Bavaria (or Bayern) is the largest state in West Germany, and is bounded by East Germany in the north, Czechoslovakia in the east, Austria in the south, and the states of Hesse and Baden-Württemberg in the west. Its capital is Munich. Bavaria was incorporated into Germany in 1871, and became a state within the Federal Republic of Germany (West Germany) in 1946. Beer is probably its most famous product, but it is also well known for glass and porcelain.

Bayeux Tapestry is an embroidered strip of linen 70 m long and 50 cm wide. It depicts the life of King Harold of England and the Norman conquest in 1066 in about 70 scenes. It begins with King Harold's visit to Normandy and ends with the English defeat at the battle of Hastings. The tapestry was probably created at the end of the 11th century. Tradition attributes its design to William the Conqueror's wife, Mathilda. It was probably made on the order of William's half-brother Odo, Bishop of Bayeux. The tapestry is a fascinating historical document which now hangs in the Museum of Bayeux in France.

Bay lynx, see Bobcat.

Bears are in the mammal order Carnivora (the meat eaters), but in fact most bears are omnivores. They eat meat, fish, berries, fruit and honey.

Brown bears live in Europe and North America, including Alaska. There are several types of brown bear, the largest being the kodiak bear. The well-known grizzly bear is also a brown bear. Black bears live in America and Asia and one, the sun bear, is the only bear found in tropical regions. Polar bears live in the freezing Arctic. They feed on seals, fish and seabirds and their eggs.

Beatles was a British pop group who achieved world-wide popularity in the 1960s. Born in Liverpool between 1940 and 1943, they were John Lennon (died 1980) and Paul McCartney – the composers of most of the Beatles' songs – George Harrison and Ringo Starr. The group was first formed in 1957 and was disbanded in 1969. Their record sales ran into millions and they made several films.

Beaver is a rodent that spends much of its time in rivers and lakes. There are two closely related species, the North American beaver and the Eurasian beaver. Both have been widely hunted for their thick, glossy brown fur, and have had to be protected by law to ensure their survival.

Beavers are intelligent animals, 75 to 100 cm (30 to 40 in) in length. They have webbed hind feet and large tails, about 30 cm (12 in) long, which make them accomplished swimmers. A beaver also uses its tail to slap the water to warn others of danger. Beavers live in colonies and often work together in groups. They feed mainly on the bark of trees, and also use wood in the form of twigs and branches to build their riverbank burrows, called lodges. To meet its needs, the beaver cuts down trees by gnawing round their bases and then floats the logs through the water to its burrow. It may use this wood, together with mud and rubble, to perform its most remarkable feat – the building of dams across fast-flowing streams to create ponds.

Becket, Thomas (circa 1118–1170), was an English churchman and royal minister. He was appointed Chancellor to Henry II in 1155, holding his office until 1162. In that year Henry made him Archbishop of Canterbury. Becket roused the King's anger by his stubborn defence of the rights of the Church against the secular power and refused to sign the Constitutions of Clarendon (1164). He fled to France, returning in 1170 after apparently being reconciled with the king. That same year he was murdered in Canterbury cathedral by four knights from Henry's court. Becket was canonized in 1172.

Beckett, Samuel (1906–), is an Irish playwright who usually writes in French. Though born and educated in Dublin, he has lived mainly in France from about 1930 and was a friend of Joyce. He has written poems, novels and stories, as well as his often mysterious plays which are part of the Theatre of the Absurd. He gained world-wide fame with *Waiting for Godot*, first performed in English in 1955. In Beckett's plays there is little or no action, and the chief impression is of deep pessimism, but he also looks at the pointlessness of life with humour.

Bedouin is an Arab of the desert in Asia or Africa. They are nomadic people, traditionally living in tents and wandering across vast areas of land with their herds of animals – usually camels, goats and sheep. In modern times, many Bedouin have been forced to abandon this way of life and work in agriculture or in towns.

Bee is an insect belonging to the order Hymenoptera. Although we usually think of bees as social insects living together in hives, most species are solitary, simply nesting in a hole in a grassy bank, or under wood.

In a beehive, the queen lays the eggs, the drones fertilize them and the sterile female workers do all the other jobs.

Bees feed themselves and their offspring on honey. First, the bees feed on the nectar produced by flowers. Some of this is stored in their stomachs and then regurgitated (spat out) by the bees to be turned into honey. Bees of all kinds – commercial honey bees and solitary bees – play a vital role in helping to pollinate flowers as they fly to and fro collecting nectar. *See also* Social insect.

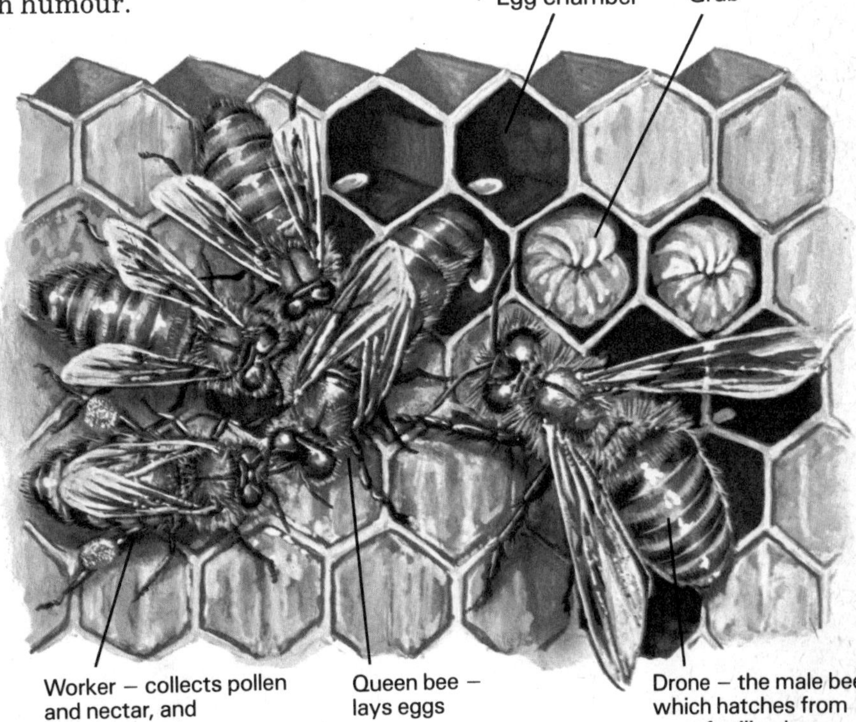

Inside a beehive.

The leaves and nut of the beech tree.

Beech trees include the common beech of Europe and western Asia, the American beech of North America, and the 'false beeches' of South America, Australia and New Zealand. Some of these Southern Hemisphere beeches are evergreen, and reach a height of 60 m (200 ft).

Beech trees prefer chalky soils, where their shallow root systems can often be seen partly above ground. The bark is usually smooth, and where trees grow close together the trunks frequently lack branches. Beech wood is easy to bend, and is often used for making furniture. The fruit of the beech tree is the beech nut – a source of food for many animals as well as the source of an oil which can be used as a butter substitute.

Beethoven, Ludwig van (1770–1827), was a German composer who came from a family of Flemish descent. He was taught by Haydn, and briefly by Mozart. In 1792 he settled in Vienna, becoming well known as a brilliant pianist with an unusual gift for improvisation. He had already composed songs and instrumental music, as well as many piano pieces, and in 1800 he conducted his first symphony in Vienna. He was always very popular, both as performer and composer, though many of the older generation of Vienna musicians were critical (and jealous). Unlike his predecessors, Beethoven never worked directly for a European ruler, aristocrat or the Church. He was financed by rich patrons, but he wrote music to satisfy his own inclinations. He was a proud, independent man, even when he began to go deaf in 1798. By 1819 he could hear nothing.

Beethoven was perhaps the most important single influence in the history of music. He brought striking new ideas to whatever kind of music he composed – from symphonies (nine of them) and opera (one – *Fidelio*), to songs and chamber music. His late works, especially the last five string quartets, were not properly understood for over a century after his death, but they are his finest compositions.

Beetles are insects of the order Coleoptera. Although beetles possess two pairs of wings, the first pair usually form a hard, protective case over the second pair. Only when a beetle is flying do the wing cases lift up to reveal the second pair of wings which are actually used for flying.

Beetles occur all over the world in every sort of habitat, including water. Many are pests because they eat people's crops and stored foods. The largest beetle is the African goliath beetle, whose body may reach a length of 10 cm (4 in). *See also* Weevil.

A two-spot ladybird and a great diving beetle.

Belfast is the capital city of Northern Ireland. It is the main seaport and centre of industry, especially linen and shipbuilding, though these are less important than they were once. There are many factories and institutions, including Queen's University and a Protestant cathedral. In recent years the buildings and citizens have suffered from terrorism and civil strife.

Belgium is a kingdom in north-west Europe, between France and the Netherlands. Capital, Brussels; area about 30 500 sq km (11 780 sq miles). The country is divided into Flemish and French-speaking regions, often a cause of internal conflict.
History The country was inhabited by a Celtic tribe when it was conquered by the Romans in the 1st century BC. In the 2nd or 3rd century AD it was invaded by Germanic peoples. It became part of the Frankish kingdom and was subsequently incorporated into Charlemagne's empire. During the later Middle Ages it was split up into a number of semi-independent principalities. It later passed to the Spanish Hapsburgs and in the 18th century to the Austrian Hapsburgs. Taken over by France in 1794, it became part of the kingdom of the Netherlands in 1815. However, in 1850 Belgium won complete independence. Occupied by Germany in both World Wars, it became a member of NATO in 1949 and the EEC, whose headquarters are in Brussels, in 1958.
Land and People In the south-east the country has wooded hills; otherwise it is mainly flat, with coastal parts no higher than sea level. Though small, Belgium is heavily populated and rich. The wealth comes mainly from manufacturing and engineering as Belgium is one of the most highly-industrialized countries in the world. The main farm products are cereals, root crops such as sugar beet, beef and dairy produce.

Belize is a republic in Central America. Capital, Belmopan; area about 23 000 sq km (9000 sq miles). Formerly British Honduras, it shares its longest border with Guatemala, which claims it. Though it became fully independent in 1981, Belize still depends on Britain for defence.

This little country has a wide coastal plain, with many lakes and cays (islands) offshore. The southern part is mountainous. There are dense tropical forests and timber products are the chief export, along with bananas from the Belize River valley, and other fruits and sugar.

Bell, Alexander Graham (1847–1922), was a Scottish inventor. As his father's assistant he became an expert in speech training. In 1870 the Bell family moved to Canada, and Alexander began to perform outstanding work in teaching deaf people to speak. In 1872 he opened a school in Boston, USA, to train teachers of the deaf. Linking his interest in speech with the study of electricity, he made a number of inventions, of which the most important was the telephone (1876).

Bellini was a family of Venetian artists: Jacopo (circa 1400–1470), Gentile (circa 1429–1507) and Giovanni (circa 1430–1516). Giovanni is the most famous; he was the outstanding painter of the early period of the great Venetian school and his career of 60 years spanned the development of the style from its beginnings as a provincial offshoot of Gothic to its High Renaissance peak. He was also the teacher of the next generation of Venetian masters, and the outstanding characteristics of the Venetian school – its rich colours (made possible by the new use of oil paints) and landscape backgrounds – are fully apparent in his work.

Ben-Gurion, David (1886–1973), an Israeli statesman, was the first Prime Minister of the independent state of Israel. He emigrated from Poland to Israel in 1906. Towards the end of the First World War he joined the Jewish Legion of the British army in the Middle East. After the war he devoted his energies to the founding of a Jewish home in Palestine and established the General Federation of Jewish Labour. After the creation of Israel in 1948 he was prime minister almost continuously for the next 15 years.

Benin, a former west African kingdom, was founded in the 13th century and was most powerful between the 14th and 17th centuries. It was in contact with the Portuguese from the late 15th century, and traded with Europeans in slaves, spices and palm oil. In 1897 British forces captured the capital, Benin City, and the kingdom was made part of Nigeria. As a result of this, Europeans became aware of the great art that had been produced at Benin – for example, the delicate, realistic bronze, brass and ivory work.

The Benin bronzes first attracted wide attention in Europe after an expedition to Benin City in 1897. Their fine artistic quality had a marked influence on European artists such as Picasso.

The city of Benin remains the capital of Benin province in Nigeria. However, another west African country bordering Nigeria, previously known as Dahomey, has adopted Benin as its official title.

Benin is a republic in West Africa. Capital, Porto Novo; area about 112 600 sq km (43 500 sq miles). It was once the centre of the powerful kingdom of Dahomey and was famous for its fierce women soldiers.

Benin is one of the smallest countries in Africa and it has no natural harbours. Lagoons behind the coastal strip give way to a lightly-forested plateau.

It is chiefly an agricultural country. Palm-tree products are a major source of revenue. Other crops include coffee, cotton and groundnuts (peanuts).

Benz, Karl (1844–1929), was a German engineer who invented the motor car. His first car, built in 1885, was a three-wheeler which could travel at just 13 km/h (8 mph). He was involved in the world's first-ever car crash, when he hit a brick wall during a demonstration drive. The company he founded became part of what is now Mercedes-Benz, which still makes cars in Germany.

Berbers were a people who inhabited North Africa before the Arab invasions that began in the 7th century AD. Most of the peoples of North Africa are now Arabs or Arabic-speaking but the various Berber languages are still spoken by about ten million people scattered over a vast area from Morocco to Egypt. The best-known surviving Berber groups are the Riff tribes of the Atlas Mountains and the nomadic Tuareg who still wander the Sahara Desert.

Berlioz, Hector (1803–1869), was a French composer. He gave up medical training to study music, despite the opposition of his family. His love for an actress he had never met inspired his famous *Symphonie Fantastique*. Later he married the actress, and worked as a critic, often under a false name which enabled him to praise his own works.

Berlioz was a Romantic in life as well as in music. Nearly everthing he composed was on a grand scale. His *Te Deum* required three choirs with a total of 800 voices. His long opera, *The Trojans*, was impossible to stage.

Bermuda is a self-governing British colony consisting of about 300 islands, islets and coral reefs. Capital, Hamilton; area about 53 sq km (20 sq miles). Only about 20 of the islands are inhabited, and there is an American naval and airforce base there. Industries include tourism, perfumes, pharmaceuticals and textiles.

Bernini, Gianlorenzo (1598–1680), was an Italian sculptor and architect. He was perhaps the greatest genius of early Italian Baroque. He gave Rome a new character with his colonnades, fountains and grand but lively buildings.

Berry is a fleshy, succulent fruit containing hard-coated seeds. Berries do not burst open when ripe, but rely instead for distribution on animals eating them and passing the seeds unharmed through their bodies. The date palm is an example of a berry which has just one seed, and the grape is an example of a berry which has many seeds. Other berries include tomatoes, cucumbers and cranberries.

Beta (β) ray is a stream of electrons or positrons. Electrons are small particles with a negative charge. Positrons are like electrons but have a positive charge. So beta rays can have a negative or a positive charge. They can move very fast, sometimes nearly as fast as light waves. They can travel a long way and can even pass through very thin pieces of metal.

Beta rays were discovered by Lord Rutherford. They are given off by radioactive atoms. When they give off beta rays, the

In the Bible, Moses presented the Hebrews with the Ten Commandments, dictated to him by God.

radioactive atoms change into the atoms of another element.

Bhutan is a kingdom in south-central Asia. Capital, Thimbu; area about 47 000 sq km (18 000 sq miles).

Once under Chinese domination, Bhutan was also briefly part of British India but has been ruled by a hereditary monarch (maharajah) since 1907. China claims some of Bhutan, and the kingdom is under a degree of Indian control, especially in foreign policy.

Situated in the eastern Himalayas, Bhutan is crossed by high mountain ridges with deep valleys. The people are related to their Tibetan neighbours and are mostly Buddhists. Their main product, besides rice and corn, is timber.

Bible is the sacred books of the Jewish and Christian religions. The Bible is divided into the Old and New Testaments. The Old Testament has religious authority for Jews and Christians although it is concerned with Judaism before the coming of Christ. It is a varied collection of poetry and prose, including myth, history, laws, songs, sermons, philosophy and proverbs, and it records the cultural life of the ancient Hebrews for over a thousand years. It reveals the development of mankind's idea of God and the gradual unfolding of God's purpose.

The New Testament records the beginnings of Christianity, containing four accounts of the life of Jesus (gospels), one book of the early history of the Church (*Acts of the Apostles*), a number of letters by apostles and disciples of Jesus, and a book of prophecy (*Revelations*).

The Bible is the fundamental authority for all branches of Christianity, though different branches have treated it in different ways. Some sects insist that every word is Truth – the Word of God revealed to mankind – while others interpret it more freely.

Bicycle – the first bicycle was called a velocipede. The rider sat on it and propelled it simply by 'walking' his feet on the ground. Such machines were in use during the 17th century. The first proper bicycle, on which the rider used pedals to drive the wheels, was invented in 1839 by a Scottish blacksmith, Kirkpatrick Macmillan – his machine can be seen in London's Science Museum.

The most famous early bicycle was the late 19th century Penny Farthing, so called because it had one huge front wheel, up to 1.5 m (4.9 ft) in diameter, on which the rider sat, and one tiny rear wheel. Both wheels were named after British coins of the time, the penny being very large, the farthing very small.

The modern bicycle, with its central pedals driving the rear wheel through a chain, was invented in 1876, with John Dunlop's pneumatic tyres being fitted in 1888 and Sturmey Archer gears in 1902.

The Penny Farthing

All bicycles have only two wheels; tricycles have three wheels (two at the back) and racing tricycles have been pedalled at over 100 km/h (62 mph). A tandem is a long bicycle designed to be pedalled by two riders.

Biennial plant is one which completes its life cycle in two years. In the first year it produces leaves only, and these leaves manufacture food by photosynthesis. The food is stored by the plant in a swollen underground stem or root. During the second year, the food produced in the first year and stored underground is used in the production of flowers, fruits and seeds. The carrot and the parsnip are two common biennial plants. The parts which we eat are the underground food stores produced during the first year.

Big bang is a theory about how the universe began. According to the theory, all the matter in the universe was once packed close together. A huge explosion, or big bang, made all this matter fly apart. All the galaxies were formed from this matter and they are still moving away from each other. Most astronomers agree with this theory.

Observations of galaxies show that they are still moving apart from each other. The universe is expanding. Some scientists have suggested another theory to explain this, known as the Steady state. For many reasons, however, most astronomers prefer the Big bang theory to the Steady state theory.

Biltong, in South Africa, is strips of lean meat dried in the sun.

Binary system is a number system in which there are only two numbers (0 and 1) instead of the ten (0 to 9) we normally use in the decimal system. The binary system works on the same principles as the decimal system. In the decimal system, numbers larger than 9 are expressed by the use of additional columns to the left of the units column; these represent tens, tens of tens (that is, hundreds), tens of hundreds (thousands), and so on. In the same way, the binary system uses additional columns for numbers above one – these represent twos, twos of twos (that is, fours), twos of fours (eights), and so on. Thus the numbers 2 to 8 in the decimal system are written in the binary system as 10, 11, 100, 101, 110, 111, 1000.

The binary system is widely used today, being employed in all computers and calculators.

Binoculars, or field-glasses, are an optical instrument that basically consists of two small, linked telescopes, one for each eye. This makes it possible for a viewer to look at distant objects comfortably with both eyes at the same time, and to see a single magnified image. There is usually a screw on the instrument with which the focus can be controlled. Conveniently portable, binoculars have been widely used during wars, but they have also added to the enjoyment of astronomy, bird- and animal-watching, sport and theatrical performances.

According to modern views, our Universe began in a giant explosion called the Big Bang, from which it has been expanding ever since. In the Big Bang theory, as the Universe expands the galaxies in it thin out.

Biochemistry is a science of the chemistry of life. It studies animals and plants by looking at the chemicals they contain. Biochemists find out what these chemicals are, and what role they perform. For example, biochemists found chemicals which carry messages from one part of the body to another in living things. These are called hormones.

Biochemists also identify the chemicals in our food and drink and find out what happens to them in the body. Biochemists have found the causes and cures of many illnesses.

Biography is the story of a person's life. If it is written by the person concerned it is called autobiography. Biography is an ancient form of literature which has been practised, in one way or another, in every age since the ancient Greeks. The first great biographer in Western literature was Plutarch in the 1st century AD. He wrote *The Parallel Lives*, describing great Greeks and Romans, which was used by Shakespeare, among others. The earliest true biography in English is a *Life of Alfred the Great*, and one of the most famous is Thomas Boswell's *Life of [Samuel] Johnson*.

Bioluminescence is the ability of certain animals, such as glow worms and some deep-sea fish, as well as some species of bacteria and fungi, to produce an intense, glowing light. The light is produced by a chemical reaction and, unlike the generation of light in an electric light bulb, there is very little heat produced.

It is mainly female glow worms which produce their greenish-yellow light, and they do it to attract males at mating time. The light is emitted from an organ underneath the abdomen. Male glow worms have huge eyes so that they can detect the light.

Deep-sea creatures which can produce light do so for a variety of purposes. For example, they may use it to signal their presence to others in the dark, or to attract inquisitive animals which they then grab and eat.

Biplane is an aeroplane with two wings, one above the other. Biplane design was very popular during the early days of aviation, because it created a large area of wing surface to provide lift. As designs became more sophisticated and speeds rose, however, the additional drag created by the second wing outweighed the advantage of its extra lift and modern aircraft are now all monoplanes.

The British biplane, the SE5, was a fighter plane during the First World War.

Birch trees are sometimes called 'lady of the woods' because of their graceful appearance. They are native to the northern temperate and Arctic regions, where they prefer light, sandy, slightly acid soils. All species are deciduous. The thin branches, papery stems and tiny leaves are characteristic features of the birches.

The silver birch grows to a height of 18 m (60 ft), and has a silvery, peeling bark. It is a native of Asia Minor and Europe. The canoe or paper bark birch is a native of North America. It gets its name from the fact that its bark was used by North American Indians for their canoes, as well as for roofing. Other species include the tiny dwarf birch of the Scottish Highlands, and the hardy white birch of the polar regions.

Bird is a vertebrate possessing feathers. Birds are the only animals which have feathers, and they use them for flight, insulation, camouflage and display. A few species of bird

– penguins and ostriches, for example – cannot fly, even though they have feathers. Birds have no teeth, but have a beak which is often used to tear off pieces of food. The feet may be clawed or webbed, depending on the bird's life-style. Birds possess extremely good eyesight. For example, an eagle can spot a rabbit from a distance of more than 3 km (nearly 2 miles). All birds produce young which hatch from eggs, and throughout the bird world there is an enormous array of bizzare and exotic courtship, nesting and parental behaviour to ensure successful breeding.

About 9000 species of bird are found throughout the world, and in every type of habitat. Over half of all bird species belong to the passerines, or perching birds, which include thrushes, robins, blackbirds and jays. *See also* Feathers.

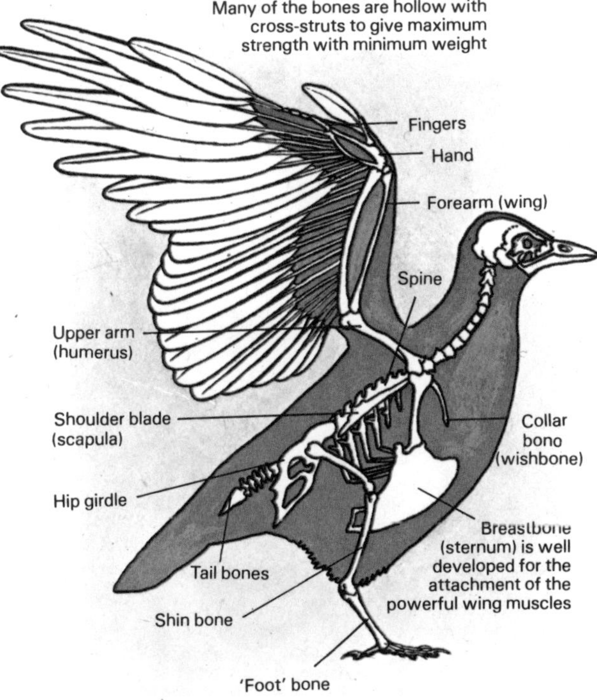

Diagram of a bird, showing the skeleton.

Biscay, Bay of, is an inlet of the Atlantic Ocean, between France and Spain. Area about 184 000 sq km (71 000 sq miles). The bay is notorious for rough seas.

Bismarck, Otto von (1815–1898), was a Prussian statesman who became first Chancellor of the German Empire. Appointed chief minister of Prussia in 1862, he defeated Denmark in war in 1864 and acquired Schleswig-Holstein. His victory over Austria two years later made Prussia the leading state in Germany. In 1870–1871 he waged a successful war against France and annexed Alsace-Lorraine. As Chancellor of a united Germany (1871) he introduced many economic and social reforms, and was a dominant figure in European politics. He was dismissed in 1890 by the Emperor William II when they disagreed over future policy.

Bison (or North American buffalo, as it is sometimes called) is a member of the large group of animals called cattle. Their huge, bearded heads and shaggy coated shoulders make it hard to mistake bison for any other animal.

The bison is an animal of the North American plains and once, before they were virtually wiped out by settlers and railroaders in the 19th century, huge herds could be seen. The total bison population, once estimated at 60 million, can be numbered nowadays in thousands only, although these are strictly protected.

Bitterns comprise 12 species of birds found throughout the world, with representatives in North America, Europe, South and Central America, west Africa and New Guinea. Bitterns are long-beaked, secretive birds, superbly camouflaged to blend into the reeds and swamps which are their home. The males of some species are more brightly coloured, however. Quite often the only indication of the presence of a bittern is its booming call, which can be heard over a great distance.

Bizet, Georges (1838–1875), was a French composer. In his own time he was most successful with incidental music, but today he is remembered chiefly for his operas, in particular his last opera, *Carmen.* It was a failure when first produced in 1875 but has since become one of the most popular operas ever written. Bizet's mastery of melody is characteristic of all his work, including piano music, songs and church music.

Black Death, a form of bubonic and pneumonic plague, ravaged Asia and Europe in the 14th century. Beginning in the Far East, it gradually spread westwards. When it reached England in 1348, it had a devastating effect. People who caught the disease generally died within a few hours and more than one-third of the population is thought to have perished. This brought about much social unrest and profoundly affected the country's economy.

Black hole is an object which astronomers think might exist in space. Nobody has found one yet, although it is thought that one particular object, called Cygnus X-1, may contain a black hole. When a star dies it may collapse to form a neutron star. This is very dense, much denser than anything found on Earth. If a very large star collapsed it would form an even denser body. This would be so massive it would have a huge force of gravity. Anything which came near it would be sucked into it. If a person went too near it they would be drawn out into a long, string-like shape as they were sucked in. Even light rays would be sucked in, so we would not be able to see it.

Black Sea is the sea between Europe and Asia, connected with the Mediterranean by narrow waterways. Area 460 000 sq km (177 000 sq miles). It has been especially important to the USSR, which has few warm-water seaports, and to Turkey, which controlled the rest of its shores until the 19th century. The Black Sea has almost no tide and is very salty, so fish and plant life is poor.

Blériot, Louis (1872–1936), was a French aircraft manufacturer – the first man to cross a sea by air successfully when he flew the English Channel in 1909. The flight, from Calais to Dover, took 37 minutes in a simple monoplane of Blériot's own design. As an aircraft designer, Blériot carried out important development on aircraft controls, inventing many of the basic systems in use today. *See also* Wright brothers.

Right: The circulatory system of blood in the human body.

Blood is a fluid which is found in most animals. It is normally carried throughout the body in a series of vessels called arteries, veins and capillaries, controlled by the pumping action of the heart. It serves a variety of purposes, and consists of several distinct parts. The watery part of the blood is called plasma. Within the plasma are red blood cells which contain the pigment haemoglobin carrying the oxygen we need in order to live; in some lowly animals the pigment is called haemocyanin and is dissolved in the plasma. Also found in the blood are white blood cells, which destroy harmful foreign bodies, and platelets, which clot the blood when we bleed, so that we do not bleed to death. In addition to these, the blood carries dissolved food to various parts of the body for nourishment, hormones – the body's chemical messengers – waste products, carbon dioxide and, very importantly, heat to keep the body warm.

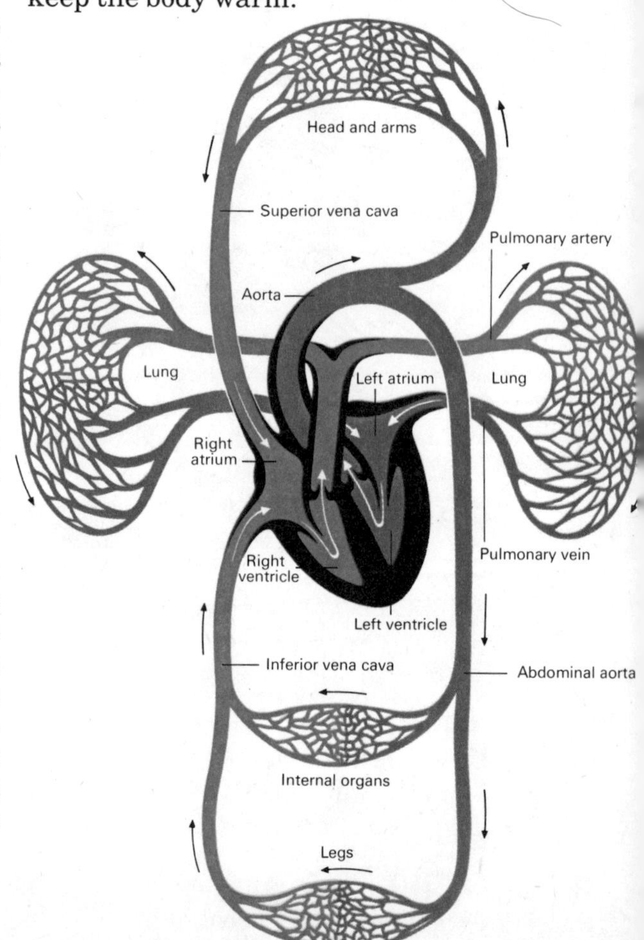

Blood circulation varies according to the animal, but in warm-blooded animals, such as humans, it is as follows. Blood is pumped from one side of the heart to the lungs, where it receives oxygen. The blood then passes back to the other side of the heart where it is pumped to the head and limbs, and organs such as the liver and kidneys. Further vessels carry the blood, now depleted of its oxygen, back to the first side of the heart, where it is pumped to the lungs again to receive oxygen.

Blubber is the layer of thick, fatty tissue lying between the skin and muscle layers of certain marine mammals, such as whales and seals. The thickness of the blubber layer may vary. For instance, when whales are swimming in the cold polar seas, the blubber is at its thickest. However, when crossing through warmer waters, the layer becomes much thinner. Without an insulating layer of blubber, it would be impossible for warm-blooded animals, such as whales and seals, to exist in the cold seas which are their home. The blubber is such a good insulator that, in some instances, the heat from the decomposing tissues of a dead whale has been contained by the blubber to such an extent that it has started to cook the whale's body!

Blue Mountains is a mountain range in New South Wales, Australia. It forms part of the Great Dividing Range, and its average height is 1000 m (3000 ft). The Blue Mountains is also the name for a low range of mountains in the USA, in north-east Oregon and south-east Washington. There is also a range of mountains, called the Blue Mountains, in Jamaica.

Bluebird, see Land speed record.

Boa constrictor is a large snake which, like the pythons and the other boas, kills its prey by wrapping its body around the victim and suffocating it. The boa constrictor is found from Mexico to Argentina in a variety of habitats, ranging from rainforest to arid lands. The boa constrictor preys on warm-blooded and cold-blooded animals. It has been known to live up to 25 years in captivity, and can be up to 3.7 m (12 ft) long.

Boadicea (1st century AD), was the British Queen of the Iceni tribe in East Anglia. She rose in rebellion when the Romans seized her husband's kingdom after his death. The Iceni sacked Colchester, St Albans and London while the Roman governor of Britain, Suetonius Paulinus, was with his army in Wales. He hastily returned and defeated her in battle, after which she committed suicide.

Boar, see Wild boar.

Boat is a small vessel for travelling on water. A boat may be powered by oars, sails or an engine. The earliest boats, used in prehistoric times, were made from either hollowed-out logs or rushwood.

Bobcat is a small member of the cat family, about 1 m (3 ft) in length, found in North America. Also known as the bay lynx, its coat varies in pattern from mottled to striped. The bobcat is adaptable, living in a variety of habitats and eating many kinds of prey, including small deer.

Boccaccio, Giovanni (1313–1375), was an Italian writer. He was one of the first scholars of the movement known as humanism, characteristic of the Renaissance, and he wrote in his native tongue rather than Latin (the universal language of European scholars in the Middle Ages). His most

Boa constrictor

famous work is the *Decameron*, a collection of stories, often humorous, sometimes scandalous, which he drew from many sources.

Boer War (1899–1902) was fought between Britain and the two Boer republics in South Africa, the Transvaal and the Orange Free State. Trouble began when the Boers refused to grant civil rights to the many foreigners who went to dig for gold in the Transvaal. In October 1899 the Boers declared war on Britain, invaded Cape Colony and Natal, and besieged the towns of Mafeking, Ladysmith and Kimberley. At first the British troops suffered heavy losses, but eventually relieved the three towns and annexed the two Boer republics. After two years of guerrilla warfare the Boers finally surrendered in 1902.

Boiling point is the temperature at which a liquid turns into a vapour or gas. For example, when water is heated in a kettle, it boils to form steam. The boiling point of water is 100 degrees Centigrade (212 degrees Fahrenheit). Different liquids have different boiling points.

Boleyn, Anne (1507–1536), the second wife of King Henry VIII, was secretly married to him before his divorce from Catherine of Aragon was complete. In 1533 she gave birth to a daughter, the future Queen Elizabeth I, but Henry was disappointed when she failed to produce a male heir. Accused of being unfaithful, she was condemned to death and executed in the Tower of London in May 1536.

Boer troops ambush British soldiers near a railway line during the Boer War.

Bolivar, Simon (1783–1830), a Venezuelan soldier and statesman, was largely responsible for freeing South America from Spanish rule. After initial setbacks which forced him into exile, he liberated New Granada (now Colombia), Venezuela and Ecuador, and subsequently Peru and Upper Peru (now Bolivia). By 1824 most of the continent was free, but Bolivar's attempts to create a unified South America were unsuccessful.

Bolivia is a republic in central South America. Capitals, La Paz (government) and Sucre; area about 1 100 000 sq km (424 000 sq miles). The ancient Bolivian civilization survived Spanish colonial rule. The country became independent in 1825, fought wars over territory with its neighbours and, more recently, suffered violent changes of government.

Bolivia is low, hot and forested in the east, with fertile valleys growing rice, sugar cane and cotton. It is very mountainous in the west, where the climate varies greatly according to altitude. Cattle and sheep are raised and, in higher pastures, llamas. Mining, especially tin, is the most profitable industry.

More than half the population are direct descendants of the people of the Inca empire, though most power and money is held by those of European descent.

Bolshoi Ballet is an outstanding Russian ballet company. It was founded in the late 18th century and, during the 19th, it led the national Russian ballet movement.

Bone is a substance found only in vertebrates, and makes up the greater part of their skeletons. Bone is composed basically of special, branching cells called osteoblasts lying in a substance known as a matrix. The matrix contains calcium and phosphate salts.

Birds have specially lightened bones for flying; these bones are almost hollow, with large air spaces and supporting struts inside.

Boomerang is a bent or curved piece of hard wood with a sharp edge, used in hunting, warfare and sport by the native Australians – the Aborigines. One type of boomerang can be thrown so it flies in an arc or circle and returns to the thrower.

Borges, Jorge Luis (1899–), is a South American writer. He was born in Argentina but spent much of his youth in Europe. Borges' 'fictions', as he called them, are set in a mysterious, frightening world something like Kafka's, which is a distorted version of the real world. The award of the important Formentor Prize in 1961 (shared with Beckett) made him suddenly famous, and today he is recognized as one of the most distinguished writers in 20th-century literature. Borges became blind in the 1950s and dictated his works to secretaries or friends.

Borgia was an Italian family of Spanish origin, infamous in the 15th and 16th centuries. Rodrigo Borgia (1431–1503), who became Pope Alexander VI, was notorious for his immorality and extravagance. He was, however, a notable patron of the arts, and it was he who divided the New World between Spain and Portugal. His ruthless and brutal son Cesare (1475–1507) tried to establish his own absolute authority in central Italy. After the death of his father he was imprisoned by the new Pope and was later killed in battle in Spain. His sister Lucrezia (1480–1519) was noted for her encouragement of art and learning.

Borneo see Brunei; Indonesia; Malaysia

Bosch, Jerome (died 1516), was a Flemish painter. He was a very odd artist indeed, whose paintings, full of weird and mysterious incidents, could be called Surrealist. No doubt their meaning was clearer in his own time, and scholars have explained some of the strange goings-on in terms of medieval folklore, humour and popular ideas.

Boston Tea Party took place on 16 December 1773, when a group of American colonists disguised as Indians boarded a ship and threw a cargo of tea into Boston harbour. This was an act of protest against the continuing British taxation of tea, since the Americans objected to paying taxes when they were not represented in Parliament. Britain retaliated by imposing stricter control on the colonies, and the ill feeling which this created brought the two countries closer to war.

Botha, Pieter Willem (1916–), is a South African politician. He has held several posts in the South African Parliament, having been the member for George, Cape Province, since 1948. He became Prime Minister of South Africa in 1978.

Botswana is a republic in south central Africa. Capital, Gaborone; area about 580 000 sq km (220 000 sq miles). A former British protectorate named Bechuanaland from 1884, it gained independence in 1966.

Most of Botswana is flat tableland, where cattle are raised. The people are herdsmen by tradition. Otherwise, agriculture is rather poor due to the dry climate. There is some mining and opportunity for more. At present, health and education are being developed, but the country's resources are small. There are no large cities and areas of the plains are almost uninhabited.

Botticelli, Sandro (1445–1510), was one of the greatest painters of the Renaissance in Florence. His paintings have a delicacy which is accompanied by a sure sense of dramatic effect and a vigorous command of line. There is also nearly always a characteristic hint of sadness, even in his paintings of joyful subjects like the *Birth of Venus*. That and his equally famous *Primavera* ('Spring') are good examples of Botticelli's creation of a new type of beauty. Among his other works are frescoes in the Sistine Chapel, illustrations for Dante's *Inferno* and many sad, passionate religious subjects.

Boyle, Robert (1627–1691), was a chemist and physicist. He was born in Munster in Ireland, but spent most of his life in England. He experimented with air and vacuums, and developed an air pump. His work on air and other gases led him in 1662 to formulate what is now called Boyle's Law. This states that, at a given temperature, the volume of a gas is inversely proportional to its pressure. For example, if the volume of a gas is doubled, its pressure is halved, according to the law.

One of his important contributions to chemistry is that he defined an element as a substance which cannot be broken down by chemical means. This helped form the basis for modern chemistry. He was a founder member of the Royal Society.

Bracken is a common fern of woodland and heathland which has a tough underground stem called a rhizome. The rhizome spreads through the soil, pushing up its familiar unfurling leaves, or fronds, at intervals. Left alone, bracken can very quickly colonize new ground. Bracken spores can be seen on the underside of the leaves in late summer, and are blown by the wind. When they land they produce a heart-shaped prothallus, which eventually produces a new plant. As autumn arrives, bracken leaves turn a golden brown colour.

Brahma, in Hindu belief, is the creator of the universe. Brahmanism is the name given to the Hindu religion in the period when it was becoming fully developed, roughly between 1000 BC and AD 200. Brahmanism itself was a development of the yet more ancient Vedic religion.

Brahma is the first being in the Hindu trinity (Trimurti) of gods. The others are

Vishnu and Siva, and these three are exalted high above all other gods. Brahma, however, was always more of an idea than an easily recognized being, like Vishnu and Siva, and he was less popular. Today he is little worshipped.

Brahms, Johannes (1838–1897), was a German composer. He earned his living from the age of 13 as a pianist, sometimes playing in dance halls and rough pubs. In 1853 he went on tour as an accompanist to a famous violinist, a major turning point in his career. He met Liszt and Schumann, who wrote an article acclaiming him as a genius. In 1863 he settled in Vienna, teaching, performing and composing. He was opposed to the 'new music' represented by Liszt and Wagner, and his greatest works followed traditional forms. He was a master of all forms of composition from symphonies to songs, but he never wrote an opera.

The Braille system of dots.

Braille, Louis (1809–1852), was a French teacher who developed a system of writing for the blind. He was blinded in an accident at the age of three and later studied at an institute for the blind. He invented Braille writing, which consists of a varying pattern of raised dots, enabling the blind to read by touch, when he was still young. He later made improvements in his system and also applied it to the reading of music.

Bracken leaves, and spores shown on the underside of a leaf.

Brain is a collection of nerve cells which receive messages (stimuli) and then cause the body to react to the stimuli. However, not all the lowly animals have true brains, and even some of the larger animals – sharks, birds or dogs, for instance – have very limited 'brain power' compared with humans, even though we often consider them to be quite intelligent.

It is in humans that the brain reaches the greatest degree of development. The human brain is made up of two greatly folded structures called cerebral hemispheres. The outer part of the cerebral hemispheres are responsible for memory and learning. Behind the cerebral hemispheres is the cerebellum, which controls certain muscular movements. The hypothalamus, seated deep inside the brain, controls glandular activity. Other parts of the brain deal with the signals which we receive when we see, hear, smell, taste and touch things. Yet other parts help to keep the body working properly – for instance, a part of the brain tells us to keep breathing when we are asleep. The brain is protected inside the bony skull, and is connected to the spinal cord, a long core of nerve tissue to which are attached nerves from various parts of the body. Messages go to and from the brain along the spinal cord, and in this way the brain is able to control the rest of the body.

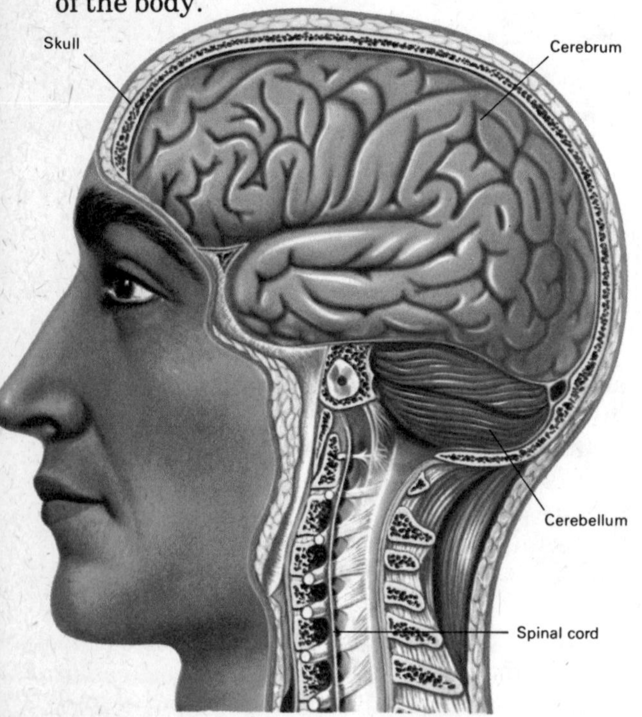

One of the most interesting results of brain study has shown that, whilst in humans the cerebral hemispheres (the part of the brain concerned with memory and learning) is well developed, the part concerned with smell is not. A bird's brain, whilst not having particularly well-developed cerebral hemispheres, has highly developed optical regions, since it needs very good eyesight for flying. Dogs, on the other hand, have brains in which the parts concerned with hearing and smell are highly developed.

Brass is an alloy of copper and zinc, which is golden or yellow in colour. It seems to have been known in ancient times – the Old Testament mentions brass musical instruments – and in the Middle Ages it was widely used for cannons. Versatile and easily worked, brass has been widely used in manufacturing, notably ships' propellers and fittings and such household items as doorknobs, fenders and lamps.

Inside some old English churches can be found at least one monumental brass – that is, a brass sheet with a figure cut into it, commemorating some local person. An impression of such a figure can be taken with black or gold wax on paper. This is called brass rubbing and is a popular hobby.

Brazil is a republic in South America. Capital, Brasilia; area about 8500000 sq km (3280000 sq miles).

History In colonial times Brazil was Portuguese rather than Spanish like the rest of South America, and Portuguese is the official language today. The Portuguese actually occupied little of the country, but in the 18th century important discoveries of gold and diamonds were made which, with the sugar and coffee plantations, brought riches to Portugal. Early in the 19th century the Portuguese king actually lived in Brazil, but in 1822 the country became independent under an emperor. After a revolution, it became a republic in 1891. In recent times it has had periods of democratic government and of dictatorship.

Land Brazil takes up roughly half of South America. It is nearly as large as the USA. The lowlands bordering the great Amazon River take up the northern third of Brazil. Most of it is jungle, much is swamp, and parts of Amazonia are very remote. The remainder of the country is mainly flat plateaux, with a number of mountain ranges, especially in the south-east. There is a narrow coastal plain, containing most of the large towns. About 75 per cent of the people live within 150 km (90 miles) of the coast, while large parts of the interior have almost no inhabitants. The foundation of a modern capital, Brasilia, in the interior in 1960 was intended as a sign of modern Brazil's determination to make the most of its own great resources and to get away from the foreign influences associated with the old, coastal capital, Rio de Janeiro.

People Brazil is a country where the races have become mingled more thoroughly than in many others. Brazilians may be of pure European, pure American Indian, or pure African descent, but most of them are a mixture. However, there are huge differences in living standards between rich and poor. The main religion is Roman Catholicism.

Economy Brazil has great natural resources including a wealth of minerals, hydro-electric power, timber and forest products. So far it has not fully developed these riches (though destruction of Brazil's forests is now causing international alarm). Farming is the biggest occupation but only a tiny part of the land is farmed. Coffee has long been Brazil's main export and is still vital to the economy, along with cotton and livestock. There are many manufacturing industries, but at present they are of minor importance.

Besides the shortage of money and skilled people, Brazil's chief problem is poor transportation. Road and railway-building is extremely difficult due to huge distances and natural obstacles. Much use is made of air transport and of the great rivers. Nearly 35 000 km (22 000 miles) of inland waterways are navigable.

Breathing, see Respiration.

Brecht, Bertolt (1889–1956), was a German playwright. A rebel from his youth, he sympathized with Communism as can be seen in most of his plays. He fled from the Nazis and lived in American in the 1940s, before returning to Communist East Berlin, where he created the Berlin Ensemble, a theatre company that became internationally famous. Brecht's influential 'epic theatre' made use of devices like songs, speech directed to the audience, printed signs and projected film to rouse the audience to a sharper awareness of social injustice. His most-often produced plays are *A Man's a Man*, *The Threepenny Opera* (music by Kurt Weill), *Mother Courage* and *The Caucasian Chalk Circle*.

Brazilian Indians obediently kiss the crosses of the Portuguese.

Brezhnev, Leonid (1906–1982), was a Soviet statesman. He served as a political commissar in the Red Army during the Second World War, subsequently holding offices in Moldavia and Kazakhstan. In 1960 he became Chairman of the Presidium of the Supreme Soviet and four years later succeeded Nikita Khrushchev as leader (First Secretary) of the Soviet Communist Party. In 1977 he was appointed President of the Presidium. The main aim of his foreign policy was to achieve nuclear arms control and a relaxation of tension with Western countries.

Britain, Battle of, was the air war fought between the Royal Air Force and the German Luftwaffe from July to October 1940. In June 1940 Adolf Hitler began to make plans for the invasion of Britain. Before this could take place it was necessary for him to destroy British air power. The Luftwaffe launched a series of attacks against south-east England, first against shipping and targets on the coast, then against airfields and finally against London and other towns. The German planes greatly outnumbered the defending British aircraft, but the use of radar gave the RAF advance warning. By the end of October the Luftwaffe had lost over 1700 planes, and the invasion was abandoned.

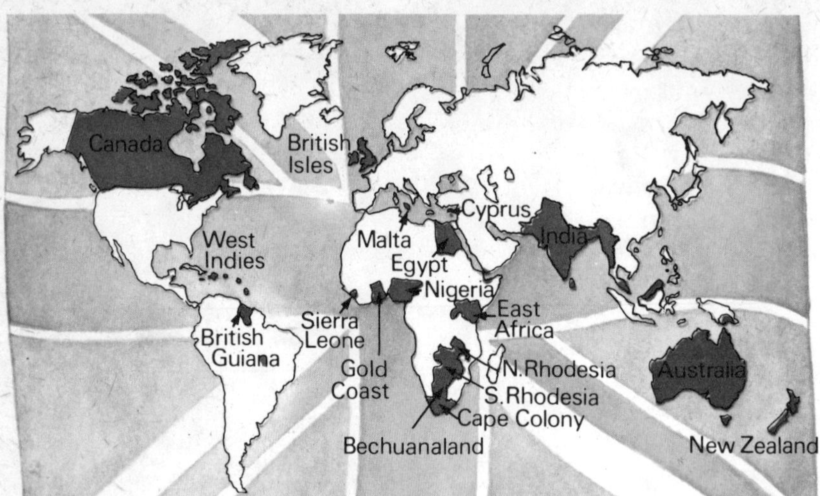

A map showing the extent of the British Empire in 1897.

British Empire was the name given to the overseas possessions acquired by Britain over a period of 400 years. The Empire really began with the founding of colonies in North America in the early 17th century. In the 18th century Britain won Canada and India from the French, but lost the 13 American colonies. After the Napoleonic Wars, Britain acquired new possessions in the West Indies, and later in the 19th century, emigration to Australia and New Zealand began. New colonies were also created in Africa. Countries like Canada and Australia became self-governing, and the Empire evolved into the Commonwealth of Nations.

British Isles are an island group in the north-east Atlantic. The British Isles include England, Scotland, Wales, Northern Ireland and the Irish Republic as well as the Channel Islands and the Isle of Man.

For details see entries on individual countries and United Kingdom.

Britten, Benjamin (1913–1976), was one of the greatest English composers of any age. He wrote mainly vocal music, and some of his most beautiful works were written for children's voices. His operas, notably *Peter Grimes* (1945), are his most famous works, together with his great *War Requiem* (1961), which was inspired by his pacifist convictions. With his friend and associate, the singer Peter Pears, he founded the music festival at Aldeburgh in Suffolk.

Bromeliads are a group of exotic plants, many of which are epiphytes, plants which live on trees, growing in the rainforests of South America. Bromeliads produce clusters of spiky leaves which grow around short stems. Some species of bromeliad bear very strange-looking flowers; these arise from the centre of the whorl of leaves, borne on a long, thin stalk. The most familiar member of the bromeliad family is the pineapple. The outer coating of the pineapple is the remains of the leaves and flowers.

Bromine is a reddish brown liquid element. It has the chemical symbol Br. Bromine is one of the very few elements which are liquid at ordinary temperatures. It gives off a strong-smelling vapour which irritates the eyes and throat. It is taken out, or extracted, from sea water, and also from a mineral called carnallite.

Bromine forms compounds called bromides when mixed with metals. Silver bromide is used in photography. Potassium bromide is used in medicine as a sedative. Bromides are also used in certain dyes and in some fire extinguishers.

Brontës were a family of English novelists. Their father was the vicar of Haworth, Yorkshire. The family consisted of three sisters: Charlotte (1816–1855), Emily (1818–1848) and Anne (1820–1849) and their brother Branwell. Besides poetry, Emily wrote only one novel, the haunting *Wuthering Heights*

(1847). It has extraordinary dramatic and emotional force, which no critic has ever been able to explain satisfactorily. Charlotte's best novel, *Jane Eyre* (1847), has great realism and insight into character, worked into a rather sensational plot. It was an instant success. Of her three other novels *Vilette* (1853) is the most popular. Anne was the least gifted, but *The Tenant of Wildfell Hall* (1848), springing from her horror at the decline, through drink and drug addiction, of her brother Branwell, is interesting.

Bronze Age was the age in the history of mankind marked by the use of metal implements. It was the first stage of human metallurgy (metalwork), when both copper and bronze were used.

The earliest really strong tools and weapons were made from stone. It was only a few thousand years ago that humans discovered how to work with metals, melting and casting copper to make far more accurate and efficient implements. Some peoples (for example, the Egyptians) used only copper, whereas others found that bronze – an alloy of copper and tin – was easier to cast and stronger than copper on its own.

A gilt-bronze shield and bowl from the 1st century BC and a mirror from the 1st century AD.

Metals were first used in the Middle East in about 6500 BC, and probably led to the rise of the earliest civilizations from about 3500 BC. Between about 3000 and 1000 BC, many flourishing big-city cultures developed in the Middle East, the Mediterranean and China, based on copper or bronze. In Britain, the Bronze Age began about 1800 BC, and rich deposits of British tin became important in European trade.

From about 1100 BC, iron began to replace bronze for most purposes, ushering in the Iron Age.

Brown, Arthur Whitten-, see Alcock and Brown.

Brown, John (1800–1859), was an American anti-slavery leader. In 1859 he led a small band of men in an attack on Harpers Ferry, Virginia, a federal arsenal, hoping to establish a base where escaped slaves could find refuge. His attempt failed, and he was hanged for treason; but his name became a rallying cry for those who wanted to abolish slavery.

Bruckner, Anton (1824–1896), was an Austrian composer. He was a famous organist in his day and began composing comparatively late in life, inspired partly by Wagner who became a great friend. His music was controversial, partly because his devotion to Wagner aroused the hostility of the supporters of Brahms in Vienna, where Bruckner lived. Nevertheless, modern critics have seen in Bruckner a continuation of the older Austrian tradition represented by Schubert. Bruckner's music is on a massive scale. His outstanding works are nine symphonies, though his church music founded in his strong religious faith, is equally impressive.

Bruegel, Pieter (circa 1520–1569), was a Flemish painter, known as 'the Elder' to distinguish him from his son, Pieter the Younger (1564–1638).

Bruegel's greatest works were paintings of ordinary peasant life, though he was an educated, widely travelled man. They also show a mastery of landscape – especially winter landscape.

Brunei is a sultanate on the island of Borneo, south-east Asia. Capital, Bandar Seri Begawan; area about 5800 sq km (2226 sq miles). Brunei is a self-governing state under British protection, within Malaysia. It was once much larger and more powerful, but it still has a fairly high income due to its oil and rubber. The people are mainly Malay, with some Chinese. Islam is the official religion.

Brunel, Isambard Kingdom (1806–1859), was a highly skilful and imaginative English engineer. He helped design the Rotherhithe tunnel under the River Thames in London, and planned the Clifton Suspension Bridge in Bristol. He also worked for Great Western Railways, designing all the bridges and tunnels for the railway line from London to Bristol. Brunel built a number of docks and three steamships. The *Great Western* was completed in 1838, the *Great Britain* in 1845 and the *Great Eastern* in 1858.

Brunel's steamship, the *Great Britain.*

Bryophytes are the group of primitive green plants which comprise the mosses and the liverworts. There are a great many species of mosses, often occurring on the tops of old walls, between paving stones, on garden lawns in autumn, and coating trees and rocks. Look closely and you may see the thin stalks of the spore-bearing capsules which arise from the green part of the plant.

There are two main types of liverwort. The leafy liverworts look rather like mosses. The thallose liverworts are usually rounded, flat, ribbon-like structures, anchored to the ground by tiny hairs. Most liverworts live in damp places such as the sides of ditches and streams, in damp woodlands or actually in water.

Buckingham Palace is the London residence of the British Sovereign, situated at the west end of St James's Park. It has served this purpose since 1837. Formerly owned by the Dukes of Buckingham, it was bought by George III in 1761. John Nash remodelled it into a 600-room palace in 1825, and Sir Aston Webb redesigned the east front in 1913.

Bud is a short, undeveloped shoot surrounded by young leaves. The winter buds of trees in temperate regions lie dormant until spring. Then the protective leaf scales fall away and the buds burst forth to produce new shoots and flowers. Many trees have structures called subsidiary buds. These are reserve buds, and they never open unless the main stem becomes damaged.

Buddha, 'the Enlightened One', (died circa 483 BC), is the founder of Buddhism. His family name was Gautama. He was a young warrior prince who, according to legend, left his family at the age of 29 to search for wisdom. One night, sitting under the sacred Tree of Enlightenment, the truth flashed into his mind. He became 'the Buddha' and

A statue of Buddha, made of sandstone.

spent nearly 50 years preaching and teaching the way of enlightenment.

The term Buddha is also used to describe a variety of Buddha figures.

Buddhism is a religion founded in India by Guatama Buddha. The aim of Buddhism is to gain *nirvana*, a state of enlightenment, gained through the extinction of all desires. The law of *karma* is concerned with reincarnation and the belief that acts in this life affect future lives.

Although Buddha is worshipped by his followers, there is no god in Buddhism and therefore no prayer. Buddhism does not recognize the soul, or spirit, in a Christian sense. Body and soul are one, and everything is connected. The life of a person is a part of the life of the universal soul, just as each wave is a part of the ocean.

Like Jesus, Buddha wrote nothing down, but his early disciples composed books (*sutras*) of his teaching soon after his death. Buddhism spread to all the countries of the Far East (though it declined in India, being re-absorbed by Hinduism) and became divided into a great many sects or branches. In modern Japan, for instance, there are at least 70 sects or sub-sects.

Budgerigar, see Parakeet.

Buffaloes are found in Europe, Asia and Africa (though the word 'buffalo' is sometimes used to describe the North American bison.) There are several species of buffalo, all resembling oxen. The domestic buffalo found in the Balkans, Italy, Egypt and the USSR is also known as the Indian or water buffalo, and a few still live wild in India and Indochina. Their milk contains twice as much cream as cow's milk. Two other Asiatic species are the tamarau of the Philippines and the anoa of Celebes.

The African buffaloes are the dwarf or forest buffalo of west Africa, and the Cape buffalo of the plains of eastern and southern Africa. Wild buffalo will charge at anything they consider to be a threat.

Bulb is a highly modified plant shoot in which the short stem is surrounded by thick, fleshy leaves. Plants which produce bulbs do so as a means of surviving the winter. Bulbs are also a means of increasing numbers vegetatively (in other words, without sexual reproduction). Within the leaves is a food store and, after the part of the plant above ground withers away, this underground part is left to await the return of spring. In spring, the buds draw on the food reserves within the leaves and produce new shoots which sprout out of the ground. As the new shoots grow, the bulb withers. However, during the warm months of the year whilst the plant is growing and producing flowers and seeds, food is stored in a new bulb ready for the coming winter. A typical bulb is the onion.

Bulgaria is a republic in south-east Europe. Capital, Sofia; area about 111 000 sq km (42 000 sq miles). The Bulgars settled here after the fall of the Roman empire, but a Bulgarian state existed only briefly, between long periods of rule by the Byzantine and, later, the Turkish Empires. The modern Bulgarian state dates from 1878.

After liberation from Axis occupation by Soviet forces in the Second World War, the Bulgarian monarchy was overthrown and a republic created.

Bulgaria is mainly a farming country, with plains, river valleys and two mountain ranges crossing its territory. A great variety of food crops are grown, especially for export to the Soviet Union, also, tobacco, mulberry trees (for silkworms) and roses (for making scent). There is not much heavy industry, and mining is also on a small scale.

Burma is a republic in south-east Asia. Capital, Rangoon; area about 678 000 sq km (262 000 sq miles).
History The ancestors of the Burmese themselves settled here nearly 2000 years ago. The country was often dominated by larger neighbours. The modern state dates from the 18th century but, after several wars, passed under British rule in the 19th century as a province of the Indian Empire. It was separated from India in 1937 and became independent in 1947.
Land and People Central Burma is formed of the basin of the Irrawaddy River and its tributaries. Much of the rest is mountainous. The climate is generally hot and humid and, in many parts, extremely wet – the tropical monsoon bringing heavy rain from May to October. The country is mainly agricultural, with rice the main crop. Fishing, forestry and mining are also important. Burma has oil deposits as well as other valuable minerals like silver, tungsten and lead.

The present population includes people of several different origins, including Chinese. Most of the people are Buddhists.

Burns, Robert (1759–1796), was a Scottish poet. A farmer's son, he was steeped in Scottish folklore, from which many of his works are fashioned. He usually wrote in the dialect of the Scottish Lowlands. Although he is most famous for poems like *Auld Lang Syne* and *Highland Mary*, his longer, satirical works like *Tam o' Shanter* are rated more highly by critics. He could not support himself by his poetry, and became a Customs and Excise officer.

Burundi is a republic in east-central Africa. Capital, Bujumbura; area about 28 000 sq km (10 600 sq miles). A former Belgian colony, Burundi has been independent since 1962. Small in area, the population is fairly large, and concentrated in a relatively small area of fertile uplands. Nearly everyone is engaged in simple farming, and development has been hindered by transport difficulties and lack of rich resources.

Bus – the first bus was a horse-drawn coach, known as an omnibus (from the Latin 'for all'), which quickly replaced the stagecoach in British towns and cities during the 1830s. An omnibus was much larger than a stagecoach, often with two 'decks' (the top deck was usually open). The development of the motorized bus followed that of the motor car and by the late 1920s buses were crossing continents at average speeds of over 40 km/h (25 mph).

Perhaps the most famous buses in the world are the red 'double-deckers' seen in London, but much larger buses have been made, including some articulated buses in Europe which can carry over 200 passengers.

Bush ballad, see Paterson, Andrew Barton 'Banjo'.

Bushbaby is a nocturnal (active at night) primate, found in Africa. It is an attractive mammal, with a long, furry tail and huge, forward-facing eyes. By day bushbabies sleep in hollow trees, but at night they come out to feed on insects, fruit and the gum that oozes from certain trees. They are extremely agile jumpers, leaping from tree to tree, and are up to 38 cm (15 in) long, excluding the tail. The smallest bushbaby, Demidoff's bushbaby, can easily fit into a person's cupped hand.

Butterflies, together with moths, make up the order of scaly winged insects known as the Lepidoptera. Butterflies are among the most beautiful of insects. They occur throughout the world in a huge array of colours and patterns. They are not all delicate creatures: some, such as the painted

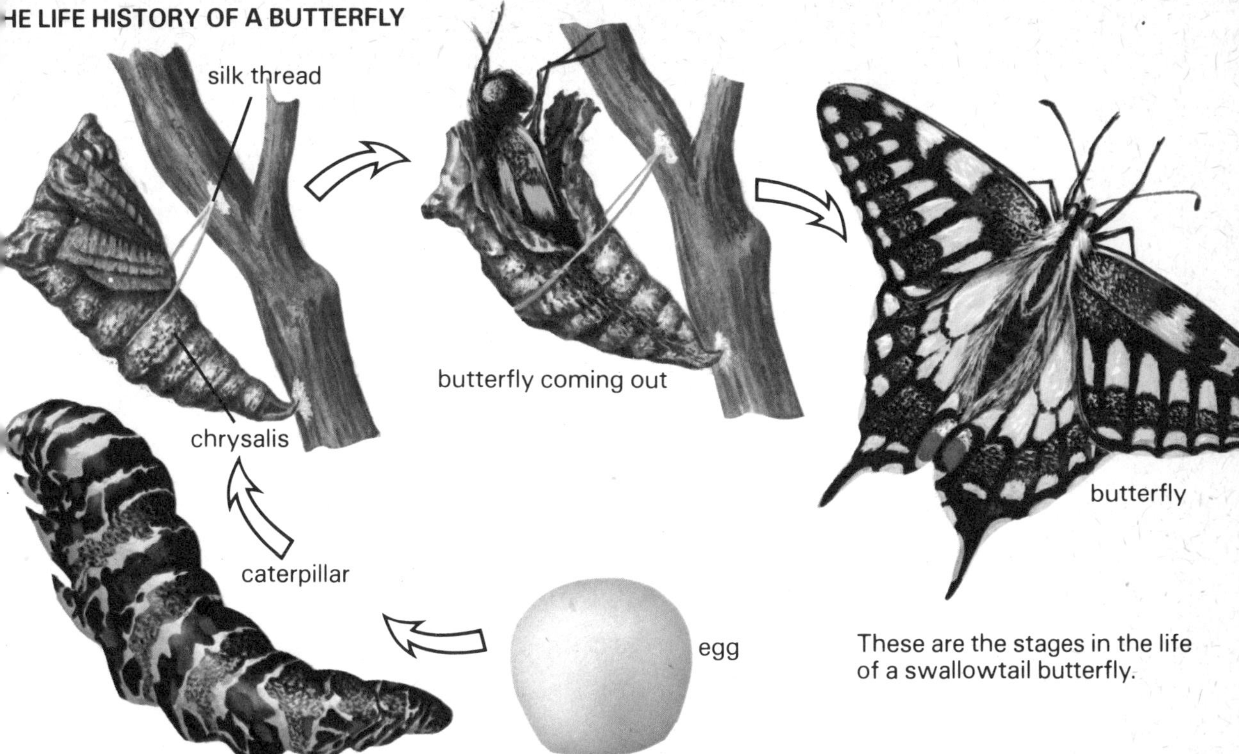

These are the stages in the life of a swallowtail butterfly.

lady, migrate all the way from Africa and Asia to breed in Europe.

Although there are exceptions, butterflies can be distinguished from moths because moths usually fly at night, have feathery antennae and fold their wings flat when resting.

The butterfly life cycle starts with an egg which hatches into a caterpillar. The caterpillar eventually turns into a pupa from which the adult emerges. *See also* Chrysalis.

Buzzards are birds of prey – in other words, they are birds which hunt and eat other animals. They are similar in appearance to eagles, with hooked beaks and strong talons. Like eagles, they can soar on broad, outstretched wings searching for prey on the ground below. When they spot a likely meal, they drop from the skies and seize the victim in their talons. They also eat dead flesh. The honey buzzard eats honeycombs and the larvae of wasps and bees.

Byron, George Gordon, Lord (1788–1824), was an English poet. Aristocratic, handsome, rich and romantic, Byron's personality had almost as much impact on Europe as his poetry, then and now. His *Childe Harold* (1812) made him immediately famous. Of later works, *Don Juan*, less romantic and more satirical, is the best. Another aspect of Byron's Romanticism was his devotion to freedom. He spent his fortune helping the Greeks in their fight for independence, and went to Greece himself where he caught a fever from which he died.

Byzantine art was the art of the Eastern Roman or Byzantine Empire, which lasted from AD 330 (foundation of Constantinople, now Istanbul) to 1453 (capture of Constantinople by the Turks). The most impressive products of Byzantine art are mosaics, a form of decoration using cubes of coloured glass or stone which was highly developed in the Roman Empire. Large, brilliantly coloured mosaics, using much gold-leaf, were made on walls, especially around the 6th and 7th centuries. Walls were also painted: there are fine examples to be seen in the churches and monasteries of south-east Europe. The other main products of Byzantine art are illustrated manuscripts and icons (religious

A Byzantine cross of the 12th century.

images).

Though originating in Western tradition, Byzantine art soon developed its own character. It was influenced by Eastern ideas, which partly explains its formal, stylized, almost abstract quality – more pattern than picture.

The greatest period of Byzantine art was the 4th to 6th centuries (when Hagia Sophia was built). For much of the 8th and 9th centuries pictorial art ceased as a result of an imperial order against making images. (Many Byzantine artists went to the West, where they influenced Gothic art.) A second 'golden age' lasted until the early 13th century (the age of the Crusades), but thereafter there was an overall decline, marked by the disappearance of mosaics.

Byzantine Empire was the name given to the eastern part of the Roman Empire after the Empire was divided into two parts in AD 395. Its capital was Constantinople. At its greatest extent the Empire included the Balkan peninsula, southern Italy, Asia Minor and North Africa. It survived long after the fall of the western Roman Empire, but gradually declined under the assaults of its enemies. It finally collapsed when the Ottoman Turks captured Constantinople in 1453. The Byzantine Empire passed on to Western Europe much of the culture and learning of ancient Greece and Rome.

Cabot, John (1450–1498), and his son Sebastian (1476–1557), were Venetian explorers in the service of Henry VII of England. They sailed west in search of a route to Asia and discovered Cape Breton Island and subsequently Newfoundland (1498). After John's death Sebastian worked as a navigator and cartographer for Henry VIII and the king of Spain. He explored the coast of South America and founded the Merchant Adventurers Company in London.

Cactus family comprises over 2000 species of unusual plants with beautiful flowers, which are found mainly in North America, with a few species in South America, Africa and Sri Lanka. Cacti grow in dry places such as deserts, and store water in their strange, thick stems. They have no real leaves, but bear spines which help to protect them from animals. One of the most unusual cacti – and now, sadly, a threatened species – is the giant cactus. This plant can live for over 250 years and stands like an enormous branched candlestick in deserts of south-west USA.

Caesar, Julius (101–44 BC), was a Roman general and statesman, who founded the

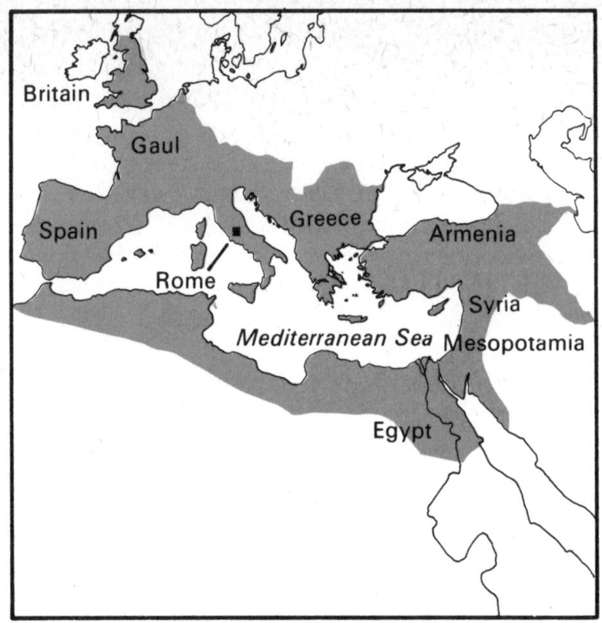

A map showing the greatest extent of the Roman Empire, founded by Julius Caesar.

Roman Empire. Although he was born into a patrician (aristocratic) family, as a young man he was a member of the popular party. He became more and more powerful politically, and in 60 BC set up the First Triumvirate (government headed by three people) with Pompey and Crassus. His successes in Gaul and his campaigns in Britain confirmed his reputation as a brilliant military leader. Then he marched into Italy with an army and defeated his rival, Pompey. After further successes he became dictator of Rome. He began a programme of important reforms, but his enemies, fearing that he wanted to become king, conspired against him. Caesar was assassinated in the Senate (supreme council of state) on the Ides of March (15 March), 44 BC.

Caimans are reptiles, very similar in appearance to alligators except that they have bony plates on their bellies instead of scales. Caimans live in Central and South America. The largest is the black caiman, which grows to a length of 5 m (16 ft).

Calcium is a silvery white metal. It has the chemical symbol Ca. It is one of the commonest metals in the Earth's crust.

It reacts easily with many other elements, and so is only found as a compound. Calcium carbonate occurs as chalk, limestone and marble. It is used in many products from toothpaste to concrete. Calcium phosphate is used in fertilizers. Calcium sulphate is found as gypsum and anhydrite. It is used in building materials, and blackboard chalk is made of calcium sulphate.

Calcium compounds cause hardness of water. Much of the food we eat contains calcium. We need it to strengthen our bones and teeth.

Calculator is a device which can add, subtract and do other calculations. The abacus was the first calculator. It has coloured beads which can be moved along wires to add and subtract.

The first calculating machine was invented by Blaise Pascal in 1642. This used toothed wheels to count. Today many people use electronic calculators. These can do complicated calculations almost instantly. Many can also store information.

Calendar is a system used for calculating time. Calendars usually divide the year into months and days. A year is the time it takes for the Earth to orbit the Sun once. A day is the time it takes for the Earth to spin around once. So we measure time by a movement in space. For this reason calendars used to be drawn up by astronomers. Calendars often show the phases of the Moon and sometimes the positions of stars and planets. There are nearly 365.24 days in a year. About 5000 years ago Egyptian astronomers divided the year into 12 months. This is the basis of the modern Christian, Jewish and Muslim calendars.

A calendar must be accurately related to natural events so that it gives the right date every year for such things as the movements of the tides and the sowing and harvesting of crops. However, over the centuries calendars have in practice got seriously out of phase with nature. The modern calendar (called Gregorian, after Pope Gregory XIII) is a corrected version of the older Julian calendar (named after Julius Caesar).

Calvinism is a form of Christian belief which began with the teaching of the reformer John Calvin (1509–1564). It is a severe form of Protestantism which insists on the sinfulness of the human race, and the predestination of all people. Only a few, chosen by God, can gain salvation; the rest are condemned to damnation.

Calvinist beliefs were especially strong in Presbyterianism, among other Protestant Churches.

Cambodia, see Kampuchea

Cambrian is a period in the history of the Earth, known from the study of rocks and the fossil remains found in them (the geological record). The Cambrian period is the first major division of the Paleozoic era and is characterized by abundant fossils. Its name comes from Cambria, the Roman name for Wales, where rocks of this period were first investigated.

The Cambrian period began about 570 million years ago and lasted for about 70 million years. It was a period when all living things were still confined to the sea but when life was becoming more diverse. In addition to plants, creatures with shells (but not yet with backbones) became common.

Camel is a large, hoofed mammal that occurs as two species: the Arabian or one-humped camel (dromedary) which is used for riding; and the Asian or two-humped camel (bactrian). The Arabian camel is now domesticated but the Asian camel still lives wild in the Gobi Desert.

Camels are known as 'ships of the desert'. Contrary to popular belief, they do not store water in their humps, although they can drink enormous amounts when the opportunity arises – 115 l (25 gals) in ten minutes has been known. Camels can go for many days without drinking, and are experts at conserving the water which is in their bodies. They can also tolerate much greater fluid losses than most other animals.

Camelot was the place where the legendary British king, Arthur, held his court. Authors of the stories of King Arthur and his Knights placed it at various different sites, including Winchester. Later, scholars believed it never existed; but more recently archaeologists have been investigating a site in Somerset, Cadbury Camp, which may have been the headquarters of the historical 'Arthur', a leader of the ancient Britons. *See also* Arthur.

Camera is a device used to take photographs. Light enters the camera through a lens. The lens concentrates the light, or focuses it, on a film at the back of the camera. The film contains special light-sensitive chemicals which can record images. To get a clear photograph, the right amount of light must enter the camera. Most cameras use a shutter and aperture to control the amount of light. The shutter normally stops any light getting in. When a photograph is taken the shutter opens and closes. The aperture is a hole through which the light has to pass. The photographer can change the amount of light going into the camera by changing the size of

Arabian camel

Asian camel

the aperture and by changing the length of time that the shutter stays open.

Cameroon is a republic in west-central Africa. Capital, Yaoundé; area about 474 000 sq km (183 000 sq miles).
History Cameroon was made a German protectorate in 1884 and later in 1922 was under joint French and British rule. It became independent in 1900.
Land and People The northern part is fairly dry, with high plains and hills; the south is humid and densely forested. Mount Cameroon (4071 m/13 356 ft) is the highest point in West Africa. In general the climate is hot: some places have an annual average of 32°C (89.6°F).

The population is descended from several related peoples and includes a few Pygmies, probably the original inhabitants. Most people live by growing only enough to feed themselves (subsistence farming). Aluminium is the only important mineral export. Other exports are coffee, cocoa and bananas.

Camouflage is the art of remaining concealed by blending into the surroundings, or even resembling part of the surroundings. Some animals are masters of the art of camouflage. The coat of the tiger is camouflage; it resembles the long grass in which the animal hunts. The plaice and the chameleon are examples of animals which can alter the colour of their bodies to suit the colour of the background against which they are hiding. Stick insects have an even more cunning sort of camouflage. As well as being the colour of twigs, they also look like twigs.

Campbell, Duncan, see Land speed record.

Camus, Albert (1913–1960), was a French writer. He grew up in poverty in French Algeria, moved to Paris in 1940 and took a brave part in the French Resistance to the Germans in the Second World War. His best-known works are the novels *The Outsider* (1942), *The Plague* (1948) and *The Fall* (1958). His beliefs were also expressed in philosophical essays, which recorded the importance of human dignity in an absurd, suicidal world.

Canada is a federal state in northern North America. Capital, Ottawa; area about 9 976 000 sq km (3 852 000 sq miles). Canada, a former British dominion, still acknowledges the British monarch as sovereign, though she has no actual powers.
History The first inhabitants of Canada were the tribes of American Indians, who came from Siberia through Alaska more than 20 000 years ago, and the small groups of Eskimos who lived along the northernmost shores and offshore islands.

The Vikings probably made settlements in Canada about 1000 and the Atlantic coast was later visited by European fishing vessels. John Cabot, sailing from Bristol, England, discovered Newfoundland in 1498 and Jaques Cartier, a Frenchman, explored the area around the Gulf of St Lawrence between 1534 and 1541. The first permanent French settlement was established at Quebec in 1608.

There was intense rivalry between the French and British for the possession of Can-

The tiger has a good camouflage. The vertical irregular stripes against the tawny background disrupt the shape of the tiger, making it difficult to see. Horizontal stripes would make it stand out.

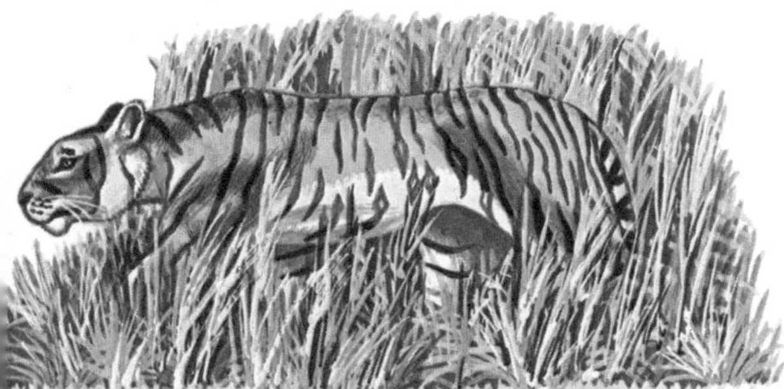

ada. Britain acquired the whole country under the Treaty of Paris (1763). The treaty followed years of fighting between the French and British, including the historic battle of the Plains of Abraham in which both the French commander (Montcalm) and the English commander (Wolfe) were killed.

In 1791 the Canada Act divided the country into Upper and Lower Canada. Upper Canada was mainly inhabited by British sympathisers; Lower Canada, by French. In the far north, however, rivalry continued between the English and French trading companies until they joined together as the Hudson's Bay Company.

In 1840 Upper and Lower Canada were joined by the Union Act and various territories were allowed by the British government to form their own governments. In 1869 Canada became a self-governing dominion, gaining complete independence in 1931.

Canadian soldiers fought on the British side in both world wars. After the Second World War Canada became increasingly prosperous and new waves of immigrants from Europe settled there. There are still, however, conflicts between the government and French separatist movements.

Prime Ministers of Canada

Sir John A Macdonald	1867–1873
Alexander Mackenzie	1873–1878
Sir John A Macdonald	1878–1891
Sir John J C Abbott	1891–1892
Sir John S D Thompson	1892–1894
Sir Mackenzie Bowell	1894–1896
Sir Charles Tupper	1896
Sir Wilfrid Laurier	1896–1911
Sir Robert L Borden	1911–1920
Aurther Meighen	1920–1921
W L Mackenzie King	1921–1926
Aurther Meighen	1926
W L Mackenzie King	1926–1930
Richard B Bennett	1930–1935

W L Mackenzie King	1935–1948
Louis S St Laurent	1948–1957
John Diefenbaker	1957–1963
Lester B Pearson	1963–1968
Pierre Elliott Trudeau	1968–

Governors-General of Canada

Viscount Monck	1867–1868
Lord Lisgar	1868–1872
Earl of Dufferin	1872–1878
Marquess of Lorne	1878–1883
Marquess of Lansdowne	1883–1888
Lord Stanley of Preston	1888–1893
Earl of Aberdeen	1893–1898
Earl of Minto	1898–1904
Earl Grey	1904–1911
HRH the Duke of Connaught	1911–1916
Duke of Devonshire	1916–1921
Viscount Byng of Vimy	1921–1926
Viscount Willingdon	1926–1931
Earl of Bessborough	1931–1935
Lord Tweedsmuir	1935–1940
Earl of Athlone	1940–1946
Field-Marshall Viscount Alexander of Tunis	1946–1952
Vincent Massey	1952–1959
Georges Philias Vanier	1959–1967
Roland Michener	1967–1974
Jules Léger	1974–1979
Edward Schreyer	1979–

Land Canada is a very large country (slightly bigger in fact than the USA), but a considerable part of the icy northern regions are uninhabited except for a few mining camps and fur traders' settlements. The largest and oldest settlements are in the south-east and along the west coast; about 90 per cent of Canada's population live within 300 km (186 miles) of the southern border with the USA.

Canada has a very long coastline, much of it ice-bound however, with many gulfs and inlets, as well as many large lakes. Two mountain ranges, the Appalachians in the east and the Rocky Mountains in the west, enclose the great central plains, or prairies. Buffalo used to roam these wide, flat plains. Now they are a major wheat producing region, with cattle ranches in the drier areas.

Provinces and Territories Canada is divided into ten provinces and two territories, which have their own governments controlling provincial affairs.

Alberta, 661 200 sq km (255 300 sq miles), capital: Edmonton. This is one of the 'prairie provinces' and produces enormous quantities of grain and meat. Alberta also has oil, gas and coal reserves.

British Columbia 948 600 sq km (366 250 sq miles), capital: Victoria. A mountainous coastal province, this is the centre of Canada's lumber industry. There are also important mineral resources.

Manitoba, 650 100 sq km (251 000 sq miles), capital: Winnipeg. A prairie province extending from fertile grain and stock producing lands in the south across a mineral rich area of large lakes to subarctic Hudson Bay.

New Brunswick, 73 400 sq km (28 350 sq miles), capital: Fredericton. Fishing is an important industry as are pulp and paper from the extensive forests. Mineral resources include silver, lead and zinc.

Newfoundland, 404 500 sq km (156 200 sq miles), capital: St John's. The first area of British settlement in Canada, Newfoundland is hilly and unsuited to agriculture but has valuable timber and fishing is an important industry.

Northwest Territories, 3 379 700 sq km (1 304 900 sq miles), capital: Yellowknife. This is a sparsely populated Arctic region extending from the Mackenzie Mountains in the west through a lake covered plateau to Hudson Bay. Fishing, fur-trapping and mining are important.

Nova Scotia, 55 500 sq km (21 400 sq miles), capital: Halifax. The first area of French settlement in Canada. Now important for fishing, lumber, coal, gypsum and salt mining.

Ontario, 1 068 600 sq km (412 600 sq miles), capital: Toronto. Ontario has large industrial centres around the Great Lakes in the south with prosperous, intensive farms around them. Further north mining (nickel, copper) and forestry are important.

Prince Edward Island, 5660 sq km (2180 sq miles), capital: Charlottetown. The smallest province, lying in the Gulf of St Lawrence. A mainly agricultural area.

Quebec, 1 540 700 sq km (594 900 sq miles), capital: Quebec. French culture dominates this province. The city of Quebec is a long-established, French speaking cultural and administrative centre. There are vast areas of forests and lakes with important mineral resources as well as major industrial centres in the south.

Saskatchewan, 651 900 sq km (251 700 sq miles), capital: Regina. A prairie province with grain and stock the main products.

Yukon Territory, 536 300 sq km (207 100 sq miles), capital: Whitehorse. A sparsely populated region with mineral resources and fur-trapping the main wealth of the region.

People The great majority of Canadians are of European descent, mainly French (especially in Quebec) and British. Canada has two official languages, French and English – all government publications are issued in both.

Economy The Canadian standard of living is generally high, thanks mainly to Canada's rich natural resources and efficient industries. The value of Canadian exports is greater than that of any other country, when measured by the number of people.

Historically, agriculture has been Canada's great money-earner. The prairie provinces of western Canada still produce huge quantities of wheat for export, as well as much beef. In general, Canada grows far more food than it needs. Forestry is also valuable: over 2 500 000 sq km (965 000 sq miles) of the country provides timber and forest products (the total area of forest is even larger). Fisheries, especially the Pacific salmon, support a big processing industry.

Power comes from hydro-electric stations on Canada's numerous fast-flowing rivers; there is enough natural gas to last for centuries in the prairie provinces, as well as large oil reserves. Canada is one of the world's leading mining countries, especially of nickel, zinc, copper, uranium and gold. Manufacturing industries are very highly developed. The value of factory products now is actually greater than the value of agricultural, fish and mining products combined. Many of Canada's products are exported over the border to the USA or shipped abroad via the St Lawrence Seaway.

Canal is an artificial inland waterway, usually of narrow construction intended for use by barges, but sometimes a large-scale waterway linking lakes or oceans, both deep and wide enough to be used by ocean-going ships. Examples of the latter include the Panama Canal and the Suez Canal, the second being the world's longest big ship canal, covering 160 km (100 miles) and being 10 m (33 ft) deep.

Canaletto (1697–1768), was an Italian painter. His finest works were architectural views of his native city of Venice. He also painted superb views of London, which he visited at the suggestion of his chief patron, the British consul in Venice.

Canary Islands are an island group in the Atlantic Ocean, off north-west Spain. Area about 7300 sq km (2820 sq miles). They make up two Spanish provinces. With their warm, dry climate, scenic mountains and beaches, they are a popular holiday resort. Formerly famous for wine and the red dye from the cochineal insect, the islands now produce big crops of tomatoes and bananas, as well as other fruits and vegetables. Irrigation is necessary as there are no rivers. There is some mining and small manufacturing industries on the larger islands. Pumice stone is a Canaries product. Many of the inhabitants are fishermen.

Canute (995–1035), was a Danish King of England. He accompanied his father, Sweyn Forkbeard, King of Denmark, when the latter invaded England in 1013. Canute shared the kingdom with Edmund Ironside until Edmund's death (1016), when he took control of the whole country. He proved a just ruler, and he became a Christian and repelled Viking attacks on England. Canute was also King of Denmark (1019–1035) and of Norway (1028–1035). On his death there was a dispute between his sons over the English throne.

Canyon is a gorge with a river running through it and high, steep sides. Canyons are normally found in arid landscapes where the river is strong enough to cut its way through soft rock, but where there is not enough rain to wear away the exposed sides. The most famous example is the Grand Canyon in the USA.

Cape Verde is an island republic in the Atlantic Ocean about 480 km (300 miles) west of Africa. Capital, Praia; area about 4000 sq km (1560 sq miles). It consists of 10 islands and 5 islets. Formerly a colony and then Overseas Province of Portugal, it was granted independence in 1975. Temperatures are high and the rainfall unpredictable. The population is of African and European descent. Products include coffee, bananas, maize and sugar cane.

Capitalism is an economic system in which commerce and industry are highly developed, and in which wealth, and the means of creating wealth, are privately owned. In Europe, capitalism has been a significant force from about the 16th century, and the dominant one during the Industrial Revolution of the 18th and 19th centuries.

Supporters of capitalism praise its encouragement of individual initiative. They claim that competition between individual producers leads to business efficiency and cheap goods. According to this view, the individual's search for profit benefits everybody.

Critics of capitalism claim that it leads to great inequalities, monopolies, and periodic crises in which industries collapse and there is high unemployment.

The most commonly proposed alternative to capitalism is socialism, ending private ownership. But most Western economies remain essentially capitalist, though subject to greater legal regulation than in the past.

Carbohydrates are widely occurring chemical compounds found in nature. Most food contains carbohydrates. Foods such as rice, sugar, bread and biscuits are mostly carbohydrates. Our bodies need them for energy.

The carbohydrates in food are changed by the body into a sugar called glucose. This is carried all over the body in the blood, giving energy to the muscles. The body can also change carbohydrates into a starch called glycogen. Glycogen is stored mainly in the liver until it is needed.

Plants contain a carbohydrate called cellulose. This is used to make their cell walls. They also store their food in a form of starch.

Carbon is probably the most important element, for it is found in all living matter. It has the chemical symbol C. It occurs naturally in the form of diamond and graphite. Coal is mainly carbon.

Diamond is the hardest natural substance known. It is used, for example, to cut other hard substances and to draw metal out into wire. When pure it is colourless. Large colourless diamonds are cut by other diamonds to be used in jewellery.

Dark grey graphite is soft and greasy. It marks paper and is the 'lead' in pencils. A good conductor of heat and electricity, it is used in nuclear reactors, for making electrodes and in many other ways.

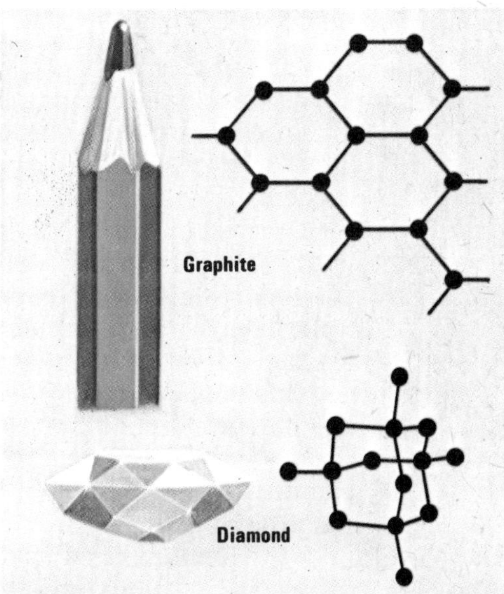

Graphite and diamond have different arrangements of carbon atoms. Graphite has layers of atoms which make it soft and slippery and it does not let light through. The arrangement in diamond makes it hard and transparent.

Graphite and diamond are crystalline. Substances which do not seem to have any crystal structures are known as amorphous. Charcoal and lampblack are examples of amorphous carbon. This is used, for example, in carbon paper, and in the manufacture of records and tyres.

There are so many carbon compounds that their study forms a separate branch of chemistry. It is known as organic chemistry.

Carbon cycle is the process by which carbon is circulated between living organisms and the environment. Carbon exists in the atmosphere in the form of the gas carbon dioxide. This carbon dioxide is taken from the atmosphere by green plants and is used to make carbohydrates by the process of photosynthesis. When animals eat the plants the carbohydrates pass to them. Predatory animals which feed on the grazing animals in turn take the carbohydrates into their bodies. When the animals breathe they return carbon dioxide to the air. When they die their bodies are broken down by bacteria into vital minerals, some of which are also eventually released into the atmosphere in the form of carbon dioxide.

Carbon dating is a scientific method of dating, for example, archaeological remains. It was devised in the 1950s by an American, Willard F. Libby, who was awarded the Nobel Prize for chemistry in 1960.

Carbon dating is based on the fact that a known amount of carbon is present in all living creatures, in particular, carbon-14 (a radioactive isotope of carbon). When a creature dies, the carbon-14 in its body decays at a fixed rate. This makes it possible to calculate the age of a human skeleton or a piece of wood, for example, from the amount of carbon-14 left in it.

There are some problems with carbon dating – for example, the amount of carbon-14 in living creatures has sometimes fluctuated – but the technique remains a valuable one. *See also* Radioactivity.

Carbon dioxide has the chemical formula CO_2, which shows that each molecule contains an atom of carbon (C) and two atoms of oxygen. It is a gas found in relatively small quantities in the Earth's atmosphere. However, it is of crucial importance in the life-cycle of the planet. Plants absorb carbon dioxide to obtain carbon, and give back to the atmosphere the oxygen which all animals need in order to live. Animals, in turn, breathe in oxygen and breathe out mainly carbon dioxide.

The gas is used industrially in, for example, refrigerators, fire extinguishers and to provide the 'fizz' in fizzy drinks.

Carboniferous is a period in the history of the Earth, known from the study of rocks and of the fossil remains found in them (the geological record). It is the fifth major division of the Paleozoic era, following the Devonian. Most of the world's coalbeds were laid down during the Carboniferous ('coal-producing') period, for during this time tremendous swamp forests of trees and ferns flourished. These were buried beneath sediment and then compressed until in time they formed coal. Amphibians, such as salamanders, and also insects, spiders and primitive reptiles, thrived in the Carboniferous period, which began about 345 million years ago and lasted for about 65 million years.

Cargo vessel is any boat or ship designed to carry freight. Perhaps the most glamorous cargo vessels ever built were the 19th century tea clippers, magnificent fast sailing ships which reached a speed of up to 40 km/h (25 mph). These ships carried tea and spices from India and the Far East, and wool from Australia to Europe and America.

Two types of modern cargo ship.

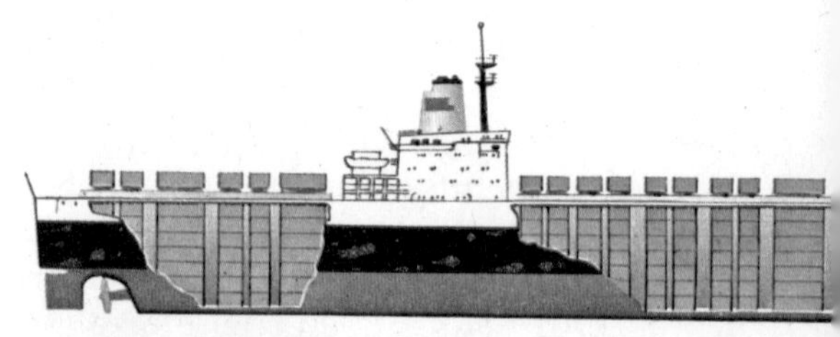

Container ship

Caribbean Sea is a large gulf of the western Atlantic, bordering Central and North America. Area about 2700000 sq km (1 042 000 sq miles). It contains many islands, large and small, known as the West Indies.

Caribou, *see* Reindeer.

Carnivores are creatures that eat meat. The term carnivore is often used to mean members of the mammal order Carnivora, the group which includes wolves, cats, bears, badgers and otters, but it can also include

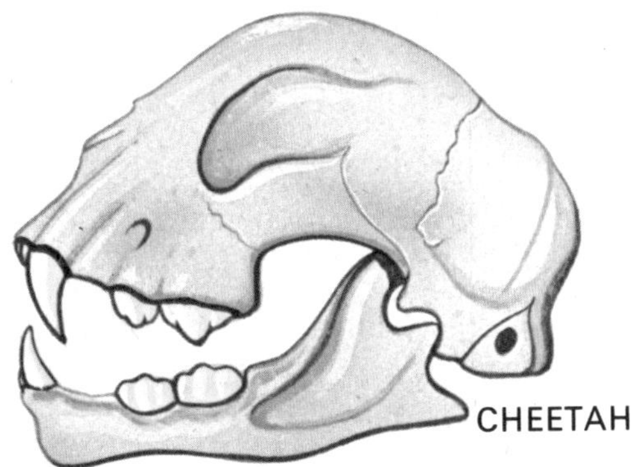

The teeth of a cheetah are for biting and cutting. The cheetah is a carnivore.

animals such as seals. Members of the Carnivora have pointed fangs known as canine teeth which are used to grab and stab their prey, as well as meat-shearing cheek teeth known as carnassial teeth. Seals have specially shaped teeth for catching slippery fish or opening mollusc shells. Some carnivores may also resort to eating berries and other vegetation.

Any other animal that eats meat can also be regarded as a carnivore, and there are even some carnivorous plants in existence! Plants such as the sundew and the Venus fly trap grow in places which are low in valuable nitrogen. By using special leaves, they trap and digest small insects, the bodies of which are rich in nitrogen. In this way the plants obtain all the nitrogen they require.

Carp

Carp are members of the fish family Cyprinidae. They occur in fresh water throughout Africa, Europe, Asia and North America, and are up to 1 m (3 ft) long. An interesting feature of carp is the substance released into the water by an injured fish; this substance warns other carp of danger. Some types of carp have sensitive feelers, called barbels, around their mouths; these help them to locate food on the bottom.

Carpel is the female reproductive organ of flowering plants. It is made up of the ovary which contains the ovules (the ovules turn into seeds after fertilization), and the stigma. The stigma is the receptive surface on which the male pollen grains land. The stigma is often borne on a slender stalk called the style. The wall of the carpel becomes the fruit after fertilization. Some fruits are hard-walled, and others are soft and juicy. The number of carpels inside the flower varies according to the species. The carpels are

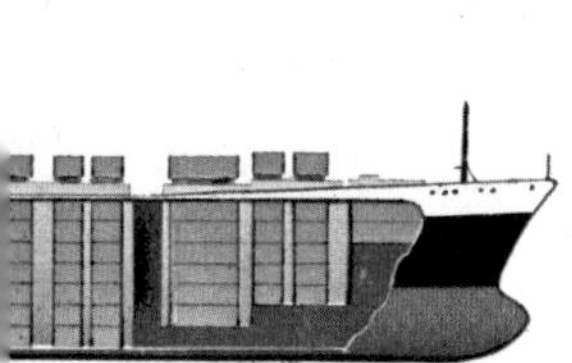

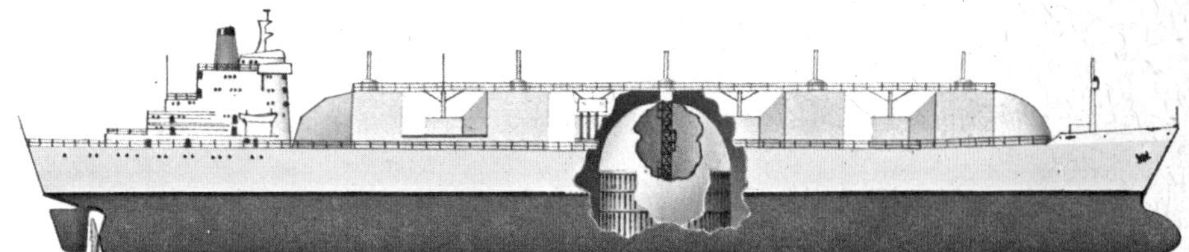

Liquified natural gas container

arranged around a part of the flower called the receptacle. The petals and the male reproductive parts, the anthers, are also attached to the receptacle.

Carrol, Lewis (1832–1898), was an English writer. His real name was Charles Dodgson, and he led a very uneventful life as a mathematician at Christ Church, Oxford. For the young daughter of a colleague he told the stories which became famous as *Alice in Wonderland* (1865) and *Alice Through the Looking Glass* (1872).

Carthage was an ancient city in North Africa, traditionally founded in 814 BC by Phoenicians from Tyre. After the capture of Tyre by the Babylonians in the 6th century BC, Carthage became the dominant Phoenician colony in North Africa and the centre of a great commercial empire. The Carthaginians made settlements in Spain, Sardinia and Sicily in the face of Greek and later Roman opposition.

By the 3rd century BC there was great rivalry between Rome and Carthage for control of the Mediterranean, which led to war. Despite the great skill of the Carthaginian general, Hannibal, Rome was victorious and Carthage was sacked in 202 BC. Because its renewed prosperity seemed to threaten Rome it was totally destroyed in 146 BC and refounded as a Roman colony. It became a centre of Christianity in North Africa until it was finally destroyed by the Muslims in AD 697–698.

Cartography is the art of making maps and charts. The earliest surviving map is Babylonian and dates from the 3rd millennium BC. The ancient Greeks, great traders and seafarers, appear to have made the first serious study of the subject. This study culminated at Alexandria in the 2nd century AD with the work of the geographer, Ptolemy. He not only tried to map the known world, but also attempted to work out the longitude and latitude of every significant place known to him.

There was virtually no further progress in cartography until the 15th and 16th centuries, when the great discoveries of Vasco da Gama, Columbus and Magellan opened up most of the world to Europeans.

In 1554 the problem of representing a roughly spherical globe on a flat sheet of paper was solved by a Flemish cartographer, Gerhardus Mercator. His solution, known as Mercator's projection, is still widely used.

Advances in astronomy and navigation made the 18th century one of the great ages of cartography. However, supreme accuracy has only been achieved in the 20th century with the aid of aerial photography, electronic measurement of distances and other precise scientific techniques. *See also* Latitude; Longitude.

Cassowary is three species of bird found in Australasia. They are powerfully built, flightless birds, standing as tall as 1.8 m (6 ft). On their forehead cassowaries have a bony crest, which helps them to batter through thick vegetation. Three to eight eggs are laid, and both parents share the task of rearing the young.

Cassowary

The keep of a Norman castle, cut away to show the inside.

Castle is a fortified residence of a king or noble, built especially in the Middle Ages. Castles were built of wood or stone and were often surrounded by a moat filled with water.

The style of castles changed. Stone towers, or keeps, surrounded by walls, were built in the 12th century. The portcullis, a grille to secure the main gate, was not introduced until the 13th century. Square towers were changed to round ones, and extra surrounding walls were built. Many castles seen today are a mixture of styles, each added by a new generation.

Castro, Fidel (1926–), is a Cuban statesman and revolutionary leader. He became an opponent of the Cuban dictator, Fulgencio Batista. After leading an unsuccessful rising in 1953, Castro was exiled. He re-entered Cuba in 1956 and began a campaign of guerrilla warfare. In 1959 Batista fled the country, and Castro took office as Prime Minister. His Marxist government introduced many social and economic reforms, and depended to a great extent on assistance from the USSR. He became President in 1976.

Cats are animals which belong to the mammal group Carnivora. They have specialized teeth and claws for hunting, and a keen sense of smell, hearing, vision and balance. A large number of different types of cat can be found throughout the world. Tigers, lions, snow leopards and jaguars are known as the 'big cats'. There are also many smaller species of cat, such as the bobcat, cheetah, puma, lynx, golden cat, European wild cat and domestic pet cat.

Catalyst is a substance which changes the rate of a chemical reaction. The compound hydrogen peroxide gives off a little oxygen. If, however, a small amount of magnesium oxide is added, then a lot of oxygen is given off. The magnesium oxide itself is unaltered during this reaction. It just makes the reaction go faster, and so is a catalyst.

Many chemical reactions take place in our body. These are speeded up by catalysts called enzymes. Enzymes are also used in 'biological' washing powders.

Catalysts are used to make most important chemicals. They speed up the manufacture of these chemicals. Some catalysts slow down a reaction. They are known as inhibitors.

Caterpillar is the larval stage of certain insects, such as moths and butterflies. Caterpillars emerge from eggs laid by the adult insect, and their job in life is simply to eat and grow. The eggs are usually laid on the food plant of their choice, so that they can begin their task straight away.

Caterpillars eat different food from the adult, which helps to ensure that there is food available for both the caterpillar and the adult to eat. After several days of eating, the caterpillar has grown considerably, and now looks for a place to pupate. During pupation, the caterpillar usually first spins a cocoon, and inside the cocoon its own body undergoes a change called metamorphosis. At the end of metamorphosis the caterpillar has turned from a wriggling caterpillar into a winged adult, which emerges from the cocoon to fly away.

Catfish number about 200 species, most of which are found in African, South American and Asian waters, although a few occur in more northerly regions. Catfish generally have long scaleless bodies, although the armoured catfish have bony plates covering

the body. Around their mouths they have long whiskers which they use for finding their way about in murky waters and for locating food. Some of the larger catfish will eat water birds and small mammals, and a few are parasitic on other fish.

Cathedrals and Abbeys were the greatest buildings of the Middle Ages, if not of all European architecture. Although cathedrals are, of course, still built today, the great age of cathedral building lasted from the 11th to the 14th century, when people were inspired to put as much money and energy as they could afford into works to the glory of God.

A cathedral is simply a church which contains the seat of a bishop. They are usually grander than ordinary parish churches.

The cathedrals of Europe display the development of European architecture from the Romanesque style (called Norman in England) through the changing forms of the grand Gothic style, with its huge windows, soaring arches and flying buttresses. The finest, or purest, examples of Gothic cathedrals are in northern France – Amiens, Chartres, Paris, Reims and other cities. Some of the largest are in Spain; some of the most interesting in England and Germany. But in Italy, for example, the Gothic style was never widely adopted.

Catherine de Médici (1519–1589), Queen of France, was Regent during the minority of her second son, Charles IX. The daughter of Lorenzo de' Medici, she married Henry II of France in 1533. She was determined to uphold royal authority during the Wars of Religion and after her husband's death (1559) was a strong influence over her sons, who became Kings of France successively as Francis II, Charles IX and Henry III. She sought at first to compromise between Catholics and Protestants, but later gave full support to the Catholics and bears a large responsibility for the St Bartholomew's Day Massacre of Protestants in 1572.

Catherine of Aragon (1485–1536), was Queen of England. The daughter of Ferdinand and Isabella of Spain, she became the first wife of Henry VIII and the mother of the future Queen Mary. Since she failed to produce a son, Henry divorced her, claiming that the marriage was invalid because she was the widow of his elder brother, Arthur. The refusal of the Pope to annul the marriage led to the Reformation in England.

Catherine the Great (1729–1796), was Empress of Russia. She became absolute ruler of the country in 1762 after her unpopular husband, Peter III, had been deposed and murdered. An energetic and capable woman, she greatly expanded Russian territory during her reign at the expense of Turkey and Poland. She made many administrative reforms, introduced Western ideas into Russia and was a patron of artists and writers. Catherine was, however, unable to abolish serfdom because of the opposition of the nobility.

Catkin is a collection of tiny flowers attached to the same pendulous stalk. It is designed for wind pollination. Plants which produce catkins bear them early in the year before the plant has developed its leaves, because the leaves would get in the way of the pollen as it was being blown away. Usually the flowers are all male, or all female. Many deciduous trees – such as hazel and birch – produce their flowers in catkins.

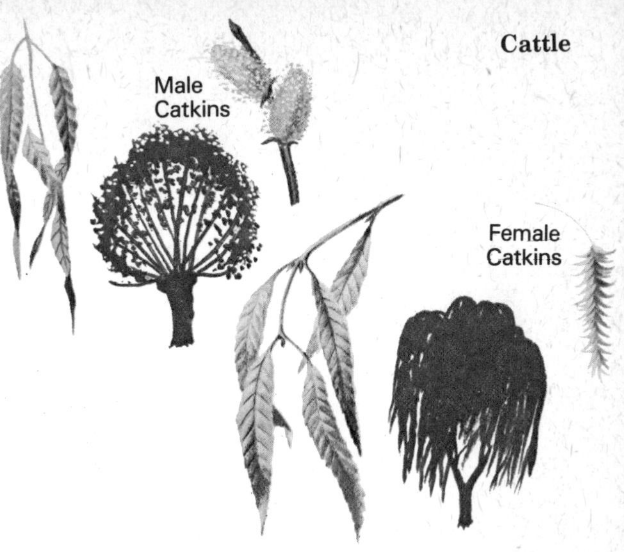

Leaves, silhouettes of the trees and catkins of the common Osier (*top*) and the weeping willow.

Cattle belong to the group of mammals known as ruminants, which also includes sheep, goats, antelopes and giraffes. Many types of cattle still live wild – for instance, the yak, Indian buffalo, anoa and the bison. Domesticated cattle are descended from the aurochs, which are now extinct.

Caucasus is a mountain region, in southern USSR, between the Black Sea and the Caspian Sea. Several peaks of the Caucasus Mountains are over 500 m (16 500 ft) high. A wild, grim region, thinly inhabited, the Caucasus has rich mineral resources and is also known for its carpets, made by hardy villagers and nomads.

Caxton, William (circa 1422–1491), was the first English printer to use movable type. A merchant by trade, he worked for many years in Bruges. About 1471 he went to Cologne, and it was there that he learnt the art of printing. In Bruges he set up his own press and printed the first book in English, *Recuyell of the Historyes of Troye* (1475). Returning to England the following year, he established a press at Westminster and printed many books, including Chaucer's *Canterbury Tales* and Malory's *Morte d'Arthur*.

Cayman Islands are a group of three small islands in the Caribbean Sea about 320 km (200 miles) north-west of Jamaica. Capital, George Town; area about 260 sq km (100 sq miles). The islands were discovered by Columbus in 1503 and became a British colony in the late 17th century. They were a dependency of Jamaica until 1959 when they became a separate dependent territory of Great Britain. Tourism is the main industry with over 180 000 people visiting the islands each year.

Cedar is a large, often majestic-looking coniferous tree whose branches spread with age. Cedar trees develop barrel-shaped cones which are borne upright on the branches, and stiff, needle-shaped leaves arranged in tufts.

Cell (electrical) produces electricity from chemicals. The first electrical cell was made by Allessandro Volta in 1801. He put two metal plates in dilute acid. He found that when wires were connected to the plates a current flowed. This is called a simple cell or Voltaic cell. The metal plates are called electrodes. The dilute acid is called an electrolyte. Since then, many electrical cells have been made using different electrodes and electrolytes.

After a time, the simple cell stops producing electricity and is useless. A new one has to be made. Cells like this are called primary cells. Some cells can be recharged by passing an electric current through them. These cells can be used again and again. They are known as secondary cells or accumulators. *See also* Battery.

Cells (plant and animal) are the tiny 'bricks' which make up the bodies of plants and animals, in the same way that a house is built of bricks. The protozoans are single-celled creatures, but larger creatures are made up of many cells. Most animals and plants are built from various types of cell, each type performing its particular role. Thus a tree has cells concerned with protection (these form the bark); cells which are responsible for drawing up water from the soil; cells which form flowers and fruit; and cells which form the leaves. Human beings have many different types of cell in their bodies. When cells are grouped together to perform a particular task they are known as tissues and organs.

Cells are usually too small to be seen without a microscope. Within a cell is a watery substance called cytoplasm, which is made from proteins and other chemicals. The cell also contains other structures, the most important of which is the nucleus. The nucleus controls all the activities of growth, food storage and so on, which go on within the cell. Cells found in plants usually possess structures called chloroplasts. These contain chlorophyll, used by the plant to trap sunlight during the process of photosynthesis.

Cellulose is the basic 'building material' of all green-plant cell walls, as well as that of certain fungi. In chemical terms it is called a polysaccharide, and it consists of long chains of molecules packed together to form a very strong and rigid material. Cellulose is an important source of carbohydrate for herbivorous animals. Their digestive systems contain special bacteria for helping them cope with what would otherwise be an indigestible food.

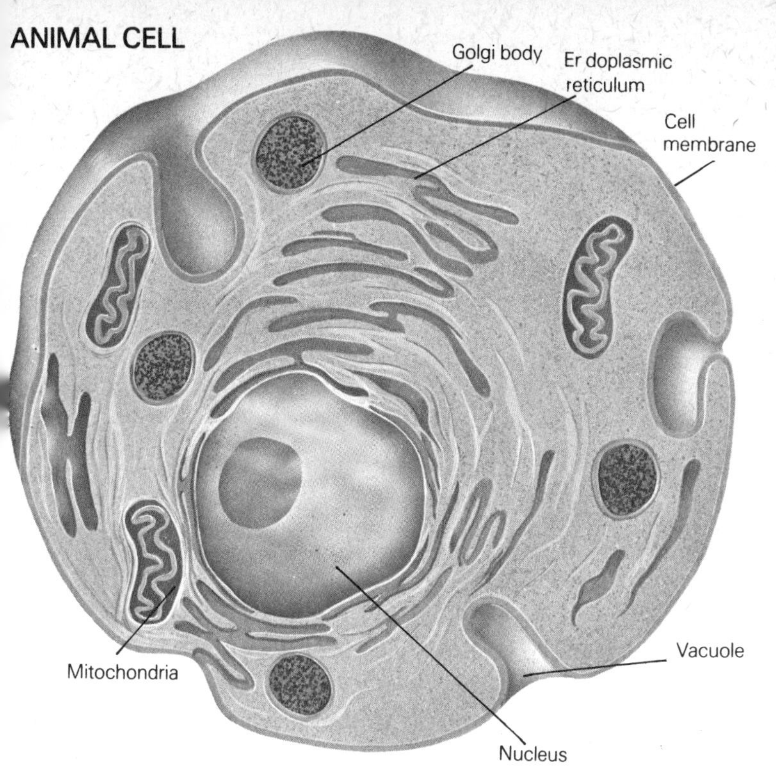

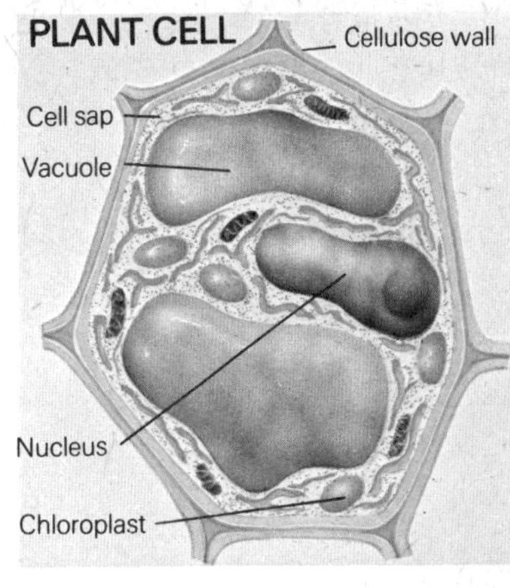

An animal cell *(left)* and a plant cell *(above)*.

Celts were a warlike people who inhabited central and western Europe from the 2nd millennium to the 1st century BC. They spread gradually westwards to reach France, northern Spain and the British Isles, and sacked Rome in 390 BC. Their warriors valued the severed heads of defeated enemies, their burials were elaborate and their priests, the Druids, demanded human sacrifice. The Celts were gradually conquered and absorbed by the Romans and by Germanic tribes, until Celtic culture remained only in the extreme western parts of Europe. They are famous for their fine craftsmanship, especially in metalwork.

Cenozoic is an era in the history of the Earth. It is the present era, the age of mammals, extending from about 65 million years

The Gaelic Celts in the Scottish Highlands went into battle with blue dye on parts of their bodies, presumably to frighten the enemy.

ago. It includes the Quaternary and Tertiary periods, and follows the Mesozoic era.

Statue of a young centaur.

Centaur was a creature in Greek myth, the top half man, the bottom half horse. Centaurs were usually wild and brutish creatures, and in many myths they are the representatives of a more barbaric age, which was overcome by Greek civilization. But there were exceptions, like the wise centaur Chiron, the teacher of many Greek heroes.

When the American Indians first saw men on horseback, they mistook them for a single creature. Perhaps the earlier belief in centaurs started in some such way.

Centipedes are predatory arthropods with long, segmented bodies. Eech segment bears a pair of legs, the number of pairs ranging from 15 to more than 170. Centipedes have heads armed with poisonous jaws, which they use to seize and kill prey, and for defending themselves. The largest centipede, which lives in South America, can reach a length of 30 cm (1 ft), but most are smaller.

Centipedes are usually active at night, when they emerge from under stones and bark to hunt insects. The largest centipedes can kill and eat mice and lizards.

Central African Republic is a nation in north-central Africa. Capital, Bangui; area about 625 000 sq km (241 000 sq miles). A former part of French Equatorial Africa, the republic became fully independent in 1960. Dry, flat savannah is the most typical scenery, with forests in the south. The country is poor and most of the people, belonging to a large number of small tribal groups, are fully occupied just growing enough food for themselves.

Transport is a major problem and trade must pass on railways through neighbouring states. Some coffee and cotton, as well as timber, are exported, and mineral resources include diamonds of high quality.

Central America is the name given to the narrow land bridge that links Mexico in North America to Colombia in South America. It is made up of seven countries: Guatemala, Belize, El Salvador, Honduras, Nicaragua, Costa Rica, Panama.

History Spanish settlements were made early in the 16th century and much of the region was conquered by the Spanish and ruled by them. After breaking away, some of it formed part of the Mexican empire, subsequently becoming a loosely united association known as the Central American Federation. In 1839 the federation split up into independent republics. The United States had important economic interests in the area and was responsible for cutting the Panama Canal (opened 1914). In the 20th century Central America has remained a poor, mainly agricultural region, marked by political instability.

Centrifuge is an instrument used to separate mixtures of chemicals. It spins around very quickly. Some centrifuges can spin as fast as 100 000 times per minute.

Anything put in a centrifuge is pulled out to the sides of the centrifuge as it spins. Denser substances are pulled harder than less dense substances. If a mixture of liquids is poured into a centrifuge, the denser liquids will move to the outside and the less dense liquids will stay nearer the middle. In this way liquids, or solids mixed with liquids, can be separated.

A spin drier is a kind of centrifuge. As it spins, wet clothes are pulled to the sides of the drier. The clothes are held by the sides of the drier, but the water can move out through holes in the sides, leaving the clothes dry. *See also* Density.

Cereals are plants in which the seeds are harvested and used by humans as food for themselves and their animals. Cereals belong to the grass family, the Graminae. From the milled and prepared seeds of cereals come proteins, oils, vitamins, starch and sugar.

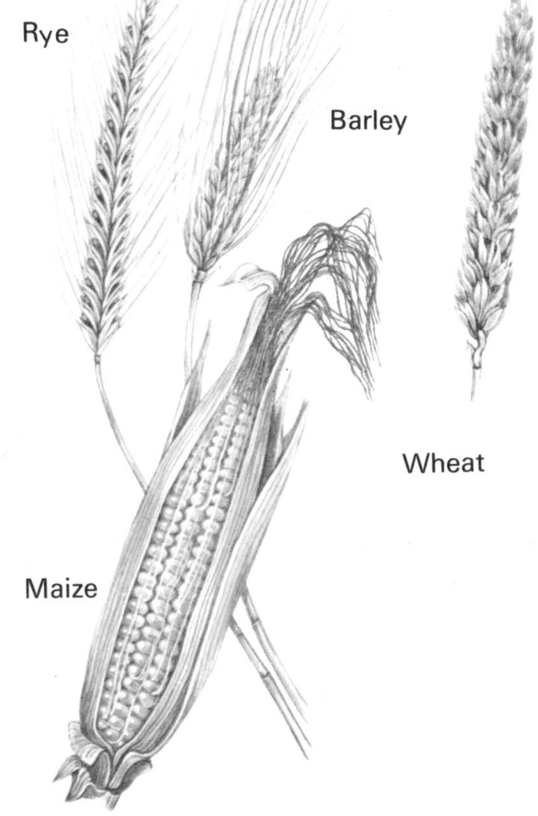

The history of cereal cultivation can be traced back to ancient civilizations. Today, among the most important are rice, the cereal of Asia which feeds half the world's population; barley and rye which grow best in the north; oats; maize, the tropical cereal which can also grow in temperate regions; and wheat, the most important cereal of Europe, North America and parts of South America.

Cervantes, Miguel de (1547–1616), was a Spanish writer. He is acknowledged as the greatest writer in Spanish literature, but outside Spain his reputation rests chiefly on one novel, *Don Quixote* (1604–1615). This story of the adventures of a clumsy, slightly crazy but well-meaning knight was intended as a comic satire on the tales of gallantry popular at the time, but it reads as a symbolic story of the hopeless struggles of the individual against the blows of Fate. Cervantes himself suffered such blows: he lost the use of an arm as a soldier in the Battle of Lepanto, he spent five years as a captive of Algerian pirates, and he was imprisoned three times.

Ceylon, see Sri Lanka

Cézanne, Paul (1839–1906), was a French painter. He has been called the 'father of modern art'. He discovered his true gifts under the influence of the Impressionists in the 1870s, which made him aware of the importance of colour and the study of nature. However, his sense of structure – 'the sphere, the cylinder and the cone' – was perhaps his most important contribution, and led towards Cubism and the modern movement in art.

Chad is a republic in central Africa. Capital N'djaména; area about 1284000 sq km (495000 sq miles). A former French colony, Chad became independent in 1960. It has since suffered from civil violence. France and, more recently, Libya have had strong influence on political events.

Much of Chad lies in the barren Sahara Desert, where only a few nomads live. Most of the people live in the savannah to the south, where they are chiefly occupied growing food such as millett, sorghum (a type of cereal grass) and wheat. Cotton is the main export crop, but Chad has serious transport problems, with the nearest seaport over 1500 km (932 miles) from its borders.

The country is named after the vast, marshy lake in the west.

Chalk is a soft, white type of limestone which consists almost entirely of calcium carbonate. Much of it was formed during the Cretaceous period from the shells and skeletons of small marine creatures. Chalk is widespread in England, where deposits are often very thick; the North and South Downs and the 'white cliffs' of Dover are well-known examples.

Chalk has various industrial and agricultural uses, but is not now used for blackboard 'chalk', which is actually made from gypsum.

Chamber music was originally music to be played in a private room (or chamber), not a concert hall, theatre or church, though nowadays most chamber music *is* performed in concert halls. The term means music for a small number of instruments, each playing an equal part with no solo instrument or voice. Frequently the group is a string quartet (two violins, viola and cello). Most major composers have written chamber music as well as works on a larger scale.

Chameleons are curious-looking lizards which move about slowly in trees searching for insects. Once a chameleon has spotted an insect, its tongue shoots out rapidly, catching the insect on the end and bringing it back to its mouth. All this happens in a fraction of a second. Chameleons can use their tails to help grip branches; they can change the colour of their bodies to match their surroundings; and each eye can swivel independently, like a miniature gun turret. This means that one eye can be looking up into the branches for food, and the other can be looking down to watch for enemies.

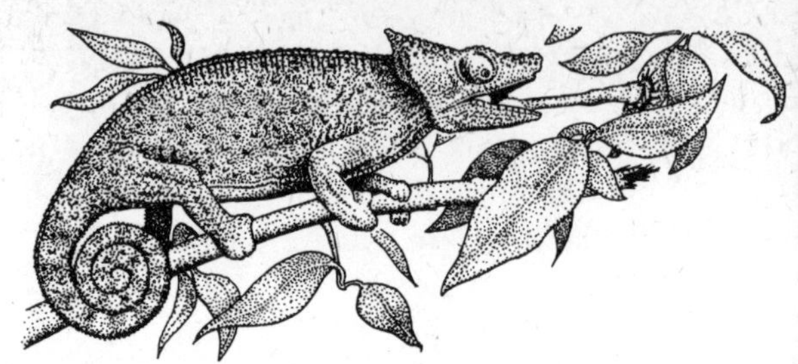

There are 85 species of chameleon, occurring mainly in Africa and Asia, although one is found in southern Europe. They are 17 to 60 cm (7 to 24 in) long.

Chandragupta Maurya (reigned circa 321–297 BC), was an Indian emperor and founder of the Maurya dynasty. He put an end to Greek rule in India and defeated attempts by the Greeks to recover their Indian possessions. He gradually extended his empire to cover the whole of India and organized a strong central government, backed by a powerful army, to keep control of his vast dominions. He abdicated in favour of his son in 297 BC.

Channel Islands are an island group in the English Channel. Area about 200 sq km (77 sq miles). Although the islands are nearer France, they have been English since 1066. They were the only part of Britain occupied by German forces during the Second World War. Famous for their breeds of cattle (Guernsey, Jersey – named after the two largest islands) and their smugglers, they are today best known as holiday resorts and producers of flowers and fruit, especially tomatoes. The Channel Islands are not part of the United Kingdom but a direct dependency of the Crown with their own legislative and taxation systems.

Chaplin, Charlie (1889–1977), was a British film actor. Born in the London slums, he was spotted touring in the United States in

1913, and became one of the most popular Hollywood stars of the silent films with his character of the little man in baggy trousers and bowler hat. He wrote and directed his own films, including *The Gold Rush* (1924) and *City Lights* (1931), and he was equally successful when sound arrived, with *Modern Times* (1936), *The Great Dictator* (1940), *Limelight* (1952), etc. Chaplin was a marvellous clown, combining knockabout comedy with pathos. In his later films especially, he often had a serious message about the freedom of the individual.

Charlemagne (circa 742–814), was King of the Franks. He inherited the Frankish kingdom, which included most of present day France and part of Germany, from his father and brother. He conquered the Saxons and Lombards and also campaigned against the Muslims in Spain. Eventually he became ruler of a large part of central and western Europe and in 800 was crowned Holy Roman Emperor by Pope Leo III. During his reign he made many legal and administrative reforms and effectively spread Christianity across much of Europe.

Charlemagne, Emperor of the Holy Roman Empire.

Charles (1948–), Prince of Wales, is the eldest son of Queen Elizabeth II and Prince Philip, and heir to the British throne. He was educated at Gordonstoun, being created Prince of Wales in 1958. He studied at Trinity College, Cambridge, during 1967–1970 and later served in the Royal Air Force and the Royal Navy. He married Lady Diana Spencer in 1981, and they had a son, Prince William, in 1982.

Charles I (1600–1649), was King of England, Scotland and Ireland. He came to the throne in 1625 on the death of his father, James I. From the very beginning of his reign his High Church doctrines, his marriage to a Roman Catholic, Henrietta Maria, and his reliance on his favourite, the Duke of Buckingham, brought him into collision with a Puritan-dominated Parliament. He ruled without Parliament for eleven years, raising the money he needed by dubious means. When Parliament met again it demanded far-reaching reforms. Charles tried unsuccessfully to arrest five of its members, and Civil War followed. After early victories the Royalists (supporters of the king) were beaten by the Parliamentary army. Charles was eventually brought to trial and found guilty of treason. He was executed on 30 January 1649.

Charles II (1630–1685), was King of England, Ireland and Scotland. After the execution of his father, Charles I, Charles II was forced to go into exile. He became king in 1660 and during the next few years was involved in disastrous wars with the Dutch. In 1670 he signed a secret treaty with France, promising to become a Roman Catholic and to convert his country to Catholicism. Charles opposed attempts by Parliament to exclude his Roman Catholic brother, James, from the succession, and from 1681 until his death he ruled without Parliament. Known as the Merry Monarch, he was popular with the people.

Charles was the patron of many institutions, such as the theatre, and during the period of his reign, know as the Restoration, many comedies were written.

Charles V (1500–1558) was Holy Roman Emperor and King of Spain. He inherited Burgundy and the Netherlands from his father and Spain and Naples from his maternal grandfather. He became Holy Roman Emperor in 1519 on the death of his paternal grandfather. This enormous stretch of territory brough him into conflict with France and the Italian states. His attempts to conciliate the German Protestants ended in failure, and he came into conflict with them. Although he defeated a Protestant army he was eventually forced to give way to most of their demands. Unable to rule the empire, he abdicated and retired to a monastery.

Chaucer, Geoffrey (died 1400), was an English poet. The first great figure in English literature, he wrote allegorical poems in the French and Italian traditions, mostly about 'courtly' (romantic) love. But his greatest masterpiece is *The Canterbury Tales*, written in rhyming couplets with lines ten syllables long. It is a collection of lively stories told by a group of pilgrims on their way to Canterbury, and was written towards the end of Chaucer's life (it is unfinished).

Cheetah is a beautifully marked hunting cat found in Africa, although it used to occur in Asia as well. The cheetah hunts mainly by day, roaming the bush looking for prey such as gazelle. Once it has spotted a likely meal, it stalks it until quite close. Then the cheetah bursts from cover and runs after the prey at great speed, pulling the victim to the ground and biting its neck. Surprisingly, cheetahs seldom eat the meat of their victims, preferring the blood and entrails instead. Over a short distance, the cheetah is the fastest animal on land, reaching speeds of up to 100 km/h (60 mph), and it is about 1.5 m (5 ft) long excluding its tail.

Chekhov, Anton (1860–1904), was a Russian playwright. A doctor of medicine, he was one of the world's greatest dramatists. He had an extraordinary gift for writing about day-to-day events, such as cutting down trees in an orchard, and producing from them a drama about the deepest concerns of the human heart. His plays, especially *The Seagull, Uncle Vanya* and *The Cherry Orchard*, have had great influence on drama in the 20th century. Chekhov also wrote short stories with the same originality and subtlety.

Chemical reaction occurs when substances combine or are broken down to form new substances. When coal is burnt, the black shiny coal changes to grey ashes. The coal joins with the oxygen in the air to form gases, such as carbon dioxide. This is called a chemical reaction. In a chemical reaction, new substances are formed which are often very different from the original substances.

When it is heated, water boils to steam. Water and steam look very different but are the same chemical. So, this is not a chemical reaction. Cooling the steam turns it back into water. It would be very difficult to turn carbon dioxide back into coal and oxygen. *See also* Oxidation.

Chemistry is the study of the composition of substances. Chemists (people who study chemistry) try to discover how the chemicals which make up everything will react.

By studying reactions, chemists have found many new chemicals. The simplest chemicals are called elements. Elements can

Cheetah

join together to form compounds. All substances are made up of elements or compounds or mixtures of these.

Chiang Kai-Shek (1887–1975), was a Chinese statesman and military leader. He took part in the overthrow of the last Chinese dynasty in 1911 and served under Sun Yat Sen in the Kuomintang (Nationalist Party). His continual conflict with the Chinese Communists was only ended by the Japanese invasion of China, when the Communists and Nationalists joined forces to fight the aggressor. After the Japanese surrender hostilities were renewed, and eventually Chiang Kai-Shek was driven out of China. He fled to Taiwan with the remnants of his army in 1949, remaining there until his death.

Chile is a republic in west South America. Capital, Santiago; area about 750 000 sq km (290 500 sq miles).

History Northern Chile was part of the Inca empire when the Spaniards arrived in the 16th century. Chile became independent in 1813 but in recent times the hostility between the extreme left (communist) and right political groups has resulted in violence.

Land Chile is confined between the Pacific Ocean and the Andes Mountains, which explains its long, thin shape. The climate varies greatly. The north is hot, almost desert, the extreme south cold and bleak, but central Chile has a pleasant, mild climate. The north provides most of the minerals which have been the chief export earner (nitrates, copper, etc.). Chile also has coal and oil reserves.

People There are few true Indians in Chile, and most people are of European or mixed descent. Roman Catholicism is the dominant religion. The average income is high for South America, but there is a huge gap between rich and poor.

Chimpanzee is an ape with many endearing characteristics. It is playful, mischievous and can be taught to perform quite complicated tasks. Scientists have even been able to talk to the chimpanzee using a form of sign language. Similarities in body shape and a high level of intelligence show that the chimpanzee is a close relative of human beings.

Facial expressions of a chimpanzee.

In the wild, the chimpanzee lives in large groups in the forests of equatorial Africa. It spends some time in the trees, especially when sleeping, but a great deal of time is spent on the ground searching for fruit, leaves, insects and small animals to eat. The chimpanzee can walk either on all fours or on its back legs only. Only one baby is born at a time, and this is cared for by the mother, even after her next baby is born. Chimpanzees are about 1.3 m (4.5 ft) tall, and live for about 50 years.

China, Great Wall of, is one of the world's greatest defensive fortifications. It was begun about 215 BC as a protection against barbarian tribes. It formed the northern boundary of the Chinese empire and covered a distance of nearly 2400 km (1500 miles). It was rebuilt from the 14th to 16th century and in recent times has been carefully restored.

China, People's Republic of, is a republic in east Asia. Capital, Peking; area about 9 597 000 sq km (3 705 000 sq miles). Measured by population, China is the largest country in the world. Despite these numbers and the long traditions of Chinese civilization, it is still in some ways a simple, undeveloped country. Most of the Chinese are engaged in farming, although only about 10 per cent of the land is cultivated.

History Chinese civilization developed in about 4000 BC along the Yellow River, but the first recorded dynasty is that of the Shang which began in about 1800 BC. The Chou dynasty (1122–221 BC) was notable for the foundation of Taoism and Confucianism. The Ch'in dynasty (221–206 BC) was a period of expansion, during which the Great Wall was built. Buddhism was introduced in the 1st century AD. Under the Sung dynasty (960–1279) art and literature flourished. In the 13th century China became the centre of the Mongol Empire, but the Mongols were eventually driven out of southern China and the Ming dynasty (1368–1644) was founded. Under the Manchus (1644–1911) China was gradually opened up to outside influence and in the 19th century was forced to grant trading rights to European countries. The dynasty was overthrown in 1911 and this was followed by anarchy, civil war, and finally, Japanese invasion. In 1949 a communist state was established under Mao Tse Tung and in 1971 China joined the United Nations.

Chinese Dynasties

Hsia	2205–1176 BC
Shang	1176–1122 BC
Chou	1122–221 BC
Ch'in	221–206 BC
Han	206 BC–AD 220
Six Dynasties	221–589
Sui	589–618
T'ang	618–906
Five Dynasties	906–960
Sung	960–1279
Yuan	1280–1368
Ming	1368–1644
Manchu	1644–1911
Rulers of the Manchu Dynasty	
Shan Chi	1644–1661
K'ang Hsi	1662–1722
Yung Cheng	1723–1735
Ch'ien Lung	1736–1795
Chia Ch'ing	1796–1820
Tao Kuang	1821–1850
Hsien Feng	1851–1861
T'ung Chih	1862–1874
Kuang Hsü	1875–1908
Hsüan T'ung	1908–1911

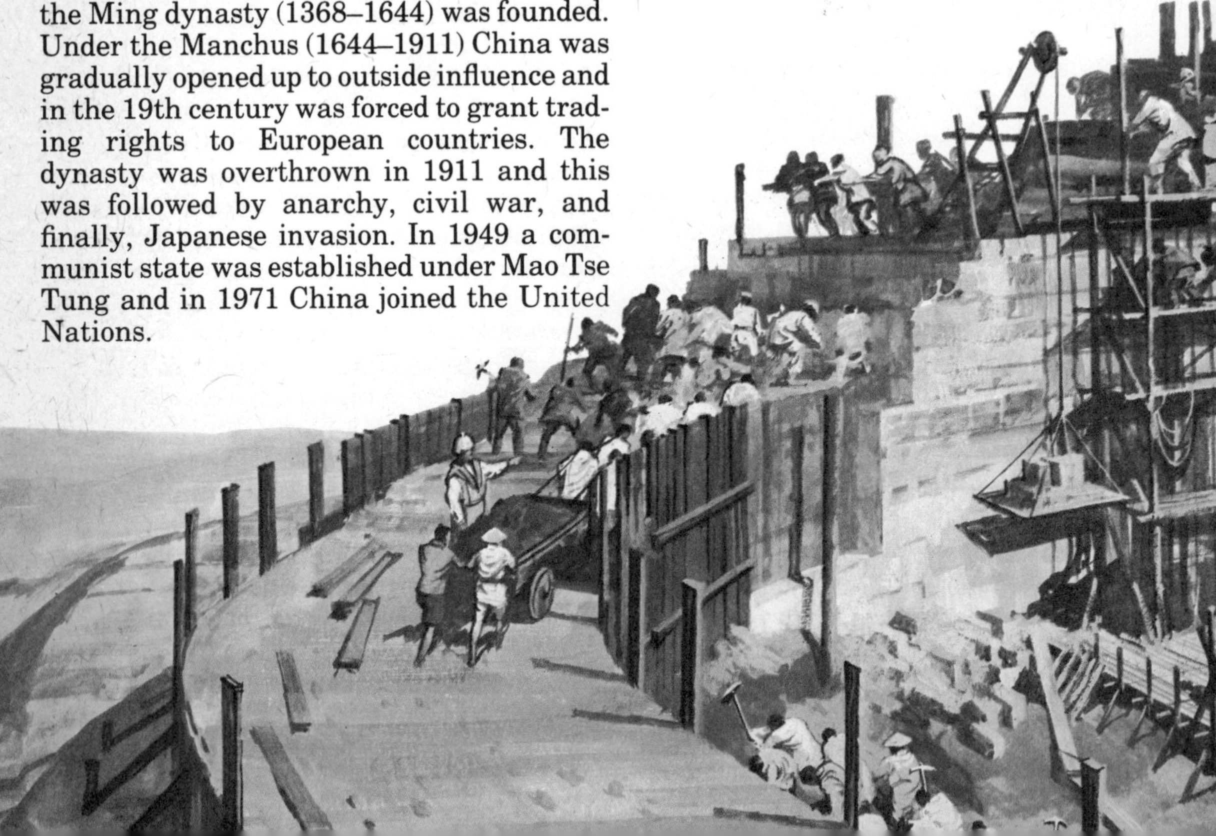

The Great Wall of China was built between 218 and 204 BC.

Land China is divided from its Asian neighbours by natural boundaries – mountains, deserts and rivers – in most places. On the east it has a long coastline, with many good harbours on the Pacific, and the great rivers, Hwang Ho (Yellow River) and Yangtse Kiang act as highways for trade.

In the north-east, the fertile plains of Manchuria are enclosed by mountains. The south is rich in minerals and is the main industrial region. The north-west is largely barren – much of it desert – and mountainous. The Gobi Desert covers a large area in the west. The wild, high plateau of Tibet stretches between the Kumlun Mountains and the Himalayas in the south; much of it is used for grazing.

Eastern China, the heart of the old empire, is the most fertile and most heavily populated region. It is divided into two by the Chin Ling Shan mountains. The climate in the region is generally mild, with the rainy season from March to October.

People The population is mostly Han ('pure') Chinese, though about 10 per cent are descended from other neighbouring peoples, such as Manchu and Mongol. There are many forms of the Chinese language, though

an official modern form is spoken by more and more people. There is no official religion, but traditional Chinese beliefs, such as Confucianism and Buddhism, remain strong.

Economy The Chinese economy is strictly controlled by the central government. The commune system is widespread in agriculture, though peasants still have their own small plots. The main crops are rice and cereals.

Industry has been rapidly expanded under the communist government, and China's place among modern industrial nations was symbolized by the successful launching of a space satellite.

There are rich mineral resources in China, including fuels like coal and oil. China's exports still tend to be mainly raw materials, while she imports much industrial machinery and equipment.

Chinchilla is an attractive rodent, about the size of a squirrel. It is much prized for its beautiful pearl-grey fur, which is very thick – in fact, no other animal has denser fur. The chinchilla lives wild among the rocky mountains of Chile, where they run about among the stones and rocks of the mountainside. Chinchilla farms throughout the world breed them for their fur and as pets.

Chipmunks are related to squirrels and are often called ground squirrels. They lack the bushy tails of true squirrels, however. Chipmunks live in holes dug around the roots of trees, and may also inhabit more open country.

The eastern chipmunk lives in coniferous forests in North America. It feeds on fruit and seeds which it stuffs into cheek pouches to be stored until it is ready to eat. Chipmunks are 13–15 cm (5–6 in) long, excluding the tail, and have a very fast heartbeat, 684 beats per minute.

Chippendale is a style of English furniture named after Thomas Chippendale (1718–1779), the most famous of all English cabinetmakers. His furniture, especially chairs, is notable for a combination of solid design and rich ornament, often in dark mahogany, and his patterns included designs in the Chinese manner.

Chlorine is a yellowish green gas which has a strong, choking smell. Its chemical symbol is Cl. The water in a swimming pool can smell of chlorine, for chlorine is often added to water to kill germs. Chlorine turns many substances white or bleaches them. Many household bleaches contain chlorine.

Chinchilla

Chlorine is usually made from sea water. It is itself used to make hydrochloric acid and other compounds. PVC, insecticides such as DDT, and chloroform are some of the many chlorine compounds.

Chloroform is a colourless liquid with a heavy vapour. Its chemical formula is $HCCl_3$. It was first used as an anaesthetic for surgery in 1847 by Sir James Simpson. Queen Victoria of England used it during the births of some of her children. It was widely used as a general anaesthetic until the 1930s, when safer substances were found. Chloroform is mainly used today as a solvent (a substance which readily dissolves other materials).

Chlorophyll is a green pigment found in nearly all plants except the fungi and a few parasitic flowering plants. Chlorophyll is usually contained in the plant cell within structures called chloroplasts. In a few primitive algae it lies free within the cells, however. Chlorophyll is able to absorb light energy which is then used by the plant to make food from carbon dioxide and water. *See also* Photosynthesis.

Cholesterol is a fat-like chemical substance which is found in certain parts of the body. It is also found in many foods, such as eggs and butter. Too much cholesterol may cause heart disease. People who have too much cholesterol in their blood may have to stop eating certain foods and lose weight.

Chopin, Frédéric (1810–1849), was a Polish-born composer and pianist. His musical gifts appeared at an early age: he gave his first concert in Warsaw at the age of eight. In 1830 he went on tour in Europe playing some of his own compositions. He was enthusiastically received in Paris, and France became his home. From that time he was more interested in composing than performing, and he produced a stream of beautiful works for the piano. His nocturnes and preludes remain among the best loved and most often played compositions in musical history, and his études require a pianist of extraordinary ability – like Chopin was himself. His more vigorous pieces, based on Polish folk music, are also popular. Chopin's private life was troubled. He died of tuberculosis.

Chordate is an animal belonging to the phylum Chordata. Chordates have bodies which are bilaterally symmetrical – that is, they can be divided into two exactly similar halves. They possess, at some time in their life cycle, a supporting rod on the back called a notochord; and the nervous system lies in a tube in the back.

Christianity is the religion founded by Jesus of Nazareth in the 1st century AD, and is centred on his life and teachings as recorded in the Bible. In the mid-1970s the number of Christians was estimated to be more than a thousand million world-wide.

Jesus Christ (the 'Annointed Saviour') intended to reform the Judaism of his time but ended in founding a separate religion. After his crucifixion, Christianity spread throughout the Roman Empire, and during the Middle Ages the Christian Church, ruled by the pope in Rome, was the most powerful institution in Europe. A separate Church, the Eastern Orthodox Church, was centred in Constantinople.

Christianity suffered a major crisis in the 16th century when there was a revolt against the authority – and some of the teaching – of the Roman Catholic Church. The result was the foundation of various Protestant Churches, differing in ritual and opposed to Rome. Meanwhile, after the fall of Constantinople to the Turks (1452), Russia became the centre of the Eastern Orthodox Church.

Christians believe in God as the creator of the world; that Jesus Christ is his son, whose perfect human life was God's way of revealing himself to mankind. However, there are great differences among the many Christian Churches.

Christian Science is a Church founded in 1879 by Mary Baker Eddy in Boston, Massachusetts. Its best-known characteristic is a belief that the miraculous powers of healing demonstrated by Jesus can be recovered by returning to the earliest form of Christianity. Christian Scientists believe that illness can be cured by spiritual means rather than modern medicine. More important, however, is the healing of sin and the improvement of people's character by true understanding of the spirit of God.

Chromosomes are tiny, paired, thread-like structures found within the nucleus of all animal and plant cells. There are usually several pairs in every nucleus, and each pair may have a different appearance to all the other pairs.

Chromosomes consist of genes which are chemicals responsible for carrying the hereditary information or 'plans' from one cell to the next. When a cell multiplies during growth, each of the two halves of a chromosome within a cell first produces an identical replica of itself, and each newly formed pair goes into each new cell. Thus, the new cell's chromosomes will have identical information to the old cell and can, when ready, produce an exact replica of itself. *See also* Genetics; Nucleic acids.

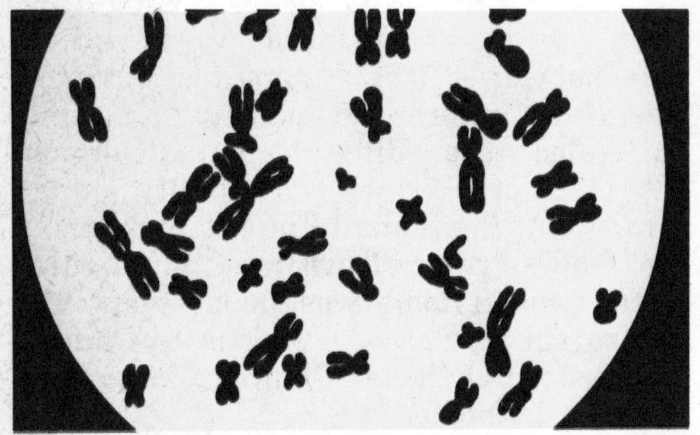

Human chromosomes (greatly enlarged).

Chrysalis is the name for the pupal stage of a butterfly or moth. Inside the protective chrysalis or pupal case, the larva changes into a winged adult which emerges to fly away. The transformation from larva to adult is called metamorphosis. Many butterflies or moths try to conceal or camouflage their chrysalises to avoid them being eaten. *See also* Cocoon.

Churchill, Sir Winston (1874–1965), was a British statesman. A descendant of the 1st Duke of Marlborough, he entered the army and took part in the Battle of Omdurman (1898). He subsequently went to South Africa as a journalist during the Boer War, was captured by the Boers and made a daring escape.

Elected to Parliament in 1900, first as a Conservative and then a Liberal, he served as Home Secretary (1910–1911) and First Lord of the Admiralty (1911–1915), subsequently holding other offices. Returning to Parliament as a Conservative in 1924, he became Chancellor of the Exchequer. Churchill was out of office during 1929–1939 and in the 1930s strongly urged Britain to rearm in face of the threat from Nazi Germany. He joined the government as First Lord of the Admiralty in 1939, becoming Prime Minister the following year. During the war he became a symbol of Britain's determination to resist Nazi aggression. He returned to office as Prime Minister in 1951, retiring in 1955 at the age of 80. At his death he was given a state funeral.

Church of England, the State Church of England, was founded in the 16th century after the English Church had broken away from the authority of the pope in Rome. The head of the Church is the monarch, the spiritual head the Archbishop of Canterbury.

The Church of England, or Anglican Church, is a Protestant Church, organized under the rule of bishops. Apart from its denial of the pope's authority and other differences in doctrine, it is closer to Roman Catholicism in practice and belief than most other Protestant Churches.

Cicada is an insect known as a bug. There are about 1500 species, found mainly in the tropics. They feed by sucking the sap from trees. The males, and in some species the females also, 'sing' by rapidly vibrating small membranes on the sides of their bodies. One American species spends 17 years in the ground as a larva before emerging as an adult.

Circuit, electric – electricity flows through a circuit. A circuit is usually a number of electrical devices joined together by wires. The wires are connected to a battery, socket or other source of electricity. Most circuits contain a switch and a fuse. When the switch is off, the wires do not meet and no electricity flows.

A television is an example of an electrical machine which contains many circuits. These have to be connected to a socket or battery. Switching on the set and the socket completes these circuits and electricity flows through to power the television.

Civet is a small mammal which looks rather like a cross between a cat and a weasel. It has a pointed face and a long, sinuous body. The civet hunts at night, usually feeding on other small mammals, although it will also eat fruit. It lives in the forests of Asia and Africa, and is 53 to 150 cm (21 to 59 in) long.

Clam is a type of mollusc which has a shell composed of two hinged halves. The body of the clam lies within the two shell halves, which can shut tightly together if danger threatens. When the shell is open the clam feeds on tiny particles in the water. The world's largest clam is the giant clam found on reefs in the Indopacific region, which can measure 1.5 m (5 ft) in length.

Classicism is a term which refers to the single most important theme in European art – the pursuit of the 'ideal' (especially an ideal type of human figure). This was the aim of the sculptors of ancient Greece, who stand at the beginning of the Classical tradition, and it was revived, with far-reaching results, in the Italian Renaissance. However, the Italian Renaissance artists achieved a new kind of perfection of their own, so that Classicism came to mean not only the ideal of ancient Greece and Rome but also the ideal of the Renaissance itself. Moreover, painters often employed Classical subjects (scenes from Greek mythology, Roman history, etc.), but painted them in a non-Classical style.

In the late 18th century the Neo-Classical movement was an attempt to revive a Classical style – harder in outline and less colourful than other styles of that period. Classicism seems to have been finally overthrown as a major theme in art by the revolutionary developments that took place in the early years of the 20th century, with the coming of Cubism and the modern movement.

Cleopatra (69–30 BC), became Queen of Egypt in 51 BC, sharing the throne with her brother/husband Ptolemy, until he expelled her from the country. With the help of Julius Caesar she defeated Ptolemy in battle and became sole ruler of Egypt. After Caesar's death she and Mark Antony became lovers. However, following their defeat at the Battle of Actium in 31 BC by Octavian, she committed suicide by allowing a poisonous snake to bite her.

Clive, Robert (1725–1774), was a British soldier and administrator, who established effective British rule in India. He joined the East India Company in 1743 and fought with distinction against the French. His victory over the Nawab of Bengal at Plassey in 1757 brought Bengal under British control.

Appointed Governor of Bengal in 1765, he carried through a number of important administrative reforms. On his return to England in 1767 he was accused of corruption. He was eventually acquitted in 1773, but committed suicide the following year.

Clock is a device used to measure time. For thousands of years, time was measured by the movement of stars, such as the Sun. The sundial is one of the earliest clocks. It measures time by throwing a shadow which moves across the ground as the Sun moves across the sky.

Mechanical clocks have been made for over 700 years. The first accurate clock was the chronometer made in 1759 by John Harrison (1693–1776). Chronometers are clocks which are used on ships, to help sailors find their way.

Today, many clocks are driven by electricity, and the most accurate clocks are atomic clocks.

Cloud is a mass of water or ice particles that floats at various heights in the atmosphere. It is formed by the condensation of water vapour on the Earth. The three main types of cloud are the puffy cumulus, the layered stratus, and the feathery cirrus. Various combinations are possible – for example, cirrostratus and stratocumulus. Where clouds are rain-bearing the word nimbus is added to the type description – for example, cumulonimbus, nimbostratus.

Club mosses are not really mosses at all, although they look rather like them, being quite small and possessing stems clothed with many tiny leaves. They are, in fact, more closely related to the ferns. Club mosses produce spores in club-shaped structures called cones, borne at the ends of upright shoots. (These cones are not true cones, like those of the cone-bearing trees, but are simply called cones because of their similar appearance.) The club shape of the cones gives club mosses their name.

Cluster is a group of stars that moves around a galaxy together. Recently formed stars may make up clusters of a hundred or more. These are known as open, or galactic, clusters. There are many open clusters in our Galaxy. The Pleiades, or Seven Sisters, are an open cluster.

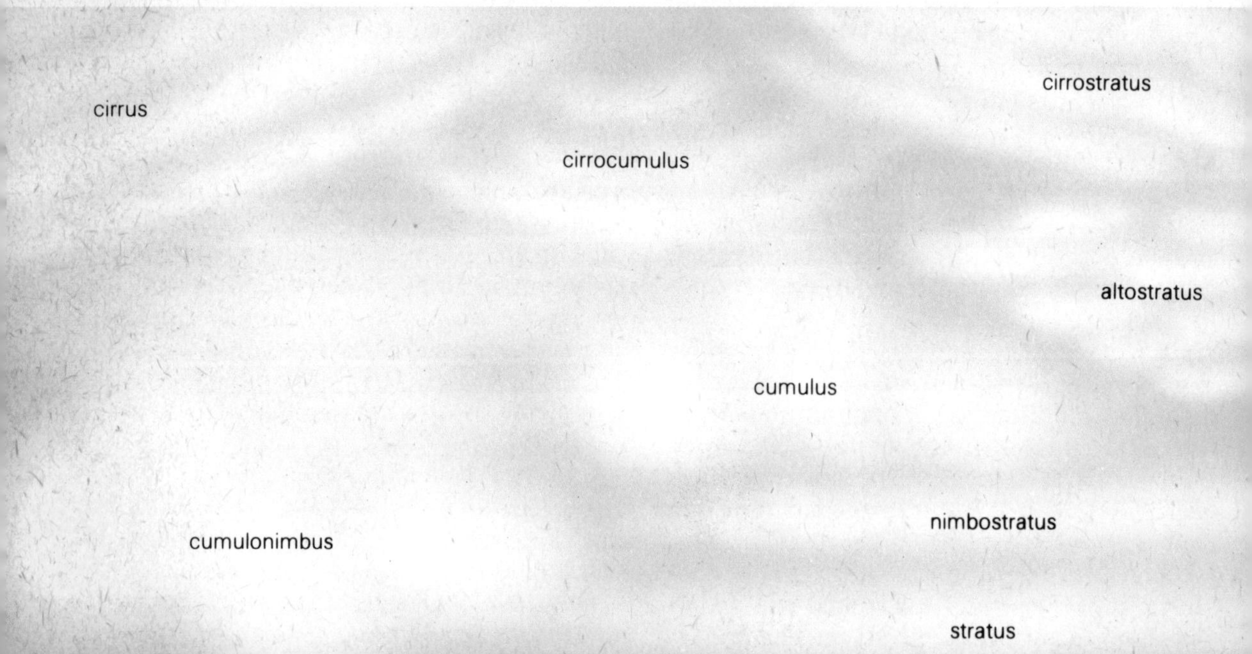

Different cloud shapes.

Old stars may form clusters of thousands of stars. These are known as globular clusters. The stars are much closer together in globular clusters than they are in open clusters. There are more than a hundred globular clusters around the outside of our Galaxy.

Coach is a more comfortable version of the bus, usually used for long-distance journeys. The name comes from the horse-drawn stagecoach, which was used for long journeys in the past. Modern coaches can travel very fast and are often very luxurious, with special seats, television, video, radio, food and drink.

Coal is the remains of trees which lived millions of years ago. These remains were buried and slowly turned into hard layers of coal. The remains of living things are called fossils, so coal is known as a fossil fuel. It is

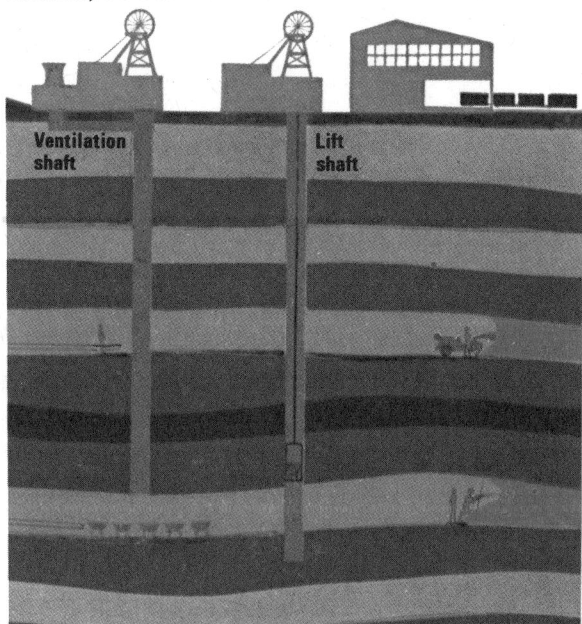

Vertical section through a coal mine.

mainly carbon, and is burnt to give heat. Many homes are heated by coal fires, and coal is used in electricity power stations to produce steam which drives turbines.

When coal is heated without air it gives coke, coal gas and coal tar. Coke and coal gas are used as fuels. Coal tar contains many valuable substances which are used to make, for example, soap, medicines, dyes and plastics.

Layers of coal, or coal seams, may be near the surface of the ground. Here, the coal can be removed very easily and the soil replaced afterwards. This is done in open-cast mines. Other seams are deep underground. Mine shafts and tunnels have to be built to reach the coal.

Cobra, found in Africa and Asia, is among the most feared of snakes. All cobras are venomous, and the African spitting cobra can actually spit venom into the eyes of an enemy from a distance of 2.4 m (8 ft). The spectacled cobra of India is the one used by snake charmers. The raised hood, which all cobras display when frightened or excited, is a flap of skin stretched between the rib bones. The hamadryad is a cobra found in India, Malay Peninsula and China. This highly venomous snake can reach a length of 5 m (16 ft), although most cobras are smaller than this. The hamadryad eats other snakes, but most cobras eat rodents.

Cockatoo is a noisy parrot, which forms large groups in the forests of Australasia. They feed on fruit and seeds, using their sharp, curved bills. Cockatoos are normally white, grey or black and have a crest of feathers on their head.

Cockerill, Christopher, see Hovercraft.

Cockroach is a fairly large, flat insect with long antennae. A few species have adapted well to human environments and occur in buildings in humid parts of the world. Here they feed on plant and animal debris, hiding away in cracks and crevices during the day. Many species never come near human dwellings. There are 3500 species, most of which are tropical, and they are 13 to 50 mm (0.5 to 2 in) long.

Coconut is the fruit of a tree called the coconut palm, which grows on many tropical coasts. The long, branchless trunks bear a crown of feather-like leaves, and the coconuts are borne at the point where the leaves join the trunk. People climb the trees to pick the coconuts, which are a valuable source of food, drink, fuel and building materials. The fibrous coat of the coconut is used to make nets and ropes.

Due to the great value of coconuts to humans, huge plantations exist in Sri Lanka, India, the Philippines and certain Pacific islands. The flesh of the coconut is exported as copra. The oil from copra is used for perfumes, soaps and fats, and the remainder is used as animal foods.

Cocoon is a protective covering for the eggs or pupae of many invertebrates, such as earthworms, insects and spiders. The cocoon of the silkworm moth is the source of silk. *See also* Chrysalis.

Cod is a fish which lives in the North Atlantic. It is yellow-brown, with a white belly, and is up to 1.8 m (6 ft) long. Beneath its chin it bears a feeler, or barbel. Cod live in shoals, feeding on crustaceans, worms and small fish. They are one of the most important fish eaten by people, forming the mainstay of the fishing industry. People have caught cod for thousands of years; bones found in ancient settlements show that they were eaten over 4000 years ago.

Coelacanth is a fish with fleshy fins and large scales, looking more like a prehistoric animal than any other fish living today. In 1938 some fishermen working off the coast of South Africa found this very curious fish in their nets. Before this, it was thought that the coelacanth had become extinct, along with all its relatives, about 70 million years ago. Since 1938 several other live specimens have also been discovered. The coelacanths so far caught have measured about 1.5 m (5 ft) in length.

Coelenterates are the group of flower-like animals, which includes the hydra, anemones, corals and jellyfish. They are all primitive animals, and have a body composed of two cell layers separated by a layer of jelly-like material. The body is usually sac-like, with a ring of tentacles surrounding the mouth. The tentacles capture animals by shooting out poisonous threads, and then cramming the prey into the mouth. Waste materials also leave the body through the mouth. Several species of jellyfish catch food by straining sea water and collecting tiny particles on strands of mucus. Some coelenterates – corals, for instance – spend the adult part of their life fixed in one place, while jellyfish drift about in the ocean currents.

Cold-blooded is a term used to describe animals whose body temperature is governed by the temperature of their surroundings. Unlike animals with feathers or fur – which can keep themselves warm and active even in cold weather – cold-blooded animals are sluggish in cold weather. Fish, reptiles and amphibians are among the most well-known cold-blooded animals. A reptile, such as a lizard, living in a cool climate can not move quickly and hunt unless its muscles are first warmed up by the sun. This is why lizards often bask on rocks in warm weather. When the air cools down with the setting sun, the

Coelacanth

lizard must seek a sheltered place to rest until the sun returns.

Coleridge, Samuel Taylor (1772–1834), was an English poet and critic. He had great intelligence and originality, though his philosophical and critical writings are today read mainly by scholars. His poems *The Ancient Mariner* and *Kubla Khan*, with their sense of exotic mystery, are still widely known. *The Ancient Mariner* was among the *Lyrical Ballads*, published by Coleridge and Wordsworth in 1798, which is regarded as the start of the English Romantic movement in literature.

Colloid is a mixture in which one substance is suspended in another. Milk is a colloid. It contains drops of fat suspended in water. Blood is also a colloid. In it, cells are suspended in a liquid called plasma. Emulsions are a sort of colloid. In these a liquid is suspended in another liquid. Emulsion paints are often used to decorate houses.

It can be very difficult to separate the substances in a colloid. The process of separation is known as dialysis.

Colombia is a republic in northern South America. Capital, Bogotá; area about 1139000 sq km (440000 sq miles). The country gained independence from Spain in 1819 under the leadership of Simon Bolivar. It was originally a larger country, including modern Ecuador, Venezuela and Panama.

Much of Colombia consists of outlying ranges of the Andes Mountains. The lowlands in the east are hot and humid. There are extensive forests, a variety of mineral resources including oil, coal, gold, silver and emeralds. Agriculture is the main occupation and about 20 per cent of the people are directly dependent on the coffee crop. Only Brazil grows more coffee. Bananas are also an important export. Most industry supplies the home market only.

Most Colombians are of mixed European and American Indian descent.

Colosseum was the amphitheatre in ancient Rome. An almost circular building, nearly 200 m (650 ft) across at the widest point, it had tiers of marble seats capable of holding 50000 spectators, with 20000 more standing. Such a gigantic structure would hardly have been possible without the Romans' knowledge of concrete.

The Colosseum was built in the 1st century AD, the fourth storey being added in the 3rd century. The lower three storeys were arcades, with statues standing in the arches. Underneath were dens for wild animals used in the bloodthirsty games which took place in the central arena. In later ages the building was plundered for building stone, but the ruins are still impressive.

Colour – light is made up of many colours. Together these are known as a spectrum. There are three main colours known as primary colours. These are red, green and blue. Mixed together in different amounts they can give any other colour. All the colours on a colour television screen are made up of red, green and blue light. If all three are mixed together equally they look white. A torch or an electric light bulb usually emits equal amounts of red, green and blue light, so its light looks white.

Most objects around us do not shine, but they have a colour. This is because they reflect some of the light that shines on them. Milk looks white because it reflects nearly all the light that falls on it. A red book looks red because it only reflects red light. It absorbs the green and blue light.

When paints are mixed together there are three colours which can make any other colour. These are also known as primary colours, but they are not the same as the primary colours for light. For paints, inks and so on, the primary colours are yellow, magenta (purple) and cyan (blue-green). If yellow, cyan, and magenta are mixed together equally they look black. These colours are used in colour printing. The colour illustrations in this book have been printed using yellow, cyan, magenta and black inks only.

Columbus, Christopher (1451–1506), was an Italian navigator who, without knowing

Columbus asks Ferdinand and Isabella of Spain for support for his voyage.

it, first discovered America. Born in Genoa, he settled in Portugal. Believing that he could reach Asia by sailing westwards, he persuaded the king of Spain to give him the financial support he needed for such a voyage. He set sail from Spain on 3 August 1492 with three ships, and landed on Watling Island in the Bahamas on 12 October. He also visited Cuba and Haiti before returning to Spain, where he received great honours. He subsequently made three other voyages during which he explored the coasts of Central and South America. Columbus made many enemies and died a disappointed man in poverty in Valladolid, Spain.

Comet is usually about 10 km (6 miles) across. It is made of ice and dust, and looks like a large, dirty snowball. There are millions of comets in space. They orbit the Sun and occur throughout the Solar System. Some have very large orbits stretching to nearby stars. Others have smaller orbits, the smallest known being that of Encke, which takes 3.3 years to complete an orbit.

Near the Sun, the heat makes part of the comet turn to gas, or vaporize. This gas forms a large head known as a coma, and a long tail. When this happens, comets can be the largest and brightest objects in the sky. One comet had a coma bigger than the Sun. Another had a tail longer than the distance from the Earth to the Sun.

Halley's comet is one of the most famous comets. It was first recorded in 86 BC, but named after Edmond Halley who noted it in 1682. It is due back near the Earth in 1986.

Comet Kohoutek photographed in 1974.

Comet was the world's first jet-powered passenger aircraft, built by the British De Havilland company and first flown in 1949. It suffered a number of disastrous crashes during its early years, but later gave good service, cutting travel time dramatically. Comet remained in regular airline service until the 1980s.

Commons, House of, is one of the two British Houses of Parliament, which are responsible for making laws. There are 635 members of the Commons, who each come from a different area or constituency. They are elected to office by the British people at elections which take place at least every five years. Members of Parliament belong to different political parties: Conservative, Labour, Liberal, Social Democrat and others. Usually the party which has the most MPs elected forms the government. The second-largest forms the opposition. The government is headed by a prime minister, who has a small advisory group of MPs called the cabinet.

The prime minister and the government are answerable to Parliament for their policies. They can introduce legislation which the Commons votes on. If it is passed in the Commons it goes to the House of Lords. When it has received the Royal Assent it becomes an Act of Parliament.

Commonwealth of Nations is an association consisting of Great Britain and countries which were formerly part of the British Empire. The Commonwealth came into existence in 1931 with the Statute of Westminster, and members of the Commonwealth accept the British crown as the symbol of their free association. In 1931 there were only four self-governing dominions, but after the Second World War many members of the Commonwealth achieved full independence. The heads of government of Commonwealth countries meet every two years, and members of the Commonwealth maintain important economic links with one another. Dominions, that recognize the British Sovereign as their queen, include Canada; republics, such as India and Malaysia, have their own heads of state.

Communications satellite is used to beam messages around the Earth. Many of these satellites have been launched into space. They orbit the Earth in a day, and travel around the Earth in the same time that the Earth spins on its axis. This means that a communications satellite is always above the same place on the Earth.

Television signals travel in a straight line, and unless they are stopped they will travel out into space. However, a communications satellite receives the signal and beams them down to another place on Earth.

Communications satellites are mainly used for telephone calls and television broadcasts. They allow television programmes to be seen all over the world at the same time.

Communism means literally, common ownership of property. Its chief modern use is to describe the ruling ideas, and the political and economic system, of the USSR and other communist countries, and also the outlook of the communist parties that exist in non-communist countries.

As an economic theory, communism is a form of socialism. But, unlike socialists, Communists have a rigid set of doctrines – Marxist-Leninism – developed from the writings of the German revolutionary Karl Marx and the Russian communist leader Nikolai Lenin. There is also a major practical difference between socialists and communists. Most socialists believe in a democratic system in which non-socialists can take part. Communists, on the other hand, believe that the control of the wealthy classes can only be ended by more drastic action. This belief is used to justify the setting up of one-party states in which the communist party is supreme.

Comoros is a federal republic, consisting of three islands in the Indian Ocean between the African mainland and Madagascar. Capital, Moroni; area about 1860 sq km (718 sq miles). Together with a neighbouring island, Mayotte, they were a French overseas territory, granted internal self-government in 1961. The three islands, Njazidja (Grande Comore), Mwali (Moheli) and Nzwami (Anjouan) voted for independence from France in 1974 which they were granted in 1975. (Mayotte voted to remain French.)

The islands have coastal mangrove

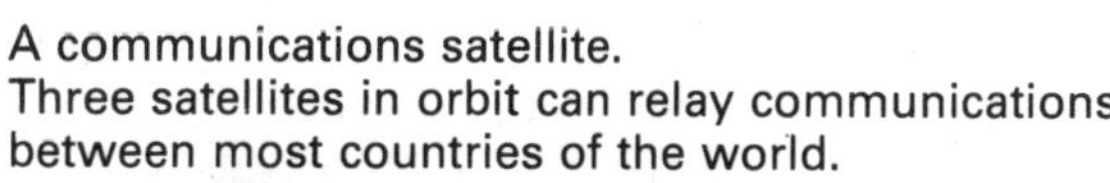

A communications satellite.
Three satellites in orbit can relay communications between most countries of the world.

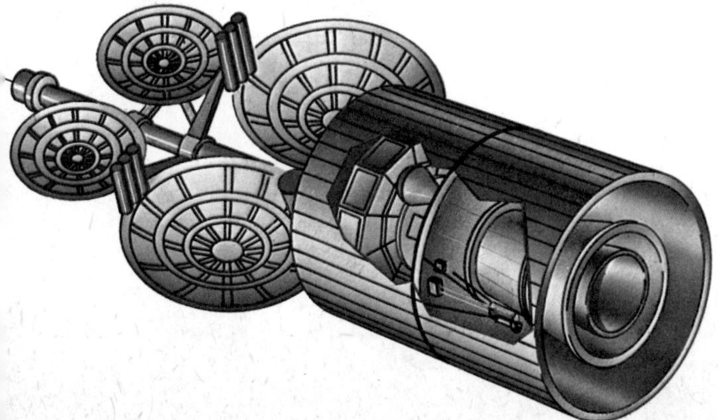

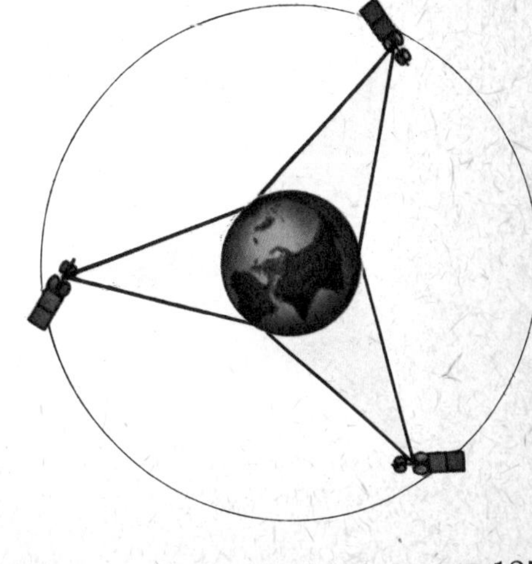

swamps, and forested or shrub-covered interiors. Mt Karthala, on Njazidja, is an active volcano that rises to 2361 m (7746 ft). The people are of mixed African, Arab, Malay and European descent. Chief exports are vanilla and essential oils.

Compass is a device used by sailors and other travellers to find their way. The Earth is like a giant magnet with magnetic poles close to the North and South geographic poles. Magnets have north and south poles too, and when they are free to turn, point toward the Earth's magnetic poles.

A compass contains a small, needle-shaped magnet, which is free to turn. This indicates north, south, etc.

Compositae is the largest family of flowering plants with more than 13 000 species world-wide. The family includes trees, shrubs, climbers and herbs. All members of the Compositae possess flower heads made up of many tiny individual flowers called florets, all attached to a common base. Each tiny floret consists of five petals joined together. The sepals are never leaf-like, but appear, instead, as hairs. They form the 'parachute' which carries the seed on the wind after fertilization. Sunflowers, daisies, dandelions, lettuce, chicory, dahlias, and ragwort are some of the more common members of the Compositae.

Compound is made up of two or more elements joined together. An element is made up of many atoms. In a compound the atoms of each element are joined together to form a molecule.

There are thousands of different compounds. Most of the substances around us are compounds. Water is a compound containing the elements hydrogen and oxygen. Each molecule of water is two hydrogen atoms and one oxygen atom joined together. Compounds are very different to the elements of which they are made. Hydrogen and oxygen are gases at normal temperatures, while water is a liquid.

Computer is like a calculator. However, it can perform much more complicated tasks than a calculator, and can do this very quickly. It can also store large amounts of information, and instructions for using it.

The instructions are called a computer program. The program is fed into the computer's memory where it is stored in the form of electric signals. To use the computer an input unit like a keyboard is operated. This sends information to the computer's central processing unit. This unit obeys the instructions in the program and uses the information to get a result. The result goes to the computer's output unit which is often a screen or printer that displays or prints the result.

Computers are used in factories, where

Daisy bush – an example of the compositae.

they can control a wide variety of machines, offices, homes and schools. Many countries use computers to control electricity, gas and telephone grids. Without computers, space travel would not be possible. In these and many other ways, computers are changing the world we live in. *See also* Hardware; Software.

Concerto is a musical composition for solo instrument and orchestra. It usually has three movements. The concerto was based largely on the older form of the sonata. In its modern form, the concerto was perfected by Mozart, who composed nearly 50 concertos for various instruments.

Concorde is the world's first supersonic passenger aircraft, developed jointly by France and Britain during the 1960s and first flown in 1969. With a cruising speed of over 2000 km/h (1243 mph), Concorde cuts journey times to half that of even the fastest conventional jets, but it uses a large amount of fuel.

Concrete is made of cement, sand and water, together with gravel and small stones. The cement slowly hardens when the water is added and holds the sand and gravel together.

Concrete is used for making buildings, paths and driveways. It may be poured into steel moulds at the building site. Sometimes the concrete is hardened in moulds elsewhere and then taken to the building site. This is known as precast concrete. Whole buildings may be made elsewhere in parts and only put together on the site. This is known as prefabrication.

Concrete is very strong when pushed or compressed, but quite weak when pulled or stretched. It can be made stronger by letting it set around stretched steel wire, or steel nets or rods. This is known as reinforced concrete. It is used for the frames of many buildings, such as high-rise office blocks and for roads, such as motorways, which have heavy traffic.

Condensation is the change of a gas into a liquid when it is cooled. For example, steam in a bathroom cools on the cold walls and windows to form trickles of water.

The condensation of water in the air forms clouds and fog. Fog occurs when water condenses on particles of dirt in the air. This is why fog often happens in areas where the air is dirty.

Condors are huge vultures found in both North and South America. They soar aloft on long, outstretched wings looking for carrion on which to feed, although they will also attack live animals. The Californian condor is an extremely rare bird since it is often shot by hunters. The Andean condor is the largest bird of prey in the world. It has a wingspan of 3 m (10 ft).

Conductor is any substance which lets either electricity or heat pass through it easily. Metals are good conductors, and copper is one of the best electrical conductors. Electricity is carried around homes through copper wires. Food is cooked in metal pots and pans so that heat can pass quickly through to the food. Bad conductors are called insulators.

Cone is the reproductive structure of the conifer or cone-bearing trees. Usually the cones are male or female, and both types are normally found on one tree. A cone is made up of a series of overlapping scales (really special leaves) attached to a central stalk. The scales of the male cones bear pollen sacs, and the female cones bear ovules (which after fertilization will become seeds). In dry weather the scales open and pollen is blown on to the female cones, which then shut. After the fertilized ovule has grown, the female cones open again and the seed, now complete with a little 'wing', is blown by the wind. It if lands on suitable ground it will germinate into a conifer.

There is another sort of cone, found in the eyes of vertebrates. These cones are light-sensitive nerve cells whose purpose is to detect colour and detail.

Confucianism, the philosophy of Confucius

Confucius teaching his disciples.

(551–479 BC), has been a powerful influence on Chinese culture for over 2000 years. Confucius taught that the individual and society should strive to gain perfect virtue by concentration on qualities such as love, courage and wisdom. It is a man's duty to try to be a 'superior man' or 'gentleman', by which Confucius meant a gentleman by character, not by birth.

Confucius told his follows to 'keep spirits at a distance'. He wanted men to be their own masters, and was not concerned with such questions as whether there is a life after death. Although his teaching was, in a sense, religious, it was not a religion as it had no organized Church nor a god to worship.

Congo is a republic in west-central Africa. Capital, Brazzaville; area about 342 000 sq km (132 000 sq miles). A former French colony, it gained full independence in 1960. It is extremely hot and humid (the Equator runs through it), and much of the land is covered by rainforest or poor savannah. The most fertile region is the Niari valley which, with the coastal plain, is the most thickly populated region.

The people belong to many different tribal groups and most are poor. Except for its forests, the country lacks resources for economic development. There are hopes of improving mineral production, but the Congo Republic, with a young and growing population, will probably remain dependent on imports for even basic foods.

Conifer is the name given to the group of plants which bear cones. Apart from the cycads, which are palm-like plants, the conifers are all tall trees found usually in the temperate or cooler parts of the world. Among the best-known conifers are the pines, spruces, larches, cedars, firs and yew. Conifers are usually evergreen, with thin, needle-like leaves. They are quick-growing trees, often planted where timber or ornamental trees are required quickly. Millions of years ago, the conifers were the dominant trees on Earth. Some now-extinct forms were even larger than the mighty redwoods – the world's tallest trees today. *See also* Cone.

Conrad, Joseph (1857–1924), was a Polish-born English novelist. He was a merchant seaman until 1894, having become a British subject ten years earlier. Most of his novels and short stories deal with the sea, though his greatest subject is human nature. Though he did not learn English until he was an adult, his prose is rich and distinctive.

His most famous novels are *The Nigger of the Narcissus* (1898), *Lord Jim* (1900) and *Nostromo* (1904). Some of his shorter fiction, for example, *Heart of Darkness* and *Typhoon* (both 1902), is equally famous.

Conservation is the protection of species to aid their survival. Due to human activities, many plants and animals are in dire danger of becoming extinct. Indeed, many species have already become extinct in recent history. To avoid the loss of even more species as their habitats become swallowed up by building and industry or just damaged by pollution, and to preserve the balance of nature, it is increasingly necessary to take special measures to protect many species.

Sometimes, in the case of rare whales or seriously depleted fish populations, all that is necessary is to control the numbers which are caught until the populations build up again, and then to ensure that they do not again reach dangerously low levels. The problem is getting all governments to agree to carry out such a measure. Quite often the only way to conserve a species is to put aside special nature reserves where it can live undisturbed. Unfortunately, even these measures have their problems. Sometimes populations build up too quickly and the reserve can not support their numbers, and sometimes they fall prey to greedy poachers. However, there are many success stories to be told, and conservation has enabled species like the Hawaiian goose – once down to only about 30 birds world-wide – to flourish again. One of the most successful techniques – used to increase, for instance, populations of the crocodile and the Hawaiian goose – is to rescue animals and breed them in captivity. The increased stocks are then released into the wild.

Constable, John (1776–1837), was an English painter. The son of a miller, he was one of the greatest painters of landscape and is famous for *The Hay Wain, Salisbury Cathedral* and *Flatford Mill*, for example. Besides careful study of his predecessors and a deep love of nature (especially his native Suffolk scenery), he possessed great technical ability. The way he broke up colour in patches influenced later French landscape painters, and Constable is sometimes seen as a forerunner of the Impressionists.

Constantine the Great (circa 285–337), was the first Roman emperor to become a Christian. He was the son of Constantius I, Roman Emperor in the West, and was himself proclaimed emperor by his troops following

Animals in danger *(Top)* Javan rhinoceros *(Above)* Hawaiian goose *(Right)* Californian Condor.

his father's death at York in 308. However, he had to defeat his rival Maxentius before he could make his position secure. In 313 he issued the Edict of Milan which established toleration of Christianity throughout the Roman Empire, and in 325 called the first General Council of the Church. He became sole emperor after defeating the Eastern Roman Emperor in 324 and moved his capital to Byzantium, a port on the Bosphorus, which was renamed Constantinople.

Constantinople was founded as Byzantium in the 7th century BC by Greeks from Megara. It was destroyed by the Persian King Darius I, but subsequently built up again by Greeks from Sparta. Changing hands several times in the course of its history, it was finally captured by the Roman Emperor Septimius Severus in AD 196. In 324 Constantine the Great chose it as his capital and renamed it Constantinople. Much enlarged and with protective walls, it was to be the capital of the Byzantine Empire for over 1000 years. Attacked many times, it was eventually captured by the Turks in 1453 and remained the capital of the Ottoman Empire until 1922. In 1928 its name was changed to Istanbul.

Constellations are patterns or groups of stars in the sky. Many groups of stars look rather like familiar objects, such as tools or animals or people. Thousands of years ago, astronomers noticed this. For example, Greek astronomers divided the stars into 48 constellations, many of which they likened to characters from their mythologies. Grouping the stars into constellations makes them easier to study. Today, we use 88 constellations. Many of them have been passed down by ancient astronomers. They are named after objects like a swan (Cygnus), an archer (Sagittarius), a net (Reticulum) and a unicorn (Monoceros).

Container ship is a modern cargo vessel designed to carry only standard-sized containers, which are also used on lorries and trains. Because these are all the same shape and size, they can be loaded and unloaded very quickly, using giant cranes, greatly reducing the time spent in harbour. Container ships are often very large, carrying many thousands of containers on each journey, and computers are used to keep track of each container to avoid it being loaded on to the wrong ship by mistake.

Continent is the name given to the main land masses. There are seven continents. In order of size they are: Asia, Africa, North America, South America, Antarctica, Europe and Australia.

Continental drift – until recently, it was thought that the continents had always been in the same place on the Earth. Now, scientists believe that the continents are moving very slowly, in a motion called continental drift.

New material from inside the Earth pushes up through the ocean floor, pushing the seabed apart. The spreading ocean floor

Diagram to show how scientists think the continents have drifted apart over millions of years.

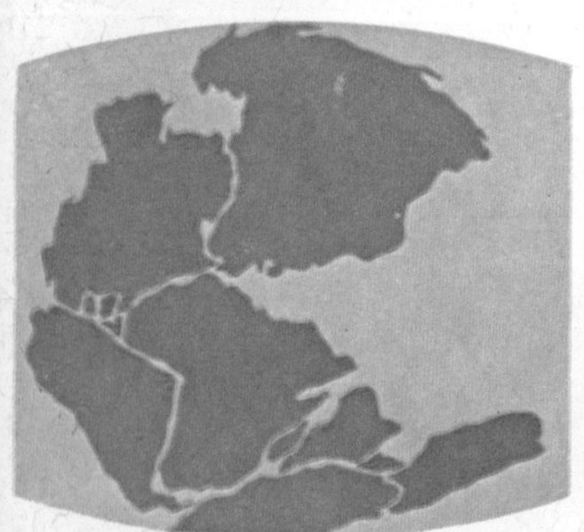

200 million years ago

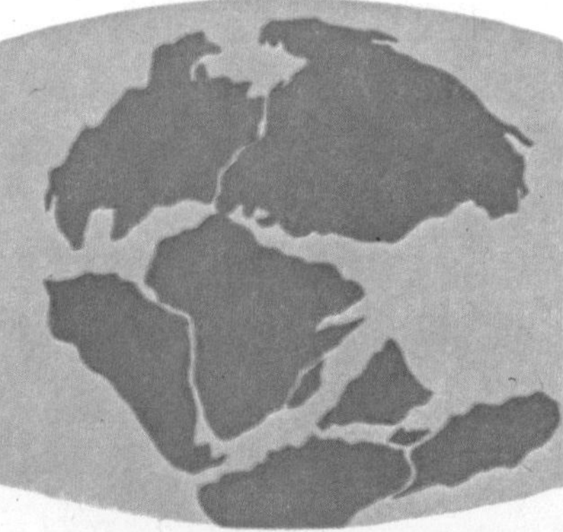

100 million years ago

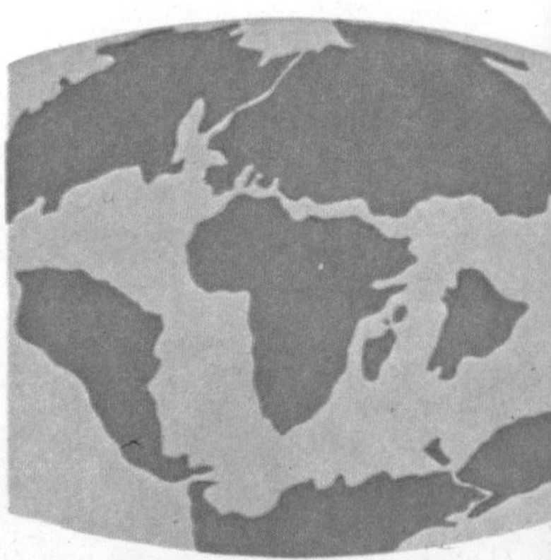

50 million years ago

Captain Cook was attacked by Maoris when he tried to land on the North Island of New Zealand.

causes the continents to drift.

The shape of the continents can be fitted together, like a jigsaw puzzle, to make one big continent. For example, the east coast of South America and the west coast of Africa fit together very well. Similar rocks and fossils are found in continents that are now very far apart. For these and other reasons, scientists think that, about 200 million years ago, all the continents were joined together in one big continent called Pangaea. Slowly this split into two pieces of land called Laurasia and Gondwana. North America, Europe and Asia have drifted apart from Laurasia. South America, Africa, Australia and Antarctica have drifted apart from Gondwana.

Cook, James (1728–1779), was an English navigator and explorer. Joining the Royal Navy in 1755, he made a survey of the St Lawrence River in Canada, and in 1768 was put in command of an expedition to the South Pacific to observe the transit of the planet Venus. He then charted the coast of New Zealand and the eastern coast of Australia. In a second voyage (1772–1775), made in search of a supposed southern continent, he discovered the New Hebrides and the Tahiti group of islands. His life ended tragically in 1779, when in the course of a third voyage he was killed in a quarrel with Hawaiian islanders.

Coots are dark-coloured water birds. They have a white beak and white head shield, which distinguishes them from the similar-looking moorhens which have red beaks. Coots build floating nests on which they lay six to nine eggs, and each parent takes a turn at brooding them. Although they do not have webbed feet, they swim well and can also dive for the water weeds on which they feed. Coots are found throughout Europe and North America, as well as parts of South America, Africa, Asia and Australia.

Copernicus, Nicolaus (1473–1543), was born in Poland. He is known as the father of modern astronomy. For 1400 years it had been thought that the Earth was the centre of the universe. The planets and the Sun were thought to move in circles around it. Copernicus put forward the idea that the Sun was the centre of the universe and that the planets, including the Earth, moved in circles around it.

He could not prove this because the telescope, which allowed more accurate observations of the planets' movements, had not yet been invented. However, his revolutionary idea led to many observations and much research. These confirmed that the Sun is the centre, not of the universe, but of our Solar System.

Copper is a red-brown metal. It has the chemical symbol Cu. It can be made into different shapes easily, and was the first metal used to make tools and weapons.

Copper is very soft, but can be hardened by mixing it with other metals. Bronze is an alloy (a special kind of mixture) of copper and tin. Brass is an alloy of copper and zinc. A lot of copper is made into bronze, brass and other alloys.

Copper is a very good conductor of heat and electricity. Most copper is used to make electric wires and cables, and water pipes.

Copper is mined in many countries including America, Russia, Zambia and Chile.

Corals form part of a group of animals called coelenterates. Almost all corals live in colonies made up of numerous individuals called polyps. Each polyp resembles a tiny sea anemone and is attached to a common skeleton. The structure of the skeleton varies: it may be chalky, horny or fleshy, depending on the species. A few species of coral, such as the Devonshire cup coral, are solitary, consisting of a simple anemone-like polyp sitting in a cup-like skeleton.

Colonial corals may form fan shapes or large stony structures called reefs. The largest collection of coral animals is the Great Barrier Reef which runs for 2020 km (1260 miles) down the eastern coast of Australia. Coral reefs provide food and shelter for many other marine animals. *See also* Atoll.

Core is the central part of the Earth, below the crust and mantle. Around the Earth's centre, the core is thought to be solid. The rest of the core is liquid. It is made of iron and nickel and small amounts of other substances.

Iron and nickel are magnetic. Magnets are often made of iron. This means that the core is like a giant magnet. The poles of this magnet are near the North and South poles of the Earth.

Cork is the protective layer of dead cells formed by the cork cambium of woody plants. The bark of a tree is sometimes composed of only cork, although some species have bark made up of cork and other dead tissues. Cork tissue is very light, and is used commercially for such items as floats.

Cormorant

Cormorants are large seabirds found throughout the world. They grow to 1 m (3 ft) long, and have long, hooked beaks and black plumage with a greenish sheen. Quite often they may be seen sitting on rocks hanging their wings out to dry, after a fishing trip. They must do this for cormorants' feathers are not waterproof, unlike those of ducks. Cormorants may also be seen flying low over the water. The Galapagos cormorant, found only on the Galapagos Islands, is a flightless species.

Corn is the name given to the seed of cereal or grain crops, such as maize, wheat or oats. *See also* Cereals.

Corsica is an island in the western Mediterranean. Area about 8700 sq km (3360 sq miles). Corsica is a department (province) of France, though it was ruled mostly by the Italian state of Genoa from 1347 to 1768. It is entirely mountainous, and the main occupation is raising sheep and goats. It was the birthplace of Napoleon. There are holiday resorts on the coast.

Cortés, Hernán (1485–1547), was the Spanish conqueror of Mexico. After taking part in the conquest of Cuba, he led an expedition to Mexico in 1519, and reached Tenochtitlan, the Aztec capital, in November of that year, with hardly any opposition. However, the Aztecs subsequently rose in revolt and Cortés was forced to abandon the capital. He returned in 1521 and destroyed Tenochtitlan and the Aztec Empire with it. Cortés took part in other expeditions before eventually returning to Spain.

Cosmic rays are charged particles moving nearly as fast as the speed of light. Most of the particles are protons, while some are alpha particles and electrons. They travel throughout our Galaxy, including the Solar System, and some strike the Earth's atmosphere. They can then be detected by instruments on the Earth. There are cosmic ray detectors in the artificial satellites orbiting the Earth.

Nobody knows how cosmic rays are formed. Some may be formed by exploding stars, or supernovae. Some may even come from outside our Galaxy.

Cosmology is the study of the universe. Cosmologists take observations made by astronomers and use these to form ideas about the universe and its birth and death. Only a thousand years ago the Earth was thought to be fixed in the centre of the universe with the heavens moving around it. Current ideas about the universe, which are based on Albert Einstein's Theory of Relativity, may seem equally strange in a thousand years' time. *See also* Big Bang; Steady State.

Costa Rica is a republic in Central America. Capital, San José; area about 51 000 sq km (20 000 sq miles). Columbus was here in 1502 and it became a Spanish province until the rebellion of 1821. It was briefly part of Mexico and then of the Central American Federation, but declared independence in 1848.

Costa Rica is crossed by mountains, which include several volcanoes. Most of the people, largely Spanish in origin, live in the central highlands. The lowlands, near the coast, are forested and swampy. Coffee is the most important export, followed by bananas, cocoa and other tropical products, as well as timber. There is little mining and industry.

Cotton is made from the white fluffy covering of cotton plant seeds. Cotton plants bear a fruit called a boll. This opens to reveal a mass of whitish fibres surrounding the seeds. The fibres are gathered and placed on a machine which separates them from the seeds. The fibres are then cleaned and baled. Once in the cotton mill, the bales are straightened, then spun or twisted into yarn for weaving into fabric.

Cotton material was made as long ago as 3000 BC in India. Today the USA and Egypt are the two major cotton-producing countries. Cotton seed, oil and meal are also produced from the fibre-extraction process, and are used for cooking, animal feed and fertilizer. The cotton boll is used as fuel.

Cotyledons are the first leaves a plant possesses. When a plant seed germinates and begins to grow, the top of the stem pulls free of the seed coat and draws with it tiny leaves or cotyledons. The cotyledons usually lack chlorophyll, and are mainly used to store food (in a few species they do later develop chlorophyll and make food using the energy of sunlight). Cotyledons are much simpler in structure than the main leaves which the plant grows later in life. Some plants – such as grasses, tulips and palms – have only one cotyledon. They are known as monocotyledons. Most plants bear two cotyledons and are called dicotyledons.

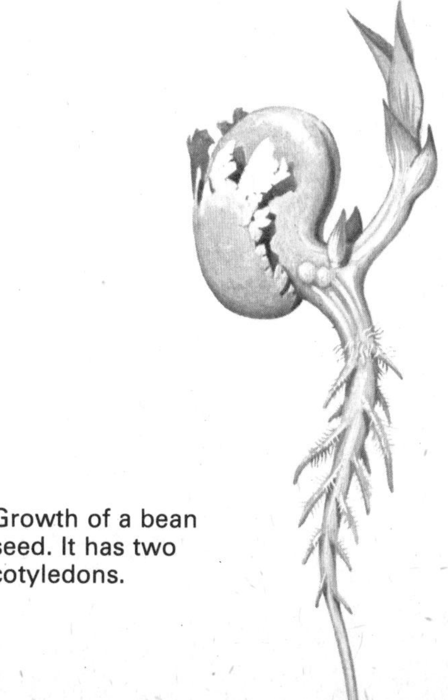

Growth of a bean seed. It has two cotyledons.

Cougar, see Puma.

Country and Western music is a form of popular music based on the folk music of poor, white rural regions of the United States. It is associated especially with Tennessee. Traditionally, the main instruments are banjo, guitar and fiddle. Together with the parallel tradition of black folk music (especially the blues), it has had some influence on pop music.

Crab most commonly seen is the one often found lurking under stones on the seashore, but there are many different kinds to be found throughout the world. Most are marine, but some can live in brackish (slightly salty) water, and others even come on to land and climb trees.

The spider crabs have long, thin legs. The largest of these (and also the largest crab) lives in the Pacific Ocean and measures 45 cm (18 in) across the body and 3.6 m (12 ft) across its outstretched legs. The hermit crabs lack the hard, protective shell, or carapace, of other crabs. They protect their soft bodies inside empty mollusc shells, trundling about the seabed in their mobile homes.

Crabs have large pincers for grabbing their food and protecting themselves. The fiddler crab also waves one pincer – much bigger than the other – to attract females for mating.

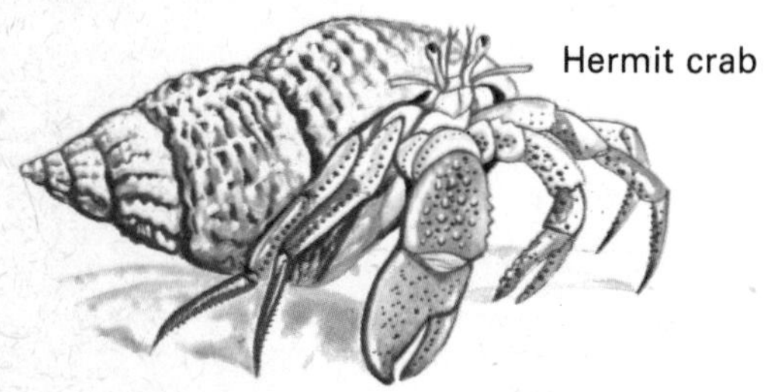

Hermit crab

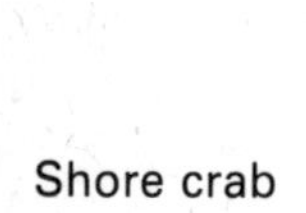

Shore crab

Crane is a tall, elegant bird found throughout the tropical and temperate regions, except South America. It is up to 1.5 m (60 in) tall. All 14 species have strong bills which they use to stab and kill small prey, although some also eat fruit. Males and females take part in dramatic courtship displays in which they dance up and down with flapping wings. Their nest is built on marshy ground. Most species migrate long distances, in huge flocks called skeins, from their summer homes to their winter homes and back again.

Cranko, John (1927–1973), was a South African-born dancer and choreographer. He came to England in 1946 and joined the Sadler's Wells Ballet (later the Royal Ballet). He choreographed many works, mainly for this company but also for other great international companies, and produced a successful revue called *Cranks*. A production in Stuttgart of his *Prince of the Pagoda* led to his appointment as director of the Stuttgart Ballet in 1961. In a few years he accomplished what was called a 'ballet miracle', creating one of the strongest dance companies in the world and producing an outstanding group of dancers.

Cranmer, Thomas (1489–1556), was an English churchman and martyr, who played an important part in the Reformation in England. He helped Henry VIII to obtain the annulment of his marriage to Catherine of Aragon in 1533, and was appointed Archbishop of Canterbury the same year. He encouraged the translation of the Bible into English; and in the reign of Edward VI issued the Prayer Books of 1549 and 1552. Following the accession of the Catholic Queen Mary he was condemned to death for treason and heresy and was burnt at the stake.

Crater is a hollow on the surface of the Earth, Moon or other planets. Meteorites crashing into the Earth's surface can dig craters. Craters are also formed by volcanoes erupting. The largest meteorite crater on the Earth, at Manicouga in Quebec, is 64 km (40 miles) across. The largest volcanic crater is at Mount Aso in Japan and is 27 km (17 miles) across.

The Moon is covered with craters, most of which are thought to have been made by meteorites. Mercury, Venus, Mars and the satellites of Mars are also known to have craters.

Cretaceous is a period in the history of the Earth, known from the study of rocks and of the fossil remains found in them (the geological record). The Latin word *creta* means 'chalk', and great beds of chalk (including the English Downs and the 'white cliffs of Dover') were laid down during the Cretaceous era.

This period is the last major division of the Mesozoic era, following the Jurassic. It began 136 million years ago and lasted for about 71 million years. The dinosaurs and other great reptiles became extinct towards its end, and at about the same time, great geological upheavals created the Rocky Mountains, USA, and the Andes, South America.

Crete is an island in the Aegean Sea (Mediterranean), and is part of Greece. Area about 8300 sq km (3200 sq miles). The advanced Minoan civilization, which existed in Crete before 2000 BC, was the forerunner of ancient Greece. Crete has never been quite so important since, and it was often a lair of pirates. After a long period of Turkish rule, the Cretans fought a long battle for union with Greece, which was successful in 1913.

Crickets are insects related to grasshoppers and locusts. They have long hind legs which they use for jumping, and strong biting mouthparts. They rub their tough wings together to produce their familiar 'song', which is used to attract mates.

Crimean War (1853–1856) was a war in which Britain, France, Turkey and (later) Sardinia fought against Russia. The causes of the war were Russian expansion in the Balkans and disagreement over the protection of the Holy Places in Jerusalem. After the Russians had sunk the Turkish fleet at Sinope, Britain and France declared war (1854). British and French forces invaded the Crimea. In 1855 they captured Sebastopol after a siege, and also fought battles at Alma, Balaclava and Inkerman. War came to an end with the Treaty of Paris in 1856. The many British troops who died from disease during the war led to formation of a proper nursing service under Florence Nightingale.

The capture of Sebastopol during the Crimean War.

Crocodiles are the largest living reptiles, the saltwater crocodile of Asia reaching a length of 10 m (33 ft). They have huge mouths armed with pointed teeth. Crocodiles are found mainly in tropical regions, where they inhabit rivers and estuaries. They live in lairs dug out of the bank until it is time to hunt. Then they slither into the water and search for fish. They may also grab animals from the bank and pull them into the water. Crocodiles may be distinguished from alligators by their teeth.

Cromwell, Oliver (1599–1658), was an English soldier and statesman and one of the most important figures in British history. He first entered Parliament in 1629 and in 1640 he became leader of the Puritans and an opponent of the policies of King Charles I. After the outbreak of the Civil War in 1642 he trained and led his troops to victory over the Royalists. At first he sought a peaceful settlement with the king, but after the 2nd Civil War of 1648 he turned against him and was one of those who signed his death warrant. From 1649 to 1650 he crushed Royalist opposition in Ireland with great cruelty and then defeated the Scots. In 1653 he became Lord Protector, ruler of England. Cromwell allowed religious toleration at home and made England a great power in Europe. At his death he was succeeded as Lord Protector by his son Richard (1626–1712), who abdicated in 1659.

Crop is a plant grown by humans. When people first started using plants as food they probably searched in a random fashion for the plants they needed. However, it soon became clear that it would be easier to grow these plants close to their dwellings, so that they would know that a source of food was readily available. Thus, trees were felled and land was made ready for growing the seeds gathered from their favourite food plants, and the cultivation of crops began.

Today, humans have learned to grow a huge variety of crops – cereals, fruit, vegetables, timber sources and other plants. They have also developed many new strains and hybrids.

Crusaders prepare for the sack of Constantinople.

Crusades were military expeditions organized in Western Europe from the 11th to 14th centuries to recover the Holy Land from the Muslims. The First Crusade (1096–1099) was launched by Pope Urban II, and the Crusaders succeeded in capturing Jerusalem and in establishing Crusader states. The Second Crusade (1147–1149) resulted in an unsuccessful siege of Damascus. The Third Crusade (1188–1192) was undertaken in response to the recapture of Jerusalem by Muslims, but the Crusaders were unable to co-ordinate their efforts. The Fourth Crusade (1202–1204) was notable for the sack of Constantinople. The later crusades were largely unsuccessful, and the Muslims retained control of the Holy Land.

Crust is the name given to the surface or outer layer of the Earth. The crust is made of solid rock. It is much thicker below the land than below the oceans. Under the continents, the crust is about 40 km (25 miles) thick. Below the oceans it is only about 6 km (3.7 miles) thick.

Pressure within the Earth beneath the crust can cause it to be pushed up to form high mountain chains, or forced down to form deep valleys. The crust rests on a layer of the Earth called the mantle.

Crustacean is an invertebrate animal belonging to the class Crustacea, which is a division of the phylum Arthropoda. There are over 26000 species of crustacean throughout the world, and they include animals such as crabs, lobsters, shrimps, water fleas, barnacles and woodlice. All crustaceans have two pairs of antennae on their head, but the number of legs and shape of the body varies, according to the species.

Nearly all crustaceans live in water, and most of them are marine. One of the few land-living crustaceans is the woodlouse.

Crystal is a solid substance found in a regular geometrical shape. The salt we use to flavour food is a white powder, but salt which occurs naturally in the Earth appears as colourless, square blocks, which are called crystals.

Even powdered salt contains tiny square block crystals. They are too small to see with the naked eye, however. Solids, whether they look like crystals or not, are usually made up of many tiny crystals.

Large crystals can be grown by dissolving a solid, such as salt, in water. The water slowly evaporates away, leaving a crystal.

Crystallography is the study of crystals. It often uses X-rays, when it is known as X-ray crystallography. X-rays passed through a crystal form a pattern on a piece of photographic film. The structure of the crystal can be found from this pattern. This method has been used to find the structure of many substances, including the DNA in the cells of our bodies.

Crystal Palace was an exhibition hall constructed for the Great Exhibition in Hyde Park, London, in 1851. It was built entirely of glass on an iron framework and designed by Sir Joseph Paxton (1801–1865), a former gardener who had previously designed large greenhouses. Some large trees in the park were contained inside it. It was the first building made of of prefabricated parts, and after the exhibition it was re-erected at Sydenham. It was destroyed by fire in 1936.

Cuba is an island republic in the Caribbean Sea. Capital, Havana; area about 114500 sq km (44200 sq miles). The largest island in the West Indies, Cuba was visited by Columbus on his first voyage. It was a Spanish colony, but a Cuban revolt against Spain in 1895 was supported by the USA, and it became a US dependency, and then a republic in 1901. Cuba was under strong US influence until Fidel Castro led a revolution and made it a communist state in 1961.

The original Cubans died out under Spanish rule; most today are of European and African descent. There is a large highland area in the east, but most of the island is fairly flat and fertile. Sugar has long been the most important product, though cigars are more famous. Sugar-processing is the largest industry, and there are good coastal fisheries.

Cubism was one of the most influential modern art movements. Invented about 1906 by Picasso and Braque, it was named by a hostile critic who described one of Braque's pictures as 'cubes'. Its origin can be traced to Cézanne and his theories of structure.

A Cubist painting aims to picture the true, three-dimensional form of its subject, as if it were seen from several angles at once. In this phase of 'Analytical' Cubism, colour was almost abandoned. In the later, 'Synthetic' phase, Cubism became less severe: colour returned and typical still-life subjects were painted, though in odd associations.

It was a short-lived movement (Picasso was not a Cubist for long). Its chief importance is not the actual works produced, but the great influence of Cubism on the way people, especially artists, look at things, and on later art movements.

Cuckoo is a parasitic bird. From its wintering grounds in Africa it flies to Europe and lays its eggs, not in a nest of its own, but in one belonging to a bird such as a dunnock or warbler. The cuckoo's egg hatches first, and the chick proceeds to eject all the rightful eggs from the nest. From then on, the new parents feed the cuckoo's chick until it grows so big that it perches ridiculously on the remains of the nest. It increases its weight by 50 times in only 3 weeks! Eventually the young cuckoo flies back to Africa, without having learned any navigational skills from its real parents (which it never sees).

There are a few species of cuckoo which are not parasitic. These include the yellow-billed cuckoo and the roadrunner of North America.

A cuckoo chick removing eggs from a reed warbler's nest.

Cuckoo pint, also known as lords-and-ladies, is a curious flower which appears in shady woods and hedgerows in Europe. It has a fleshy green sheath enclosing a long, fleshy stalk. Lower down the stalk, hidden by the sheath, are tiny male and female flowers. The cuckoo pint attracts flies with its foetid smell. These flies crawl inside the sheath towards the flowers, where they are trapped by tiny hairs. As they crawl about trying to get out, they become dusted with pollen from the male flowers. They may also brush pollen – previously collected from another flower – on to the female flowers. Soon the sheath withers and the flies escape, ready to pollinate another plant. In autumn the plant produces very poisonous red berries.

Cultivation is the method of growing plants under the control of humans. This means that the plant or crop can be given the conditions of soil, water, temperature and so on that best suit it, and so will give the best possible yield. Cultivated plants are often grown together in large groups for easier harvesting, and so that diseases and competition from other plants or animals can be controlled. *See also* Crop.

Curie, Pierre (1859–1906) **and Marie** (1867–1934, **née Sklodowska**), were a husband and wife who studied radioactivity and magnetism. They started the investigation of radioactive elements. Pierre was born in Paris and became Professor of Physics at the Sorbonne, Paris. Marie was born in Poland.

They discovered that a mineral called pitchblende contained the radioactive elements polonium and radium. With their friend Antoine Henri Becquerel (1852–1908), the Curies received a Nobel prize in 1903 for this work. After Pierre's death in a street accident, Marie Curie became Professor of Physics at the Sorbonne. She continued working on radioactive elements and managed to obtain pure samples of polonium and radium. She was awarded another Nobel prize in 1911.

Current is a movement of water or air. The

Surface currents of the world's oceans.

word is used to describe the surface movements of the ocean, which are mainly caused by prevailing winds or differences in temperature or salt content between different bodies of water. Major currents, such as the Gulf Stream, can have an important influence on climate.

Current electricity is caused by electrical charges which are moving. There are two sorts of current electricity: direct current (DC) and alternating current (AC). The batteries which power torches and radios produce direct current.

Most of the electricity we use is alternating current. This lights and heats homes and factories and powers most electrical machines. It is produced by generators, usually in power stations. The generators are driven by the heat from coal or nuclear reactions, or by water. Wind and energy from the Sun, called solar energy, are also used to make alternating current.

The alternating current is taken by overhead or underground cables to homes and factories. Copper wires carry electricity around the home to sockets and light switches.

Electricity can be very dangerous. For example, touching a metal wire carrying electricity causes an electric shock, which can kill. All electrical equipment, including wires, sockets, switches and plugs, must be kept in good condition and used carefully.

Cuttlefish are molluscs, related to the octopus and squid. Unlike most molluscs which have a shell outside their bodies, cuttlefish are active swimmers with only a tiny shell inside their bodies. The body has a fin around its edge, and the head bears eight short and two long, suckered tentacles. The long tentacles are used to catch fish and shrimps. Cuttlefish swim by means of their fin, but they can also shoot about rapidly by squirting jets of water from their body. They can change colour and squirt jets of ink to deceive their enemies.

Cutty Sark was a sailing ship built at Dumbarton, Scotland, in 1869. She was one of the famous tea clippers, used to rush tea and spices from India and the Far East, and wool from Australia, to Britain in the late 19th century. *Cutty Sark* completed a round-the-world journey from Australia to Britain in 72 days, a feat which even modern racing yachts have failed to achieve. *Cutty Sark* is preserved at Greenwich, London.

Cybernetics is the scientific study of the way people, other animals and machines communicate with each other and make decisions. This information is used to make machines, such as computers and robots, which can do a wide range of jobs on their own. It is also used to learn more about the way people and other animals think and act.

Cycads are conifers, but they look very different from the tall trees which make up the majority of the conifers. Also unlike most other conifers, cycads grow in the warmer parts of the world. Cycads usually have short, unbranched stems (although a few grow quite tall), at the top of which is a crown of large ferny leaves. They are sometimes regarded as living fossils, having changed little over millions of years.

Cyclone is a violent and destructive tropical storm. It is a form of whirlwind, with tremendously strong winds blowing round the centre or 'eye' of the storm, which may itself be quite calm. Thunder, lightning and torrential rain accompany cyclones. They occur in the Arabian Sea, the Bay of Bengal, the China Seas (where they are called typhoons) and the West Indies (where they are called hurricanes). *See also* Hurricane.

Cyclops, in Greek myth, was a one-eyed giant. In Homer's *Odyssey* cyclopses were hideous wild shepherds who lived on an island and ate humans. Their leader was Polyphemus, from whom Odysseus and his companions escaped after blinding the monster's single eye. In some later stories, they were the assistants of Hephaestus, the blacksmith-god, and worked in his forge.

The *Cutty Sark.*

Cypresses are a group of evergreen coniferous trees. Most species originate in North America or Japan, but many have now been planted in other countries as decorative trees, or as quick-growing evergreen hedges. The Monterey cypress is a majestic tree with a wide-spreading crown, rather like that of a Lebanon cedar. Another popular species, the nootka cypress, grows more like a 'Christmas' tree.

Cyprus is an island republic in the eastern Mediterranean. Capital, Nicosia; area about 9250 sq km (3570 sq miles). It was conquered by the Turks in 1571 and controlled by Britain from 1887 until its independence in 1960.

Cyprus has suffered as a result of its division between Turkish and Greek inhabitants and the rivalry of Greece and Turkey. Since 1974 the north has been controlled by Turkey, following a military invasion, and many Greek Cypriots are refugees.

The island is very attractive to tourists thanks to its warm climate, mountains, beaches, historic buildings and archaeological remains. Agriculture is the main occupation. Wine, fruit and vegetables and olive oil are important exports.

Cyrus the Great (599–530 BC), was King of Persia and creator of a vast empire. He won control of Medea and Lydia, and conquered Babylon in 539 BC. He then added Syria and Palestine to his empire.

Czechoslovakia is a communist republic in central Europe. Capital, Prague; area about 128 000 sq km (50 000 sq miles).

History Czechoslovakia was created in 1918 out of territories which had been formerly part of the Austro-Hungarian Empire. Although the country achieved considerable economic progress in the 1920s and 1930s it encountered problems with its large German minority group in the Sudetenland. This was annexed in 1938 by Nazi Germany, which in the following year seized the rest of the country. After the Second World War, in February 1948, a communist government was formed.

Land and People Parts of Czechoslovakia, especially the north-west, are mountainous and forested. There are also wide river valleys and plains, especially in the south. The climate is 'continental' – warm summers, cold winters.

There are many different peoples in Czechoslovakia, but the majority are of course Czechs, who come from Bohemia in the west, and Slovaks. Slovakia, in the east, is largely a farming region. Industry is mainly concentrated in the ancient and beautiful capital, Prague, and other Bohemian cities. The country is highly industrialized and exports cars, armaments, machinery and chemicals, chiefly to countries of the Soviet bloc. Beer is another famous Czech product. There are large coal reserves, and forestry is also of some importance.

The city of Prague, Czechoslovakia.

Dada was a movement of defiance among artists and writers, originating in Zurich, Switzerland, about 1916. It was provoked largely by disgust at the First World War. The Dadaists (their name, characteristically, means nothing in particular) attacked every generally accepted institution and idea. When they put on an art exhibition, they provided axes for the spectators to hack the pictures. Dada might have been quickly forgotten had it not developed into the movement of Surrealism.

Daddy Long Legs, see Fly.

Dalai Lama is a Tibetan Buddhist leader, considered by his followers to be divine and to be the reincarnation of the previous Dalai Lama. As head of Tibetan Lamaism (the Tibetan form of Buddhism) he has authority over believers in Tibet and Mongolia. The present Dalai Lama was born in 1935. After a Tibetan revolt against the Chinese Communists, he went into exile in India in 1959.

The Dalai Lama.

Dali, Salvador (1904–), is a Spanish artist. He became one of the leading Surrealist painters, producing pictures of weird and irrational subjects, sometimes gruesome ones. His work owed something to Freud's theories about the working of the unconscious mind and the importance of dreams. Apart from his subject-matter, Dali's pictures were painted with deliberate, detailed realism, recalling the technique of the Pre-Raphaelites. He also produced, with Buñel, two notable Surrealist films, and kept himself in the public eye by a series of wildly outrageous acts and statements.

Dalton, John (1766–1844), was an English chemist who put forward an atomic theory. According to this theory, all matter consists of small particles called atoms. All the atoms in any one element are the same and have the same weight. The atoms of different elements are not the same and differ in weight.

Compounds are formed by atoms of different elements combining in simple proportions. This atomic theory was very important to the development of chemistry.

He worked with gases and put forward the law of partial pressures which is often known as Dalton's Law. He also studied the weather, and was the first to describe colour blindness, from which he suffered.

Dam is a barrier built across a river or sea which is high enough to stop the water flowing over it. In a river dam, the water which is held back forms a reservoir. Fresh water from this can be sent through pipes to homes for drinking and washing, or used to water crops. The water can also be used for hydro-electric power schemes.

Today, artificial dams are made of rock and clay or concrete.

(Right) Darwin making notes about iguanas he found on the Galapagos Islands.

Dams have been built for more than 5000 years. The highest dam is the Rogunsky dam in Russia, which is 325 m (1066 ft) high. The largest concrete dam is the Grand Coulee Dam across the Columbia River in the USA. It is 167 m (550 ft) high and 1272 m (4140 ft) long. *See also* Water power.

(Below) The Kariba dam on the river Zambesi on the Zambia–Zimbabwe border.

Dante Alighieri (1265–1321), was an Italian poet. One of the greatest figures in European literature, Dante, a native of Florence, spent much of his life in political exile. His greatest work, the *Divine Comedy*, is a long semi-religious poem. The poet is guided through heaven and hell by Beatrice, who is both a symbol of religion and a re-creation of a girl Dante loved. It expresses medieval ideas about God and mankind, and has been enormously influential.

Danube is the second longest river in Europe. Length, 2850 km (1770 miles). The Danube rises in the Black Forest of West Germany and flows through Austria and east Europe to the Black Sea. The upper Danube valley is very beautiful and associated with many colourful events in history and literature. It has long been a major highway for trade. Among other fish, it contains the Danube salmon, or hüchen.

Darius I (circa 548–486 BC), was King of Persia. Elected by the nobles in 521 BC, he restored order in a rebellious empire and reorganized the administration, dividing his land into 20 satrapies. He pushed Persia's frontier eastward into India and crushed a revolt of the Ionian city-states. He determined to punish the Greeks for supporting the Ionians and sent two expeditions against them. The first was partly successful, but the second ended in the disastrous Persian defeat at Marathon (490 BC). Darius died while preparing a third expedition.

Darling is a river in south-east Australia. Length, 2720 km (1690 miles). It eventually flows into the River Murray. The flow is irregular, according to season, and several dams have been built.

Darwin, Charles (1809–1882), was born in Shrewsbury, England and studied at both Edinburgh and Cambridge Universities. In 1831 he was invited to join the survey ship HMS *Beagle* as naturalist. For five years HMS *Beagle* sailed on an expedition of discovery through the waters of the Southern Hemisphere. It was on this voyage that Dar-

win first encountered the vast array of different animals and plants that were to stir him to write his most famous book, *The Origin of Species by Means of Natural Selection*, which was published in 1859. This book made it necessary to re-think many of the religious and moral views held at that time. It also described for the first time how all plants and animals arose from their ancestors, and how the process of natural selection enabled the fittest to survive and produce new generations. *See also* Evolution.

David was king of Israel (reigned circa 1000–962 BC). What we know of him comes chiefly from the Bible. He is shown as an ideal ruler – poet, warrior and statesman, and is believe to be the author of many of the Psalms.

Originally a simple shepherd, he was chosen to be king by the prophet Samuel. Stories told of him include his victory over the giant Goliath, his conquest of Jerusalem and his love for Bathsheba (whose husband he had – indirectly – killed). It is difficult to separate the historical David from the legends, but he was clearly responsible for turning a beleaguered band of shepherds into a powerful kingdom.

Day is the average time it takes the Earth to spin around once on its axis. Clocks measure the day from midnight of one day to midnight the next day, dividing the day into 24 hours. Each hour is divided into 60 minutes and each minute is divided into 60 seconds. Days are grouped into weeks, months and years.

Astronomers use a slightly shorter day. It is 4 minutes shorter than a 24-hour day, and is called a sidereal day.

The word day is also often used for the number of hours of daylight. The rest of the time is called night.

Dead Sea is a salt lake in south-western Asia, between Israel and Jordan. Area, 1000 sq km (386 sq miles). The Dead Sea is the lowest surface anywhere on earth, 395 m (1296 ft) below the level of the nearby Mediterranean. It is extremely salty and therefore provides salt for the region.

Death cap is the sinister name given to a particularly deadly poisonous fungus. Unfortunately, it bears a resemblance to the edible mushroom, and so is often mistakenly picked and eaten. The death cap has been responsible for over 90 per cent of all deaths caused by eating poisonous fungi. It appears in deciduous woods during late summer and autumn. It has a white stalk upon which is borne an olive-yellow cap. The gills are also white.

Debussy, Claude (1862–1918), was a French composer, sometimes described as an 'impressionist'. The painters of Impressionism influenced him, and the supposed lack of form in his *Prélude à l'Après-midi d'un Faune* (1894) caused very hostile criticism. More important, Debussy was an innovator, who prepared the way for many new features in modern music and escaped entirely from the powerful Germany influence of Wagner (whom he nonetheless admired). He described himself as a 'French musician', with emphasis on the adjective.

December is the twelfth month of the year in the modern calendar, and lasts for 31 days. In the ancient Roman calendar it was the tenth month, and so its name comes from the Latin *decem* meaning 'ten'. Christmas Day is celebrated on 25 December.

Deciduous is the name given to trees which do not carry their leaves all year, but shed them at the onset of autumn. From buds, new leaves develop the following spring. Typical deciduous trees include most species of oak, the maple and the birch.

Deciduous teeth are milk teeth (the first of the two sets) of a mammal.

Deer are all herbivorous mammals. They range in size from the pudu of Chile which is only 35 cm (14 in) high, to the North American moose which reaches 2.2 m (7 ft) at the shoulder. In most of the 40 species the males bear horns known as antlers. These are shed each year to be regrown the next. The musk deer and water deer have tusks instead of antlers. Most deer live in herds, but a few species are solitary. Among the most common deer are red deer, fallow deer and reindeer.

Roe deer

Degas, Edgar (1834–1917), was a French painter. He is regarded as one of the leading Impressionists, though he was not an 'outdoor' painter. His chief interest was in the human figure caught in unusual poses, and his subjects included washerwomen, ballet, café and racing scenes. A great draughtsman, he produced many swift and brilliant chalk drawings. In recent years, his small sculptures, often made as studies for his pictures, have become very highly esteemed.

De Gaulle, Charles (1890–1970), was a French soldier and statesman. He served in the army in the First World War and during the 1930s became a strong advocate of mechanized warfare. Appointed a general in 1940, he refused to accept France's defeat by the Germans, and formed the 'Free French' forces in Britain. After the liberation of France he returned home as head of the provisional French government and served as President until 1946. He was recalled in 1958 as Prime Minister to deal with the crisis over the proposed independence for Algeria. Elected President of the newly created Fifth Republic, he successfully negotiated the French withdrawal from Algeria. His presidency brought France a period of stability and he was re-elected in 1965. He withdrew France from NATO and opposed British membership of the EEC. His position became weaker following the unrest of 1968, and he resigned after his government's defeat in a referendum on constitutional reform in 1969.

Charles De Gaulle

Delacroix, Eugène (1798–1863), was a French painter. He is often regarded as Romantic rather than Classical, though he disliked being categorized in that way. He shared the Romantics' love of liberty (some of his finest works celebrate the Greeks' fight for independence), of poetry and the theatre (his famous *Death of Sardanapalus* was inspired by the work of the Romantic poet, Byron), of exotic settings (his stay in Morocco influenced his art), and of nature in the wild. He was also a highly intelligent critic of art, his own included.

Delius, Frederick (1863–1934), was an English composer. Family pressure forced him to go into business, but he was determined to be a musician. He was of German descent and lived much of his life abroad, but he was a very 'English' composer. He wrote six operas and several large orchestral works (though he disliked traditional forms like the symphony or sonata), but his shorter works and songs have proved most popular.

Delphi is a town in ancient Greece. A sacred place from the earliest times, Delphi became linked with the worship of Apollo. It was especially famous for the oracle in the temple of Apollo, where the words of the gods were spoken through a prophetess, called the Pythia.

The oracle at Delphi was consulted on important matters by both individuals and statesmen. Unfortunately, the replies given were usually expressed in mysterious phrases whose meaning could be interpreted in more than one way. *See also* Apollo.

Democracy is a political system of government by the entire people, rather than by an élite (aristocracy) or by one person (monarchy or dictatorship). The word was coined by the Greeks (the Greek word *demos* means 'people'), and the Greek city-state of Athens was the most famous democracy of the ancient world.

Although democratic ideas were occasionally put forward in later times, actual democratic systems of government only began to emerge in the late 19th century – and in most

A council of 500, elected by the people, was part of the first democratic government in Athens.

countries applied exclusively to adult men. In Britain, for example, adult women only gained equal political rights with men in 1928.

Unlike ancient Athens, modern democracies are so big that all their citizens could not possibly come together and pass laws. Instead, the citizens vote to elect people to pass laws and run the government for them. This is representative democracy, in which elections become contests between people and parties of different political opinions.

Denmark is a kingdom in north-west Europe. Capital, Copenhagen; area about 43 000 sq km (16 630 sq miles).

History From about AD 800 Denmark was occupied by Vikings who then raided England, France and regions around the North Sea. By the 11th century Denmark, now converted to Christianity, was an empire comprising Denmark, England and Norway, ruled over by King Canute. However, his empire collapsed soon after his death in 1035.

In 1397 Denmark, Norway and Sweden joined together in the Union of Kalmar, although Sweden subsequently broke away. The house of Oldenburg was established on the throne in 1448, and in 1536 Lutheran Protestantism became the accepted religion. Denmark was involved in wars with Sweden in the 16th and 17th centuries. In 1814, having supported Napoleonic France against England, Denmark was forced to hand over Norway to Sweden. In 1866 it lost the German duchies of Schleswig and Holstein to Prussia. Occupied by Germany during the Second World War, Denmark joined NATO in 1949 and the EEC in 1972.

Land Denmark consists of a large peninsula (Jutland) and many islands in the Baltic Sea. It is generally very flat, the highest point being only about 150 m (492 ft) above sea level. It has no large rivers and few large lakes, but with an irregular coastline it has many fiords and off-shore lagoons.

Economy Denmark is quite heavily populated, with 25 per cent of the people living in Copenhagen. An advanced welfare state, it is highly industrialized, but agriculture is the most important economic activity. Large amounts of meat and dairy products are exported to other members of the EEC. Fishing is also very important for the Danes. Among a great variety of manufacturers, goods like furniture have given the Danes a reputation for high standards of design and production. The standard of living is very high, though taxes are too.

Density is the mass of an object divided by its volume. For example, lead is denser than glass, and a lead marble would feel much heavier than a glass marble of the same size. So lead is said to have a higher density than glass. Most solids have a higher density than liquids. Gases have very low densities.

Dentistry is the prevention and treatment of tooth and gum disorders. Teeth sometimes hurt because of tooth decay and gum diseases. The dentist can drill away the decay and fill the hole with amalgam, or a metal such as gold. If a tooth has to be removed, the dentist can put an artificial or false tooth in its place. This is not painful because a dentist uses an anaesthetic.

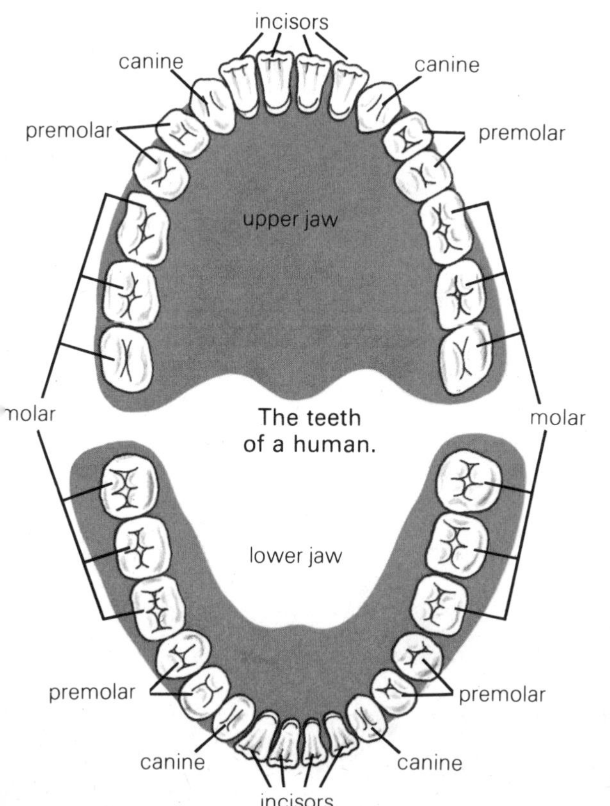

The teeth of a human.

Desert is an arid area in which there is not enough rainfall (or other moisture) to support vegetation on a scale useful to humans. However, deserts do support some vegetation and a number of other life forms. Among the world's great deserts are the Sahara in north Africa, the Kalahari in south-west Africa, the Arabian in Egypt, the Gobi in east Asia and the Australian Deserts.

Detergent is a substance which is used to remove dirt and grease. Unlike soap, detergents do not form a thin layer of scum on the surface of water.

Soap and detergents remove dirt and grease in a similar way. When dissolved in water, they form long molecules. Part of each molecule clings to dirt and grease. Another part clings to the water. As the water moves it pulls away the molecule along with the grease and dirt. In this way, clothes, skin, dishes, etc can be cleaned by washing.

De Valera, Eamon (1882–1975), was an Irish statesman. Born in New York, the son of an Irish mother and a Spanish father, he took part in the Easter Rising in Ireland in 1916. Sentenced to life imprisonment, he was released under an amnesty and became President of Sinn Fein. Rearrested, he escaped to the United States, returning to Ireland in 1920. He refused to accept the treaty of 1921 which created the Irish Free State and in 1926 founded the Fianna Fail opposition party. In 1932 he became Prime Minister of Ireland, holding office for nearly 20 years, and during this time he made Ireland a complete sovereign state. He was President of the Republic from 1959 to 1973.

De Valois, Dame Ninette (1898–), is an Irish-born dancer and choreographer. She was a soloist in Diaghilev's Russian Ballet before founding her own school in London in 1926. With Lillian Baylis, proprietor of the Old Vic Theatre, she founded the Vic-Wells Ballet, the direct ancestor of the company now known as the Royal Ballet, and was its director until 1963. She also founded a second company, originally known as the Sadler's Wells Opera Ballet.

Devonian is a period in the history of the Earth, known from the study of rocks and of the fossil remains found in them (the geological record). The name is taken from the county of Devon, England, where rocks of this period were first studied seriously.

The Devonian period is the fourth major division of the Paleozoic era, following the Silurian. It began about 395 million years ago and lasted for about 50 million years. It is sometimes called 'the age of fishes', since their fossils are well-represented in many Devonian rocks. It was also the age in which the first animals (creatures like salamanders) began to live on land.

Diaghilev, Serge (1872–1929), was a Russian ballet director. Diaghilev had great success in 1905–1908 organizing Russian art exhibitions and concerts in Paris. Despite his preference for opera, he turned to ballet in 1909, partly because of his belief in the genius of the choreographer Fokine and the dancer Nijinsky. He created an independent company, the Ballets Russe, which astounded Paris and other capitals with its splendid performances of classics like *Swan Lake* and *Giselle* as well as new works. Diaghilev had a wonderful ability to get the finest artists to work for him and to get the best out of them. His influence on the development of ballet in the West was enormous.

Diamond, see Carbon.

Dias, Bartolomeu (circa 1450–1500), was a Portuguese explorer. In 1486 King John II of Portugal entrusted Dias with the task of exploring down the west coast of Africa. In 1488 he discovered the Cape of Good Hope, although he could not sail round it because of the terrible storms. He had, however, shown that there was a route to India around the southern tip of Africa.

Diatoms are tiny, single-celled plants which occur in both fresh and sea water. They form part of the plankton and can swim about. A diatom's cell wall is composed of a chemical called pectin, and is made up of two halves, one half overlapping the other. The cell walls of some diatoms are very beautiful, being drawn out into unusual shapes. Some diatom species occur singly, while others occur together in chains or colonies.

Skeletons of diatoms, seen under a microscope.

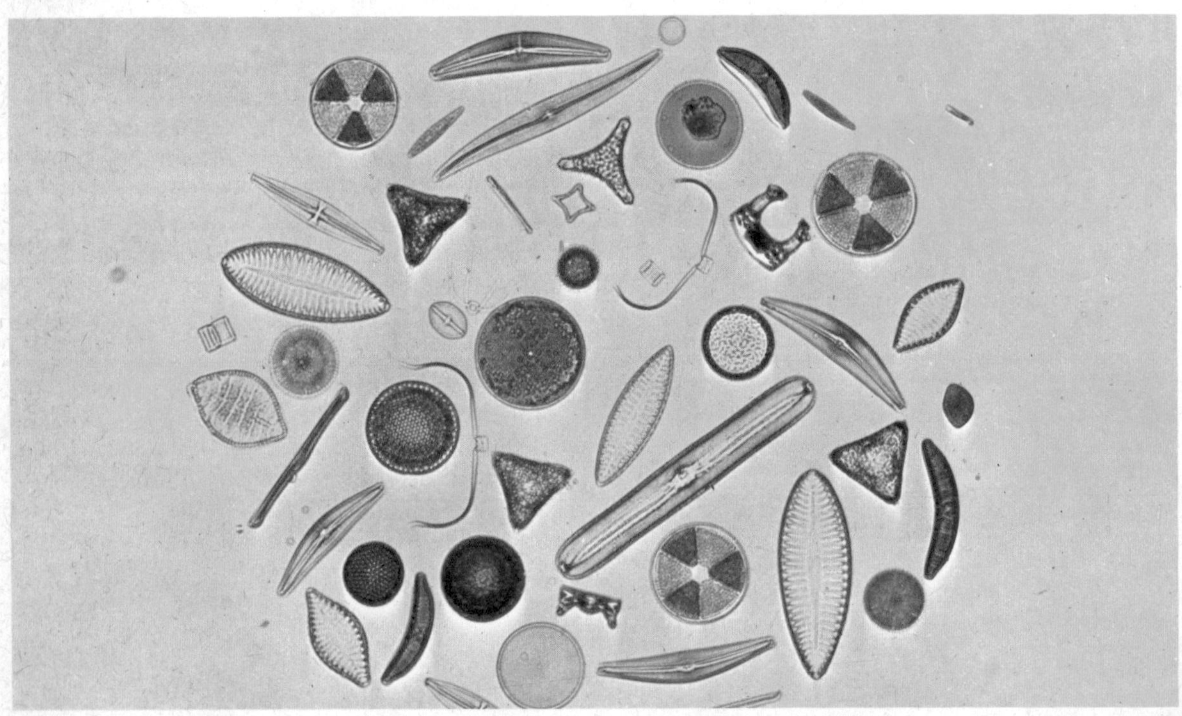

Dickens, Charles (1812–1870), was an English novelist. He began his writing life as a journalist and all his novels – the most popular novels in English literature and the most widely known abroad – first appeared as serials in magazines. *Pickwick Papers* (1836–1837) is a very funny account of the adventures and mishaps of the plump and endearing Mr Pickwick, which made Dickens famous. Later novels grew more serious: many of them were powerful attacks on unjust or unpleasant aspects of English life. Among his most popular novels are *Oliver Twist* (1838), *Nicholas Nickleby* (1839), *Martin Chuzzlewit* (1844), *David Copperfield* (1850; based partly on his own boyhood), *Bleak House* (1853), *A Tale of Two Cities* (1859; set in the French Revolution), and *Great Expectations* (1861).

Head of *Tyrannosaurus.*

Dicotyledon, see Cotyledons.

Digestion is the process during which food is broken down by chemicals called enzymes into simpler substances, so that they can be absorbed by the body tissues. *See also* Pancreas; Saliva; Stomach.

Dingaan, see Shaka.

Dinosaurs were a group of prehistoric reptiles which ruled the Earth from the Triassic period (225 million years ago) until the end of the Cretaceous period (66 million years ago). The word dinosaur means 'terrible lizard' but although some dinosaurs were large, fearsome creatures, others were very small – about the size of chickens.

Dinosaurs have been divided into two groups, the Saurischia (lizard-hipped dinosaurs) and the Ornithischia (bird-hipped dinosaurs), according to the arrangement of the bones in the pelvis. The Saurischia included *Apatosaurus* (once called *Brontosaurus*), and *Tyrannosaurus* – a huge 6 m- (20 ft-) high meat-eater or carnivore with terrifying jaws and pointed teeth. The Ornithischia included the armour-plated *Stegosaurus* and the horned *Triceratops*, both of which were plant-eaters or herbivores. The heaviest dinosaur was *Brachiosaurus*, a swamp-dwelling herbivore weighing 51 tonnes and measuring 24 m (79 ft) from head to tail.

No clear evidence is available as to why these creatures, successful for so long, suddenly disappeared – almost overnight in evolutionary terms. Many theories, from cosmic radiation to a rapid cooling of the Earth, have been suggested, but the truth remains a mystery.

A typical lizard-hipped dinosaur.

Disciples was the name given to the first followers of Jesus, including the twelve apostles chosen to be his close companions, and figures such as St Paul, who became the early missionaries of Christianity.

Disraeli, Benjamin (1804–1881), was a British statesman. Of Jewish origin, he was baptized a Christian in 1817. He entered Parliament in 1837 and led the 'Young England' group of radical Tories (Conservatives). He put forward his political views in his novels such as *Coningsby* (1844) and *Sybil* (1845). He was Chancellor of the Exchequer in three Conservative governments and played a major part in passing the Reform Act of 1867 which extended the franchise. In 1874 he became Prime Minister and carried through many useful reforms. Disraeli also pursued a vigorous foreign policy. He bought Britain a controlling interest in the Suez Canal company (1875) and effectively stopped Russian advances into Turkish territory and towards India. He also had the title of Empress of India conferred on Queen Victoria.

Dissolution of the Monasteries in England took place between 1536 and 1539, under the supervision of Thomas Cromwell, Henry VIII's chief minister. It followed the Act of Supremacy of 1534 which made Henry VIII 'supreme head of the Church and clergy of England'. Cromwell sent commissioners to close the monasteries, and their wealth and property was taken by the king.

Distillation is a process used in chemistry to separate mixtures of liquids and solids. For example, drinking water can be made from sea water by distillation. Sea water is salt and other substances dissolved in water. When sea water is heated, the water boils into steam, leaving the other substances behind. The steam is cooled to form pure water. The many substances in petroleum are separated by distillation. The petroleum is heated. Each substance is collected as it boils, and is cooled to a pure liquid or solid.

Djibouti is a republic in north-east Africa. Capital, Djibouti; area about 23 000 sq km (8880 sq miles). It was a French colony until 1977 and still depends on French and international support, being very small and rather poor. The capital, near the entrance to the Red Sea, is an important seaport for regions in the interior and is the main source of income.

DNA is the accepted abbreviation for deoxyribonucleic acid. This is a vital component of the cells of living things. The DNA molecule is important, above all, as the means by which characteristics are passed on from one generation to the next. It carries the 'genetic code' that determines inheritance.

One of the greatest breakthroughs of modern biochemistry was made in 1953, when two British scientists, James Watson and Frances Crick, identified the structure of DNA – that is, the way in which its components were arranged and the shape of the molecule.

Dodo

Dodo was a swan-sized, flightless bird related to the pigeons and doves. It lived on Mauritius Island in the Indian Ocean. Because of its trusting nature, and the fact that it could not fly, it was caught for food in such large numbers by sailors who landed there that it became extinct by the end of the 17th century.

Dog is a carnivore or meat-eater, related to the wolf, jackal and fox. The familiar domestic dog possibly arose as a cross between the wolf and the jackal. There are also several

Three kinds of dogs:
Dachsund *(Right)*
Alsatian *(Far Right)*
Dingo *(Above)*.

types of true wild dog which are not just domestic dogs gone wild, although this is believed to be how the Australian dingo came into existence.

The Indian wild dog looks like a shaggy Alsatian, but has more teeth than a domestic dog. The Cape hunting dog lives in Africa and is a pack hunter. It will attack and kill antelopes. The bush dog is a South American animal which lives in the forests of Brazil and Guyana.

Doge's Palace was the palace of the elected ruler (doge) of the republic of Venice. It stands next to St Mark's church and overlooks the lagoon. Building of the present palace began in the 14th century in the distinctive Venetian version of the Gothic style. The walls of pink and white marble and the windows are decorated with sculpture.

Dolomites are a mountain range in northeast Italy. They are a continuation of the Alps. The highest peak in the Dolomites is Marmolada at 3342 m (10965 ft). They contain marvellously coloured rocks, attractively shaped peaks and many resort towns for skiers and holiday-makers.

Dolphin is a small whale. It is not a fish – although it looks rather like a fish and spends the whole of its life in water – but a mammal. Dolphins usually have beak-like jaws armed with rows of pointed teeth. Usually they are found in warm and temperate waters where they feed on fish. They are highly intelligent creatures, and are often the star attractions of marine aquaria.

Domesday Book was a survey of the land of England carried out on the instructions of King William I in 1085–1086. The two-volume book, arranged in counties, showed the distribution, ownership and value of every piece of land in the country. It includes the social status of each village's inhabitants, and the number of plough-teams or value of crops. It was intended to be used for taxation and administration purposes, but provides a record of economic conditions in medieval times.

Dominica, Commonwealth of, is an island republic among the Windward Islands, West Indies. Capital, Roseau; area about 750 sq km (290 sq miles). A former British colony, Dominica became formally independent in 1978. The people are mostly of African descent.

Small but exotic, Dominica has steep, volcanic mountains up to 1200 m (3940 ft) with waterfalls, geysers, tropical forest and rich plant life. It exports cocoa, bananas, citrus fruits, coconut products and spices.

Dominican Republic is a state occupying the eastern part (about two-thirds) of the island of Hispaniola, West Indies. Capital, Santo Domingo; area about 48500 sq km (18700 sq miles).

History Santo Domingo was the first capital of Spanish America. Having numerous coves and inlets, it became a great haunt of pirates. The western third of the island (now the Republic of Haiti) passed to France in 1697. The Dominicans, aided by Britain, declared their independence in 1809, but there were periods of Spanish and Haitiian rule until 1865. The republic was politically and economically unstable, resulting in US control from 1905 and dictatorial rule. The first free elections for nearly 40 years were held in 1962.

Land and People The country has rich soil on the plains north and south of the central mountains, and considerable mineral resources. Agriculture is most important, and the main export crop is sugar, followed by coffee and cocoa.

The people are mostly Spanish-speaking and Roman Catholic.

Don is a river in USSR. The Don, or Duna, rises south of Moscow and flows for 1870 km (1162 miles) to the Sea of Asov (a gulf of the Black Sea). It has played a large part in Russian history and literature. The Don is fairly shallow, with excellent fishing.

Donatello (circa 1386–1466), was an Italian sculptor. He was one of the leaders of the early Renaissance in Florence and his work shows the steady development away from the late Gothic style and towards the Classical style of the Renaissance, inspired by the sculpture of ancient Rome. His *David with the Head of Goliath* (circa 1408) is often quoted as a landmark in the history of sculpture. Donatello tried to bring the spectator and the work of art closer together. His statues, like *St George*, are of individuals, and make a powerful, realistic impression.

Donkey is descended from the African wild ass. Smaller than a horse, it has a large head and big ears. Donkeys are normally good-tempered, friendly creatures with the ability to work hard. In many countries they are used to carry farm produce, or even people, and their sure-footedness makes them particularly popular in hilly regions.

Dormouse is a furry rodent inhabiting Europe, Asia and Africa. The smallest species measures about 10 cm (4 in) long, and the biggest, about 30 cm (1 ft). They resemble squirrels, and most of them are good climbers.

Dostoevsky, Fyodor (1821–1881), was a Russian novelist. A young man of middle-class background with socialist sympathies, he was sentenced to several years in prison and the army. Later he became more conservative. An unsuccessful publishing venture and his incessant gambling left him in debt until his second wife managed his affairs and, in his late years, he became a respected writer. Dostoevsky's philosophic ideas are dramatized in his novels, of which the most famous are *Crime and Punishment* (1866) and *The Brothers Karamazov* (1880). He believed that man is a self-destructive creature of conflicts – good and evil, love and hate.

Dragonflies are the 'fighter pilots' of the insect world. They may often be seen hovering over water or resting on waterside plants. Dragonflies have large, often colour-

ful bodies, with a wingspan of up to 17 cm (7 in). Their heads have huge, bulging eyes that can spot other insects from a very long distance. Once they see a victim, they close in at great speed, catching the prey on the wing. Even the aquatic pre-adult stage – called a nymph – is predatory, creeping up on other aquatic creatures before suddenly grabbing them.

Drake, Sir Francis (circa 1540–1596), was an English seaman and navigator. As a young man he took part in slave-trading expeditions and subsequently in attacks upon Spanish towns in the West Indies and Panama. In 1577–1580 he began a major voy-

Drake's ship *The Golden Hind.*

age, rounding South America by the Straits of Magellan and raiding Spanish shipping off the west coast. He went on across the Pacific to Java, returning home by the Cape of Good Hope. Knighted by Queen Elizabeth for his exploits, in 1587 he attacked Spanish warships in Cadiz Harbour, thus delaying the departure of the Armada, in whose defeat he later played an important part. He died on board his own ship off the coast of Panama.

Drakensberg is a mountain range in the east part of the Republic of South Africa. It reaches its maximum height of 3482 m (11 425 ft) above sea level in Lesotho and stretches for about 1100 km (680 miles). The range forms two distinct parts of the South African Great Escarpment, or plateau edge. Very steep on the coastal side, the mountains slope gently on the interior. There are several parks and game reserves in the region.

Drama is a form of art in which the story is acted out on a stage.

Drama began as religious ritual. Its continuous history in the West dates from the 6th century BC, when solemn tragedies were performed in outdoor theatres in Greece. Comedy originated a little later.

In other cultures drama developed in different ways. In the Far East, it was bound by strict conventions of style, enforced by ancient tradition.

Medieval drama in Europe was mainly religious, with mystery plays performed by groups of amateurs, sometimes on a travelling stage.

The Renaissance was a glorious period for European drama. In Spain and England the golden age was dominated by Lope de Vega and Shakespeare. In Italy the tradition of comedy known as *commedia dell'arte* flourished. France's greatest age was the 17th century, with the Classical tragedies of Corneille and Racine and the comedies of Molière. In Britain, after Charles II was returned to the throne, Restoration drama flourished with works by Dryden, Congreve and others. Eighteenth-century drama was less distinguished. Romanticism produced at least one great playwright, the German Schiller, but developed into melodrama, with fancy scenery and simple plots in which good always defeated evil.

The age of realism arrived with Henrik Ibsen (1828–1906) in Norway and Chekhov in Russia. From it was born the many contemporary styles of drama. Some, like the US theatre of Eugene O'Neill (1888–1953) and Arthur Miller, were basically realistic. Some, like the 'epic theatre' of Brecht, used devices from other media. Others, like the so-called Theatre of the Absurd, were more experimental. Film and television greatly broadened the appeal of drama.

Dromedary, see Camel.

Drought is a period of dry weather, caused by lack of rain. There are four different kinds of drought: permanent drought, found in arid and semi-arid regions; seasonal drought, which occurs in climates with definite dry and rainy seasons; unpredictable drought, where normal rainfall has failed to come; and invisible drought, when even frequent showers do not restore sufficient moisture to the land.

Drugs are substances used in medicine to prevent or cure illnesses. Once, most drugs were made from parts of plants. Drugs made from plants are called herbal drugs, and thousands are known. Today, most drugs are made in factories from chemicals. Making drugs is called pharmacy, and the factories which produce drugs are part of the pharmaceutical industry. Through the efforts of this industry, a huge range of drugs is available for millions of people.

Drum is a musical instrument. Sound is produced by striking a skin stretched over a hollow body. All human societies have used drums. The earliest were probably hollow tree trunks, still seen in some Pacific islands. In Africa particularly drumming became a highly developed art as well as a means of communication. Drummers in modern orchestras and bands use a variety of instruments, including the big bass drum, sometimes worked by a foot pedal; the copper kettledrums or *timpani*, which are of Arabian origin; snare drums, with strings instead of a skin; and jingling tambourines.

Dublin is a city and port, capital of the Republic of Ireland (Eire). Dublin is at the heart of Irish history and literature, and contains many fine buildings and squares, especially of the 18th century. It is the main Irish business and industrial centre, especially famous for its beer, or stout, and its textiles.

Ducks are waterbirds which occur throughout the world. They have webbed feet, dense, waterproof plumage, and, usually, broad, flat beaks. The males are generally brightly coloured, particularly during the breeding season.

Duckweed is a group of tiny freshwater flowering plants, including the smallest of all flowering plants. All are floating plants, consisting of a tiny green disc-like structure 1–2 mm (less than 1 in) across. Some species have roots which hang down from beneath the disc. Duckweed is found throughout the world, and can occur in some ponds in such huge numbers that the whole surface looks as though it is covered in a solid green carpet.

Dugong, see Sea-cow.

Duncan, Isidora (1872–1929), was a US dancer. Rebelling against the strictness of ballet training, she developed her own form of free dancing, which supposedly rep-

A military drum.

resented the dancing of ancient Greece. She had great success touring Europe, though less in the United States where her love affairs and sympathy for Communism caused resentment. A powerful personality, she had some influence in encouraging freer and more expressive movement in dance.

Dunkirk is a port in northern France which in May and June 1940 was the site of the evacuation of about 350 000 French and British troops, during the Second World War. The rapid German advance through France had cut off Allied forces in the north from the main French army further south, and left them in danger of being encircled and captured. Ships of all shapes and sizes came from Britain to rescue the men, and despite repeated German air attacks, the vast majority of the soldiers were safely returned to England.

Dunlop, John, see Bicycle.

Dürer, Albrecht (1471–1528), was a German painter and engraver. He was the outstanding artist of the Renaissance in northern Europe. His art combines the Gothic tradition and craftsmanship of the North with the new Classicism and learning of the Italian Renaissance. His greatest gift was for line, and he is best known for his engravings and drawings.

Dvořák, Antonin (1841–1904), was a Czech composer. A butcher's son, he showed early musical talent. His first compositions were heavily influenced by Wagner, and he first became well known for works inspired by nationalist feelings and Bohemian (Czech) folk music, such as his *Slavonic Rhapsodies and Dances*. He became especially popular in England and, later, in the United States. There he composed his famous *Symphony in E Minor (from the New World)*, which showed that his appreciation of folk music could take in other cultures as well as his own.

Dye is a substance used to colour many different materials, such as textiles, paper and wood. Dyes have been used for thousands of years, and used to be made from parts of animals and plants. For example, a yellow dye was made from a crocus, a red dye from a kind of beetle, a purple dye from a kind of snail and blue dyes from indigo and woad plants. Dyes from plants are still sometimes used.

Today artificial dyes are more common. These give a wider range of brighter colours, which do not fade as easily as natural dyes.

Dylan, Bob (1941–), is a US pop singer and songwriter. He became well known in the early 1960s when he was a leading figure in the pop revival of folk song and a representative of the movement among young people of protest against modern society. *Blowin' in the Wind* was his most famous number from this period. Later his style changed considerably, going through a period of free-wheeling rock and roll, influenced by the blues.

E

Eagle is a bird of prey with a strong, hooked beak and powerful, grasping claws, or talons. Its wings are usually rectangular in shape, and this shape, together with the huge size of many species, makes eagles easy to spot as they soar around the skies searching for animals on which to prey. The golden eagle is found in the mountainous regions of Europe, Asia and North America, and has a wingspan of over 2 m (6 ft). The bald eagle is the emblem of the USA. The many other species include sea eagles, and eagles that specialize in hunting for fish, monkeys or bats.

Above: A golden eagle attacking a curlew. Eagles can catch other birds in mid-air.
Below: Structure of the human ear, with inset showing bones of the ear.

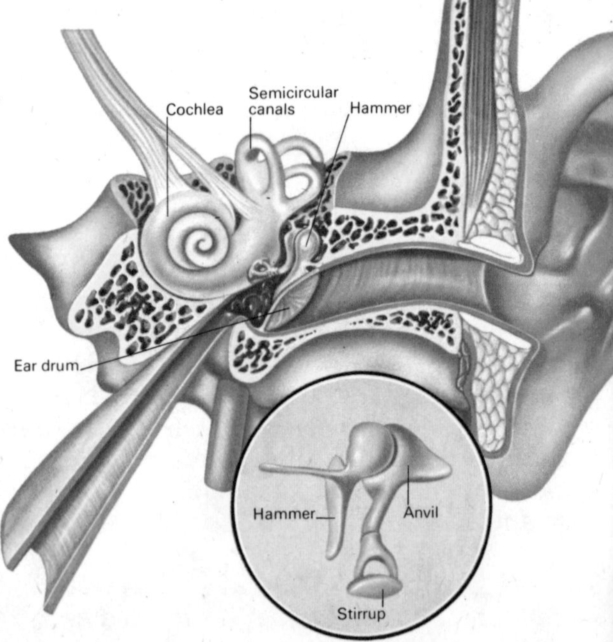

Ear is one of a pair of structures found on either side of the head of vertebrates. Ears are concerned with both hearing and balance. The only part of the ear that we can see – the external ear or pinna – locates and directs the sound into the inner ear. Here the sound waves are turned into nerve impulses and are passed to the brain. Some animals have no external ears, but, of course, this does not mean that they cannot hear.

The parts of the ear which control balance are called the semicircular canals. Movements of the head cause fluid in the semicircular canals to swirl over tiny cells within the canals, telling the animals when it is 'out of balance'.

Earth, our planet, is the third farthest from the Sun, and orbits it in 365.24 days. The Earth rotates on its axis in about 24 hours. The Earth is made up of three main parts: the core, the mantle and the crust. The core is mainly iron and nickel, and it is the metals of the core which give the Earth its magnetic field. The crust is the surface of the Earth. It rests on a layer called the mantle. The crust and mantle move very slowly, and their movement has created rift valleys and mountains. Oceans cover about 60 per cent of the crust and the continents cover the rest. The Earth has an atmosphere mainly of nitrogen and oxygen. It is the only planet in the Solar System with plenty of liquid water and a lot of oxygen in the atmosphere. The Earth has one satellite, the Moon. *See also* Continental drift; Plate tectonics; Seasons.

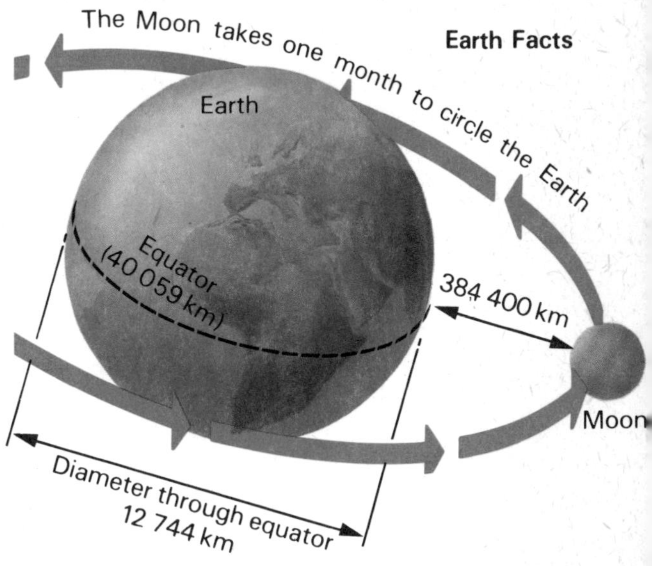

Earthquake is a sudden movement below the surface of the Earth. It can make the Earth's surface shake, causing great damage. Huge cracks in the ground, landslides of rock and avalanches of snow can result from earthquakes. Large numbers of buildings can be destroyed and many people killed. In 1556, an earthquake in China killed about 830 000 people.

Earthquakes can also cause giant waves in the sea, called tsunami. One tsunami in the Western Pacific Ocean was 85 m (280 ft) high.

Earthquakes are recorded and measured on instruments called seismographs. There are about half a million earthquakes each year. Very few of these are serious enough to cause damage to people or buildings, however.

Earthworm is an animal with a long, rounded body divided into compartments known as segments. As earthworms burrow through the soil, they swallow mouthfuls, digesting tiny food particles and passing the waste out behind them, leaving the familiar worm casts. The worms help to mix soil and leaf litter as they burrow through it. In Australia there are giant earthworms which can reach a length of 3 m (10 ft).

Easter Island is in the central Pacific, about 3700 km (2300 miles) off the coast of Chile, which owns it. Area about 165 sq km (64 sq miles). An isolated volcanic island, it was discovered on Easter Day, 1722, by the Dutch explorer, Roggeveen. The original inhabitants were Polynesians, but now the islanders are of mixed descent. The island is famous for its large, mysterious statues. The main occupations today are sheep-rearing and fishing.

Eastern Orthodox Church, the Christian Church in the East, became divided from the Roman Church when the Roman Empire itself was divided, with its eastern capital at Constantinople. During the Middle Ages it developed separately from the Roman Church. There were disagreements over basic beliefs such as the origin of the Holy

Spirit and the authority of the pope, and there was a complete break in the 11th century.

Eastern Orthodox Christianity extended into North Africa and Eastern Europe and was adopted by Russia, the main source of its strength in modern times.

Easter Rising was an armed rebellion against the British government which took place in Dublin in April 1916. It was led by Irish nationalists who wanted to achieve independence for their country. On Easter Monday 1916 they occupied key points in the city, including the General Post Office, and proclaimed the establishment of an Irish Republic. After fierce fighting, the rebels surrendered, and 15 of their leaders were executed.

East Germany, see German Democratic Republic.

East India Company was an English commercial company which was granted a charter by Queen Elizabeth I in 1600, giving it a monopoly over trade with the East. Driven out of the East Indies by the Dutch, it concentrated on trade with India, where it gradually achieved considerable political influence. After Robert Clive's successes against the French in the Seven Years' War (1756–1763), the Company administered a large part of India. However, after the Indian Mutiny of 1857 the British crown assumed complete control of the government of British India, and the East India Company ceased to exist in 1873.

Echidna is an extremely strange mammal which lives in Australia and New Guinea. Also known as the spiny anteater, it has a rounded, furry body covered with spines. The short legs have strong claws which are used for digging out worms, ants and other insects. The long, narrow jaws enclose a very long tongue, which whips out to lick up food. The echidna may grow to a length of 46 cm (1.5 ft). The most unusual feature of echidnas is the fact that they lay eggs, like the platypus, instead of bearing live young.

Echinoderms are invertebrate animals with spiny skins. They are all marine creatures, and include the starfish, brittlestars, sea-urchins, sea-cucumbers and featherstars. Echinoderms have a curious arrangement of tubes projecting through their skins. These tubes are called tube feet, and they are connected to a series of water-filled canals within the animals' body. Muscles within the echinoderm's body enable water pressure to be exerted on the tube feet, causing them to move and so the animal can crawl about. Tube feet are also used to grip objects.

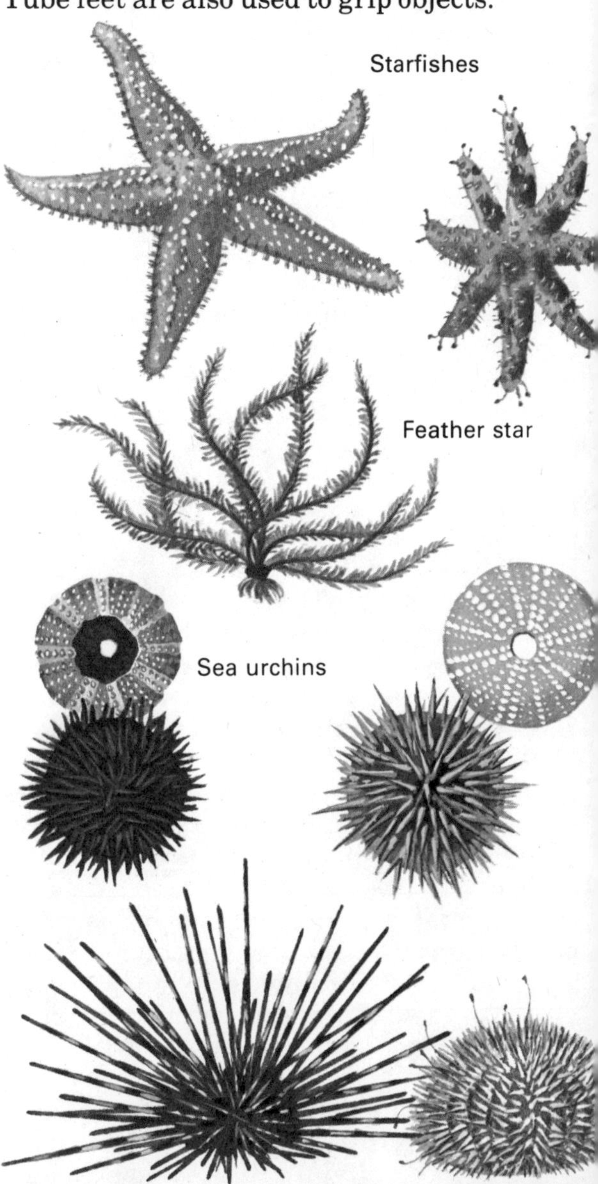

Some kinds of echinoderms.

Echo sounder is an instrument used in sonar. *See also* Sonar.

Eclipse, in astronomy, is when the light of a satellite is obscured when a primary planet comes between it and the Sun. The Moon moves around the Earth and the Earth moves around the Sun. In its orbit, the Moon sometimes passes in front of the Sun, blocking off its light. This is known as an eclipse of the Sun, or a solar eclipse. It occurs when the Sun, Moon and Earth are in line, with the Moon in the Middle.

If they are in line with the Earth in the middle, the Moon is in the Earth's shadow. This means that the Earth stops the Sun's light reaching the Moon. This is known as an eclipse of the Moon, or a lunar eclipse.

Ecology is the study of plants and animals in relation to their natural surroundings, and in relation to each other.

Ecuador is a republic in north-west South America. Capital, Quito; area 270679 sq km (104500 sq miles).
History Ecuador was part of the Inca empire until the Spanish conquest in 1534. The region became independent in 1822. The modern republic was founded in 1830. Its history has been turbulent, and it has been involved in conflicts with neighbours.
Land and People The scenery and climate vary immensely as a result of variations in altitude. Quito is on the Equator, yet its height in the Andes give it a year-round climate like an English spring. A few kilometres away on the coastal plain, the temperature may be 25°C (77°F) higher. The Ecuadorians are mostly Roman Catholics of mixed Spanish/Indian descent, who live by farming.
Economy The coastal lowlands produce tropical crops like cocoa, bananas and sugar cane, with coffee on mountain slopes. Industry and mining are not highly developed and communications are difficult. Ecuador, and not Panama, is the source of Panama hats and most of the world's balsawood.

Edinburgh is a city and capital of Scotland. Standing on hills south of the Firth of Forth and built largely in stone, Edinburgh is one of the most handsome cities in Europe. The castle and Holyrood Abbey (Canongate) date back to the early Middle Ages. An important political capital in the 15th and 16th centuries, Edinburgh's most glorious period was the 18th century, when its artists and writers earned it the nickname, 'the Athens of the North' and the splendid New Town was built. The annual festival held in August and September continues this artistic tradition.

Edward I (1239–1307), was King of England (1272–1307). The son of Henry III, he defeated the rebel barons at the Battle of Evesham (1265), and killed their leader, Simon de Montfort. After his accession he undertook the conquest of Wales (1276–1284), but was less successful in his efforts to subdue the Scots. He put down a revolt led by William Wallace (1298), and was on his way to Scotland to crush another rebellion, this time by Robert Bruce, when he died. His main achievements in England were reforms which weakened the feudal powers of the nobility and established a parliamentary system.

Edward II (1284–1327), was King of England (1307–1327). He was created Prince of Wales in 1301, the first to bear the title. An incompetent ruler, he was dominated by his favourites, and his attempt to pursue his father's policy of conquering Scotland ended in defeat at Bannockburn (1314). His conduct roused the hostility of the barons and of his wife Isabella. With the help of Roger Mortimer, Earl of March, she led a force of exiled nobles in an invasion of England (1326). Edward II was deposed and subsequently cruelly murdered.

Edward III (1312–1377), was King of England (1327–1377). He took the government of the country out of the hands of his mother, Queen Isabella, and Mortimer, Earl of March (1330), and subsequently pursued a successful campaign against the Scots. During his reign the Hundred Years' War with France began, and Edward won a notable naval battle at Sluys (1340). With the help of his son Edward, the Black Prince, he went on to further victories at Crécy (1346) and Poitiers (1356). The expenses of the war, the extravagance of his magnificent court and the economic effects of the Black Death brought severe financial problems and increased the power of Parliament. In his last years Edward's son, John of Gaunt, was a dominant influence over him.

Edward IV (1442–1483), was King of England (1461–1470 and 1471–1483). He was the son of Richard, Duke of York. With the help of Richard Neville, Earl of Warwick, he defeated the Lancastrians (who supported Henry VI) at the Battle of Mortimer's Cross (1461) and became the first Yorkist to ascend the throne. He was exiled for a short time in 1470 when the Earl of Warwick restored Henry VI to the throne, but returned to defeat Warwick next year at the Battle of Barnet. The rest of his reign was peaceful.

Edward V (1470–circa 1483), was King of England in 1483. Following the death of his father, Edward IV, he was placed in the Tower of London by his uncle, Richard, Duke of Gloucester. Richard subsequently had himself proclaimed King, and Edward, together with his brother, the Duke of York, was murdered some time afterwards.

Edward VI (1537–1553), was King of England (1547–1553). The son of Henry VIII and Jane Seymour, he was still a boy when he came to the throne, and so the government of the country was in the hands of his uncle, the Duke of Somerset, and later the Duke of Northumberland. Edward had been brought up as a Protestant, and during his short reign the Reformation made much progress in England.

Edward VII (1841–1910), was King of Great Britain and Ireland (1901–1910), in succession to his mother Queen Victoria. During her reign he was not permitted to take any part in politics. He did, however, lead an active social life and was a keen traveller and sportsman. As monarch he was able to play an influential part in bringing about the *Entente Cordiale* with France in 1904, and enjoyed great popularity with his subjects.

Edward VIII (1894–1972), was King of Great Britain and Northern Ireland (1936). As Prince of Wales he travelled widely throughout the British Empire and also took a keen interest in social problems at home. He became King in January 1936 on the death of his father, George V, but abdicated later the same year in order to marry a divorced American woman, who would not have been acceptable as Queen. He was governor of the Bahamas during 1940–1945 and later lived in France.

Edward the Confessor (circa 1002–1066), was King of England. The son of Ethelred the Unready, he was brought up in Normandy. He succeeded to the throne in 1042 on the death of Hardicanute, the last Danish King of England. A weak and pious man, he was at first much influenced by his Norman advisers. Later his father-in-law, Earl Godwin, and Godwin's son, Harold, dominated him, and Edward left the government of the country in their hands. He was buried in Westminster Abbey, which had been rebuilt during his reign. At his death both Harold and William, Duke of Normandy, laid claim to the throne.

EEC, see European Economic Community.

Eels are long-bodied fish found in both sea water and fresh water. Freshwater eels spend most of their lives in rivers and lakes, but migrate to the sea to spawn in huge numbers. They will eat almost anything, but prefer animal food.

Another type of eel, the conger eel, lives in the sea all the time. Conger eels have huge teeth and grow very big. They like to live among rocks and old sunken vessels. Also found in the sea, but in warmer waters, is the moray eel. This bad-tempered fish is very aggressive. It lies in a coral or rock crevice and darts out to catch fish swimming by.

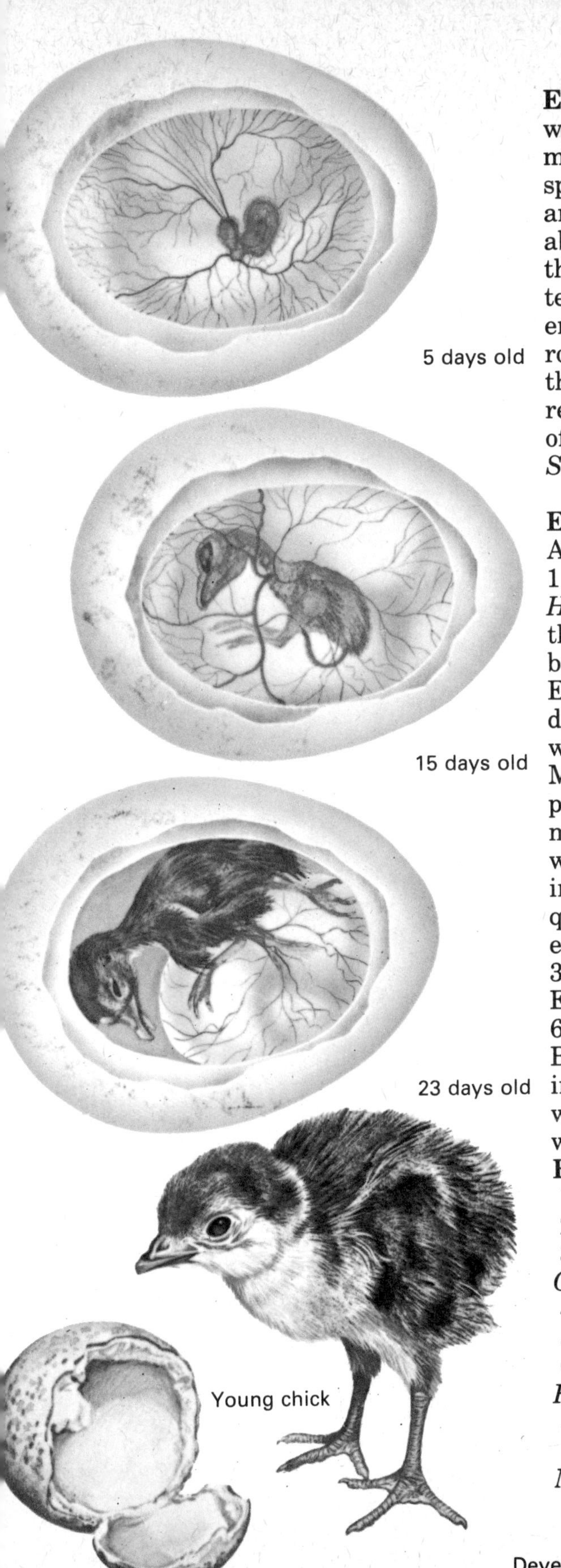

Development of a turkey chick inside the egg.

Egg is the structure produced by the female which, when fertilized by the sperm of the male, eventually produces young, or offspring. Eggs can vary considerably in size and shape. Those with which we are probably most familiar are chicken eggs, where the developing chick is encased within a protective shell. Frog spawn is the eggs of frogs, encased in a protective jelly-like layer, and roe is the eggs of fish. Many animals – and this includes humans – produce eggs that remain within the body until the developing offspring is ready to be born into the world. *See also* Yolk.

Egypt, Arab Republic of, is in north-east Africa. Capital, Cairo; area about 1 000 000 sq km (386 198 sq miles).
History The recorded history of Egypt, one of the great civilizations of the ancient world, begins with the union of Upper and Lower Egypt about 3100 BC. During the Old Kingdom (2610–2180 BC) the pyramids at Gizeh were built. After a period of anarchy the Middle Kingdom (1990–1785 BC) was a period of expansion and artistic achievement. A period of decline began and Egypt was occupied by a series of foreign rulers, including Assyrians and Persians. Its conquest by Alexander the Great led to the establishment of the Ptolemaic dynasty. In 30 BC Egypt was absorbed into the Roman Empire. It was conquered by the Arabs in AD 640 and by the Turks in 1517. Declared a British protectorate in 1914, it became an independent kingdom in 1922. A republic was established in 1953. Conflict with Israel was ended with a peace treaty in 1979.

Egyptian Dynasties

1st Dynasty	3100–2890 BC
2nd Dynasty	2890–2670 BC
3rd Dynasty	2670–2610 BC
Old Kingdom	
4th Dynasty	2610–2500 BC
5th Dynasty	2500–2350 BC
6th Dynasty	2350–2180 BC
First Intermediate Period	
7th, 8th, 9th, 10th and 11th Dynasties	2180–1990 BC
Middle Kingdom	
12th Dynasty	1990–1785 BC

Second Intermediate Period	
13th, 14th, 15th, 16th and 17th Dynasties	1785–1570 BC
New Kingdom	
18th Dynasty	1570–1320 BC
19th Dynasty	1320–1200 BC
20th Dynasty	1200–1090 BC
End of New Kingdom	
21st Dynasty	1090–945 BC
22nd Dynasty	945–745 BC
23rd, 24th and 25th Dynasties	745–663 BC
26th Dynasty	663–525 BC
Persian Period	
27th Dynasty	525–404 BC
28th Dynasty	404–399 BC
29th and 30th Dynasties	399–343 BC
Ptolemaic Period	
Ptolemy I–XI	323–51 BC
Ptolemy XII	51–47 BC
Ptolemy XIII	47–44 BC
Cleopatra VII	51–30 BC

Land and People A small part of Egypt, the Sinai peninsula (the only mountainous region) is in Asia, separated from the rest of the country by the Suez Canal. The heart of Egypt is the Nile valley. The Nile flows the length of the country north to south. The great majority of people live in the Nile delta, known as Lower Egypt. Most of Egypt is desert, though there are some large oases. Except on the coast, rainfall is very low, and the Nile provides nearly all water.

There are still some nomads living in the

The pharaoh of Egypt and his queen, making their way through one of their temples, around 1250 BC.

desert. Most Egyptians are fellahin, or peasants, but about 40 per cent live in towns or cities.
Economy Egypt is largely agricultural. Parts of the delta are so fertile they produce three crops a year. Cotton is the main money-earning crop, followed by food crops such as rice, corn and dates. Improvements such as the building of the Aswan Dam and the creation of Lake Nasser have made more land available for farming, but the total fertile area is still small.

Manufacturing has increased in recent years, mainly in Cairo (the largest city in Africa) and Alexandria. But Egypt has no great reserves of oil like its Arab neighbours, and the country lacks the resources to pay for large industrial expansion. Profits from tourism and the Suez Canal are some help.

Einstein, Albert (1879–1955), was a German-born physicist and mathematician. He became a Swiss citizen in 1901, and an American citizen in 1940. One of the greatest scientists, he revolutionzied physics, particularly because of his ideas about the universe and the atom. He published his Special Theory of Relativity in 1905 while working at the Swiss Patent Office. In 1916 he published his General Theory of Relativity. He became a Professor at Zurich university in 1909, and later at Prague and Princeton, USA. In 1921 he won the Nobel prize and was elected to the Royal Society. *See also* Relativity.

Eire see Ireland

Eisenhower, Dwight David (1890–1969), was an American soldier and statesman. During the Second World War he was commander of the Allied forces in North Africa and Italy (1942–1943). In 1943 he was appointed supreme commander of all the Allied forces in Europe and helped to plan the invasion of Normandy in June 1944. After the war he became military commander of NATO. Enjoying great popularity, he was elected President of the USA in 1952, being re-elected in 1956. During his presidency relations with the USSR improved, and troops were used in the USA to bring about racial integration in schools.

El Cid (circa 1040–1099), was a Spanish nobleman and warrior, whose real name was Rodrigo Diaz de Vivar. He became the hero of the struggle between Christians and Muslims in Spain in the 11th century, but his exploits are so obscured by legend that it is difficult to separate truth from fiction. He was exiled from the court of Alfonso VI of Castile about 1080 and subsequently fought for both Christians and Muslims as a soldier of fortune. In 1094 he captured Valencia, which he ruled until his death.

Electricity is a form of energy manifested in a large variety of magnetic, chemical, thermal, visual and mechanical phenomena. Electrically-charged bodies either repel or attract each other, depending on the nature of the charge. Similar charges repel each other, while unlike charges attract. Bodies can be charged in this way by rubbing. The nature of a charge depends on the structure of the body's component atoms, in which positive and negative charges are normally balanced. Electrons charge an atom negatively. When they exceed the positive protons the atom is negatively charged, and when they are less the atom is positively charged. When charged particles such as electrons and protons are set in motion, an electric current results. Some metals, e.g. copper, permit a more rapid flow of electrons and are said to be good conductors.

A current may be generated either by a chemical process such as immersing copper and zinc strips in diluted sulphuric acid, or by rotating a coil of wire in a magnetic field (dynamo). If a conductor offers considerable resistance to the flow of current, heat results. If the heat is sufficiently intense, and the conductor strong enough to withstand the high temperature, light is produced.

Electrolysis is a process used in chemistry to split up certain substances. It does this by using electricity. The substance to be split, called an electrolyte, must be a liquid or a solid dissolved in a liquid. Two plates or rods,

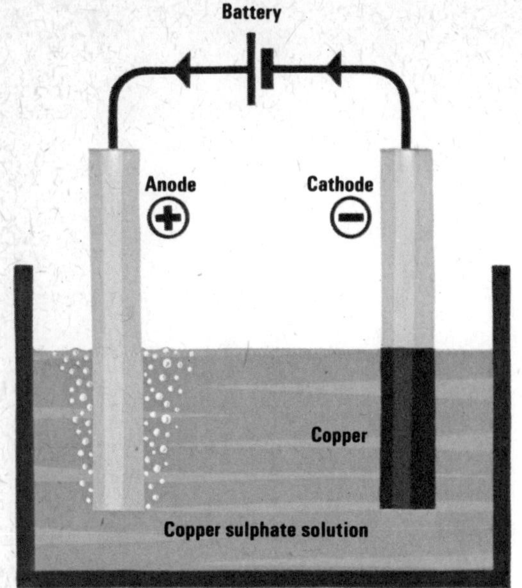

In this example of electrolysis, an electric current is passing through a solution of copper sulphate – the electrolyte. One electrode becomes coated with copper. Oxygen gas is given off at the other.

called electrodes, one negative and one positive, are put into the electrolyte. Electricity flows from a battery through the electrolyte via the electrodes. The electrolyte is split up into ions. The ions travel to the electrodes and become coated on them.

Salt (sodium chloride) can be split by electrolysis. The sodium coats one electrode and chlorine coats the other. Some metals are split from their ores by electrolysis. The metal moves to one electrode and coats it. The metal will also coat a spoon, fork, or other object on the electrode. This is called electroplating. *See also* Ion.

Electromagnet is a wire wound around a piece of iron. When an electric current is passed through the wire, the iron becomes a strong magnet. Its magnetism disappears when the current is switched off. Electromagnets are used for lifting heavy pieces of metal. They are also used in doorbells, telephones and many other pieces of equipment.

Electromagnetic radiation consists of electro and magnetic fields vibrating at right angles to each other. Light is a sort of electromagnetic radiation or ray or wave. All electromagnetic waves travel at the same speed. They are known by different names according to their wavelengths. Electromagnetic waves with long wavelengths are used to send signals around the Earth. They are known as radio and television waves. As the wavelengths get shorter, they are known as microwaves and infra-red waves and light. Waves with a shorter wavelength than light are ultra-violet waves, X-rays and gamma rays.

Light is the only electromagnetic radiation that our eyes can see. Infra-red rays can be felt as heat. Special equipment has to be built to detect the other waves. All electromagnetic waves travel through space. We receive all of them from the planets, stars and galaxies around us. They are also produced by equipment on Earth.

Electron is a negatively charged particle which moves around, or orbits, the nucleus of an atom. It is the lightest particle in the atom. (A proton is about 1836 times heavier than an electron.) The number of electrons in an atom is always the same as the number of protons, which have a positive electrical charge. The electrons and the protons cancel each other out, and thus the atom has no electrical charge.

If an atom loses or gains an electron, it becomes an ion and has an electrical charge. This causes static electricity. A moving electron causes current electricity and magnetism.

Radioactive substances give off a stream of electrons known as beta-rays.

Electronics is a type of science that uses electrons. Moving electrons can produce electricity, radio waves, television waves, X-rays and many other signals. They can be used to make sounds in radios and electronic musical instruments, and can form pictures on television screens. They can also carry information in electronic calculators and computers.

Elegy is a lament in poetry for someone who has died. Often, however, the term is used in a less strict sense of any poem in a serious and thoughtful mood. Thomas Gray's 'Elegy in a Country Churchyard' is a famous example. In ancient times an elegy was simply a poem written in a particular metre.

Element, in chemistry, is the simplest substance there is. There are ninety-two natural elements, and others have been made artificially.

An element is made up of identical atoms. Different elements have different atoms. Symbols are used for all the elements because some of their names are quite long; for example, molybdenum has the symbol Mo, and silver has the symbol Ag. Each element also has an atomic number. Elements are often referred to by their symbol and atomic number. The thousands of different substances in the world are all made from these few elements. Some substances, like gold, exist as pure elements. Most, like table salt, are compounds (elements joined together chemically). Substances such as the air are a mixture of elements and compounds. *See also* Atomic number; Periodic table.

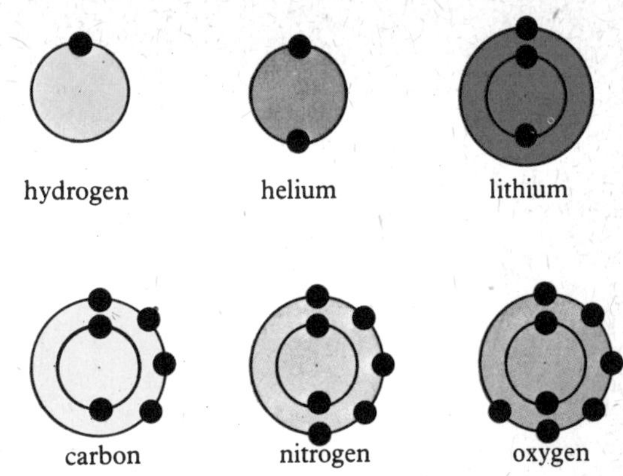

Atoms of six of the lightest elements, showing the number of electrons in orbit round the nucleus. This gives the atomic number of the element.

Elephants are strict vegetarians, despite their huge size. They are the largest living land animals, and the African elephant is larger than the Indian elephant. A fully grown African bull (adult male) can reach a weight of 6 tonnes. Elephants live in herds of up to 100 consisting of babies and their mothers, young bulls, and the herd leader, which is either an old bull or an old female (known as a cow).

Elephants have long tusks, which are actually the incisor teeth of the upper jaw. Sadly, these are much prized by hunters who kill the elephants just for their tusks. Elephants also have long trunks which they can use for breathing, smelling, sucking up and squirting water, and for putting food into their mouths. African elephants have larger ears than the Indian species, for they spend more time in the hot open bush. The large ears can flap backwards and forwards to help fan the animal, and they also lose heat from the blood vessels in the ears.

An Indian elephant *(left)* and an African elephant *(right)*.

Elgar, Sir Edward (1857–1934), was an English composer. Until middle age he earned his living chiefly as a violin teacher, but about 1900 he was hailed as the greatest English composer since Purcell. His *Enigma Variations* (1899) helped make his name, while his oratorio *The Dream of Gerontius* (a failure in England) led to his music being frequently performed in Germany. Soon he became as popular with ordinary people as with music critics – a result of his song *Land of Hope and Glory* (1902) which was derived, on the suggestion of King Edward VII, from one of his *Pomp and Circumstances* marches. It became an alternative national anthem.

El Greco, 'the Greek' (1541–1614), was a Spanish painter of Greek origin. He was trained in the tradition of Byzantine art in his native Crete and, after a long stay in Italy, finally settled in Spain. El Greco was a highly individual artist, as a result of his mixed background and his own genius. The Byzantine element was always evident in his work, yet his passionate intensity of emotion is very un-Byzantine. It was achieved largely by disregarding normal rules. His figures are strangely stretched, and his colours full of sharp discords. He paid little attention to perspective, or to normal effects of light and shadow.

Eliot, George (1819–1880), was an English novelist, whose real name was Mary Anne Evans. Her early novels – *Adam Bede* (1859), *The Mill on the Floss* (1860), *Silas Marner* (1861) – were concerned with contemporary life in the English Midlands, pictured with sharp observation, imaginative sympathy and humour.

Later novels, especially *Middlemarch* (1872), were more profound, dealing with the relationship of the individual to society. George Eliot is generally regarded as one of the greatest and most intelligent English novelists.

Eliot, Thomas Stearns (1888–1965), was a US-born poet who lived in England from 1914. He was awarded the Nobel Prize for literature in 1948. The experimental technique and pessimism of his early work reached their most powerful expression in *The Waste Land* (1922), probably the most influential poem of the century (and extremely difficult reading for most people). Eliot's grim view of contemporary society brightened after his acceptance of Christianity in 1927. His *Four Quartets* (1943), which made use of the Anglican prayerbook, were calmer and more hopeful.

T. S. Eliot believed that poetry should be 'useful', and he was therefore drawn to the theatre. His *Murder in the Cathedral* (1935), on the martyrdom of St Thomas Becket, is a moving experience, though other verse plays (e.g. *The Cocktail Party*, 1943) were less successful.

Elizabeth I (1533–1603), was Queen of England (1558–1603). The daughter of Henry VIII and Anne Boleyn, she came to the throne on the death of her half-sister, Mary I. She re-established Protestantism in England, but rejected the more extreme form of Puritanism. She had to deal with several plots by Roman Catholics to place her cousin Mary Queen of Scots on the throne, which eventually led to Mary's execution (1587).

A contemporary portrait of Queen Elizabeth I.

Long hostility between Spain and England ended in war, when Philip II of Spain despatched the Armada in an unsuccessful attempt to conquer England. Elizabeth was a capable and popular ruler, and her reign was marked by a growth in commerce and trade, the founding of colonies and a flowering of literature, music and architecture.

Elizabeth II (1926–), is Queen of Great Britain and Northern Ireland. She married Prince Philip, Duke of Edinburgh in 1947, coming to the throne in 1952 after the death of her father, King George VI. As a constitutional monarch and head of the Commonwealth of Nations, Queen Elizabeth has many important duties to perform. In 1977 she celebrated the Silver Jubilee of her accession, which was an occasion for national celebration. She has four children, Charles, Anne, Andrew and Edward.

Elk, *see* Moose.

Elm is a popular, stately tree found in Europe, Asia and eastern North America. Elms have tall trunks bearing upward-pointing branches clothed with serrated leaves. When the seeds develop, they are enclosed within a papery, wing-like structure. Elm wood is highly prized for fine craft work such as furniture and panelling, and is also used in structures, such as bridge supports, where durability is required.

Sadly, the landscape of America and parts of Europe has been marred by the deaths of millions of elm trees, victims of a fungus which blocks the water tubes of the trees. The disease, carried by a beetle, is called Dutch elm disease.

El Salvador is a republic in Central America. Capital, San Salvador; area about 21400 sq km (8260 sq miles). Though very small, El Salvador has been an independent republic since the 1840s and is the most thickly populated and industrialized state in Central America. In the early 1980s it was the scene of a brutal civil war between Right-wing government forces and Left-wing guerrillas.

The country has two ranges of volcanic mountains, but is mostly high plateau. Coffee is an important crop, and other crops such as sisal and sugar cane grow well in the rich soil. El Salvador produces most of the world's balsam (used in perfume). The mainly light industry includes hats, cigars and leather goods.

Embryo is the name given to an animal or plant during its early development, when it is just past the stage of a fertilized egg.

Emu is a large, flightless bird found in Australia. Standing 1.8 m (6 ft) in height, it is second only to the ostrich in size. On its long legs the emu can run at speeds of up to 50 km/h (30 mph). The plump body is covered with brown feathers, and the long neck has patches of blue skin. Emus live in open grassland where they feed on vegetable matter.

Energy – all matter has mass and volume, but there are some things which do not have mass or volume. These include electricity, sound, light and heat. They are called energy, and each one is a form of energy.

Energy can be changed from one form into another. In a power station, heat is changed into electricity. In a television, electricity is changed into light and sound.

Energy is measured in units called joules. *See also* Matter.

Engine is a machine that burns fuel to make heat, which is turned into energy to produce motion. In the case of a bicycle, the 'engine' is actually the rider, whose fuel (food) is turned into energy to power the bike. Most engines use fuel such as petrol, coal, oil or electricity.

The internal combustion engine is very common, used in cars, lorries, buses, motorcycles, small boats and many trains and aircraft.

The electric motor is used to power trains, a few road vehicles and many smaller machines, such as fans, record players, washing machines, drills, etc. Power is taken either from a battery or by wires from the power station. Electric motors are very efficient and clean.

George Stephenson's steam locomotive, *The Rocket.*

The steam engine, invented in approximately 1712 by Englishman Thomas Newcomen, is sometimes referred to as an external combustion engine. It was commonplace on railway locomotives and ships, and is still in widespread use to turn electrical generators in power stations.

The jet engine, or gas turbine engine, is one of the simplest and most efficient types of power unit. It can be used to power a large propeller, allowing gas turbine engines to be used for high-speed propeller aircraft and for helicopters, as well as for ordinary jet aircraft. Such engines are very efficient and can be very powerful – thrusts of over 50 000 kg (110 250 lb) are common on military aircraft – but they require large amounts of fuel.

The rocket motor is the simplest of all engines in principle. It works in the same way as a blown-up balloon whose neck is released and which then rushes through the air until it becomes deflated. Unlike other combustion engines, a rocket does not need oxygen from the air to help burn its fuel – it carries its own oxygen, either in a separate tank or as a chemical part of the fuel itself. It can therefore fly in the airless vacuum of outer space. Most modern rockets, such as those used to carry people into space, are powered by liquid fuel, which is ignited in a combustion chamber. This was invented by a Russian, Konstantin Tsiolkovsky, in 1903.

The nuclear engine is usually only a steam engine, the nuclear reaction being used to heat water into steam, which is then used to drive pistons or turn turbines in the same way as steam engines whose water is heated by oil or coal.

Engineering is a branch of science concerned with making machines, buildings, roads and many other things. They are invented, designed, built and maintained by engineers. There are many different sorts of engineering. For example, chemistry is used by chemical engineers to make huge amounts of drugs, fertilizers and other substances. Civil engineers build bridges, roads and docks. Electronic engineers design and build scientific instruments and systems.

England is part of the United Kingdom of Great Britain and Northern Ireland. Capital London; area 130 357 sq km (50 331 sq miles).

History England was inhabited by Celtic tribes in pre-Roman times. Invaded by Julius Caesar in 55 and 54 BC, it remained under Roman rule during the 1st–5th centuries AD. Successive waves of Angles, Saxons and Jutes reached England in the late 5th century and the country was subsequently divided into a number of small kingdoms, which were gradually converted to Christianity. From the 8th century onwards Danish invasions began and the country was for a time ruled by Danish kings. The Norman Conquest (1066) introduced a centralized government and gave England extensive possessions in France, all of which were finally lost at the end of The Hundred Years' War. The country was torn by dynastic conflict during the Wars of the Roses, but the accession of the Tudors brought stability, the establishment of Protestantism and the development of overseas trade. For subsequent history *see* United Kingdom.

Rulers of England

Saxons

Egbert	828–839
Ethelwulf	839–858
Ethelbald	858–860

Ethelbert	860–865
Ethelred I	866–871
Alfred the Great	871–899
Edward the Elder	899–924
Athelstan	924–940
Edmund	940–946
Edred	946–955
Edwy	955–959
Edgar	959–975
Edward the Martyr	975–978
Ethelred II, the Unready	978–1016
Edmund Ironside	1016
Danes	
Canute	1016–1035
Harold I Harefoot	1035–1040
Hardicanute	1040–1042
Saxons	
Edward the Confessor	1042–1066
Harold II	1066
Normans	
William the Conqueror	1066–1087
William II Rufus	1087–1100
Henry I	1100–1135
Stephen	1135–1154
Plantagenets	
Henry II	1154–1189
Richard I	1189–1199
John	1199–1216
Henry III	1216–1272
Edward I	1272–1307
Edward II	1307–1327
Edward III	1327–1377
Richard II	1377–1399
Lancaster	
Henry IV	1399–1413
Henry V	1413–1422
Henry VI	1422–1461
York	
Edward IV	1461–1483
Edward V	1483
Richard III	1483–1485
Tudor	
Henry VII	1485–1509
Henry VIII	1509–1547
Edward VI	1547–1553
Mary	1553–1558
Elizabeth I	1558–1603

(For rulers after 1603 see United Kingdom.)

Land England comprises more than 55 per cent of the area of Great Britain. Its principal mountain range is the Pennine Chain in the north-west, stretching from the Cheviot Hills on the Scottish border southwards to Derbyshire. The Lake District, between the Pennines and the coast of the Irish Sea, is famous for its lake and mountain scenery: it includes Scafell Pike (977 m/3205 ft), England's highest mountain.

In the south – between the valleys of England's longest rivers, the Severn and the Thames – are two ranges of low hills, the Cotswolds and the Chilterns. Both are known for their beautiful countryside and villages. To the south of the Thames lies the rolling chalk land of the Weald and the Downs. In the far south-west is the peninsula of Devon and Cornwall, with its sheltered coves and fishing villages.

Economy See United Kingdom.

Counties of England

County	Area sq km	sq miles
Avon	1346	520
Bedford	1234	476
Berkshire	1255	485
Buckinghamshire	1882	727
Cambridgeshire	3409	1316
Cheshire	2329	899
Cleveland	583	225
Cornwall	3546	1369
Cumbria	6808	2629
Derbyshire	2631	1016
Devonshire	6711	2591
Dorset	2654	1025
Durham	2436	941
Essex	3674	1419
Gloucester	2642	1020
Hampshire	3782	1460
Hereford and Worcester	3926	1516
Hertford	1634	631
Humberside	3512	1356
Kent	3732	1441
Lancashire	3040	1174
Leicestershire	2553	986
Lincoln	5886	2273
London, Greater	1580	610
Manchester, Greater	1284	496
Merseyside	646	249
Norfolk	5356	2068
Northampton	2367	914
Northumberland	5033	1943
Nottinghamshire	2164	836
Oxfordshire	2612	1008
Salop	3490	1347
Somerset	3450	1332
Staffordshire	2716	1049
Suffolk	3807	1470
Surrey	1679	648
Sussex, East	1795	693
Sussex, West	2016	778
Tyne and Wear	540	208
Warwick	1981	765
West Midlands	899	347
Wight, Isle of	381	147
Wiltshire	3481	1344
Yorkshire, North	8309	3208
Yorkshire, South	1561	603
Yorkshire, West	2039	787

English Civil War (1642–1651) was the war between Charles I and Parliament. For some years there had been bitter opposition between the King, who claimed to rule by divine right, and Parliament, which wanted a greater share in the government of the country. This hostility came to a head when the King, whose financial position was desperate, was forced to recall Parliament in 1640. Charles refused to agree to Parliament's demands, and war broke out. At first the Royalists won several battles, but eventually the Parliamentarians were able to train a well disciplined army, which gained a series of important victories at Marston Moor (1644), Naseby (1645) and Preston (1648). After Charles I had been executed, his son Charles II renewed the war with Scottish support, but was finally defeated at the Battle of Worcester in 1651.

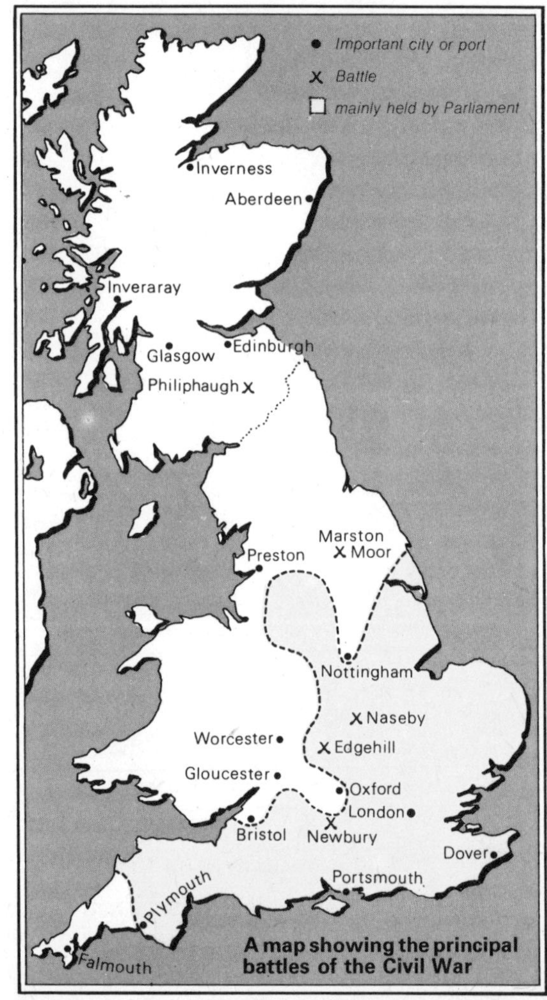

A map showing the principal battles of the Civil War

Environment of a plant or animal is all the external conditions under which it lives – for instance, light intensity, temperature, water, other organisms and food availability.

Enzymes are proteins which have the ability to change the rate at which chemical reactions occur within a plant or animal. At the end of the reaction, the enzyme remains unchanged, although the reaction may have produced new substances. Many of the chemical processes in living organisms can only occur in the presence of enzymes. An example of an enzyme found in the human body is amylase. Amylase converts starch in foods into a sugar called maltose. Another enzyme, maltase, converts maltose into glucose.

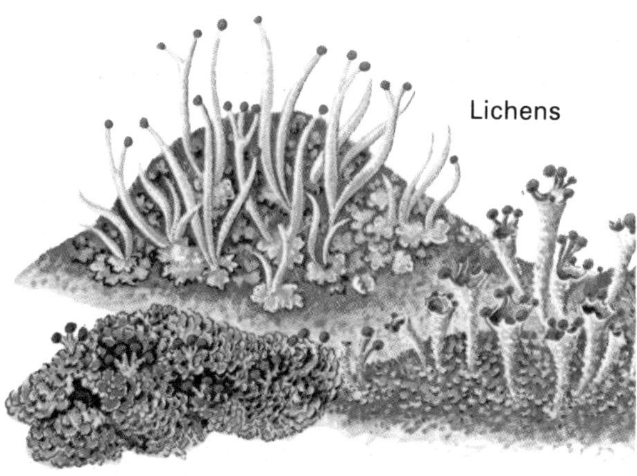
Lichens

Epiphyte is a plant which grows upon the surface of another plant. It is not a parasite, but merely uses the plant to support itself. Epiphytes are common in many tropical rainforests, where exotic bromeliads and orchids perch on the trunks and stems of the forest trees. Other common epiphytes include lichens and mosses.

Equator is an imaginary line round the Earth's, or any other planet's, surface, at an equal distance from each of the poles. It is the longest parallel of latitude (0 degrees). The Earth's equator measures 40 059 km (24 892 miles).

Equatorial Guinea is a republic in West Africa, consisting of the islands Bioko (formerly Fernando Poo) and Pagalu (formerly Annobon) and the continental province, Rio Muni. Capital, Malabo; area about 2805 sq km (10 830 sq miles). Formerly Spanish Guinea, it gained independence in 1968.

Bioko has fertile soil and high rainfall and coffee and cocoa are the main products. The mainland lacks the rich volcanic soil and is largely forested. Timber and bananas are exported from the coastal plain.

Equinox is the time when the Sun is directly overhead at the equator. At other times, the Sun is overhead in the northern or southern tropics. At equinox, day and night are each twelve hours long everywhere on the Earth. At other times of the year, day and night differ in length. In the winter, the night is longer than the day. In the summer, the day is longer than the night.

There are two equinoxes each year.

Ermine, see Stoat.

Eros, in Greek myth, was the god of love. The Romans identified him with Cupid, who was usually represented as a beautiful, but mischievous, boy with wings. Originally, however, Eros was a more dignified figure.

Eros was the son of Aphrodite (Venus). He delighted in shooting his magic arrows into both gods and humans, causing them to fall in love – sometimes with unsuitable people. Later, his name came to mean sexual love, as distinct from other kinds of love like mother love or the love of God.

Erosion is the wearing down of land by forces such as wind or water, which carry away soil. Erosion by water may occur through rainfall, through the impact of the tides on a coastline, or through the action of a river or stream. Another important agent is the movement of glaciers, since gigantic masses of ice create and carry along quantities of rock fragments called moraine.

Erosion is generally a slow process, only producing large effects over several centuries. However, human activity sometimes causes rapid and disastrous changes, especially where the soil is stripped of the vegetation which holds it in place. Such activities include felling all the trees in an area and exhausting the soil by overcultivation (as in the American 'dust bowl' areas). Soil conservation has become an important study in recent years, involving replanting of trees and improved agricultural techniques.

Eskimos are a people living in Alaska, the northern parts of Canada and Greenland, and (a very few) in eastern Siberia. The small, copper-skinned Eskimos are a completely separate people from the American Indians. They arrived in America much later than the Indians, apparently crossing from Asia to Alaska in about the 1st century AD, and spreading from there across Canada to Greenland by about the 10th century.

The traditional Eskimo way of life was very well adapted to their cold, hostile surroundings. With ivory, wood and whalebone they made highly effective weapons, such as the harpoon, which they used to fish and to hunt whales, seals, walruses, reindeer and other animals. Whale and seal oil provided fuel and food, and the oiliness of the Eskimos' diet built up a layer of fat beneath their skin that protected them against the extreme cold. Their houses, called igloos, were carefully insulated, and included the well-known snow houses built by some Canadian Eskimos as temporary dwellings during hunting expeditions. Other features of Eskimo life were sleds and teams of dogs, whale-boats and one-person kayaks made from animal skins.

Eskimos used to build igloos like this to live in while on hunting trips.

Today the total Eskimo population only numbers a few tens of thousands, and the Eskimo way of life has been much modified by contact with other people.

Ethanol is a colourless liquid made from petroleum. Its chemical formula is C_2H_5OH. Ethanol is often called ethyl alcohol or simply alcohol. It is used to dissolve many substances. Perfumes are often dissolved in ethanol, and it is also used to produce methylated spirits.

Ethanol can also be made from foods such as potatoes, malt, grapes, wheat, honey and apples. Ethanol is produced when these foods are fermented to make drinks such as wine, beer, cider and whisky.

Ethelred the Unready (968–1016) was King of England (978–1016). During his reign England was under continual threat from the Danes, and Ethelred attempted to buy off Danish raiders by paying them tribute (Danegeld). He was exiled after being deposed in 1013 by Sweyn Forkbeard, but was restored to the throne in the following year.

Ethiopia is a republic in east-central Africa. Capital, Addis Ababa; area about 1 000 000 sq km (395 000 sq miles).

History Formerly Abyssinia, Ethiopia became the first Christian country in Africa in the 4th century AD. In the 7th century, Christianity only survived in the interior where rugged mountains protected the people from the powerful Islam force on the coast. After centuries of conflict the country was reunited under Theodore II in the 19th century. Annexed by Italy in 1936, it regained independence in 1941. The monarchy was overthrown in 1974.

Land and People The climate in Ethiopia varies a great deal with the rapid changes in altitude. Cattle-rearing has long been the most important occupation, though a large variety of crops are grown. Ethiopian coffee is famous for its quality.

Mineral resources are large but little exploited due to transport problems and political difficulties. Water power also has great potential, but industry in general is underdeveloped.

Ethiopia contains a great variety of people. The Galla, mainly farmers and herdsmen, are the most numerous. The Amhara, the traditional ruling class, make up about 10 per cent.

Ethylene is a colourless gas made from petroleum. Its chemical formula is CH_4. It is also called ethene. Ethylene is used to make ethanol and antifreeze. Antifreeze is put in the water of car radiators to stop the water freezing in cold weather.

Ethylene molecules can be joined together to form a long chain. This changes the ethylene from a gas into a waxy solid, known as a plastic. This plastic is called polyethylene or polythene, which can be made into any shape such as a jar, bottle or bowl.

Etosha Pan is a vast bowl-like depression, area about 6000 sq km (2300 sq miles), in the Etosha National Park, Namibia. For most of the year it is a parched wasteland, but during the rainy season, it is briefly filled with water, and then animals such as zebras, wildebeests, lions and flamingoes migrate to it in their thousands.

Etruscans were an ancient people who settled in central Italy in the 8th century BC. For several centuries, Etruscan city-states flourished and produced fine works of art, notably tomb decoration, wall-paintings, pottery and sculpture. The power of the Etruscans began to decline in the 5th century BC under attacks from Gaul, the Greeks in southern Italy and the Romans.

Eucalyptus trees are native to Australia, but have been planted in many other parts of the world. They are by far the most dominant trees in Australia, occurring on mountains, in semi-arid regions and in hot, steamy rainforests. They are very varied; some are tall, straight species, while others are short with widespread crowns. Their leaves are evergreen, greyish in colour and are leathery.

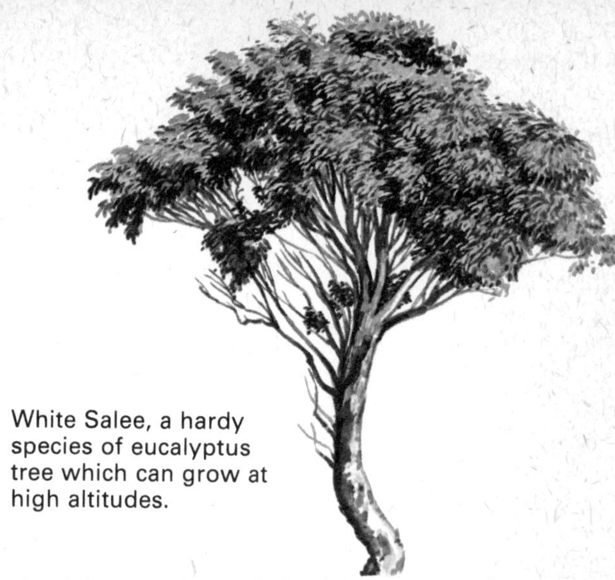

White Salee, a hardy species of eucalyptus tree which can grow at high altitudes.

Euglena, see Animals; Protozoan.

Euphrates is a river in south-west Asia. It rises in the Armenian mountains and flows about 2850 km (1770 miles) to join the Tigris in Iraq, before reaching the Persian Gulf.

Europe is a continent lying between Asia and the Atlantic Ocean. Area about 10 500 000 sq km (4 054 000 sq miles). It is the second smallest continent yet it is the second most highly populated (after Asia). Europe is divided into many different countries. Individual entries on these countries give greater detail of history etc.

History Europe has played a dominant role in the modern history of the world. Europeans, including European settlers in other continents, controlled almost the whole globe, directly or indirectly, in the late 19th and early 20th centuries. Many of the practical, political and economic ideas of people throughout the world today are of European origin.

The countries of Europe belong to various smaller international associations. The European Economic Community (EEC) includes most of Western Europe. The communist countries of Eastern Europe are bound by common allegiance to the Soviet Union.

Land Europe has a great variety of scenery

Arctic Ocean
Arctic Circle
Reykjavik
ICELAND
Faeroe Is.
Shetland Is
Orkney Is.
Atlantic Ocean
NORWAY
Oslo
Stockholm
SWEDEN
FINLAND
Helsinki
SCOTLAND
Edinburgh
North Sea
Nth. IRELAND
Belfast
Dublin
IRELAND (EIRE)
WALES
ENGLAND
London
DENMARK
Copenhagen
Baltic Sea
U
S
Hague
Amsterdam
NETHERLANDS
Brussels
BELGIUM
Bonn
LUXEMBOURG
Rhine
Elbe
Berlin
GERMANY (EAST)
Vistula
Warsaw
POLAND
Prague
CZECHOSLOVAKIA
CARPATHIAN MTS
Paris
Loire
FRANCE
GERMANY (WEST)
Vienna
AUSTRIA
Budapest
HUNGARY
Bern
SWITZERLAND
Bay of Biscay
ROMANIA
Danube
Bucharest
Belgrade
YUGOSLAVIA
BULGARIA
Sofia
PYRENEES
Ebro
PORTUGAL
Lisbon
Madrid
Guadiana
SPAIN
Gibraltar
Po
APENNINE MTS
Adriatic Sea
ITALY
Rome
Corsica
Sardinia
Sicily
Tirana
ALBANIA
GREECE
Athens
Aegean Sea
Crete
Mediterranean Sea
0
750 km
0
500 miles

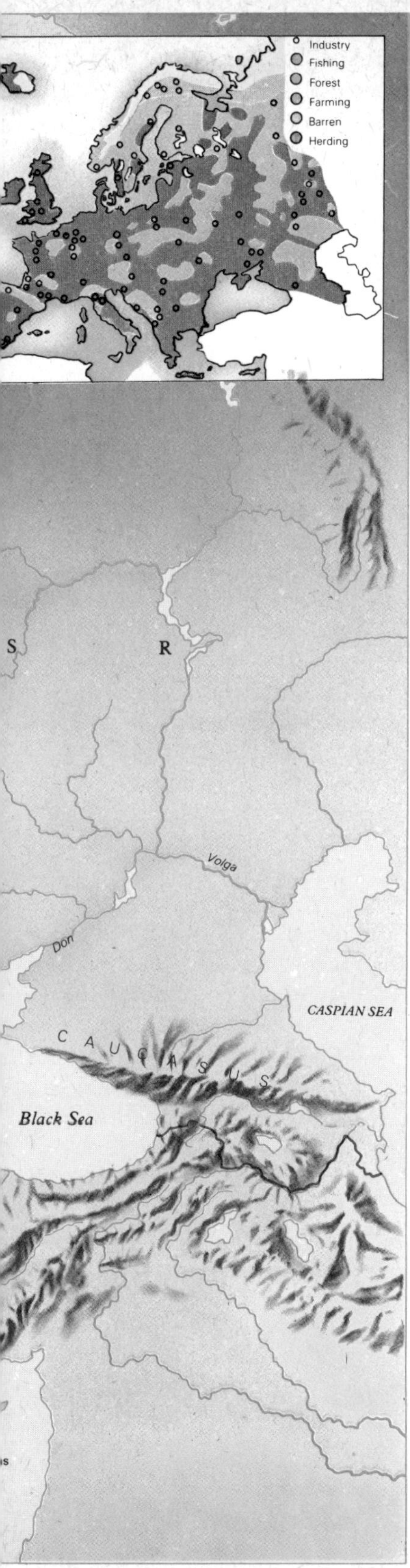

and climate. There are many mountainous regions, (the largest being the Alps), broad plains, especially in Russia and Spain, thick forests, marshlands and lakes. However, there is practically no desert and the climate, though extremely severe in the Arctic north, is generally temperate, with few areas of really low rainfall or extreme heat. The west, however, is more temperate, and more prosperous, than the east. The proportion of land suitable for human settlement is higher than in all other continents.

Europe has been more altered by the works of people than other continents. The forests which once covered most of it have been greatly reduced, and there are few large animals left in the wild.

People Although there is a great variety of races and nations, most Europeans share a common descent. They are all known as Caucasoid, and their languages are related (Finnish is one exception). Various forms of Christianity are found in all parts of Europe. Although it began in Asia, Christianity has been essentially a European religion.

Economy Europe is rich in coal and iron, but many other minerals have to be imported by most of the countries. In farming, productivity is not very high except in a few countries such as Britain, Denmark and the Netherlands.

Europe is the most highly industrialized continent. A greater proportion of its people live in large towns and work in industry rather than agriculture. Manufacturing is especially strong, and the countries of Western Europe, particularly, have an economy based on importing raw materials and exporting manufactured products. The creation of the EEC has made a wider market, and industry in EEC countries is increasingly organized for an international market.

European Economic Community (EEC) is an organization of Western European countries established by the Treaty of Rome in 1958 in order to encourage economic co-operation and development, and political unity. The members of the organization – France, West Germany, Italy, Belgium, the Netherlands and Luxembourg – lowered customs duties among themselves and set up a common market with a single tariff on imports from all other countries. In 1973 Britain, Denmark and the Republic of Ireland became members, and Greece joined in 1981.

Evaporation occurs when a liquid is heated and part of it becomes a gas called a vapour.

The Sun heats water in the rivers and oceans. Some of this evaporates into the air. It then cools and falls back to the Earth as rain or snow.

Everest, Mount, is the world's highest mountain at 8848 m (29 029 ft), in the Himalayas, central Asia. Standing on the remote borders of Nepal and Tibet, Mount Everest is chiefly famous as the target of mountaineers. The first successful attempt to reach the top was in 1953 by a British expedition led by Sir Edmund Hillary and Tenzing Norgay.

Evergreen is the name given to a plant which bears leaves all the year round. Although the plant may shed leaves from time to time, it is never without leaves. The best-known evergreens are the coniferous trees, such as the pines and larches. *See also* Conifer; Deciduous.

Evolution is the process by which all the animals and plants that we see around us today have come about. Hundreds of millions of years ago the first forms of life were simple creatures rather like bacteria. Slowly, as conditions on Earth changed, chance genetic mutations gave rise to new, more complicated creatures. Some of these flourished for a while and then died out; some gave rise to other groups of animals and plants; and a very few are still unchanged even to this day. Eventually, plants and animals evolved sufficiently to leave the seas, rivers and marshes and conquer the land.

Evolution is still taking place. The creatures we see around us today – including ouselves, humans – may look nothing like the creatures inhabiting the Earth in the distant future. *See also* Fossils; Prehistoric animals.

Exoskeleton is a skeleton outside the body which some animals possess, unlike human beings, who have a skeleton inside their bodies. An exoskeleton forms the protective body covering of arthropods (insects, spiders and crabs), molluscs (snails and clams) and tortoises, as well as providing an anchorage for muscles and other organs. Arthropods can shed their exoskeletons and form new ones as they grow bigger. *See also* Skeleton.

Explorers

3000 BC	Minoans from Crete explored the Mediterranean.
600 BC	Pheonicians sailed into the Atlantic and reached Britain.
500 BC	Hanno the Carthaginian voyaged down the west coast of Africa.
circa 340 BC	Pytheas the Greek explored coasts of Spain, Gaul and Britain, and possibly reached Arctic.
circa AD 982	Eric the Red reached Greenland from Iceland.
circa 1000	Leif Ericson probably reached coast of North America.
1271–1295	Marco Polo travelled to China.
1420–1446	Henry the Navigator directed voyages of discovery to West Africa, the Cape Verde Islands, etc.
1487–1488	Bartolomeu Dias sailed round Cape of Good Hope.
1492	Christopher Columbus reached the West Indies.
1497	Vasco da Gama sailed round Africa to reach India.
1497–1498	John and Sebastian Cabot sailed across North Atlantic to reach Newfoundland.
1500	Pedro Cabral discovered northern coast of Brazil.
1513	Vasco de Balboa led expedition across Panama and discovered Pacific Ocean.
1519–1521	Ferdinand Magellan

	commanded first expedition to sail round the world.
1519–1521	Hernán Cortés discovered and conquered Mexico.
1531–1535	Francisco Pizarro explored Peru.
1535	Jacques Cartier sailed up the St Lawrence River in Canada.
1596–1597	Willem Barents discovered Spitsbergen Island while seeking North-west Passage.
1607	Henry Hudson explored Hudson Bay while seeking North-west Passage.
1642	Abel Tasman discovered Tasmania and New Zealand.
1768–1779	James Cook made extensive voyages in the South Pacific and charted eastern coast of Australia.
1785–1788	Comte de la Pérouse explored Pacific coasts of Asia.
1795–1796	Mungo Park explored course of Niger in Africa.
1804–1806	Meriwether Lewis and William Clark led expedition across Rocky Mountains, USA, to Pacific.
1819–1821	Fabian von Bellinghausen circumnavigated Antarctica.
1849–1873	David Livingstone explored Zambezi and discovered Victoria Falls and Lake Malawi in Africa.
1853–1858	Sir Richard Burton explored Arabia and East Africa.
1860–1861	Robert Burke and William Wills crossed Australia from south to north.
1858	John Speke discovered Lakes Tanganyika and Victoria in Africa.
1909	Robert Peary was the first man to reach the North Pole.
1911	Roald Amundsen was the first man to reach the South Pole.
1957–1958	Sir Vivian Fuchs led first expedition across Antarctica.

The Victoria, shown here in front, was the only ship in Magellan's fleet that completed the voyage round the world.

Explosive is a solid or liquid chemical that can suddenly change into a large amount of gas. This rapid expansion is called an explosion and can, for example, split rocks in half and cause a loud bang.

Explosives have many uses, such as destroying buildings which are no longer wanted, making holes in the ground for mining and quarrying, and tunnelling through mountains for roads and railways. They are also used in wars in bombs, shells and other weapons.

The first explosive was gunpowder. Later, dynamite and gelignite were used. Today, there are many powerful explosives, such as cyclonite, TNT and liquid oxygen.

Explosives are set off by detonators. A detonator produces the explosion by first producing a flame, an electrical spark or a small explosion.

Expressionism was a movement in modern art, chiefly in Germany, in the early years of the 20th century. The German Expressionists mostly belonged to two groups – the 'Blue Rider' and the 'Bridge'. An expressionist painting aims to express the feelings of the artist, which are usually powerful and often spring from some intense emotional or mental concern. The result is exaggeration or distortion of normal appearances. Among the German Expressionists, this often took the form of very strong colours as well as non-realistic shapes. But expressionism is a feature of much art, not merely of the painters labelled 'Expressionist'.

Extinction is the process during which a population or species of plant or animal ceases to exist. Once this point is reached, the organism has gone forever. Recent extinctions include the dodo, a large flightless bird, and the great auk, another bird. During the process of evolution many plants and animals became extinct as a result of an inability to compete with newly evolving forms of life, or because they could not adapt to changing environmental conditions. Sadly, most recent extinctions of animals or plants have been caused by over-hunting or destruction of their habitat by humans.

Scientists sometimes say a population or species is extinct if it no longer exists in a certain place, even though it may occur elsewhere. *See also* Conservation; Evolution.

Extraterrestrial life is life on a planet other than the Earth. Science fiction books and films have imagined many different worlds with strange forms of life. It was once thought that people lived on Mars, but when Viking spacecraft landed on Mars in 1976 they could find no trace of life. Nothing on Earth could live on Mars. There does not seem to be life on any other planet in the Solar System either.

However, the search for extraterrestrial life continues. Astronomers think that one in every 10 stars has planets, which means that there are thousands of millions of stars in our Galaxy with planets. Some of these may have life. Signals are sent out from Earth which could be picked up by one of these planets, and there is equipment on Earth to detect signals which may come from another planet.

Eyes are found in a large number of animals, and are essentially structures for receiving light. The simplest types of eyes are to be found in animals like clams. Rows of tiny eyes set along the edge of the shells will cause the shells to shut if a shadow falls upon them.

Other animals have eyes which can detect shape, movement and colour. The most well-developed eyes are to be found in vertebrates such as birds, some of which can detect an animal as small as a mouse on the ground whilst they themselves wheel in the sky far overhead. Vertebrate eyes have a cornea and lens which focus light on to the retina to form an image. The retina, stimulated by the light, sends messages to the brain along the optic nerve.

Insects are unusual in that they have both simple, light-receptive eyes called ocelli, as well as image-making compound eyes. Chameleons also have peculiar eyes. Each eye can rotate entirely independently of the other. Thus, one eye can be looking up into the trees for prey, whilst the other can be keeping a look out for predators from below.

F

Fable is a story with a moral, or lesson. The characters are often animals which represent some quality (the fox = cunning, the donkey = stupidity, etc). The earliest and most famous fables are those of Aesop.

Faeroe Islands are a small island group in the north-east Atlantic. Capital, Thorshavn; area about 340 sq km (520 sq miles). The Faeroes are a self-governing part of Denmark. They are hilly and rather bleak. Some of the smaller islands are uninhabited. Sheep-raising and fishing are the main occupations.

Falcons are the birds of prey which make up the family Falconidae. (The other large family of birds of prey is the one containing the eagles, hawks, buzzards and vultures. A third family contains the osprey.) Falcons usually hunt by flying after prey at great speed, and their long, narrow wings are built for fast flight. The most unusual falcon is the South American caracara. It spends most of its life running on the ground. More common falcons include the kestrel, hobby, merlin, gyr falcon and peregrine falcon.

Peregrine falcons

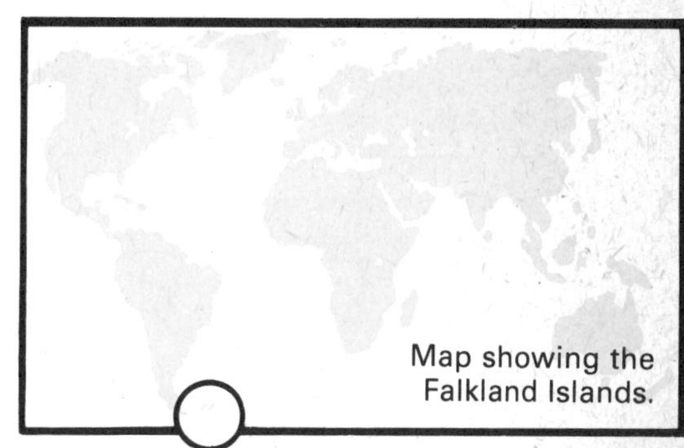
Map showing the Falkland Islands.

Falkland Islands are an island group in the south-west Atlantic. Capital, Stanley; area (including dependencies of South Georgia and South Sandwich group) about 16 000 sq km (6180 sq miles). A British colony since the early 19th century, they are claimed by Argentina, as the Malvinas. In 1982 Argentine troops took the islands by force but were driven out by a strong British force after a short campaign. The Falklands are bleak and treeless; sheep-rearing is the main occupation.

Faraday, Michael (1791–1867), was an English chemist and physicist. He studied science while working as an apprentice bookbinder, becoming Sir Humphrey Davy's assistant in 1813. In 1827 he took over from Davy as Professor of Chemistry at the Royal Institution, where he was a very popular lecturer. Lectures for children, known as Faraday lectures, still continue.

Faraday studied the effect of passing an electric current through certain solutions. From this he formed his laws of electrolysis. In 1831 he showed how a magnetic field can produce an electric current. This is known as electromagnetic induction. He made the first electric motor and the first electric generator.

Far East is an unofficial name for the countries of eastern Asia. Normally this means China and Japan and their smaller neighbours, plus eastern Siberia (Soviet Union). However, lands as far west as India and Pakistan are sometimes included.

Fats are an important part of the food we eat. They give us energy and enable us to produce heat to keep the body warm. Fats can also be stored in the body. Eating too many fats can make people overweight.

Fats are normally solid. When they are liquid they are called oils. Plants and animals contain both fats and oils. Animal fats include butter, which is made from milk, and lard. Margarine is made from animal and vegetable fats. Plant oils, such as linseed oil, are used to protect wood, some are used to make soap, and some, such as olive oil, are used as food.

Faulkner, William (1897–1962), was a US novelist. He lived most of his life in rural Mississippi, in the 'Yoknapatawpha County' of his books. Faulkner's main theme was the brutal decline of the South in the period after the American Civil War, combined with the psychological conflicts of individuals. The best-known works are *Sanctuary* (1931) and *Intruder in the Dust* (1948). His last book, *The Reivers* (1962), was different from his others – light-hearted and funny.

Fault is a fracture or break in the Earth's crust which has allowed the rocks on either side of it to move in different directions during periods of geological stress and upheaval. For example, the crust on one side of a fault may have risen, fallen or even tilted at some period. Where this has exposed the strata (levels making up the rock, each representing different ages in the history of the Earth), it has provided much valuable geological information. Faults may be vertical, horizontal or, indeed, at any angle between the two.

A famous example of a fault is California's San Andreas fault. It has often been predicted that Earth movements will cause earthquakes along the San Andreas fault line, bringing disaster to California and its major cities.

The San Andreas Fault.

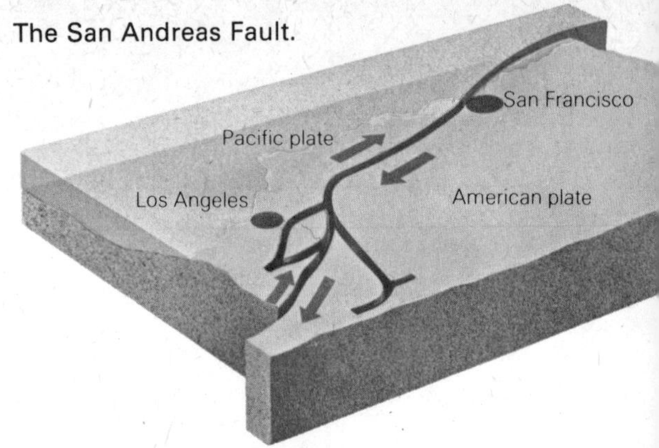

Fawkes, Guy (1570–1606), was an English conspirator. A convert to Roman Catholicism, he served with the Spanish army in the Low Countries in the 1590s. On his return to England he became involved in the Gunpowder Plot (5 November 1605) to blow up the Houses of Parliament, when the King, James I, and the members of both Houses were sitting together at the beginning of a new session. The plot was discovered, and Fawkes and the other ringleaders were executed.

Feathers are found only on birds. They are produced as outgrowths of the skin, and help to insulate the bird against the cold, streamline the body, act as camouflage or display, and are used in flight. A typical flight feather, like the ones often seen discarded by birds in woodlands, consists of a central shaft bearing a vane on either side. Each vane is made up of rows of branches called barbs. The barbs bear smaller right-angled branches called barbules. The barbules lock together by means of tiny hooks called barbicels.

The number of feathers found on different species of bird varies: thrushes only have about 2000 feathers, whereas a swan may have 25 000. It is the wing feathers which are concerned with flight; the long feathers on the outer part of the wing are used for pushing the bird through the air, and the feathers on the inner part of the wing provide lift. The tail feathers help to steer the bird and act as an air brake when landing. Other, smaller feathers scattered over the body help to give the bird its streamlined shape and cut down wind resistance.

Birds must ensure that their feathers are kept in good condition, and so they spend many hours preening their feathers – oiling them, stroking them back into shape with their beaks, and bathing in dust or water to remove parasites from them. *See also* Moult.

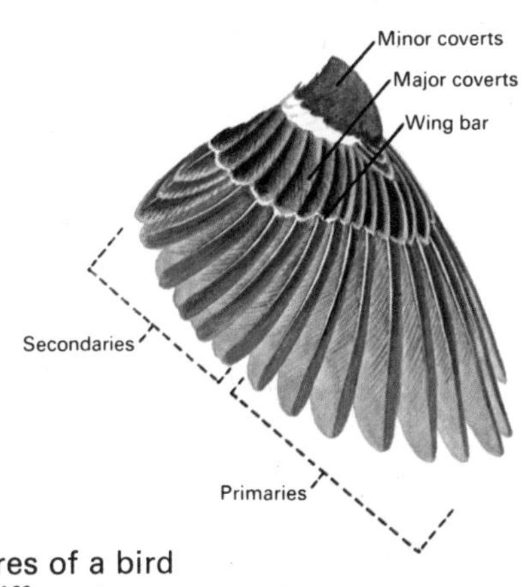

External features of a bird showing the different feathers.

February is the second month of the year in the modern calendar, named after the ancient Roman month *Februarius*. It lasts for 28 days except during a leap year (every fourth year), when it lasts for 29.

Feisal I (1885–1933), was King of Iraq (1921–1933). As a young man he took a prominent part in the Arab nationalist movement. During the First World War he led Arab armies in revolt against Turkish rule. He was King of Syria briefly in 1920 before being compelled to abdicate by the French. In 1921 he was made King of Iraq under a British mandate, obtaining complete independence for his country in 1932.

Fermentation is the breakdown of certain animal and plant substances by chemicals called enzymes, found especially in bacteria and yeast. Food, such as yoghurt, and alcoholic drinks, such as beer and wine, are made by fermentation. *See also* Enzymes.

Ferns are an ancient group of non-flowering plants, common in woods, on heathlands and by streams and other damp or shady places. Although the majority of ferns grow in the soil, a few species grow as epiphytes on the trunks of trees. Some species seem to sprout out of rocks, but their roots are embedded in tiny pockets of soil within the crevices of the rock.

Millions of years ago giant ferns were the dominant plants on Earth. Their crushed and long-buried remains have turned to coal and oil – the fossil fuels we find so valuable today. Present day ferns are usually quite small, although there are a few tropical species of tree fern which can reach a height of 15 m (50 ft).

Ferns produce spores in special cases called sporangia. At certain times of the year these may be seen as brown dots on the tips or undersides of the leaves, which are known as fronds. The spores are released and develop into a flat green structure called a prothallus. Male and female gametes are produced from the prothallus. After fertilization, the egg which is formed develops into a new fern.

There are about 9000 species of fern. Some, like the maidenhair fern, are very beautiful. The staghorn fern gets its name from its fronds which look like a stag's antlers. One of the most common ferns is bracken.

Hard fern

Ferret is a semi-domesticated form of polecat. The ferret usually has white fur and pink eyes. It has been used for hundreds of years to hunt rabbits and kill rats. A muzzled ferret is put down a rabbit burrow, and frightened rabbits are caught in nets as they escape from another burrow entrance. *See also* Polecats.

Ferry is a vessel designed to carry passengers, often with their cars, over short stretches of water, such as rivers or narrow sea straits. A ferry can be very small, sometimes consisting of no more than a wooden raft propelled by a pole; or it can be a large ship – the world's biggest ferry, *Finlandia*, carries over 300 cars and 1200 passengers across the Baltic Sea, and is powered by gas turbine engines very similar to those fitted to Concorde aircraft.

Fertilization is the joining of two special cells called gametes during sexual reproduction. Fertilization produces a single cell called a zygote. The male gametes are called sperms and the female gamete is called an ovum, or egg. Fertilization sometimes occurs *externally*, where gametes are shed into water. This occurs in animals such as starfish. *Internal* fertilization takes place in most land-living plants and animals. *See also* Egg; Pollination.

Fertilizer is a substance which is added to the soil to improve plant growth. The soil contains many chemicals, such as potassium, nitrogen and phosphorus, which plants need for healthy growth. As crop after crop is harvested, these chemicals are used up. Fertilizers contain these chemicals, and are put in the soil to replace them. Most fertilizers are manufactured, though other natural substances, such as manure and bonemeal, are fertilizers.

Fertilizers allow farmers to grow far more food, and over 60 million tonnes of fertilizers are used each year around the world.

Feudal system was a social and military system. A nobleman would grant the use of land to a vassal (tenant or servant) in return for service, often military, and homage. It originated during a period of disorder in western Europe in the 9th century and lasted until the 14th century. The king would distribute land to the higher nobility, who in their turn granted land to the lesser nobles and so on, each person pledging service and homage to the person from whom he received the land. The feudal system in the later Middle Ages declined for a variety of reasons, including the growth of towns outside the system and the centralization of royal authority.

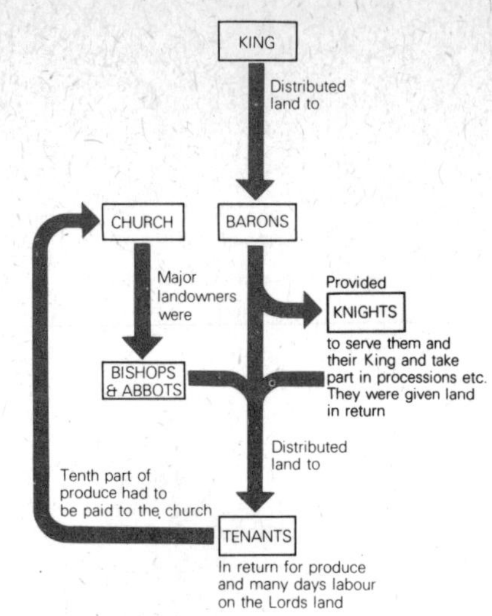

Fiji is an island group in the west Pacific Ocean. Capital, Suva; area about 18300 sq km (7070 sq miles). Fiji was a British colony until it became an independent republic in 1970. There are many islands, some too small for people to live on.

Fiji is a big producer of sugar, coconuts and bananas. The original inhabitants are Melanesians, but the largest group is Asian in origin, descendants of plantation workers brought from India.

Film is used in a camera when taking photographs. It is usually a special sort of paper coated with chemicals. Some substances, such as silver compounds, become dark when light falls on them. They are called light-sensitive substances and are used to coat the film. When photographs have been taken, the film is removed from the camera and other

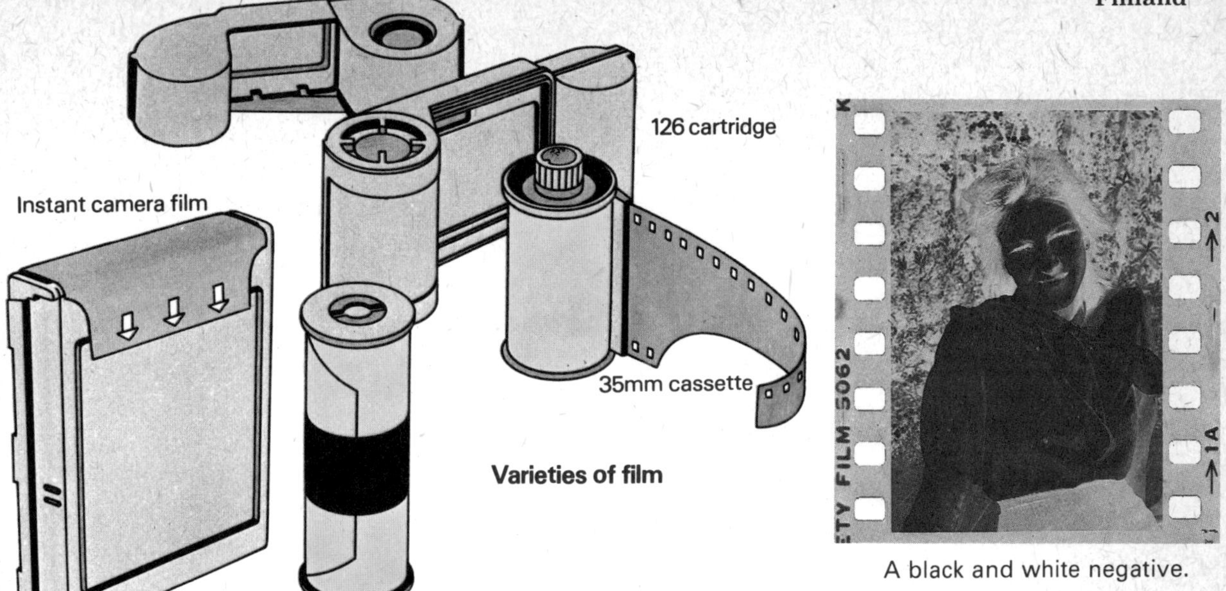

Varieties of film

A black and white negative.

chemicals are added to it. This is called developing and fixing, and the processes produce a negative. On a negative the light areas of the scene appear dark, and the dark areas appear light. In other words, everything is back to front. A photographic print is made by shining light through the negative onto a light-sensitive piece of paper. This makes the light areas of the scene light and the dark areas dark. The developing, fixing and printing of films is called processing.

Finch is a small, mainly tree-dwelling bird. Various species occur in North and South America, Eurasia and Africa, and they have been introduced to Australasia, too. Finches are seed eaters, and are well suited to this diet, for they have strong, conical bills which can deal with the toughest seeds. The crossbill has a specially shaped bill for extracting seeds from pine cones. The woodpecker finch of the Galapagos Islands is unusual: it uses a twig to extract insects from holes.

Fingerprint is the pattern of skin on the end of fingers and thumbs. The surface of the skin is covered with hundreds of tiny lines, and the tips of fingers have very clear lines which form curves and swirls.

By putting ink on the fingertips and then pressing them on a piece of paper, the pattern of these lines can be seen more easily. These are known as fingerprints. Everybody has slightly different fingerprints. Even identical twins do not have the same fingerprints.

In the days when many people could not write, fingerprints were often used instead of signatures. Now they are used to find criminals. The police keep records of the fingerprints of people who have committed crimes. Any fingerprints found at the scene of a crime can be checked against these records.

Finland is a republic in north-west Europe. Capital, Helsinki; area about 305 500 sq km (117 950 sq miles).
History The country was settled by Finnish people in prehistoric times. It was conquered by Sweden in the 12th century and the inhabitants were converted to Christianity. In the 18th century part of the country was annexed by Russia and in 1809 the rest of Finland came under Russian control with the status of an autonomous grand duchy. It declared itself an independent state in 1917 and became a republic two years later. After being defeated by the Soviet army in war in 1939–1940 and again in 1944 it was forced to cede certain territories to the USSR. After the Second World War Finland maintained a policy of careful neutrality.
Land and People Finland is a land of many lakes – they cover 10 per cent of the total area – but few mountains. It has extensive

forests, and timber is the main export. The long Baltic coast provides many good harbours. Finland has abundant water power, thanks to numerous, fast-flowing streams, and some mineral resources.

Less than 25 per cent of the people now depend on agriculture, and the standard of living is high.

Fins are the 'arms and legs' of water-dwelling animals such as fish and whales. In fact, although they are not truly arms and legs, they are supported by the same bones which make up arms and legs. Fins have flattened, oar-like shapes, and are used by the animal for balance, or sometimes to propel itself through the water by using the fin to literally push against the water.

Fish normally have two sets of paired fins. The pectoral fins near the front, behind the gills, and the pelvic fins underneath the body, help keep the fish level in the water. They also have single fins – dorsal on the back, anal near the tail and the tail fin itself – which help prevent the fish rolling from side to side. The tail is also used to propel the fish along. Some fish, the perch for instance, have two dorsal fins.

Fiord is a long, narrow, steep-sided inlet in a coastline. Fiords were created by the action of glaciers during the Ice Ages. The best-known fiords are those along the coast of Norway (the word *fjord* is Norwegian), but others occur in Greenland, Scotland, Canada, New Zealand and elsewhere.

Fire of London raged between 2 September and 5 September 1666. Beginning in a baker's shop in Pudding Lane, it spread very rapidly among the wooden buildings, destroying more than 13 000 of them, including old St Paul's Cathedral. London was so badly damaged that it had to be largely rebuilt, but the fire did succeed in cleansing the city of the infection left by the Plague in the previous year.

Fireworks were probably first made in China, where they were used to scare off enemies or evil spirits. They are now usually used for entertainment. In Britain, fireworks are lit on 5 November to celebrate the fact that a plot by Guy Fawkes to blow up the Houses of Parliament in 1605, failed.

Fireworks often contain a small amount of gunpowder and metals. When lit, they explode, producing sparks and bangs. Other substances in the fireworks burn with brilliantly coloured flames. For example, barium compounds burn with a green flame and strontium compounds burn with a red flame.

Firs of the genus *Abies* (true firs) are tall, dense, conical-shaped coniferous trees. Many are important to humans in the production of wood, paper and oils, and as ornamental or Christmas trees. The needle-shaped leaves of true firs grow singly, and leave a clean, round scar if detached. Those of the similar spruces tear, bringing a small strip of bark with them. True fir cones are borne upright on the branches, and leave a central core attached to the branch when the scales fall away. Some of the most common fir trees are the silver fir, the giant fir and the balsam fir of North America, and the nikko fir of Japan.

Fish are the most primitive vertebrates. Indeed, some living fish have hardly changed at all since the Devonian period (395 to 345 million years ago) when they were the dominant life forms on Earth. The coelacanth is a living representative of a group of fish which was thought to have become extinct more than 70 million years ago. Because fish live in water, they have developed gills with which to breathe and fins with which to propel themselves about.

Living fish are usually divided into three groups. The first group, lampreys and hagfish, look like, but are not related to, eels. They have a skeleton composed of cartilage, do not possess jaws, and have only rudimentary fins. The hagfish are all parasitic – usually on other fish – and some of the lampreys are parasitic also.

The second group is the sharks and rays. These fish have a skeleton composed of cartilage, but possess proper jaws. Sharks are the supreme hunters of the fish world, eating all kinds of living and dead animals.

The last group of fish is the bony fish. These also possess jaws, and they have a skeleton composed of bone, not cartilage. They include the most advanced fish, and are present in both sea water and fresh water. The bony fish include the eels, the deadly piranhas, the strange lungfish, and familiar ones like pike, cod, herring, guppies, trout and sturgeon.

Fitzgerald, F. Scott (1896–1940), was a US novelist. He was the spokesman of the 'Jazz Age' during the 1920s, a period of frivolity and extravagance which came to an end with the world slump of 1929. *This Side of Paradise* (1920) made the dashing, debonair Fitzgerald a popular success, but a much finer book, *The Great Gatsby* (1925) established him as a great writer. *Tender is the Night* (1934) and the unfinished *The Last Tycoon* (1941), as well as many fine short stories, confirmed his reputation. Heavy drinking led to his death at 44.

Flag is a coloured design, usually on cloth, which serves as the symbol of a country or of some other organization.

Flamingo is a beautiful bird with red or pink tinted feathers. It has long, slender legs, and large, down-curved bills on the end of a long neck. The bill has a sort of strainer which retains tiny food particles as the bird probes about in the water. Flamingos live and breed on shallow lakes and lagoons in tropical and sub-tropical Europe, Asia, Africa and America.

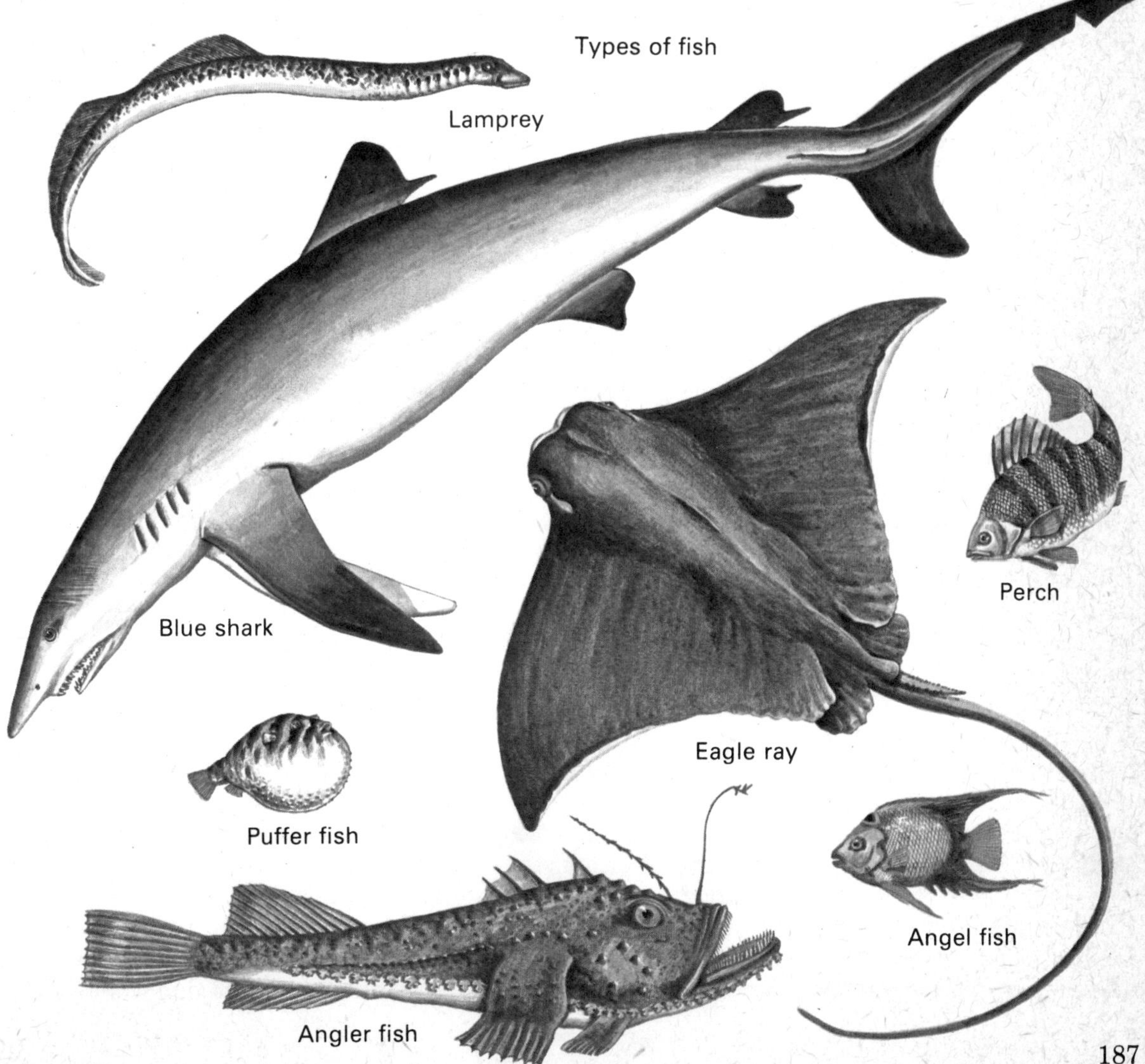

Types of fish

Flaubert, Gustave (1821–1880), was a French novelist. He is regarded as one of the world's greatest novelists and the founder of the realistic modern novel; but this reputation rests chiefly on one work, *Madame Bovary* (1857).

Flea is a tiny, flattened, wingless, parasitic insect. It feeds on the blood of warm-blooded animals (called the host) and has a spiky body which prevents it falling from, or being scratched from, its host's fur. Eggs are laid where a suitable host will rest. When the young fleas hatch, they wait for the host, and then they 'jump aboard'. Fleas have an amazing ability to jump, reaching up to 130 times their own height in one leap. They are up to 1 cm (0.4 in) long.

Fleming, Sir Alexander (1881–1955), was a Scottish scientist who discovered the antibiotic penicillin in 1928. Although he was already investigating substances that might resist bacteria, Fleming's actual discovery happened because of an accident. He was growing a tray of bacteria and found that it had become contaminated by a green mould. He noticed that the bacteria was failing to establish itself near the mould, and realized that the mould must be the antibacterial agent he was looking for. Even when heavily diluted, the mould – which Fleming called penicillin – continued to kill bacteria.

Fleming's discovery won him the Nobel Prize. It began the medical revolution which has made antibiotics one of the most important ways of treating infections.

Flower is the part of certain plants which is concerned with reproduction. Although flowers vary considerably in shape and colour, they all consist of a central axis called the *receptacle* into which are inserted four sets of parts. Outermost are the *sepals*. These are protective, but may sometimes be colourful to help attract insects. Next come the *petals*, whose job it is to attract insects and provide a landing platform when they come to visit a flower. Petals often produce sweet nectar too. Inside the petals are *stamens*. Each stamen consists of a stalk supporting a pollen bag. The stamens are the male flower parts. The female parts are called *carpels*. Each carpel consists of an ovary containing an ovule, and a stalk called the style. The tip of the style is called the stigma, and this is where pollen from the stamens is deposited during pollination. After fertilization, the ovule becomes a seed.

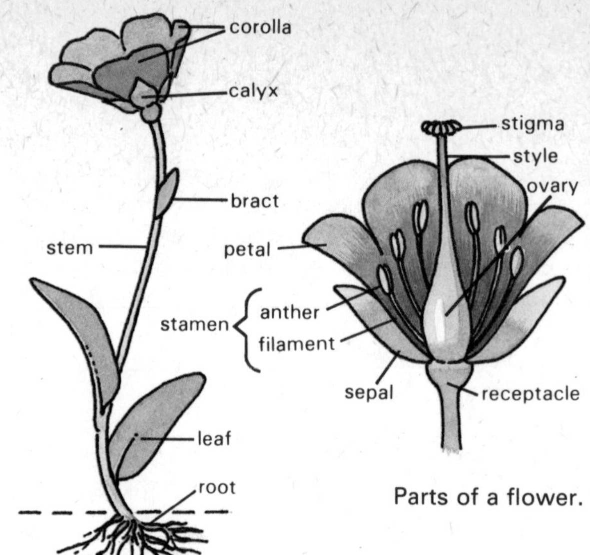

Parts of a flower.

Some flowering plants have flowers in which the various parts are highly modified, reduced or even lacking, depending on their life style. Thus, wind-pollinated plants do not need colourful flowers with bright, showy petals, and so these parts are missing. Other flowering plants have flowers which have only male or female parts. For fertilization to occur, the pollen must be carried to a different flower, or even a different plant.

Fluke is a parasitic member of a group of creatures known as flatworms. Some species live in the liver, gut, lung or blood vessel of vertebrates, and others live externally on the animal, or host. Flukes have flattened bodies armed with suckers which they use to cling to their host whilst they absorb food from it. Some, such as the internal parasite known as the liver fluke, can cause great damage to the host, even killing it.

Fluorine is a pale yellow gas with a strong smell. Its chemical symbol is F. Fluorine reacts more easily than any other chemical. It combines with nearly every element to form compounds called fluorides.

Bones and teeth contain fluorine, and fluorides are often added to drinking water or toothpaste to strengthen teeth.

Fly is an insect belonging to the order Diptera. Diptera means 'two-winged', and all flies have only one pair of wings. Behind the wings, some species of fly have a small pair of balancing organs called halteres.

Many flies are dangerous carriers of disease. The tsetse fly causes sleeping sickness, and even the common housefly can cause illness through its habit of feeding on animal faeces as well as human food.

Fly agaric is one of the most familiar of the wild fungi, and one that is often depicted in fairy tales. The fly agaric is so named because an extract made from it was formerly used as a fly poison. It is poisonous if eaten by humans, causing sickness.

Flying boat is an aircraft designed to take off and land on water. A large flying boat usually has a boat-shaped hull and extra floats under each wing. Such aircraft were very popular for a few years during the 1930s when long air routes were being developed, but there were very few airfields on which to land. As land-based aircraft became more reliable and could fly further, flying boats became less popular. Smaller seaplanes, usually light aircraft with floats fitted in place of wheels, are used in many remote parts of the world where a shortage of prepared landing strips makes water landings necessary. *See also* Aeroplane.

Flying doctor is a service started in the remote regions of Australia in 1926, intended to serve a population living on scattered farms far from medical aid. Today's Royal Flying Doctor Service has a large fleet of specially equipped aircraft, capable of landing on unprepared ground and fitted out as mobile ambulances, which can cope with many medical emergencies on the spot, or ferry casualties to hospital. Organizations similar to the RFDS have been set up in other remote parts of the world, such as Africa and South America.

Flying fish cannot truly fly, but they can leap from the water and glide above the waves for long distances. Flying fish are herring-like, and feed on plankton in tropical seas. They swim rapidly to the surface by means of their powerful tails – often at speeds of up to 32 km/h (20 mph). As they break the surface they spread their enlarged pectoral fins (and in some species their pelvic fins as well) and soar over the waves in a glide which may extend for many metres. Flying fish grow to about 45 cm (18 in) long.

Flying fox is not really a fox at all, but a fruit-eating bat, up to 40 cm (16 in) long. Flying foxes are found in Asia, Australia and on many Indian and Pacific Ocean islands. They get their name from their fox-like faces.

Flying Scotsman is a famous express train which ran from London's King's Cross station to Edinburgh every day. The name was also given to a powerful steam locomotive which was named after (and used to haul) the *Flying Scotsman* train. This locomotive, built in 1922, is preserved at Britain's National Railway Museum in York and is still used occasionally.

Foetus is the name given to young mammals which are still developing within their mother's womb, but in which features such as limbs, eyelids, and so on are recognizable.

Fokine, Mikhail (Michel) (1880–1942), was a Russian dancer and choreographer. He was one of the most powerful reforming influences on classical ballet.

Fokine wanted greater integrity in ballet – greater unity of music, dancer and decoration, less empty gestures and more use of the whole body. When Diaghilev formed his Ballet Russe, Fokine gained his opportunity. His most famous choreographic works included *Les Sylphides*, *Firebird* and *Daphnis and Chloe*.

Fokker, see Triplane.

Folk music consists of songs and dances with no known composer which are passed from one generation to the next. Folk music is associated particularly with country people, but the reason is probably that most folk music is older than cities.

In the 20th century scholars in many countries have carefully collected their local folk music, which was in danger of being forgotten as times changed. Many composers, such as Bartok or Dvořák, have made use of folk music in their own works.

Fonteyn, Dame Margot (1919–), is a British dancer. One of the outstanding ballerinas of the 20th century, she danced nearly all the major roles for ballerinas for the Royal Ballet during her long career, and created many new parts (the first in 1935, the last in 1972). Frederick Ashton made many ballets for her, and she was often partnered by Rudolf Nureyev.

Dame Margot Fonteyn and Rudolf Nureyev.

Food is needed by all animals and plants in order to live, for food provides the energy necessary for growth, movement and reproduction. Most plants make their own food out of water and carbon dioxide by a process called photosynthesis. Animals have to eat plants or other animals to obtain their food. Animals which eat plants are called herbivores. Animals which eat other animals are called carnivores.

People usually eat both plants and animals. Food must contain certain substances to keep us healthy. These are called carbohydrates, proteins, fats, vitamins and minerals. If people do not eat enough of any of these they become ill. This condition is called malnutrition. Many people in the world suffer from malnutrition, because they either do not have enough food to eat or do not have the right sort of food.

Food web is a term to describe how the animals and plants in a habitat feed, and how many of them are food for other creatures, and also how they vary their food requirements according to the seasons. Suppose a small creature such as an aphid eats a leaf, and a ladybird eats the aphid, which in turn is eaten by a bird, and then the bird is eaten by a cat. This sequence is called a food chain, for food has passed, in a chain-like fashion, from the leaf to the cat. In nature, many such chains exist, but normally the chains are linked, invisibly of course, to other food chains. For instance, the aphid in our example may be eaten directly by a bird which is already part of another food chain. This complicated series of connecting food chains is called the food web.

Force is anything which changes the motion of an object. A ball thrown into the air is pulled back to the ground by a force called gravity. A magnet can pull metal objects

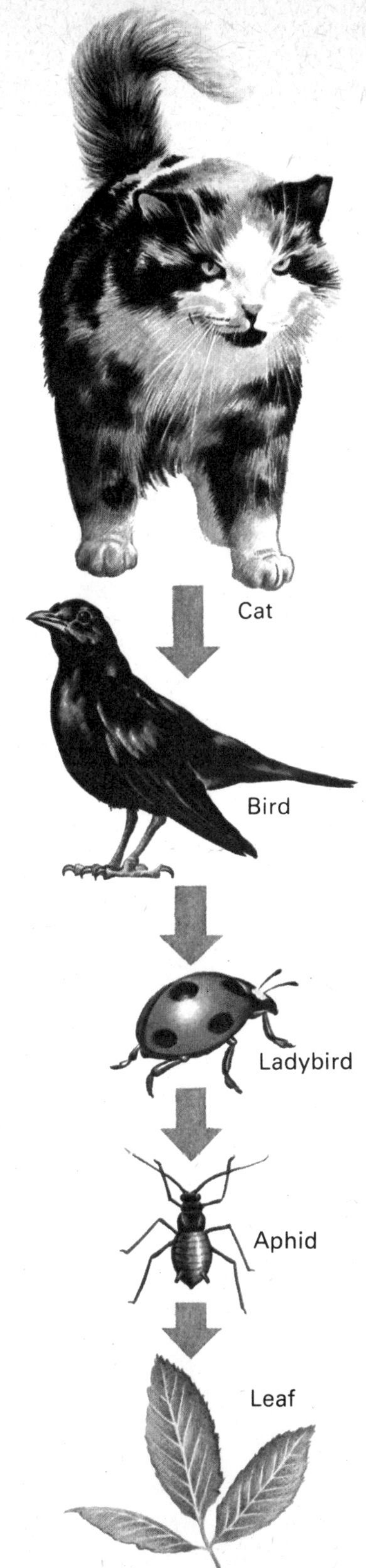

A food chain

towards it by a force called magnetism. A cyclist going down a steep hill can stop the bicycle by using a force called friction when the brakes are applied. There are many different forces.

The ways in which forces move objects was first studied by Sir Isaac Newton, and forces are measured in units called newtons.

Ford, Henry (1863–1947), was an American automobile manufacturer who invented modern methods of mass production to produce cheap and reliable cars. His process was introduced in 1908 to make the Model T, which was built from standard parts on a moving production line, halving the assembly time for each car. In this way, Ford made over 15 000 000 Model Ts and the car stayed in production until 1927. One of Ford's instructions was to simplify the paint scheme, leading to his famous slogan: 'You can have a Model T any colour you like, so long as it's black'.

Forensic medicine and science is a combination of medicine or science and legal matters. The skill of a doctor is sometimes needed to investigate a crime. This branch of medicine is called forensic medicine.

For example, if somebody has a wound a doctor will clean and try to heal the wound. If the wound may be due to a crime, a forensic doctor will also try to say what object made the wound, when it was made and whether it could have been an accident.

Scientists also help to investigate crimes. For example, tiny amounts of substances, such as blood and hair, found at the scene of a crime can be examined. These may give information about the criminal.

Forest is a large community of trees and shrubs. Usually it also supports a varied collection of other plants as well as animals such as birds, mammals, reptiles and insects. Thus, forests are an example of a habitat.

Throughout the world, there are several types of forest. The conifers grow in the cool parts of the Northern Hemisphere. Temperate regions support forests of deciduous hardwood trees such as oak, ash, elm and maple. Another group of hardwoods, including mahogany, ebony and teak, grow in tropical regions.

Formula, in chemistry, is symbols and figures used to express chemical compounds. A compound's formula shows which elements are in the compound and how much of each element is in the compound.

For example, table salt is sodium chloride and its formula is $NaCl$. This means that one molecule of table salt contains one atom of sodium (Na) and one atom of chlorine (Cl).

The formula for sulphuric acid is H_2SO_4. This shows that a sulphuric acid molecule contains two atoms of hydrogen (H), one atom of sulphur (S) and four atoms of oxygen (O).

Fossils are the remains or traces of animals and plants in rocks. When animals and plants die, they may become buried in soft ground, which later hardens into rock. Parts of the animals and plants can harden into rock or leave marks in the rock. This is called fossilization.

Whole animals and plants may be fossilized. Usually fossils are just parts of them, such as teeth, bones, shells, leaves or even footprints.

Fossils can be hundreds of millions of years old. Most are of animals and plants which no longer exist. Huge dinosaurs, and large elephants, called mammoths, are only known from their fossils.

The study of fossils is called palaeontology, and palaeontologists use fossils to trace how animals and plants have evolved.

Fox is a carnivore, in the same group as the wolves, jackals and dogs. Foxes are usually night hunters, feeding on birds, insects, lizards and small mammals, although they will also eat fruit and berries. The red fox of Eurasia, North America and North Africa generally hunts alone, but a pair may hunt together.

The fennec fox of the North African desert has a pale coat and large ears, which allow it to detect the smallest sound. The Arctic fox has a grey-brown coat in summer, and a white coat in winter. It feeds on birds, fish, seal pups and lemmings.

France is a republic in western Europe. Capital, Paris; area about 544 000 sq km (210 000 sq miles). The largest country in western Europe, France is one of the most prosperous industrial nations, and a leader of the EEC. Her imperial past and unequalled traditions in the arts make her still one of the most influential nations in the world. French cooking, French wine and French fashion lead all others, and Paris is one of the world's most attractive capital cities.

History The country was conquered by Julius Caesar in 51 BC, and remained a Roman province until it was overrun by Germanic tribes during the 3rd–5th centures AD. The Franks (after whom the country is named) settled in the north and the Goths and Burgundians in the south. The Franks became dominant and the Frankish empire under Charlemagne included much territory outside France.

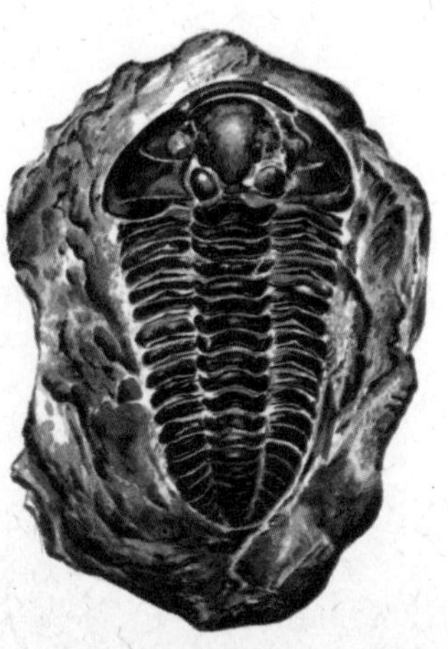

Some different fossils. *From left to right:* Ammonite (Jurassic period), Trilobite (Devonian period), Fern leaves (Carboniferous period).

General de Gaulle at the head of a triumphal procession in Paris, after the city was liberated from German occupation in 1944.

After the Norman Conquest of England in 1066 the kings of France had great difficulty in maintaining their authority over the whole country in the face of English claims to French lands and the power of the feudal nobility. However, royal power was gradually strengthened despite the setback of the Hundred Years' War.

During the 16th century the country was divided by religious wars but under Louis XIV France became the leading European power. During the 18th century there was a decline in the influence of the monarchy which ended with the Revolution of 1789 and the proclamation of a republic.

Under Napoleon's First Empire (1804–1814), France was briefly dominant in Europe, but during the 19th century under the restored monarchy, she experienced a series of political upheavals and the monarchy was overthrown in 1848. The Second Empire (1852–1870) collapsed when the French army was defeated in the Franco-Prussian War and was replaced by the Third Republic.

France suffered enormous casualties in the First World War and was occupied by Germany in the Second World War. In the postwar period France encountered serious problems with its overseas possessions, first in Indo-China and later in Algeria. The establishment of the Fifth Republic in 1959 with Charles de Gaulle as president, brought a period of stability. In 1981 a Socialist government led by François Mitterrand took office.

Rulers of France since 987

Capetian Line	
Hugh Capet	987–996
Robert II	996–1031
Henry I	1031–1060
Philip I	1060–1108
Louis VI	1108–1137
Louis VII	1137–1180
Philip II	1180–1223
Louis VIII	1223–1226
Louis IX	1226–1270
Philip III	1270–1285
Philip IV	1285–1314
Louis X	1314–1316
John	1316
Philip V	1316–1322
Charles IV	1322–1328
House of Valois	
Philip VI	1328–1350
John II	1350–1364
Charles V	1364–1380
Charles VI	1380–1422
Charles VII	1422–1461
Louis XI	1461–1483
Charles VIII	1483–1498
Louis XII	1498–1515
Francis I	1515–1547

Henry II	1547–1559
Francis II	1559–1560
Charles IX	1560–1574
Henry III	1574–1589
House of Bourbon	
Henry IV	1589–1610
Louix XIII	1610–1643
Louis XIV	1643–1715
Louis XV	1715–1774
Louis XVI	1774–1792
The First Republic	
National Convention	1792–1795
The Directory	1795–1799
The Consulate	1799–1804
The First Empire	
Napoleon I	1804–1814
The Restoration	
Louis XVIII	1814–1824
Charles X	1824–1830
Louis Philippe	1830–1848
The Second Republic	
Louis Napoleon (president)	1848–1852
The Second Empire	
Napoleon III	1852–1870
The Third Republic: Presidents	
Adolphe Thiers	1871–1873
Marshal MacMahon	1873–1879
Jules Grévy	1879–1887
Sadi Carnot	1887–1894
Jean Casimir-Périer	1894–1895
François Felix Faure	1895–1899
Emile Loubet	1899–1906
Armand Fallières	1906–1913
Raymond Poincaré	1913–1920
Paul Deschanel	1920
Alexandre Mulerand	1924–1931
Gaston Doumergue	1931–1932
Paul Doumer	1931–1932
Albert Lebriun	1932–1940
Vichy Government	
Philippe Pétain (head of state)	1940–1944
The Fourth Republic: Presidents	
Vincent Auriol	1947–1954
René Coty	1954–1959
The Fifth Republic: Presidents	
Charles de Gaulle	1959–1969
Georges Pompidou	1969–1974
Valery Giscard d'Estaing	1974–1981
François Mitterand	1981–

Land and People The landscape varies greatly. It includes high mountains on the eastern and southern borders, especially the Alps and Pyrennees – the high plateau of the Massif Central towards the south-east, and the productive lowlands of north and west. The climate is generally mild – on the Mediterranean coast throughout the year, although winter on the Massif Central can be very cold.

In spite of the long and proud traditions of French culture, there are strong differences among the French themselves. Brittany is a Celtic land with its own language, and there are many other minorities, including North Africans (mostly Algerians). Differences in the food from one region to another are one sign of the continuance of strong local traditions. The majority of French people are Roman Catholics.

Economy Agriculture is very important and a wide variety of crops is grown. However, it is still largely organized in small units. Wine is a major export, and so is cheese, of which there are hundreds of distinct types.

In natural resources, France lacks some of the resources of neighbours like Germany. There are large reserves of iron ore and aluminium, but fuels are in short supply. France has therefore been a world leader in exploiting other sources of power, such as hydro-electric power and, experimentally, energy from the movement of the tides. Manufacturing industry is widely developed – from motor vehicles to silk scarves.

Francis of Assissi, Saint (1182 – 1226), was an Italian friar. The son of a rich merchant, his life was changed by two dreams during an illness when he was in his twenties. He gave his money to the poor and took up a life of prayer, poverty and service in imitation of Jesus Christ. He founded the Franciscan order of friars, but eventually retired to live as a hermit with a few companions. St Francis regarded all creatures as God's work; many stories are told of his love of animals.

Franco, Francisco (1892–1975), was a Spanish soldier and statesman. In his youth he served with the army in Morocco and achieved rapid promotion. Appointed chief of

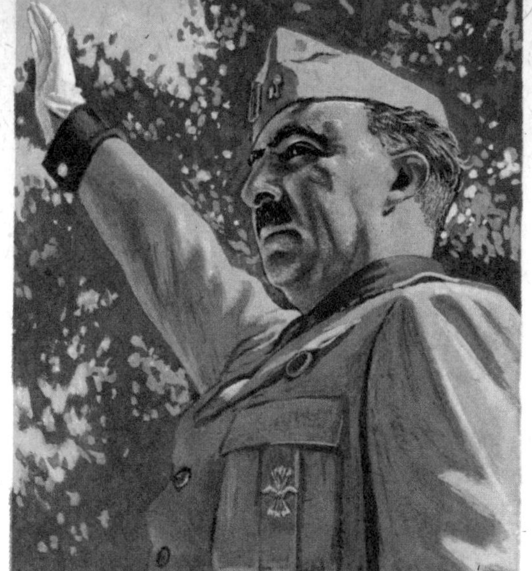

Francisco Franco

the general staff in 1935, he joined the conspiracy against the Popular Front government. When Civil War broke out in 1936, rebel forces in Morocco led by Franco invaded Spain and quickly occupied large areas of the country. However, it took nearly three years of ruthless fighting for Franco to bring the whole country under his control. When the war ended with the surrender of Madrid in 1939, Franco became head of state, a position he held until his death. He achieved considerable economic progress for his country, but ruled as a dictator until his death.

Frederick the Great (1712–1786), was King of Prussia (1740–1786). His military genius made Prussia one of the leading European powers. In the War of the Austrian Succession (1740–1748) he defeated Austria and gained Silesia. His victory in the Seven Years' War (1756–1763) made Prussia the dominant military force in Europe, and in the First Partition of Poland (1772) he acquired further territories. At home he introduced important legal, financial and military reforms, and was a great patron of artists and writers, including Voltaire.

Freezing point is the temperature at which a liquid changes to a solid. This happens when a liquid is cooled to a certain temperature. For example, water, when it is cooled, freezes to solid ice. Different liquids have different freezing points. The freezing point of water is 0 degrees Centrigrade (32 degrees Fahrenheit).

French Guiana is a French province in north-east South America. Capital, Cayenne; area about 91 000 sq km (35 135 sq miles). Once famous for its prison on Devil's Island, it has been reorganized as a *departement* (province) since 1946. It is mostly a low-lying, steamy country, with forested mountains in the interior. The population is a mixture of people of South American, African and European descent. Agriculture is limited to a small coastal region, but there are valuable minerals, including gold, and a large shrimp fishery.

French Revolution was the political upheaval in France from 1789 to 1799 which led to the overthrow of the monarchy and the establishment of a republic. During the 1780s France was in a desperate financial state, and in 1789 King Louis XVI was forced to call a meeting of the Estates General (nobility, clergy and Third Estate, or common people) to find some way to pay the country's debts. When the meeting was held at Versailles the people refused to let themselves be dominated by the nobility and clergy. They broke away to form a National

The fall of the Bastille, an infamous fortress and prison in Paris, during the French Revolution.

Assembly, representing the majority of the French people.

Events followed quickly: the Bastille was stormed, there were riots in Paris and the royal family were forced to leave Versailles and live in the capital. In 1791 a new constitution was introduced after the King had attempted unsuccessfully to flee the country.

The Revolution then took a more extreme course. A National Convention was appointed which declared France a republic. In January 1793 the King was executed and later that year a Reign of Terror began, in which thousands of people were executed. This ended in 1794 with the downfall of Robespierre. A Directory was established in 1795, and the Revolution finally ended in 1799 when Napoleon Bonaparte took charge of the country.

Frequency is used to describe sound, light and other waves. It is measured by the number of waves which pass a given point each second. The frequency is expressed as Hertz. High-frequency waves can pass through many substances. X-rays and gamma rays are like light, but have much higher frequencies. High-frequency sound waves are called ultrasonic sound. Ultrasonics, X-rays and gamma rays can go into the human body, and are used in medicine. *See also* Wave; Wavelength.

Fresco is a method of painting on plaster – usually a wall. Frescoes differ from murals (ordinary wall paintings) because the paint is applied when the plaster is still wet (*fresco* means 'fresh'). The paint becomes part of the plaster which, as it dries, forms a protective layer to preserve the colours. Fast working is necessary: the masters of fresco made careful sketches and a full-size drawing, or cartoon, before they started. Although fresco existed in ancient times, it is particularly characteristic of the Renaissance in Italy.

Freud, Sigmund (1856–1939), was an Austrian doctor. He is the father of much modern psychology and psychiatry. He believed that there are parts of the mind of which we are not usually aware. He called these parts the unconscious mind. Freud said that many thoughts and feelings, particularly sexual feelings, were pushed away into the unconscious minds of most people. These could sometimes make people act in strange ways and cause illnesses of the mind.

Freud tried to get his patients to release these thoughts and feelings, and was particularly interested in their childhood memories and dreams. The method he used to treat patients is known as psychoanalysis. His ideas were not accepted until about 1930, and have been developed and altered by many other psychologists.

Friction is what happens when two surfaces rub or move against each other. Friction

The Raising of Lazarus, a detail from the fresco painted by Giotto in 1305–9.

slows down or stops movement, and makes the surfaces that rub together hot. Bicycle brakes use friction. They push against the bicycle wheel, and the friction between the brakes and the wheel stops the bicycle. Cars going around corners are held to the road by the friction between the tyres and the road.

Friction can be harmful. Machine parts rubbing against each other can cause wear, slow the machine down and make it hot. Machines are oiled to reduce friction.

Frog is an amphibian which, like the toad, has adapted well to life on land. There are frogs which climb trees and others which live in deserts, as well as many kinds which live in forests, woods or by grassy banks. Although most frogs must return to water to breed, a few species have reduced this dependence to a minimum, even carrying the eggs in moist pockets on the adults' bodies.

Frogs are often distinguished from toads by the fact that they have smooth skins (unlike the warty skin of toads). They can usually jump well, using their long back legs. Frogs eat almost anything they can swallow – usually insects and worms. The tongue can shoot out at great speed to catch flying insects. Frogs range in colour from the greens and browns of many tree or forest-dwelling species, to the brilliant reds and blues of the arrow-poison frogs of South America. The largest frog is the goliath frog, an African rainforest species which grows to a weight of 3 kg (7 lb). *See also* Tadpole.

Marsh frog

Frond is the leaf of a fern. Fern fronds are often divided into many smaller leaflets.

Frond is also the term for the main part of the body of a seaweed, such as a wrack or kelp. The frond of a seaweed is usually attached to a flexible stalk called the stipe, and this is itself anchored to a rock.

Fruit – after fertilization has taken place in a flower, the ovule within the carpel becomes a seed, and the ovary wall swells. The sepals, petals and stamens all wither and drop off. The swollen or ripened ovary wall enclosing the seed is now called a fruit. There are several different kinds of fruit. Succulent fruits are called berries, and after the juicy ovary has been eaten by an animal the seed passes unharmed through the body. Sometimes the fruit is hard, however, and forms a nut.

Fuel is a substance which is used to make energy. Coal, petroleum and natural gas are burnt to give heat, and are called fossil fuels. Petrol and diesel oil, which are made from petroleum, are common fuels. They are used to fuel cars, planes and ships. Uranium is a fuel. It is not burnt, but is used to make electricity in nuclear reactors. Electricity can be made from water and wind so they, too, are sometimes fuels. *See also* Energy; Nuclear reactor.

Fungus is a member of the large group of non-flowering plants which includes the mushrooms, toadstools, rusts and moulds. Fungi do not make their own food, for they do not possess chlorophyll. Instead, they must obtain their food ready made, and so they live on living or dead animals and plants (called hosts), absorbing nutrients through the walls of their cells.

A fungus has no stem, roots or leaves. Instead, the body of a fungus – called a mycelium – consists of minute threads called hyphae. These branch in all directions and run between and into the body of the host. At certain times of the year the fungus reproduces by producing spores in structures called fruiting bodies. Fruiting bodies vary greatly according to the species, but among the more common are those of mushrooms and toadstools. The fruiting body erupts from the ground as a long stalk upon which is a flattish cap. From beneath the cap millions and millons of spores rain down from either tiny thin plates called gills, or from minute tubes. When these spores land in a suitable place they form a new mycelium.

Fungi are a very widespread and important group of plants. Nearly a third of all known plants are fungi. They are helpful to humans in the brewing and baking industry, and as a source of antibiotics. They also aid the whole of nature for they break down dead matter and release valuable nutrients. However, some fungi can cause diseases – to crops for instance – and must be controlled by spraying with fungicides.

Fur, see Hair.

Fuse is a safety device put into an electrical circuit. Electricity can make substances hot. If too much electricity flows through a wire, it can become too hot and start a fire, or damage televisions, radios and other electrical appliances.

A fuse stops too much electricity flowing through. It is a thin piece of wire which melts easily. Too much electricity makes the wire melt, breaking the circuit. The fuse then has to be replaced. Plugs and many electrical devices have fuses in them. *See also* Circuit.

Fruiting bodies of some fungi.

G

Gabon is a republic in west-central Africa. Capital, Libreville; area about 267 000 sq km (103 300 sq miles). Formerly part of French Equatorial Africa, Gabon has been independent since 1960. Much of the country is covered with dense, equatorial forest, which also provides the most valuable exports. The main item is okoumé wood, used for plywood.

The majority of the people live by simple farming, but Gabon is comparatively fortunate with its natural resources. Besides timber, these include manganese (one of the world's largest deposits), gold, uranium and a host of other valuable minerals.

The Gabonese belong, traditionally, to a large variety of smallish tribal groups, the Fang being the most numerous. There are still strong links with France.

Gagarin, Yuri (1934–1968), was the first man in space – he completed one orbit of Earth on 12 April 1961 in the Russian Vostok 1 capsule. Before becoming a cosmonaut, Gagarin was a Soviet air force test pilot.

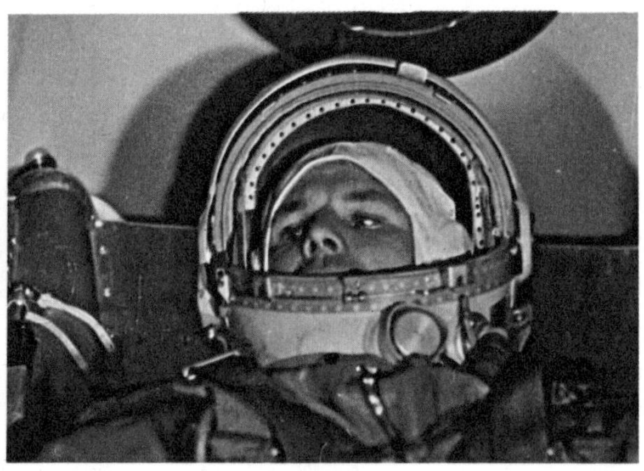

Yuri Gagarin in his Vostok spacecraft.

Gainsborough, Thomas (1727–1788), was one of the greatest English painters. His two main subjects were portraits and landscapes. He painted portraits to make money and landscapes because that was his greatest interest. Often he managed to combine the two by painting his portrait subjects in the open air – but he conscientiously devoted as much care to the human figures as to the scenery. His best-known painting is probably *The Blue Boy*, a token of Gainsborough's respect for Van Dyck.

Galapagos Islands are a small group of islands belonging to Ecuador in the eastern Pacific. Total area about 7850 sq km (3030 sq miles). The Equator runs through the islands, but ocean currents make the climate temperate. There are few inhabitants; mostly fishermen and their families.

The Galapagos are famous for their unusual wild life, such as the giant tortoises. Charles Darwin visited them in 1835, gaining ideas for his future work on evolution.

Galaxy is a huge number of stars grouped together. Our Galaxy contains about 100 000 million stars. It looks like a disc with a fat centre and spiral arms. From the front it looks like a slowly spinning Catherine Wheel. From the side it looks like a convex lens. The Sun is about two-thirds of the way from the centre of the Galaxy. The Sun takes 225 million years to travel around the Galaxy. Because of its shape, our Galaxy is classed as a spiral galaxy. Other galaxies have different shapes and sizes. The nearest galaxies to our Galaxy are the Magellanic clouds. *See also* Hubble classification; Magellanic clouds.

Galileo Galilei (1564–1642), was an Italian astronomer, physicist and mathematician, a pioneer of experimental science.He realized that a pendulum can be used to measure time. With his pendulum, he was able to study motion. His many discoveries formed the basis for Newton's laws of motion.

Galileo also made the first thermometer and the first telescope which could be used for astronomy. Using this, he discovered four moons of Jupiter and described the Milky Way. He supported Copernicus's views that the Earth moved round the Sun.

Gama, Vasco da (circa 1469–1524), was a Portuguese navigator, the first person to sail from Europe round Africa to the East. His expedition, which was sponsored by the king of Portugal, set off in 1497, rounded Cape of Good Hope and sailed up to East Africa. He was then guided across the sea to India, reaching Calicut in May 1498. His voyage opened up trade with the East Indies and also led to the foundation of Portugal's overseas empire.

Gambia, The, is a republic in West Africa. Capital, Banjui; area about 10 600 sq km (4090 sq miles). The Gambia, formerly a British colony, became independent in 1965 and is the smallest country in Africa. Political disturbances led to the formation of a close defensive connection with neighbouring Senegal.

The country consists of little more than the valley of the Gambia River. Rice is grown on what used to be mangrove swamps, and peanuts are the main export. The capital, formerly called Bathurst, is an attractive city; but upstream, the climate is very hot and humid.

Gamma (γ) ray is an electromagnetic ray. (Light is another sort of electromagnetic radiation but it has a longer wavelength.) Gamma rays travel at the same speed as light, and have very short wavelengths. They can pass through as much as 25 cm (1 ft) of metal. Gamma rays are given off by radioactive elements.

Gamma rays can be harmful, and so the radioactive elements which emit them are kept in thick metal containers. These protect the people handling them from the radiation.

Gamma rays are used in medicine to diagnose illnesses and to treat cancer, and some artificial satellites contain gamma-ray telescopes. Gamma rays are also given off by stars, and are studied by astronomers.

Gandhi, Indira (1917–), became India's first woman Prime Minister in 1966, succeeding Lal Bahadur Shastri. She was the daughter of Jawaharlal Nehru. Following India's defeat of Pakistan in a war in 1971, she won a notable victory in a general election. In 1975 she declared a state of emergency in India. Defeated in the election of 1977, she was returned to power in 1980.

Gandhi, Mohandas Karamchand (1869–1948), was an Indian political and religious leader. After studying law in London he went to South Africa, where he campaigned for rights for Indians living there. Returning to India he took up the cause of independence for his country, which he wanted to achieve by non-violent means. Imprisoned by the British on various occasions for civil disobedience, he played a prominent part in the various conferences held to discuss India's future. A saintly man, he campaigned on behalf of the untouchables (the lowest Indian class) and tried to reconcile Hindus and Muslims. He was assassinated by a Hindu fanatic.

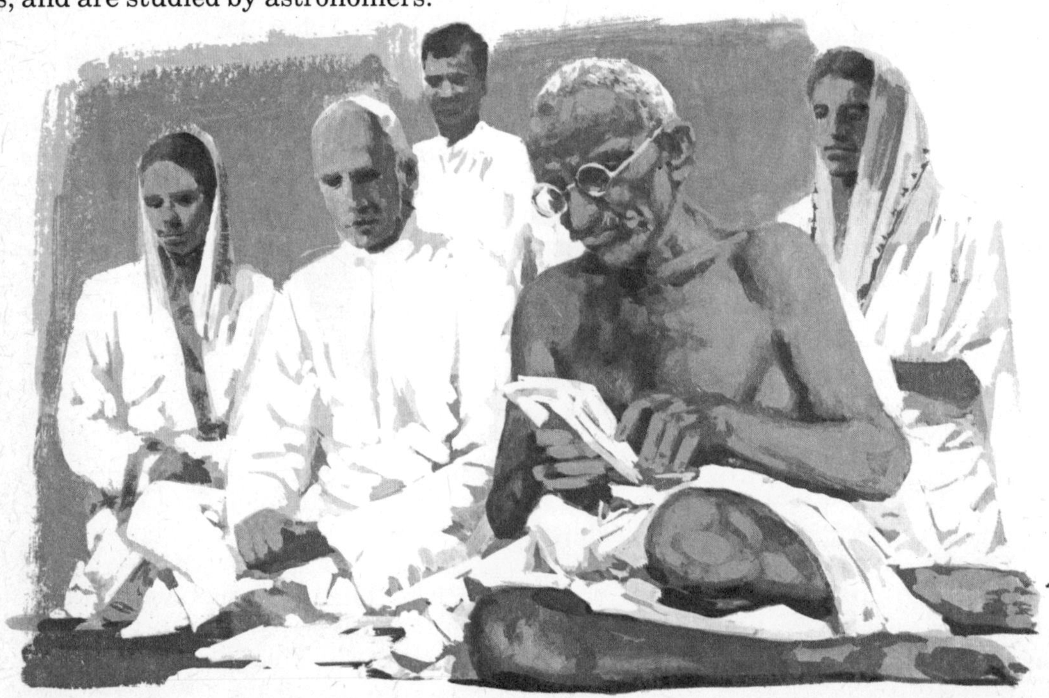

Gandhi fasting in protest against the delay in India's progress towards independence.

Ganges is a river in the Indian sub-continent. It rises in the Himalayas and flows for about 2500 km (1553 miles) to its junction with the Brahmaputra in Bangladesh. Its valley is extremely fertile and supports a large population on the adjacent plains.

The Ganges is a sacred river for Hindus, and pilgrims flock to the shrines on its banks, notably at Benares.

Garibaldi, Giuseppe (1807–1882), was an Italian soldier and patriot who played a leading part in the movement for the unification of Italy. Forced to leave Italy because of his political views, he returned to take part in the revolution of 1848, when he fought against the Austrians. He subsequently defended Rome against the French. In 1860 with a band of 1000 volunteers he conquered Sicily and Naples, which afterwards became part of the new kingdom of Italy.

Gas is the name given to a substance which has no fixed shape or volume. Particles of gas can move to fill any space and form any shape. Air is a gas, which fills all the space around us.

If a gas is cooled it turns into a liquid. Steam is a gas, which cools to form water. All substances become gases if they are heated. Even iron melts to form a liquid and eventually boils to a gas when heated to a very high temperature.

Gas cloud is a huge cloud of gas and dust. There are many in our Galaxy. Most of the gas is hydrogen. These gas clouds are known as nebulae. We know very little about them, although astronomers have put forward certain theories about them.

Stars could be formed from these clouds. A large gas cloud could form hundreds of stars. Some gas clouds, like Orion, are bright. They contain young stars. Others are dark. Inside these, stars may be forming.

When an old star explodes, gas is thrown out into space. Some of this may form part of another gas cloud. So a new star could be formed from the remains of an old one.

Gauguin, Paul (1848–1903), was a French painter of the Post-Impressionist school. He is remembered especially for the paintings of his last years, when he lived in poverty in Tahiti. Gauguin adopted a simplified design in his pictures which, with his rich colours, made him a major influence on modern art.

Gazelle is a delicate antelope, species of which are found in Africa and Asia. They are about 60–75 cm (2 ft–2 ft 6 ins high). The males have long, curved horns, but the females have only very short horns. They both have a white streak down either side of the face. Most gazelles roam in herds on the plains, looking for grass and other vegetation to eat, but always alert to danger from predators such as lions.

Gecko is a lizard which can climb up walls and even walk upside down over ceilings. This ability is due to muscular suction pads on their feet which enable them to grip the smoothest of surfaces. Geckos live in warm countries, and are often seen in houses where they hunt for insects. They make a noise that sounds like 'gecko', from which they get their name. There are about 650 species of gecko, which are from 3 to 15 cm (1 to 6 in) long.

Gemini project was the second major space programme undertaken by the USA, following their successful Mercury project. Gemini

Gemini 10 approaches an Agena rocket prior to docking with it.

spacecraft, as the name implies, carried two astronauts who pioneered most of the systems which would be needed for the trip to the Moon in Apollo. Space 'walking' (to perform tasks outside the capsule in space), rendezvous and docking of spacecraft, manoeuvring in space and spending enough time in space (eight days) for the lunar trip were all tried out on the 12 Gemini missions.

Gemstone is a cut and polished mineral which is used in jewellery and ornaments. Usually only rare, beautiful and hard minerals are used to make gemstones. They are cut and polished so that they shine and sparkle in the light.

Gemstones are also called precious stones. Their value depends on their colour and size – diamonds, rubies, sapphires and emeralds are among the most valuable.

Generator is a machine used to make, or generate, electricity in a power station. If a magnet is rotated within a coil of wire, an electric current flows in the wire. If the coil of wire is moved instead of the magnet an electric current also flows.

A generator contains coils of wire called an armature. The armature is rotated within magnets, and an electric current flows in the armature. The armature itself is turned by another machine called a turbine.

Genetics is the study of heredity, and the resulting variations. Any plant or animal has a number of features by which it can be recognized. Some of these features are physical, and others physiological (in other words, to do with the way the organism functions). Discovering which of these features are transmitted from parent to offspring, and how, is what scientists call heredity. *See also* Mendel, Gregor.

Geneva is a city in west Switzerland. It occupies most of the canton (state) of Geneva, and spreads along the shores of Lake Geneva.

Genghis Khan (circa 1162–1227), was a Mongol chieftain and military genius. After a long struggle he gained control of Mongolia (1206). He went on to conquer northern China (1213–1215) and large areas of central Asia, reaching as far west as Persia and southern Russia. At his death his empire

A map of Genghis Khan's empire.

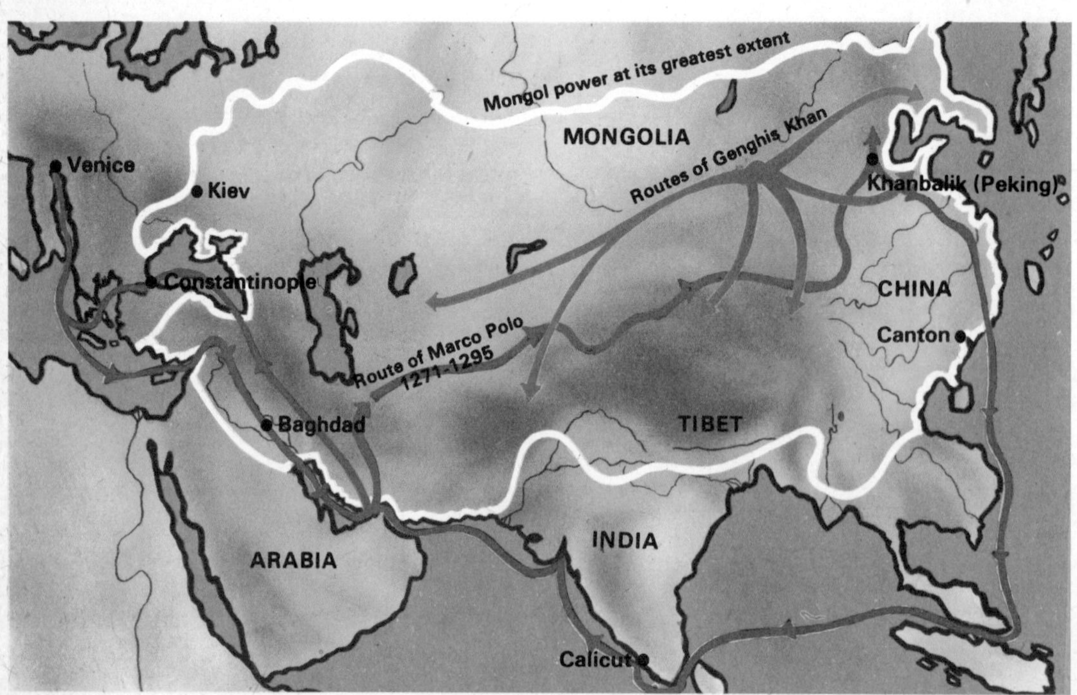

stretched from the Yellow Sea to the Black Sea.

Geological time scale measures the time from the Earth's formation to the present. It is divided up into eras, periods and epochs. The Earth is thought to have been formed about 4500 million years ago. The oldest rocks on the Earth are nearly 3800 million years old. Life is thought to have started on Earth about 3400 million years ago.

Geology is the study of the structure of the Earth. Since the Earth was formed, its surface has been constantly changing, and mountains and valleys have been forming. Many different animals and plants have lived on Earth. Geologists study the Earth's changes and find out what may have caused them. Many of the Earth's changes are explained by the theory known as plate tectonics.

Geologists particularly study the rocks and minerals near the Earth's surface. Many of these contain metals and other valuable substances. The oil and coal in the Earth are also needed. Geologists investigate where these can be found. *See also* Plate tectonics.

George I (1660–1727), was King of Great Britain and Ireland (1714–1727) and Elector of Hanover (1698–1727). He was the first Hanoverian monarch of Britain under the Act of Settlement of 1701. He did not play much part in British affairs, and did not speak English; he left the administration of the country to his ministers.

George II (1683–1760), was King of Great Britain and Ireland (1727–1760). Like his father, George I, he continued to rely on the ministers in his government. This encouraged the evolution towards a constitutional monarchy. He was the last British king to lead his troops into battle – at Dettingen in 1743.

George III (1738–1820), was King of Great Britain and Ireland (1760–1820), in succession to his grandfather, George II. He attempted to assert greater control over the government of the country and strongly supported the war against the American colonists. He was also opposed to Catholic emancipation and other reforms. When he became ill in 1811 a regency was established under his son.

George IV (1762–1830), was King of Great Britain and Ireland (1820–1830). He became King on his father's death in 1820, having held the position of Regent for nine years. His dissipated extravagant lifestyle made him unpopular, and his attempt to divorce his wife, Caroline of Brunswick, lowered the prestige of the monarchy.

George V (1865–1936), was King of Great Britain and Northern Ireland (1910–1936), in succession to his father Edward VII. Early in his reign he had to face constitutional crises over the reform of the House of Lords and Home Rule for Ireland. In 1917 the royal family's name was changed from Saxe-Coburg-Gotha to Windsor. He became popular through his Christmas Day radio broadcasts.

George VI (1895–1952), was King of Great Britain and Northern Ireland (1936–1952). The second son of George V, he succeeded to the throne on the abdication of his brother, Edward VIII. During the Second World War he and the royal family stayed in London and endured the worst German bombing, which boosted the morale of his subjects.

Georgian is a general term used to describe the style in architecture etc. in Britain during the 18th century (strictly, from 1714, when George I came to the throne). It is perhaps most distinguished for its plain but elegant town housing (like Edinburgh's New Town). Larger buildings were generally in the Classical style of Palladio with, later, the enchanting decoration of Robert Adam.

German Democratic Republic is the official name for East Germany in central Europe. Capital, East Berlin; area about 108 000 sq km (42 000 sq miles). Since 1949 it has been a communist state, one of the Soviet

Union's most loyal allies.

Land The north is mostly a low, sandy plain, with small hills, shallow lakes and marshes. In the south it is more mountainous, and, on the Czechoslovak border, rises to 1244 m (4081 ft) in the Erzgebirge ('Ore Mountains'). The Elbe flows from south-east to north-west across the country and another river, the Oder, forms part of the eastern border.

Economy East Germany is highly industrialized, and the majority of people live in towns and cities in the industrial region of the south and south-west. The country is the world's largest producer of lignite, a type of coal; other important minerals are potash, copper and iron ore.

Agriculture is also well developed, with large crops of sugar beet, potatoes and cereals.

Germany is a former nation that was divided into two independent countries after the Second World War. (*See* German Democratic Republic; Germany, Federal Republic of.)

History The region was inhabited by Germanic tribes from earliest times. It came under Frankish domination in the 6th and 7th centuries AD, and was converted to Christianity. Germany began as a distinct entity after its separation from France in 843 to form the Kingdom of the East Franks.

The German empire was the successor to the Roman Empire, but the struggle between the papacy and the Holy Roman emperors (a title revived by the German King, Otto I) over the continuing domination of Italy and Rome (the centre of the Christian faith) led to increased power among local princes. There was eastward expansion under the Hapsburg emperors, Prussia being conquered in the 13th century. However, the difficulty in establishing a centralized monarchy was made worse by the Protestant Reformation, which split Germany up into Catholic and Protestant states.

The country suffered greatly during the Thirty Year's War, but in the 18th century Prussia became a dominant power in Europe at the expense of Austria (also part of the empire). In the 19th century Prussia led the movement for German unification which was finally achieved after the Franco-Prussian War (1870–1871). Germany rapidly became an important industrial power and acquired colonies overseas.

In 1914 Germany's support for Austria helped to bring about the First World War and after Germany's defeat in 1918 a republic was established. This was followed by the rise to power of the Nazis under Adolf Hitler whose expansionist policies brought about the Second World War. After the war Germany was divided into West and East Germany.

Germany, Federal Republic of, is the official name for West Germany in central Europe. Capital, Bonn; area about 248 600 sq km (96 000 sq miles). It originated as the area occupied by British, French and US forces after the defeat of Germany in the Second World War, East Germany being the Soviet-controlled zone.

Land and People The north is mostly flat or rolling country, becoming more hilly in the centre and mountainous in the south, towards the Alps. Much of the mountains is also densely wooded. The Black Forest is a mountainous region which is heavily forested. The Rhine, one of the great rivers of

The German Emperor Wilhelm II (1859–1941).

Europe, flows through south-west Germany into the Netherlands. The Ems, Weser and Elbe, all flowing into the North Sea, are important waterways in the north, and the Danube rises in the Black Forest and flows across the south.

As Germany was only united in the 19th century, there are strong regional differences, particularly between north and south. Saxons, Rhinelanders and Prussians (north) tend to be tall and fair. Bavarians and Swabians (south) to be short and dark. The north is predominantly Protestant, the south Roman Catholic.

Economy After the Second World War, the economy had to be almost totally rebuilt. It soon became the most efficient and productive in Europe. The standard of living is higher than in any other EEC country.

Heavy industry is concentrated in the coal-producing region of the Ruhr. Manufactures include steel, motor vehicles, industrial machinery, electrical goods and a great variety of other products. The factories are among the most up-to-date, in terms of technology, in the world.

Agriculture is also efficient, especially on the fertile plains, though farms are mostly small. The traditional German fondness for pork makes pig-farming a major industry, though beef and dairy products are also important. Some of the world's most esteemed white wines come from the valleys of the Rhine and Mosel.

Germination is the process whereby plant seeds or spores 'come to life' and begin to produce a new plant. Germination will only take place if the seed or spore lands in a suitable place and has the correct temperature, water and oxygen conditions.

Let us look at what happens to the seed of a flowering plant. First, in the presence of water it begins to swell, and the now softened seed coat bursts. From the seed a tiny root grows. No matter which way up the seed has landed, the root grows downwards. Then the first shoot appears, pulling with it the first leaves, the cotyledons. The shoot always grows up towards the light. Whilst the seed is germinating it relies on food stored in the seed or the cotyledons, but soon it produces leaves which can make their own food.

Gettysburg, Battle of, was the most important battle of the American Civil War. It was fought in July 1863 in Pennsylvania, when a Confederate army led by Robert E. Lee was defeated by a Northern army under George Meade. It marked a turning point in the war and inspired President Abraham Lincoln to deliver his famous Gettysburg Address later the same year.

Geyser is a hot spring which intermittently sends up great jets of hot water, accompanied by clouds of steam. These spurt up through a crack or hole in the ground, at regular or irregular intervals. In some cases the jet reaches a height of 70 m (230 ft) or more.

The word 'geyser' comes from the Icelandic word *geysir* meaning 'gusher'. There are many geysers in Iceland, on New Zealand's North Island and at the Yellowstone National Park, USA. Yellowstone's 'Old Faithful' is probably the best-known geyser, erupting with great force every half- to one-and-a-half hours.

Geysers are found in volcanic areas. Their channels run deep into the Earth, where the water that seeps into them is subjected to intense heat. It suddenly converts to steam, which flings out quantities of water at the top of the channel.

Ghana is a republic in West Africa. Capital, Accra; area about 238 000 sq km (92 000 sq miles).

History Ghana was first settled by the Portuguese in the late 15th century. Coastal forts were built by the British, Danes and Dutch in the 17th and 18th centuries. The country was made a British colony called the Gold Coast in 1874, and gained independence in 1957.

Land and People The scenery ranges from rainforest in the south to tropical savannah in the north. There are no hills above 1000 m (3280 ft). The climate is hot and humid most of the year. The background of the people is varied; and over 30 languages or dialects are

spoken. Islam is strong in the north, Christianity in the south.
Economy The largest export crop is cocoa, but some gold is still produced and, more recently, diamonds, as well as more ordinary but valuable minerals such as bauxite (aluminium). However, fuel is short. The land is generally poor, but supports many cattle. Fishing is a major occupation on the coast, and developments on the Volta, the chief river, have provided more opportunities for manufacturing industry.

Gibbons are apes, related to humans, chimpanzees, gorillas and orang-utans. The six species of gibbon all live in the forests of south-east Asia. They have slender bodies and very long arms, with which they swing from tree to tree with great ease. They live in family groups and spend the day searching for fruit, eggs or insects to eat. At night they sleep in the trees. Gibbons are from 41 to 66 cm (16 to 26 in) tall.

Gibraltar is an island in the western Mediterranean, at the southern tip of Spain. Area 6.5 sq km (2.5 sq miles). It has been British since 1713 but is claimed by Spain. It is really one great rock, with a town at the base – a useful fortress guarding the entrance to the Mediterranean. There is no agriculture and water is scanty. Many of the people, of Spanish or Italian descent, work at the naval base.

Gilbert and Sullivan Opera is English light opera with words by Sir W. S. Gilbert (1836–1911) and music by Sir Arthur Sullivan (1842–1900). Witty, light-hearted and full of clever musical parodies, these works (e.g. *Pirates of Penzance*, 1879, *The Mikado*, 1885, and *The Gondoliers*, 1889) are still popular. Unfortunately Sullivan, a serious musician, believed such work was beneath him and, after a quarrel with Gilbert (concerning a new carpet for the Savoy theatre, according to legend), their partnership broke up in 1889.

Gills are used by some animals for breathing. Human beings obtain the oxygen they need from the air by means of their lungs, but most aquatic animals have to obtain their oxygen from the water using gills.

Gills usually consist of a series of plate-like structures over which water, with its dissolved oxygen, passes. As it passes over the gills, oxygen is absorbed from the water into the blood supply of the gill, and waste carbon dioxide leaves the blood and enters the water.

The gills of fish are situated behind the eyes, and are protected by a bony plate called the operculum. The fish takes water into its mouth and pushes it over the gills, and it leaves by a slit underneath the operculum. Some insects, such as damselflies, have aquatic larvae whose gills look like little lace bags at the rear of their bodies.

There is another kind of gill found in the living world which has nothing to do with breathing. There is a large group of fungi called gill fungi. They get their name from the fact that underneath the head, or cap, of the fungus lie rows of vertical plates also called gills, radiating out from the centre just like the spokes of a bicycle wheel. Mushrooms are common gilled fungi. The gills have minute projections bearing spores. The spores drop from the gills in their millions, to produce new fungi.

Giotto (circa 1266–1337), was an Italian painter. He was the first great artist of the school of Florence – that brilliant flowering of talent in the early Renaissance. Very little is known of him apart from his work. Outstanding are his frescoes illustrating the life of St Francis, in Assisi, and those on the life of Christ and the Virgin Mary, in Padua. In a majestic but simple style, with realistic human figures, his pictures tell their stories with human sympathy and drama. They foreshadow the great achievements of Florentine artists over a century later.

Giraffe is the world's tallest animal. A fully grown giraffe can reach the leaves growing on trees as high as 5.8 m (19 ft), for giraffes have very long legs and necks. In fact, their legs are so long that a giraffe has to almost 'do the splits' when it wants to drink water, otherwise its head cannot reach the ground. It roams the African bush in herds, searching particularly for acacia bushes. Only the giraffe can reach the tops of these so it has little competition for food from browsing animals.

Giraffes grazing from the high foliage on the African plains.

Glacier is a mass of ice that moves slowly down a valley, continually supplied from a source in the mountains. Sizes of glaciers vary enormously; the largest known to exist at present is in Antarctica and is 400 km (250 miles) long.

During the Ice Ages much of the Northern Hemisphere was periodically covered with glaciers and ice sheets. Because the movement of a glacier smooths out rock surfaces and carries away masses of loose rock (called moraine), glaciation has had a profound effect on the landscape.

Gladstone, William Ewart (1809–1898), was a British statesman. He entered Parliament as a Tory but joined the Whigs (later the Liberals) after the repeal of the Corn Laws. As Chancellor of the Exchequer he reduced government expenditure and promoted free trade. As Prime Minister he introduced several important reforms including secret ballots at elections, an Education Act and measures to protect Irish tenants.

William Ewart Gladstone. He was Prime Minister four times.

Glands are cells, or collections of cells, which expel, or secrete, substances from themselves. In animals, there are many kinds of glands. Some, such as the sweat glands which are found in our skin, secrete water on to the surface of the skin. This evaporates, and cools us down. Other types of glands are found within the body and secrete their contents directly into the blood stream.

The hormones which control many of our activities are secreted by glands.

Plants have glands, too. The scent of flowers, such as lavender, is secreted by glands, and so is the nectar that attracts insects.

Glass is the substance used to make windows, milk bottles, drinking glasses, lenses, mirrors and many other things. It is usually colourless, but can be coloured by adding substances such as copper. Different substances, such as sand, soda-ash and lime, are used to make many sorts of glass. Some break very easily. Others are so tough that they are not broken by a bullet and are called bullet-proof glass. Blowing air or steam into hot glass forms long threads of glass called glass fibre. This is used as an insulator.

Glendower, Owen (circa 1359–1416), was a Welsh prince. He led a revolt against English rule in Wales in 1400, allying himself with the enemies of the English King, Henry IV. In four years he gained control of most of Wales, but was gradually driven back by English forces, who eventually reconquered the whole country. Glendower disappeared in 1416.

Glider is a craft which is heavier than air and flies in a similar way to a powered aeroplane, but has no engine. The forward speed needed to create lift from the wings is obtained by towing the glider, or by launching it from the top of a hill. A glider can remain aloft for many hours by using rising warm air currents. The first gliders were based on kites.

Glow-worm is a lampyrid beetle belonging to the same family as the fireflies. They get their name because they emit a cold yellowish-green light, the females usually producing the greater brilliance. This light usually helps the sexes to locate each other. However, the glow-worms from the caves of Waitomo, New Zealand, (*Arachnocampa luminosa*) use their light to attract tiny midges for food.

Adult glow-worms seem to feed very little, but the larvae eat snails and slugs.

Gnu is a large antelope found on the African grasslands. There are two sorts of gnu: the brindled gnu or wildebeest, and the white-tailed gnu. Gnus have bearded heads bearing horns rather like those of a cow, and slender bodies up to 2.4 m (7.8 ft) long. Their sense of smell and hearing is very keen. They gather in herds as they roam about looking for feeding grounds and water holes. They are always on the alert for their greatest enemy, the lion.

Gobi Desert is a largely barren region in central Asia, mostly in Mongolia. Area about 1 300 000 sq km (500 000 sq miles). It lies in a high plateau region, fringed by mountains. It is sandy in the south-west, but other parts are marshy or stony, with salt lakes. Ancient caravan routes and a modern railway run across it. In the central parts almost nothing grows and no one lives.

God is a being whom people worship. In this wide sense, a god can be almost anything, including a spirit. Early myths and religions had many gods, some great and powerful, some no more than a kind of supernatural guardian.

However, in the Christian, Jewish and Muslim religions, there is only one God, a supreme being who is the creator of all things in the universe and possesses unlimited power and wisdom. The Bible and other holy books describe the characteristics of God, though they do not prove that God exists.

Goethe, Johann Wolfgang von (1749–1832), was a German poet, writer and thinker. He was, and is still, the greatest German cultural hero. He spoke five languages at the age of eight and qualified in law at 22; he was also an able scientist.

His earliest writings were love poems to his landlord's daughter, and his first big success was the sentimental, Romantic novel, *The Sorrows of Young Werther* (1774). The following year he settled at Weimar, the chief cultural centre in Germany, where he began *Faust*, his greatest literary work which occupied him, off and on, for over fifty years. He came to reject the *Sturm und*

Drang ('Storm and Stress') movement, rooted in Romantic nationalism, after a visit to Italy during which he wrote his great drama *Egmont* (1788). Meanwhile he was producing novels and poems, as well as scientific works (especially on the study of optics) which occupied most of his time for several years. The poet Schiller brought him back to literature about 1794. His novel *Elective Affinities* (1809), sometimes described as the first psychological novel, was the greatest work of his later years.

Gold is a shiny, rare yellow metal. It has the chemical symbol Au. Gold is soft, and can be made into many different shapes. For these reasons it has always been highly valued. Gold ornaments and jewellery have been made for thousands of years. Early chemists, known as alchemists, tried to make other metals turn into gold.

Gold has caused many people to rush great distances to discover it. Famous gold rushes were to California, USA in 1848, and to Klondike in Alaska in 1896. Gold is found mainly in Australia, Russia, America, and southern Africa, especially South Africa. Some of the deepest mines in the world are gold mines, though gold is also found on river beds.

Gold is often hardened by adding other metals to form an alloy. The amount of gold in the alloy is measured in carats. Pure gold is 24 carats. Nine carat gold has nine parts of gold and 15 parts of other metals.

Gordon, Charles (1833–1885), was a British soldier. He saw service in the Crimean War and then in China, where his part in the defeat of the Taiping rebellion (1854) earned him the name 'Chinese' Gordon. During 1877–1880 he was Governor of the Sudan. In 1884 he was sent back to the Sudan to evacuate the Egyptian garrison and Europeans who were threatened by the revolt of the Mahdi. Gordon was beseiged in Khartoum for ten months and was killed before a relieving force could reach him.

General Gordon faces Sudanese rebels in Khartoum.

Gorilla is the largest of the primates. This mighty animal lives in the forests of west Africa in family groups led by an old silverback male. (The name silverback comes from the silver-grey hairs which appear on the back and shoulders of old males.) Despite its ferocious appearance, the gorilla is a shy, retiring creature, only becoming aggressive when threatened or irritated. A gorilla warns of a likely attack by performing a display of chest-beating.

The gorilla feeds during the day, on leaves, pulling branches or even small trees towards it with its powerful arms. By night, the family sleeps in a tree. Only one baby gorilla is born at a time, and this is nursed and cared for by the mother. Gorillas are up to 1.75 m (nearly 6 ft) high.

Gothic describes the general style in European art and architecture from about 1100 to 1500. The name was originally an insult, meaning that Gothic art failed to obey the Classical principles of ancient Greece and Rome.

The outstanding survivals of the Gothic period are the great religious buildings of the Middle Ages. Striving for greater height, medieval builders discovered the principle of the pointed arch – the main feature of Gothic architecture. With the support of flying buttresses, this enabled them to raise the roof to a great height and to fill the walls with huge windows of stained glass.

In sculpture and painting, the Gothic style strayed from realism. For example, Gothic artists were uncertain about the human body, though they excelled in fashioning the swirls of clothing it wore. Gothic art is rich in detail and shows a love of bright colour and ornament. The finest examples, until the late Gothic period, are illuminated (illustrated) manuscripts.

Gothic was not really one style but many. It was constantly evolving, and it varied greatly from one country to another.

Goths were a Germanic tribe which moved out from southern Scandinavia in the first century BC and settled in the region around the Black Sea by the 3rd century AD. They began to encroach upon the Roman Empire and were converted to a form of Christianity. In the 4th century, they split into two groups. The Visigoths later sacked Rome (in 410) and went on to found a kingdom in Spain. The Ostrogoths settled in Hungary and subsequently established a kingdom in Italy.

Goya, Francisco de (1746–1828), was a Spanish painter. A major figure in European art, he was a contradictory artist. He was a court painter, and produced sumptuous portraits of upper-class subjects but also quite savage ones of the unattractive royal family. He was a patriot and a revolutionary who was horrified by the war in Spain, as seen in his famous etchings showing the beastliness of war and the stupidity of people. Although he only painted one female nude (the *Nude Maja*), it is one of the most famous examples in all art.

Graham, Martha (1894–), is a US dancer, one of the most important figures in modern dance. She founded her School of Contemporary Dance in 1927, and formed a company from her pupils, also dancing herself. She developed an original technique in her 'dance plays' and created about 150 works of different lengths and styles. Many of the most famous modern dancers were her pupils at some stage, and an offshoot of her school, the London Contemporary Dance Theatre, was formed in England in 1967.

Grand Canyon is a deep steep-sided gorge in Northern Arizona, USA. Length about 320 km (200 miles); depth about 1.5 km (1 mile). It has been carved by the Colorado River and it's tributaries for about 10 million years, and heat, cold and frost have also helped to erode it. It is a popular tourist spot and some people canoe down the river, shooting the rapids. Scientists also explore the canyon, as each layer of rock shows a part of Earth's history, containing fossils of each era – including those of prehistoric animals.

Granite is an extremely hard, durable, usually light-coloured rock, so coarse-grained that its crystals are visible to the naked eye. Most of the Earth's very abundant granite originated as molten volcanic rock which gradually cooled and solidified. Quartz and feldspar are its main constituents, and its strength has made it a popular building material.

Grant, Ulysses S. (1822–1885), was an American general and statesman. Appointed Commander-in-Chief of the Federal armies in 1864, he gradually wore down the resistance of his Confederate opponents. He received their surrender at Appomatox court house in 1865, thus ending the Civil War. Elected President of the United States in 1868, he was re-elected in 1872. Although Grant was an honest man himself, he failed to deal with the corruption which was widespread in his government.

Grass family, or Graminae, is one of the most widely distributed and important of all plant families. Several thousand species are known, including cereals such as wheat, oats, rice and sugar cane, bamboo and millet. As well as the grasses that humans eat, there are grasses which feed vast herds of herbivorous animals.

Grasses normally have hollow stems surrounded by thin leaves. Grass flowers are usually arranged in clusters called spikes. Each spike is composed of numerous small flowers called spikelets. The flowers are wind pollinated and, thus, have no colourful petals or sepals. The seed of the grass is called grain. The grain of cereal grasses such as wheat, barley, rice and oats are vital foods for humans.

Grasshopper is an insect with long back legs, which jumps about grass and other foliage during the summer months. As well as being able to jump very well, it can also fly. Grasshoppers are usually green or brown in colour and so, despite the noise they make by rubbing their back legs against their wings to attract mates, they are often very difficult to spot. Grasshoppers are found in many countries, where they feed on foliage.

Gravity is the force that holds us to the Earth. Sir Isaac Newton showed that any two objects are drawn towards each other by gravity. The closer the objects are and the more mass they have, the stronger the force. For us, the most massive thing nearby is the Earth itself. So we are pulled towards it. Without this pull we would float around as people do in space. The Earth's gravity also pulls the Moon, making it orbit around the Earth. The Earth orbits around the Sun, pulled by *its* gravity.

Great Barrier Reef is a ridge of coral off the coast of Queensland, Australia. The largest area of coral in the world, it stretches about 1900 km (1180 miles) to the coast of New Guinea. The shallow waters on the landward side are very clear and contain colourful fish and plants. They are a great recreation area. It has always been a danger to shipping, and Captain Cook ran aground on it in 1770.

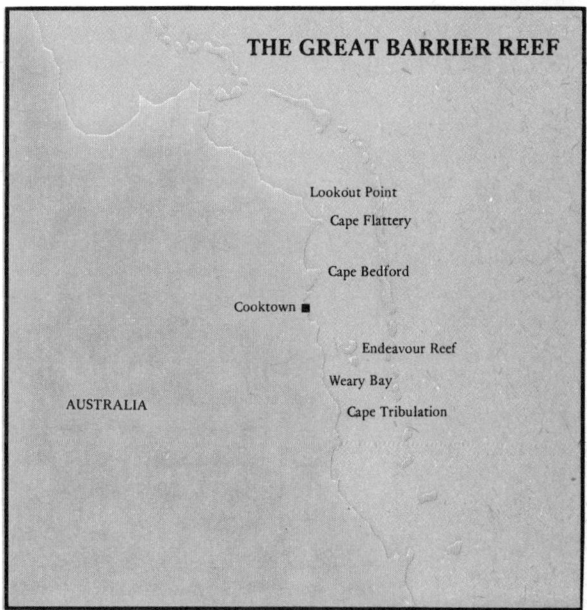

Great Britain is the island made up of England, Scotland and Wales. It is the largest island in Europe and the main part of the United Kingdom of Great Britain and Northern Ireland. *See also* United Kingdom; England; Scotland; Wales.

Great Dividing Range is a mountain system running north-south near the eastern coast of Australia. In places, the mountains cover an area over 300 km (186 miles) wide. In the south-east, the mountains are known as the Australian Alps and include the country's highest peak, Mount Kosciusko at about 900 m (2950 ft) high. There are several areas for winter sports.

Great Lakes are five large lakes connected by rivers in North America. Total area about 247 000 sq km (95 000 sq miles). They lie on the border between the USA and Canada and are linked to the sea by the St Lawrence Seaway. Ocean-going ships can reach them, except in winter. In order of size they are: Lake Superior, Huron, Michigan, Erie and Ontario. Together they form the largest body of fresh water in the world. They are surrounded by a rich industrial, mining and agricultural region.

Great Rift Valley is a series of gigantic clefts that cut through the eastern side of Africa. The Great Rift Valley runs northwards from the mouth of the River Zambezi (in Mozambique) to the northern end of the Red Sea. It then extends into south-west Asia. In Tanzania, the valley divides into branches, which unite again before it enters Ethiopia. Lake Victoria, Africa's largest lake, lies between the branches. For much of the valley's course, the deep trenches that form it are occupied by bodies of water. The largest of these is the Red Sea. The edges of the Great Rift Valley are spectacular in places, with rocky escarpments towering above the valley floor. Volcanic peaks rise along both sides of the valley; they include Mts. Kilimanjaro, Kenya, and Elgon.

Great Trek, The, was the migration of Afrikaner (Boer) farmers in South Africa during the 1830s and 1840s away from Cape Colony northwards across the Orange and Vaal rivers. Their aim was to escape restrictions which British rule in Cape Colony had imposed upon them, and they also needed more land for their cattle. Eventually they established Boer republics: the Transvaal and the Orange Free State.

Greece is a republic in south-east Europe, forming the southern tip of the Balkan peninsula. Capital, Athens; area about 132 000 sq km (51 000 sq miles).

History In Bronze Age Greece the Mycenaean civilization developed in the 2nd millenium BC. After its collapse a network of city-states grew up during the 8th–6th centuries BC. These states established colonies in Asia Minor and around the eastern Mediterranean. Persian attempts to conquer Greece were finally defeated at the Battle of Plataea in 479 BC. An Athenian empire was established in the 5th century BC, but was destroyed by the Peloponnesian Wars. Macedonia became dominant in the 4th century, but the whole of Greece was under Roman control by 133 BC. Greece later formed part of the Byzantine Empire until its eventual conquest by the Turks in the 15th century. It achieved independence from Turkey in the 1820s. A monarchy from 1832 to 1924, it was a republic during 1924–1935, becoming a monarchy again in 1935. Occupied by German forces during the Second World War, it was involved in a civil war from 1946–1949. The government was overthrown by the army in 1967 but civilian rule was re-established in 1973, when the country became a republic. It joined NATO in 1951 and the EEC in 1981.

Land and People Greece includes many islands in the Aegean Sea. The country is mountainous and was once forested, but grazing goats have put an end to the trees. The climate is hot and dry in summer, mild and wet in winter.

The Greeks are of mixed descent, the ancient Greeks being only one set of ancestors. The majority belong to the Greek Orthodox Church. Living standards are rather low, though Greece is not heavily populated.

Economy Greece has a grave lack of natural resources: the soil is generally poor, communications are difficult, and mineral deposits rather small. Fishing and shipping are important, but more than half the people are peasant farmers, working mainly with hand tools. However, the rich plains of Thessaly and Macedonia produce export crops such as olive oil and fruit. Among other exports are

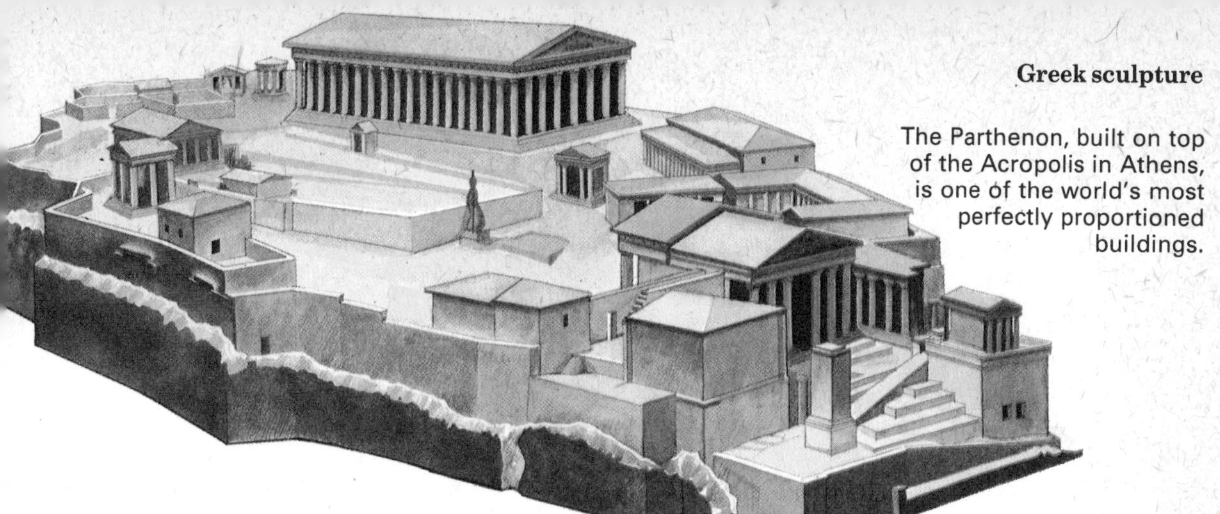

The Parthenon, built on top of the Acropolis in Athens, is one of the world's most perfectly proportioned buildings.

wine and cotton. Tourism is a vital source of government income.

Greek architecture was the most influential style in building until the beginning of the 20th century. The Greek architects tried to discover unchanging rules of form and proportion – to create an ideal style. History shows that they succeeded better than anyone else. The Parthenon at Athens has been called the most nearly perfect building ever constructed.

The Greeks did not use the arch, though their successors, the Romans, did. Theirs was an architecture of straight lines, based on the column and entablature – the horizontal element across the capitals (tops) of the columns, which were decorated with sculpture. There are three 'orders' of Greek architecture; Doric, Ionian and Corinthian, of which the earliest, Doric, is the most important. They are most easily recognized by the shape of the capitals, very simple in Doric, scroll-form in Ionic and a more complex, leaf-like pattern in Corinthian.

Greek sculpture is the outstanding art of ancient Greece. Few paintings have survived, except on vases, from this period; nevertheless, the Greeks do seem to have regarded sculpture as the highest form of art.

Greek sculpture can be divided into three periods: archaic, Classical and Hellenistic.

In the archaic period, from the late 7th century BC, Greek sculpture was similar to the work of older Mediterranean cultures such as Egypt. Human figures are rather stiff, the faces mask-like and the arms usually straight down at the sides because the sculptor had not yet gained the confidence to separate arms from body.

The Classical period dates from about the end of the Persian Wars, 480 BC. The most striking changes are much greater realism

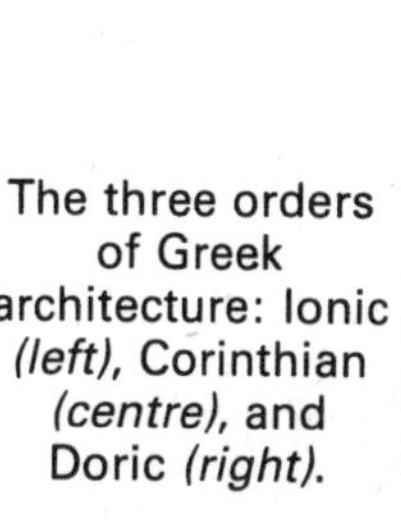

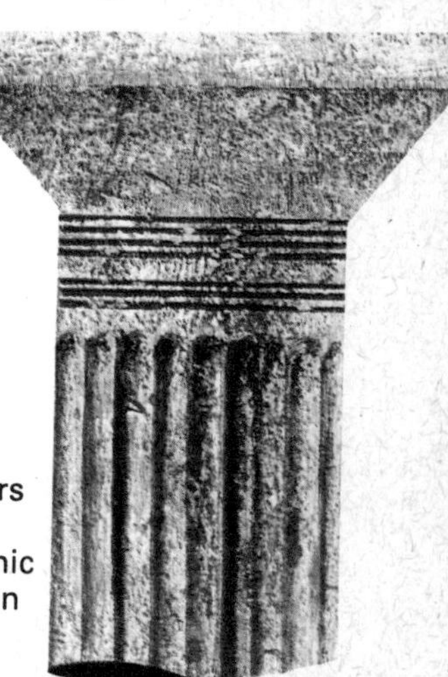

The three orders of Greek architecture: Ionic *(left)*, Corinthian *(centre)*, and Doric *(right)*.

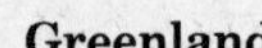

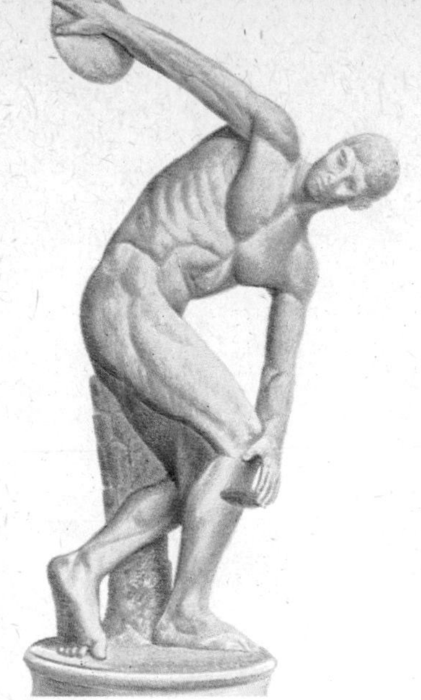

The Discus Thrower (The Discobolos), a statue sculpted by the Greek artist Myron in 5 BC.

and willingness to experiment. Sculptors soon gained an extraordinary mastery of human anatomy, and produced figures in complex, athletic poses. The sculpture of the Parthenon (mid-5th century BC) shows a sense of form, of overall design and technical ability seldom equalled. The nude human figure, in which the Greek artists tried to attain a divine perfection, has never been more beautifully represented than in Classical Athens.

The Hellenistic period dates from the time of Alexander the Great. Greek art ceased to be exclusively Greek, as Alexander's conquests spread Greek culture all over the known world, though it was still mainly created by Greek artists. Sculpture became much more varied, and less serious. Some of the finest – certainly the most skilful – masterpieces (like the *Venus de Milo*) date from this period. But the purity and sincerity of Classical Greece was gradually lost.

Greenland is an island in the Atlantic and Arctic oceans, off north-east North America. Area 2 175 000 sq km (846 000 sq miles). Greenland is part of Denmark, though it has internal self-government. Most of it is covered permanently by an ice cap over 2000 m (6560 ft) thick. Its small population lives mostly by fishing and hunting in the south-west. There is also some mining.

Greenwich mean time (also known as GMT) is standard time, used for calculating the time all over the world. It is the time at the Greenwich Royal Observatory, London, which is situated on the Greenwich meridian. A meridian is an imaginary line around the Earth passing through the North and South poles. The Greenwich meridian is the line that passes through the poles and Greenwich.

A standard time makes it easier for people in one country to work out what time it is in another country. All countries compare their time with the standard time at the Greenwich meridian. For example, Japan is nine hours ahead of GMT. This means that when it is noon in England, it is 9 pm in Japan. Trinidad is four hours behind GMT. When it is noon at Greenwich it is 8 am in Trinidad.

Grenada is an island republic of the Commonwealth in the south-eastern Carribean Sea. Capital, St George's; area about 344 sq km (133 sq miles). It consists of Grenada and the smaller islands of the Southern Grenadines. It was discovered by Columbus in 1498, and then became a French colony until 1783 when it was ceded to Britain. It was granted independence in 1974. Exports include cocoa, spices (especially nutmegs, mace and cloves) and bananas.

Grey, Lady Jane (1537–1554), was Queen of England for nine days. She was a great-grand-daughter of Henry VII and a cousin of Edward VI. When Edward was dying he had been persuaded by the Duke of Northumberland, who effectively controlled the government of the country, to make Jane his successor instead of his half-sister, Mary. Jane was proclaimed Queen in July 1553, but Mary had popular support and soon secured possession of the throne. Jane was found guilty of treason and beheaded.

Grieg, Edvard (1843–1907), was a Norwegian composer who was 12 when his first work was performed. He was determined to bring independence and national character to Norwegian music, which was at that time dominated by German. In works like the two

Peer Gynt suites (1876) he expressed the mystery and grandeur of the Norwegian countryside; and he often used Norwegian folk music in his songs. He was very popular in England, where he and his wife, a singer, gave many recitals, and his *Piano Concerto in A Minor* (1868) is one of his most famous works.

Grimm, Jacob (1785–1863) and **Wilhelm** (1786–1859), were German scholars and writers, authors of *Grimm's Fairy Tales* (1812–1815). The brothers Grimm were learned students of ancient German culture, especially language. Their famous collection of fairy stories grew out of their studies. Outside Germany, it is their most famous work.

Guatemala is a republic in Central America. Capital, Guatemala City; area about 109000 sq km (42000 sq miles). After 300 years of Spanish rule, Guatemala became an independent republic in 1839. It had a succession of strong presidents, effectively dictators, but recent political history has been turbulent.

Guatemala is largely mountainous. Coffee, the most valuable product, grows on the mountain slopes. Mahogany and other hardwoods come from the upland forests, and bananas from the coastal lowlands. The soil is fertile and Guatemala has usually managed to grow most of its own food. The majority of Guatemalans belong to the ancient Maya nation.

Guillemot is a black and white seabird. It feeds in the northern seas, especially around Iceland and Greenland, although it also lives further south. Guillemots nest on cliffs, packed tightly together in noisy groups. They are small birds, up to 43 cm (17 in) long.

Guinea is a republic in West Africa. Capital, Conakry; area about 246000 sq km (95000 sq miles).

Guinea became a French colony in 1891 but gained independence in 1958. It has a hot and humid region near the coast; the rest is mainly savannah, with intervening tropical forest. There are many rivers, providing hydro-electric power. Among natural resources, the most important is bauxite (aluminium). There are also large coal reserves and some gold and diamonds.

More than half the inhabitants belong to either the Fulah (Fulani) or Malinke peoples. Farming is the chief occupation, and several crops, including peanuts, bananas, coffee and pepper, are grown for export.

Guinea-Bissau is a republic in West Africa, between Guinea and Senegal. Capital, Bissau; area about 36000 sq km (14000 sq miles). It was discovered by the Portuguese in 1446 and became a Portuguese colony in 1879. It gained independence and became a republic in 1974.

It is a small country, and much of it is low and marshy. Rice is grown near the coast, where rainfall is highest. Peanuts and cattle are raised farther inland.

Top: Common Guillemot *Bottom left:* Brünnich's Guillemot *Bottom right:* Bridled Guillemot

Guineafowl are seven species of plump-looking birds found in Africa. They have no feathers on their heads, but often bear tufts of bristly quills instead. They have very strong feet and legs, which they use for running and scratching about in the soil for food. Guineafowl are often farmed by natives, both for their eggs and meat. The birds are up to 50 cm (20 in) long.

Gulf Stream is a warm ocean current that has an important influence on climate. It begins in the Gulf of Mexico and moves north-eastward along the coast of the USA. Its warmth gives Bermuda its famous mild winters, and off Florida it is actually visible as a bright blue band in the cold grey waters of the North Atlantic Ocean. It meets the cold Labrador current off Newfoundland, creating dense mists in the area, then moves east towards Europe. In mid-ocean it divides into branches, one of which passes along the north-west coasts of Great Britain. The warmth of the Gulf Stream contributes greatly to the relatively mild winters in Great Britain and north-western Europe.

Gull is probably the best-known of all sea-birds. Its raucous cries and mewing sounds make it instantly recognizable. On the coast gulls live by catching fish and other animals in the sea, as well as scavenging on the seashore. Some species (for example, the herring gull) have moved far inland to feed on such places as rubbish tips and ploughed land.

Gulls have webbed feet and swim well, although they do not dive. They often hover over the sea to catch fish swimming near the surface. The largest gull is the Arctic glaucous gull, and the smallest is the little gull.

About 40 species of gull are found throughout the world, but mostly in the northern hemisphere. They live in noisy colonies, nesting on cliffs, buildings and dunes. The nest is often made of seaweed and two or three eggs are laid. About five or six weeks after hatching, the young are able to look after themselves.

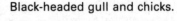

Black-headed gull and chicks.

Gum tree is any tree that exudes gum, including the eucalyptus, the sweet gum, the sour gum, etc. *See also* Eucalyptus.

Guppy is a small freshwater fish that is often kept in aquaria, although its real home is the waters of northern South America. Many attractive varieties of guppy have been bred, with bright colours and fancy fins. They are up to 6 cm (2.5 in) long.

Gutenberg, Johannes (circa 1400–1468), was a German printer, generally regarded as the inventor of printing with movable metal type. He began his first experiments with printing in the late 1430s, and by 1455 had produced the first printed Latin Bible – known as the Gutenberg Bible. Gutenberg fell into debt and was compelled to hand over his printing press in order to pay off his creditors.

Guyana is a republic in north-eastern South America. Capital, Georgetown; area about 216 000 sq km (83 000 sq miles). Formerly British Guiana, it became independent in 1966 and a republic in 1970. Except in the flat coastal region, where most of the population live, the land is covered by tropical forest and savannah. The people are of mixed descent, mainly Indian, Africa, Chinese and European. The main products are sugar cane, rice and peanuts, alumina and bauxite.

Cones of different pine trees. Conifers are gymnosperms.

Gymnosperms are the group of seed-bearing plants which includes the conifers, the cycads and the ginkgo. Unlike the other major group of seed-bearing plants, the angiosperms, the gymnosperms produce seeds which are not enclosed within an ovary, but are borne 'naked'. The largest group of gymnosperms is the conifers, most of which are tall, elegant, evergreen trees found in the colder parts of the world.

Gyroscope, see Navigation.

Habitat is an environment containing certain plants and animals, each depending in some way on the habitat to provide food and shelter. Some of the more common habitats are deserts, deciduous forests and lakes. Within the habitat, conditions may vary. For instance, the top of a rocky shore will be exposed more often to the air than the lower shore. Therefore, some of the plants and animals found at the top of the shore will differ from those found at the lower shore, depending on their ability to cope with the differing conditions. Within a habitat are smaller units called microhabitats. The underneath of a stone is a typical microhabitat, containing minute fungi, bacteria, mites and other small creatures. *See also* Environment.

Hades, in Greek myth, was the god of the Underworld. It was also the Underworld (the equivalent of hell) itself. A brother of Zeus, Hades is a grim but not evil figure. Besides ruling the Underworld, he is also the god of wealth, and in that aspect he was called Pluto. He appears in few myths, and the most famous story about him concerns his quarrel with Demeter after he had stolen her daughter, Persephone, as his wife.

The kingdom of Hades, somewhere below the Earth, was reached by a ferry across the River Styx – the river of the dead. It was guarded by Cerberus, a three-headed dog. The spirits of bad people were tortured in Tartarus.

Hadrian's Wall is a barrier which was built on the northern frontier of Roman Britain to keep out the Pictish tribes, who were constantly raiding across the border. The wall was begun at the orders of the Emperor Hadrian in AD 120. It stretched from the Tyne to the Solway, a distance of about 120 km (75 miles). It incorporated an elaborate system of forts and proved an effective defence. The wall was, however, finally abandoned about AD 383. Only parts of it still stand.

Hair is a thread-like outgrowth arising from the skin of mammals. Collectively hairs are often referred to as fur. Hair consists of dead cells containing pigments which give it its colour. Hairs are fixed into pockets in the skin called follicles. Each hair is normally attached to a muscle called an erector muscle, which can make it stand up or lie flat. The most important job which hair has to do is keep the animal warm. It does this by trapping air, which is then warmed up by the animal's own body heat. Hair also keeps cold air away from the body. It can be used to make the animal appear invisible in its surroundings, while in some animals it is used for just the opposite purpose – areas of coloured fur are used to attract mates or signal danger. Animals, such as cats, can make their hair 'stand on end', giving the impression to enemies that they are bigger.

Plants sometimes have hairs, too. They arise from the epidermis, the outermost layer of the plant. One of the most familiar plant hairs is the root hair. These tiny, delicate hairs greatly increase the surface area of the root so that it can take up more water from the soil. *See also* Moult.

Haiti is a republic in the West Indies occupying the eastern third of the island of Hispaniola. Capital, Port-au-Prince; area about 27 750 sq km (10 700 sq miles). A French colony from 1697, it was the scene of a famous revolt of slaves (1791) and was afterwards ruled by men of African descent, such as Toussaint l'Ouverture, who dominated the whole island in 1800. It has been a republic since 1820, but it has suffered dictatorial and corrupt government.

Haiti is extremely poor, though much of the soil is rich. Sugar is the largest crop, followed by coffee and cocoa from the upland areas. There are mineral resources, but economic development is slow.

Haley, Bill (1925–1982), was a US pop singer and bandleader. He made his first recording in 1945, but his fame dates from *Rock Around the Clock* (1954). He was the first popular success in white rock-and-roll music.

Halibut are three species of marine fish found mainly in the North Atlantic, North Pacific and Arctic waters. They are the largest of the flatfish, all of which have both eyes on one side of the body and lie on the seabed. In many ways halibut are unlike other flatfish, however. For example, they have rounder bodies and they often swim actively in the water, chasing other fish and squid, which they eat with their toothed jaws. Halibut are an important food for people.

Hals, Franz (1580–1666), was a Flemish-born painter. He settled in Holland and became the greatest portrait-painter (after Rembrandt) of the Dutch school. He had a remarkable ability to give his subjects a happy or lively expression; the best-known example is *The Laughing Cavalier* (he is not actually laughing but *about to* laugh, a much more subtle expression). Hals painted only portraits.

Hammurabi (died 1750 BC) was King of Babylon (1792–1750 BC). The founder of the Amorite dynasty, he enlarged and unified his kingdom. He is best remembered for his Code of Laws, the first in history. It was a very harsh code, dealing with the social structure, industries, law, economic conditions and family life.

Handel, Georg Friedrich (1685–1759), was a German-born composer who became an English subject in 1726. His early works, operas in the Italian style, gained him a good reputation. Recognizing the opportunities available in England, he settled there and was director of an 'academy' devoted to Italian opera. However, this was a declining fashion, and Handel turned to writing the oratorios which are his best-known works. The most famous, the *Messiah*, was first produced in Dublin in 1742.

Hannibal (247-circa 182 BC), was the commander of the Carthaginian army in Spain. He brought about the Second Punic War by his attack upon Saguntum in 219 BC. With an army which included a number of elephants, he then crossed the Alps into Italy and defeated the Romans at Trasimene (217 BC) and Cannae (216 BC). He was, however, unable to capture Rome and was eventually recalled to Carthage to defend it against a Roman invasion. Defeated by the Romans at Zama (202 BC), he went into exile and later committed suicide to avoid falling into Roman hands.

Hannibal's army crossing the Alps.

Hapsburg was a European royal family which played a dominant part in European politics for more than 600 years. During this period its members were at various times Holy Roman Emperors, Kings of Spain and rulers of the Austrian Empire.

The family first became prominent when Rudolf I was elected German King in 1273 and thereafter steadily acquired more territories including Austria, Styria and Carniola. In 1438 another Hapsburg, Albert II, became German King and Holy Roman Emperor. After this the Hapsburgs held the imperial title almost without interruption until it was abolished in 1806. In 1516 Charles V added Spain, the Spanish overseas empire, Italy and the Netherlands to the Hapsburg possessions. His brother, who succeeded him as Emperor, acquired Bohemia and Hungary. The Spanish branch eventually died out in 1700, but the Austrian Hapsburgs ruled Austria and Hungary and various subject races (Czechs, Poles, Slovaks, etc) until 1918.

Hardie, Keir (1856–1915), was a British Labour leader. Born in Scotland, he worked in the mines as a boy before becoming a trade unionist and the founder of the Independent Labour Party. In 1892 he was the first Socialist to be elected to Parliament, and he later helped in the formation of the Labour Party. He was a convinced pacifist.

Hardware is the name given to the machines used in the computer industry. The part of a computer that does the calculations is called the central processing unit (CPU). This also controls all the other parts. Information can be stored on discs or tapes. This store is called the memory.

Machines which are used to put information into the computer and to get answers out are called input and output devices. They may be keyboards on which information is typed. They may be visual display units (VDU), printers or other machines. A visual display unit shows information on a screen, like a television screen. These devices may be many kilometres away from the computer, connected by telephone.

A microcomputer may have all its parts in one box no bigger than a television, but a large computer may fill several rooms. *See also* Software.

Hardy, Thomas (1840–1928), was an English novelist and poet. The son of a Dorset craftsman, he remained very close to the land and people of Dorset. The decline of this traditional society, and the emotional conflicts within himself, especially the loss of his religious faith, were expressed in his 'Wessex' (i.e. south-west England, especially Dorset) novels. They include *Far From the Madding Crowd* (1874), *The Return of the Native* (1878), *The Mayor of Casterbridge* (1886) and *Tess of the D'Urbervilles* (1891). Hardy was a poet by instinct. He wrote novels because they made money whereas poetry did not, but in his late years he gave up novel writing altogether.

Hare is related to a rabbit. However, unlike rabbits they have long legs and large ears, and are not social animals, but rest alone during the day in a depression in grass called a form. They venture forth at night to feed on crops and other vegetation. Hares have remarkable powers of hearing and smell, and bound away at great speed if danger threatens. They are up to 76 cm (30 in) long.

The brown hare lives all over Europe except northern Scandinavia and Russia. The mountain hare lives in alpine regions in Europe. The Arctic hare is found in Canada, Alaska and Greenland. Also found in America are the varying hare and the Californian jack rabbit (a hare despite its name).

Harold II (circa 1022–1066) was the last Anglo-Saxon King of England. The son of Earl Godwin, he was apparently named as heir to the throne by Edward the Confessor. However, his claim was challenged by Duke William of Normandy and Harold III of Norway. Harold III invaded England in 1066, but was defeated and killed at the Battle of Stamford Bridge. King Harold then had to march rapidly south to meet the Norman invasion, and was killed at the Battle of Hastings.

Harrier, see VTOL aircraft.

Harvey, William (1578–1657), was an English doctor, who discovered that the blood in our bodies circulates. It had been thought that the liver made blood all the time. The blood was supposed to be used up by the body, as a motor car 'uses up' petrol.

William Harvey showed that the blood is pumped by the heart around the body. It is then pumped back to the lungs, to pick up oxygen, and is pumped around the body again.

Hastings, Battle of, took place on 14 October 1066 near Hastings in East Sussex. After fierce fighting, an invading army, led by

Duke William of Normandy, defeated an English force commanded by King Harold, who was killed in the battle. Duke William assumed the crown as William I and went on to conquer England for the Normans.

The Normans fight their way up Senlac Hill at the Battle of Hastings.

Hawaii is an island group in the central Pacific, forming a state of the USA. Capital, Honolulu; area about 17000 sq km (6560 sq miles). Colonized by Polynesians about 500 AD, the islands were discovered by Captain Cook in 1778. In 1893 the Hawaiians asked to become part of the USA.

Hawaii is best known for its beauty (including volcanoes in spectacular action). It is a major tropical tourist resort, but also a naval base. (Pearl Harbor, near Honolulu, was the scene of a Japanese attack in 1941). It produces tropical crops like pineapples, sugar cane and coffee. There are big processing plants for these products and many flourishing businesses, but no heavy industry.

Hawk, together with the kite, eagle, harrier, buzzard and Old World vulture, makes up one of the largest families of the birds of prey. Although there are several other birds of prey called hawks – the marsh hawk and Harris' hawk, for instance – true hawks are placed in a separate group known as the subfamily Accipitrinae. They are found in many parts of the world and include the various species of sparrowhawks and goshawks. True hawks are broad-winged, long-tailed birds which live and hunt in forests.

Haydn, Franz Joseph (1732–1809), was an Austrian composer. A prolific genius whose gifts were noticed when he was a small child, he went to Vienna and for 30 years lived in the household of an aristocratic patron, Prince Esterházy. Although he had many other duties there, Haydn composed at a great rate and soon gained an international reputation. He was an admirer of the young Mozart, and Beethoven was briefly his pupil.

Haydn has generally been regarded as inferior to these two, perhaps unjustly. His vast output included over 100 symphonies, but he mastered and expanded every form of music, never lacking new ideas. Today his work, especially his operas, is still being rediscovered.

Hearing, see Ear.

Heart is simply a pump made of muscle. It pumps blood around the body by rhythmic contractions. A system of valves ensures that blood is always kept flowing in the right

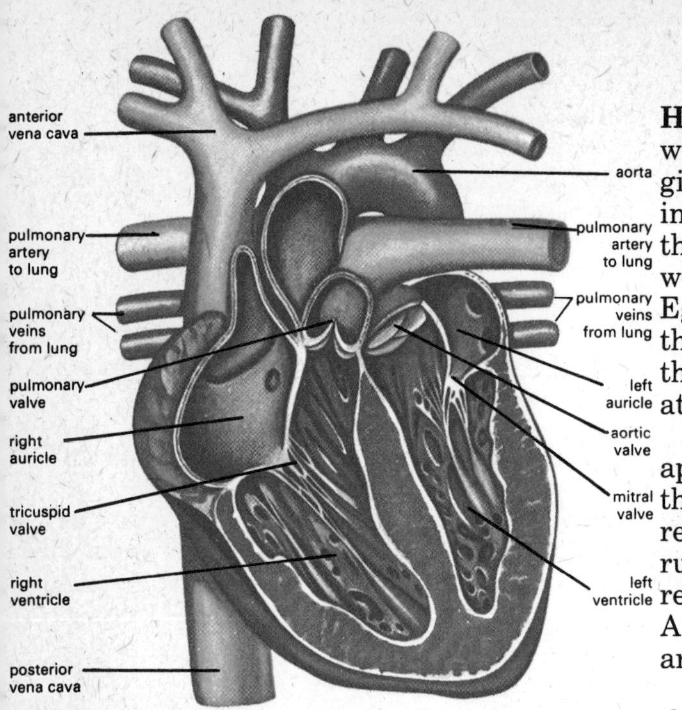

Section of the human heart showing chambers, major vessels and valves.

direction. In more simple animals the heart may be little more than an expanded portion of a blood vessel. Earthworms have a series of hearts. In the vertebrates the heart is divided into a series of chambers. In mammals the heart consists of four chambers: the left auricle, the right auricle, the left ventricle and the right ventricle.

The rate of contraction is controlled automatically by the nervous system. Anxiety or exercise causes the heart to beat faster, supplying more blood to various parts of the body. After activity, the heartbeat rate drops automatically to what is known as the resting rate. In humans this is about 72 beats per minute. You can feel your own heartbeat rate, or pulse, if you place your fingers on the blood vessels at the side of your neck, underneath your jaw, or on your upturned wrist.

Heat is a form of energy. It is used in many ways, for example, to warm homes, to cook food, to power cars and trains and to cut metals. Burning coal, oil and gas are used to heat homes. Electricity can make substances hot. It heats coils of wire in electric fires. The Sun also gives heat. Temperature, or how hot an object is, is measured using an instrument called a thermometer. *See also* Energy.

Hebrews are the Jews of the Old Testament, who spoke Hebrew and belonged to the religion of Judaism. They were a nomadic people in Palestine about 1000 BC. Some (or all) of them lived for a time in Egypt, where they were persecuted. Their departure from Egypt under the leadership of Moses marked the real beginning of the Hebrew nation and the Judaic religion. A national state was created under King David.

In 586 BC the Hebrew state of Judaea disappeared with the Babylonian conquest, but the scattered people kept their culture and religion in small colonies. Under Persian rule, a national revival was marked by the rebuilding of the temple in Jerusalem (516). A theocratic state – government by priests – arose.

Hebrew culture was next seriously threatened by the influence of Greece and the power of Rome. Judaism survived, but eventually Palestine came under Roman rule. Jesus of Nazareth was born in this period. Revolts against Rome resulted in the final destruction of the state and the dispersion of the Jews in the 2nd century AD.

Hebrides, or Western Isles, are islands in the Atlantic off western Scotland. Area about 8000 sq km (3090 sq miles). They are usually divided into the Outer Hebrides (including Lewis, Harris, North and South Uist) and Inner Hebrides (including Skye, Mull and Islay). They passed to Scotland from Norway in the 13th century. They are mostly rocky or mountainous and damp, with little good soil. Distilling whisky, fishing, livestock-raising, stone-quarrying and tourism are important, and the most famous Hebridean product is Harris tweed.

Hedgehog is a mammal whose sides and back are covered with a dense layer of prickly hairs. This helps to protect it from predators, such as foxes, especially when the hedgehog rolls into a ball. Hedgehogs eat insects, worms and other small creatures, although they will also take fruit. They are suprisingly immune to snake poison, and the European hedgehog has been known to kill an adder without suffering any ill-effects if

bitten. Hedgehogs are active mostly at dusk, shuffling along in the undergrowth, and sometimes they hunt through the night. Several species of hedgehog are found throughout the world. Those in colder climates must hibernate during the winter.

Helicopter is an aircraft lifted by one or more large horizontal propellers, instead of using wings. The main attraction of such a machine is that it can take off and land vertically, so needing no long runway or airport. A helicopter can also hover in the air, making it ideal for rescuing people from cliffs, sinking ships or burning buildings. It is usually considered that the first practical helicopter was designed by the German Heinrich Focke (founder of the Focke-Wulf company) in 1936. Since the Second World War, development has been rapid and has followed that of winged airplanes, so that the latest helicopters are powered by gas turbine jet engines. The largest models can lift 40 tonnes, while the fastest travel at more than 450 km/h (280 mph). The helicopter is expensive to make, is noisy and uses a great deal of fuel, so that its use is limited to situations where the ability to take off vertically or to hover is essential. One of the helicopter's most common modern uses is to supply offshore oil rigs, which are too small for aircraft and are often situated in seas too rough to permit regular supply by ship.

Helium is a colourless gas, which does not usually react with any other substance. Its chemical symbol is He. After hydrogen, helium is the lightest and most common element in the universe. On Earth, however, it is quite rare. It is taken from natural gas found in America. Radioactive substances called alpha rays give off helium.

Because it is light, and does not explode like hydrogen, helium is used to lift balloons and airships.

Hemingway, Ernest (1899–1961), was a US writer. At 19 he volunteered to serve in the First World War and was wounded – the first of a series of violent episodes in his life which ended with his self-inflicted death by shooting. The subjects of his books include bull-fighting (*Death in the Afternoon*, 1932) and big-game hunting (*The Green Hills of Africa*, 1935). Besides his brilliant short stories, his most admired novels are *The Sun Also Rises* (1926), *A Farewell to Arms* (1929) and *For Whom the Bell Tolls* (1940). His lean prose style, where not a word is wasted, had an enormous influence on younger writers.

Hemlock is a white-flowered plant of the parsley family used by the Greeks to produce a poison which they also called hemlock. Hemlock trees get their name from the smell of their crushed leaves, which resembles the smell of hemlock. They are coniferous trees, some of which are native to China, Japan and British Columbia. They are now planted in many other parts of the world. Hemlock trees have needle-like leaves and brown oval cones. Their timber is used for fencing, carpentry and in the paper industry.

Hengist and Horsa (5th century AD), were two semi-legendary chieftains and brothers from Jutland. They were apparently invited to England in order to help the British chieftain, Vortigern, to fight off Pictish invaders. They then turned on the Britons and were constantly at war with them. Horsa was killed in AD 455, but Hengist made himself King of Kent, not dying till AD 488.

Henry I (1069–1135), was King of England (1100–1135). The youngest son of William I, he succeeded to the throne on the death of his brother, William II. He resisted the claims of his elder brother, Robert II, Duke of Normandy, forced Robert to recognize him as King and eventually seized Normandy as well. Henry is remembered for his important reforms in law and administration.

Henry II and the Archbishop of Canterbury, Thomas à Becket.

Henry II (1133–1189), was King of England (1154–1189). The son of Matilda, daughter of Henry I, and Geoffrey of Anjou, he succeeded Stephen as King. Having already inherited extensive French possessions, he gained still more land in France through his marriage to Eleanor of Aquitaine. He carried out reforms in government which greatly strengthened the central power at the expense of the barons. Henry's attempt to curb the power of the Church ended with the murder of Thomas à Becket.

Henry III (1207–1272), was King of England (1216–1272). He came to the throne at the age of nine on the death of his father, King John. The government of the country was in the hands of Hubert de Burgh, until Henry began to rule in person through favourites. His extravagance and autocratic rule caused great discontent among the nobles and led to the Barons' War of 1263 under the leadership of Simon de Montfort. The King was defeated at Lewes (1264). However, in the following year his son, Edward, won a decisive victory over the barons at Evesham. Henry then left affairs to Edward.

Henry IV (1367–1413), was King of England (1399–1413). The first Lancastrian monarch, he seized the throne from Richard II, who had previously exiled him for life. Many disputed his claim to the crown, and he had to face serious rebellions by Owen Glendower, the Scots and the Percy family. His last years were troubled by poor health.

Henry V (1387–1422), was King of England (1413–1422). Succeeding his father, Henry IV, he reopened the Hundred Years' War with France and won a decisive victory at Agincourt (1415). He eventually controlled much of northern France and married the daughter of the French king, who recognized him as his heir.

Henry VI (1421–1471), was King of England (1422–1461 and 1470–1471). He succeeded his father, Henry V, when only a baby, and the country was governed by a regency until he came of age. He was crowned King of France in 1431; but inspired by Joan of Arc, the French gradually ousted the English from their country. The loss of French territory made Henry VI personally unpopular, and he also began to suffer attacks of madness, which increased his ineffectiveness as a ruler. The outbreak of the Wars of the Roses led to his deposition by Edward IV (1461). Briefly restored to the throne in 1470, by the Earl of Warwick, he was defeated in battle the following year and murdered.

Henry VII (1457–1509), King of England (1485–1509), was the first Tudor monarch. He won the throne by defeating and killing Richard III at the Battle of Bosworth in 1485 and, himself a Lancastrian, united the houses of York and Lancaster by his marriage to the daughter of the Yorkist, Edward IV. Henry was an able administrator, who successfully restored the royal finances and created a strong central government.

Henry VIII (1491–1547), was King of England (1509–1547). His marriage problems led eventually to the Reformation in England. Coming to the throne in succession to his father, Henry VII, he some became involved in war against France, defeating the French at the Battle of the Spurs (1513), while in his absence English forces crushed the Scots at Flodden. The failure of his Chancellor, Cardinal Wolsey, to obtain the annulment of his marriage to Catherine of Aragon, led to Wolsey's downfall. Henry achieved his divorce, with the help of Thomas Cromwell, by repudiating papal authority and by making himself supreme head of the Church in England. He next married Anne Boleyn, who was executed for adultery, and then Jane Seymour, who died after giving birth to the future Edward VI. His marriage to Anne of Cleves ended in divorce and his fifth wife, Catherine Howard, was executed in 1542. His last wife, Catherine Parr, outlived him.

Hephaestus, in Greek myth, was the god of fire and the crafts, especially the craft of the blacksmith. He was the son of Hera and, in some versions of the myth, of Zeus also; and the husband of Aphrodite. He was not one of the great figures of Olympus (the home of the gods) and he often appears as a figure of fun. He was lame, perhaps as a result of being thrown out of heaven for a time, but he made many marvellous things in his workshop, such as the armour of Achilles.

The Romans identified him with Vulcan, but Vulcan was not a blacksmith, merely the god of fire in its destructive form.

Hepplewhite is the style of English furniture made according to the design of George Hepplewhite (died 1786), originating in his very influential *Cabinet-Makers' and Upholsterers' Guide*. Hepplewhite is a little more conventional than his contemporaries, Chippendale and Sheraton, and closer to English tradition, though some of his early furniture especially was influenced by French rococo. Chairs were Hepplewhite's speciality; he is said to have been the originator of the winged chair.

Hera, in Greek myth, was the wife (and sister) of Zeus and thus the senior goddess on Mount Olympus. Her Roman equivalent was called Juno. She was widely worshipped as the protector of brides, wives and mothers, and she represented the Greek idea of the female virtues.

However, some writers, particularly Homer in the *Iliad*, pictured her as a spiteful, shrewish creature, quarrelsome and jealous, who spent much of her time persecuting the numerous lovers of Zeus and their children.

Herakles, or Hercules, was the greatest hero of ancient Greek legend. A son of Zeus by a mortal woman, he was persecuted by Hera, who forced him to become the slave of King Eurystheus. He had to perform Twelve Labours. These were: capturing Cerberus, the watchdog of Hades; stealing the golden apples of Hesperides; killing Geryon; stealing Hippolyte's girdle; killing the Nemean Lion and the Hydra; catching the Erymanthian boar and the Cerynean hind; driving away the Stymphalian birds; cleaning the Augean stables; catching the Cretan bull and Diomedes' horses.

Herb is any flowering plant which does not have parts existing above ground all year. Thus, daffodils, daisies and buttercups are herbs, but shrubs, like the rhododendron, and trees are not. Some herbs such as thyme, mint and parsley are used in cooking.

Herbivores are animals which only eat plants. Cows, rabbits, sheep, horses, elephants, giraffes, deer and gazelles are just a few of the many species of herbivorous animal. Whereas meat-eaters, or carnivores, can eat plant matter as well, herbivorous animals cannot chew meat. They have flattened teeth which are well suited for chewing grass, but which are totally useless for eating meat.

Hermes, in Greek myth, was the messenger god, equivalent to the Roman Mercury. A son of Zeus, he is a minor figure among the gods, junior to his half-brother, Apollo. He carries a staff, the symbol of his role as herald or messenger.

Hermes was very popular among ordinary people, especially young men. Among the myths told of him are how he stole Apollo's cattle and made them walk backwards so Apollo would follow their footprints in the wrong direction; how he invented the lyre; and his love affair with Aphrodite, from which was born Hermaphrodite, a being half-male and half-female.

A statue of Hermes, messenger of the gods.

Heron is a bird found throughout the temperate and tropical regions of the world. Some, like the European grey heron, are tall birds with long legs, necks and beaks. They grow up to 1.8 m (6 ft). Others, such as the squacco heron of Europe, Asia and Africa, are more pigeon-like although they, too, have a long beak. Herons feed by the waterside, wading into the shallows to grab at fish which swim by or to snap at passing insects, or at amphibians and crustaceans.

Grey heron

Herschel, Sir Frederick William (1738–1822), was a German-born English astronomer. He made a reflecting telescope and later built a 12-m (40-ft) long telescope. He discovered Uranus and two of its satellites, and studied Saturn, discovering two of its satellites.

Herschel's greatest work was in recording many of the stars he could see. From these observations he thought that the Milky Way was shaped like a convex lens, which was later shown to be correct. He also drew up a famous star catalogue, and was astronomer to the English King George III.

Hibernation is a kind of deep sleep in which an animal lives off the layers of fat it has built up before the onset of winter. In cold climates, when winter comes, there is too little food to be found to keep many animals alive. These animals either die, leaving eggs to turn into new individuals in the spring, or they hibernate.

Hibernation occurs in some mammals, reptiles, amphibians and birds. Mammals such as bears look for snug caves in which to hibernate, bats look for caves or the roofs of buildings and dormice seek the shelter of hedgerows. Reptiles and amphibians usually burrow into holes in the ground or under stones. There is a species of bird which hibernates, too. This is the poor will. When scientists first discovered a hibernating poor will they thought it was dead, for no one had ever seen a hibernating bird before. When they brought it back to the warmth of the laboratory it revived, thinking spring had arrived.

Hieroglyphic writing is a form of writing in which pictorial symbols are used to represent living beings, objects, words or sounds. Hieroglyphics were used by the Egyptions from about the middle of the 4th millennium BC, generally as inscriptions on monuments. They were also used by other ancient peoples, notably the Hittites and Cretans, and then by the Aztecs and Mayas of Mexico.

Hillary, Sir Edmund (1919–), is a New Zealand mountaineer and explorer. In 1953 he and Tenzing Norgay, a Nepalese guide, were the first men to climb to the summit of Mount Everest. Hillary received a knighthood for his exploit. In the later 1950s he took part in a trans-Antarctic expedition to the South Pole.

Himalayas are a mountain range in central Asia. The greatest mountains in the world, reaching a record height on Mount Everest (Chomolungma), they are really a series of parallel ranges up to 250 km (155 miles) wide. They extend for about 2500 km (1553 miles) across the north-east of the Indian subcontinent, and parts of them are practically unknown. For the past 100 years, the Himalayas have been a great attraction for mountaineers. Many great rivers begin here, all flowing south. *See also* Everest.

Hinduism is the main religion and social system in India. Hinduism has no known founder and no firm creeds or articles of belief, though it has much sacred literature. It is based not so much on belief as on birth and behaviour. It has many complex forms which, however, do share some basic principles. It is notably tolerant towards other religions.

The origins of Hinduism are in Vedic literature, over 3000 years old. Later, it developed a more ceremonial form called Brahmanism, when the caste system, dividing people into rigid social categories, appeared. During the past 2000 years Hinduism has developed in several directions, with different sects devoted to different gods; and religions such as Buddhism are, in a way, offshoots of it.

Hippocrates (circa 460–377 BC), was a Greek doctor who lived and worked on the

Hillary and Tenzing reach the top of Mount Everest.

Adolf Hitler arrives at a huge rally of his supporters at Nuremburg in 1937.

island of Kos. He studied the body and its illnesses very carefully, and made a number of important discoveries. He is often called the father of modern medicine. Before practising medicine, many doctors take an oath called the Hippocratic oath.

Hippopotamus, or 'river horse' as it is sometimes known, is the third largest land animal after the African and Indian elephants. The hippopotamus may reach a length of 4.3 m (14 ft) and a weight of 4 tonnes. It lives in the rivers of Africa south of the Sahara, swimming about in the water by day, and coming on to land to feed on vegetation at night. Although the hippopotamus often just wallows about in the water with its huge mouth open, it can swim at speeds of 48 km/h (29 mph) when necessary and can also walk along the river bed.

Hiroshima is a city in Japan which was almost completely destroyed on 6 August 1945 by the first atomic bomb ever used in war. More than 70000 people were killed, and many injured. Hiroshima has now been largely rebuilt. The Peace Memorial Park was created in memory of the victims.

Hitchcock, Alfred (1899–1980), was a British-born film director. He made his name in the British cinema with a succession of thrillers, and in 1939 moved to Hollywood. He claimed to be no more than an entertainer, but his distinctive style made him a hero of a younger generation of film makers and critics. His most successful films were sophisticated, suspense thrillers, usually involving an innocent person caught up in mysterious events. Among them are *The Man Who Knew Too Much* (1934; new version

1956), *The Lady Vanishes* (1939), *Strangers on a Train* (1951), *To Catch a Thief* (1955), *North by North-West* (1959), *Psycho* (1960), *The Birds* (1963) and *Frenzy* (1972).

Hitler, Adolf (1889–1945), was a German Nazi leader and dictator of Germany from 1923 to 1945. Born in Austria, the son of a customs official, he served in the German army in the First World War. In 1919 he joined the German Workers' Party (later the Nazi Party), of which he soon became leader. After an unsuccessful attempt to seize power in Bavaria in 1923, he was imprisoned. While in prison he wrote a book which set out his ideas about German racial superiority, his hatred of Jews and of Communism.

The economic depression of the late 1920s greatly increased the popularity of the Nazi Party and in 1932 they won a majority of the seats in the German Parliament. In 1933 Hitler became Chancellor and in 1934 Führer (leader) with the powers of a dictator. He established a totalitarian government, set up concentration camps for Jews and other people he considered his enemies and began a massive programme of rearmament. His aggressive foreign policy brought Czechoslovakia and Austria under German control, and his invasion of Poland in September 1939 led to the outbreak of the Second World War.

At first the German armies were successful, but they suffered a major defeat at Stalingrad in Russia in 1942–1943. Hitler survived an attempt to assassinate him in 1944, but committed suicide when the Russians entered Berlin.

Hittites were an ancient people who dominated much of Anatolia (Asia Minor) during the 2nd millennium BC. They probably came from lands beyond the Black Sea, entering Anatolia about 2000 BC. They built up an empire centred on their capital at Hattusas, reaching the zenith of their power in the 14th century BC, when they challenged Egypt for control of Syria and Palestine. The Hittite empire was overthrown by the Sea Peoples in the 12th century BC.

Ho Chi Minh (1892–1969), was a Vietnamese Communist leader, who played an important part in freeing his country from French rule. As a young man he lived in London and Paris, where he joined the French Communist Party. He was trained in revolutionary methods in Moscow, returning to

The Hittites contributed to western civilization by the discovery of iron.

Vietnam in 1941. There he formed the Viet Minh which waged guerrilla warfare against the French after the Second World War, securing independence for North Vietnam in 1954. He then pursued a policy of reunion with South Vietnam by supporting Communist guerrilla movements there, although he did not live to see both countries reunited.

Hockney, David (1937–), is a British artist. From a promising group of young British artists, mostly at the Royal College of Art about 1960, Hockney emerged as the most successful. 'I paint what I like, when I like and where I like,' he said (1962), though his versatility and his ability in basics such as drawing were recognized only slowly. He was associated with the Pop art movement, painting subjects like Hollywood swimming pools in a deliberately simple style, but he later extended his range in many directions – for example, in designing stage sets.

Hogarth, William (1697–1764), was an English painter and engraver. He was the great illustrator of London life whose satirical, sometimes savage, pictures of human foolishness and vice were very popular as prints. A great patriot, he criticized the art snobs who only admired French or Italian old masters obscured by dirty varnish. Though his satirical prints are more famous, he was also an outstanding portrait painter.

Holland, see Netherlands

Hollywood is a suburb of Los Angeles, California. It has been the centre of the American film industry since the early silent films, because of its fine weather. Supposedly one of the richest and most glamorous places on earth, Hollywood's greatest days were the 1930s and 1940s – the era of the great film stars and the big film-producing studios. It is now a tourist spot and, although still the centre of film making, much of its work is designed for television. Nowadays more feature films are made on location.

Holocaust is the name given to the extermination of nearly six million Jews by the Nazis during the Second World War. The Jews came from all the countries in Europe which were under German occupation. They were herded into concentration camps, of which the most notorious was Auschwitz, where they were systematically killed.

Holography is a form of photography which uses laser light. Photographs are usually flat. They are called two-dimensional images. Using lasers, photographs can be made which are not flat but have the same shape as the objects photographed. They are called three-dimensional images. They are taken using a photographic plate called a hologram. When laser light is shone through the hologram a three-dimensional image can be seen. *See also* Laser.

Holst, Gustav (1874–1934), was an English composer. He is especially remembered as a teacher of music and as the composer of *The Planets*, an orchestral suite on a large scale. He wrote much choral music, often showing sensitive awareness of folk-music traditions, and four operas, as well as orchestral music.

Holy Roman Emperors

Frankish Kings and Emperors	
Charlemagne	800–814
Louis I, the Pious	814–840
Lothair I	840–855
Louis II	855–875
Charles II, the Bald	875–877
Throne vacant	877–881
Charles III, the Fat	881–887
Arnulf	887–899
Louis III, the Child	899–911
Conrad I, of Franconia	911–918
Saxon Kings and Emperors	
Henry I, the Fowler	919–936
Otto I, the Great	936–973
Otto II	973–983
Otto III	983–1002
Henry II, the Saint	1002–1024
Frankonian Emperors	
Conrad II	1024–1039
Henry III	1039–1056
Henry IV	1056–1106

Henry V	1106–1125
Lothair II	1125–1137
Hohenstaufen Kings and Emperors	
Conrad III	1138–1152
Frederick I Barbarossa	1152–1190
Henry VI	1190–1197
Philip of Swabia	1198–1208
Otto IV (rival to Philip)	1198–1215
Frederick II	1215–1250
Conrad IV	1250–1254
The Great Interregnum	1254–1273
Rulers from Different Houses	
Rudolf I of Hapsburg	1278–1291
Adolf of Nassau	1292–1298
Albert I of Austria	1298–1308
Henry VII of Luxembourg	1308–1313
Louis IV of Bavaria	1314–1347
Frederick of Austria (co-regent)	1314–1326
Charles IV of Luxembourg	1347–1378
Wencelaus of Bohemia	1378–1400
Rupert of the Palatinate	1400–1410
Sigismund	1411–1437
Hapsburg Emperors	
Albert II	1438–1439
Frederick III	1440–1493
Maximilian I	1493–1519
Charles V	1519–1556
Ferdinand I	1556–1564
Maximilian II	1564–1576
Rudolf II	1576–1612
Mathias	1612–1619
Ferdinand II	1619–1637
Ferdinand III	1637–1657
Leopold I	1658–1705
Joseph I	1705–1711
Charles VI	1711–1714
Charles VII of Bavaria	1742–1745
Hapsburg-Lorraine Emperors	
Francis I	1745–1765
Joseph II	1766–1790
Leopold II	1790–1792
Francis II	1792–1806

Holy Roman Empire was a loose federation of central European states roughly covering the area occupied by Germany, Austria, Switzerland and northern Italy, although its boundaries shifted from time to time. It was considered to be a continuation of the western part of the ancient Roman Empire.

The name was first used by Charlemagne to describe his dominions, but the empire was really founded by the German King, Otto I, who ascended the throne in 936. He had himself crowned Emperor in 962, and after that all emperors were to be elected by German princes. The empire gradually lost much of its territory and had real power only when it was ruled by exceptionally strong Emperors. It was weakened by the Reformation and the Thirty Years' War and was finally abolished by Napoleon in 1806.

Homeopathy is a type of medicine. Homeopathic doctors give patients tiny amounts of a drug which causes effects or symptoms similar to those which are being treated. For example, a patient with a fever may be given a tiny amount of a drug which causes that fever, in the belief that these drugs will encourage the body to fight the illness.

Homer was an ancient Greek poet who lived about the 8th century BC. He wrote the epic poems the *Iliad* and the *Odyssey*. The first describes the last stages of the Trojan War, the second the adventures of Odysseus (Ulysses) on his way home from Troy. These magnificent poems are not the only first works in Greek – and therefore European – literature, they are also among the greatest.

Honduras is a republic in Central America. Capital, Tegucigalpa; area about 112 000 sq km (43 200 sq miles). Part of the ancient Maya empire, it was claimed for Spain by Columbus in 1502. The present republic was founded in 1838, and survived attacks from neighbours with US support. In the present century it has suffered frequent political disturbances.

Apart from coastlands and river valleys, the country is mountainous. Bananas are the chief product, while the extensive forests provide valuable hardwoods. Silver has been mined for centuries from Rosario mine, but the rich mineral wealth is hard and expensive to obtain.

Honey is the sweet, thick fluid made by bees from the nectar they obtain from flowers. It is stored in their nests or hives to be used as food. The honey we eat is produced by honey bees, which store the honey in special structures called combs.

Honey bear, see Kinkajou.

Hong Kong is a British colony on the Chinese coast. Area about 1000 sq km (386 sq miles). It was ceded to Britain by China in 1841; and the New Territories were added on a 99-year lease in 1898. China is expected to claim sovereignty over the whole in 1998.

Hong Kong has a fine harbour and is an important point of contact between China and the West. It is best known for its prosperous manufacturing industries – textiles, toys, electronic goods, etc – which are exported in large quantities. The numerous population is mainly Chinese. Land is in short supply and water is often rationed.

A junk. Many of these boats can be seen around Hong Kong, used as cargo vessels and also as homes.

Hops are a small family of climbing herbs which are cultivated to grow up strings attached to poles. The male and female flowers are separate. The bunches of female flowers, which look rather like cones, are dried and used in beer. Hops give beer its bitter flavour. They are native to Europe, North America and Asia, but are also grown in South America and Australia.

Hormone is a chemical messenger produced by one part of an organism and carried to another part of the organism where it acts to control growth, sexual activities or other processes. Both animals and plants produce hormones. Plant hormones for example, help to promote growth by stimulating the cells to divide and enlarge. Animal hormones are very varied. One of the best-known is adrenalin, which is produced when an animal is frightened. Adrenalin tells the body to produce glucose, which quickly gives the animal energy in case it must fight or run. It also increases the heartbeat. The feeling of 'butterflies in the stomach' we get when we are nervous is caused by adrenalin.

Horse differs from the other horse-like animals, such as the donkey, ass and zebra, in having small ears, round hooves and hairs which grow the whole length of its tail. The true wild horse is the Mongolian horse or Przewalski's horse, although there are many kinds of domestic horse which are allowed to live a wild, or semi-wild existence. Horses have been domesticated by people for 4000 years, and during this time they have been bred to carry out many tasks. Massive shire horses can pull great loads, delicately built thoroughbreds can gallop extremely fast, and sturdy ponies can be used for many different purposes.

Horse chestnut tree is believed to be a native of Greece and Albania. This tree is now planted in many other parts of the world, usually for its ornamental appearance. The fruit of the horse chestnut is the familiar 'conker' – a brown nut enclosed in a large, green, prickly case. Although some animals can eat these nuts, they are not favoured by horses, and are far too bitter for humans to eat. The chestnut which we eat is from the sweet (or Spanish) chestnut tree, which is not related to the horse chestnut.

Horsetail is a non-flowering plant related to the ferns. Several hundred million years ago the horsetails were represented by many species – some of them giant plants up to 30 m (100 ft) tall. Today, however, there are only about 25 species living, and they are all quite small, rarely reaching a height of more than 1 m (about 3 ft).

Hot-air balloon – on 21 November 1783 a human being flew for the first time, on a platform suspended beneath a bag filled with hot air from a fire on the ground. The craft, named *Montgolfière* after its inventors, the French brothers Joseph and Etienne Montgolfier, travelled approximately 8 km (5 miles) in about 25 minutes.

The sport of ballooning briefly became popular, but the craft were always at the mercy of the wind and could only remain aloft while the air inside the bag remained warm. In recent years there has been a revival of hot-air ballooning, using lightweight propane gas burners which can be carried with the passengers to keep re-heating the air.

A hot-air balloon being prepared for take-off.

Hovercraft is a flat-bottomed vessel which travels on a cushion of air, held in place by a flexible 'skirt' around the base of the vessel. Forward propulsion is by means of propellers mounted on top of the craft. A hovercraft can travel over land and water, but is hard to steer accurately, limiting its use at present to areas where there is ample space. It is especially useful for crossing marshland, where few other vehicles can go. The largest hovercraft in regular use carry over 50 cars and over 400 passengers at a time over the English Channel, a crossing which they can complete in 35 minutes, compared to almost two hours taken by ships.

The same principle is also used by hovering lawn mowers. Hovercraft were invented in 1955 by Englishman Christopher Cockerill. *See also* Hydrofoil.

Hubble classification is the classification of galaxies. Millions of galaxies can be seen from the Earth. They have many different shapes and sizes. An American astronomer, Edwin Powell Hubble (1889–1953), studied some of these galaxies. In 1925 he classified galaxies which looked the same into three main groups. In the first group are galaxies which look like an ellipse, or a squashed circle. In the second group are galaxies which are shaped like catherine wheels. These are known as spiral galaxies. Our Galaxy is a spiral galaxy. All other galaxies are in the third group and are known as irregular galaxies. Each of these groups is divided into many types.

Hugo, Victor (1802–1885), was a French writer. His early work included Romantic poetry, drama and *The Hunchback of Notre Dame*, a novel inspired by his love of Gothic architecture. In the 1840s he stopped writting and took up politics. Becoming a stern republican, he resisted the Emperor Napolean III in 1851 and spent 20 years in exile in Guernsey, where he renewed his literary activities. He wrote prolifically, including essays, political satires, a collection of legends, religious works, poetry and his great historical ten-volume novel, *Les Misérables*.

Huguenots is the name given to the French Protestants, most of whom were followers of John Calvin, in 16th- and 17th-century France. Their numbers grew rapidly in the mid 16th century and their rivalry with the Catholics led to the outbreak of the Wars of Religion. When Henry IV came to the throne he issued the Edict of Nantes (1598) which granted some degree of religious toleration and brought the wars to an end. However, during the reign of Louis XIV, the Huguenots were increasingly persecuted, and when the Edict was revoked in 1685 many of them fled abroad.

Hummingbird is a tiny, delicate bird found throughout the New World. Most of the 300 or so species are brilliantly coloured. They get their name from the noise their wings make as they beat them – sometimes at rates of up to 100 beats per second – whilst they hover at flowers sucking up the nectar with their long beaks. They dart among the flowers like flying jewels, and can even fly backwards. The smallest hummingbird is the Cuban bee hummingbird. It is only 5.6 cm (2.2 in) long – even smaller than some insects – and its nest is the size of a thimble. Despite their small size, hummingbirds can migrate long distances. The rubythroated hummingbird flies 800 km (480 miles) across the Gulf of Mexico without stopping.

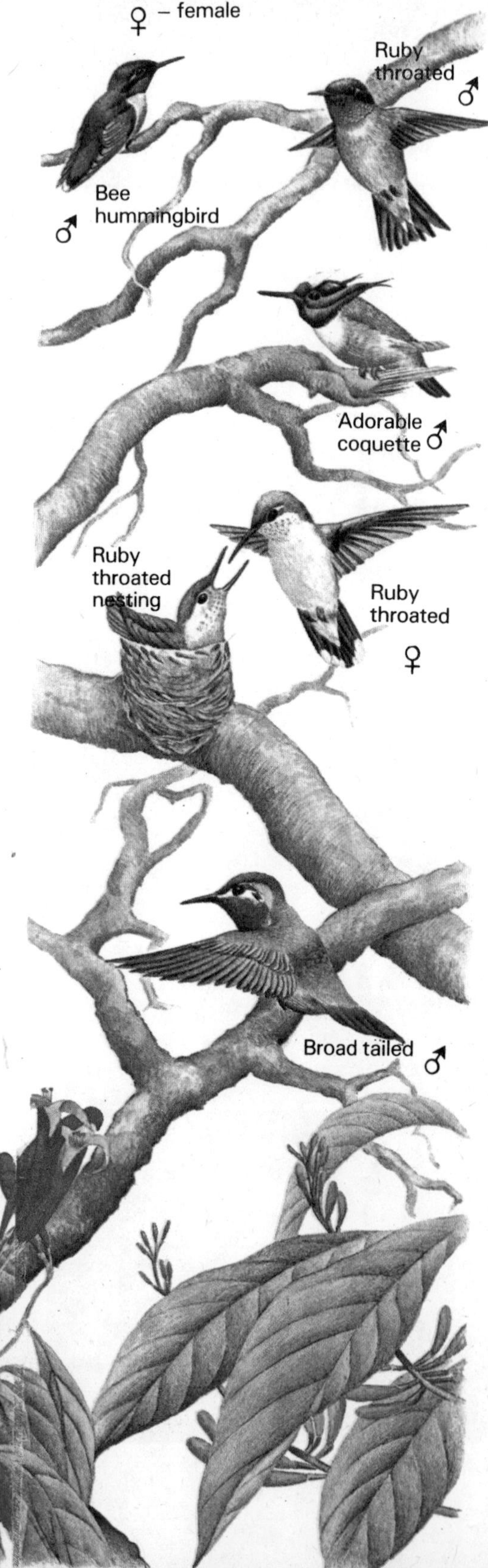

Hundred Years' War, between England and France, lasted intermittently from 1337 to 1453. It began when Edward III laid claim to the French throne, and the English won victories at Sluys (1340), Crécy (1346) and Poitiers (1356). Later the French forced the English to relinquish most of the territory they had conquered. After a long truce the conflict was renewed by Henry V, who defeated the French at Agincourt (1415) and conquered Normandy. However, the tide of war turned against England after Henry's death, when the French, led by Joan of Arc, gained a series of victories. The French King made peace with Burgundy, England's ally, and by 1453 the English had lost all their French possessions except Calais.

Hungary is a republic in central Europe. Capital, Budapest; area about 93 000 sq km (36 000 sq miles).
History The area was settled by Magyar tribesmen in the late 9th century AD. Hungary became an independent kingdom from about AD 1000, adopting Christianity. Defeat by the Turks at Mohass in 1526 brought much of the country under Turkish sovereignty, the rest being ruled by Austria. In 1699 the whole of Hungary became part of the Hapsburg Empire. During the 19th century there was an upsurge of nationalism, but a revolt in 1848 was suppressed by the Austrians. In 1867 Hungary became self-governing within Austria-Hungary. After the collapse of Austria-Hungary in 1918 Hungary became briefly a Communist republic. However, in 1920 it was made a constitutional monarchy. It became a republic again after the Second World War and in 1949 came under Communist rule. An uprising in 1956 was ended by Soviet troops.
Land and People The country is mainly level plain, with a highlands region in the north. The Danube and its tributaries are the main river system.

Most of the Hungarians are Magyars, whose ancestors arrived in the 9th century, but there are several groups of different national background, including gypsies.
Economy The soils of the Danube plain are mostly very fertile, and Hungary is still chiefly an agricultural country. Thanks to the Carpathian Mountains in the north, the climate is fairly mild and, although rainfall is adequate for crops, there is a lot of sunshine. Hungary is a major producer of cereals, potatoes and sugar beet; many other crops, such as grapes, are grown. Rapid industrial development has taken place since 1945, and there are important resources of coal, aluminium, oil and natural gas.

Huns were a nomadic Mongol people who originated in central Asia. They invaded Europe in the 4th and 5th centuries AD, compelling other barbarian tribes, such as the Visigoths, to flee before them across the frontiers of the Roman Empire, which they subsequently invaded. Their remarkable horsemanship and their bloodthirsty reputation created terror in more peaceful peoples. Under the leadership of Attila they ravaged western Europe.

Hurricane is a violent and destructive tropical storm that usually travels west across the West Indies and then north along the Atlantic coasts of Mexico and the USA. It is a form of whirlwind and is, in effect, the American version of the cyclone. It is accompanied by storms and torrential rain. A hurricane-force wind is one with a speed of more than 125 km/h (78 mph).

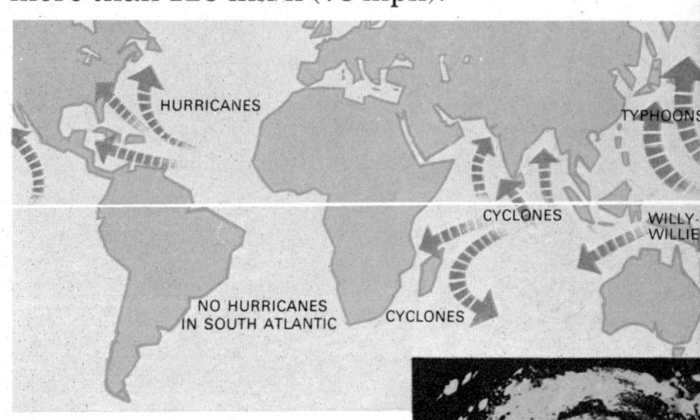

Above: Hurricane areas.
Right: In a hurricane, violent winds circulate. In the very centre of the hurricane is an area of clear sky and light winds, called the 'eye of the storm'.

Hybrid is an animal or plant produced as the result of a cross between genetically unlike parents – such as different species. The mule is a hybrid of a horse and a donkey. Many plants are bred as hybrids, for this can ensure that the best characteristics of two different plants are contained in the hybrid.

Hydra is a small, freshwater coelenterate, which is common in ponds and slow-moving streams. Like other coelenterates it has a sac-like body with a mouth at the top, surrounded by tentacles. The body, usually attached to a rock or plant, can stretch and shorten as the hydra sways about searching for tiny creatures to catch on its tentacles. It can also 'swim' by looping along or rolling along 'head-over-heels'. Hydra reproduces by releasing from the body a fertilized egg which develops into a new individual, or by growing a bud, which also turns into a new hydra.

Hydrofoil is a device used to make boats much faster. The hydrofoil is mounted on pylons beneath the boat's hull and raises the hull clear of the water, so reducing friction. The Russians have many hydrofoil vessels, including a fleet of 100-seat passenger craft which travel at 56 km/h (35 mph), and a 400 tonne warship which uses gas turbine engines to travel at over 110 km (68 mph). *See also* Hovercraft.

A hydrofoil

Hydrogen is a gas with no taste, colour or smell, and is the simplest substance there is. Its chemical symbol is H. Astronomers think that there is more hydrogen in the universe than any other element. On the Earth, hydrogen is a component of water, petroleum, sugar and many other substances.

Because hydrogen is so light, it was once used to lift huge airships which carried passengers across the Atlantic Ocean. Unfortunately, mixtures of hydrogen and air explode if they are lit and several airships exploded. Now helium is used to lift airships instead.

Hydrogen bomb is the most dangerous weapon yet made. It can cause more damage than millions of tonnes of explosives, such as TNT. The first hydrogen bomb was exploded by the USA in 1952.

A small atom bomb is used to set off a hydrogen bomb. It is called a hydrogen bomb because its energy comes from the joining together, or fusion, of hydrogen nuclei. *See also* Nuclear fusion.

Hyena is a carnivorous mammal with a powerful neck and shoulders. Its teeth are strong enough to bite through and eat the largest bones. There are three species; the striped, brown and spotted hyenas. They live on open grassland in Africa and parts of Asia. By day, they act as scavengers, attending the kills of the big cats after they have eaten their fill, and greedily ripping the carcass apart to feed on the remains. By night, however, they are hunters, travelling in packs to track down and kill young wildebeest, antelope and zebra.

Brown hyenas

Ibex are wild goats living in rocky or mountainous regions from Spain to Mongolia. They migrate to the lower slopes during winter. They have typical goat-like bodies but have enormous, backward-curving horns.

Abyssinian ibex

Ibn Saud (1880–1953), was the founder of the kingdom of Saudi Arabia. The son of the Sultan of Najd, he was forced into exile by a rival, but recovered his lands in 1902. He gradually brought the whole of Arabia under his control, taking Hejaz in 1924. In 1932 he became King of a united country, which was renamed Saudi Arabia. During his reign exploitation of the region's enormous oil resources began.

Ibsen, Henrik (1828–1906), was a Norwegian playwright, and the dominant figure in European drama during the second half of his life. He wrote many verse plays (notably *Brand* and *Peer Gynt*), but his greatest impact was as a realist, exposing the hypocrisy and injustice of 19th-century society. *A Doll's House* (1879) was particularly important in showing how women were denied opportunities to develop their own personalities and opinions. Later still, Ibsen turned to psychological and mysterious, poetic subjects. Among his many famous plays are *Ghosts*, *The Wild Duck*, *Hedda Gabler* and *When We Dead Awaken*.

Icarus was a figure in ancient Greek mythology. He was the son of the great craftsman, Daedalus, and was imprisoned with him by King Minos in Crete. Daedalus made wings out of wax and feathers with which they escaped. But Icarus ignored his father's warning not to fly too near the Sun. As a result, the wax melted and he fell into the Sea of Icarus, where he drowned.

Ice is solid water. Water freezes to ice and ice melts to water at 0 degrees Centrigrade (32 degrees Fahrenheit). Most substances shrink when they freeze, but water expands slightly when it freezes. This means that ice floats on water, and a frozen pond usually has water under the ice. Animals and plants can live through the winter in the pond protected from the cold by the ice. It also means that water pipes can crack when the water in them thaws after freezing. The cracks are discovered when the ice melts, and water pours out of them.

Parts of the Arctic and Antarctic continents and the tops of high mountains are always covered in ice. Snow, hailstones and frost are all forms of ice.

Ice Age is a time when much of the Earth is very cold, and sheets of ice cover large parts of the land. During the last Ice Age, ice covered much of Europe and North America.

An icebreaker in the Baltic.

It disappeared about 10 000 years ago. The last Ice Age might not have truly finished, however. Many scientists believe we may be living through a warm spell in the Ice Age.

Ice Ages have changed the shape of the land, because moving ice, known as a glacier, cuts through and erodes rocks.

If the Earth moves away from the Sun it becomes colder. Dust from volcanoes can cover the Earth, blocking out some of the Sun's heat. These and other factors may have caused the Ice Ages.

Iceberg is a floating mass of ice (*berg* is German for 'mountain') which has broken off from a glacier and drifts in the world's oceans until it melts. Most icebergs come from the great ice-sheets covering Greenland and Antarctica. Antarctic icebergs are the largest, usually several kilometres (miles) long. However, Greenland icebergs are a greater menace, endangering ships on the busy North-Atlantic routes.

One of the worst disasters at sea occurred in 1912 on the ocean liner *Titanic's* maiden voyage. The ship collided with an iceberg and went down with great loss of life. This led to the establishment of the International Ice Patrol, which is still engaged in tracking icebergs and warning any shipping in the area.

Icebreaker is a ship which is specially shaped and strengthened so that it can cut through icefields which would stop or crush an ordinary vessel. The largest such ship is the 134 m (440 ft) Russian *Lenin*, which can travel at 33 km/h (approximately 20 mph) – she was also the world's first nuclear-powered ship.

Iceland is an island republic in the north Atlantic. Capital, Reykjavik; area about 103 000 sq km (40 000 sq miles).

History The island was first settled by Vikings in AD 874. A parliament was established in the 10th century, and Christianity was adopted soon after. In 1262 it was united with Norway, coming under Danish rule in 1380. In the 19th century it received its own constitution and in 1918 became almost completely independent of Denmark except for foreign affairs. Iceland eventually received full independence as a republic in 1944, joining NATO in 1949. It was involved in fishing disputes with Britain in the 1950s and the 1970s.

Land and People The coast is very jagged and much of the interior is mountainous, with many hot springs, geysers and active volcanoes. Though so far north, warm ocean currents keep the summers mild, but much of Iceland is still bleak and the population is small. Fishing is the main occupation.

Icon is a religious painting as used in the Eastern Orthodox Church. It is usually a figure of Christ or a saint. The icon originated in the wooden panels painted with such subjects in Byzantine art. Later, it was often metal, with ornamental jewels and sometimes gold plate. Russia was the great centre of icon production, though the early Russian icons were often the work of Greek (Byzantine) artists.

Igneous rock is one of the three types of rock making up the Earth's crust (the other two are metamorphic and sedimentary rocks). The term comes from the Latin *igneus* meaning 'fiery', and igneous rocks consist of solidified molten rock or lava.

There are many kinds of igneous rock, depending on the chemical composition of the original lava, and on the pressure under which it solidified, beneath or above the ground. Granite and basalt are examples of igneous rocks.

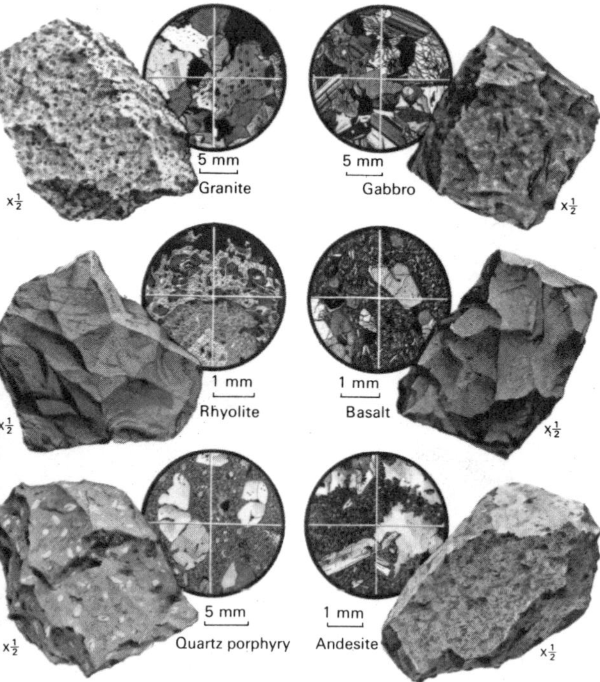

Some examples of igneous rocks, showing also what they look like under a polarizing microscope.

Iguana is a lizard found in the New World. One iguana, the basilisk of Central America, can run on its hind legs. Some iguanas live in trees, but the marine iguana is the only lizard living in or near the sea. It can dive under water, and feeds on seaweed.

Imago is the name given to the adult, sexually mature form of an insect. During its life, an insect undergoes several changes of shape, and each is given a different name.

Immunization is a process that results in increasing resistance to infection. It may occur naturally (for example, babies acquire certain immunities through their mothers' milk) or through deliberate human action.

The most important kind of intentional immunization is vaccination. Due to this, many once-dreaded diseases, such as smallpox, have virtually disappeared.

Vaccination was discovered by an English physician, Edward Jenner. Another great pioneer of immunology was the French scientist Louis Pasteur. *See also* Vaccine.

Impressionism was a movement in French art which began in the 1860s and was at its peak in the 1870s. The Impressionists were a group of mostly very young artists who wanted to get away from the dull and lifeless tradition of 'official' art. The chief characteristic of Impressionism was a concern with the effects of light. The Impressionists painted from nature in the open air, rather than in a studio, and achieved their effects by the use of broken patches of colour. They were influenced by earlier landscape painters, especially Corot, and by realists like Manet, who became their hero and was often found among them at the Cafe Guerbois in Paris. The group included Monet, Renoir, Degas, Pissarro and Cézanne, who all eventually developed in different ways but had many convictions in common.

An Impressionist painting is a vivid glimpse of a scene, not a studied gaze. The surroundings are often blurred – just as they are when the eye is looking at an object.

A later phase, called Post-Impressionism, included such great painters as Cézanne, Gauguin and Van Gogh, who all used techniques owing something to Impressionism but modified by their individual genius.

Although early reactions to the movement were hostile, Impressionism produced many of the best-loved pictures in European art. It was also of great historical importance as a forerunner of the revolution in art which occurred in the early 20th century.

Chandragupta, the founder of the Mauryan dynasty in India, reviews his army.

Incas were South American people of the southern Andes who established a capital at Cuzco about the 11th century AD. They gained control of an extensive region, and by the early 15th century their empire stretched from Peru and Ecuador to Chile. Inca civilization, which lacked the wheel and knowledge of writing, was a remarkable one, notable for its splendid buildings, extensive system of roads and fine pottery, textiles and metalwork. It crumbled rapidly, however, following the sacking of Cuzco in 1533 by the Spaniards under Pizarro and the overthrow of its king, Atahualpa.

Atahualpa, King of the Incas, offered for his own ransom, a room filled with gold *(right)*. The Spaniards did not release him however, and put him to death *(below)*.

India is a republic, forming the major part of the Indian sub-continent, south-central Asia. Capital, New Delhi; area about 3 288 000 sq km (1 269 500 sq miles).

History The Indus Valley civilization (circa 2300-circa 1750 BC) was the first to be established in the Indian sub-continent. From about 1700 BC the first waves of Indo-Europeans entered India from the northwest and pushed the inhabitants, the Dravidians, southwards. These Indo-Europeans gradually developed Hinduism which has remained India's dominant religion. Alexander the Great invaded in 327 BC and his successors were driven out by Chandragupta, who founded the Mauryan dynasty.

The Gupta dynasty created a new empire in northern India in the 4th century AD. Muslims began to invade India in the 11th century, the first Muslim dynasty being established about 1200. In the 16th century the Mogul rulers founded an empire covering most of northern and central India. Euro-

pean trading posts were established in the 16th and 17th centuries, and after 1765 the British East India Company obtained a control of large parts of the country. After the Indian Mutiny (1857) India passed to the British Crown, and was proclaimed an empire in 1877.

It achieved independence in 1947, the subcontinent being partitioned between India and Pakistan. India followed a policy of neutrality in world affairs, but had to cope with the problem of an enormous population and intermittent hostility with its neighbours: Pakistan and China.

Land Despite the mighty Himalayas in the north, India is mostly flat. South of the mountains are the great fertile plains of the Indus and Ganges. Most of the interior of the peninsula is occupied by the Deccan plateau, bounded by mountain ranges, the West and East Ghats, beyond which lie coastal plains. The climate is dominated by the monsoon, which brings the summer rains. Temperatures are very variable. It can be extremely hot on the Ganges plain while freezing in the northern hills. There are still large forests in mountain areas.

India has many unusual animals – elephants, tigers (now rare) and various poisonous snakes – and beautiful tropical flowers.

People More than one seventh of all the people in the world live in India. The country contains a great variety of people. One way of measuring this is by language; over 800 languages and distinct dialects are still in use. The official language is Hindi, and many Indians speak English.

Most of the people are classed as Hindu in religion. India is also the home of Buddhism, though there are few Buddhists now. Other minority religious groups are Muslims, Jains and Parsees (Zoroastrians).

By Western standards, most Indians live in poverty. The average Indian eats two-thirds of what the average American eats, and for most people meat is rare. The cow is a sacred animal to Hindus, who therefore do not eat beef.

Economy Though India has several large cities, most of the people live in small villages and are directly dependent on farming. About 75 per cent of the agricultural land is used for food crops. Rice is the main one, but not enough can be grown to meet home demand, and other staple foods, like wheat, must also be imported. Cotton and jute, tea, coffee and rubber are the main crops grown for export. The worst problems are poor land and lack of water. The monsoon is unreliable, and if it comes late, crops may wither. However, a growing quantity of land is irrigated.

Great developments have taken place in raising living standards and improving economic performance, but India's problems are enormous and likely to last a long time. The rising price of oil, nearly all of which is imported, has hindered development, and the rapidly rising population constantly outgrows economic expansion.

India has some very large mineral resources, including iron and bauxite (aluminium) as well as scarcer substances like ilmenite – for making titanium. For many centuries it was the only producer of diamonds. Though the mines are now nearly worked out, fine jewellery is made.

Cotton textiles are the largest manufactured product. The development of recent years has made India a truly industrial country, but workers are mostly employed in small enterprises – craftsmen's workshops rather than factories.

Prime Ministers of India

Jawāharlāl Nehru	1947–1964
Lal Bahadur Shastri	1964–1966
Indira Gandhi	1966–1977
Morarji Desai	1977–1979
Charan Singh	1979–1980
Indira Gandhi	1980–

Presidents of India

Dr Rajendra Prasad	1950–1962
Dr S Radhakrishnan	1962–1967
Dr Zakir Hussain	1967–1969
Shri V V Giri	1969–1974
Fakruddin Ali Ahmed	1974–1977
Sanjiva Reddy	1977–1982
Zail Singh	1982–

States and Territories of India

States	*Capital*	*sq km*	*sq miles*
Andhra Pradesh	Hyderabad	276814	106878
Assam	Disspur	78523	30318
Bihar	Patna	173876	67134
Gujarat	Ahmedabad	195984	75670
Haryana	Chandigarh	44222	17074
Himachal Pradesh	Simla	55673	21495
Jammu and Kashmir	Srinagar	101283	39105
Karnataka	Bangalore	191773	74044
Kerala	Trivandrum	38864	15000
Madhya Pradesh	Bhopal	442841	170982
Marharashtra	Bombay	307762	118827
Manipur	Imphal	22356	8632
Meghalaya	Shillong	22489	8683
Nagaland	Kohima	16527	6381
Orissa	Bhu	155782	60148
Punjab	Chandigarh	50362	19445
Rajasthan	Jaipur	342214	132130
Sikkim	Gangtok	7298	2818
Tamil Nadu	Madras	130069	50220
Tripura	Agartala	10477	4045
Uttar Pradesh	Lucknow	294413	113673
West Bengal	Calcutta	87853	33920
Union Territories			
Andaman and Nicobar Islands	Port Blair	8293	3202
Arunachal Pradesh	Shillong	83578	32270
Chandigarh	Chandigarh	114	44
Dadra and Nagar Haveli	Silvassa	491	190
Delhi	Delhi	1485	573
Goa, Daman and Diu	Panaji	3813	1472
Lakshadweep	Kavarath	32	12
Mizoram	Aijal	21087	8142
Pondicherry	Pondicherry	480	185

(Opposite) Mangul Pandy, an Indian sepoy, tries to lead an insurrection of the native guard against the English, in 1857.

Indian Mutiny was a rebellion by Indian soldiers (sepoys) in British service. It began with a massacre of Europeans in Meerut in May 1857 and rapidly spread throughout central India. Delhi was captured by the rebels, Lucknow was besieged, and many discontented people, including dethroned princes, joined in the mutiny. However, large sections of the Indian army remained loyal to the British, and by the end of 1858 the rebellion was virtually over. One important result was that the British crown took over the administration of the country from the East India Company.

Indian Ocean is the smallest of the world's three great oceans, and lies between Africa and Australia. Area about 73 427 000 sq km (28 350 000 sq miles). It is linked to the Mediterranean by the Red Sea and Suez Canal. The average depth is about 4000 m (13 000 ft) though it is twice as deep south of Java.

The Indian Ocean was the first to be regularly sailed by people. When the Europeans reached it in the late 15th century, they found ancient shipping routes in existence. Traffic increased greatly after the opening of the Suez Canal in 1869.

Indians, American, inhabited North and South America before the arrival of the Europeans. It is thought that their remote ancestors entered America from Asia, by way of Alaska, in successive migrations, starting about 20000 years ago. The people vary greatly in physical appearance, and probably did not originally belong to one racial group. American Indians also showed a great cultural diversity ranging from the primitive societies of the Brazilian jungle to the advanced Aztecs and Incas.

Indonesia is an island republic off south-east Asia. Capital, Jakarta; total area about 1919000 sq km (741100 sq miles). It consists of the islands of Sumatra, Java, Madura, Sulawesi (Celebes), Kalimantan (most of Borneo) and thousands of smaller islands. Irian Jaya (the western half of New Guinea) also belongs to Indonesia.

History It was ruled by the Dutch East India Company from 1602 and then by the Netherlands government. During the Second World War, the islands were occupied by the Japanese. In 1945 Indonesia declared independence, which was eventually recognized by the Dutch in 1969. Under the dashing leadership of Sukarno, Indonesia increased its territory by taking over western New Guinea (Irian Jaya) in 1969. Sukarno was eventually overthrown by military leaders and thousands of people, mainly Chinese, who were suspected of supporting him were massacred.

Land and People Parts of Indonesia are extraordinarily fertile. Food crops such as rice and rubber, tea, coffee, sugar cane and tobacco are grown in plantations. The forests produce valuable hardwoods. There are large tin mines and oil reserves. The majority of Indonesians are of Malay origin and speak a language similar to Malay. They are mostly Muslims. *See also* Bali, Java, Sumatra.

Indus is a river in central Asia. It rises in Tibet and flows for about 3060 km (1900 miles) before reaching the sea in Pakistan. It is an important source of water for India as well as Pakistan.

The Indus valley was the site of the ancient Mohenjo-Daro civilization. It also provided a route through the mountains for many invaders of the sub-continent. Its course sometimes changes, and it contains many islands and sandbanks.

Industrial Revolution was the transformation of Britain from a mainly agricultural society to a predominantly industrial one, in the period from about 1760 to 1840. The revolution began in the textile industry with a series of inventions, such as the flying shuttle and power loom, which speeded up the manufacturing process and improved the quality of the goods produced. This meant that work could no longer be carried out in people's homes, but had to be done in large factories. The invention of the steam engine was another vitally important stage in the change to an industrial society. In the 19th century the Industrial Revolution spread to western Europe and the USA.

The Indians of North America built canoes from birch bark.

Infection is the diseased condition found in both animals and plants when harmful micro-organisms, such as bacteria, enter the tissues of the victim and multiply. Trees often become infected when the bark is damaged by grazing animals or through the loss of a branch. Spores enter the tree and can cause deformities, fruit loss or even death. Infections can also occur when the roots become damaged, allowing entry to soil-borne organisms. Animal infections can be caused by wounds. Some infections of humans are passed in the tiny water droplets that are produced when we sneeze. The common cold is transmitted in this way, and is caused by a virus which infects the cells of our mouth, nose and throat. Some infections are cured by the victim's own defence, but others require treatment with medicines such as antibiotics.

Inflation, in economics, describes a situation in which the general level of prices rises significantly and persistently for a period of several years or more. It also means that the value of money falls since, for example, a peseta or dollar will buy less at this year's higher prices than it did the year before.

Inflation has been taking place in most Western countries since the Second World War. After the steep rise in prices during the 1970s it came to be seen as a major economic problem.

The causes and cures of inflation remain a subject of fierce argument involving economists and politicians. It seems that policies simply reversing the trend (deflationary policies) make matters worse rather than better, by creating mass unemployment.

Infra-red radiation consists of rays which are similar to light rays, but which are invisible. Although they cannot be seen, they can be felt as heat. All hot objects give off infra-red rays. Infra-red heaters are used for drying in factories, and infra-red lamps are used in many homes.

Satellites take photographs of the infra-red rays from the Earth. These photographs can show which parts are densely populated and which parts have mainly plants growing on them – they can even show the different plants growing. Military satellites can detect the heat given off by rockets and submarines. *See also* Electromagnetic radiation.

Insecticides are used to kill insects. Some insects harm crops and spread disease. Insecticides are sprayed over crops, and are used in homes, hospitals, etc. Their use allows more food to be grown and fights diseases, such as malaria.

However, most insecticides kill helpful as well as harmful insects. Some, such as DDT, can build up to dangerous levels in the soil and in the animals which eat them. Chemists are now developing safer insecticides.

Insectivores are animals such as bats and shrews which eat mainly insects. They have small, pointed teeth for crunching up the insects' bodies before swallowing them. Sometimes the word insectivore means any mammal belong to the order Insectivora although, confusingly, many members of the Insectivora, such as moles and hedgehogs, eat several other food items apart from insects.

Two examples of insectivores: a horseshoe bat *(top)*, and a shrew *(above)*.

Insects are arthropods whose body is divided into three sections: head, thorax and abdomen. The head bears feelers (antennae), eyes (usually light-detecting eyes called ocelli and also image-forming compound eyes), and mouthparts. The thorax bears three pairs of jointed legs and two pairs of wings. The abdomen bears breathing holes called spiracles and, in females, an egg laying tube called the ovipositor. In many species some of these parts are lost or altered to suit the lifestyle of the particular insect. Thus the parasitic fleas and lice, which spend most of their lives attached to a host, have lost their wings.

There is no place that insects have not been able to colonize, and they are the most numerous animals. In terms of numbers and choice of habitats, they are the most successful animals on Earth. Over three-quarters of all known animal species are insects, and together all the insects in the world would outweigh every other animal in the world put together.

Insulator is a substance which does not let either electricity or heat pass through it easily. Plastic, rubber, air and paper are good insulators. Electrical wires and equipment are often covered with plastic. This stops the electricity leaking out, and protects people from electric shocks.

Fur and wool keep animals warm because they hold a lot of air which stops heat leaving the animal's body, insulating it from the cold. Bad insulators are called conductors.

Insurance is a means of avoiding or keeping down the cost to the victim of accidents or misfortunes. By paying a relatively small sum (called the premium) to an insurance company, people can arrange cover for the unexpected cost of, for example, breaking a leg, crashing a car, or their house burning down. The insurance company operates on the principle that such accidents will only occur to a small percentage of its customers each year, so that it will emerge with a profit. Insurance can cover such things as business ventures, property, ships, life and theft.

Invertebrates are animals which do not have backbones or, more precisely, invertebrates are all the animals which are not members of the Vertebrata (the Vertebrata are the mammals, birds, reptiles, amphibians, and fish). Although the invertebrates are usually small animals, often living secretive lives, they make up more than 90 per cent of the Animal Kingdom. They include sponges, jellyfish, worms, snails, insects, spiders and crabs.

THE VARIETY OF INVERTEBRATES

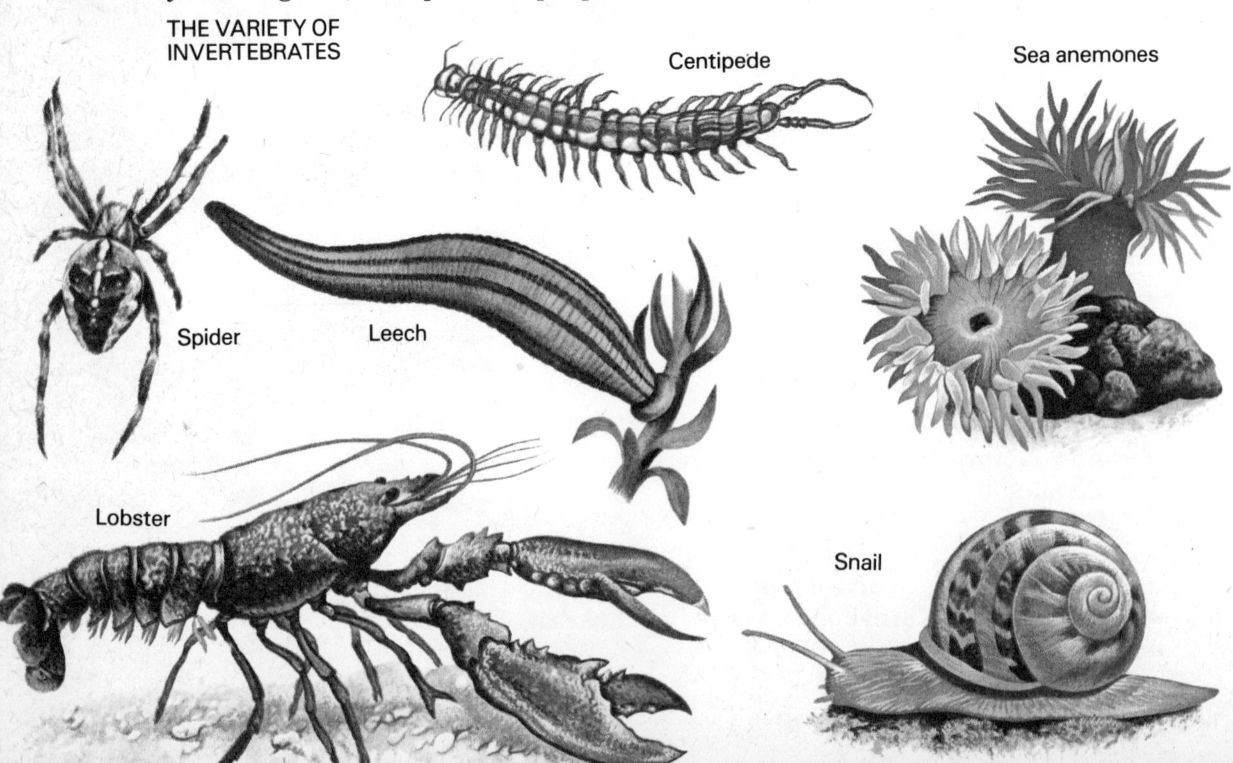

Ion is an atom which has lost or gained electrons. An ion has an electrical charge. When atoms are changed to ions, it is known as ionization. Some substances become ionized when they are dissolved in liquids, and radiation can ionize gases. *See also* Electrolysis.

Ionosphere is a deep, outer part of the Earth's atmosphere. It has three layers. It is called the ionosphere because the gas atoms in it are ions. An atom becomes an ion when it gains or loses electrons. When the Sun's rays hit the Earth's outer atmosphere they knock electrons out of the gas atoms. The ionosphere is ionized by the Sun.

The ionosphere is very important in world-wide communications. Radio waves travel in a straight line. So, instead of travelling around the Earth, they go straight out into the Earth's atmosphere. The ionosphere bounces them back to the Earth. In this way radio waves can zigzag around the Earth. This allows people to send radio messages anywhere in the world.

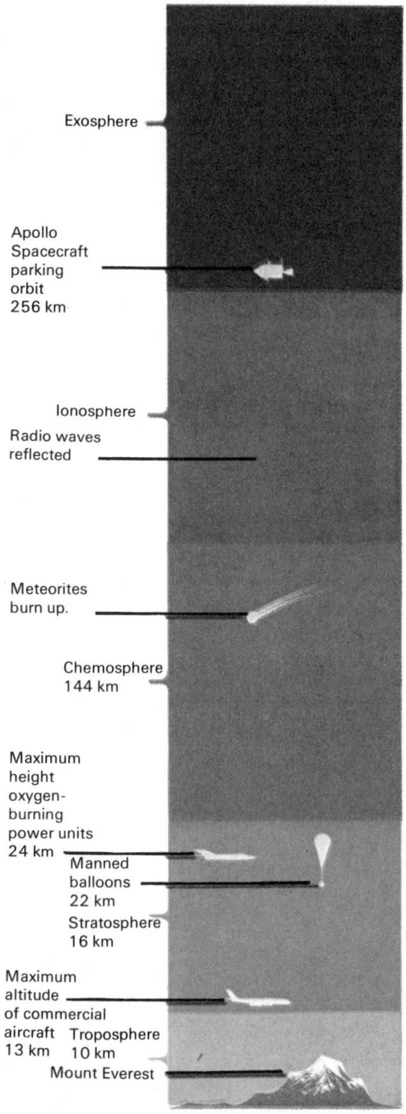

The Earth's atmosphere, showing the ionosphere and other layers.

Iran is a republic in south-west Asia. Capital, Tehran; area about 1 648 000 sq km (634 000 sq miles).

History The country was settled by Aryan tribes from about the 9th century BC. The kingdom of the Medes was established about 730 BC, when Iran broke away from the Assyrian Empire. In the 6th century BC the Medes were overthrown by Cyrus the Great who began the creation of a vast empire, which was destroyed by Alexander the Great in 330 BC. Iran subsequently passed under Parthian control and then, in the 3rd century AD, flourished once more under the Persian Sassanid dynasty. This period ended with the Arab invasions of the 7th century.

Arab rule lasted until the 13th century when Iran was conquered by the Seljuk Turks and then by Genghis Khan and the Mongols. It enjoyed a period of expansion under the Safavids (1502–1736). The Kajar dynasty ruled from 1796 to 1925, when the Pahlavis came to power. In 1980, the Shah, Mohammed Reze Pahlavi, was forced to go into exile when a revolutionary Muslim regime came to power.

Land Much of Iran consists of a great plateau, flanked by the Zagros Mountains on the west and south and the Elburz in the north. The plateau itself has mountain ridges and barren areas. Most of Iran is desert or semi-desert, and cities like Tehran grew from oases. There are few rivers or forests, except in mountain regions. The climate is very variable, and in most parts the days are hot and the nights cold.

People Only about 65 per cent of the population are true Iranians, or Persians, and members of the Shi'ite branch of Islam. The numerous racial minorities include Kurds in Kurdistan and Baluchis in the south-east. Among many social conflicts in modern Iran, there is a general hostility between people who live in the plains and those who live in the mountains.

Economy Iran has huge oil reserves, by far the most important economic factor. There are other mineral deposits, but they are unimportant by comparison, and there is little heavy industry, though many types of manufacturing. Perhaps the most famous export, after oil, is carpets, some of which are still hand-made by the old methods. Cotton textiles are also exported in large quantities.

Iraq is a republic in south-west Asia. Capital, Baghdad; area about 438000 sq km (171000 sq miles).

History The modern state of Iraq, descendant of the ancient civilization of Mesopotamia, was founded as an Arab kingdom in 1921, supervised by Britain under a League of Nations mandate until 1930. The monarchy was overthrown and a republic established in 1958. Quarrels with the Islamic regime in Iran led to war between these neighbours in the early 1980s.

Land and People Iran is mainly fairly flat, except in the north, and parts of the west and south-west are desert. The central plain – 'Land of the Two Rivers' – is crossed by the Tigris and Euphrates. The climate is hot in summer and warmish in winter. Frost in Baghdad is rare, though not unknown. Most of the people are Arabs, with more Shi'ite than Sunni (orthodox) Muslims. There is a large minority of Kurds.

Agriculture is now reasonably prosperous in Iraq, thanks to extensive irrigation. Manufacturing has flourished but is mainly small in scale. The most important natural resources are oil and natural gas.

Ireland (Eire) is a republic in north-west Europe, forming most of the island of Ireland. Capital, Dublin; area about 69000 sq km (26600 sq miles).

History Ireland was invaded by Celts about 500 BC and converted to Christianity in the 5th century AD. Invasions by Norsemen started in the late 8th century, but were effectively stopped by Brian Boru at the Battle of Clontarf (1014). Anglo-Norman invasions began in the 12th century, but English rule was restricted until Tudor times when a policy of conquest was adopted. English and Scottish settlements called plantations were set up, and after Cromwell's expedition of 1649–1650 to suppress a rebellion, English rule was established. The Irish bitterly resented this, and there were frequent rebellions. In 1801 the Act of Union gave Ireland representation in the British Parliament. The population suffered severely from the potato famine of the 1840s, and agitation for Home Rule grew. An act granting Home Rule was passed in 1912 despite opposition of Irish Protestants in Ulster. The Irish Free State was established in 1921, but the six counties of Ulster, mostly Protestant, remained part of the United Kingdom as Northern Ireland.

The protestant king of England, William III, defeated the former Catholic king, James II, at the Battle of the Boyne in Ireland in 1690.

Ireland became fully independent in 1948, joining the United Nations in 1955 and the EEC in 1973.

Land and People Ireland is known as the 'Emerald Isle' because it is so green, thanks to the generally mild, damp climate. Central Ireland is mostly gently rolling country; the north-west is more mountainous, with steep – though not very high – granite peaks. There is another upland area south-west of Dublin, including the Wicklow Mountains, and many lakes and rivers. Nearly all the old forest has gone, but there are still areas of bogs – a source of peat. Most of the people are Roman Catholic.

Economy Agriculture is still the most important section of the economy. Although some parts are very fertile, livestock-raising and dairy farming are more important than crops. Potatoes are less vital than they were in the 19th century. Large industrial development has taken place in recent years, and there is a wide range of manufacturing.

Otherwise, there are few natural resources, and though Ireland enjoyed a boom after joining the EEC, it is basically a poor country economically. *See also* Northern Ireland; United Kingdom.

Prime Ministers of Ireland

William T Cosgrave	1922–1932
Eamon de Valera	1932–1948
John A Costello	1948–1951
Eamon de Valera	1951–1954
John A Costello	1954–1957
Eamon de Valera	1957–1959
Seán Lemass	1959–1966
Jack Lynch	1966–1973
Liam Cosgrave	1973–1977
Jack Lynch	1977–1979
Charles J Haughey	1979–1981
Garret Fitzgerald	1981–1982
Charles J Haughey	1982–1983
Garret Fitzgerald	1983–

Counties of Ireland

Counties and county boroughs	*Area sq km*	*sq miles*
Province of Leinster		
Carlow	896	346
Dublin County Borough	116	45
Dublin	790	305
Dun Laoghaire Borough	18	7
Kildare	1694	654
Kilkenny	2062	796
Laoighis	1720	664
Longford	1044	403
Louth	821	317
Meath	2339	903
Offaly	1997	771
Westmeath	1764	681
Wexford	2352	908
Wicklow	2025	782
Total of Leinster	19638	7582
Province of Munster		
Clare	3188	1231
Cork County Borough	36	14
Cork	7423	2866
Kerry	4700	1815
Limerick County Borough	18	7
Limerick	2668	1030
Tipperary, N.R.	1997	771
Tipperary, S.R.	2258	872
Waterford County Borough	10	4
Waterford	1828	706
Total of Munster	24126	9315
Province of Connacht		
Galway	5934	2293
Leitrim	1525	589
Mayo	5397	2084
Roscommon	2463	951
Sligo	1795	693
Total of Connacht	17120	6610
Province of Ulster (part of)		
Cavan	1891	730
Donegal	4830	1865
Monaghan	1290	498
Total of Ulster (part of)	8011	3093

Celts, during the Iron Age, made tools and weapons out of iron. Here, a chieftain watches as his sword blade is forged.

Iron is the commonest metal in the Earth's crust, after aluminium. Its chemical symbol is Fe. Most countries have iron mines. It has been mined for thousands of years and is still the most useful metal.

Iron is found in ores such as magnetite and hematite. These are heated in blast furnaces until the iron becomes liquid. The liquid iron used to be allowed to trickle into containers called pigs, and iron from a blast furnace is still known as pig iron. Pig iron contains small amounts of other substances, which are removed before the iron is made into wrought iron or steel.

In the presence of air and water iron forms red compounds known as rust. Iron objects have to be covered with paint or another metal to stop this forming.

The iron ore, magnetite, is magnetic, and iron is used in electromagnets.

Iron Age was the third great stage in the history of humans as tool and weapon makers, coming after the Stone Age and the Bronze Age. Techniques of working iron were developed in Asia Minor (now part of Turkey) by about 1500 BC and had arrived in the Middle East and south-east Europe before 1000 BC. After this they spread quickly, for example reaching China by 600 BC and Britain by about 550 BC. In America, iron remained unknown until the arrival of Europeans in the 15th century AD.

Iron Curtain was an expression first used by Sir Winston Churchill in a speech at Fulton, Missouri, USA in 1946. It described the ideological barrier which had arisen after the Second World War between the democratic West on the one hand and the USSR and the Communist-dominated countries of eastern Europe on the other.

Isis was a goddess of ancient Egypt. She was the wife (and sister) of Osiris and mother of Horus. While Osiris was absent, she governed Egypt wisely and well. The tears she wept after her husband's death were said to explain the annual flooding of the Nile, which was the basis of Egypt's prosperity.

Islam is the religion of the Muslims. 'Islam' means 'obedience to God' and also 'peace'. There is one god, whose name is Allah, and his word is revealed in the Koran, the sacred book of Islam. Islam also has some respect for the Bible and acknowledges such figures as Abraham, Moses and Jesus as prophets.

The greatest of the prophets, however, is Muhammad, the true founder of the Muslim religion in the 8th century. He made Mecca the Holy City of Islam and ruled all Arabia by the time he died.

The Arabs carried their religion abroad with extraordinary speed. Within a century Islam stretched from India to northern Spain. The contest between Islam and Christian Europe was one of the main themes of the Middle Ages. *See also* Allah; Koran.

Isle of Man is an island off north-west England, and is a self-governing dependency of the Crown. Capital, Douglas; area 572 sq km (227 sq miles). It has a parliament, the Tynwald, which is 1000 years old, and its own ancient laws.

Isotopes are atoms of the same element which have different numbers of neutrons. Atoms of the same element always have the same number of protons in their nucleus, but the number of neutrons may vary.

The mass of an atom depends on the number of protons and neutrons. A hydrogen atom usually has a mass of 1, and has one proton. There are hydrogen atoms, which have masses of two. These still have one proton, but also have one neutron in their nucleus. Hydrogen atoms with a mass of three have one proton and two neutrons in their nucleus. They are written as H^1, H^2 and H^3 and are isotopes of hydrogen. Every element has isotopes. Some of these are radioactive. They are known as radioisotopes and are used in medicine and industry.

Israel is a republic in south-west Asia, bordering the Mediterranean. Capital, Jerusalem; area about 21 000 sq km (8000 sq miles).
History The state of Israel was established in 1948 following the partition of Palestine. It was immediately invaded by the armies of neighbouring Arab states, who were successfully repulsed. During the next 30 years Israel's population grew rapidly with the influx of Jews from all over the world.

Israel was at war with its Arab neighbours in 1956, in 1967 and 1973. It considerably expanded its frontiers, annexing the Jordanian part of Jerusalem in the process. In 1979 Israel and Egypt signed a peace treaty, but Israel still faced the hostility of other Arab states and the Palestine Liberation Organization.
Land and People The sandy coastal plain, including reclaimed marshes, gives way to central uplands and rugged hills. In the east is a lowland valley region, containing the Dead Sea and Sea of Galilee. In the south is the Negev Desert. The north and west have a warm, Mediterranean climate. In the south

and east the summers are very hot.

The people are mainly Jews whose families immigrated in recent years, but there is a large Arab minority.

Economy Agricultural development in Israel has been little short of miraculous. Formerly barren areas now yield rich crops thanks to irrigation, and Israel is a big exporter of citrus fruit. Many farms are run on a co-operative system. The best-known type of organization is the kibbutz, where all property is owned, and all work shared by the people equally.

Israel is the most highly industrialized nation in the Middle East, but lacks fuels and many minerals. The most valuable export by far is diamonds which, however, are first imported in the natural 'rough' state and then processed in Israel.

Italy is a republic in southern Europe consisting of a peninsula and the islands of Sicily and Sardinia. Capital, Rome; area about 301 000 sq km (116 000 sq miles).

History After the collapse of the Roman Empire, Italy was invaded by Ostrogoths and Lombards in the 5th–6th centuries AD. From 774 it formed part of the Carolingian Empire, and from 962 it was part of the Holy Roman Empire, when the German King, Otto I, was crowned in Rome. Northern Italy was divided into city-states which became caught up in the conflict between Pope and Emperor. During the 16th century Spain became the dominant power in Italy, ruling most of the country directly or indirectly. In the 18th century Spanish control of Italy passed to Austria. The 19th-century movement for independence led to complete reunification in 1871 under a monarchy. In 1922 a Fascist regime under Benito Mussolini was established, which lasted until 1943. Italy became a republic in 1946 and was a founder-member of the EEC.

Land and People The Alps form Italy's northern boundary, and their offshoot, the Apennines, run down the peninsula like a spine. In the north is the broad, fertile plain drained by the River Po. Coastal plains lie on either side of the Apennines, fairly narrow on the Adriatic Sea. Sicily and Sardinia are similar to southern Italy, with rugged mountains rising in the interior from a coastal plain.

Benito Mussolini, ruler of Italy from 1922 to 1943. He was executed by Italian patriots.

Although Italy is fairly small, it is a great distance from north to south, and this is reflected in differences in the climate (the south being hotter) and in the people. Southerners tend to be shorter and darker. The country is quite heavily populated, especially on the North Italian Plain. Practically all Italians are Roman Catholics.

Economy Considering how much of the country is mountainous, a large proportion of Italy is used for farming and grazing. Wheat is the biggest crop, and Italy is the one country of the EEC to grow rice. It is also a big wine producer. Farming, and life in general, is less prosperous in the south.

Minerals generally are in short supply. The lack of coal hindered early industrial development, though northern Italy is now one of Europe's most highly industrialized regions. Milan is the largest industrial centre and the business capital of Italy. As many raw materials and foods must be imported, Italian manufactures are essential in preserving a reasonable balance of trade. Another important source of income is tourism. The climate, food, entertainment and cultural interest of Italy are a great attraction.

Ivory is a type of dentine (the material which teeth are made of), forming the teeth or tusks of the elephant, hippopotamus, walrus, warthog, wild boar and some whales.

Ivory has been used for decorative work since prehistoric times, when people carved or scratched designs on mammoth tusks. Demand for ivory remains so great that many African elephants continue to be killed illegally for their tusks – a situation which may eventually threaten them with extinction.

Ivory Coast is a republic in West Africa. Capital, Abidjan; area about 322 000 sq km (124 000 sq miles). Formerly part of French Equatorial Africa, the Ivory Coast has been independent since 1960, but it maintains close links with France.

The Ivory Coast is mainly flat. Beyond the low coastal belt there are plains and plateaux, with areas of extensive forest towards the south and dry savannah in the east. The north-west is hilly. The climate is generally hot and humid.

The people belong to a variety of small tribes and they are mostly rather poor. Industrial potential is limited, and the main products are crops such as peanuts, tropical fruits and millet. Cocoa, coffee, cotton and coconuts are also grown for export.

(The capital of Ivory Coast is to be moved to Yamoussoukro, the birthplace of the President.)

Ivy family contains trees, shrubs and climbers, most of which are tropical. They bear small, often drab flowers, usually clustered together in bunches. An ivy, common throughout much of Europe, is often seen growing on tree trunks or adorning the sides of houses. It climbs by means of tiny, sucker-like roots which sprout from the stem to maintain a grip as the plant grows.

Jackal is a member of the dog family. Three species live in Africa; one of them also lives in parts of Europe and Asia. Jackals look like small wolves, and they live in pairs, hunting rats, gazelles and other animals by night, but will also feed on carrion and fruit.

Jaguar, the largest of the American wild cats, ranges from the southern USA to Argentina. Its coat is spotted but, unlike the leopard's spotted fur, the jaguar's coat has a central spot inside each group or rosette of spots. It is up to 1.8 m (5.9 ft) long, excluding its tail.

Jamaica is an island state in the West Indies. Capital, Kingston; area about 11 500 sq km (4400 sq miles). It was discovered by Columbus and occupied by the Spaniards until seized by Britain in 1658. It became part of the Federation of the West Indies (1958–1962) before gaining independence in 1962. It retains links with Britain since many Jamaicans have emigrated there to find work.

Jamaica is largely mountainous – very rugged in the Blue Mountains – with small but fertile plains and a coastal strip. The people are mostly descendants of former African slaves, and sugar is still the main crop, as it was in colonial times. People were brought by force from Africa to work the sugar plantations, and this led to Jamaica being overpopulated. Other export crops are bananas, coffee, cocoa, fruits and nuts. There are good fisheries off the coast and valuable timber in the forests. Tourism is also important.

James I (1566–1625), was King of England and Ireland (1603–1625) and, as James VI, King of Scotland (1567–1625). He succeeded to the Scottish throne on the abdication of his mother, Mary Queen of Scots, and to the English throne on the death of Elizabeth I. He was much influenced by favourites, and his attempt to assert the divine right of Kings brought him into conflict with Parliament. A notable achievement of his reign was the publication of the Authorized Version of the Bible.

James II (1633–1701), was King of England, Scotland and Ireland (1685–1688). He ascended the throne on the death of his brother, Charles II, after the failure of attempts to exclude him from the succession because of his Roman Catholicism. Having crushed the Monmouth rebellion, he ruled in an arbitrary manner and attempted to appoint Roman Catholics to high offices. The growing opposition to his rule led to the Glorious Revolution of 1688. James fled the country and was succeeded by William III and Mary, James II's daughter. James' attempt to regain the crown was defeated at the Battle of the Boyne (1690).

James, Henry (1843–1916), was a US-born novelist, who settled in England in 1875. The conflict between American and European society was a theme of his early novels, such as *The American* (1877) and *The Europeans* (1878). Later works became more experimental in technique, and included unsuccessful plays, but he returned to his original interest with his last and most subtle novels, like *The Ambassadors* (1903). The son and brother of famous philosophers, James is a thinking person's novelist. As a critic he had a great influence on the modern novel. Today his ghost story, *The Turn of the Screw*, is one of his most popular works.

January is the first month of the year in the modern calendar, beginning with New Year's Day. January lasts for 31 days. In ancient Roman times it was sacred to Janus, the two-headed god of doorways, and beginnings and endings, and was named after him.

Japan is an island kingdom off east Asia. Capital, Tokyo; area about 372 000 sq km (143 000 sq miles). There are four main islands: Honshu, Hokkaido, Kyushu and Shikoku, and many hundreds of small ones. *History* The Yamato dynasty was established by the mid-4th century AD. In 1192 Minamoto Yorimoto set up the first of the shogunates (military governments) which were to rule Japan for 650 years, the emperors remaining in the background. The first Europeans arrived in the 1540s and introduced Christianity. In the early 17th century the Tokugawa shogunate expelled all foreigners, stopped all trade and forbade Christians to worship. Japan's seclusion ended in the 1850s when the first treaty with the United States was signed. The Meiji restoration of 1868 returned power to the throne and abolished the feudal system. Japan then underwent a period of expansion and rapid industrialization, invaded China in 1931 and fought against the Allies in the

A traditional costume from Hokkaido, the most northerly of the Japanese islands.

Second World War. After the war the emperor became a constitutional ruler and Japan achieved great economic prosperity.
Land Most of Japan is hilly or mountainous. The plains regions are small, yet they support most of the large population and grow nearly all the food. Most of the main cities are on the irregular Pacific coast, which provides many good harbours, and is sunnier in winter. The climate is temperate, with plenty of rain and marked changes in seasons. There are often severe storms in autumn.
People Nearly 75 per cent of the people live on the island of Honshu. The Japanese are renowned for their sense of honour, duty and hard work. There is still much formality in Japanese life, which helps the Japanese to live in their very overcrowded cities. The two main religious systems are Shintoism, which is associated with veneration of ancestors, and Buddhism, which has several popular modern sects in Japan. The sharp divisions in social class of the past have been abolished; nevertheless, there is a large minority of poor, underprivileged people.
Economy The Japanese economy is one of the marvels of the modern world. Japan is short of raw materials and depends heavily on imports. However, supplies are mostly nearby, and Japanese industrial enterprises are the most efficient and profitable in the world. Only the Soviet Union and the USA – both vast countries by comparison – have a larger total economic output.

Precision engineering is the key to Japan's most profitable industries. Exports have concentrated on watches and cameras, motor cars and electronic equipment. The government has shown skill in recognizing the best industries to support financially, allowing them to capture large foreign markets. To begin with, Japan's great economic boom was based on the low cost of its manufactures, but it is quality rather than cost which explains the continuing success in trade.

Agriculture is highly intensive, due to scarcity of land, and Japan manages to produce about 80 per cent of its food, rice being much the largest item. There is little livestock. The Japanese eat more fish than meat and fishing is a major occupation.

The Samurai of Japan were military guards with a special code of behaviour and discipline. They guarded the emperor until the 16th century.

Japanese drama is the traditional theatre of Japan. The oldest form, Nō drama, developed from religious dancing in the 16th century and is mystical in content. It is performed according to strict conventions; actors wear masks and make symbolic movements and gestures, accompanied by music and dance.

In Jōruri, which was at its height in the 17th and 18th centuries, the 'actors' are puppets.

Kabuki, the most popular form, replaced Jōruri and borrowed some techniques from both its predecessors. It is violently melodramatic, with exotic make-up and costumes, spectacular scenery and an exaggerated style of acting.

All three forms still exist, together with modern drama of the Western type.

Jason was a hero of Greek legend. In order to regain his kingdom, he had to obtain the Golden Fleece (the pure gold coat of a magic ram) from Colchis on the eastern shore of the Black Sea. He built a boat, the *Argo*, on which he sailed with his fellow Argonauts, including other legendary heroes like Herakles and Castor and Pollux. He was aided by various goddesses and also by the witch Medea, whom he married. She later murdered their children to avenge herself on Jason who had abandoned her for Creusa, the daughter of the king of Corinth.

Java is an island in south-east Asia and is part of Indonesia. Area about 126000 sq km (48500 sq miles). It is the most heavily populated and most productive island of Indonesia, containing the capital, Djakarta, and other large cities. Java was once part of a Hindu empire stretching from Malaya to the Moluccas. New invaders in the 16th century were Muslims, and most people today are Muslim. Under the Dutch in the 17th century, Batavia (Djakarta) was the headquarters of the Dutch East India Company.

Though largely mountainous, with many active volcanoes, the rich soil and constantly warm and wet climate make Java ideal for agriculture. It is one of the most densely populated regions in the world, and has more than 5000 species of plants. Rice is the largest crop, and various agricultural products such as palm oil and tea are exported.

Jays number 40 or so species, and are colourful members of the crow family. They have longer tails than crows, and many have crests on their heads. Eurasian jays eat mainly acorns, which they bury in autumn to use later. They are noisy birds, uttering a harsh call, except during the breeding season when they remain quiet so that they do not give away the position of the nest. The American blue jay lives in eastern North America and is quite common in parks and gardens.

Jays

Below: This jay is allowing ants to crawl over its body. It is thought that formic acid produced by the ants protects birds from lice.

Jazz is a form of music which developed in the Southern United States in the late 19th century. New Orleans is considered the home of jazz, and its early exponents were mainly black. Jazz has many styles, but its main characteristics are emphasis on a style of rhythm known as the beat, and improvisation by the performer. The ancestors of jazz can be found in West African music and popular American religious songs (spirituals).

The earliest forms of jazz as it was known around 1900 were syncopated piano music, called ragtime, and the type of vocal lament called the blues. Dixieland or 'traditional' jazz developed from a combination of the two; it is usually played by a group of about six people, led by a trumpet. An outstanding performer of this type of jazz was Louis Armstrong.

After 1920 jazz became more sophisticated. In the 'big band' era there was less room for improvisation, though individual bands (e.g. Glenn Miller's) developed distinctive styles. Duke Ellington emerged as a composer of jazz, though the Ellington band still improvised.

The later developments were known as swing (mainly big bands) and so-called 'modern' jazz, which incorporated a large range of styles from the 'bebop' musicians Charlie Parker and Dizzie Gillespie to the very 'cool' jazz of Miles Davis and Stan Getz. In the 1960s jazz faded from the public eye with the rise of pop music, itself owing much to jazz.

Many musicians, including composers like Debussy, Gershwin and Stravinsky, sometimes combined jazz and traditional styles in their music.

Jehovah, or Yaweh, is the holy name of the god of the Hebrews in the Old Testament.

Jehovah's Witnesses is a Christian sect founded in the United States in 1884. Jehovah's Witnesses believe that all human institutions, including governments and Churches, are bad, and they look forward to the coming of God's kingdom, which they believe will be soon. Their energetic attempts to gain converts have sometimes caused ill feeling in other Christian Churches.

Jellyfish are coelenterates which, unlike most other coelenterates, do not remain fixed in one place but float about in the ocean currents. They can also swim up and down by contracting their umbrella-shaped body. Jellyfish are well named, and 95 per cent of their body consists of water. They feed by catching animals with their trailing tentacles or by straining tiny organisms caught on strands of mucus. The smallest jellyfish are only a few millimetres across, but the largest have tentacles 20 m (65.6 ft) long and measure 2 m (6.5 ft) across the body.

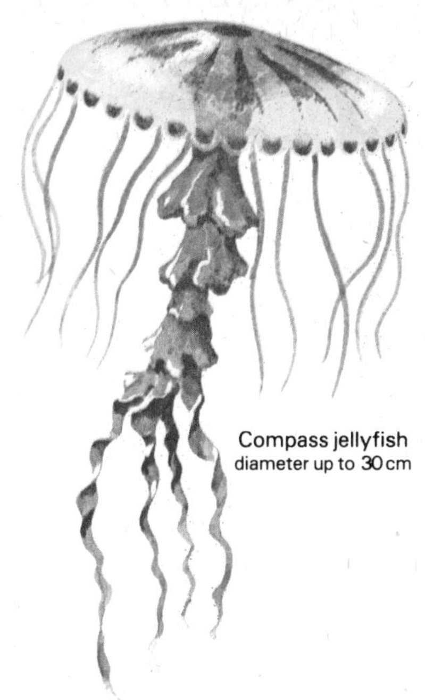

Compass jellyfish
diameter up to 30 cm

Jesus (5–6 BC – circa AD 29), was the founder of Christianity. Little is known of the life of Jesus the man except during his last two years. He was born in Bethlehem, Judaea, the son of Mary, wife of a carpenter of Nazareth. When he was about 30 he began his ministry after being hailed by the prophet St John the Baptist as 'the Lamb of God'. His preaching and teaching during the next two years, recorded in the Bible, is the foundation of the Christian religion.

Jesus earned the hostility of the Jewish authorities, whom he fiercely criticised, and at their insistence he was crucified (nailed to a cross until dead) by the Roman rulers of Palestine. According to the Bible, he returned from the dead after three days and 40 days later rose into heaven.

Christians believe that Jesus was both man and God. He described himself as the Son of God: the Christian God is a trinity of Father, Son and Holy Spirit. Even non-Christians acknowledge that Jesus was one of the most influential people in all history. Two thousand years after the Crucifixion, more than half the population of the world call themselves Christians.

Jews are a people who believe themselves to be descended from Abraham, who emigrated from Mesopotamia to Canaan about 2000 BC. His descendants, known as the 12 tribes of Israel, settled in Egypt where they were enslaved. Led out of Egypt by Moses in about the 14th century BC, they eventually settled in Palestine. Conquered by the Assyrians and Babylonians, they were taken into captivity, being allowed to return by Cyrus the Great. After the destruction of Jerusalem by the Romans, they were dispersed to many different countries. Jews have suffered intermittent persecution through the ages. Anti-Semitism revealed itself at its worst when nearly six million Jews were exterminated by the Nazis during the Second World War. After 1948 many Jews emigrated to their new homeland in Israel.

Joan of Arc (1412–1431), was a French patriot, known as the Maid of Orleans. A peasant girl, she believed that she heard the voices of saints urging her to help the Dauphin Charles to drive the English out of France. She led an army which raised the siege of Orléans in 1429, thus enabling Charles to be crowned King of France. After being captured by Burgundians, she was handed over to the English. Condemned as a heretic and a sorceress, she was burnt at the stake. She was canonized in 1920.

John (1167–1216), was King of England (1199–1216). He succeeded to the throne following the death of his brother, Richard I. During his reign England lost many of its French possessions, and the King came into conflict with the Pope, to whom he eventually had to submit. A dispute with the barons ended when John was forced to seal the Magna Carta at Runnymede. His attempts to go back on his word led to war with the barons, during which he died.

The barons force John to sign the Magna Carta.

Johnson, Amy (1903-1941), was a pioneer English aviator who became, in 1930, the first woman to fly alone from England to Australia. She went on to break flying records all over the world, worked as an air ferry pilot during the Second World War and became a national heroine.

Johnson, Samuel (1709–1784), was an English writer. He was one of those literary figures who dominate their age through personality as much as their writing. His biography by his Scottish admirer, Thomas Boswell, partly explains his fame today, and his conversation partly explains his prestige in his own lifetime. He was a great critic, who produced an edition of Shakespeare and the critical-biographical *Lives of the Poets*. His deep moral beliefs appear in *Rasselas* (1759) and in the essays he wrote for *The Rambler*, a magazine. Above all, he produced *A Dictionary of the English Language* (1775) which was the first work of its kind.

John the Baptist, Saint, was a prophet of Israel, the forerunner of Jesus. He lived in the desert until beginning his powerful ministry, in which he shook the country with his demands for repentance and forecasts of the coming Kingdom of God. He first adopted the practice of baptism, and baptized Jesus, whom he described as his superior and eventually acknowledged as the long-awaited Messiah – the saviour sent from God. Imprisoned by King Herod, he was beheaded as a result of a trick by Herod's wife and her daughter, Salome.

John the Evangelist, Saint, was one of the Twelve Apostles of Jesus, probable author of the fourth gospel (account of Jesus) and three epistles (letters) as well as (perhaps) the book of *Revelation* in the New Testament. He was a fisherman by trade and is described as 'the apostle whom Jesus loved'. He alone was with Jesus at the Crucifixion.

St John's Gospel is very different from the other three. It is more theological, seeking to show Jesus as 'the Word of God made flesh' – the universal God, not just the Jewish Messiah. It is more concerned with the spiritual meaning of events than with historical facts.

Jones, Inigo (1573–1652), was an English architect. Sometimes regarded as the first professional architect in the modern sense, he brought the Classical style from Italy to England, where Gothic still lingered, and transformed English architecture. His most famous surviving building is the Banqueting Hall in Whitehall, London, which shows the overwhelming influence of Palladio yet remains thoroughly English, not Italian. He was essentially a court artist, and he devised many extravagant sets and costumes for the masques (a kind of musical play) performed at court.

Jordan, The Hashemite Kingdom of, is an Arab kingdom in south-west Asia. Capital, Amman; area about 98000 sq km (38000 sq miles). Without very valuable natural resources (such as oil), Jordan is one of the poorer Arab nations. It is unusual in still being ruled by a monarch.

History The country was occupied by Nabataeans from the 7th century BC, becoming part of the Roman Empire in AD 106. Conquered by the Muslims in 636, it came under the control of the Crusaders in the 12th century. It was ruled by Ottoman Turks from the 16th century until the end of the First World War. With the name of Transjordan, an emirate was created in 1921 but was under British protection. It achieved full independence as the kingdom of Jordan in 1946, but lost its territory west of the Jordan river to Israel in 1967.

Land Most of the centre and east of Jordan is desert, and irrigation is necessary for agriculture. Without irrigation, the land is useful only for grazing, mainly sheep and goats. Jordan has deposits of manganese and iron, and phosphates and potash from the Dead Sea are important exports.

Joyce, James (1882–1941), was an Irish novelist. He lived abroad from 1904 but all his works are centred on Dublin. His originality appeared in *A Portrait of the Artist as a Young Man* (1916) and in *Ulysses* (1922), the record (in 730 pages) of one day in the life of a group of Dubliners. In his last book, *Finnegan's Wake* (1939), the language is fused together, resulting in words not found in a dictionary which make their effect by setting up suggestions or allusions in the reader's mind. No one doubts it is a brilliant achievement, but unfortunately, for most people, it is impossible to understand.

Juan Carlos I (1938–), is King of Spain. His family lost the throne in 1931, but Juan Carlos was chosen by the fascist dictator General Franco to succeed him. He became head of state on Franco's death in 1975. However, he supported the new democratic régime, and acted as a strictly constitutional monarch.

Judaism is the religion of the Jews. Its origins and early development are recorded in the Old Testament of the Bible. Unlike most religions, it has no single great figure but a succession of prophets (of whom Moses is the greatest). In Judaism, the law and custom are more important than any human figure. It has proved a very powerful religion, surviving for nearly 4000 years in spite of the fact that the Jews had their own, independent state for only a brief period (recently revived in the modern state of Israel). On the other hand, Judaism has never sought converts from non-Jews.

Judaism aroused the hostility of Christians throughout history because the Jews were held responsible for killing Jesus, the Christian Son of God.

Jews believe in one God, who is to be worshipped through acts of justice, love and charity. The Jews are a 'chosen people', but this places on them a special responsibility to make the world a better place. The load they bear is illustrated by the sorrows and troubles which the Jews have suffered throughout history.

Judas Iscariot was the apostle of Jesus who betrayed him to the Jewish authorities in exchange for 30 pieces of silver. Repenting later, he killed himself. His treachery made him one of the most hated figures in history.

July is the seventh month of the year in the modern calendar, and lasts for 31 days. It is named in honour of the Roman Julius Caesar.

Jump-jet, see VTOL aircraft.

June is the sixth month of the year in the modern calendar, and lasts for 30 days. Its name comes from the ancient Roman month *Junius*, probably so called in honour of Juno, the goddess of wisdom.

Juniper is an evergreen conifer which grows as a bush or small tree. It occurs throughout the temperate and subtropical parts of the Northern Hemisphere. It has spiky leaves arranged along the twigs in groups of three. The leaves are blue-green with a waxy coating. In spring, the juniper has tiny yellow male flowers and small, bud-like female flowers. By autumn the female flowers have turned into dark blue 'berries'. Birds eat the 'berries', passing out the black seeds which are thus helped in their dispersal. Juniper wood burns with a resinous scent, and is sometimes used to smoke cheeses and hams.

Common Juniper tree and its leaves and cones. The cones are fleshy and look like berries.

Top: The sizes of Jupiter *(left)* and Earth *(right)*, compared.
Above: The cloud belts of Jupiter.

Jupiter is the fifth planet from the Sun. It takes 11.9 years to orbit the Sun. Jupiter rotates on its axis in just under ten hours. Although small in comparison with the Sun, Jupiter is a giant among the planets. Its diameter is 11 times that of the Earth. Its mass is greater than that of all the other planets put together.

Jupiter is very different to the four, solid, inner planets. Like the Sun, it is mainly composed of hydrogen and helium. The atmosphere contains many different gases. These form the coloured belts of cloud that are seen from the Earth. Many spots can be seen as well, including a red spot three times as wide as the Earth. Jupiter gives out more heat than it receives from the Sun, and has a strong magnetic field.

Jupiter has at least 16 satellites. Four of these, Io, Europa, Ganymede and Callisto, are similar in size to Mercury and the Moon.

Jurassic is a period in the history of the Earth, known from the study of rocks and of the fossil remains found in them (the geological record). It is named after the Jura Mountains in Switzerland.

The Jurassic period is the second major division of the Mesozoic era, following the Triassic. It began about 190 million years ago and lasted for about 54 million years. Reptiles were the dominant animals in the sea and on land and dinosaurs, such as *Apatosaurus* (once called *Brontosaurus*) and *Diplodocus*, grew to enormous sizes. Flying reptiles appeared, as did the earliest bird, *Archaeopteryx*. The Jurassic also included the earliest plants to have survived unchanged down to the present day.

Archaeopteryx, the earliest bird, from the Jurassic period.

Kafka, Franz (1883–1924), was a Czech-born Austrian writer. He suffered from depression and poor health (dying at 41). Despite this, he wrote a great deal, and his reputation rests chiefly on two disturbing allegorical novels *The Trial* and *The Castle*, both unfinished and published after his death. They are written in a clear style which contrasts with the vagueness of the plot, in which the characters struggle unsuccessfully with inexplicable fate.

Kalahari is a large region of semi-desert, mainly in Botswana and Namibia. Its area is about 906 500 sq km (350 000 sq miles). The annual rainfall varies from 50 cm (20 in) in the north-east to 12 cm (5 in) in the south-west. Its few inhabitants are Bushmen, one of the world's oldest races, and Bantu tribes live on the outskirts of the region.

Kampuchea, Democratic (formerly Cambodia), is a republic in south-east Asia. Capital, Phnom Penh; area about 181 000 sq km (71 000 sq miles). It was part of French Indochina, becoming independent in 1954. It was involved in the Vietnam War and suffered political upheavals as a result of contesting groups inside and outside the country. The men who seized power in 1979, inspired by a mixture of ideologies and personal ambitions, are said to have been responsible for massacres on a large scale. Many people attempted to leave the country by sea.

The lowlands of the Mekong valley are very fertile. Rice is much the largest crop. With its monsoon climate, much of the country is covered by dense forest which could be a valuable source of future revenue. Fishing is an important occupation, and there is little industrial or mining development.

A female kangaroo with a young one in her pouch.

Kandinsky, Wassily (1866–1944), was a Russian-born painter, a very influential figure in modern art. In Germany he was one of the group of Expressionists who formed the 'Blue Rider' school, but by 1910 he was producing wholly abstract paintings. He is the founder of the modern school known as Abstract Expressionism, which reached its height in the United States during the 1950s. The Abstract Expressionists emphasized the actual act of painting, and believed that the painting communicates the feelings of the artist, quite apart from representing an object or decorating a surface.

Kangaroo is a marsupial (pouched) mammal living in the forests and on the plains of Australia. There is also a tree kangaroo which lives in New Guinea. Kangaroos are placed in the family Macropodidae, which means 'big-footed', and with their huge feet and long legs kangaroos are able to jump great distances. Some species can cover 6 m (20 ft) in one leap. Kangaroos also have long tails and slightly mule-shaped heads.

Kangaroos rest in the grass by day, but become active at dusk. They are herbivores, pulling grass towards their mouths with their forelimbs. The musky rat kangaroo of the Queensland rainforests also eats small animals, and it is the smallest kangaroo, 40 cm (16 in) in length. The largest are the red and grey kangaroos of the open bush, which stand 2 m (6 ft) high.

Karroo is made up of two distinct basins, named the Great Karroo and the Little Karroo, in the Cape of Good Hope Province, South Africa. It is about 259000 sq km (100000 sq miles) in area; and about 900 to 1200 m (3000 to 4000 ft) high above sea level. It forms two successive terraces between the south coast and the high veld of the interior of Cape Province.

Keats, John (1795–1821), was an English poet. A contemporary of Byron and Shelley, he was influenced by Wordsworth and Coleridge. Apart from *Endymion* (1818), nearly all his greatest work was written in the year 1819, including the long narrative poems, *The Eve of St Agnes*, *La Belle Dame sans Merci* and *Hyperion*, as well as his famous odes *To a Nightingale*, *On a Grecian Urn*, etc. He died of tuberculosis when he was only 26 years old.

Kelvin, Lord William Thomson (1824–1907), was a Scottish physicist. He became a Professor at Glasgow University in 1846, and President of the Royal Society in 1900.

Kelvin studied mainly electricity and heat. He suggested a scale of temperature based on absolute zero, which is known as the Kelvin scale, and the units used for it are known as kelvins.

His research in electricity led to the laying of the first transatlantic telegraph cable in 1858. He designed many meters for measuring electricity, and the present-day mariner's compass is still much as he designed it.

Kennedy, John Fitzgerald (1917–1963), was an American statesman and President of the USA (1961–1963). The son of businessman and diplomat, Joseph Kennedy, during his presidency he compelled the USSR government to withdraw its missiles from Cuba (1962). Later he negotiated a Nuclear Test-Ban Treaty with the Soviet leader, Nikita Khrushchev, which brought about a relaxation of tension between the USSR and the USA. Kennedy also increased American involvement in Vietnam. He was assassinated in Dallas, Texas, in November 1963.

John F Kennedy

Kenya is a republic in East Africa. Capital, Nairobi; area about 583000 sq km (225000 sq miles). In 1895, Kenya became a British protectorate and then a colony in 1920. It gained independence in 1963.

Land and People Kenya lies on the Equator, and a large area in the north is semi-desert, but the highlands which extend across the interior contain fertile plateaux. Kenya is famous for its wild life, and there are many game reserves. Mount Kenya (5200 m/17000 ft) is almost on the Equator, but is permanently snow-capped.

Kenyans are a mixture of peoples, but the most numerous are the Kikuyu, the Masai and the Luo. The Masai are nomadic herdsmen by tradition, the Kikuyu and Luo farming people. There is a large Asian minority, mainly shopkeepers, businessmen or labourers, and a sprinkling of Europeans, including plantation owners in the highlands. Despite troubles in late colonial times, Kenya has remained friendly towards Western Europeans, and attracts many tourists.

The main products are tea, coffee, sisal and tropical food products. There are also mineral reserves; Kenya produces large quantities of soda ash.

Kenyatta, Jomo (circa 1891–1978), was a Kenyan statesman and nationalist leader. He studied in England before returning to Kenya after the Second World War. He was imprisoned in 1953 because of his part in the Mau Mau rebellion. Released in 1959, he was elected leader of the Kenya African National Union in 1961. He became Prime Minister of independent Kenya in 1963, and President in 1964.

Kepler, Johann (1571–1630), was a German astronomer. In 1600 he went to Prague to work with the Danish astronomer Tycho Brahe (1546–1601). Brahe had made many observations of the planets and their movements. From these, Kepler realized that the planets move in ellipses around the Sun. It had previously been thought that the planets moved in circles. He also showed that the speed of a planet depends on its distance from the Sun.

These findings showed that in some way the Sun controlled the movement of the planets. Newton later showed that the Sun controlled the planets by the force of gravity.

Kestrel is a small bird of prey, which usually hovers above the ground looking for prey moving below. Once a likely meal is spotted, the kestrel drops quickly down, grabbing the prey in its talons. Kestrels feed on insects, worms, small rodents, lizards and other birds. The lesser kestrel catches its insect prey in the air. There are several different species of kestrel, found in places such as Africa, Europe and Asia. The Mauritius kestrel is probably the rarest bird of prey. Kestrels are up to 30 cm (12 in) long.

Kestrel

Khomeini, Ayatollah (1900–), is Iranian spiritual head of his country's Shi'ite Muslims. Exiled to Iraq and later to France for his outspoken criticism of the Shah of Iran, he became the acknowledged focus of all opposition to the Shah's government. After the Shah left the country early in 1979, Khomeini returned home to lead the Islamic Revolution. He banned Western customs, censored the press and executed many people who either sympathized with the old regime or opposed the new one.

Nikita Khrushchev

Khrushchev, Nikita (1894–1971), was a Soviet statesman. He succeeded Joseph Stalin as First Secretary of the Soviet Communist Party in 1953, becoming Prime Minister from 1958 to 1964. In 1956 he publicly denounced Stalin's regime and adopted a policy of peaceful co-existence with the West. He was forced to withdraw Soviet missiles from Cuba to avoid a confrontation with the USA in 1962. During his period of office the USSR's relations with China grew worse. He was deposed in 1964.

Khyber Pass is a gorge in the mountains on the Afghanistan-Pakistan border. It is practically the only pass suitable for military movements on the north-west frontier of the Indian sub-continent, and has been used by invaders throughout history. Since the 1920s a railway, with 34 tunnels, has run through the Pass.

Kidney is one of a pair of organs which are found in the bodies of vertebrates. Kidneys act as filters. They take chemicals, which are valuable to the body, from the blood as it passes through them, as well as water which the body also needs. Eventually the soluble waste products which are left form urine, which is passed out of the body.

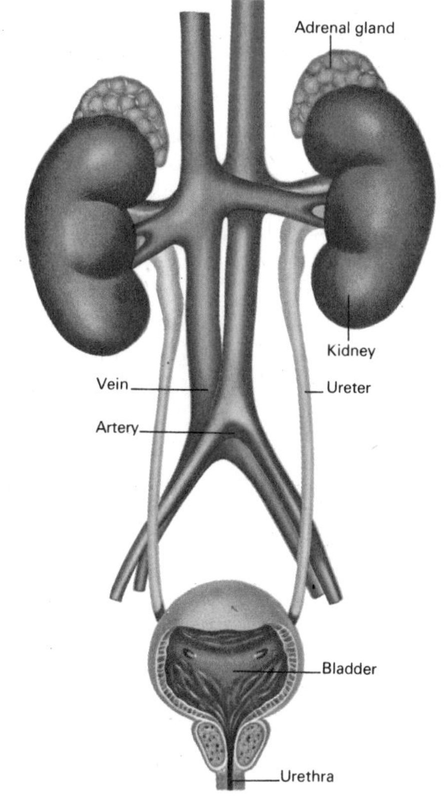

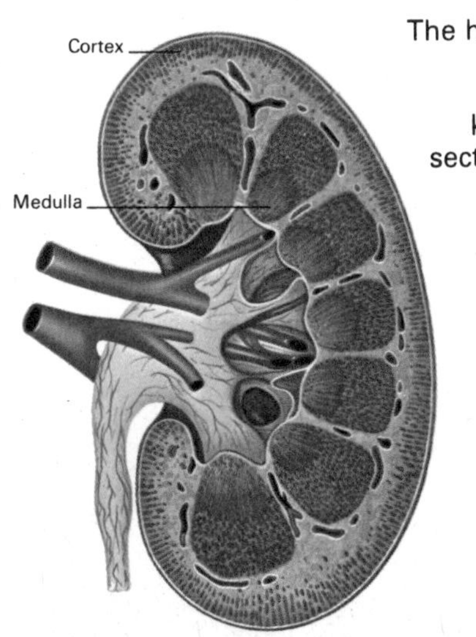

The human urinary system *(top)* showing the kidneys, and a section through a kidney *(left)*.

Kilimanjaro, Mount, in East Africa, is the highest mountain in Africa. It has two peaks, the higher being 5895 m (19340 ft). It is a dormant volcano, and is not extinct.

Kingfisher is a small, stocky bird, with a large head, long beak and short legs. It often has brilliantly coloured plumage. It is found world-wide, except in the polar regions and on some islands.

King, Martin Luther (1929–1968), was a black American clergyman and civil rights leader. He led a nationwide non-violent campaign to secure racial equality for black people in the USA. His actions did much to bring about the passing of laws to end black segregation. Awarded the Nobel Peace Prize in 1964, he was assassinated in Memphis, Tennessee four years later.

Kinkajou is a small, bear-like mammal related to the raccoons. It is about 30 cm (1 ft) long and has golden-brown fur. The kinkajou and the binturong are the only members of the order Carnivora which have prehensile tails. (Prehensile tails are ones which can twist round and grip branches to help the animal when climbing about in trees.) Its tail is about 45 cm (18 in) long. The kinkajou lives in parts of South America up to southern Mexico. It feeds among the trees on fruit, insects, nuts and leaves, and relishes honey. In fact, it is often called the honey bear.

Kipling, Joseph Rudyard (1865–1936), was a British writer, born in India. His short stories, as in *Plain Tales from the Hills* (1887), *Debts and Credits* (1926), and most of all his children's stories, *The Jungle Book* (1894–1895), *Just So Stories* (1902) and *Puck of Pook's Hill* (1906), are still popular. In his poetry, such as *Barrack-Room Ballads* (1892), he displayed his remarkable gift for using the language of ordinary people, such as British soldiers. The quality of his work varied, and his novels, except *Stalky and Co.* (1899) and *Kim* (1901) are less successful.

Kiribati is a republic in Micronesia in the central Pacific Ocean, consisting of three groups of coral islands. Capital, Tarawa; area about 684 sq km (264 sq miles). Formerly the Gilbert Islands, it was a British colony until independence was achieved in 1979 as a republic.

Kirov Ballet is an outstanding Russian ballet company, together with the Bolshoi Ballet. In its present form it dates from the 1880s, though its forerunners in St Petersburg (now Leningrad) go back to the early 18th century, with the ballet school founded for the children of the tsar's servants. It reached its height under the direction of Marius Petipa in the late 19th century, and many of its finest dancers were recruited by Diaghilev for his Ballet Russe. In the 1920s it took on new life as the leader of experimental ballet, but later it became less creative. Though it made a great impression on foreign tours after 1960, a number of Kirov dancers chose to remain in the West, where they found more challenging artistic opportunities.

Kitchener, Horatio Herbert, 1st Earl (1850–1916), was a British soldier. Joining the Egyptian army in 1882, he became its Commander-in-Chief ten years later. In 1898 he defeated the Mahdi's forces at Omdurman, thus completing the conquest of the Sudan. Kitchener commanded the British forces during the latter part of the Boer War. As Secretary of State for War in 1914 he undertook a successful recruitment campaign. He was drowned while on a journey to Russia.

Kite is a bird of prey, related to the buzzards, eagles and Old World vultures. Because kites have lighter bodies than the other members of their family, they can soar about on thinner, more pointed wings. Many also have forked tails.

The red and black kites of Europe hunt over hills, plains, meadows and marshes looking for birds to eat, but they will also scavenge on carrion. North America has several species of kite including the snail kite or Everglades kite, which has a long, thin, hooked beak for reaching snails inside their shells. The honey buzzard is really a kite, and is found in Eurasia in the summer, and Africa and southern Asia in the winter. It feeds on the grubs and honey of wasps and bees, but will also take birds and small mammals. The square-tailed kite of Australia flies low when hunting, and feeds on birds and reptiles.

Kiwi is a chicken-sized, flightless bird found in New Zealand. There are three species, and their rounded bodies are carried on short, strong legs. They are nocturnal birds, hunting in the forest for invertebrates. These are located in the ground by means of a powerful sense of smell, with the nostrils positioned at the tip of the long, pointed bill. The female, larger than the male, lays one or two eggs, which are incubated mainly by the male.

Klee, Paul (1879–1940), was a Swiss painter. He was among the 'Blue Rider' group of Expressionists in Munich and was influenced by a wide variety of earlier artists, but his own style of paintings, drawings and etchings is unique. He once compared what the painter makes out of life to the way in which a tree turns the soil into leaves and branches. The working of the subconscious mind was important to him, but he believed plain observation and technique to have their place too. His works, not always easy to understand, reveal a gentle charm and a highly original imagination.

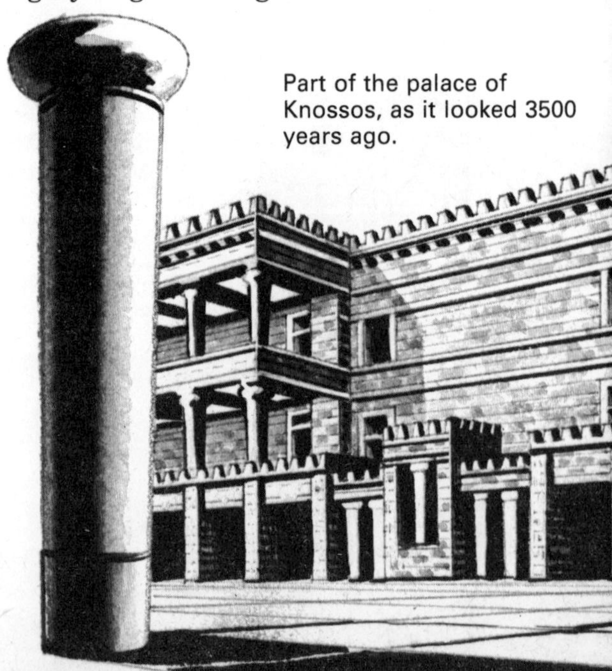

Part of the palace of Knossos, as it looked 3500 years ago.

Knossos was the main centre of the Minoan civilization in Crete. At its height, about 1500 BC, it was a forerunner of Mycenean civilization and, through the Myceneans, of Classical Greece. The palace of Knossos, excavated by Sir Arthur Evans in 1900–1908, was built at various times before 1400 BC. It consists of rooms arranged around an open courtyard. The walls are decorated with painting of remarkable quality, with realistic animals, plants and scenes of a mysterious ceremony in which people jumped over bulls.

A koala with a young one clinging to her back.

Koala looks rather like a small grey bear. It has a large head and nose, and big hairy ears. It lives in the eucalyptus forests of eastern Australia and feeds at night on the leaves and bark of the trees, over 1 kg (2.2 lb) of food being eaten each day. Koala means 'no drink', and the animal obtains all the moisture it requires from the leaves and bark. The young, carried initially in the mother's pouch, eventually climbs out and is carried about on her back. The koala is up to 85 cm (33 in) long.

Kookaburra is also known as the laughing jackass because of its loud, laughing call. It is an Australian kingfisher which no longer feeds on fish, but instead eats snakes, lizards, rats, mice and insects. It has a short body with a large head and beak, and is larger than other kingfishers, being about the size of a raven. It makes its burrow in termites' nests, but is often seen scavenging around towns.

Koran is the sacred book of Islam. It consists of God's revelations to the Prophet Muhammad. These were usually writen down as he reported them to his followers, and were put together in the Koran soon after his death in 632.

Korea, North is a Democratic People's Republic occupying the northern half of the Korean peninsula in east Asia. Capital, Pyongyang; area about 122000 sq km (47000 sq miles).

A Chinese-influenced Communist state, it has been divided from South Korea ever since 1945, when American and Russian forces entered Korea to enforce the surrender of the Japanese troops who were there. They divided the country, for convenience, into two portions. In 1950–1953 a war was fought with the South.

It is a mountainous country, especially in the north, where hydro-electric stations harness the rivers for power. There are large reserves of coal and iron, as well as other minerals, and the country is highly industrialized. Before the division of Korea, most of the food was produced in the south, but there is now extensive farming, organized on a communal system, in North Korea.

Korea, South is a republic in east Asia occupying the southern half of the Korean peninsula. Capital, Seoul; area about 98 500 sq km (38 000 sq miles). A former Japanese colony, Korea was divided after the Second World War. North Korea, with Soviet and Chinese support, attempted to force reunification, but was checked by South Korea with United Nations support, in 1950–1953.

South Korea is largely mountainous, though the mountains are not very high. The lowland areas and river valleys are fertile, but there is a lack of important minerals – tungsten being an important exception. Industry has expanded very rapidly in recent years, especially around Seoul, and the South Koreans have learned valuable economic lessons from the Japanese, especially in gaining a foothold in Western markets.

Korean War (1950–1953) – in this war United Nations forces came to the aid of South Korea after it had been invaded by North Korea. The North Korean attack, which began in June 1950, was condemned by the United Nations, and many member nations sent troops, although the vast majority were Americans. After much fierce fighting, in which the North Koreans were later supported by the Chinese Communists, the war ended inconclusively and an armistice was signed in July 1953.

Krill are the small, shrimp-like crustaceans which live in the plankton, the floating layer of tiny sea creatures. Krill are present in the cold oceans of the world in enormous numbers, and are the vital food source for baleen whales.

Marco Polo, the famous Venetian traveller, visits Kublai Khan at Peking in 1275.

Krishna is a Hindu god. Krishna is the eighth *avatar* or incarnation of Vishnu. He is associated with peasants and workers, and one of the most widely worshipped Hindu gods. Originally a cowherd, Krishna has a colourful mythology, with stories of miracles and conquests over demons, notably Kamsa, whose activities were the cause of Vishnu's rebirth as Krishna.

Kruger, Stephanus Johannes Paulus (1825–1904), was a South African statesman. He was loved by many Afrikaners who regarded him as the symbol of Afrikaans resistance to British imperialism. He was born in the Cape Colony in South Africa, but emigrated to the Orange River area in the Great Trek. He helped to found the state of the Transvaal and this was recognized as independent in 1852.

In 1877, the Transvaal was annexed by Britain following difficulties between the Boers and the British. A Boer rebellion followed, led by Kruger. When it was over he was made President. It was a difficult time: the Boers and the British were unable to solve their differences, and in 1899 the Second Anglo-Boer War broke out. But Kruger was too old to take part, though he did travel around Europe looking for support for the Boer cause. *See also* Boer War.

Kublai Khan (circa 1215–1294), was Mongol Emperor of China (1260–1294). The grandson of Genghis Khan, he completed the Mongolian conquest of China. He established Peking as the capital of an empire which stretched from the China Sea to the borders of Europe. However, his efforts to conquer South-east Asia and Japan were unsuccessful.

Kuwait is an independent state in south-west Asia, at the tip of the Persian Gulf. Capital, Kuwait; area about 24 000 sq km (9000 sq miles). Kuwait is a very small country. It was a British protectorate, achieving independence in 1961. It is mostly desert and its very existence has been challenged by the claims of larger neighbours, notably Iraq. What makes it so valuable is its huge oil reserves. In terms of income divided by population, Kuwait is one of the richest states in the world.

Lake is an inland expanse of water more or less permanently occupying a large hollow in the Earth's surface. However, some lakes – for example, Lake Eyre in south Australia – may shrink dramatically or disappear completely during a dry season.

Lakes may be freshwater or saline (salty) like the Great Salt Lake, Utah, USA and the Dead Sea, Israel. They may also be artificial, such as Kariba Lake, formed behind the Kariba Dam in southern Africa.

Land speed record – in order to qualify as official holder of the world land speed record, a car must cover a measured distance (one mile or one kilometre) in both directions, with only a limited time allowed between runs. The average speed achieved on the two runs is what counts. Over the years, the speed has risen from the 100 km/h (62 mph) of the earliest attempts, to the 690.9 km (429.7 mph) achieved by Donald Campbell's *Bluebird* in 1964, which remains the highest speed by a wheel-driven car. Since then, however, cars powered by pure jets and rockets have been allowed, and these have taken the record to over 1019 km/h (633 mph). Several organizations are now preparing to attempt to exceed the speed of sound, circa 1220 km/h (758 mph).

Laos is a republic in south-east Asia. Capital, Vientiane; area about 237 000 sq km (91 500 sq miles). In recent years Laos has had its share of the terrible conflicts of the south-east Asian peninsula. Formerly French, it became independent in 1949. A Communist republic was declared in 1975.

Laos is a mountainous country with no sea coast and a small population. There is plenty of timber, and rapid streams provide hydro-electric power. But there is little or no industry and not much mining except for tin. Most of the people live in river valleys, growing rice and other crops to feed themselves. The Laotian people are of mixed descent, and there is some conflict between different groups, especially lowlanders and tribal mountain people.

Lapland is a region extending through northern Scandinavia into the Soviet Union. Area about 388 000 sq km (150 000 sq miles). All of Lapland lies north of the Arctic Circle and it is very thinly inhabited. The Lapps are a people of Asian origin, who are nomadic reindeer herders and fishermen. Nowadays, there is some forestry and mining.

Lapps tending reindeer.

Lapwing, also called the green plover or peewit, is a glossy green and white bird found throughout Europe and central Asia. It is up to 30 cm (12 in) long. On the back of its head it bears a distinctive crest of feathers. The lapwing lives on marshes, meadows and cultivated land, and by rivers and coasts. During the breeding season males put on an elaborate aerial courtship display, when they wheel, roll and turn in the sky. About four eggs are laid, and the newly hatched young are able to move about on their own after only a few days.

Larva is a stage which many animals pass through in their life cycle. In animals which have a larva, the larva hatches out from the egg. It can feed independently and looks different from the adult form that it will eventually become. Some of the more common larvae that you may have seen, apart from caterpillars (the larvae of butterflies and moths), are tadpoles (the larvae of frogs) and maggots (the larvae of flies). Some common seashore animals, such as starfish and winkles, also have larvae, but these are tiny and swim in the sea.

Laser is an instrument which produces a beam of light. However, laser light is much more powerful than ordinary light. It has such high energy that it can cut through very hard substances such as metal and diamond. Metals are also joined together, or welded, using lasers.

Lasers are used in medicine. Very narrow beams of laser light are used to operate on the eye, acting as precision tools, or are used in cancer treatment.

Laser beams can measure distances, such as the distance from the Earth to the Moon, and are used in a form of photography called holography. *See also* Holography.

Latex is the fluid – usually appearing as a milky juice – which exudes from the cut stems of certain plants. It is stored in a series of tubes running throughout the plant, and consists of proteins, oils, sugars and mineral salts. Its function is not fully known, but it is believed to be a kind of food store. It may also have some wound-healing properties. The latex which comes from the cut stems of rubber trees is used to make commercial rubber.

Other latex-producing plants include the dandelion and common spurge.

Latitude is part of a geographical measuring system which, in combination with longitude, makes it possible to locate anything on the Earth's surface. It has been of immense importance to map-makers and navigators.

The latitude of a given spot is determined by the angle it makes at the centre of the Earth with the equator. It is expressed in degrees, minutes and seconds north or south of the equator. The equator itself has a latitude of 0 degrees. Most world maps are marked with lines of latitude, called parallels, at intervals of 10 degrees.

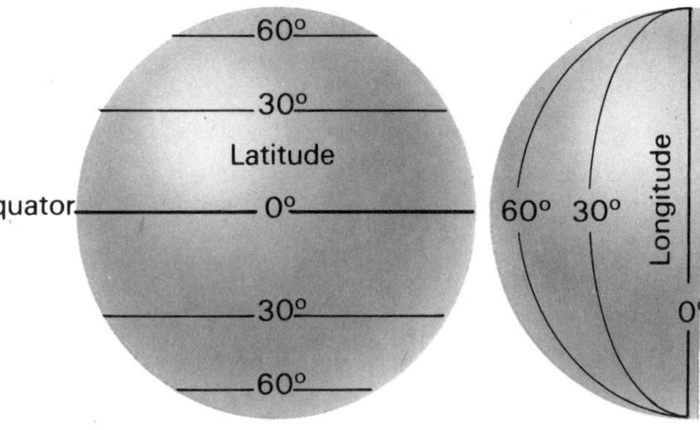

Knowing its latitude makes it possible to locate, for example, a ship along an imaginary east-west line running round the globe. A similar system, longitude, locates it on an imaginary north-south line. The point at which these two lines cross indicates the exact location of the ship. *See also* Longitude.

Lava is molten rock, thrown out on to the Earth's surface through the crater or vents of a volcano. The same molten rock beneath the Earth's crust is known as magma. Much of the present landscape was once lava.

Lavoisier, Antoine Laurent (1743–1794), was a French chemist. He is best known for disproving the phlogiston theory. Substances which burn were thought to contain something called phlogiston. When they burned they released the phlogiston into the air. He found that metals gain weight when they burn. He showed that this was because they combine with oxygen. His oxygen combination theory replaced the phlogiston theory.

Lavoisier showed how oxygen is used in breathing and how it joins with hydrogen to form water. After his discoveries chemistry advanced rapidly.

He also worked in the tax office, and for this he was sent to the guillotine during the French Revolution.

Lawrence, David Herbert (1885–1930), was an English novelist. The son of a coal miner, he was a controversial writer in his own time, but his reputation has grown steadily. He was critical of English society and after 1912 spent his life mostly abroad.

D. H. Lawrence believed passionately that in modern society human nature is being damaged by the division between mind and feelings. His best-known novels are the autobiographical *Sons and Lovers* (1913), *The Rainbow* (1915), *Women in Love* (1921) and – mainly because it was banned for 30 years – *Lady Chatterley's Lover* (1928). He also wrote excellent short stories, poetry and criticism, and his published letters show the power and range of his mind.

Lead is a soft, heavy blue-grey metal which is easy to shape. Its chemical symbol is Pb. Although lead is not common it has been used for thousands of years. The Romans used it to make water pipes.

Lead is found in an ore called galena. Many alloys are made from lead. Type metal, used to make the letters for printing presses, is lead mixed with tin and antimony.

Lead is used in buildings, for example, in roofs, paints and pipes. It is also used in car batteries and petrol.

Lead stops much of the radiation from radioactive substances. It is thus used to shield people from radiation.

The amounts of lead in the air and in water are carefully checked. Too much lead can cause lead poisoning.

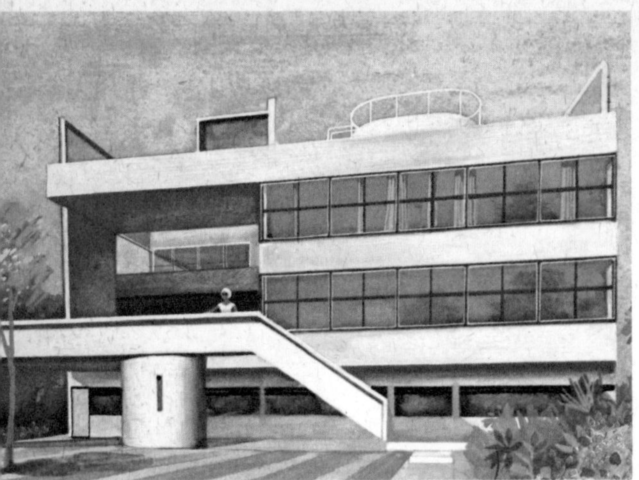

Maison Stein at Garches, France, designed by Le Corbusier in 1929.

Le Corbusier, Charles-Edouard (1887–1966), was a French architect. One of the most brilliant and influential of 20th-century architects, Le Corbusier was very inventive, as well as being an excellent salesman of his own ideas. He was an early pioneer of 'mass-production' housing and town planning, but also built unusual private houses, white and cube-like. His early buildings were smooth glass and metal (such as the UN building in New York), but he later turned to a rougher style, exposing concrete beams still marked by the planks in which the concrete had set.

League of Nations was an international organization which was established in 1920 after the First World War, with the aim of keeping peace among nations. The USA refused to join, which reduced the League's efficiency. Although the League performed many important tasks, it proved powerless in the face of aggression by strong countries in the 1930s. It came to an end in 1946, being replaced by the United Nations.

Leaves are vital parts of a green plant. They perform a variety of tasks, the most important of which is to manufacture food. They do this from carbon dioxide and water, using the energy of sunlight which is trapped in the leaves by the pigment chlorophyll. In addition, tiny pores in the leaves called stomata allow carbon dioxide and oxygen to diffuse in and out of the plant. They also allow water to evaporate from the leaves. This evaporation not only helps to cool the plant in hot weather but is also part of a steady 'pull' which begins with the drawing of vital moisture from the soil through the roots, and provides the plant with water to keep it alive and healthy.

Sometimes the leaves perform other roles. The leaves of the stinging nettle are armed with poisonous hairs which help ward off would-be grazers, for instance. Carnivorous plants such as the pitcher plant and the Venus fly trap catch and devour insects using their leaves for traps. In some species the leaves are used to store food. An onion is really a short stem surrounded by special food-storing leaves.

When the weather becomes cold, deciduous trees shed their leaves and await the return of spring before bursting forth with new leaves. *See also* Photosynthesis; Transpiration.

Lebanon is a republic in south-west Asia, on the Mediterranean. Capital, Beirut; area

Reedmace *(left)* and alpine rose *(above)* showing their different shaped leaves.

10 000 sq km (3860 sq miles).
History The country was part of the Phoenician Empire before coming under Persian and later Greek control. Occupied by the Romans in 64 BC, it then became part of the Byzantine Empire, but in the 7th century AD was overrun by Arabs. In the 16th century it formed part of the Ottoman Empire, coming under French influence in the 19th century. Lebanon was ruled by France under a mandate from 1920, and was occupied by British and French forces during the Second World War. It achieved full independence in 1946, became a base for Palestinian guerrillas in the 1960s and was in a state of intermittent civil war in the 1970s and 80s.
Land and People It is largely mountainous, with a wide, fertile valley lying between the two main ranges. The people are Arabs, including a minority of Christian Arabs who, in the past, have generally held most of the power and wealth.
Economy Beirut's position as the major business centre of the Middle East has been damaged by recent civil conflicts, and industry and tourism have also suffered. Citrus fruits, maize, olives and vegetables are the chief agricultural products.

Lee, Robert E. (1807–1870), was an American soldier who commanded the Confederate army during the Civil War. He was an outstanding military leader and won important victories in the early years of the war. He suffered a severe defeat at Gettysburg in 1863, after which the Confederate army was on the defensive. His surrender to General Grant at Appomatox in April 1865 brought the war to an end.

Legume is a member of the flowering plant family called the Leguminosae. The Leguminosae includes the vetches, peas, clovers, gorse and groundnuts. The fruit of a legume is called a pod. It is a dry fruit produced by a single carpel which splits into two halves along both the top and bottom, to reveal the seeds within. A typical legume pod is that of the garden pea.

Lemming is a small, hamster-like mammal which lives in the colder regions of the Northern Hemisphere, such as Lapland. In years when food is plentiful, lemmings breed very quickly to produce enormous populations. When this happens, thousands migrate away from their main breeding grounds due to overcrowding. As they migrate, many fall prey to foxes, snowy owls, stoats and other predators. During this mass migration, and perhaps to try and escape the predators, many lemmings fall into rivers and over the edges of cliffs into the sea, giving rise to the popular myth that they commit suicide.

Lemur is a primate which lives on Madagascar. Its size ranges from that of a mouse to that of a dog. They have fox-like faces, woolly coats and long, thick tails. They eat insects, leaves and fruit. One of the most common lemurs is the ring-tailed lemur, which has a black-and-white-ringed tail. The tail is used to signal to other ring-tailed lemurs, and is also used as a 'scarf' when the animal sleeps.

Two members of the lemur family: an aye-aye *(above)* and an indris *(below)*.

Leonardo da Vinci at work in his studio.

Lenin, Vladimir Ilich (1870–1924), was a Russian revolutionary leader, who brought about the Bolshevik Revolution. Strongly influenced by the writings of Karl Marx, he was convinced of the necessity for revolution in Russia. He became leader of the left wing of the Russian Social Democratic Party, subsequently known as the Bolsheviks. He was living in exile in Switzerland when Revolution broke out in Russia in 1917. Returning home he overthrew the provisional government and established a Communist regime. Two years of civil war (1918–1920) ended with the founding of the Soviet Union, of which Lenin became first head of state. He became ill in 1922 and died in January 1924.

Lens is a curved piece of glass, plastic or any clear substance. It is used to refract light. Some lenses are curved so that they are thinner in the middle than at the edge. These are concave lenses and spread light out. Others

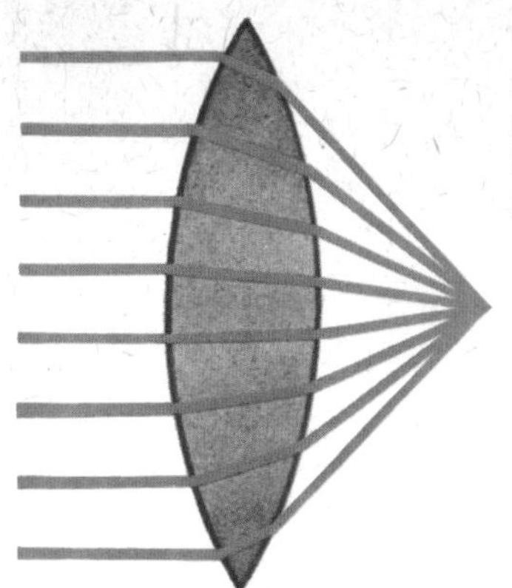

A convex lens brings parallel rays of light to a point, called the point of focus.

are flatter in the middle than at the edge. These are called convex lenses and bring light closer together.

Lenses are used in spectacles, for correcting eyesight. They are also used in telescopes, microscopes, cameras and many other optical instruments. *See also* Refraction.

Leonardo da Vinci (1452–1519), was one of the greatest figures of the Italian Renaissance. He was a true 'Renaissance Man' or 'universal genius' – there seems to have been no limit to his abilities. He painted some of the most famous pictures in the world, including the *Mona Lisa*, but he is equally well known for the remarkable studies in engineering and science, revealed by his notebooks. He had ideas about aeroplanes, submarines, split-level roads, town-planning and numerous other subjects centuries before their time.

Leopard is one of the big cats. Its coat is tawny yellow with black spots. The leopard has become very rare in many of the parts of Africa and Asia which it used to inhabit. It is a powerful and agile climber, and carries its prey into the trees so that other predators can not reach it.

Lesotho is a kingdom entirely surrounded by South Africa. Capital, Maseru; area about 30 000 sq km (11 700 sq miles). It was formerly the British colony of Basutoland. A small, mountainous country, it is inevitably dependent on South Africa and many of the people work in South African mines. It is largely an agricultural country, livestock-raising being especially important.

Lever is a sort of machine. There are many different types of levers, but they all consist of a solid object able to turn about a point called the fulcrum. A see-saw is a lever. It is a plank of wood balanced, usually in the middle, at the fulcrum. If two people of the same weight sit, one on each end, it is level. If somebody heavier sits at one end, the fulcrum has to be moved nearer to them to make the see-saw level. If the fulcrum is moved very close to a heavy person, a light person at the other end can lift them up. This same principle is used to enable heavy weights to be lifted by people, using a lever.

A crowbar is a lever with the fulcrum very close to one end. A heavy weight on this end can be lifted by pushing the other end. Pliers, wheelbarrows, nutcrackers and bottle openers are other examples of levers. Many levers are used in homes and factories.

Lianas are tropical rainforest plants which have long, woody, rope-like stems. Because light does not penetrate far down in the dense rainforests, they climb up to reach it. They do this by twining around the trunks of trees until the tops of their stems are near the top of the trees.

Liberia is a republic in West Africa. Capital, Monrovia; area about 113 000 sq km (43 000 sq miles). It was founded as a settlement for freed slaves from the USA in 1822 and became an indpendent republic in 1847. A huge section was granted to a US company in 1926 for rubber plantations.

From the beaches and mangrove swamps of the coast, the land rises to an undulating plateau, largely forested. There are mountains, containing iron ore, in the north. Timber, rubber and iron ore are the main exports. There are also gold and diamonds. Descendants of the original colonists are few in number and have recently become more integrated with the original inhabitants.

Libya is an Islamic republic in North Africa. (Official name: Socialist People's Libyan Arab Jamahiriyah.) Capital, Tripoli; area about 1 760 000 sq km (679 000 sq miles). Libya has been occupied since ancient times by the Phoenicians, Greeks, Romans, Vandals and Ottoman Turks. From 1911 it was an Italian colony. It eventually became an independent kingdom in 1951. The monarchy was overthrown in 1969 by army officers led by Colonel Gaddafi, who became president of the new republic. He established a radical, though not totally undemocratic, regime which was hostile to both the West and the communist bloc, and was often accused of supporting terrorist organizations in other countries.

Though it is large in area, Libya has a small population, as most of it is desert. The only areas capable of being cultivated are the coastal strip, up to 80 km (50 miles) wide, and scattered oases. Most of the people are of mixed Arab and Berber descent. Islam is the state religion.

Libya was a poor country, dependent on foreign aid, until the discovery of its immense oil reserves. The export of oil, making up more than 99 per cent of exports, has allowed rapid development, including irrigation schemes to increase the available farming land.

Lichen is a plant which exists in the form of a partnership between a fungus and an alga. The fungus provides shelter and attachment, and the alga makes food by photosynthesis. The fungus gives the lichen its shape, and acts as a covering for the algal cells which lie just beneath the surface.

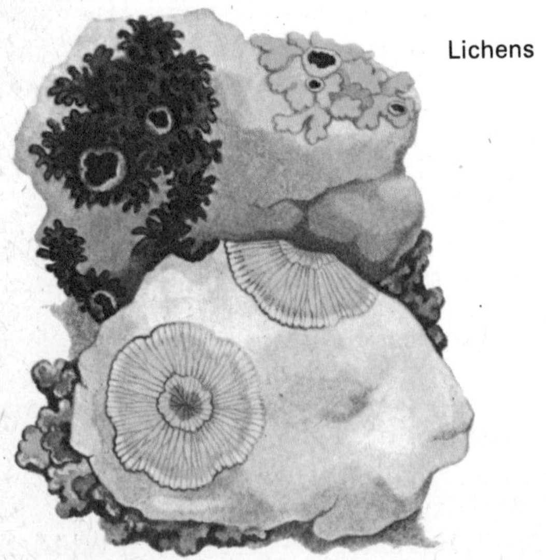

Lichens

There are over 6000 species of lichens throughout the world, and they can be found from the Arctic to the tropics. Most species cannot withstand pollution, however, and so are generally absent from towns.

Lichens are often the first plants to colonize bare rock. They help to break down the surface of the rock by the acids they produce, so that other plants can, in time, colonize the surface too.

Liechtenstein is a principality (ruled by a prince) in central Europe, between Switzerland and Austria. Capital, Vaduz; area about 160 sq km (62 sq miles). Liechtenstein is a historical freak, a tiny strip of land along the Rhine which has not been absorbed by larger neighbours. It has farming, winemaking and small manufacturing industries, and tourism brings in revenue.

Lie detector is an instrument used to measure whether somebody is telling the truth or lying. When somebody lies they may become tense. Tension can make the palms of the hands wet, dry the mouth, and quicken the heartbeat and breathing. A lie detector can measure changes in one or all of these things as a person answers questions.

The results of a lie detector may not be correct, however. Many factors, besides lying, can make people tense.

Life cycle of an animal or plant is the sequence of changes which it undergoes from fertilization (the joining of the gametes), through development, growth and maturity, to the same stage in the next generation.

Light is a form of energy. Light travels as rays. When we look at an object, we see it because the light rays bounce off the object and enter our eyes.

Stars, such as the Sun, are tremendously hot and so give off light. During the day, light comes to us from the Sun. At night, there is sunlight reflected from the Moon and light from other stars. Hot wood, coal and other substances give light when they burn. Hot filaments in electric light bulbs glow to provide light.

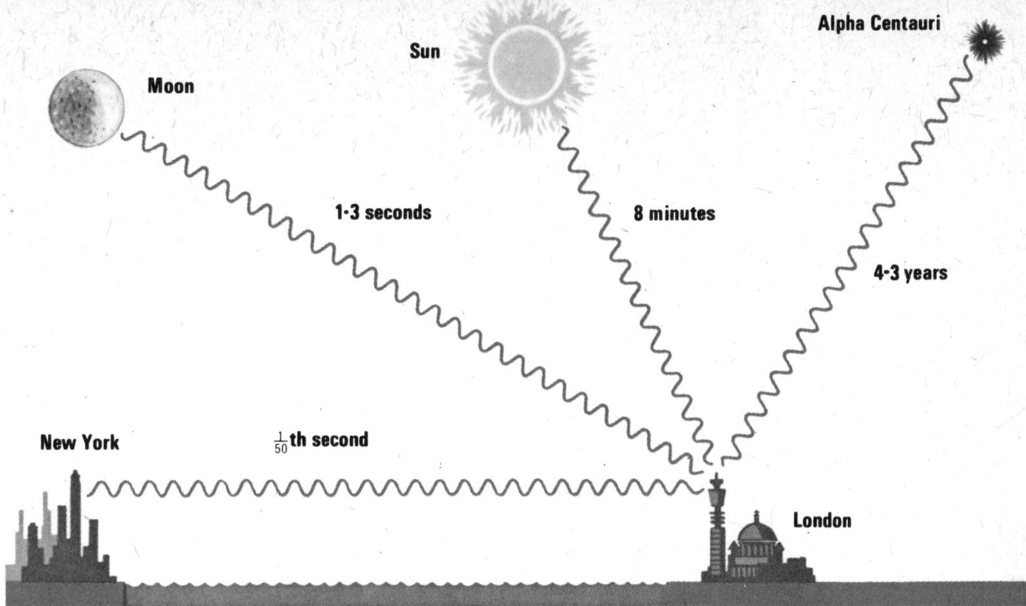

A diagram to show how long it takes light to reach London from different places.

Lightning is a flash or flashes of light, seen during a thunderstorm. It is caused by a build up of electrical charges and is actually the flash of an electrical discharge between clouds, or between a cloud and the Earth. Thunder is the name given to the sound created by the discharge. Since the speed of light is so much faster than that of sound, lightning is usually seen before the thunder is heard. By measuring the time between seeing the lightning flash and hearing the thunder, it is possible to work out how far away the storm is: every five seconds represents about 1.6 km (1 mile).

Light year is the distance that light travels in one year: 9.5 million million km (6 million million miles). The light year is used to measure the distances to other stars. Our nearest star, Alpha Centauri, is 4.3 light years away. If this distance was written in kilometres it would be a very long number. Star distances are so great that a large unit is needed.

Light travels so fast that we see something that happens on Earth at almost exactly the same time as it happens. Light can travel seven times right around the Earth in less than one second. However, stars are so far away that we can not see things that are happening there as they happen. The fact that Alpha Centauri is 4.3 light years away, also means that we are seeing it as it was 4.3 years ago.

Limerick is a form of comic verse in five lines. For example:

There was an old man of Darjeeling
Who travelled from London to Ealing.
It said on the door
Do not spit on the floor,
So he carefully spat on the ceiling.

Limestone is rock that consists mainly of calcium carbonate. Much of the Earth's limestone originated as the shells of sea creatures, subjected to great pressures over the ages. There are a number of varieties of limestone, including marble and chalk.

Limpets are aquatic molluscs with a conical shell, which feed by grazing seaweeds and other vegetation. They have powerful muscles which can clamp the animal and its shell to a rock making it difficult to remove.

Lincoln, Abraham (1809–1865), was an American statesman and President of the USA (1861–1865). Of humble origins, he became a lawyer and entered Congress in 1847. He soon became prominent through his strong opposition to slavery, and his election as President caused the Southern states, in which slavery was an institution, to break away from the rest of the country. Lincoln was determined at all costs to preserve the

USA as one country, and Civil War broke out. In 1863 Lincoln proclaimed the abolition of slavery. Re-elected President in 1864, he was assassinated in the following year by a Southern fanatic.

Lion is probably the best-known of the big cats. Although the lion once roamed over the whole of Africa and southern Asia, it is now restricted to Africa south of the Sahara and a small part of India. Male lions are easy to recognize for they have long, shaggy manes. Lions live in groups called prides, consisting of females and their cubs, and several males. They hunt antelopes and zebras. Usually a group of lions lies in wait for prey by a water-hole. All the pride feeds on the kill, after which they may be so full that they do not need to feed again for several days or more.

Liquid is a state of matter between a gas and a solid. A liquid does not have a definite shape, but takes on the shape of its container. For example, a liquid such as milk can be poured from a bottle into a jar or pan, and it then takes on the shape of the jar or pan. Although their shapes change, liquids always take up the same amount of space.

Water is the commonest liquid. When it is very cold, water freezes to form solid ice. Heated water boils into the gas, steam. All liquids change into solids or gases if they are cooled or heated to certain temperatures.

Liszt, Franz (1811–1886), was a Hungarian-born composer and pianist who showed tremendous ability even as a child. He gave recitals all over Europe, and became court musician at Weimar, Germany, in 1848. He sponsored the work of many young composers, including Berlioz and Wagner (who married his daughter). At Weimar he wrote much of his music, including his Hungarian Rhapsodies. He invented a new form, the tone poem (a work of one movement in the form of a symphony).

Liszt was a leader of the progessive 'new music' of the 19th century which culminated

Abraham Lincoln with an officer from the Union army.

in Wagner. He also extended the range of the piano, both by his compositions and by his own brilliant performances.

Liver is a large, lobed, red-coloured organ found in the bodies of vertebrates. It is the largest organ in the body by far, accounting for nearly a quarter of the total bulk of all the organs in the abdomen. Large blood vessels connect the liver to other parts of the body. All the blood in the body passes through the liver every two minutes, and the liver's main task is to control the level of chemicals in the blood. As well as doing this, it also stores food and produces bile which is used in digestion.

Livingstone, David (1813–1873), was a Scottish missionary and explorer. After studying medicine and theology, he was sent by the London Missionary Society to Bechuanaland (now Botswana). He led an expedition across the Kalahari Desert to discover Lake Ngami (1849), and then decided to penetrate northwards in order to open up central Africa to European civilization and to put an end to the slave trade. He travelled up the Zambezi River, discovering the Victoria Falls and Lake Malawi. In the 1860s and 1870s he tried to find the source of the Nile, and in 1871 had his famous meeting with H. M. Stanley.

Lizards are a group of reptiles which have been on Earth for about 180 million years. They are the most numerous and most adaptable of the reptiles, having invaded habitats on land and in the sea. There are tree lizards, burrowing lizards, gliding lizards and marine, seaweed-eating lizards. Lizards cannot live in very cold climates, however, since they are cold-blooded, and those that live in temperate regions often hibernate for the winter. Although there are many species of poisonous snake (snakes are close relatives of lizards), only two species of lizard are poisonous. These are the gila monster and beaded lizard of the deserts of Arizona and

Stanley greets Livingstone near Lake Tanganyika.

New Mexico. The largest lizard is the ferocious Komodo dragon, which grows to a length of over 3 m (10 ft).

Llama is a South American mammal used as a beast of burden, especially in the Andes. It has a long, shaggy coat which is white, brown or grey, and a long neck. The llama is descended from the guanaco, a wild South American relative of the camel.

Llewelyn I (Llewelyn ap Iorwerth; circa 1175–1240), was a Prince of North Wales who succeeded in extending his rule over the whole of Wales. He joined the English barons in their rebellion against King John, whose daughter he had married, and managed to have recognition of Welsh independence included in the terms of Magna Carta.

Llewelyn II (Llewelyn ap Gruffydd; circa 1246–1282), was a Welsh Prince, the grandson of Llewelyn I. He was the only native Prince of Wales to be officially recognized as such by the English. He helped the English barons in their conflict with Henry III, and refused to do homage to Edward I on his accession in 1272. Edward invaded Wales in 1276 and forced Llewelyn to acknowledge him as overlord. However, in 1281 Llewelyn rebelled again and was killed. Edward then annexed Wales entirely.

Lloyd George, David, 1st Earl (1863–1945), was a British statesman, born in Manchester of Welsh parents. He became a solicitor and was first elected to Parliament in 1890. As Chancellor of the Exchequer (1908–1915) he introduced a number of far-reaching social reforms including old-age pensions and national insurance, and his 'people's budget' of 1909 brought him into conflict with the House of Lords.

In 1916 he became Prime Minister of a wartime coalition government, and proved a vigorous leader in his efforts to bring the war to a successful conclusion. He also played an important part in drawing up the Treaty of Versailles (1919) at the end of the First World War. He ceased to be Prime Minister in 1922, but remained an MP until 1944.

Lobster is a large crustacean armed with fierce-looking claws with which it catches prey and also defends itself. Lobsters live in the sea, some species inhabiting deep water and others shallow water. They are mainly active at night, and fishermen catch them by lowering baited baskets called lobster pots on to the sea bed. The lobster climbs into them to reach the bait, but cannot get out again. Lobsters are blue when alive, only turning red when boiled.

Lock is used on canals or rivers to raise or lower ships from one level to another. A portion of the canal is closed off by gates and water is pumped in or out of the enclosed space to make it level with the other end of the lock. The world's largest single lock, near Antwerp in Belgium, is 500 m (1640 ft) long and 57 m (187 ft) wide.

Locomotive is the part of a train containing the engine, which is used to haul passenger carriages or goods wagons along the rails. It may be powered by steam, diesel or electricity.

The first self-propelled rail locomotive was built in 1804 by Englishman Richard Trevithick; it carried 70 passengers and 10 tonnes over 14.5 km (9 miles). By 1825, George Stephenson's *Locomotion* was hauling almost 50 tonnes at 24 km (15 mph) on the Stockton & Darlington Railway. Four years later George and Robert Stephenson built *Rocket*, the first modern steam locomotive, on which all subsequent designs were based. The fastest speed ever achieved by a steam locomotive was 202.8 km (125.9 mph), by the streamlined *Mallard*, again in England. (*Locomotion*, *Rocket* and *Mallard* all survive and can be seen in museums.)

Since the 1960s, steam locomotives have been replaced by diesel and electric

machines, which have gone even faster. British high speed trains with diesel engines travel regularly at 200 km/h (124 mph), while the French TGV electric trains manage 260 km/h (161 mph) on special railway tracks.

Locust is a large, herbivorous insect related to the grasshopper and cricket. It is found in many parts of the world, but Africa, Australia and North America are the continents where locusts do most damage. During periods when the populations of these insects build up, they undertake long swarming flights, devastating any crops or vegetation on which they settle to feed.

London is the capital of the United Kingdom. There was a Roman settlement here, and the city became the English capital early in the Middle Ages. In the 19th century it was something like a world capital, through its domination of world banking, insurance and business and as the heart of a large empire. The population is about the same as that of Scotland and Wales combined.

Central London consists of three main areas: the City (the oldest) which is the business centre; the West End (shopping and entertainment); and Westminster (government). Most of the medieval city was destroyed in the Great Fire (1666) and, architecturally, the most attractive parts of London are 18th and early 19th century.

The remainder of Greater London consists of a large number of connected 'villages', varying greatly in character. There is little heavy industry but almost every other type of manufacturing. London is also an important, though declining, port, and receives the major part of British imports.

Longitude is part of a geographical measuring system, in combination with latitude.

The longitude of a given spot is determined by the angle it makes at the centre of the Earth with the Greenwich meridian (an imaginary line running north-south through Greenwich, England). Longitude is expressed in degrees, minutes and seconds east or west of the Greenwich meridian. The meridian of Greenwich has a longitude of 0 degrees. Most world maps are marked with lines of longitude, all known as meridians, at intervals of 10 degrees. *See also* Latitude.

Lords, House of, is one of the two British Houses of Parliament, which are responsible for making laws. Its members are the British peers (dukes, earls, barons and so on) and the two archbishops and 24 senior bishops of the Church of England.

Once more important than the House of Commons, the House of Lords has steadily lost authority in democratic Britain since its

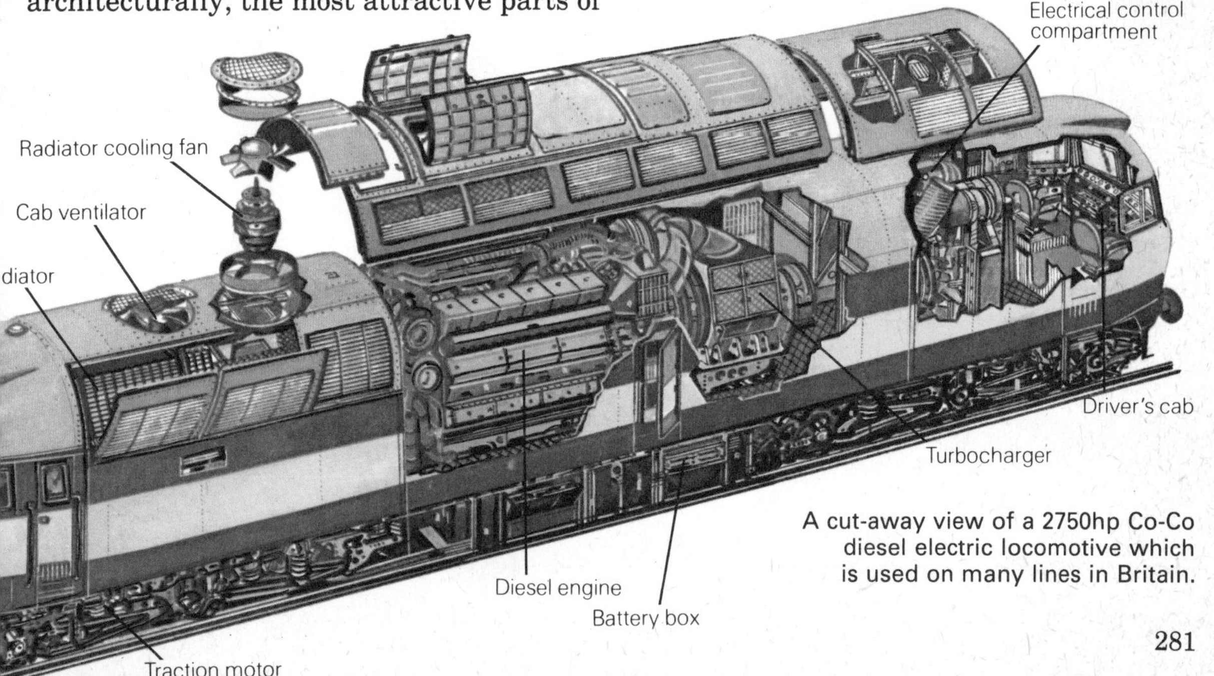

A cut-away view of a 2750hp Co-Co diesel electric locomotive which is used on many lines in Britain.

members are not elected and the overwhelming majority of peers have simply inherited their titles. Today the House of Lords only has the power to delay for a year the passing of any bill that the House of Commons is prepared to insist on.

Since 1958 there have also been some Life Peers in the House. These are appointed in recognition of their achievements, but do not pass their titles on to their heirs.

The House of Lords acts as the highest court of law in Britain. Appeals are heard by the Law Lords.

Louis XIV (1638–1715), was King of France (1643–1715). He succeeded to the throne on the death of his father, Louis XIII. Until 1661 the country was ruled by Cardinal Mazarin, but after his death Louis took personal charge of his country's affairs, with the assistance of able ministers, such as Colbert. France grew prosperous, Louis built a magnificent palace at Versailles and the arts flourished. As absolute monarch of the most powerful state in Europe, the ambitious King embarked on a series of wars with Spain, Holland and England. By the end of his reign, France was financially exhausted.

Louis XVI (1754–1792), King of France (1774–1792), was the grandson of Louis XV. During his reign France was on the edge of bankruptcy. His finance ministers tried to introduce much needed financial reforms, but this was frustrated by the opposition of the nobility and his wife, Marie Antoinette. In 1789, in an effort to deal with the crisis, Louis called a meeting of the Estates-General (nobility, clergy and Third Estate, or common people). This lead to the French Revolution. Louis made an unsuccessful attempt to escape abroad, but was deposed and subsequently guillotined after having been found guilty of treason. *See also* French Revolution.

Louse (plural lice) is a small, wingless, flat, parasitic insect. The word is also used to describe booklice (which are non-parasitic insects living in barns, houses and among debris), and whale and fish lice (which are parasitic crustaceans).

True insect lice are parasitic on the bodies of birds and mammals, clinging on to them with hooked claws. They have either biting

Louis XIV and his court, where extravagances seemed unlimited.

or sucking mouthparts, depending on the species, and feed on the host's blood or skin tissues. The adults remain on the host all the time, and the eggs are cemented to the hairs or feathers. Young lice hatch out which are miniature versions of the adults.

Luke, Saint, was the (probable) author of one of the gospels (accounts of Jesus) and also of the book called *Acts of the Apostles* in the Bible. Little is known of him except that he was a Gentile (a non-Jew) and a doctor, who accompanied St Paul on some of his journeys. His is the only gospel which tells of Jesus' boyhood.

Luminosity is the amount of light emitted by an object. If something shines it is said to be luminous. A star is luminous. To help find out more about stars, astronomers try to work out their degree of luminosity.

If you look down a street at night the street lamps will seem to get dimmer the farther away they are. They are all equally luminous, in fact, but they seem to have different luminosities because they are at different distances from you.

Stars are different distances away from the Earth. Unlike street lamps they also have different luminosities. To find their luminosity, their brightness (or apparent luminosity from the Earth) and their distance from the Earth must be measured. This luminosity is called their absolute magnitude.

Lung is one of a pair of sac-like organs found in the chest cavity of air-breathing vertebrates, such as humans, and including whales. There is even one type of fish, the lungfish, which breathes using a lung.

Air enters the lungs through a tube which is connected to the back of the throat. As air enters the lungs, oxygen diffuses into the tiny blood vessels that run through the lungs. Waste carbon dioxide leaves the blood and enters the lungs. It is expelled from the body when the animal breathes out.

Lutheranism is a form of Christian belief that began with the teaching of Martin Luther (1483–1546), the monk who led the Reformation. The main emphasis of Lutheranism is on religious faith in God, which is nourished by the Bible. Through faith, and faith alone, a believer can gain salvation and forgiveness.

Martin Luther nails a list of his arguments with the Church to the church door at Wittenberg in 1517.

Luther was the most influential of all the Protestant reformers of the 16th century, and Lutheranism remains the most important ingredient of Protestantism today. However, there is no single, authorized form of Lutheran worship, and even Churches which call themselves Lutheran may have slightly different forms of service.

Luxembourg is a grand duchy (ruled by a Grand Duke) in western Europe, bordering France, Germany and Belgium. Capital, Luxembourg; area about 2600 sq km (1000 sq miles). Centuries of rivalry amongst surrounding powers left Luxembourg independent, though it is closely linked with Belgium and the Netherlands (the Benelux countries). It is hilly and wooded, mainly agricultural, but possesses a very large iron and steel industry. The native language is

Lyrebirds build a nest of sticks on a ledge or on the ground.

Superb Lyrebird male

related to German but most Luxembourgois also speak French; most are Roman Catholic.

Lynx is a wild cat which has a short tail, long legs and tufted ears. The northern lynx is about 1 m (3 ft) long and lives in the forests of Eurasia and North America. The Canadian lynx has longer fur and broader feet than the northern lynx. Other species include the bay lynx of the southern parts of North America, and the rare but beautiful caracal lynx of North Africa and Asia.

Lyrebird is a bird which lives in the rainforests of eastern Australia where the two species feed on seeds and insects. The name comes from the shape of the tail, which in the male is very long and during courtship is thrown forward to resemble an old-fashioned lyre. The birds are about the size of a chicken, but the tail feathers are 60 cm (2 ft) long. The two outer feathers form the frame of the lyre and the delicate, inner feathers look like silvery strings.

M

Macao is a Portuguese territory in southeast China, near Hong Kong. Area about 16 sq km (6 sq miles). Consisting of a picturesque peninsula and two small islands, Macao has been Portuguese since the 16th century, though Portuguese sovereignty was not recognized by China until 1887. In recent years there has been some Communist opposition to Portuguese rule. Macao is a centre for tourists and is famous as a gambling centre.

Macaw is the largest, noisiest and most colourful of all the parrots. Macaws live in the tropical forests of Central and South America. They feed on fruits and nuts, easily splitting them open with their big, powerful beaks. The most familiar of these birds is the scarlet macaw, which reaches a length of 1 m (3 ft) including its long tail.

MacDonald, James Ramsay (1866–1937), was a British statesman and the first Labour Prime Minister. One of the founders of the Labour Party, he was elected to Parliament in 1906. He was Prime Minister and Foreign Secretary in the Labour government which briefly held office in 1924. MacDonald became Prime Minister again in 1929, but the Labour government collapsed during the economic crisis of 1931. He then headed a National government supported by Conservatives and Liberals, resigning in 1935.

Machiavelli, Niccolò 1467–1527), was an Italian statesman and political theorist

Niccolo Machiavelli.

whose ideas had great influence. He held office in the republic of Florence until the return to power of the Medici family in 1512 forced him to go into exile. In his book *The Prince*, published in 1513, he stated that a ruler was entitled to use any means, however ruthless, in order to maintain power and keep his country peaceful.

MacMillan, Kenneth (1929–), is a British dancer and choreographer. He worked for the company which became the Royal Ballet, becoming resident choreographer in 1965 and director in 1970. As a choreographer, he was a master at revealing the private ambitions and emotions that lurk below the surface of modern society, conveyed entirely through movement. Many MacMillan works were unusual in both form and content, but they remained faithful to the classical ballet tradition.

Macmillan, Maurice Harold (1894–), is a British statesman. He was Foreign Secretary briefly in 1955, and Chancellor of the Exchequer from 1955 to 1957. He succeeded Sir Anthony Eden as Prime Minister in 1957 and helped to restore the morale of the Conservative Party after the Suez Crisis (1956). During his period of office many British colonies were granted independence, and he tried unsuccessfully to negotiate Britain's entry into the EEC.

Madagascar is an island republic off south-east Africa. Capital, Antananarivo (Tananarive); area about 594000 sq km (229000 sq miles).

It was made a French colony in 1898 and a French overseas territory in 1946. It gained independence in 1960.

The 'great red island' of Madagascar is mostly highland, with upland plateaux and high peaks near the centre. In the east the land falls to a narrow but fertile coastal plain; in the west the slope is more gradual. In the highlands the climate is fairly temperate, but it is very dry in the south-west. The people are mainly a mixture of African and Indian descent; many are nomadic herdsmen.

Madagascar has remarkable wildlife. In particular, it has various species of lemur – many now extinct in the wild. Lack of resources plus transport problems hinder industrial growth. Valuable exports are vanilla beans, coffee and other tropical produce, including oils used in perfume.

Madrigal is a musical composition for several voices, usually unaccompanied. The madrigal came originally from medieval Italy. It was revived in the 16th century and reached its finest form in the work of Monteverdi. A number of composers in Elizabethan England wrote madrigals, but in the 17th century the madrigal was succeeded by the more dramatic form of the cantata, with instrumental accompaniment.

Magellan, Ferdinand (circa 1480–1521), was a Portuguese navigator and explorer. After undertaking voyages to India and Africa, in 1519 he set off from Spain with five ships and sailed westwards to try to find a route that would take him to the East Indies. He rounded the coast of South America and reached the Philippines, but was killed there (1521). One of his ships returned to Spain in 1522, thus completing the first circumnavigation of the globe.

Magellanic Clouds are the nearest galaxies to our own Galaxy. There are two of them, known as the Large and Small Magellanic Clouds. They are named after the Portuguese explorer Ferdinand Magellan (1480–1521), who was the first person to travel around the Earth.

In southern skies Magellanic Clouds look like faintly shining clouds. They cannot be seen by people north of the equator.

The Large Magellanic Cloud is about twice as wide as the Small Magellanic Cloud. They both contain thousands of millions of stars. They are part of our Local Group of galaxies. There are nearly thirty galaxies in our Local Group.

Magma is hot melted rock, usually found far below the Earth's surface. It can sometimes force its way up to the surface, however, where it cools to form rocks. These are known as igneous rocks.

Magma can also erupt out of volcanoes. It is then called lava.

Liquid magma may contain gases and solid rock. These gases can be trapped in the rock when it cools, forming a light, spongy rock called pumice.

Magna Carta was a charter which King John sealed at Runnymede in 1215 under pressure from barons and churchmen. Its chief aim was to protect the feudal privileges of the nobility and the rights of the Church against the extension of royal power. It also provided some safeguards, such as freedom from arbitrary arrest, for the humbler members of society. In later ages it was seen as the foundation stone of English liberties.

The Magna Carta was signed in 1215.

Magnesium is a white metal. Its chemical symbol is Mg. It is found in many ores such as magnesite and dolomite, and in sea water. Magnesium burns in air with a brilliant white flame, and is used in fireworks. It is very light weight, and is used with other metals, such as aluminium, to make aircraft and cars.

Magnesium compounds are used in medicines, such as 'milk of magnesia'.

Magnet is usually a straight, or horseshoe-shaped, piece of steel. The ends of a magnet, called its poles, can attract other metals, such as iron. Hung from a piece of string, a magnet always points in the same direction – north-south. The end which points north is called the north pole and the other end is called the south pole.

If one magnet is brought near another one, it may push it away or pull towards it, depending on whether or not the two similar poles of each magnet are nearest each other. North poles push away from each other. North and south poles are pulled towards each other.

Magnets have many uses. Recently, trains have been made which travel above, rather than on, railway lines. The trains are pushed above the lines by magnets. *See also* Compass.

Magritte, René (1898–1967), was a Belgian Surrealist painter. He specialized in producing unusual images which deliver a shock to the sense of reason. His usual method was to put two or more unlikely objects together – a train steaming out of a fireplace, a businessman with an apple for a head, etc. These disturbing, provoking images were painted in a realistic way, and seem to make fun of all forms of visual communication.

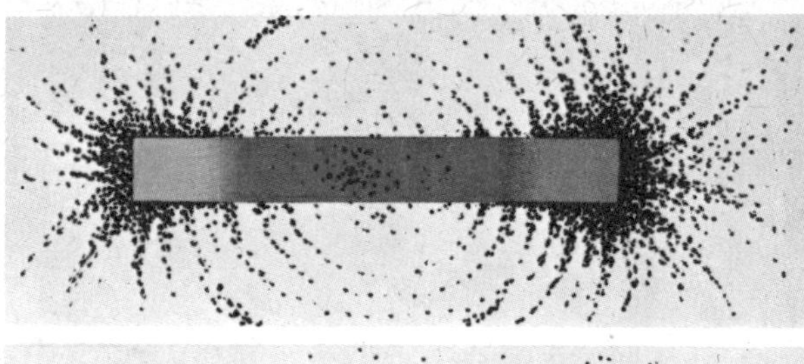

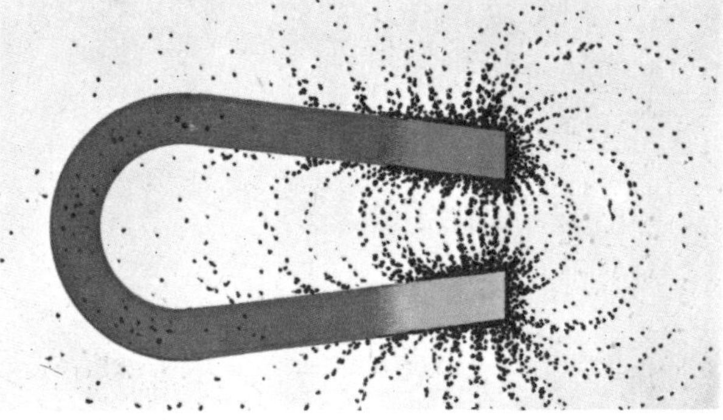

A horseshoe magnet *(below)* showing the poles. Iron filings show the magnetic field of magnets *(left)*, the region a magnet can have an effect on.

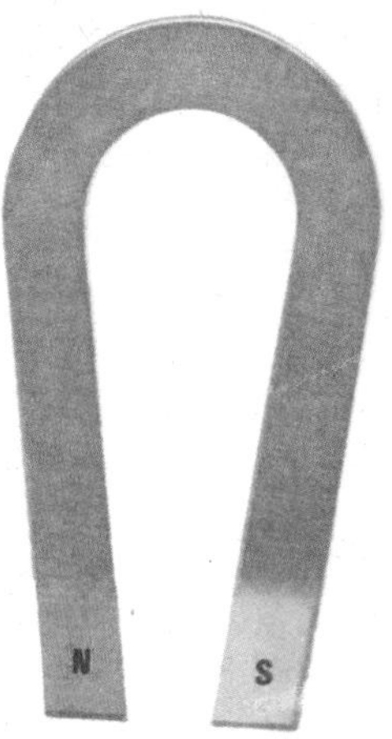

Mahler, Gustav (1860–1911), was an Austrian composer and conductor. He gave his first piano recital at the age of ten, and as a young man was associated with Bruckner. In 1880 he began his very successful career as a conductor, which continued for the rest of his life.

Despite praise from Strauss, Mahler's own music aroused hostility. For many years he was admired only by a small but enthusiastic minority, who recognized both his powerful romantic appeal and his significance as a musical innovator. Mahler did not become widely popular until after the Second World War. His chief works are his ten grand symphonies, his songs and 'song symphony', *Song of the Earth* (1911).

Maize is an important cereal crop, which originated in the Americas. In North America it is called corn. It is a member of the Graminae, or grass family. The maize cob is a collection of female flowers which have turned to seed. Various varieties of maize are grown – for instance, pop corn and sweet corn. Maize is also used to produce animal feed, corn syrup, corn oil, and in the paper industry.

Malawi is a republic in south-central Africa, along the Great Rift Valley. Capital, Lilongwe; area about 94 000 sq km (36 000 sq miles). It was made the British protectorate of Nyasaland in 1891 until it gained independence under Dr Hastings Banda in 1964.

The enormous Lake Malawi lies in the east, and there are high plateaux to the west, where the climate is less hot. Water supply is fair by African standards, and parts of Malawi are heavily populated. The people belong to a variety of nations, including the Chewa and Ngoni but tribalism is not a major problem.

Most people grow maize, rice, etc for their own use. The main plantation crops are tea, cotton, coffee and tobacco. Mineral resources are rather slight, and industry is restricted to manufactures for the home market.

Malaysia is a federated state in south-east Asia, consisting of 11 states on the Malay peninsula and two on the island of Borneo – Sarawak and Sabah. Capital, Kuala Lumpur; area about 330 000 sq km (128 400 sq miles).

History Malaysia was part of the Hindu and Buddhist Kingdom of Sri Vijaya and ruled from Sumatra for 500 years up to the 13th century. Subsequent rulers included Javanese, Thais and the Malay ruler of Malacca from where the religion of Islam spread. The Portuguese, Dutch and British all had trading interests in the region in the 16th and 17th centuries, but, by the beginning of the 18th century, the Sultanates in the Malay peninsula were coming under British control. In 1826 the British colony of Straits Settlements was formed although Johore, the last state to join, held out until 1914.

The Japanese occupied Malaya during the Second World War. After the war the idea of a federation (the joining together of separate states) grew in popularity, particularly under the leadership of Tunku Abdul Rahmau – the first prime minister when the Malay peninsula became independent in 1957.

In 1963 Sarawak, Sabah and Singapore joined the Federation of Malaysia, but Singapore left again in 1965.

Land Rich natural resources make the Federation of Malaysia one of Asia's most prosperous countries: it is the world's largest producer of tin, natural rubber, and palm oil. The country has two distinct regions: West Malaysia, or Malaya, which is the southern part of the Malay Peninsula; and East Malaysia, which comprises the territories of Sabah and Sarawak on the northern coast of the island of Borneo. An artificial causeway, built across the narrow Strait of Johore, connects West Malaysia to the island country of Singapore in the south.

Both West and East Malaysia are mountainous: their mountains, though separated by sea, belong to the same formation. The two parts of the country are also alike in that they are heavily forested: more than two-thirds of the total area is thick tropical rain forest.

In West Malaysia, wide coastal plains fringe the mountains of the interior. The mountain ranges hamper communications between the western and eastern sides of the peninsula. The longest of the peninsula's many rivers are the Pahang and the Perak.

The country's climate varies little: almost all areas have equatorial monsoon conditions, with high temperatures and rain all the year round.

People Malaysia has suffered from rivalry between its two main ethnic groups, the Malays and the Chinese. Minority groups include Indians and Pakistanis, as well as the Dasuns in Sabah and Dyaks in Sarawak.

Economy Economically, West Malaysia is dominant; it provides 90 per cent of the national income. The most important food crop is rice. Cash crops include pineapples and tea. Rubber, tin, and timber are the chief earners of foreign currency.

Maldives, Republic of, is a group of about 2000 coral islands in the Indian Ocean. Capital, Malé; area about 298 sq km (115 sq miles). The British took possession of the islands from the Dutch in 1887 until independence in 1965. Only about 200 of the islands are inhabited and most of the people are Muslims of Arab descent. The Maldives have a hot, humid climate. The economy is based on fishing, bonito (a mackerel-like fish) being the chief export. Coconut products are also important.

Mali is a republic in West Africa. Capital, Bamako; area about 1 240 000 sq km (479 000 sq miles). Formerly known as French Sudan, it became independent in 1960, taking the name of a medieval African empire. Though large, it has few people. The north is part of the Sahara, and it is dry everywhere except in the marshy region of the Niger River, where most people live.

The inhabitants belong to many African nations, the Mande and Fulbe (Fulani) being the most numerous. Nomadic Berber peoples inhabit the north. The great majority of people are farmers and herdsmen, who produce only enough for themselves. Islam is the chief religion.

The chief export crops are rice, peanuts and cotton. The Niger is rich in fish, and Mali also sells smoked and dried fish to its neighbours. Transportation and lack of valuable resources are major problems.

Malta is an island republic in the western Mediterranean, about 100 km (62 miles) south of Sicily. Capital, Valetta; area 246 sq km (949 sq miles). Malta has a colourful history, and has been attacked or conquered by most of the Mediterranean powers of the past 2000 years. The British were the last holders, and Malta was an important

naval base until it became independent in 1964.

The Maltese are a distinct race who trace their ancestry to the ancient Phoenicians. Their three inhabited islands have no rivers or mountains, but the many bays and beaches, and the warm climate, attract tourists, who are the main source of income.

Mammals are warm-blooded vertebrates which have hair on their bodies, and usually suckle their young on milk produced inside the mother's body. There are 4200 species of mammal world-wide, and nearly two-thirds of all these are rodents. Mammals are the most highly advanced animals, with an efficient four-chambered heart which allows great activity, and an advanced brain reaching its highest level of intelligence in human beings. Unlike reptiles which have teeth that are all similar, mammals may have several different kinds of teeth. There are incisors for rasping, nibbling and nipping, canines for stabbing and holding prey, and molars for chewing.

Some examples of mammals. All these mammals live in fir and pine forests of the north. They grow an extra-thick fur in the bitterly cold winters.

Although there are fewer mammals than any other group of animals, they live in almost every type of habitat. They have evolved a huge array of body shapes to exploit the chosen habitat – for example, bats and gliding squirrels in the air, whales and seals in the sea, moles underground, hippopotamuses and manatees in the rivers, and elephants, lions, giraffes, rats, kangaroos, rhinoceroses, horses, cats, and dogs on the ground.

Mammals are divided into three groups. The monotremes are primitive mammals that still produce young by laying eggs. The only monotremes are the platypus and the echidna or spiny anteater. The marsupials give birth to live young, but the young are very undeveloped, and must crawl into the mother's pouch to continue development. Marsupials include the kangaroo, bandicoot and koala. The placental mammals are the most advanced group. The young grow inside the mother's womb and are not born until they are well developed. All other mammals, including human beings, are placental mammals.

Mammoth was one of the animals which lived during the Ice Ages. About two to three million years ago, at the end of the geological period known as the Pliocene, the Northern Hemisphere became much colder than it had previously been. Great sheets of ice came to cover much of the land. In time, these melted and there followed a warm period, which itself was followed by another freezing ice age. There were four such ice ages, and one of the animals which lived during them was the mammoth. The mammoth was a huge, shaggy coated elephant which browsed on conifers, birch and lichens. It had huge tusks, and stood over 3 m (10 ft) high. Sometimes mammoths are found still frozen in the icy wastes of Siberia – perhaps having been driven into lakes thousands of years ago by carnivorous animals or early humans.

Mammoth

Manatee, see Sea-cows.

Mandrill, see Baboons.

Manet, Edouard (1832–1883), was a French painter. He was one of the most important artists of the 19th century, the hero of the future Impressionists. He was no rebel by nature, and his constant failure to get proper recognition from the art 'establishment' disappointed him. His technique – using areas of flat colour with little 'modelling' – was criticized as crude, and his subject-matter condemned as scandalous. The works which aroused the loudest protests were actually based on old masterpieces by Venetian painters. What gave offence was Manet's realistic style: his nudes looked like real women, not Greek statues.

Mangroves are trees which occur along the swampy coasts of America, Africa, India and the Philippines. Most trees can not tolerate salt water, and none can survive with their roots permanently submerged and thus starved of oxygen. Mangroves have evolved a cunning way to solve this problem. The mangrove's dense tangle of roots send up through the mud special 'air tubes' called pneumatophores. These take in the necessary oxygen from the atmosphere.

Mann, Thomas (1875–1955), was a German writer who became a US citizen in 1944. The greatest German novelist of the century, he became famous with *Buddenbrooks* (1901), the story of the decline of a wealthy family. Mann was concerned with conflicts, especially the conflict between the creative, artistic spirit and a staid, conservative society. This was one of the themes of his greatest novel, *The Magic Mountain* (1927). Of his many other works, perhaps the best known are *Death in Venice* (1913) and his series about the world of the Bible, beginning with *Joseph and His Brothers* (1933).

Mannerism, in art, is an exaggeration of style (or manner). The word is applied especially to 16th-century Italian painting between the Renaissance and the Baroque periods. Its characteristics included elongated or very muscular figures (this originated with Michelangelo), violent colour and exaggerated gestures.

Man-powered flight – the earliest pioneers of aviation, in the 18th and 19th centuries, dreamed of flying like birds by attaching artificial wings to their arms and flapping them. They quickly discovered that human muscles were simply not powerful enough, a problem which also prevented all other attempts at man-powered flight in heavier-than-air craft (usually involving pedals turning a propeller).

In the late 1970s, an American engineer, Dr Paul MacCready, constructed *Gossamer Condor* from the very latest synthetic materials, using a carbon fibre framework, a polythene-type covering for the wings and plastic control lines. This made the whole machine extremely light – under 100 kg (221 lb) with the pilot on board – and meant that one person could produce enough power through a pedal-driven propeller to make the machine fly. A later machine, *Gossamer Albatross*, flew over the English Channel in 1979. *Albatross* was an enormous aircraft – its 28 m (92 ft) wingspan was greater than that of many passenger jets – but its weight, including the pilot, was only 97 kg (214 lb). *Albatross* crossed the English Channel at a height of only 0.76 m (2.49 ft) in three hours.

Mantis, or praying mantis as it is sometimes called, is a cunning, predatory insect occurring mainly in the tropics. With their long, twig-like bodies, mantises closely resemble the branches on which they lie in wait. However, as soon as an unsuspecting insect comes close, they shoot out their spiny front legs and impale the insect on the spines. They are called praying mantises because they hold up their front legs whilst waiting for a meal, as though they are praying.

Mantle is one of the Earth's three layers. Around the centre of the Earth is a layer called the core. Around the surface of the Earth is a layer called the crust. Between the core and the crust is a layer called the mantle. The mantle is the biggest part of the Earth.

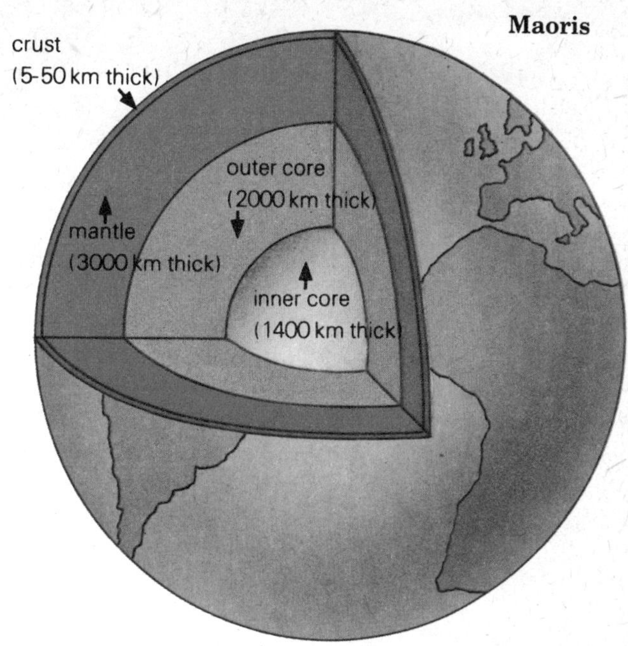

Most of the mantle is fixed and cannot move, but near the crust there is thought to be a part of the mantle which can move. Above this is a thin, fixed layer of mantle. This last part of the mantle is thought to be divided up into a series of large plates.

The continents were once all joined. Slowly, they drifted apart into their present shapes.

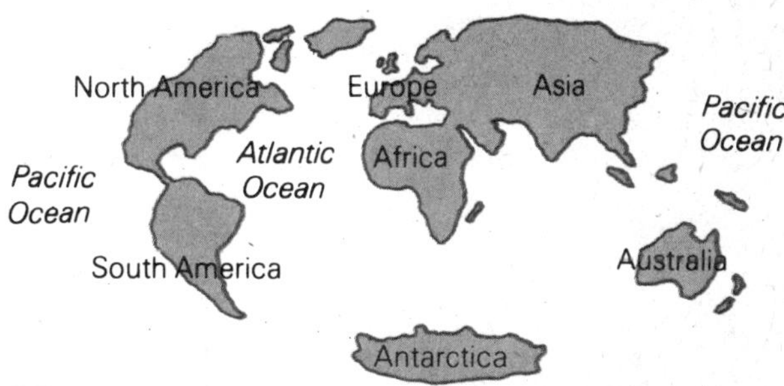

Maoris are the Polynesian people who live in New Zealand. They have been there since before the arrival of the Europeans – it is thought that they arrived about the middle of the 14th century. By the early 19th century their population may have numbered as many as 200 000. Divided into tribes, they lived in villages and engaged in agriculture, and also showed great skill in stone and wood carving. By the Treaty of Waitangi (1840) the tribal chiefs yielded sovereignty

Maoris in traditional costume. This is still worn on ceremonial occasions.

to the British crown. Many Maoris now live in the towns, and their numbers are again increasing after a period of decline.

Mao Tse Tung (1893–1976), was a Chinese Communist statesman and political theorist. One of the founders of the Chinese Communist Party, he became its leader in 1927. After quarrelling with the Chinese Nationalists, he was forced to go on the 'Long March' to avoid capture by them. The civil war between Nationalists and Communists was temporarily ended in order that both sides could combine to fight the Japanese invaders in the Second World War. The Civil War was resumed in 1945 and by 1949 the Nationalists had been defeated and forced to flee to Taiwan. Mao Tse Tung became chairman of the People's Republic of China and began building a Communist society in China. In 1966 he was the leading spirit of his country's Cultural Revolution.

Mao Tse Tung as a young man.

Marble is a hard, shiny stone, found in a variety of colours and capable of being brilliantly polished. It is a more or less crystalline form of limestone, which has been subjected to intense heat and pressure in past geological ages. It has been used for building and sculpture since ancient times.

March is the third month of the year in the modern calendar, and lasts for 31 days. Its name comes from the ancient Roman month *Martius*, which was sacred to Mars, god of war. In Britain, 25 March was regarded as the first day of the year until 1752, when 1 January became New Year's Day.

Marconi, Guglielmo (1874–1937), was an Italian inventor who pioneered radio. Using morse code, he transmitted the first radio message in 1895. After improving the range of his equipment, he sent a radio message from France to Britain in 1899, and in 1901 he sent the first intercontinental message from Cornwall to Newfoundland.

Marconi was awarded the Nobel prize for Physics for his work in 1909. In 1916 he started experimenting with short radio waves. He played a large part in the development of telegraph, telephone and broadcasting systems.

Marie Antoinette (1755–1793), was Queen of France (1774–1792). The daughter of the Emperor Francis I and Maria Theresa of Austria, she married Louis, later Louis XVI of France, in 1770. Her extravagance and her frivolity, together with her opposition to the reforms of her husband's ministers, made her very unpopular. She attempted secretly to obtain help from Austria to crush the French Revolution. Found guilty of treason, she was imprisoned and executed in 1793.

Mark, Saint, was the probable author of one of the gospels (accounts of Jesus) in the Bible. He was known to some of Jesus' closest disciples, though he was a much younger man, and his gospel (if it *is* his) was probably the first to be written, about AD 70. It places special emphasis on the power of Jesus as a worker of miracles.

According to tradition, St Mark became the first bishop of Alexandria. He also has a connection with Venice, of which he is the patron saint.

Marlowe, Christopher (1564–1593), was an English poet and playwright. His plays – *Tamburlaine* (two parts), *The Jew of Malta*, *Dr Faustus* and *Edward II* – are his most famous works. They were written from 1587 to 1593, just before Shakespeare's plays, and clearly influenced Shakespeare greatly though he also mocked Marlowe's high-flown language. Marlowe died mysteriously in a fight in an inn. He may have been a government secret agent.

Marie Antoinette waiting for her execution.

Marmoset is a small South American monkey. They scurry along the branches of their tropical forest homes, with claws rather than finger nails on the ends of their fingers to help them grip. Marmosets have shrill voices and act rather like squirrels. The most brightly coloured living mammal is the golden lion marmoset which has a shimmering bright red-gold coat. Marmosets usually give birth to twins, which are cared for by the father except at feeding time.

Mars is the fourth planet from the Sun. It orbits the Sun every 687 days. A Martian 'day' is about 40 minutes longer than a day on Earth. Mars is about half the size of the Earth, and because its atmosphere is thin, its surface can be seen from the Earth.

The iron oxide in Mars's surface gives the planet a red colour. The atmosphere is mainly carbon dioxide. The average temperature is over 40 degrees Centigrade below freezing, and ice forms permanent polar caps, and some cloud and fog. The surface of the planet has craters and channels, and two major features are a series of canyons about

A picture of the surface of Mars taken at the landing site of Viking 1.

4000 km (2486 miles) long, and the biggest volcano known in the Solar System, 26 km (16 miles) high.

Many spacecraft have investigated Mars. Some of the American Viking spacecraft landed and took samples of the surface. From these samples it is thought that there is no life on Mars.

Mars has two satellites, Phobos and Deimos.

Marsupials are primitive mammals which get their name from the Latin word *marsupium* meaning pouch. In fact, marsupials are often called pouched mammals. Only females possess the pouch, and it is used as a nursery for the young. Marsupials give birth to tiny, undeveloped young which crawl into the pouch where they cling on to a teat, and then continue their development. Even when they are quite well grown, they will often hop back into the pouch for safety.

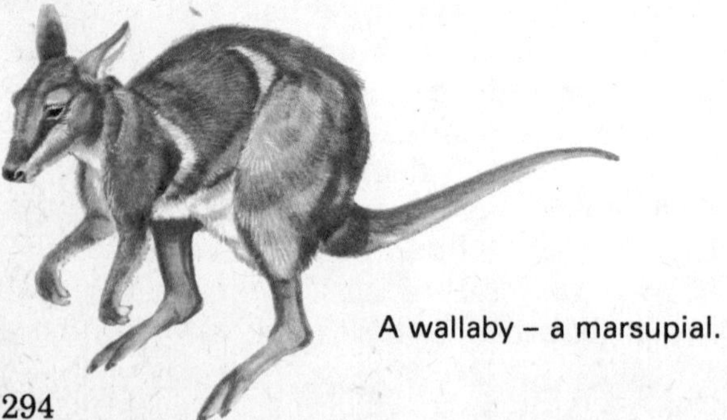

A wallaby – a marsupial.

The majority of marsupials are found in Australia, although Tasmania, New Guinea and South America also have a few. North America has the Virginian opossum. The most familiar marsupials are probably kangaroos, but koalas, wallabies, Tasmanian devils, wombats and numbats are also marsupials.

Martinique is an island in the Windward Islands, West Indies. Capital, Fort-de-France; area about 1100 sq km (420 sq miles). A mountainous island, it has been a French colony since 1635 and is now an overseas province of France. The people are mainly of African descent and speak a Creole dialect, though French is the official language. Sugar is the main crop, and sugar and rum the chief exports.

Martins are dark, slender birds with long, pointed wings and, often, a forked tail. They feed on insects which they catch on the wing, for they are very clever fliers. Many species, such as the European house martin, migrate

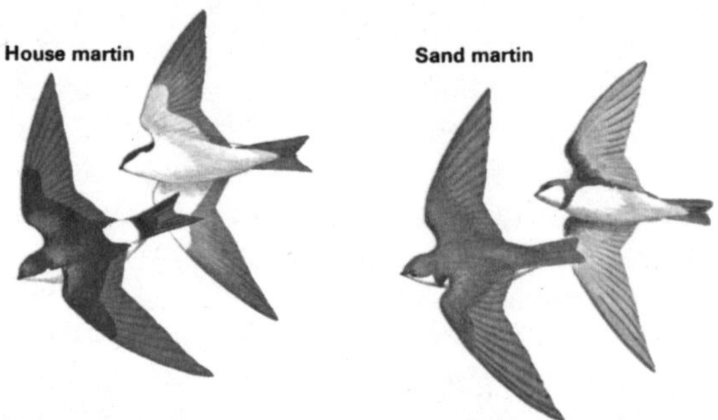

from Africa to breed in Europe before returning in the autumn. The house martin glues a mud nest to the eaves of houses, and the sand martin builds a nest with a long, narrow entrance in sandy banks. The grey-breasted martin ranges from Texas to Argentina.

Marx brothers were US comedy actors. The most famous is 'Groucho' (1895–1977), followed by 'Chico' (1891–1961) and 'Harpo' (1893–1964), though there were originally five brothers. They made their name and developed their style on the stage, moving into films in 1929. Among their most successful films are *Horse Feathers* (1932), *Duck*

Soup (1933), *A Night at the Opera* (1935) and *A Day at the Races* (1937). Groucho always played the antisocial, wisecracking leader; Chico based his character on an Italian street pedlar; while Harpo was the amiably crazy one who never spoke.

Marx, Karl (1818–1883), was a German philosopher and economist. He left Germany in 1843 after the Prussian government had banned a radical newspaper which he edited. In 1848, together with Friedrich Engels, he published the *Communist Manifesto*, in which he first put forward his ideas about socialism. Living in London from 1849, he continued to develop his theories, which were eventually published in his most famous work, *Das Kapital*. Marx believed that all human society goes through various historical stages from feudalism and capitalism to communism. His ideas were to have an enormous influence on the history of the 20th century.

Karl Marx

Mary I (1516–1558), was Queen of England (1553–1558). The daughter of Henry VIII and Catherine of Aragon, she was brought up as a Roman Catholic. She succeeded to the throne on the death of her half brother, Edward VI, after the conspiracy to make Lady Jane Grey queen had failed. Her determination to re-introduce Catholicism, her ruthless persecution of Protestants, her marriage to Philip II of Spain and finally the loss of Calais all combined to make her very unpopular.

Mary Queen of Scots (1542–1587), was Queen of Scotland (1542–1567). She succeeded to the throne shortly after her birth following the death of her father, James V. She was brought up at the French court and was briefly Queen of France as the wife of Francis II. Returning to Scotland in 1561 after the death of her husband, she as a Roman Catholic had to face the growing strength of Protestantism. In 1565 she married Lord Darnley, who was murdered two years later. Mary then married the Earl of Bothwell, who was suspected of having killed Darnley, and she was compelled to abdicate in favour of her infant son. She fled to England where she was imprisoned by Elizabeth I. After many years in prison she was implicated in a plot against Elizabeth (Mary had a strong claim to the English throne) and executed.

Mary, Saint, was the Mother of Jesus, called the Virgin Mary or Our Lady. According to the Bible the birth of Jesus was forecast by an angel and took place in a stable at Bethlehem, where the Three Wise Men and the Shepherds came to worship the infant Jesus.

The Bible contains some information about Mary, but not a complete life story. She was with Jesus at the Crucifixion, when he was

Mary, Queen of Scots, prepares for her execution.

deserted by all his disciples except St John.

In the early Eastern Church Mary became the subject of intense worship. She was hailed as the 'Mother of God' – not merely of the human Jesus – and became the most important being in Christianity after God. In the West this happened later: the cult of devotion to Mary was not fully established until well into the Middle Ages. However, most of the great Gothic cathedrals were dedicated to her.

Many of the beliefs and practices in the worship of Mary were rejected by the Protestant reformers in the 16th century, and to this day Mary stands much higher in the Roman Catholic Church than in Protestant Churches.

Mass is the amount of matter in an object. It is measured by weighing the object. However, mass and weight are not the same. Weight measures how much an object is pulled by the Earth. If you weighed yourself on Jupiter you would be over twice as heavy as on Earth. In space you would have no weight at all. But the amount of matter or mass of your body stays the same. Mass is measured in units called grams. *See also* Gravity.

Mathematics is a science which studies numbers, shapes and other abstract things. A form of mathematics that deals with numbers is called arithmetic. Adding up the cost of purchases in a shop and subtracting to find how much change the shopkeeper will give are examples of arithmetic.

All the buildings and instruments around us were invented and made by people who used mathematics. For example, before making a table, a carpenter needs to know its size, to know how much wood to buy. Working out areas and volumes of shapes is part of another form of mathematics, called geometry. Thousands of years ago, the Egyptians used geometry to design and build huge pyramids.

Matisse, Henri (1869–1954), was a French painter. He tried various styles and was interested especially in Post-Impressionist experiments with colour. In 1905 he and a group of like-minded artists were named the Fauves ('wild beasts'). Although he told his pupils to study nature, Matisse continued to paint ultra-vivid colours and simplified but distorted forms. His pictures may have first appeared violently sensational, yet Matisse's art was always directed towards refinement, simplicity and order. Although best known as a painter, he was also a sculptor, engraver and architect.

Matter is the name given to the substance of which everything is made. Everything in the universe – animals, plants, rocks, televisions, the Earth – is made of matter. There are four kinds of matter: gas, liquid, solid and plasma. These are called states of matter.

All matter is made up of atoms or ions. The amount of matter in an object is called its mass. The amount of space it takes up is called its volume. All matter has mass and volume.

Matthew, Saint, was one of the Twelve Apostles of Jesus, believed to be the author of the first gospel (account of Jesus). He was a tax collector employed by the Roman government, and Jesus attracted much criticism for associating with such hated people. Nothing is known for certain about St Matthew's later life. His gospel emphasizes that Jesus is the Jewish Messiah, who will restore Israel, and concentrates on Christ's teaching, notably the Sermon on the Mount (Chapters 5–7).

Mauritania is a republic in western Africa. Capital Nouakchott; area about 1 030 000 sq km (398 000 sq miles). The first European (Portuguese) base in West Africa was on an island off the coast. The region fell under French influence and became a colony in 1920. It became independent in 1960.

Mauritania is mostly desert, though there are rich soils and more rainfall in the Senegal valley, in the south-west, where most of the people live. The majority of the inhabitants are of Berber descent and are Muslims. Herding and agriculture are the main occupations, but large deposits of iron ore exist in the north-west, and this provides the most valuable export at present.

Mauritius is an island in the Indian Ocean, east of Madagascar. Capital, Port Louis; area about 1860 sq km (720 sq miles). Now independent, it was a British colony after 1814 and was previously French. A volcanic island, subject to cyclones, it supports a large population of mixed origin, mainly French-speaking. Agriculture is very productive. Mauritius produces large amounts of sugar as well as other tropical products.

Maximilian (1832–1867) was Emperor of Mexico (1864–1867). The brother of the Austrian Emperor, Francis Joseph, he was offered the Mexican crown by Napoleon III after the French invasion of Mexico in 1862. When the French withdrew their troops, Maximilian was left without any real support. He was captured by the troops of Benito Juarez and executed.

May is the fifth month of the year in the modern calendar, and lasts for 31 days. Its name comes from the ancient Roman month *Maius*, probably so called in honour of the goddess Maia, mother of Hermes.

Mayas were an American Indian people who settled in the Yucatan peninsula in southern Mexico possibly as early as 2500 BC. Mayan civilization, which reached its peak between the 4th and the 10th centuries AD, had evolved a hieroglyphic system of writing and possessed a remarkable knowledge of mathematics and astronomy. The Mayas gradually came under the influence of the Toltecs, and their civilization declined. It finally crumbled when the Spanish arrived in Mexico in the 16th century.

Mayflower was the ship which carried the Pilgrim Fathers from England to America in 1620. The *Mayflower* set sail from Plymouth on 16 September carrying 102 passengers. After a dangerous voyage, it landed at New Plymouth, Massachusetts, on 26 December of that year, where the first English colony in New England was founded.

Medici was a family which played a dominant part in the history of Florence during the 14th to 18th centuries. They acquired an enormous fortune by banking and money-lending and first achieved political power under Cosimo de' Medici (1389–1464). Thereafter the government of Florence was effectively in their hands. Cosimo's grandson, Lorenzo the Magnificent (1449–1492), was a patron of the great artists of the Italian Renaissance. The Medicis were expelled from Florence on several occasions, but after 1530 they became hereditary rulers with the title of Duke. Two Medicis became Popes and two, Catherine de Médicis and Marie de Médicis, Queens of France.

Mediterranean Sea is a sea almost enclosed by land, bordered by Europe, Asia and Africa. Area about 2504000 sq km (966750 sq miles). It is connected with the

A Mayan ceramic figure from Campeche, Mexico.

Atlantic by the narrow Straits of Gibraltar and includes a number of lesser seas (Adriatic, Aegean, etc). There are also many islands: large (Sicily, Sardinia, Cyprus, Crete, etc) and small. The Suez Canal links it with the Red Sea and Indian Ocean.

The Mediterranean has been the centre of Western civilization for thousands of years, and the chief avenue for contacts between Europe, the Middle East and North Africa.

It has little tidal movement. The climate of the region is mild in winter and hot in summer, with much sunshine, making this a popular region for holidays. The sea grows saltier towards the east, and fishing is therefore better in the western half. Pollution is now a worrying problem.

Medusa was one of the three Gorgons in Greek myth. Originally she was a beautiful girl, but she offended the goddess Athena, who turned her hair into serpents. Medusa was so horrible to look at that the sight of her turned people into stone. She was eventually killed by Perseus, who avoided this fate by looking only at her reflection in his shield as he cut off her head.

Mekong River is in south-east Asia. It rises in Tibet, flows through China, forms the border between Laos and Burma and Laos and Thailand, and runs through Kampuchea and Vietnam to the Gulf of Tongking. Length about 4500 km (2790 miles).

Melanesia is the name given to the islands in a region of the western Pacific, including the Solomons, Santa Cruz, New Hebrides, New Caledonia and Fiji.

Mendel, Gregor (1822–1884), was an Abbot of Brünn (now Brno in Czechoslovakia) who created the science of genetics. He was the first person to carry out selective breeding experiments (he started by using peas) to show that the characteristics of parents were inherited by their offspring.

Mendeleev, Dmitri Ivanovich (1834–1907), was a Russian chemist. He was appointed Professor of Chemistry at St Petersburg (now Leningrad) in 1866.

Mendeleev drew up a periodic table of the elements in 1869. He arranged elements in order of atomic weight, and then grouped those with similar properties. From his table he was able to predict the properties of some undiscovered elements. This helped them to be found: gallium was discovered in 1875 and germanium was discovered in 1885. Both had the properties predicted by Mendeleev. The element with atomic number 101 is called mendelevium after him.

Mendelssohn, Felix (1809–1847), was a German composer and conductor. By the age of 12 he had given his first recital, composed numerous works and become the friend of the

Diagram to show the laws of inheritance, as researched by Gregor Mendel.

72-year-old Goethe. A prolific composer, he was a great success in Britain, where the Scottish Highlands inspired his *Hebrides* overture. Active as a conductor, teacher and publicist (notably for Bach), he continued to compose at such a rate that he ruined his health.

In the late 19th century there was a reaction against Mendelssohn, and the Romantic elegance of his music was regarded as a sign of shallowness. More recently his reputation has risen, and his five symphonies, violin concerto, chamber music, songs and oratorios (especially the great *Elijah*) are popular again.

Menuhin, Yehudi (1916–), is a US-born violinist, who gave his first recital at the age of eight. In 1932 he recorded Elgar's Violin Concerto with the composer conducting. Later, he settled in England, where he founded a school of music and became an occasional conductor. One of the most famous of modern violinists, he is also a man of great charity and wide sympathies.

Menzies, Sir Robert Gordon (1894–1978), an Australian statesman, was Prime Minister over a period of nearly 20 years. He entered Parliament in 1934, becoming Prime Minister for the first time in 1939 to 1941. In 1944 he formed a new political group, the Australian Liberal Party, which he led to victory in the general election of 1949. During his second term of office as Prime Minister (1949–1966), Australia experienced a remarkable economic expansion, and Menzies played a notable part in international politics.

Mercury (chemical) is a silvery coloured liquid. Its chemical symbol is Hg. The ore cinnabar is mined for mercury. Mercury is the only metal which is liquid at ordinary temperatures. If it is spilt on, say, a table, it forms small droplets which slide quickly across the table. For this reason, mercury is also known as quicksilver.

It is used in barometers and thermometers. Mercury joins or mixes with other metals to form amalgams.

Mercury (planet) is the closest planet to the Sun. It takes 88 days to travel around it. Mercury rotates on its axis in 59 Earth days. Its closeness to the Sun makes it difficult to see from the Earth, and the spacecraft Mariner 10 discovered much of our present knowledge about it. Mercury is small: only about one and a half times bigger than the Moon. It looks very like the Moon, being covered with craters.

Mercury's surface is very hot on the side facing the Sun, and very cold on the other side. It has a thin atmosphere of helium. No forms of life that we know could live there.

Except for the Earth, it is the densest planet. It has a magnetic field, and is thought to have a core made of iron and nickel.

Mercury project was the first manned space programme undertaken by the USA. The Mercury capsule was a small, one-person spacecraft which on 5 May 1961 carried the first American into space, when Alan Shepherd completed a 190 km (118 miles) 'straight-up-and-down' mission. The first American to orbit Earth was John Glenn in 1962, and later Mercury missions were used simply to prove that humans could travel into space and back safely. During the years of the Mercury project, the Russians held a commanding lead in spacecraft design and

A picture of the surface of Mercury, taken by Mariner 10 in 1974.

achievement. The Mercury project was followed by the Gemini and Apollo projects. *See also* Apollo project; Armstrong, Neil; Gemini project; Saturn rocket.

Merlin was the legendary court magician of King Arthur in Celtic myth. According to one version of the story, Merlin actually made the Round Table of King Arthur and his knights for Arthur's father, Uther Pendragon. Merlin was famous for his prophecies about the future of Britain.

Mesopotamia was the name given by the ancient Greeks to the region between the Tigris and Euphrates rivers. In this fertile land the world's first known civilization was created by the Sumerians, who settled here about 4000 BC. They flourished during 3000 to 2000 BC, creating a number of city-states. The Sumerians laid the foundations for later civilizations which developed here, including the Babylonian and Assyrian empires. The region subsequently came under Persian, Greek and Roman domination, before being conquered by the Arabs in the 7th century AD. It now forms part of Iraq.

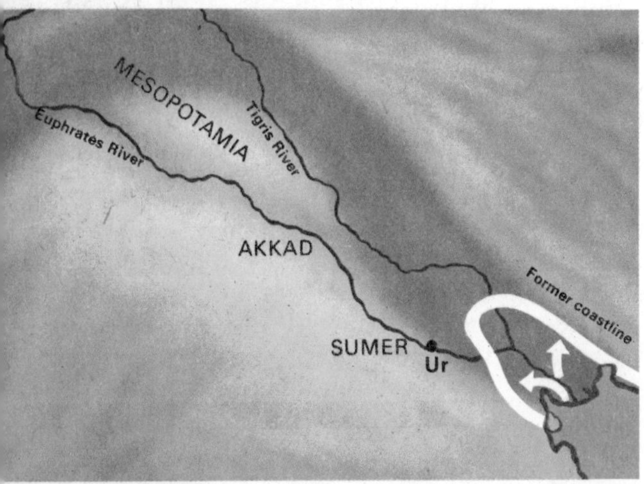

A map showing Mesopotamia situated on a fertile crescent of land which spreads from the Persian Gulf to the Mediterranean Sea in the west.

Mesozoic is an era in the history of the Earth, known from the study of rocks and of the fossil remains found in them (the geological record). Mesozoic means 'middle-living', and it is so called because it falls between the other two great geological eras, the Paleozoic and Cenozoic.

The Mesozoic era began about 225 million years ago and ended about 65 million years ago. It was the age when reptiles, including dinosaurs, dominated the Earth.

Metal – elements are divided into two groups called metals and non-metals. Most elements are metals. Metals are usually shiny solids. They can be made into many differnt shapes, such as large sheets or thin wires. Electricity and heat usually pass easily through metals.

Metals are found in minerals called ores. Some metals are also found on their own, and are called native metals. Gold and copper are native metals. They were the first to be used by people. They were made into ornaments, tools and weapons.

Now many ores are mined and their metals are taken out, or extracted, and used. They are used to make buildings, trains, spacecraft, factory machines, money, electrical wires and many other things.

The most common metals in the Earth are aluminium and iron. Platinum and gold are amongst the rarest.

Metamorphic rock is one of the three types of rock making up the Earth's crust (the other two are igneous and sedimentary rocks). Metamorphic means 'to do with change'. Metamorphic rocks originated as igneous or sedimentary rocks, which changed physically or chemically under the pressure of Earth movements and through exposure to intense heat. Marble and slate are examples of metamorphic rock.

Meteor is a tiny, dust particle weighing less than a gram. When a comet passes near the Sun, parts of it vaporize and it loses gas and dust. The dust particles burn up if they enter the Earth's atmosphere. We see this as a streak of light, and each burning dust particle is known as a shooting star or meteor. A comet leaves a trail of dust particles behind it. Therefore, many shooting stars may be seen close together. This is known as a meteor shower.

If a comet has recently passed there may

be a dense cloud of dust particles. For example, in 1966, 150000 meteors an hour were recorded. This is known as a meteor storm.

Meteorite is a large piece of stone and metal which crashes into the Earth. It is thought that meteorites may be parts of asteroids. The largest meteorite known is one that fell in Hoba West in Namibia, Africa. It was mainly iron and nickel and weighed about 60 tonnes.

Because a meteorite is moving at a fast speed it will cause a hole or crater in the ground. These craters are similar to the ones on the Moon, most of which are believed to have been formed in this way. A meteorite crater in Quebec is 64 km (40 miles) wide.

A meteorite crater near Winslow, Arizona, USA, about 1 km (0.6 miles) in diameter.

Methane is an invisible gas with no taste or smell. Its chemical formula is CH_4. It burns in air, and mixtures of methane and air can explode.

There are large quantities of methane, coal and petroleum in the Earth. They were all formed from plants and animals that lived millions of years ago. Methane, coal and petroleum are known as fossil fuels.

Methane is found with coal and oil, and is also found alone. It is used to heat homes, when it is called natural gas. Methane found with coal is often called fire-damp. When uncovered flames were used in coal mines, fire-damp caused explosions and many injuries.

Methane is also found near ponds and marshes, where it is made by rotting plants. This methane is known as marsh gas. *See also* Natural gas.

Methodism is a movement in Christianity which began in the meetings of John and Charles Wesley and a few friends in Oxford in 1729. The regularity of their meetings for prayer, religious study and charity work earned them the nickname Methodists.

John Wesley was a priest in the Church of England, but he became dissatisfied with its dullness and lack of zeal. He began preaching up and down the country to crowds of people who normally never went to church, and gradually built up a new religious movement. Wesley himself never left the Church of England, but after his death the Methodists broke away, organizing their own Church and appointing their own ministers.

Methodism, with its popular sermons and hymn-singing, appealed most strongly to the lower classes in society and made many converts among industrial workers. It spread rapidly throughout the British Empire, including North America, splitting up into many different, though associated, bodies.

John Wesley preaching Methodism to American Indians.

Metric system is a decimal system of weights and measures. Devised by the French in 1791, the metric system is used internationally by scientists and has now been adopted for general use by many countries. *See also* SI units.

Mexico is a federal republic in southern North America. Capital, Mexico City; area about 1967000 sq km (761500 sq miles).

History Mexico was the site of three important civilizations during the first millennium (one thousand years) AD – the Mayas, the Toltecs and the Aztecs. After the Spanish conquest (1519–1521) Mexico became part of the viceroyalty of New Spain. The revolution against Spanish rule began in 1810, leading to independence in 1821. After the short-lived empire (1822–1823), Mexico became a federal republic. In the 1840s it lost California, Texas and New Mexico to the United States. In 1864 the French installed Maximilian as emperor, but he was overthrown and executed. After the long presidency of Porfirio Diaz there followed a period of political unrest (1911–1920). Since 1920 Mexico has been governed by the Institutional Revolutionary Party.

Land and People Mexico has long coasts on the Atlantic and Pacific. Two ranges of mountains, extensions of the Rockies, are divided by a high central plateau, averaging 2000 m (6560 ft) above sea level and occupying more than half the country. The Yucatan peninsula is flat and low. Here and on the coastal plains the summer is very hot, but at Mexico City on the central plateau, where most people live, the climate is one of the finest in the world.

The majority of the people are of mixed Indian and European descent. There is a small, largely white, ruling class of landowners, but the majority of people are poor. Roman Catholicism is the chief religion.

Mexico has developed a distinctive culture which is a blend of Indian and Spanish traditions. The arts in particular owe a strong debt to the ancient Indian inhabitants.

Economy Although half the people live in towns, agriculture is the main occupation. However, very little of the land is suitable for intensive farming. Land ownership is still one of Mexico's main social problems. Maize is the chief food crop and beans are also important. Coffee, bananas and vegetables are exported, and Mexico is the main producer of the fibre called henequen, which is used for making such things as rope and coarse fabrics.

Mexico has important mines, which produce more than half the world's silver, as well as sulphur, lead, mercury, copper, zinc and gold. There are also oil reserves and timber, including mahogany. Manufacturing industry in the Mexico City area and other centres is very varied. Mexico's main trading partner is the USA, and many American tourists go to Acapulco and other resorts.

Michelangelo Buonarroti (1475–1564), was one of the greatest artists of all time – painter, poet, architect and sculptor. Born in Florence, he created most of his greatest works in Rome, and he lived long enough to see the emergence of Mannerism which was greatly influenced by his own later works.

Michelangelo's most famous works are his paintings of *The Creation*, in which the story is told entirely through the pose and gesture of human figures, and *The Last Judgement*, in the Sistine Chapel. It was in sculpture that Michelangelo's greatest genius lay: these include the *Pièta* in St Peter's Rome; the great figure of *Moses* for the tomb of Pope Julius II; and the *David* in his native city.

Michelangelo designed the great dome of St Peter's and also several Roman palaces. Few artists have had greater influence. He and his rival, Raphael, can be seen as the originators of separate lines of development in European art down to the end of the 19th century.

Micronesia is the name given to island groups in the western Pacific, including the Caroline, Mariana and Marshall islands. Area about 1800 sq km (700 sq miles). Most of the islands belong to a US dependency, the Federated States of Micronesia (formed 1979). Some, including Kiribarti (formerly the British Gilbert Islands) are independent. They are mostly very small and of coral formation, though the Carolines and Marianas are volcanic. The climate is tropical. The Micronesians, with Melanesians and Polynesians, are the three main groups of Pacific island people.

Microscope is an instrument used to look at tiny objects. A light microscope uses lenses to make the objects look much bigger. This increase in size is called magnification. Light passes through the object which is being viewed and enters the eye of the observer. Under a light microscope pond water, for example, can be seen to contain hundreds of small animals and plants, which are usually invisible to the eye.

To look at even smaller objects an electron microscope is used. This produces a highly magnified picture of the objects by using electrons instead of light rays.

A microscope

Microwaves are a form of electromagnetic radiation. Microwaves are used to measure the distances of objects. They are also used to cook foods by causing the food molecules to vibrate very fast, causing heat. In microwave ovens, food is cooked from the middle outwards in only a few seconds. *See also* Electromagnetic radiation; Radar.

Midas was a king in Greek legend. As a result of his kind treatment of one of the attendants of Dionysus, he was told by the god that he could have anything he wished. Midas asked that everything he touched might turn into gold, but soon regretted his unthinking greed. His food turned to gold before he could eat it, and he begged to have the gift taken away. He was told to wash in a river, which freed him from his golden touch, though the river is supposed to have contained gold ever since.

Middle East is a convenient term for the countries of south-west Asia. It is not a precise term, but usually includes Egypt and Libya and sometimes countries as far east as Burma, though usually no farther than Iran.

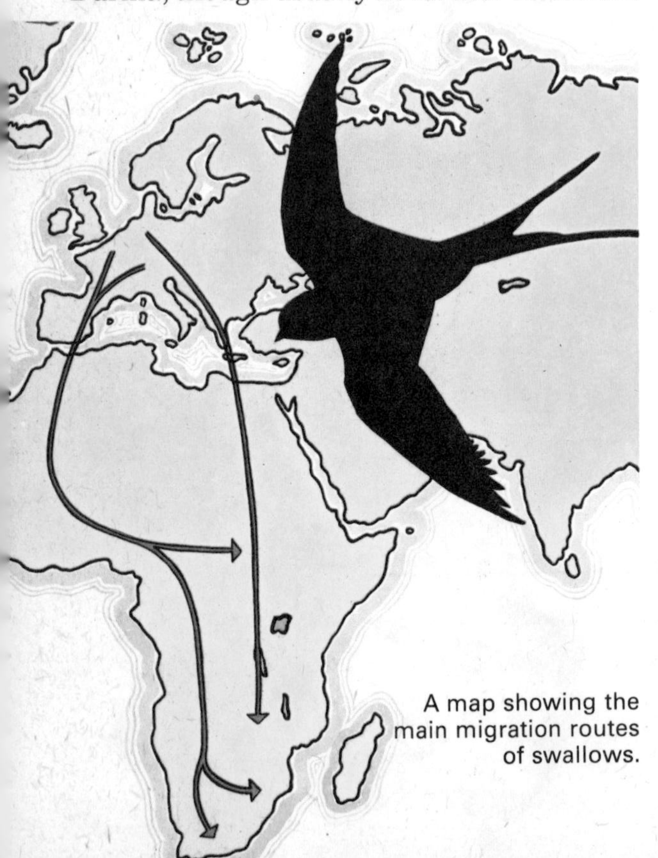

A map showing the main migration routes of swallows.

Migration is the instinctive movement of an animal population (or part of it) from one place to another, and then back again. Animals which migrate do so because their sources of food are not available all the year round in one place. You may have noticed that some of the birds you see at one time of the year are not present at another time of the year. They have migrated. Swallows are among the 5000 million birds which undertake the journey from Europe and Asia to spend the winter in Africa.

Not only birds migrate, however. The great herds of wildebeest found on the African plains are just one of several types of mammals which migrate in search of fresh water and pastures. Many bats, whales and fish – even some insects – also migrate. It is hard to believe that delicate butterflies migrate, but some species like the painted lady fly from Africa to Britain – a journey of thousands of kilometres. The longest migration is that of the arctic tern, however. This small bird breeds in Alaska near the North Pole and then flies all the way down to the Antarctic to spend the winter.

Milky Way is the narrow band of light that can be seen across the sky on a clear night. In a Roman legend, the milky way was the milk spilt when the goddess Juno fed her baby, Hercules. This gave it its name. The narrow band is actually thousands of stars, which are all part of our Galaxy.

Miller, Glenn (1904–1944), was a US bandleader and composer. A trombonist, he led one of the most famous 'big' bands of the swing era in jazz. Besides writing a large number of hits (e.g. *Moonlight Serenade, In the Mood*), he produced a distinctive sound from his band which, from 1941, was a US Air Force band. He died in a plane crash between England and France.

Millipede is an arthropod with a long, thin segmented body, each segment carrying two pairs of legs. Millipedes are slow-moving creatures found all over the world, usually under decaying vegetation or burrowing underground where they eat plant material.

They defend themselves by squirting a foul liquid from glands in the sides of the body.

Milton, John (1608–1674), was an English poet. His greatest work is *Paradise Lost*, an epic on the Biblical Fall of Man. It was published in 1667, after he had lost his sight – he dictated to his daughter. It is written in blank verse of extraordinary grandeur, and is divided into twelve books. It was followed by *Paradise Regained* and *Samson Agonistes* (1671). Milton's 'sublime' style had great influence on English poetry, not always for the best. Some of his shorter poetry – e.g. the elegy *Lycidas* (1637) and the sonnet *On the Late Massacre in Piedmont* (1655) – is equally fine.

Milton was a republican who served in the government of Oliver Cromwell. He also wrote much prose propaganda e.g. *Areopagitica* (1644), an appeal for freedom of speech.

Mime is a form of acting in which the story is told by movement and gesture, without words. In ancient Greece and Rome, mime was simply a form of low, clowning comedy, including speech.

Mineral is every substance on earth which is not made from animals and plants. All substances not made from minerals are made from animals and plants. Rocks are made up of many minerals.

Apart from mercury, all minerals are solid at normal temperatures. They are made up of many tiny crystals. Sometimes these crystals grow into beautiful shapes and are used as ornaments or gemstones.

Some minerals are mined for their metals or other substances. These are called ores.

Mining is the industry concerned with taking metals, coal, oil and other substances from the Earth. Metals are found in minerals called ores. Open-cast mines and quarries are used to take ores which are near the surface. The earth is removed by machines and the ore is dug out. The earth can then be replaced.

For deeper ores, a hole, called a shaft, is dug down to the ore, with tunnels running off it. The ore is then dug out, broken up and carried to the surface.

Some ores, such as salt, are mined by pumping a liquid down to dissolve them. They are then pumped to the surface.

Gold is sometimes mined by sending down strong jets of water. These break up the gold, which is then pumped to the surface.

Mink are sinuous-bodied, small, carnivorous mammals related to the weasel. They dig a burrow by the banks of wooded lakes and rivers, and form a lair under roots or other vegetation. Mink have partially webbed feet and waterproof fur, which equip them to hunt in and around water, for frogs, fish and other water animals. The American mink is farmed for its beautiful fur, and many have escaped from captivity to form wild mink populations in places where they were not originally native.

Minoan civilization flourished in Crete from about 3000 to 1200 BC. Named after the legendary King Minos, it was the first real European civilization. By about 1700 BC the Minoans had achieved an advanced Bronze

A bronze dagger blade and an earthenware jar, both from the Minoan period, found at Phaestos in Crete.

Age culture, and Crete was the centre of a maritime empire, with splendid palaces at Knossos and Phaestos. Excavations have revealed the remarkable naturalness and lifelike treatment of subjects in Cretan art and sculpture. Crete's prosperity was destroyed about 1400 BC probably by an earthquake and by an invasion by the Myceneans.

Minotaur, in Greek legend, was a monster with a man's body and a bull's head, kept by King Minos of Crete in a labyrinth. As revenge for the killing of King Minos's son, every nine years seven young boys and seven girls were sent from Athens for the Minotaur to eat. The monster was finally killed by the hero Theseus, who found his way through the labyrinth by following a string.

Mirror is a smooth surface that reflects light. Metals are good reflectors of light, which is why many metals look shiny. Most mirrors are made of a sheet of glass with a thin coat of metal, such as silver or aluminium, on one side. The metal is often covered with paint to protect it.

Mirrors can be flat or curved. Curved mirrors make objects look bigger or smaller. For example, a shaving mirror may be curved so that the face looks bigger. Mirrors are used in telescopes and other instruments. *See also* Reflection.

Mississippi River flows almost the length of the USA, north–south, from Minnesota to the Gulf of Mexico. Length about 3780 km (2350 miles). It is navigable for large vessels from the delta up to Minneapolis and was an important waterway in earlier times, sailed by the famous Mississippi paddle steamers. It still carries even more cargo than the Panama Canal.

With its tributaries, the Mississippi drains the whole central region of the USA between the Appalachians and the Rockies, about 2 500 000 sq km (965 000 sq miles).

Mistletoe is an evergreen plant which lives semi-parasitically on trees in temperate regions. Although it produces its own food by photosynthesis, it obtains its water supply by sending suckers into its host's sap and drawing the fluid up. In early spring, mistletoe bears tiny, wind-pollinated flowers. Juicy white berries are produced in the following winter, and these are eaten by birds. If a bird rubs the berry on to another tree, the seeds of the mistletoe lodge in crevices and sprout the following spring to begin the life cycle again.

Mistletoe is said to have magical properties, and was a sacred symbol to the ancient Druids. Even today, hanging mistletoe in a porch or doorway is supposed to be a sign of peace.

Mite is an arthropod related to spiders and scorpions. They are usually very small creatures, and they sometimes occur together in huge numbers. Some live in the soil, and millions may exist in 0.4 hectare (1 acre) of soil. Other mites are parasites of plants and other animals. The itch mite causes the skin disease known as scabies in humans and domestic animals.

Mitterand, François (1916–   ), is a French statesman. A Socialist, he held positions in a number of French governments after the Second World War and was an unsuccessful candidate in 1965 and again in 1974 in the election for the presidency. Mitterand finally became President in 1981, defeating Valery Giscard d'Estaing.

Moguls were a Muslim dynasty which ruled India from 1526 to 1858. The dynasty was founded by Babar, a descendant of Genghis Khan. It was considerably expanded under his grandson Akbar the Great, who ruled much of northern and central India as well as Afghanistan, and reached its greatest extent under Aurangzeb (reigned 1658–1707). In the 18th century the Mogul Empire began to decline, and the effective control of the country passed to the British, who deposed the last ruler in 1858.

Mole is a small, furry mammal related to the hedgehog and shrew. Moles spend most of their lives underground, digging tunnels with their powerful front legs and large claws. Their tiny eyes are hidden by fur. Sometimes a mole will clear soil from its tunnels by heaping it on to the surface, forming the familiar mole hill. Moles eat earthworms, which they detect by smell and hearing. They bite and paralyse those that they do not need immediately to eat later.

Molecule is the smallest part of a compound that there can be. When chemicals react to form compounds, their atoms join together to form molecules. All the molecules in a compound are the same.

Different compounds have different molecules. For example, two hydrogen atoms and an oxygen atom can join to form a molecule of water. A hydrogen atom joined to a chlorine atom forms a molecule of hydrochloric acid. So, changing the atoms in the molecule has changed the compound from water which we bathe in to hydrochloric acid which burns the skin very badly.

Some molecules, such as those in plastic and rubber, are very large. They can contain thousands, or even millions, of atoms.

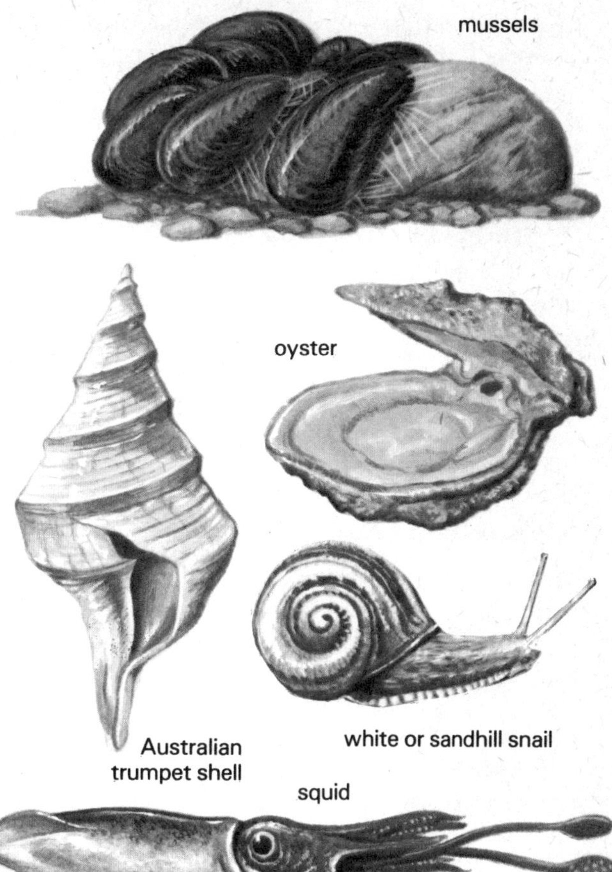

Molière (1622–1673), was a French playwright whose real name was J-B. Poquelin. He directed his own plays, and sometimes played the leading role himself. He was the author of the finest comedies in European literature – *The School for Wives* (1662), *Tartuffe* (1664), *The Misanthropist* (1666) and about 30 others. The founder of the 'comedy of manners', in which social customs are mocked, he introduced realistic characters instead of the crude simplifications of earlier comedy. Although Molière offended many important people, he generally enjoyed the favour of King Louis XIV. His last play, *The Hypochondriac* (1673) was a satire on doctors written when Molière was ill. He played the title role on stage, collapsed, and died a few hours later.

Molluscs are the second largest group of invertebrates, after the arthropods. They include snails, slugs, clams, limpets, oysters, mussels, squid, cuttlefish and octopuses.They have invaded all parts of the sea and fresh water, and several species of snail are perfectly suited to a life on land.

Molluscs are extremely variable in shape, size and behaviour and have only a few features in common. The body consists of a head, a muscular foot and the part containing the body organs. A sheet of skin called the mantle produces the shell which most molluscs have. The shell gives protection, anchorage for the body muscles and, in some species, is used to bore into rock or wood. Some molluscs – octopuses and seaslugs, for example – lack a shell. Most species breathe through gills lying between the mantle and the body. Many molluscs feed on vegetation which they rasp off with a horny tongue called the radula, but predators, such as the octopus, have a beak like a parrot's. The bivalve molluscs, such as the clams, feed by sucking in fine food particles through tubes called siphons. The foot, which forms a smooth surface upon which molluscs such as snails and whelks creep along, also forms the tentacles of the octopuses, squid and cuttlefish.

Moluccas is an island group in east Indonesia. Capital, Amboina; area about 841 000 sq km (32 000 sq miles). These were the 'Spice Islands' sought by Europeans in the 15th century and found by the Portuguese. They were later taken by the Dutch. The Moluccans are Indonesian under protest. They attempted to form an independent republic in 1950 but were checked by Indonesian forces.

Most of the islands are mountainous, with dense forest and plant life. Spices (nutmegs, cloves, etc) are now less important than sago, copra, forest products and pearls.

Monaco is a principality (country ruled by a prince) in south-east France. Area 190 hectares (467 acres). Though independent, it is closely linked with France, which surrounds it on three sides (the fourth side being on the Mediterranean). It contains the town of Monte-Carlo, famous for gambling, and is mainly a resort. Only a minority of the people are native Monegasques.

Mondrian, Piet (1872–1944), was a Dutch painter. He was the chief figure of the De Stijl ('The Style') group, founded in 1917, which aimed to unify all fine art and design, based on simple principles of rectangular shapes and primary colours. Mondrian's paintings are less simple than they look: they are entirely abstract and mathematical, and are related to contemporary architecture. The ideas of the De Stijl group had some influence on the founders of the Bauhaus school. *See also* Bauhaus.

Monet, Claude (1840–1926), was a French painter, a leader of the young Impressionists during the 1860s. By about 1870 he had developed his method of creating the effects of light with colour. His interests in changes of light led him to paint series of pictures of the same subject, such as Rouen Cathedral. In his studies of the water lilies in his garden pond, his vision of air, water and light resulted in paintings that are almost abstract.

Money is a type of payment, providing a medium of exchange through which goods and services can be valued and traded. The use of money developed because barter (exchange of goods) is cumbersome even in quite simple situations.

Money need not be valuable in itself, although it has tended to be so until recent times. Cattle, bars of iron, and, more often, gold and silver have been valued and have served as money.

The banknote was originally a kind of cheque rather than money. Today banknotes, like modern 'silver' and 'copper' coins, are simply tokens without having a value in themselves.

Bank deposits are also a form of money, huge quantities of which are manipulated and transferred without ever becoming visible as notes or silver.

Mongolia, officially the Mongolian People's Republic, is in central-east Asia. Capital, Ulan Bator; area about 1 565 000 sq km (604 250 sq miles). The historic region of Mongolia is larger, part now being within China, and Mongolians are widely scattered through central Asia.

The modern republic, territory once disputed by the Russians and the Chinese, dates from 1924. The present government is Communist. The land is mainly flat and poor, with mountains and desert regions. The Gobi Desert occupies much of the centre and south-east of the country. The climate is cold and dry. The Mongolians are traditionally nomadic, and stock-raising is still very important. Crops are grown mainly in the south, and there are large mineral resources.

Mongols are a nomadic central Asian people who came into prominence in the 13th century when they were united under the leadership of Genghis Khan. He created a vast empire which eventually stretched from the Yellow Sea to the Black Sea. After his death his empire was divided among his sons, but the Mongols were gradually driven out of the territories they had conquered, and their empire had disappeared by the beginning of the 15th century.

The Mongol ruler, Genghis Khan.

Monkey puzzle tree is a curious-looking conifer native to Chile, where it is known as the Chilean pine. In its native country, the monkey puzzle tree is grown for its timber, but in other parts of the world it is grown as an ornamental tree.

The tall stem bears many forked branches densely covered in spiky leaves. On closer inspection these leaves appear as dark green, pointed, overlapping scales. The tree is said to have got its name because climbing it would puzzle even a monkey!

Monkeys are divided into two main groups: the New World monkeys of the Americas and the Old World monkeys of Africa and Asia. Both types are primates, related to the lemurs, the chimpanzee, the gorilla and ourselves.

New World monkeys have wide noses and round heads. Their long tails can be used by some species as an additional 'hand' to grip on to branches. The smallest monkeys are the marmosets, which are found in the Amazonian region of South America. Howler monkeys live in South and Central America, and their calls can be heard for several kilometres.

The Old World monkeys have narrower noses than New World monkeys, and they can not use their tail to grip objects. Unlike New World monkeys, which spend their life in trees, some Old World monkeys – for instance, the baboon – spend their life on the ground. Other Old World monkeys include macaques, langurs and mandrills.

Monocotyledon, see Cotyledons.

Monorail is a railway system using only one rail instead of the normal two. Usually the train hangs from an overhead rail, and railways built like this exist in Japan, West Germany and the USA, but they have not been commercially successful. A much more revolutionary system is being developed in several countries in which the train 'hovers' above a single rail which carries powerful magnets, both to keep the train in the air and to propel it along the track. This system promises to allow trains to travel at very high speeds, perhaps 500 km/h (311 mph).

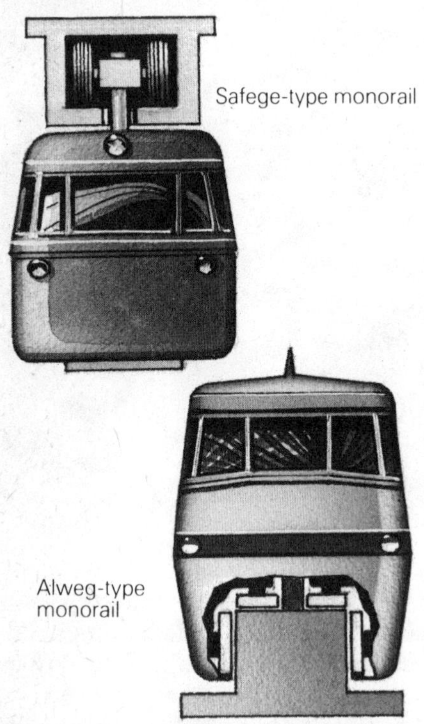

Monroe, Marilyn (1926–1962), was a US film star. An orphan from a poor background, she was taken up by Hollywood and turned into a symbol of the glamorous, desirable woman. Though often cast as the traditional 'dumb blonde', she displayed real ability as a comic actress in films such as *The Seven Year Itch* (1955) and *Some Like It Hot* (1959). The stress of having to live up to the image that her studio created for her led to her death from an overdose of drugs.

Monsoon is a word generally used to describe the rainy season in southern Asia which lasts from about April to September. It arrives at each place at virtually the same time every year, often accompanied by violent storms. Geographers apply the term 'monsoon' more widely, employing it to describe the wind pattern of the area, which is responsible for the abruptness of the seasonal changes. For six months (roughly October to March), a cold, dry wind blows from the north-east. Then there is a complete reversal as a warm, moist wind advances from the south-west, ushering in the rainy season.

Monteverdi, Claudio (1567–1643), was an Italian composer. In 1613 he became Master of Music of the republic of Venice, and produced many beautiful religious works. He entered the Church himself in 1632. He also composed operas and madrigals, but unfortunately much of his work has been lost.

Monteverdi was famous in his own time and is admired today, but in the interval he was less widely appreciated. Now he is seen as one of the great innovators, who dominates Renaissance music. He was the first, for example, to make use of a full orchestra in opera, and though he did not 'invent' any new forms, he extended and enriched the music of his time in every way.

Montezuma (circa 1466–1520), was the last Aztec Emperor of Mexico (1502–1520). He was not a strong ruler, and his country was troubled by internal warfare. When the Spanish headed by Cortés arrived in Mexico in 1519, Montezuma did not resist them and he allowed himself to be taken prisoner. When the Aztecs finally attacked the Spanish, Montezuma was killed in mysterious circumstances, possibly by his own people.

Montgolfier, Étienne and Joseph, see Hot-air ballon.

Montezuma prepares to greet Hernan Cortés outside Tenochtitlan, in Mexico.

Montgomery of Alamein, Bernard, 1st Viscount (1887–1976), was a British soldier. During the Second World War he commanded the army which defeated the German forces at Alamein (1942), and went on to take charge of the British army in Sicily and Italy (1943). He headed the land forces in the Allied invasion of Normandy in 1944, and received the German surrender at Luneberg Heath in May 1945. After the war he was Chief of the Imperial General Staff (1946–1948) and Deputy Supreme Commander of NATO (1951–1958).

Month is a twelfth of a year. Our months are the same lengths as those used by Julius Caesar in the Julian calendar drawn up in 45 BC. The names of the months are also similar to those in the Julian calendar, except that July and August have been renamed after Julius and Augustus Caesar.

Months are divided into weeks and days. A week has seven days. Most months have 31 days. April, June, September and November have 30 days. February usually has 28 days with an extra day every 4 years. Years in which February has 29 days are known as leap years.

The length of time from one new moon to the next is known as a lunar month. It is about 29.5 days long.

Montserrat is an island in the Leeward Islands, West Indies. Capital, Plymouth; area about 106 sq km (39 sq miles). It was discovered by Columbus in 1493 and is now a British crown colony.

Moon is the Earth's only satellite. It orbits the Earth in about 27.3 days. It also rotates on its axis in about 27.3 Earth days. This means that we always see the same side of the Moon.

It seems to shine because it is lit by the Sun. As it orbits the Earth, different parts of the side visible to us are illuminated. This is why we see the Moon as a crescent shape growing to a half circle, full circle and then back again. These are known as phases of the moon.

The moon is, on average, about 384 000 km

(238 400 miles) away from the Earth. Many spacecraft have landed on it, and astronauts have explored parts of it and brought back samples of its surface. Much is now known about it, and there are more detailed maps of the Moon's surface than of some parts of our Earth.

The Moon has no air, no water and no magnetic field. The surface is covered with craters, which are thought to be due to the impact of meteorites. From Earth, the Moon appears to have light and dark areas. The light areas are known as terrae or highlands, and the dark areas as maria. The other side of the Moon is nearly all highlands. The maria are lowland areas which are covered with lava.

Moore, Henry (1898–) is a British sculptor. The son of a Yorkshire coalminer, he became widely recognized as an outstanding sculptor after his one-man exhibition at the New York Museum of Modern Art in 1947 and his winning of the International Sculpture Prize at the Venice Biennale in 1948. His most powerful theme, in his larger works especially, is the female – as woman, mother and earth-goddess. He is notable also for his close relationship with his materials, whose natural characteristics (like the grain in wood) are often brought out in his work.

Moose, also called the elk in Europe, ranges across Eurasia and North America. It is the largest member of the deer family, standing 2.2 m (7 ft) at the shoulder, with huge dished antlers and a large beard under the chin. The moose lives in forests but also likes watery places, often wading up to the neck to feed on water plants.

More, Sir Thomas (1478–1535), was an English statesman and scholar. He succeeded Cardinal Wolsey as Lord Chancellor in 1529, but resigned in 1532 because he could not agree to Henry VIII's divorce from Catherine of Aragon and his marriage to Anne Boleyn. In 1534 he was imprisoned for his refusal to conform to the Act of Supremacy which made Henry VIII head of the Church in England. More's conscience would not allow him to repudiate the authority of the Pope. He was found guilty of treason and beheaded.

Thomas More

Mormons are a religious group whose proper name is the Church of Jesus Christ of Latter-day saints. It was founded in the United States in 1830 by Joseph Smith, on the authority of a supposedly ancient text called the Book of Mormon. The organization and beliefs of the Mormons aroused public hostility. Under Brigham Young they founded a new colony at Salt Lake, Utah (1847), still the Mormon headquarters.

Morocco is a kingdom in north-west Africa. Capital, Rabat; area about 660 000 sq km (255 000 sq miles). The country has an ancient and fascinating history. Once a Roman province, it became the centre of western Islam in the Middle Ages, home of the Almoravids who conquered Spain. In 1912 it was divided into French and Spanish sections, but regained independence as a constitutional monarchy in 1956.

Morocco has fertile coastal plains backed by the Atlas Mountains. To the south it becomes desert. The people live mainly on the coast. They are mostly Berbers by descent but speak Arabic and their religion is Islam.

Agriculture is the chief occupation, though variable rainfall and locusts are problems. There are vast numbers of sheep and goats. Mining is the second largest occupation, phosphates being especially important. Other exports are cork, sardines and various minerals. Morocco has little heavy industry except mining but is famous for its handicrafts, especially leather goods and textiles. The coastal resorts are popular with Europeans.

Morse Code is a code used for signalling or for sending messages by telegraph. It was devised by the American Samuel F.B. Morse (1791–1872). It uses two signals, which were written down as a dot or a dash, the dash-signal lasting three times as long as the dot-signal. By various groupings of dots, dashes and spaces, the code represents each letter of the alphabet, numbers and punctuation.

Morse Code

A	·—	M	——	Y	—·——
B	—···	N	—·	Z	——··
C	—·—·	O	———	1	·————
D	—··	P	·——·	2	··———
E	·	Q	——·—	3	···——
F	··—·	R	·—·	4	····—
G	——·	S	···	5	·····
H	····	T	—	6	—····
I	··	U	··—	7	——···
J	·———	V	···—	8	———··
K	—·—	W	·——	9	————·
L	·—··	X	—··—	0	—————

Distress signal (SOS)	···———···
Attention signal	—·—·—
Break	—···—
Understood	···—·
Received	·—·
Position report	—·—·
End of message	·—·—·
Finish of transmission	···—·—

Moscow is the capital of the Soviet Union. Founded in the 12th century, Moscow is the historic heart of Russia. Most of it was burned down during the French invasion of 1812, but the Kremlin, which contains the seat of government, and many ancient churches and palaces, remained. It was chosen, instead of Leningrad, as the capital of the Soviet Union in 1918 and has been expanding rapidly ever since. It is the largest Soviet city and is a huge industrial complex as well as the centre of government.

Moses was the founder of the ancient Hebrew (Jewish) nation, the 'children of Israel'. Abandoned as a baby, he was brought up (according to the Bible) in Pharoah's court, but fled after killing an Egyptian official who was mistreating a Hebrew slave.

As a result of a vision in which the voice of God spoke from a burning bush, Moses led the children of Israel from their Egyptian slavery. God inflicted a series of disasters on Egypt to persuade the Pharaoh to let them leave. When the Pharoah's army set off in pursuit, God parted the Red Sea so the Israelites could escape.

At Mount Sinai God delivered to Moses the Ten Commandments, the fundamental law. Eventually, helped by other miracles, the Israelites reached the Promised Land of Israel. Moses saw it from a mountain top but, according to God's prophecy, he died before his people entered Israel. *See also* Ten Commandments.

Moses with the Ten Commandments.

Mosque is a Muslim temple. The original mosque built at Medina by Muhammad in 622 was a square enclosure with high walls, partly roofed. Later and grander buildings, throughout the Islamic world, follow the basic form established in the 7th century. The original open court was usually covered by a dome. Interiors show the Muslim delight in making solid walls and pillars seem to disappear by a wealth of intricate decoration. Decorations are usually abstract, geometric designs because the Islamic faith forbids the imitation of Gods' creation.

Mosquito is a two-winged insect related to the fly. Male mosquitoes feed on plant sap and nectar, but the females feed on the blood of other animals. When they take blcod they sometimes infect the victim with a disease which they are carrying in their saliva. Malaria and yellow fever are two diseases that are transmitted to people in this way. Mosquitoes breed and lay their eggs on water, and the larvae cling to the surface film whilst they turn into adults.

Mosses, together with liverworts, make up the large group of non-flowering plants called the Bryophyta. Mosses are common almost everywhere there is a crack or crevice and where moisture is obtainable.

Mosses consist of a simple stem covered in many tiny leaves. Some species of moss grow upright, while others form dense cushions. Mosses reproduce by means of spores liberated from a spore case borne on the end of a thin stalk. When the spore lands and germinates, it first forms a thin green structure called a protonema. This then develops the upright leafy shoots of a new moss plant.

Moth is an insect, placed together with the butterfly in the order Lepidoptera. Moths usually fly at night, have feathery antennae and hold their wings horizontally when resting. Like butterflies, moths' wings are covered in scales, often producing beautiful patterns and colours. Adult moths are often very striking in appearance, and the caterpillars of many species are bizarre and colourful. The atlas moth of the rainforests of Asia has the largest wingspan of any insect, up to 30 cm (1 ft) across. *See also* Chrysalis.

Adult pine hawk moth and caterpillar.

Motion is the name given to any movement. Sir Isaac Newton examined the way in which things move, and found that changes in movement were caused by forces. He drew up three laws of motion, to explain what he saw. The study of motion is called mechanics. *See also* Force.

Motorcycle is basically a bicycle propelled by an internal combustion engine, although the first ever motorcycle, built in France in 1868, had a steam engine and could travel at 14 km/h (8.7 mph) – but only for ten minutes. Until the First World War, the motorcycle was regarded only as a bicycle with a detachable engine, but wartime use by dispatch riders on both sides, together with post-war racing successes, did much to change the image. Soon after the Second World War, Japanese companies started producing cheap motorcycles, and quickly grew to dominate the world motorcycle market.

Triumph Bonneville (744 cc).

Vespa 200 Rally (198 cc).

Motor scooter is a term used for a motorcycle with an 'apron' and a floor to offer some protection against the weather. It became popular in Italy during the 1950s and is still common in southern Europe.

The moped, or motorized pedal cycle, is a return to the original concept of the motorcycle, and features a tiny (usually 50 cc) engine which needs human assistance on pedals to start or climb hills. A moped can rarely travel at more than 50 km/h (31 mph).

Mould is a fungus. It often grows on stale bread or on boxes and suitcases left in damp places. Moulds may appear as a whitish or greenish 'fluff'. The fluff is really the masses of tiny hyphae which make up the body, or mycelium, of the fungus.

Moult is the seasonal process whereby, for example, birds lose their feathers and mammals their fur, to be replaced by new feathers or fur. In birds, the replacement feathers may be brightly coloured to attract a mate; at other times of the year these breeding feathers may be moulted to be replaced by new feathers that will ensure that the bird is fit for a long migration flight. The stoat moults its summer coat and grows a white coat for winter. The white coat enables it to remain concealed in the snow.

An Arctic hare, showing the summer and winter coat.

Arthropods (insects, crustaceans, etc) also moult. From time to time they split off their hard exoskeleton; underneath is a new, soft exoskeleton which hardens after the animal has enlarged its body. Snakes and lizards moult their scaly skins as they grow, too.

Mountain lion, see Puma.

Mountain-building is the geological process which leads to the creation of mountain chains. It occurs through the upthrust or folding of the Earth's crust under the immense pressures built up by interior stresses. These processes usually occur very slowly, whereas the eruptions of volcanoes sometimes create mountains out of lava within the space of a few years. *See also* Plate tectonics.

Mozambique is a republic in south-east Africa. Capital, Maputo; area about 785 000 sq km (303 000 sq miles). The ancient Monomotapa kingdom disappeared about the time the Portuguese arrived in the late 15th century. Mozambique became a Portuguese colony in the 16th century and was created an overseas territory of Portugal in 1951. It gained independence in 1975.

Mountainous in the north, it is mostly low-lying with a hot and – near the coast – humid climate. It has two good harbours and the Zambezi River provides hydro-electric power, but the tsetse fly and tropical diseases limit human settlement, and the land is mostly poor. The people belong to a number of tribal groups such as Makonde and Ndau. Portuguese is spoken by many, though a large number of people cannot read or write. Mozambique has some mineral resources, including oil, but the main exports are agricultural produce. It is the world's largest producer of cashew nuts. Sugar, cotton and tea are also exported.

Mozart, Wolfgang Amadeus (1756–1791), was an Austrian composer, born in Salzburg. He is one of the greatest figures in Western music. He began composing at the age of five and wrote operas, 41 full-scale symphonies, concertos, sonatas and piano and chamber music at a prolific rate for the rest of his short life.

The sheer quantity of Mozart's music, the extraordinary quality of nearly all of it, and the range of musical forms he employed, makes it almost impossible to describe his work with justice. Music to him seems to have been an instinct, like breathing. Perhaps his greatest contribution was in opera (*Don Giovanni*, *Cosi fan Tutte*, *The Magic Flute*, etc) and the concerto.

Muhammad (570–632), was the founder of Islam. He was born in Mecca, Arabia, where he was known as al-Amin, 'the trustworthy'. During a period of prayer and fasting he received a divine message – that he should preach the unity of God and the need for people to live virtuously.

His own people persecuted him, but his teaching took root in Medina. In 622 (the first year in the Muslim calendar) he made his *hegira* (flight) to Medina. Within a few years he was able to march into Mecca, where he destroyed the idols to pagan gods and, by the time of his death, he was the unquestioned leader of a united, Muslim Arabia – the first Arab nation.

The words of God as revealed to Muhammad during his ministry are recorded in the Koran. *See also* Islam; Koran.

Murray River flows in south-east Australia. It rises in the Australian Alps, New South Wales, and flows west to the Indian Ocean. Length about 2200 km (1300 miles). It is the longest river in Australia, and with its tributaries drains about 15 per cent of the continent and provides irrigation and hydro-electric power.

Muscle is a tissue. The bodies of most animals are made up of cells. When groups of these cells join together they form tissues and organs. Muscle has an unusual property – it can contract. When the muscles which are attached to part of an animal's body contract, that part of the body moves, and these muscular movements are what enables worms to wriggle, insects to fly, snails and slugs to creep, and a person to raise and lower their arm. In vertebrates the muscles are attached to the bones by tendons, and are usually arranged in pairs. When lifting an arm up, for example, one set of muscles relaxes while the other contracts, and when the first set relaxes and the other set contracts, the arm is lowered again. Muscles also line the walls of blood vessels, the digestive system and the skin.

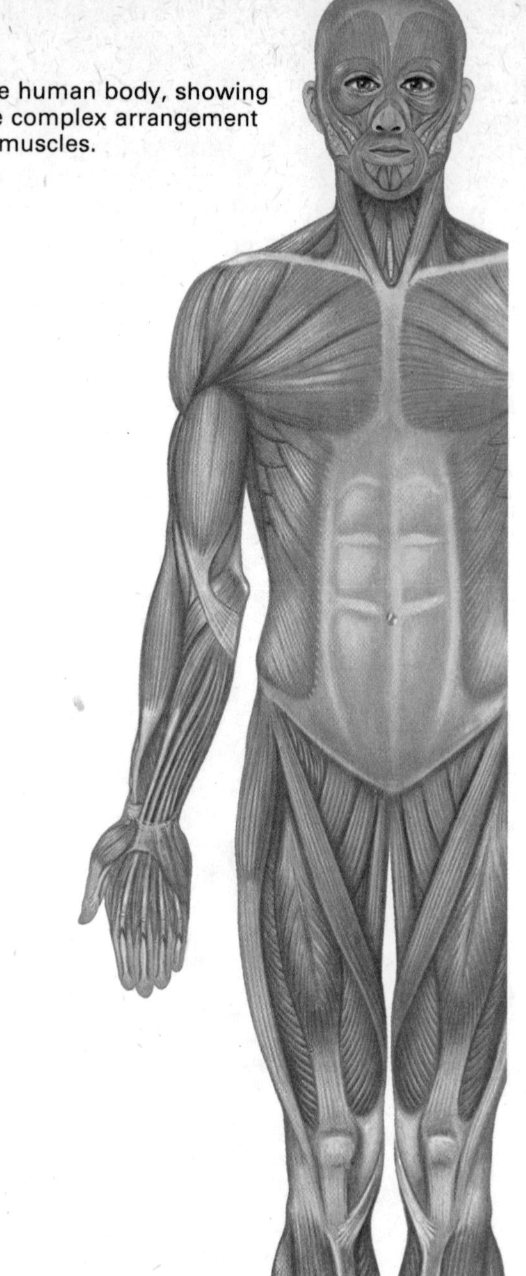

The human body, showing the complex arrangement of muscles.

Muses, in Greek myth, were nine minor goddesses, the daughters of Zeus by Mnemosyne ('Memory'). They were the patrons of arts and learning: Clio the muse of history, Thalia of comedy, etc, though in the early myth they did not have these separate identities. Like other gods and goddesses, they were jealous, and any mortal who dared to compare his talent with theirs was likely to be struck dumb.

Mushroom is the popular name given to the reproductive or fruiting body of several of the larger species of fungi. A fruiting body usually consists of a stalk, on top of which is the spore-bearing cap. Often the stalk and cap of edible fungi is called a mushroom, whereas the stalk and cap of poisonous fungi is called a toadstool. However, going by those common names is a very unreliable way to decide whether a fungus is really edible or not, and the only mushrooms safe to eat are those bought in shops for that purpose.

Mussel is a bivalve mollusc, and some kinds are an important food source in many parts of the world. Mussels live in huge groups known as beds, attaching themselves to rocks or piers by means of special threads which they secrete from their bodies. Their shells are two havles hinged together. In the common mussel and the horse mussel they are roughly oblong in shape, tapering slightly at one end. The fan mussel has shells shaped like a partly opened fan. Mussels feed by filtering small food particles from the water. Some mussels – the swan mussel, for instance – live in fresh water.

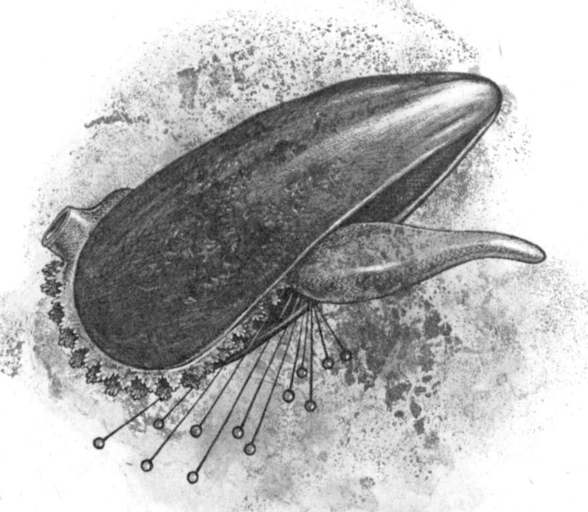

Mussolini, Benito (1883–1945), was an Italian Fascist dictator. He began his political career as a Socialist, but after being expelled from the Socialist Party went on to found the Fascists (1919). He came to power as Prime Minister following the famous 'March on Rome' in 1922. Mussolini subsequently established a totalitarian dictatorship, conquered Ethiopia (1935–1936), joined in the Spanish Civil War on the side of General Franco and in 1939 annexed Albania. In 1940 he brought Italy into the Second World War as an ally of Nazi Germany, but was overthrown in 1943 after a series of military defeats. Rescued by Germans in order to become head of a puppet government, he was eventually captured by his own people and shot.

Mutualism, see Symbiosis.

Mynah is a large, sparrow-like bird found in southern Asia. It usually lives in flocks, feeding on fruit and insects, and it nests in holes in the trees. The most well-known mynah is the Indian hill mynah or Indian grackle. This bird is black with white wing patches, and has an orange bill and yellow legs. It is a popular cage bird, for it can imitate the human voice.

Namib Desert is an arid region in southwest Africa. It lies along the coast of Namibia, between the Atlantic Ocean and the interior plateau. The area is very dry, receiving less than 1 cm (0.5 in) of rain each year, and very little vegetation grows here. Its area is 170 000 sq km (66 000 sq miles).

Napoleon (1769–1821), was a French soldier and statesman, and Emperor of France (1804–1805). Born in Corsica, he became an artillery officer, and put down a rising against the National Convention in Paris in 1795. In the Italian campaign of 1796–1797 he defeated the Austrians, but his Egyptian expedition ended when his fleet was destroyed by Nelson (1798). He overthrew the French government in 1799 and became First Consul, later having himself created Emperor.

Napoleon's greatest achievement in France was the codification of laws, known as the *Code Napoléon*, which is still the basis of French law. During the years from 1800 to 1808 he won a series of brilliant military victories which made France supreme in Europe, though his invasion of Russia in 1812 was a disaster. He was forced to abdicate in 1814, and was exiled to Elba. However, he escaped, returned to France and reassumed power. He was finally defeated at

Waterloo in 1815. He was exiled by the British to St Helena where he died.

Narcissus, in Greek myth, was the son of a minor river god and the water nymph Leiriope. He was extremely beautiful and the nymph Echo fell in love with him. Cold-hearted Narcissus rejected all lovers, and Echo gradually faded away with grief, until nothing but her voice was left.

Narcissus, leaning over to drink from a spring, fell in love with himself when he saw his reflection in the water. So intense was his self-love that he could not tear himself away from the water. He wasted away, until he was changed into the flower named after him.

NASA stands for National Aeronautics and Space Administration. This is the organization which develops and controls space research in the USA. It was set up in 1958, and has launched many rockets and satellites since then. These are launched at Cape Canaveral in Florida, and are carefully watched from huge NASA control rooms during their voyages.

The launchings include the rockets of the famous Apollo programme which landed the first man on the moon, and the Mariner spacecraft which have explored many of the planets in the Solar System.

The American flag is set up on the Moon by Apollo 17 astronauts.

Napoleon retreats from Moscow. When his army reached Moscow in 1812, Napoleon found the Russians had burnt the city and deserted it. His men were cold, hungry and sick, having suffered terribly from the harsh Russian winter, and he was forced to retreat.

Nash, John (1752–1835), was an English architect. His output was enormous, and his designs were in every possible style from thatched cottage to 'Gothic' castle. He is best remembered as London's finest town planner. His major work was the planning of Regent's Park, with its magnificent surrounding terraces of houses. His chief patron was George IV whose death in 1830 ended Nash's employment on the rebuilding of Buckingham Palace.

Nasser, Gamal Abdul (1918–1970), was an Egyptian statesman and army officer. He took part in the military coup in 1952 which overthrew King Farouk and made Egypt a republic. He was Prime Minister from 1954 to 1956, and President from 1956. His nationalization of the Suez Canal led to the Anglo-French attack on Suez in 1956. His championship of Arab nationalism made him unpopular in the West, but he was the acknowledged leader of the Arab world.

NATO stands for North Atlantic Treaty

Organization. This is an alliance formed in 1949 by a number of western European countries and the USA in face of the growing hostility of the USSR. The treaty which established the alliance was signed by delegates from 12 countries and provided for mutual assistance against aggression.

Natural gas is methane mixed with other gases. It is used as a fuel for heating homes, shops and factories, and is found underground or under the sea bed. Holes are drilled in the Earth, up to several kilometres deep, to obtain natural gas. Gas wells under the sea bed are drilled from floating rigs.

Millions of kilometres of pipes carry natural gas from the rigs to homes and factories. Gas can be compressed into a liquid for storage.

Natural gas is used in many parts of the world including Africa, America, Europe and USSR. It can also be made from coal or oil.

Sometimes natural gas has no smell. Other substances must then be added to it to give it a smell, so that gas leaks can be noticed. Gas leaks must be mended quickly because they can cause explosions. *See also* Methane.

Nauru is an island republic in the western Pacific Ocean. Area about 2130 hectares (5263 acres). First annexed to Germany, it came under a mandate to Australia after the First World War. After the Second World War it was made a trusteeship of the United Nations and gained independence in 1968, becoming the smallest independent republic in the world.

Navigation is the means by which travellers keep track of where they are and know which way to go to reach their destination. On land, navigation is usually done by means of a map, although remote regions may also require the use of stars (such as the Pole Star, which is always to the north in the Northern Hemisphere) or a magnetic compass (which always points to the North or South Pole). Stars and compass were also used by early sailors and pilots, but modern navigation at sea and in the air is by means of radio beams (sometimes from satellites). Some craft are also fitted with inertial navigation systems, which use tiny gyroscopes to detect every movement of the craft. *See also* Radar; Satellite.

Nazis were a political party founded in Germany in the early 1920s by Adolf Hitler. They were strongly nationalistic, believed the Germans to be a master race and were filled with hatred of the Jews. The Nazis

Nazi German soldiers take Jewish children to a concentration camp.

became more powerful in Germany during the economic depression of the late 1920s and early 1930s, achieving power in 1933 until the end of the Second World War. Their belief in the unification of all German-speaking peoples led to the annexation of Czechoslovakia and Austria. During the Second World War the brutal persecution of Jews and others led to mass exterminations in concentration camps.

Nebuchadnezzar II (died 562 BC), was King of Babylon (605–562 BC). He defeated the Egyptians at Carchemish and extended his empire to include Palestine, Syria and part of Anatolia. In 586 BC he destroyed Jerusalem and forced the Jews to go into exile. He rebuilt Babylon and created the famous hanging gardens which became one of the Seven Wonders of the World.

Nebula is a huge cloud of gas and dust. It may be as wide as 30 parsecs (astronomical unit of distance: one parsec is about 3.3 light years). Some nebulae shine because they contain bright stars. Others are dark, blocking off all the light from farther stars. Our Galaxy has hundreds of nebulae. They are named after the shapes they resemble. For example, the North American nebula in Cygnus has the rough shape of that continent. It is thought that stars may be formed from nebulae.

A planetary nebula is a ring or circle of gas with a star in the middle. They are called planetary because some of them look like planets.

Other galaxies are sometimes called nebulae.

Nectar is a sugary fluid produced in certain plants by special glands. The glands are usually situated at the base of the petals, and the nectar is used by insect-pollinated plants to attract, for example, butterflies and bees. When the insects come to drink the nectar they brush their bodies against the stamens and stigmas and thus pollinate the plant.

Nefertiti (died circa 1350 BC), Queen of Egypt of the 18th Dynasty, was the wife of Akhenaten who began the worship of the sun god. A bust of Nefertiti, made of painted limestone and showing her exceptional beauty, was found at Tell el-Amarna in Egypt.

Head of Nefertiti, made of painted limestone.

Nehru, Jawaharlal (1889–1964), an Indian statesman, was the first Prime Minister of India after the country's independence from Britain. Educated in England, he returned home to take an active part in nationalist politics. Becoming head of the Indian National Congress, he was repeatedly arrested by the British for his involvement in civil obedience. After the Second World War he played an important part in the negotiations which led to the creation of independent India and Pakistan. As Prime Minister (1947–1964) he pursued a policy of neutrality in world affairs.

Jawaharlal Nehru

Nelson, Horatio, Viscount (1758–1805), was a British naval commander. He played an important part in the defeat of the Spanish fleet off Cape St Vincent in 1797. In the following year he destroyed a French fleet at the Battle of the Nile, which effectively ended Napoleon's plans to conquer Egypt. Nelson won another brilliant victory at Copenhagen in 1801 when he routed a Danish fleet. This made him a national hero. In 1805 he attacked and utterly defeated a combined French and Spanish fleet at the Battle of Trafalgar. He was killed in the battle.

The death of Nelson at the Battle of Trafalgar.

Nepal is a kingdom in the central Himalayas, between India and China. Capital, Kathmandu; area about 141 000 sq km (54 600 sq miles). Nepal has a long history as an independent state. Its independence was recognized by the British rulers of India in 1923, and it has been a constitutional monarchy since 1951.

Nepal is extremely mountainous in the north but flatter in the south, especially in the Vale of Kathmandu. Most of the country is too rugged for wheeled vehicles. The people, who include the Gurkhas, are mostly of distant Mongol origin, and Buddhism is the most common religion. The more favourable regions are densely settled and grow a variety of crops. Trade and industry are at a low level, but tourism has increased recently.

Neptune is the eighth planet from the Sun. It orbits it every 165 years. It is very similar to Uranus, but is slightly smaller, and looks green because its atmosphere contains methane. The planet is mainly rock, ice and hydrogen. Its two satellites are Triton, which is larger than the Moon, and Nereid. Neptune was discovered by the German astronomer Galle in 1846.

Nero (AD 37–68), was a Roman Emperor (AD 54–68). He was adopted by his stepfather Claudius, whom he succeeded as Emperor. His reign gradually became more despotic and brutal: he murdered Claudius' son, Britannicus, his own mother Agrippina, and his first wife, Octavia, in order to marry Poppaea Sabina, whom he also later murdered. Nero used the fire which destroyed Rome in 64 as an excuse for the persecution of Christians. He committed suicide when the Governors of the provinces and his personal guard revolted against him.

Nerve is a collection of special cells called neurons which are able to transmit messages to the brain and to transmit messages from the brain to sets of muscles. Nerves allow an animal to react to the messages it receives. The messages travel along the nerves as a series of tiny electrical impulses. There are 13 000 million nerve cells in the human body. *See also* Brain; Spinal cord.

Netherlands, The, is a kingdom in north-west Europe. Capital, Amsterdam, Seat of Government, The Hague; area about 41 000 sq km (15 800 sq miles).
History The region was occupied by the Romans from the 1st century BC. In the 5th century AD Frankish tribes invaded and in the 9th century it became part of Lotharingia, a region in Charlemagne's empire named after his descendant Lothair II. The whole area then came under the control of the Dukes of Burgundy in the 14th century. In 1504 it passed to the Spanish Hapsburgs but in 1568 the northern provinces rebelled against Spanish rule, finally achieved independence in 1648, and The Netherlands became an independent republic. It was overrun by the French in 1795, and Napoleon created the kingdom of The Netherlands in 1806, but later made it part of France. The Dutch gained independence again in 1815 and The Netherlands, Belgium and Luxembourg were united under one king. However, in 1830 the southern part rebelled and formed the kingdom of Belgium, and Luxembourg broke away in 1890.

The Netherlands were under German occupation during 1940–1945. It joined NATO in 1949 and the EEC in 1957.
Land and People The Netherlands, sometimes called Holland (the major province), is very flat and low-lying. Much land has been reclaimed from the sea by building dykes and these areas are known as polders. The largest area of polder is around the Ijsselmeer, a large lake which was formerly part of Zuider Zee, an inlet of the North Sea. The mouths of three large rivers, Rhine, Meuse and Scheldt, form deltas in the south-west. There are low hills, up to 300 m (980 ft) high in the south-east.

The Netherlands is very heavily populated. The Dutch have a reputation for hard work and initiative, and have made their small country extremely prosperous. There are slightly more Protestants than Roman Catholics.
Economy The polders provide rich farmland and although comparatively few people are engaged in farming, agriculture, especially dairy products like cheese and butter, is a very profitable activity. Almost as important are bulbs: the Dutch tulip fields are famous.

Mineral and fuel deposits are not large, but industry is highly developed, though it depends largely on imported raw materials. Rotterdam-Europort is one of the largest and most modern ports in Europe. There is a large Dutch merchant fleet.

The cheese market in Alkmaar, Holland.

Neutrino is a very small particle. It has no electrical charge, and travels at the speed of light. Nuclear reactions, such as those in the Sun, produce neutrinos. The number of neutrinos produced by the Sun can tell us about these nuclear reactions. This is why astronomers are interested in them.

Neutrinos can pass through any material. Cosmic rays cannot. To shield neutrino detectors from cosmic rays, they were put at the bottom of gold mines, the deepest mines. During experiments using these shielded neutrino detectors, fewer neutrinos were found than had been expected.

Neutron is one of the two particles in the nucleus of an atom. The other is a proton. They are known as subatomic particles. For many years it was thought that the atomic nucleus contained only protons. The neutron was discovered in 1932. It has about the same mass as a proton, and has no electrical charge.

Atoms of the same element often contain different numbers of neutrons. These are known as isotopes.

The neutron can split the nucleus of certain atoms, which led to the development of the atom bomb and nuclear energy.

New Guinea is a large island in the west Pacific, divided between Irian Jaya, (which belongs to Indonesia) in the west and the state of Papua-New Guinea in the east. Area about 885 000 sq km (342 000 sq miles). New Guinea is very mountainous, with several active volcanoes, and most is covered with dense forest. Some parts have not been thoroughly explored, but there is a rich animal life, especially birds.

The people are divided into two main groups, Papuans, who occupy most inland areas, and Melanesians, on the coasts. The people are mostly farmers, growing mainly root crops and keeping pigs. Some remote tribes are very primitive and still fight amongst each other.

Crops like copra (part of the coconut), coffee and rubber are grown on plantations. There is some mining, though not fully developed; timber is more important. Transport is very difficult throughout New Guinea.

Newt, like the related salamander, is an amphibian with a tail. Unlike the frogs and toads, some species of which only return to water to breed, newts often spend much of their lives in water, including breeding.

Newts occur mainly in the temperate regions of North America and Eurasia, where they hunt insects and other small animals. Some species of newt perform elaborate courtship displays in which the males develop bright breeding colours to attract the females. *See also* Tadpole.

Male *(top)* and female smooth newt.

Newton, Sir Isaac (1642–1727), was an English mathematician and physicist. He was one of the greatest scientists. He was also a member of Parliament twice, and was master of the Mint from 1699.

It is said that watching an apple falling from a tree started Newton's investigation into gravity. He published his laws of gravity in 1687 in the book *Principia*.

By placing a prism in a beam of sunlight he also showed that light is made up of a spectrum of colours. He built the first reflecting

telescope. These and other discoveries about light were published in the book *Optiks* in 1704.

The three laws of motion were put forward by Newton, and he also developed the science of calculus. The unit of force, the newton, is named after him.

New York is a city in New York State, USA. It is the business and cultural capital of the USA, a major port and industrial centre, and the chief port of entry on the Atlantic. It is divided into five boroughs, the heart being Manhattan. Originally bought from the Indians by Dutch settlers, Manhattan Island (actually a peninsula) contains the business section, the main entertainment and shopping centre, and the headquarters of the United Nations. There are many colourful neighbourhoods like Chinatown and Greenwich Village. The other four boroughs are mainly residential and industrial.

New Zealand is in the south-west Pacific, and consists of two large islands (North and South Island) with several smaller ones. It is an independent state acknowledging the British monarch. Capital, Wellington; area about 269 000 sq km (104 000 sq miles).

Wellington, on the south coast of North Island, is an important seaport and commercial centre, exporting meat, wool and dairy products. Other major towns on North Island include Auckland, Hamilton and Rotorua. Auckland is the centre of New Zealand's major industrial and commercial region. Hamilton, on the Waikato river, is an important road and rail junction and an agricultural research centre. Rotorua, situated on a volcanic plateau, attracts many tourists. The biggest city on South Island is Christchurch – a port and market centre for the Canterbury Plains. These are a great expanse of rolling grasslands where sheep are reared and wheat grown.

History The country was first settled by Maoris from Polynesia, probably during the 14th century AD. It was discovered by the Dutch navigator Abel Tasman in 1642 and visited by the British explorer Captain Cook in 1769. In the early 19th century whaling stations and trading posts were set up. By the Treaty of Waitangi (1840) the Maori chiefs yielded sovereignty and New Zealand became a British colony. Many British settlers then arrived, and quarrels over land led to war with the Maoris.

Christchurch Cathedral, New Zealand.

Lake Tekapo in the Southern Alps, New Zealand.

New Zealand became a dominion in 1907, achieving full independence in 1931. New Zealand forces fought in both world wars and after the Second World War the country's mining and manufacturing industries expanded considerably.

Land New Zealand is mountainous, especially in South Island, with many forests, lakes and fast-flowing rivers. In North Island there are central volcanoes and an extraordinary region of hot springs around Rotorua. The coasts are irregular, with many good harbours and spectacular fiord scenery in South Island. The climate is generally temperate with mild winters and cool summers, and in general, quite heavy rainfall. It has many distinctive plants and animals, such as the kiwi, a large flightless bird.

People The original inhabitants, the Maori, are now a small minority and well integrated with the rest of the population who are the descendants of mainly British settlers. The standard of living is high, with an advanced form of welfare state. New Zealanders have a great reputation as games players, especially rugby football.

Economy Traditionally, New Zealand is a great farming country, well-known for sheep and dairy products. These products still make up most of the country's exports. There is coal and other mineral deposits, and in recent years industry has grown considerably, helped by the use of hydro-electric and geothermal (using heat from beneath the earth's crust) power.

Niagara Falls are waterfalls in North America, on the US-Canada border. At present there are two main falls – American and Horseshoe (Canadian) Falls. The shape of the falls changes from time to time. A dam was built upstream in the 1950s to prevent erosion, and provide hydro-electric power. Horseshoe Falls are about 57 m (187 ft) high and 750 m (2460 ft) wide; American Falls 59 m (193 ft) high and 300 m (984 ft) wide. They are a famous tourist attraction, and in the past, bold individuals have crossed them on a tightrope or gone over them in a barrel!

Nicaragua is a republic in Central America. Capital, Managua; area about 148 000 sq km (57 000 sq miles). After 300 years of Spanish rule, Nicaragua became independent in 1823, but it has suffered many political crises.

The west is mountainous, with many lakes, volcanoes and earthquakes. The east is swampy, and the centre is broken plateau. In general Nicaragua is lightly populated, and in the recent past immigrants, including Chinese, were encouraged. Most people are of American Indian, Spanish and African descent.

Agriculture is the main occupation and coffee the chief cash crop. Other exports include turtles. The large forests provide timber products and some gold is mined. There are other rich mineral resources not yet fully developed.

Nicholas II (1868–1918), was Tsar of Russia

(1894–1917). He succeeded his father, Alexander III, and followed his reactionary policies, but was a weak, indecisive ruler. Russia's defeat in the Russo-Japanese War of 1904–1905 revealed the incompetence of the government and led to the 1905 Revolution. Nicholas allowed the formation of a representative parliament, but then severely reduced its powers. After the outbreak of the First World War he took command of the Russian army, leaving the court in the hands of his wife and her adviser Rasputin. When the Russian Revolution broke out, Nicholas abdicated. He was later shot by the Bolsheviks, together with his family.

Nickel is a strong, hard, magnetic metal. Its chemical symbol is Ni. Nickel ore, called pentlandite, is mined in Canada, USSR and Australia. Nickel is silvery coloured.

Metals are often coated with nickel to protect them, and many alloys are made from nickel. It is often added to iron and steel to strengthen them, and is used in stainless steel. The alloy cupronickel is made of nickel mixed with copper. Cupronickel is used to make 'silver' coins.

The alloy nickel silver is a mixture of nickel, copper and zinc. Cutlery often has the initials EPNS on it. This stands for electroplated nickel silver.

Niger is a republic in West Africa. Capital, Niamey; area about 1 186 000 sq km (458 000 sq miles). Formerly part of French West Africa, Niger has been independent since 1960. It is landlocked, and most of the north and centre are desert, though there are scattered oases and grazing on the Air Massif. The south is more productive, with fertile land on the flood plain of the Niger River.

Except in the extreme south, Niger is very thinly populated, by nomadic Tuareg and Teda peoples. The farming groups in the south are not closely related, and speak quite different languages (Fulbe, Hausa, etc). Islam is the chief religion though there is a large Christian minority.

Some cash crops are raised, notably peanuts. Minerals are scarce though there is some uranium and, apparently, diamonds.

Nigeria is a federal republic in West Africa. Capital, Lagos; area about 924 000 sq km (357 000 sq miles). In 1976 it was announced that the federal capital would be moved inland to Abuja in the centre of the country.

History A Yoruba kingdom existed in AD 1000s. In the 1500s, Lagos became part of the kingdom of Benin. Europeans began to explore the country from the 16th century onward. Britain extended its rule over the whole of Nigeria during the 1860s and it became a British colony in 1914. The states were united in a federation in 1954 and Nigeria became an independent federal republic in 1960. Between 1967–1970 there was a civil war.

One in six of all Africans is a Nigerian, and the Nigerian Federation has a larger population than any other country in the continent. Its economic prosperity is based on the diversity and value of its resources. In recent years, it has done much to develop and modernize its industry.

Land The country takes its name from the River Niger, which enters Nigeria in the north-west and flows southwards to its wide, swampy delta on the Gulf of Guinea. The valleys of the Niger and its tributary the Benue form a broad Y-shaped trough, separating the three major highland and plateau regions that make up most of the country.

The largest region lies to the north of the rivers. Much of it consists of the high plains of Hausaland, with sparse woodlands and rough grass.

The region to the south and west of the River Niger includes the vast Yorubaland Plateau. Many of Nigeria's largest cities lie in this region. The third natural region, to the south and east of the Niger-Benue valleys, has plains and plateaux that rise to the Adamawa Highlands on the border with Cameroon.

Mangrove swamps line Nigeria's coast. To their north is a belt of dense rainforest and oil-palm, which merges into a zone of wooded savannah.

Nigeria lies completely within the tropics, and the whole of the country is hot. The highest temperatures occur in the north, but the heaviest rainfall is in the south. During the

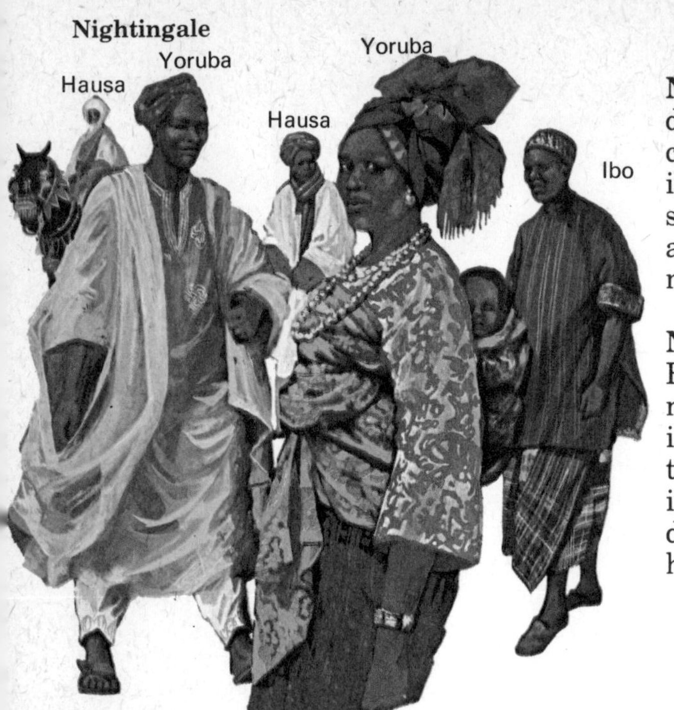

Traditional costumes worn by some of the tribal groups in Nigeria.

dry season, the dusty north-east trade wind, the *harmattan*, blows from the Sahara.

People The people of Nigeria belong to about 250 different ethnic groups. The four largest are the Yoruba in the south-west; the Ibo in the east; the Hausa (a people of Hamitic origin) in the north-west and north-centre; and the Fulani in many parts of the north.

The pattern of life varies throughout the country, and provides great contrasts. Nigeria has picturesque ancient towns, such as the walled inner city of Kano. It also has fine modern cities, with splendid public buildings and spacious residential areas. Outside the cities, most people follow traditional ways of village life.

Economy Nigeria's most important economic resource is petroleum, found mainly in the south. The country is Africa's largest producer, and petroleum accounts for most of its export earnings. Other valuable mineral products are tin, iron, and tantalum, mined in the Bauchi Plateau. Manufacturing industry is of growing importance. However, four people out of five live by cultivating crops, herding livestock, or forestry. Food crops include cassava, millet, maize (corn), and rice.

Nightingale is a shy, thrush-like bird whose drab brown plumage helps it to remain concealed in the undergrowth, where it feeds on insects. It winters in African savannah scrubland, and breeds across most of western and central Europe. It is best known for its melodious song which it delivers at night.

Nightingale, Florence (1820–1910), was a British hospital reformer and the founder of modern nursing. After being trained in nursing in London, she took a group of nurses to the Crimea in 1854 and began the task of improving both the standard of care and the dreadful sanitary conditions in British army hospitals. Her work achieved remarkable

results, and she drastically reduced the death-rate in hospitals. She was called 'the Lady with the Lamp'. On her return to Britain she established a training school for nurses which was to set the pattern for all nursing standards in the future. In 1907 she became the first woman to receive the Order of Merit.

Nightjars comprise nearly 70 species of birds living in tropical and temperate parts of the world. The common nightjar is a migratory bird, spending the summer in Europe and Asia, and the winter in Africa. Like most other nightjars, it rests by day among leaves and bark, its brown, mottled feathers hiding it from view. By night it fills the air with its strange calls as it flies slowly about catching insects on the wing in its huge, bristle-lined mouth. Usually two eggs are laid directly on to the ground, and the male helps with the incubation.

Nijinsky, Vaslav (1888–1950), was a Russian dancer, perhaps the most brilliant dancer in the history of ballet. The son of dancers, he was a sensational success before he turned 20. Diaghilev made him the star of his Ballet Russe, and he astonished Western European audiences in the classics as well as in new works by Fokine.

Vaslav Nijinsky dancing with Tamara Karsavina.

Nile is a river in north-east Africa. It rises in East Africa and flows north through the Sudan and Egypt to the Mediterranean. With a total length of about 6700 km (4160 miles) it is probably the longest river in the world. Since ancient times, the Nile has been vital to Egypt, and supported an early civilization in its valley and delta region. It is still the main source of water for Egypt and the Sudan. It is navigable from Upper Egypt to the delta and contains many species of fish, including the large Nile perch. Above Khartoum, it is divided into the White and Blue Niles.

Nitrogen is a gaseous element with no taste or smell. Its chemical symbol is N. All animals and plants need nitrogen. Nearly 80 per cent of the air we breathe is nitrogen, but our bodies only make use of the oxygen which is present in the air.

Plants can obtain nitrogen from compounds in the soil, and humans obtain nitrogen by eating plants and animals. Eventually, the nitrogen in plants and animals goes back into the soil. This is known as the nitrogen cycle. Nitrogen compounds, such as nitrates, are added to the soil by farmers. These help to put nitrogen into the soil more quickly than can be achieved by the nitrogen cycle.

Nitrogen compounds are also used in explosives, such as TNT, plastics, dyes and many other things. *See also* Fertilizer.

Nixon, Richard M (1913–), is an American politician. He became vice-president of the USA during the presidency of Dwight D. Eisenhower (1953–1961). He was the Republican Party candidate for the presidency in 1960, but was defeated by John F. Kennedy. Then, after a period of retirement, he made a comeback, becoming President in 1969.

As President, Nixon established better relations between the USA and China, and also improved American relations with the USSR. He ended the costly and demoralizing American involvement in the Vietnam War, withdrawing all American troops by 1973.

In 1972 Nixon was re-elected president, but his career was ruined by the Watergate scandal. This started when a burglary was committed on the premises of the rival Democratic Party. Nixon's attempts to cover up links between the burglars and the Republican Party and himself, and other illegalities, became known, and he resigned his office in August 1974. He is the only president of the USA to have done so.

Nkomo, Joshua (1917–), is a Zimbabwean politician. In the 1970s he was one of the leaders of the guerrilla war waged against the white-dominated government of the country (then called Rhodesia). Nkomo led the Zimbabwe African People's Union (ZAPU), which collaborated in a 'Patriotic Front' with Robert Mugabe's Zimbabwe African National Union (ZANU) while the war lasted.

When black majority rule was achieved, ZAPU did badly in the elections and Mugabe became Prime Minister. In 1982 Nkomo was invited to become Minister of Home affairs, but he left the government, and relations between the two leaders and their parties became dangerously strained.

Nkrumah, Kwame (1909–1972), was a Ghanaian statesman. After studying in the USA and Britain he returned home to form the Convention People's Party in 1949. He became Prime Minister in 1952 and led his country to independence in 1957. In 1960 he took office as President. Nkrumah pursued a strongly anti-colonialist policy, but his dictatorial regime in Ghana led to his being deposed by the army while on a visit to China in 1966. He died in exile in Romania.

Nobel, Alfred (1833–1896), was a Swedish chemist who invented dynamite and other explosives. He was opposed to war and hoped that his discoveries might actually stop warfare by making it too destructive for any nation to embark on. A synthetic chemical element, nobelium, is named in his honour.

Nobel left most of his enormous fortune to finance prizes, known as Nobel prizes, for human achievement.

Nobel Prize is a prize which is given for outstanding work. Six awards are given each year to people for work in medicine, chemistry, physics, literature, peace and economics. A Nobel Prize is the highest award that anybody in these fields can receive.

Norman Conquest was the conquest of England by William, Duke of Normandy. The Normans landed at Pevensey in Sussex without opposition in 1066. The English, led by King Harold, who had just repelled an invasion from Norway in the north, hastened south, but were defeated by the Normans at Hastings. William had himself crowned King of England. Risings against the Normans took place in various parts of the country, but by 1172 they had all been suppressed. Feudalism was imposed upon the English people, the English nobility was replaced by a Norman nobility and French became the language of government.

Normandy invasion was the landing of Allied troops in German-occupied northwest France, which began on 6 June 1944. The biggest seaborne invasion in history, it took place after months of careful preparation, and nearly 5000 ships were used to carry the British, American and Canadian forces and their equipment across the Channel from England. Within a few days, over a million troops had been landed, and the struggle to liberate western Europe began.

North America is the third largest continent, covering some 24 248 400 sq km (9 362 400 sq miles). It extends from the Arctic Circle to the Tropic of Cancer. In the south the narrow land chain of Central America links North and South America. In the north the frozen waters of the Arctic Ocean contain a great many islands. The most important of these is Greenland (an overseas territory of Denmark), which is the world's largest island. In the extreme northwest only 90 km (56 miles) of sea (the Bering Strait) separates North America from Asia.

A great mountain chain dominates the western side of North America, the largest part of this being the Rocky Mountains range, which runs from Alaska into northern Mexico. Two large countries occupy most of North America: the United States of America and Canada. The USA is slightly smaller than Canada but has a much larger population. *See also* Canada and United States of America.

Northern Ireland is a province of the United Kingdom of Great Britain and Northern Ireland, formed of the six counties of Ulster. Capital, Belfast; area about 14 000 sq km (5400 sq miles).

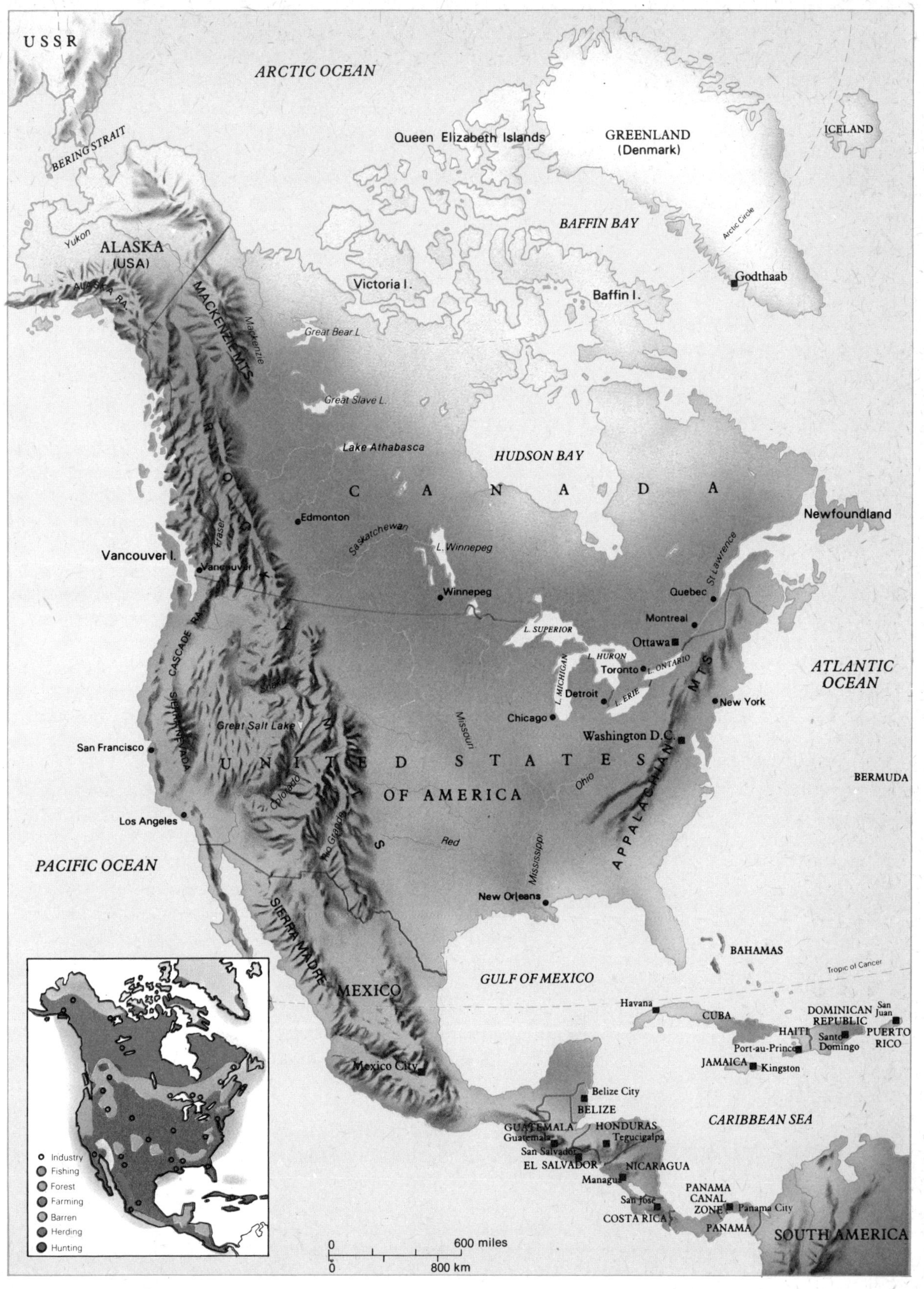
USSR
ARCTIC OCEAN
BERING STRAIT
Queen Elizabeth Islands
GREENLAND
(Denmark)
ICELAND
BAFFIN BAY
Arctic Circle
Yukon
ALASKA
(USA)
ALASKA RA.
MACKENZIE MTS
Mackenzie
Victoria I.
Baffin I.
Godthaab
Great Bear L.
Great Slave L.
Lake Athabasca
HUDSON BAY
C A N A D A
Newfoundland
Edmonton
Saskatchewan
L. Winnepeg
Fraser
Vancouver I.
Vancouver
Winnepeg
St Lawrence
Quebec
Montreal
Ottawa
L. SUPERIOR
L. HURON
L. MICHIGAN
L. ONTARIO
L. ERIE
Toronto
Detroit
Chicago
ATLANTIC
OCEAN
New York
Washington D.C.
CASCADE RA.
SIERRA NEVADA
Snake
Great Salt Lake
Missouri
San Francisco
U N I T E D S T A T E S
OF AMERICA
Ohio
BERMUDA
Colorado
APPALACHIAN MTS
Los Angeles
Rio Grande
Red
Mississippi
PACIFIC OCEAN
New Orleans
SIERRA MADRE
BAHAMAS
Tropic of Cancer
GULF OF MEXICO
MEXICO
Havana
CUBA
DOMINICAN
REPUBLIC
San
Juan
HAITI
Santo
Domingo
PUERTO
RICO
Port-au-Prince
JAMAICA
Kingston
Mexico City
Belize City
BELIZE
CARIBBEAN SEA
GUATEMALA
Guatemala
HONDURAS
Tegucigalpa
San Salvador
EL SALVADOR
NICARAGUA
Managua
PANAMA
CANAL
ZONE
Panama City
San José
COSTA RICA
PANAMA
SOUTH AMERICA
0
600 miles
0
800 km
Industry
Fishing
Forest
Farming
Barren
Herding
Hunting

History It originated when a majority of the people, who are linked historically to Britain in religion, economics and politics, voted to remain British rather than become part of independent Ireland (1922). Extremist groups among both the Protestant, 'loyalist' majority and the Catholic, republican minority, brought Northern Ireland close to civil war in 1969, resulting in direct rule from London and the sending of British troops to maintain order. Acts of terrorism and murder have continued.
Land Northern Ireland consists of plains surrounded by low mountains near the coast. On the northern coast of Antrim is the famous formation of about 40 000 polygonal blocks of basalt known as the Giant's Causeway. They stretch for nearly 10 km (6 miles). In the centre of Northern Ireland is Lough Neagh, the largest lake in the British Isles.
Economy The political crisis has damaged Northern Ireland's economy, especially through lost investment and high unemployment. About one-quarter of the people are directly involved in farming (less than the republic of Ireland). There are few minerals or fuels, but large and varied manufacturing industries, especially in Belfast and Londonderry. *See also* Ireland; United Kingdom.

Counties of Northern Ireland

Counties and county boroughs	*Area* hectares	acres
Antrim	304 526	752 500
Armagh	132 697	327 901
Belfast CB	7305	18 051
Down	246 624	609 420
Fermanagh	185 097	457 384
Londonderry	210 782	520 946
Londonderry CB	1044	2585
Tyrone	326 550	806 987

North Korea see Korea, North

North Pole is the northernmost point of the Earth, in the Arctic Ocean, about 700 km (435 miles) from the tip of Greenland. The first man to reach the North Pole was the American explorer, Robert E Peary, in 1909.

North Sea is part of the Atlantic, between Britain and continental Europe. Area about 600 000 sq km (232 000 sq miles). Shipping has been heavy throughout history, and there are valuable fisheries, now somewhat smaller (the huge herring fishery almost disappeared). More recently, valuable undersea deposits of oil and natural gas have been exploited. In prehistoric times, the North Sea was a dry plain linking Britain with the continent.

Norway is a kingdom in north-west Europe, forming the western part of Scandinavia. Capital, Oslo; area about 324 000 sq km (125 000 sq miles).
History The country was occupied by Germanic tribes in the 1st millennium (one thousand years) AD and was first united under one ruler in the 10th century, when it was converted to Christianity. Norway was united with Sweden, and then with Denmark, remaining under Danish rule until 1814. In that year it was joined to Sweden, but the union with Sweden was dissolved in 1905, and Norway became an independent kingdom. It was under German occupation 1940–1945. It became a member of NATO in 1949, and enjoyed increasing prosperity through the development of its oil and natural gas resources.
Land and People Norway is the most mountainous country in Europe, and one-third is north of the Arctic Circle. Much of the interior is too cold and barren for people to live. Most people live in cities like Oslo and Bergen, near the west coast, where the Gulf Stream keeps the climate suprisingly mild. The country has a spectacular coast line, cut by steep fiords. Fast-flowing rivers descend from the mountains, providing ample hydroelectric power as well as magnificent salmon fishing. The exciting scenery attracts many tourists.
Economy There is a shortage of fertile land in Norway. Many farmers are also part-time foresters or fishermen. In the far north there are reindeer herds kept by the nomadic Lapps. There are mineral resources, but there are mainly small and expensive to work, though North Sea oil and gas have

given the Norwegian economy a helpful boost. Thanks to cheap hydro-electric power, manufacturing industry is well developed, though fish and timber products are the largest exports. The merchant fleet is large, as in a country with limited natural resources, trade is especially important.

Nova means new. Ancient astronomers thought that novae were new stars. They are really faint stars that suddenly become thousands of times brighter. This brightness fades away slowly over days or even years.

It is thought that gas from the faint star is drawn away to a neighbouring white dwarf or neutron star. The gas then explodes. We see this explosion as a nova.

After fading, nova sometimes flare up again after a few months or years. Many novae have been seen near the middle of our own galaxy.

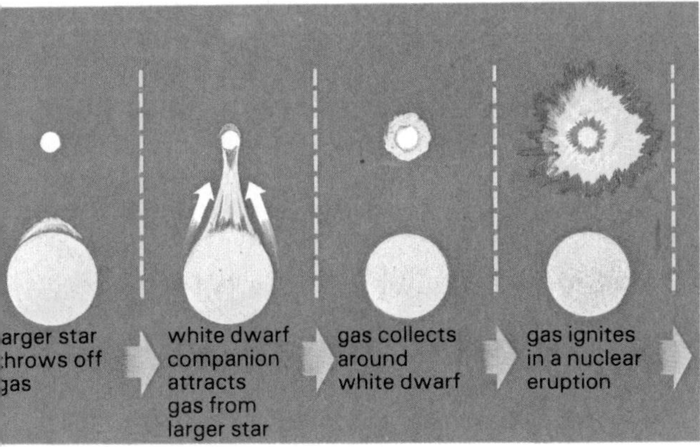
arger star
:hrows off
jas
white dwarf
companion
attracts
gas from
larger star
gas collects
around
white dwarf
gas ignites
in a nuclear
eruption

Novel is a work of fiction which tells a story in prose. Although a novel can be about anything, the usual subject-matter is human beings and their relationships – with themselves, with others, with society. Story-telling is an ancient occupation, and it is impossible to say when the novel began. However, it became a distinct form of literature in the 18th century, with the rise of authors like Defoe, Richardson, Fielding and Sterne, and a new, middle-class reading public. Most critics would say that the greatest age of the novel was the 19th and early 20th centuries, with Dickens, Thackeray, George Eliot, Hugo, Balzac, Goethe, Dostoyevsky, Tolstoy, Hawthorne, Twain and others.

November is the eleventh month of the year in the modern calendar, and lasts for 30 days. In the ancient Roman calendar it was the ninth month, and this accounts for its name: in Latin, *novem* means 'nine'.

Nuclear energy is energy from the nucleus of an atom. It is used in weapons, such as the atom bomb, and also to make electricity.

Nuclear fission, is the splitting of a large nucleus, such as a uranium or plutonium nucleus. It produces energy and two or more neutrons. These neutrons can cause more nuclear fission and more neutrons. As more and more nuclei are split, a huge amount of energy is produced.

This energy is used in an atomic weapon, and can be used to make electricity.

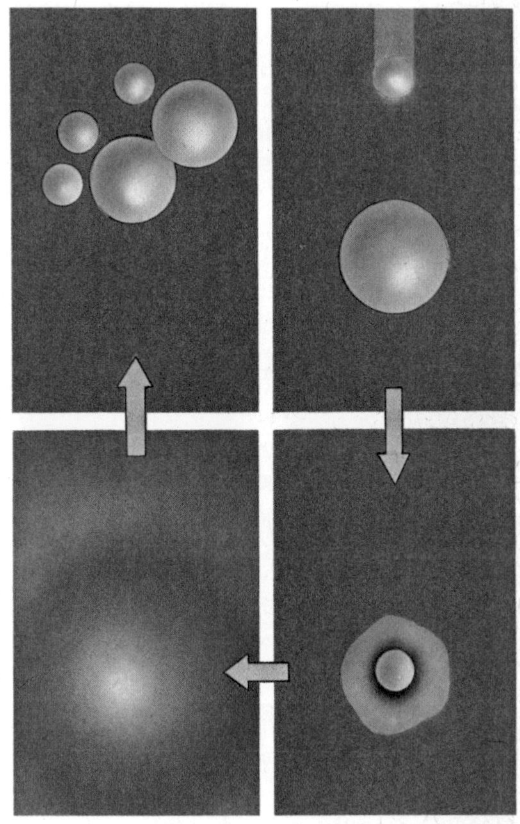

A diagram showing nuclear fission. A fast-moving neutron collides with the nucleus of a uranium atom. The nucleus becomes distorted and then breaks in two, releasing energy in the form of an explosion. Two lighter nuclei and three free neutrons result from the explosion.

Nuclear fusion is a joining together of nuclei. Small nuclei can join together to form one big nucleus; for example, four hydrogen nuclei can join to form one helium nucleus. Nuclear fusion produces huge amounts of energy, far more than is produced by nuclear fission.

Nuclear fusion happens at very high temperatures. The centres of stars are very hot. The heat and light of stars, such as the Sun, are thought to come from nuclear fusion in their centres.

An atom bomb exploding produces enough heat for nuclear fusion. Scientists are trying to find other ways of bringing about nuclear fusion so that it can be used to make electricity. *See also* Hydrogen bomb; Nucleus.

Nuclear reactor is a device which makes electricity from the nuclear fission of substances such as uranium. The heat from the nuclear fission is used to heat water, which boils into steam. This pushes around a turbine to produce electricity.

Nuclear fission produces harmful rays, such as gamma rays. The uranium is surrounded by thick walls of steel and concrete which stop the rays. Dangerous waste substances are also formed in nuclear reactors.

Nucleic acids are chemical compounds found within the cells of all living organisms. Their structure is very complicated, and they take the form of long chains of molecules. There are two types of nucleic acids. Deoxyribonucleic acid (DNA) is found mainly in the chromosomes of the cell nucleus, and contains the hereditary information of the organism. Ribonucleic acid (RNA) is found mainly in the cytoplasm (the fluid part of the cell) and its main function is to control the formation of proteins.

Nucleus (biology) is part of all living cells except viruses. It is the most obvious structure in the cell, usually appearing as a large, spherical or oval, dark-coloured structure. The nucleus contains the chromosomes, and controls the cell's activities, for when the nucleus is removed the rest of the cell soon dies. *See also* Cell.

Nucleus (physics and chemistry) lies at the centre of an atom and is surrounded by electrons. The nucleus of a hydrogen atom is a proton. The nuclei of all other atoms contain protons and neutrons.

Protons and neutrons are much heavier than electrons. So, the weight of an atom is almost the same as the weight of its nucleus. All other nuclei are heavier than hydrogen nuclei. Uranium has a very heavy nucleus. It contains 92 protons and many more neutrons. The protons and neutrons in any nucleus are held together by huge forces.

Nureyev, Rudolf (1938–), is a Russian-born dancer. As a soloist with the Kirov Ballet from 1958, he was often in conflict with the authorities. In 1961, after a great success in Paris, he defected to the West. For several years he was the principal partner of Margot Fonteyn in the British Royal Ballet, but he also danced with many other international companies. His athletic technique and powerful personality as a performer, plus his creation of many new roles, made him the outstanding dancer of the 1960s and 1970s.

Nut is a hard-coated fruit containing one seed. Typical nuts are those found on oak trees, beech trees and sweet chestnut trees.

Nyerere, Julius (1922–), is a Tanzanian politician. He was the first Prime Minister of Tanganyika in east Africa when it gained independence from Britain in 1961. In 1962, when the country was declared a republic, Nyerere became President.

In 1964 Tanganyika and Zanzibar united to form the new state of Tanzania, and Nyerere has been president of this ever since. His policies of socialism and economic independence have impressed many people. He has supported independence movements in southern Africa, and in 1978 Tanzanian forces overthrew the tyranny of Idi Amin in neighbouring Uganda.

Nylon is the best-known artificial material. The American scientist, William Carothers, wanted to make a material like silk, and discovered nylon in 1935. It is made from the chemicals found in petroleum or coal.

Nylon threads are twice as strong as silk. They can be stretched and will go back into their original shape. So they are used to make stockings and tights. Nylon can also be made to look like other natural materials, such as wool and silk. Clothes, carpets and fishing nets are all made of nylon.

Nylon is a plastic. Instead of being spun into thread it can be set in moulds. Moulded nylon is used to make gears, combs, screws, belts and many other items.

Nymph is the miniature version of the adult which hatches from the egg of some insects, cockroaches for example, whose life cycle does not include a larval stage. On hatching, nymphs are complete except they do not have fully developed wings and do not have the ability to reproduce. By a series of skin sheddings called moults they grow larger, wings developing with each moult.

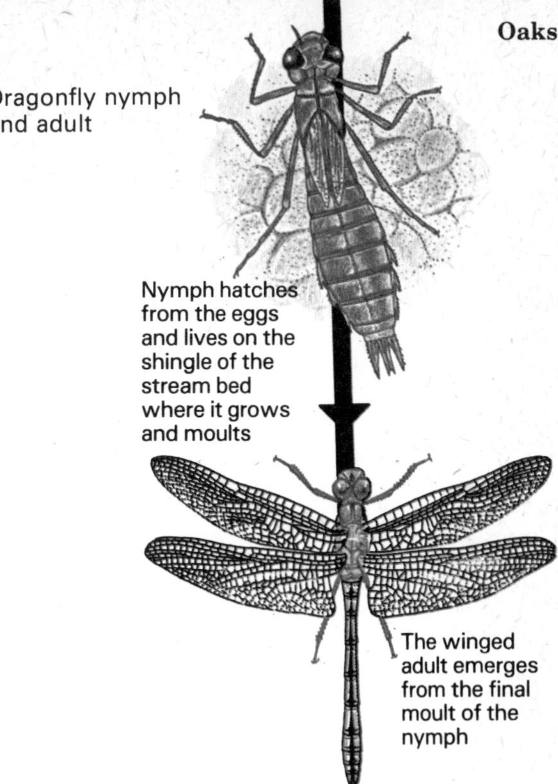

Nymph hatches from the eggs and lives on the shingle of the stream bed where it grows and moults
The winged adult emerges from the final moult of the nymph

Dragonfly nymph and adult

O

Common oak tree

Oaks are the most important, the most widely distributed and the biggest genus of hardwood trees to be found in the Northern Hemisphere. There are also species growing in such places as Japan, China and Africa. Most oaks are deciduous, shedding their leaves during winter. However, some – such as the holm oak and the cork oak – are evergreen. All species bear acorns, although the shape and arrangement of these varies from species to species.

Oaks are justly famous for their durability. Many species grow to a great age and produce wood which is used for a wide variety of purposes. Throughout history the oak has provided humans with charcoal, and timber for ships, building materials and furniture. Not only humans benefit from the oak, however. The acorn is eaten by birds, pigs and many other animals. In addition, the generous spreading boughs of an oak tree can literally teem with animal and plant life. Birds, insects, spiders, mites, fungi, ferns and lichens – all these organisms and more feed on and among the oak tree. Perhaps this bountifulness is the reason why oaks have often been revered in religion.

Oasis is a fertile place in the middle of a desert, with a spring or some other source of water. Date palms are particularly associated with oases, providing a food source and so making human settlement possible.

For centuries, oases have provided a vital element in trade and travel on the caravan routes across great desert areas such as the Sahara. In some places water does not appear naturally on the surface but has to be pumped up, often from great depths.

Oceania is a general term used to include all the islands in a vast area of the Pacific, from New Guinea to Australia and New Zealand, and as far north as Hawaii.

Ocean liner is a passenger-carrying ship nowadays used for luxury cruises. The name comes from the fact that such ships used to be part of a liner service running on fixed routes, regularly. The first such ship was probably the 72 m (236 ft) British paddle steamer *Great Western*, launched in 1838.

The *Normandie* (1932) captured the Blue Riband on her maiden voyage.

The heyday of the ocean liner was the years immediately before and after the Second World War, when ships fought for the Blue Riband, awarded for the fastest crossing of the North Atlantic before air travel really took over.

The fastest liner of all was the *United States*, whose 1952 crossing of the Atlantic in the time of 3 days 10 hrs 40 mins (at an average speed of 66 km/h (41 mph) has never been beaten by a passenger ship. These years also saw in service the largest ocean liners ever built, including the famous British 'Queens' – *Queen Elizabeth* and *Queen Mary* – and the longest ever, the 315.6 m *France*.

October is the tenth month of the year in the modern calendar, and lasts for 31 days. In the ancient Roman calendar it was the eighth month, and so was named after the Latin *octo* meaning 'eight'.

The October Revolution in Russia (1917) led to the setting up of the present Communist state, the USSR (the Union of Soviet Socialist Republics or Soviet Union).

Octopus is a mollusc which has eight tentacles or arms surrounding a beak-like mouth. They also have well-developed eyes and brains, but no shell. All octupuses are marine, feeding on other molluscs and crabs which they catch or envelop with their suckered tentacles. The shells are dealt with by the jaws, and the meat is scooped out by the tongue. Most octopuses are quite small. They normally stay hidden out of sight under stones or in crevices until it is time to feed or mate. The blue-ring octopus is an extremely venomous species living in Australian waters.

Odin, or Wotan, Woden, etc, was the chief god in Germanic and Norse (Scandinavian) myth. He was primarily a god of battle, though he also became a god of wisdom after giving up one of his eyes for the gift of wisdom. He reigned from Valhalla in Asgard, home of the gods, attended by the Valkyries. His spear, Gungnir, never missed its mark.

Odysseus, in Greek legend, was one of the warriors at the siege of Troy, whose later adventures are told in Homer's *Iliad.* His Latin (Roman) name is Ulysses.

Among the Greeks at Troy, Odysseus was not the greatest warrior but he was the cleverest. All his cunning was needed on his voyage from Troy, during which he was involved in a series of adventures, such as his escape from the Cyclops, Polyphemus, and a visit to the witch, Circe, who turned his men into pigs. He eventually reached home in Ithaca, where his patient wife Penelope was still waiting for him.

Oil, see Petroleum.

Oil tanker is a ship designed specially for carrying crude oil, which is refined to produce petrol, diesel and other liquid fuels. The biggest oil tankers, known as supertankers, are the largest cargo vessels ever built – weights of up to 250 000 tonnes are common and several mammoth ships are twice that size. Such ships are so large that the crew use bicycles to get around the decks and the ships can take over 3 km (1.9 miles) to stop.

Okapi is an African herbivorous mammal related to the giraffe. It has a reddish brown body with white stripes on the legs. The head is a little like a giraffe's, but it has a much shorter neck. The okapi lives in the forests of Zaire, and was only discovered by Europeans about 80 years ago. It is up to 1.6 m (5.2 ft) tall at the shoulder.

Olympic Games is the greatest international festival of sport. The Games are a revival of the ancient Greek games of Olympia, the first Olympiad dating from 776 BC, although games had been held in Olympia for hundreds of years before then. The ancient games, like today's, were held every four years, the last being 393 AD. They were then prohibited by the Emperor, and Olympia declined rapidly.

The revival of the Olympics was the inspiration of Baron Pierre de Coubertin, a Frenchman, and the first modern Games was held at Athens in 1896.

Athletics has always been the principal sport at the Olympics, the most important event in the ancient games being the marathon. The modern games include a variety of other sports, from association football, boxing, gymnastics and swimming to those less widespread such as shooting, volleyball and weightlifting. Other sports have been included and discarded, among them cricket, croquet, rugby and polo.

The Olympic ideal has been very important, the words of Coubertin appearing now on the electronic scoreboards: 'The most important thing . . . is not to win but to take part . . .' All competitors must be amateurs, but the definition of amateurism is latterly causing great concern. Other aspects causing concern are the vast expense of staging the games and the opportunity they afford for terrorism and demonstrations.

Okapi

Olympus is the highest mountain in Greece. In Greek myth, Mount Olympus is often the home of the gods (sometimes called the Olypians), though in some versions they live in the sky.

Oman is a sultanate in the south-east Arabian peninsula. Capital, Muscat; area about 272 000 sq km (105 000 miles). Once the centre of a considerable Arab empire, it was known as Muscat and Oman before 1970. It has historic links with Britain.

Much of the land verges on desert, but there is a fertile coastal plain, and cereals are grown in hilly areas. The population is mainly Arab, but very mixed on the coast. Since the discovery of oil in 1964, Oman has grown rich. Other industries and products are far less important.

Omnivore is the name given to animals which eat both plants and animals. Omnivorous animals include humans and badgers.

A badger – an omnivore.

O'Neill, Eugene (1888–1953), was a US playwright. He began to write one-act plays during an illness in 1912, and his first full-length play, *Beyond the Horizon* (1920), won an important prize for drama. His early work was often cruelly realistic, but later plays were more symbolic, inspired by the conflict between the human spirit and the pressures of ordinary life. His greatest works are *Mourning Becomes Electra* (1931), *The Iceman Cometh* (1946) and the autobiographical *A Long Day's Journey Into Night* (1956). The first US playwright of international fame, O'Neill opened the door for a generation of gifted younger playwrights.

Opal is a silica mineral, found in a wide range of colours. The more attractive and rarer opals have been used as gem stones at least since Roman times. In precious opals, minute, water-filled cracks refract the light, creating a beautiful play of colours, and the white opal has a milky, pearly appearance. Also valuable are fire opals (red, orange or yellow) and the very rare black opals. In modern times the finest gem opals have come from Mexico, and from Queensland and New South Wales in Australia.

Op art is a trend in modern art in which striking effects or optical illusions are created to deceive or intrigue the eye of the observer. These effects were often created with the aid of advanced technology, such as computers. Op (short for 'optical') art was connected with Pop art, and although a few artists specialized in creating this type of image in the 1960s and later, Op art was not an exclusive school or movement, and it became merged with other developments in contemporary art.

OPEC stands for the Organization of Petroleum Exporting Countries. This was set up in 1960, and its members are Nigeria, Algeria, Saudi Arabia, Iran, Iraq, Kuwait, Libya, Abu Dhabi, Qatar, Indonesia and Venezuela. Oil production in these countries was started, and for a long time effectively controlled,. by Western companies, whose policies ensured a constant supply of cheap energy for the Western world. This situation changed gradually as the oil-producing countries sought greater benefits for their own peoples. In December 1973, OPEC enforced massive price increases, revealing Western dependence on the oil producers and creating an 'energy crisis'.

A conference is held every two years to work out OPEC policies, prices, and to discuss other related matters.

Opera is drama set to orchestral music and sung. In opera the music is the most important ingredient of the drama; in a sense it *is* the drama. There is little or no speech. Opera began in 16th-century Italy. It developed rapidly in the 17th century through Monteverdi, who used more instruments and wrote arias for the singers, and later Scarlatti. The Italian opera was introduced into France and Germany and in the early 18th century reached new heights in the works of Handel. In the 18th century the form was changed and the orchestra became increasingly important. Mozart wrote *The Marriage of Figaro* (1786) and *Don Giovanni* (1787), fine examples of the classical style.

The Romantic movement in Germany, of which Wagner represents the peak, transformed the form once more. Wagner, who preferred the term 'music drama', abandoned the old form of aria and recitative (sung narrative) in favour of a more symphonic construction. The older style was retained, however, by Verdi.

In the late 19th century there was a move for greater realism in opera (which can be seen in Puccini, for example), and a growth of national opera, most notably in Czechoslovakia but later in England and the United States.

Most composers have regarded opera as the greatest challenge, though some (e.g. Brahms, Bruckner) never attempted it. Beethoven wrote only one (*Fidelio*). In addition opera, which usually requires splendid costumes and sets, has attracted great painters as designers.

Virginian opossum

Opossum is the only marsupial mammal living in America. There are about 65 species, of which the most successful is the Virginian opossum. This opossum, once confined to South America like the other American opossums, has now spread northwards to the southern parts of North America.

Opossums are rat-like creatures up to 50 cm (20 in) long. They live in woods and hunt at night for invertebrates and other small animals, as well as fruit and seeds. The phrase 'playing possum' comes from the opossum's habit of pretending to be dead when confronted by a predator.

Optics is the study of light. It is part of a branch of science called physics. Instruments which use light, such as telescopes and microscopes, are called optical instruments.

Orang-utan is a large ape with long, reddish brown hair, which lives in the rainforests of Borneo and Sumatra. Its name means 'man of the woods'. It is in great danger of becoming extinct because forests are being destroyed. Males, which are larger than females, stand 1.5 m (5 ft) high. The orang-utan swings through the branches of its forest home using its very long arms. Small family parties live together, searching for fruit, although they also eat insects and birds eggs.

Orbit is the path which the Earth follows as it moves around the Sun, held by the force of gravity of the Sun. All the planets, asteroids and comets in the Solar System orbit the Sun. The Moon and artificial satellites orbit the Earth, held by its force of gravity.

All orbits were once thought to be circles. In 1609, Johann Kepler showed that these orbits are ellipses. (An ellipse is like a flattened circle.) He also showed that the speed of a planet varies as it travels along its elliptical orbit. It travels faster when it is close to the Sun, and slower when it is far from the Sun.

Orchestra is a combination of musical instruments playing together and (in modern times) controlled by a conductor. There are various types of orchestra, but the typical symphony orchestra consists of about 100 players and is divided into four sections: strings, woodwind, brass and percussion.

The orchestra began with the string section in the 17th century. Various instruments were added during the next century, and the brass section was established in the 19th century.

The development of the orchestra depended largely on composers, who came to exploit its possibilities with growing subtlety in the 19th century. Towards the end of the century the demands of composers like Wagner, Strauss and Mahler greatly enlarged the orchestra.

Orchids are beautiful and unusual insect-pollinated flowering plants found in the tropics as well as in colder regions. There are about 17 000 species world-wide. Some live as epiphytes, attached to the branches of trees; others are saprophytes, feeding on decaying matter in the soil.

Many orchids are named after animals, for the shape of their petals often resembles a particular creature. Thus, there are bee orchids and fly orchids which look like these insects, and probably use their shapes to attract insects to come and pollinate them. There is also a frog orchid and even a man orchid, which has petals shaped like a man, complete with arms and legs.

One kind of orchid.

Ordovician is a period in the history of the Earth, known from the study of rocks and of the fossil remains found in them (the geological record). It is named after an ancient Welsh tribe, because early investigations of Ordovician rocks were carried out in Wales.

The Ordovician period is the second major division of the Paleozoic era, following the Cambrian. It began about 500 million years ago and lasted about 70 million years. Most Ordovician fossils are marine invertebrates (creatures without backbones) although it was also the period when the first fish, which were also the first vertebrates (creatures with backbones) appeared.

Organ, in music, is a keyboard instrument. Its notes are sounded by air blown through pipes. Its history goes back to the 3rd century BC. Some of the largest organs were made in the Middle Ages and some of the most beautiful in the 18th century. The organ, sometimes called 'king of instruments', can reproduce an almost unlimited range of sounds at very loud or soft volume.

Electric organs were first widely made in the 1930s and became popular in homes as well as cinemas, dance halls, etc. Some modern varieties, producing sound by electro-mechanical means, are capable of extraordinary effects.

Organ is a group of animal or plant cells which carry out a definite task. The leaf is a plant organ. Its job is to allow carbon dioxide and oxygen to enter and leave the plant. The leaf also manufactures food by trapping the energy of sunlight and using it to produce sugars. Animals have many organs. The heart is an animal organ whose job is to pump blood around the body, and it is composed mainly of special muscle cells. Other animal organs include the kidneys, the skin and the eyes.

Organic chemistry is the study of carbon compounds. At one time, it was the study of the chemistry of living organisms. This is why it is known as 'organic'.

All things contain carbon. Petroleum, rubber and plastic are some of the many familiar

The great organ of Ste Clotilde, Paris.

substances made with carbon compounds.

Carbon forms hundreds of thousands of compounds, far more compounds than those of all the other elements put together. This is because its atoms can join together to form long chains or rings.

Orkney is a group of 67 islands separated from the north Scottish coast by the 10 km (6 mile) wide Pentland Firth. Area 905 sq km (349 sq miles); capital, Kirkwall. Dairy farming, fishing, distilling and tourism are the main industries. The island of Flotta has an oil pipeline and tanker terminal.

Ormer, see Abalone.

Orwell, George (1903–1950), was a British writer, whose real name was Eric Blair. He came from a privileged background, but had socialist sympathies. He fought for the Republicans in the Spanish Civil War, and wrote *Homage to Catalonia* (1938) as a result. Later, his horror of totalitarianism inspired his most famous books, *Animal Farm* (1945), in which a farm falls under the rule of a Stalinist pig, and *1984* (1949), a frightening picture of a future society under totalitarian rule. He wrote a number of other novels and many critical essays. Orwell was widely admired for his moral courage and honesty.

Oscar is the name given to the gold statuettes awarded by the American Academy of Motion Picture Arts and Sciences for outstanding achievements in the cinema. Oscars, or Academy Awards, have been presented every year since 1929 for the best film, best director, best musical score and so on, of the previous year. Candidates for awards are nominated by members of the Academy. Even a nomination that does not win an Award is regarded as an achievement worth advertising. The statuettes are said to have been nicknamed after the Academy Librarian's uncle Oscar.

Osiris, a god of ancient Egypt, was husband (and brother) of Isis. At first he was a simple nature god, who died in the winter and was reborn in the spring. Later he was worshipped as the god of the dead, and he became the most important of the Egyptian gods. Legend has it that he gave the people their laws, their knowledge of farming, and their religion. Having established himself in Egypt, he then went on to conquer the world.

Osiris was killed by his evil brother Set, but Isis restored him to life. However, he preferred to give up his earthly rule and retired to reign over the dead.

Osprey, or fish hawk, is a mainly brown and white bird of prey, which hunts for fish. It soars above rivers, lakes and coastal waters, and plunges from a height of 30 m (100 ft) to grab fish in its talons. The talons have special spiky scales on them to prevent the slippery prey from escaping. The osprey is 51 to 61 cm (20 to 24 in) long. It lays its eggs in a nest built high in the trees.

Osteopathy is a type of medical treatment started by an American doctor, Andrew Still. Our bodies are each supported by a skeleton of bones. Dr Still thought that all illnesses were caused by faults in this skeleton. Today, doctors think that only some illnesses can be helped by osteopathy.

Osteopaths massage or manipulate the body to try to find any faults and to correct them. They may also look at the bones using X-rays.

Ostrich is the largest bird in the world, a fully grown male standing 2.4 m (8 ft) tall. It cannot fly but is the world's fastest running bird. With its long legs and clawed feet it can outpace many other animals, too. Male ostriches have black and white plumage, and females have brown plumage. Both sexes have large, round bodies carried on naked legs, for feathers would get in the way when running. The head and most of the neck is also featherless. The ostrich inhabits the open plains and scrublands of eastern and southern Africa, and used to live in Asia.

Otter is an aquatic, carnivorous mammal related to the weasel. It is much bigger than the weasel, however, with a broader, flattened face and small ears. Most species have webbed hind feet to aid swimming. Otters catch most of their food in the water, and their diet is mainly fish. The common otter of Eurasia builds a den in the river bank and comes out at night to hunt. It is a playful animal, and family groups often spend much time sliding down the bank into the water. The sea otter is an almost entirely marine animal, only coming ashore to give birth. It eats clams, crabs and fish. To get inside tough shells, it lies on its back in the water, places the crab or mollusc on its stomach, and hits it with a stone held between its paws.

Ottoman Empire was a Muslim Turkish state which ruled Anatolia (Asia Minor), south-eastern Europe, the Middle East and a large part of North Africa from the 14th to the 20th centuries. The empire was founded in the 13th century by Osman I as a small Turkish state in north-western Anatolia, but rapidly expanded over the whole peninsula and into Greece. In 1453 the Ottomans captured Constantinople, which they made their capital, thus putting an end to the Byzantine Empire. In the 16th century they brought Egypt, Syria and Algeria under their control, but suffered their first serious defeat at the Battle of Lepanto (1571). In 1683 they reached Vienna, but from this period the empire went into a decline, gradually losing its territories. It finally collapsed in 1922 when Turkey became a republic.

Mahomet II, the Ottoman sultan who captured Constantinople in 1453.

Owl is a bird of prey with a large head, forward-facing eyes and a short tail. Its feathers have special edges that prevent them rustling as it flies. Like other birds of prey, owls have powerful talons for grasping their prey, but they do not possess large powerful beaks because they usually swallow their prey whole, instead of tearing pieces off. Most owls hunt by night, lying in a tree hole or disused building by day. They have extremely good hearing, and can detect the faintest sound made by a small animal. There are over 120 different species of owl, ranging in size from the sparrow-sized elf owl to the eagle owl which is 76 cm (30 in) long.

Oxidation is the joining, chemically, of a substance with oxygen. Compounds, such as oxides, are formed. For example, if a piece of iron is left outside it becomes rusty. The iron has combined with oxygen in the air to form a red substance. When substances such as coal burn, they combine with oxygen. The oxygen we breathe in, joins with compounds in the blood. These are all examples of oxidation reactions.

Other chemical reactions, such as those in which substances lose hydrogen, are also called oxidation reactions.

Oxygen has the chemical symbol O. This element is a colourless gas with no taste or smell. About one-fifth of the air is oxygen. All living things need oxygen. Humans breathe it in from the air; fishes use the air dissolved in water to breathe and plants take in oxygen in a compound called carbon dioxide.

There is more oxygen than any other element in the Earth's crust. Nearly half of the crust is oxygen in compounds. Oxygen forms many compounds, for example, water is a compound of hydrogen and oxygen.

High in the air there is not enough oxygen to breathe, and deep underground the air is often not pure enough to breathe. So climbers, underwater swimmers and sometimes miners, carry cylinders containing oxygen and other substances.

Many substances burn in air to form compounds with oxygen. Some gases, burnt in oxygen, produce a flame hot enough to cut through metals. Substances are burnt in oxygen to launch and drive space rockets. *See also* Acetylene; Ozone

Oyster is a bivalve mollusc – that is, its shell consists of two halves, or valves. It lies on the seabed with its shell slightly open, and pumps water and tiny food particles into its body. Some kinds of oyster are vaulable food sources for people; and the pearl oyster is important because it produces pearls. Pearls begin as tiny grains of sand or other foreign bodies which become lodged under the oyster's shell. The oyster then covers the particle with layer upon layer of a lustrous material called nacre, eventually producing a pearl.

Oystercatchers are coastal birds, all six species being similar in shape and life style. They feed on shellfish, using their tough bills to stab their way into the shell to reach the animal inside. The European oystercatcher is a striking black and white bird, with an orange bill and pink legs. Its 'kleep-kleep' call is often heard. Other oystercatchers occur in North America and Australia. Male oystercatchers perform a dance before a female during mating time. Sometimes two males try to 'outdance' each other to win the favours of the female.

Ozone is a form of oxygen. When three oxygen atoms join together, they form an ozone molecule. Like oxygen, it is a colourless gas, but it has a slight smell. It can be made by passing electric sparks through oxygen. Electric motors sometimes smell of ozone.

There is a layer of ozone in the atmosphere. This stops harmful radiations from the Sun reaching the Earth.

Ozone kills germs, and is sometimes used to clean drinking water and to clean the air in crowded places such as underground railway stations. Ozone also makes many substances turn white and is used as a bleach.

P

Pacific Ocean is the world's largest ocean, lying between Asia and the Americas. Area about 165 000 000 sq km (64 000 000 sq miles). In the Marianas Trench, it is over 11 000 m (36 000 ft) deep. The Pacific contains a great many islands, Australia being the largest. Although it covers one-third of the Earth's surface, it was unknown to Europeans until the 16th century. Magellan sailed across it (1520) but it was not properly explored until the days of Captain Cook, in the 18th century. The Pacific is surrounded by volcanic mountain ranges and receives few great rivers. Probably the world's richest fishing grounds are in the North Pacific.

Paddle steamer is a ship or boat propelled by large rotating paddle wheels, either one on each side of the hull or one at the rear. The first system was most popular on early steamships, because one paddle wheel could be reversed while the other turned forward, making the ship very manoeuvrable. The invention of the screw propeller in 1835 led to a rapid end of paddle ships, because the screw, being totally underwater, is much more efficient and less vulnerable to accidental damage. A few paddle steamers survive, however, and are used for pleasure cruises at holiday resorts.

Pakistan is a republic of Asia, occupying the north-western corner of the Indian sub-continent. Capital, Islamabad; area about 803 940 sq km (310 400 sq miles).
History Pakistan was created an independent state in 1947 from the predominantly Muslim regions of the former Indian Empire. It consisted of two parts, West and East Pakistan, separated by 1450 km (900 miles) of India. The constitution was suspended in 1956 and in 1962 a presidential type of gov-

A woman in traditional Pakistani dress.

ernment came into force. In 1971 the eastern province withdrew from the alliance and, after a bitter war involving India, became the independent state of Bangladesh. Pakistan left the Commonwealth of Nations in 1972 and after a period of civilian rule the army assumed control of the country in 1978. (For history previous to 1947 see India.)
Land Pakistan has a varied landscape. There are mountains, plains, swamps and deserts, but it is predominantly a dry region. The River Indus which crosses the country, is a life-line providing water for the towns, irrigation for crops and also some hydro-electric power.
People The people are of mixed descent, but there are several distinct groups. The largest is the Punjabis (60 per cent). Another important group is the Sindhis (13 per cent). Urdu is the official language but English is used in business and government.
Economy Pakistan has deposits of natural gas, and some coal, iron ore and other minerals. Most of the people are occupied in farming and the main crops are wheat, cotton, maize, sugar cane and rice. There are some industries including textiles, food processing and chemicals.

Palaeontology is the study of the animals and plants that have lived on the Earth in the past. Palaeontologists look at the preserved remains of living things, called fossils. Fossils can show when things lived and what they might have looked like.

Fossils also show how much the Earth has changed over the hundred of millions of years since life started. For example, fossils of sea creatures can be found in inland rocks, which shows that these rocks must have been under water in the past. Fossils of tropical plants can be found in cold countries, which shows that these countries must have been much hotter in the past.

Paleozoic is an era in a history of the Earth, known from the study of rocks and of fossil remains found in them (the geological record). Paleozoic means 'ancient life', and the era begins with the first abundant and well-preserved fossils, about 570 million years ago. It ends about 225 million years ago with the beginning of the great age of reptiles. There were many developments over this huge era, culminating in the establishment of life on land.

Palestine was a country in south-west Asia, roughly equivalent to the modern state of Israel which has taken its place. Area about 26000 sq km (10000 sq miles) – the Holy Land of Palestine in the Bible was somewhat larger. Palestine was governed by the British, under the Mandate of the League of Nations, from 1920 to 1948. In 1948 the independent State of Israel was proclaimed and many Palestinian Arabs left and became refugees in neighbouring countries. Many have waged violent campaigns to regain their homeland.

Palladio, Andrea (1508–1580), was an Italian architect. He revived ancient Roman ideas on harmony of proportions, which depended on a relationship between architecture and music (e.g. if two strings, one half as long as the other, are plucked, the shorter string gives a note one octave higher; this means that a ratio of 1:2 is a 'good' proportion). Palladio aimed to recapture the glory of ancient Rome, and built villas that look like Classical temples. He was extremely influential, especially in England where the Neo- ('new-') Classical style in the 18th century was named 'Palladian'.

Palms comprise 2500 species of tree distributed throughout the warmer countries of the world. All palms have tall trunks, bearing at the top a crown of feathery, frond-like leaves. Many species of palm are of economic importance. Dates, coconuts, sago and oils are some of the more valuable products that come from palms.

Pampas are the huge grassy plains in Argentina, extending from the Andes to the Atlantic Ocean. The western plains are mainly arid, but the eastern pampas are temperate, well-watered and fertile. Their most striking natural feature is abundant pampas grass, which often stands as high as a tall person. Today they are peaceful farming areas used for the production of cereals and flax, and the raising of sheep and cattle for Argentina's meat industry.

Pan was a minor god in Greek myth. He was the son of Hermes and therefore grandson of Zeus, and the god of flocks and fields. He was pictured as part man and part goat, often playing his pipe, or syrinx (a kind of mouth organ). Pan was a simple, crude and vigorous character, the companion of shepherds. He often chased after women, and had the ability to make people in a crowd feel sudden, unreasonable fear, or 'panic'.

Panama is a republic in Central America, occupying the Isthmus of Panama. Capital, Panama City; area about 77 000 sq km (30 000 sq miles). It became part of Colombia in the 19th century but gained independence in 1903.

Panama is mountainous, with narrow coastal plains. The volcanic soil is fertile but scarce, and the mountains are forested. The Panama Canal is an important source of income, and coffee, sugar and bananas are exported. Fishing is imporant, but raw materials are in short supply. Panama has a huge, foreign-owned merchant fleet because of its low ship registry fees.

Panama Canal is a canal which crosses the isthmus of Panama and connects the Atlantic and Pacific Oceans. Construction of a canal was begun in 1881 by a French company under Ferdinand de Lesseps but came to an end when the company went bankrupt. In 1903 the United States negotiated an agreement with Panama, which gave it the right to build a canal, and to control the land on either side of it (the Canal Zone). The canal was eventually opened in 1914. In 1979, under a new treaty, Panama re-gained sovereignty over the Canal Zone. The canal is 82 km (51 miles) long.

Pancreas is a gland found in most vertebrates, and its job is to aid the digestion of food. It is connected to the small intestine by a tube, or duct. It produces a substance called pancreatic juice, containing enzymes which break down proteins, starch and oils.

Also found within the pancreas is a collection of cells called the Islets of Langerhans, which produce insulin. Insulin controls the amount of glucose in the blood. When there is too much, insulin prevents any more being produced from glycogen in the liver. *See also* Glands.

Panda is a mammal related to the raccoon. The giant panda is a large, black and white, bear-like animal. It is up to 1.5 m (5 ft) tall, and it sits up and rolls playfully about. The giant panda lives in the bamboo forests of Tibet and China, and eats mainly the shoots and stems of bamboo. It may spend as long as 12 hours a day just sitting and eating.

The red panda lives in the mountainous regions of Nepal and China. It has red fur and a cat-like face. It lives in the trees, and eats fruits, buds and leaves.

Giant panda

Pankhurst, Emmeline (1858–1928), was a British suffragette. In 1903 she founded the Women's Social and Political Union in order to agitate for the right of women to vote. She was actively assisted by her two daughters, Christabel and Sylvia, and increasingly used more violent tactics to draw attention to her cause. Emmeline was imprisoned several times and released after hunger strikes. During the First World War she brought her campaign to a halt and devoted her energies to the war effort. All women in Britain over the age of 21 received the right to vote in 1928, the year of her death.

Papaw is a giant-sized herb with a crown of large, many lobed leaves. It is native to South America, but is also grown in tropical and subtropical Asia, Africa and Australia. The plant can reach a height of 7.6 m (25 ft), and produces a yellowish melon-shaped fruit weighing up to 1.8 kg (4 lb). The fruit is rich in vitamin A, and is used to make drinks, jams and preserves. Even the latex of the plant is useful – it contains an enzyme used in medicine.

Paper is a substance used for writing on, printing, wrapping and so on, which is manufactured from vegetable matter. It was invented in about 3500 BC by the ancient Egyptians, who used strips from the stems of papyrus grass reeds. These strips were flattened, laid out in a criss-cross pattern, dampened and pressed into sheets.

In AD 105 something closer to modern paper was invented in China by Ts'ai Lun, who beat plants, nets and rags until they were broken down into a pulp that could be flattened and dried out. Knowledge of Ts'ai Lun's discovery travelled very slowly, reaching the Arabs in the 8th century and northern Europe by the late 14th century. After the invention of printing, paper was often in short supply but no significant improvements occurred in paper-making until early in the 19th century. Then wood-pulp became the main material used, and machines began to do much of the work.

Today, nearly all paper is made from fast-growing trees such as fir, pine and spruce. The tree logs are cut into thin pieces and heated with water and other chemicals. This forms a soft mixture called wood pulp, which is cleaned and whitened. It then flows on to a wire mesh where it is pressed and dried to form paper sheets or rolls.

Waste paper, with the ink or dye removed, is used to make recycled paper.

Emmeline Pankhurst speaking to her followers.

Parable is a story which contains a moral or lesson. It is similar to a fable, but is usually religious – as in the parables of Jesus recorded in the Bible.

Paraguay is a republic in central South America. Capital, Asunción; area about 407 000 sq km (157 000 sq miles). After independence from Spain (1811) it lost territory in border disputes with its larger neighbours.

Divided by the Paraguay River, much of the land is low, wooded plains and swamp, but is more hilly in the east. The population is mainly of mixed Indian and Spanish descent, and most people live in the fertile lands bordering the Paraguay River, where the soil is rich. Cattle, twice as numerous as people, provide the chief exports, followed by timber. Minerals are scarce and industry limited.

Parakeet is the name given to small, long-tailed members of the parrot family. The Carolina parakeet was once common in North America but is now extinct. The best-known parakeet is the budgerigar. In Australia budgerigars live in flocks in the wild. The plumage of wild budgerigars is green and yellow; other colours, such as blue, are only found in captive-bred birds.

A hagfish, an external parasite, boring into a haddock

Parasite is an animal or plant which lives upon another organism (called the host) and feeds upon its tissues for food. A parasite may be *facultative*, (it is usually free-living or in the case of plants, lives on dead material, but can become parasitic if the opportunity arises); or it may be *obligate* (it cannot survive without a particular host). Parasites may also be *external*, in which case they cling to the outside skin of their host, or *internal*, where they live within the body of the host.

Lice are external parasites which feed on the blood of their hosts. The eel-like hagfish is another external parasite. The protozoan which causes the disease malaria is an internal parasite living in the blood of the host. The disease of crops called rust is caused by an internal parasitic fungus.

Paris is the capital of France. It has been the capital since the 10th century and has been at the heart of French history every since.

One of Europe's most attractive cities, it is a port on the River Seine. The cathedral of Notre Dame is on an island in the river. Paris is the chief cultural centre and seat of government and also the leading industrial city in France. The city is very popular with tourists who flock to the theatres, art galleries, palaces, fashion shows and restaurants. The Eiffel Tower, although only built in 1889 is the best-known symbol of Paris. Many of the famous streets, squares and monuments also date from the 19th century.

Parliament in Britain developed from the Great Council of the Realm, which was an advisory body to the monarch consisting of nobles and high churchmen. In the 13th century representatives of other classes were also summoned, and Parliament has been based at Westminster, London, since that time. By the reign of Edward III the two groups had become divided into Lords and Commons, each meeting separately. Gradually Parliament began to increase its powers and during the reign of Elizabeth I it demanded a still greater voice in the country's affairs. In the reign of Charles I the conflict between King and Parliament for supreme power came to a head and ended in Civil War. The Bill of Rights (1689) acknowledged the supremacy of Parliament, and the 18th century saw the development of political parties. The power of the House of Lords was severely reduced in the 19th century, and by the early 20th century the Commons was elected by universal suffrage. Most other parliamentary systems in the world are based on the British Parliament. *See also* Commons, House of; Lords, House of.

Parnell, Charles Stewart (1846–1891), was an Irish nationalist leader. Elected to Parliament in 1875, he soon became leader of the Home Rule movement for Ireland, and also associated himself with the popular agitation for land reform, which culminated in the Irish Land Act of 1881. He gave his support to the Prime Minister, W E Gladstone, on the promise that Gladstone would attempt to pass a Home Rule Bill through Parliament. However, the Bill failed in 1886, and Gladstone's Liberal Party was permanently divided. Parnell lost the leadership of the Irish nationalists in 1890 when he became involved in a divorce case.

Parrots (not including other members of the parrot family such as macaws, lorikeets and cockatoos) are generally stocky birds with large, hooked beaks, long wings and squarish tails. Parrots are found mainly in Australia, New Guinea, Africa and South America, and are from 7.5 to 90 cm (3 in to 3 ft) high. They live in the trees, often in noisy flocks, and feed on fruit and seeds, tearing the food apart with their powerful beaks. The best-known parrot is the African grey parrot. This bird, which has a beautiful red tail, is very intelligent and can be taught to imitate the human voice.

New Zealand also has three species of parrot. One, the kakapo, is very rare, and is unusual in that it does not fly and is nocturnal.

African grey parrot

Parsec is a unit used in astronomy to measure the distances of stars. It is 3.3 light years or 31 million million km (19 million million miles). It is often written as pc. For very distant stars, even bigger units are used. The kiloparsec or kpc is one thousand parsecs.

The megaparsec or mpc is one million parsecs. The most distant object from the Earth that can be identified is 55 000 megaparsecs away. If this were written in kilometres or miles, the figure would have 25 numbers. This is why another larger unit is used.

Parthenon is an ancient Greek temple. It is one of the most famous and beautiful of all buildings, and stands on the Acropolis.

In 480 BC the Persians destroyed the fortifications and temples of the Acropolis, which the Athenians – then reaching the height of their ancient glory – rebuilt in even more splendid style. The Parthenon, dedicated to the goddess Athena Parthenos (the Virgin Athena), was the largest of these new buildings. It survived the decline of Athens and remained in good condition until 1687, when it was blown up by the Venetians.

Inside the Parthenon stood a huge ivory and gold statue of the goddess by the sculptor Phidias, but this has long since vanished. Other statues and carvings in relief decorated the outside of the temple, and many of these were brought to England by Lord Elgin, in about 1812. These, the 'Elgin Marbles', are now in the British Museum, London.

Pasteur, Louis (1822–1895), was a French chemist, who became Professor of Chemistry at the Sorbonne, Paris. He is best known for his work on tiny living things known as bacteria. His work formed the basis for bacteriology, the study of bacteria.

He showed that bacteria cause many common diseases. He inoculated sheep and cows against anthrax, which led to inoculations being used to prevent diptheria, cholera and other common human diseases.

In many countries, milk is pasteurized (treated) by being kept at a high temperature for a period of time before it is drunk. This treatment kills the bacteria in the milk.

Patagonia is a region in southern South America. Area about 805 000 sq km (311 000 sq miles). It is a high, dry, bleak plateau region, mostly in Argentina, partly in Chile. Many of the people are of Welsh origin. It is used mainly for grazing, but there are coal and oil reserves.

Patent is a form of protection stopping anybody, except the inventor, making or selling an invention. Only inventions which can be built and used, such as machines and gadgets, can be patented. Other discoveries are not protected in this way. In some countries, certain drugs, medicines and special health-foods may be patented.

Paterson, Andrew Barton 'Banjo' (1864–1941), was an Australian poet and writer. He was famous for bush ballads, including *Waltzing Matilda* (1917). Bush ballads are early Australian ballads, often with a recurring chorus and lively rhythm, which celebrate the exploits of early Australian pioneers and settlers. They were transmitted orally, and are part of Australian folklore.

Patrick, Saint (circa 389–461), is the patron saint of Ireland. He was born in Scotland, captured by pirates and sold as a slave in Ireland. He escaped to Gaul (France) but felt a call to return to Ireland as a missionary.

There are many legends about his mission, like his ridding Ireland of snakes or his use of a shamrock leaf to explain the Trinity. He does seem to have been responsible for turning a mainly pagan country into a Christian one, and he founded many churches and monasteries.

Paul, Saint, was an apostle of Christianity, originally called Saul. He died a martyr in Rome in AD 64 or 65. Originally a persecutor of Christians, he was suddenly converted on the road to Damascus, when the voice of Jesus spoke to him.

He is known as the 'apostle to the Gentiles', for he was largely responsible for spreading knowledge of Jesus and his teaching to non-Jewish peoples, and he freed Christianity from Jewish law and custom. On his missionary journeys, which are recorded in the *Acts of the Apostles*, he made numerous converts and founded many churches. He is sometimes regarded as the co-founder of the Christian religion.

St Paul was a man of extraordinary intelligence and inspired energy, who would even preach to the guard when he was in prison. Many of his letters to the new churches he founded are preserved in the New Testament.

Pavlova, Anna (1881–1931), was a Russian dancer. One of the outstanding figures in the history of ballet, her first great success was in *The Dying Swan* (1907). It was choreographed by Fokine, whose efforts to make ballet more expressive and more natural she greatly assisted by her grace and sensitivity as a performer. Her greatest fame as a dancer resulted from her appearances on tour with Diaghilev's Ballet Russe and with her own company. From her base in London she became a great ambassador for classical ballet, and her name was known to people who were not interested in ballet.

Peacock, see Peafowl.

Peafowl live in the jungles and forests of India and China. The male bird, called a peacock, is famous for its beautiful array of tail feathers which it raises to attract the female, producing a shimmering fan of blue, green and bronze colours. The female is called a peahen, and is a much less colourful bird. Peafowl are omnivorous, gobbling up all manner of food items with their stout, hooked bills. Their bodies are 75 cm (30 in) long.

Pearl is a precious stone formed by certain bivalve molluscs, particularly some oysters. When a grain of sand or some other irritant becomes lodged inside the oyster's shell, the creature may neutralize it by surrounding it with layer after layer of nacre (composed mainly of calcium carbonate), which forms a pearl.

Pearls vary greatly in size and shape. The most precious are perfectly round and unblemished, lustrous, translucent and iri-

The Japanese attack Pearl Harbor, Hawaii.

descent. The finest are usually found in the Persian Gulf and the Indian Ocean.

Cultivated pearls are produced by inserting irritants into oysters and then allowing the pearl-making process to take place. Imitation pearls are made from glass or plastic.

Pearl Harbor was an American naval base in Hawaii. The Pacific Fleet of the USA was there when it was attacked by Japanese aircraft on 7 December 1941. The attack, which came as a complete surprise to the Americans, was launched from Japanese aircraft carriers in the Pacific Ocean and resulted in the sinking of several American battleships and the destruction of more than 200 aircraft. Its result was to bring the USA into the Second World War.

Peasants' Revolt was a rebellion which took place in south-east England in 1381. Growing discontent among the people at the miserable conditions in which they were forced to live reached a climax when they were compelled to pay a poll tax. A large number of peasants led by Wat Tyler and John Ball marched on London. The young King Richard II, met them at Smithfield and granted all their demands. At a later meeting with the King, Tyler was stabbed to death by the Lord Mayor of London. The rebellion was then brutally suppressed, and the concessions made by the King were withdrawn.

Peat is the accumulation of dead plant material in conditions which are lacking in oxygen. Because of the lack of oxygen the plant material does not fully decompose. Peat is especially common in upland boggy or lowland fen areas. The peat may form a layer several metres deep. Near the bottom it is a brown, solid material, but near the surface it is possible to see plants like sphagnum moss, which thrives in these damp, acid conditions. In countries such as Ireland, peat is cut out of the ground and dried for use as fuel.

Peccary is a South American pig. Unlike other pigs, its upper tusks curve downwards and its hind limbs have only three toes rather than four. Peccaries live in family groups of over 100 individuals. They root around at the edges of forests for fruit, seeds and the occasional insect, worm or other small animal. Peccaries are common prey for big cats and snakes.

Peel, Sir Robert (1788–1850), was a British statesman. Elected to the House of Commons in 1809, as Home Secretary (1822–1827 and 1828–1830) he introduced important prison reforms, established the Metropolitan Police (1829) and secured the passage of the Catholic Emancipation Act through Parliament (1829). His Tamworth Manifesto of 1834 laid the foundations of the Conservative Party. As Prime Minister in the 1840s he made further reforms, including the repeal of the Corn Laws in 1846, which caused his party to split. Those who supported repeal subsequently joined the Liberal Party.

Pegasus, in Greek legend, was a winged horse. He sprang from the body of Medusa when Perseus cut off her head. Another hero, Bellerophon, tried to catch him, but no earthly bridle would hold him. Then Athena provided a heavenly bridle, and Bellerophon was able to ride Pegasus, enabling him to defeat the monster called the Chimera. Later, Pegasus threw him off when he tried to ride up to heaven.

Peking is the capital of China. The old walled city dates from Kublai Khan's time (1215–1294). Part of the old city, the Forbidden City, contains the imperial palaces, and is now a museum area. Though it is not the largest city in China, it is the chief cultural centre and seat of government. In Peking today, there is extensive industrial development in the east, since the Communist revolution, and the main, modern, residential area is to the west. Peking is perhaps more correctly spelt Beijing.

Pelican is a large, fish-eating water bird which is found throughout the warmer regions of the world. With its long neck and huge beak, it is rather ungainly on land, but can swim and fly very well. Beneath the beak is a large extendable pouch. When fishing for food, pelicans use this pouch as a net, swimming along with their beak open in the water, and scooping up fish as they go.

Penguin is a flightless bird found in the Southern Hemisphere. No other group of birds is so well adapted to a life spent in and around water. The tiny wings are used for swimming, but penguins are so graceful when they swim that they appear to be flying through the water. They use their tails and webbed feet for steering, as they glide about searching for fish to eat. Penguins can live in the coldest places, huddled together on the frozen ice floes to keep warm, although some species live in fairly warm climates. King and Emperor penguins grow to 1.2 m (4 ft) tall.

Penicillin is an antibiotic discovered in 1928 by the Scottish scientist Sir Alexander Fleming. He discovered that penicillin killed bacteria and might, therefore, be used to treat infections. Penicillin was not developed as an effective medicine until the Second World War. Now it can be made synthetically, and is used to fight many different infections.

Penny Farthing, see Bicycle.

Percussion is a family of musical instruments which are played by striking a surface, usually with a stick. Drums are the most obvious example. Others are the xylophone and the triangle. Percussion is probably the oldest kind of musical instrument. Some modern composers have written music for percussion of curious kinds, such as motor horns and even typewriters.

Perennial plant is one which continues to grow year after year. In some perennial plants – known as herbaceous perennials – the parts above ground wither and die at the onset of winter, and the plant sprouts new stems and leaves the following spring. Examples of herbaceous perennials are daffodils and irises. Woody perennials keep their stems all through the year, although some species may lose their leaves. Trees and shrubs are woody perennials.

Pericles (circa 495–429 BC), was an Athenian statesman whose powers of leadership and superb oratory made him a dominant figure in Athens during the period of its greatest glory. He introduced important reforms, tightened control of his country's maritime empire and was a notable patron of the arts and drama. He was responsible for the construction of the Parthenon and other notable buildings. Pericles foresaw that conflict between Athens and Sparta was inevitable and took defensive precautions, but was unable to prevent the disaster that was to follow in the course of the Peloponnesian War. He died of the plague.

Periodic table is a table which lists and groups together the elements that make up all the substances in the world. There are 92 elements in or on the Earth. More have been made by machines. Each element is known by a symbol, which is often a shortened form of its name. Each element also has a number called its atomic number.

The periodic table shows the elements listed in the order of their atomic number, starting with number 1, hydrogen. Similar elements are grouped, one below the other, in the table.

A 'battery' of drums and percussion effects.

Darius I King of Persia, 521–486 BC

Permian is a period in the history of the Earth, known from the study of rocks and of the fossil remains found in them (the geological record). It is named after Perm, USSR, where such rocks occur.

The Permian period is the last major division of the Paleozoic era, following the Carboniferous. It began about 280 million years ago and lasted for about 55 million years. It was the period when reptiles became widely established on land. They survived the upheavals that marked the end of the Permian and became the dominant animals in the Triassic period, which followed it.

Perseus, a hero in Greek legend, was the son of Zeus by a mortal princess, Danae. Perseus' most famous adventure was killing the Gorgon Medusa. He was helped by gods and goddesses, who gave him winged shoes, a shield like a mirror (so that he would not have to look directly at the Gorgon) and a cap which made him invisible.

On his way home with Medusa's head in a bag, he rescued Andromeda, who was chained to a rock as a sacrifice to a sea monster.

Persian Empire was founded in 549 BC by Cyrus the Great. In the 6th century BC Cyrus became King of the Persians while they were still a small tribe and persuaded them to overthrow their overlords the Medes. Within a few years he had freed Persia completely and went on to found a vast empire. Before his death in 530 BC he had conquered Anatolia (Asia Minor), Babylon, Syria and Palestine. Under his son, Cambyses, the empire was extended to include Egypt. Darius I brought Thrace into the empire and pushed its boundary as far as north-western India, but failed in his efforts to conquer the Greeks. The empire finally collapsed in 331 BC when it was attacked by Alexander the Great.

Persian Gulf is part of the Arabian Sea, between Arabia and Iran. Area about

233000 sq km (90000 sq miles). There are many islands and shoals. The area of the Gulf contains many large oil fields and a large proportion of the world's known oil reserves.

Peru is a republic in western South America. Capital, Lima; area about 1285000 sq km (496000 sq miles). Peru was the centre of the Inca empire, but it was conquered in 1533 by the Spaniards who held it until 1824. Since then it has engaged in local wars over territory and suffered periods of dictatorial rule. In the 1980s it had a democratically elected government.

Beyond the coastal desert plain, the Andes rise. To the west a hilly region descends to the low-lying plain of the upper Amazon. The cold Humboldt (Peru) Current chills the dry coast, but the lowlands are generally hot and wet. About half the Peruvians are pure Indian; the other half is of mainly European descent. Agriculture is the chief occupation, though farming land is scarce; potatoes are an important food crop.

Llamas and alpacas, as well as sheep, are raised for wool. Fishing and forest products are important, and there are various mineral resources, including some oil. Hydro-electric power has great possibilities. Peru is famous for textiles, and its scenery and ancient ruins attract many tourists.

Petal is one of the parts of a flower. Petals are formed from modified leaves. Together, the collection of petals on a flower is called a corolla. Petals vary greatly from one species of flowering plant to another. However, they are usually brightly coloured, for their job is to advertise the presence of the flower so that insects and other animals will visit the flower and pollinate it. To make the visit worthwhile, many petals provide sugary nectar at their bases, which the visiting animals drink.

Peter, Saint, was the first of the Twelve Apostles of Jesus, who died a martyr in Rome, circa AD 67. His original name was Simon. Jesus named him Peter, meaning 'stone', and called him the rock on which the Church would be built. With his fellow fisherman Andrew and the brothers James and John, he was one of Jesus' earliest followers and often acted as the spokesman for the apostles. A vigorous, powerful, but impetuous man, he once said he would never deny Jesus but later, in fear of arrest, he did so.

After the Crucifixion, St Peter was the effective leader of the Christians. He travelled widely as a missionary, and two epistles (letters) in the New Testament are believed to be his. He is regarded as the first bishop of Rome and therefore the founder of the Papacy.

Peter the Great (1672–1725), was Tsar (1682–1721) and later Emperor (1721–1725) of Russia. After gaining an outlet for Russia to the Black Sea by defeating the Turks, he travelled extensively in Europe to gain knowledge of Western institutions. On his return he began to modernize Russia, introducing reforms in administration, education, trade and the army, and he also founded a navy. His victory over the Swedes in 1709 gave Russia access to the Baltic. By the time of his death he had, by the use of often ruthless methods, laid the foundations of a modern state and made Russia an important European power.

Petrarch (1304–1374), was an Italian poet, one of the forerunners of the Renaissance. He spent much of his life travelling on diplomatic missions for Italian princely families, but his best work was written in Vaucluse, France. Though he wrote more in Latin, his fame depends on works in Italian. Much of his poetry was inspired by a mysterious woman called Laura.

Petrarch perfected the form of the sonnet, adopted by later poets. A famous scholar, he collected ancient manuscripts from all over Europe (there were no printed books at that time) and modelled his writing on Classical authors.

Petrochemical is a chemical made from petroleum. In a refinery, petrol, paraffin, diesel oil and other substances are taken out of the petroleum. Petrochemicals are made from what is left. These are used in the manufacture of many things, including plastics, rubbers, drugs, dyes and cosmetics.

Petroleum or crude oil, is a thick black liquid. It is thought to be the remains of plants and animals that were buried millions of years ago. The petroleum then rose up through the Earth until it was trapped in pockets in the rocks. These pockets are called oil fields. Petroleum is often found with natural gas.

To get the petroleum, wells are drilled up to several kilometres (miles) deep. Wells may be drilled under the sea or on land.

The petroleum is taken, often by large ships called oil tankers, to refineries for processing.

Phalanger is one of the numerous marsupials which live in Australasia. They are nocturnal, living in trees, and are mainly herbivorous, but also eat insects and small animals. The family includes mouse-like, squirrel-like and lemur-like forms and the teddy-bear form, the koala.

The brush-tailed phalanger is the most widely distributed Australian marsupial, being found over most of the country.

The Australian opossums were given their name by Captain Cook in 1770, because of their superficial resemblance to the American opossum. Today the Australian ones are often called 'possums' to distinguish them. The more suitable name phalanger refers to the adaptation of some of the phalanges (finger and toe bones) to help climbing.

Philip II (1527–1598), was King of Spain (1556–1598). The son of the Emperor Charles V, in 1554 he married Mary I, Queen of England. During his reign Spain was the dominant power in Europe, and in 1580 he added Portugal to his possessions. However, his intolerance and repressive policies drove his Dutch subjects into open rebellion. Philip's failure to conquer England with the Armada in 1588 marked the beginning of Spain's decline, and when he died his country's resources had been exhausted by continual wars.

Philippines, Republic of the, is an island republic in south-east Asia. Capital, Manila; area about 300 000 sq km (116 000 sq miles). The Philippines were discovered by Magellan and were mainly under Spanish rule until the Spanish-American war brought them under US control in 1898. Following Japanese occupation, they became independent in 1946.

There are over 7000 islands, of which Luzon and Mindanao are the largest. They are generally mountainous, with broad plains and valleys in the larger islands. Despite the sea, temperatures are high and so is rainfall, and cyclones and earthquakes are frequent dangers. The people are a mixture, but most are of Indonesian and Malay descent. Roman Catholicism is the chief religion, but there is a Muslim minority. The typical Filipino is a small farmer, and the main exports are coconut products, sugar and natural fibres, such as Manila hemp. Forestry and mining are also significant.

Phoenicia was an ancient country comprising a group of city-states along the narrow coastal plain of Syria. The Phoenicians were a seafaring Semitic people who settled in the region some time during the second millennium (2000) BC and founded cities, of which Tyre and Sidon were the most important. In the early part of the 2nd millennium they ventured further westward and established colonies and trading posts at Carthage and in southern Spain. Their commercial activities covered the whole Mediterranean world: they exported cedar wood, textiles, purple dyes and glassware. Phoenicia was never a strong power and in turn came under Assyrian, Persian, Greek and finally Roman domination. One outstanding Phoenician contribution to civilization was the invention of the alphabet, which was later developed by the Greeks.

Phosphorus has the chemical symbol P. This element has a number of forms or allotropes. The yellow solid called white phosphorus bursts into flames in the air, so it has to be kept under water. It is very poisonous and has been used to kill rats. White phosphorus glows in the dark. When heated, it turns into a red-brown powder called red phosphorus which is not poisonous and is used to make matches.

Phosphorus occurs, as phosphates, in many minerals, eg. apatite which has calcium phosphate. Our bones are mainly calcium phosphate and much of the food we eat contains phosphates. Large amounts of phosphates are mined and used as fertilizers.
See also Allotropy; Fertilizer.

Photography uses light to make a permanent image of an object or scene, on treated paper or film. The photograph is taken with a camera.

Photography started in 1826, when Joseph Niepce formed a picture on a coated metal plate. Later, photographs were taken on coated glass plates. The first colour photographs were taken in 1891. Today, much lighter strips of coated plastic film are used, and cameras have become much smaller and lighter.

Photography is also used to make television and cinema films.

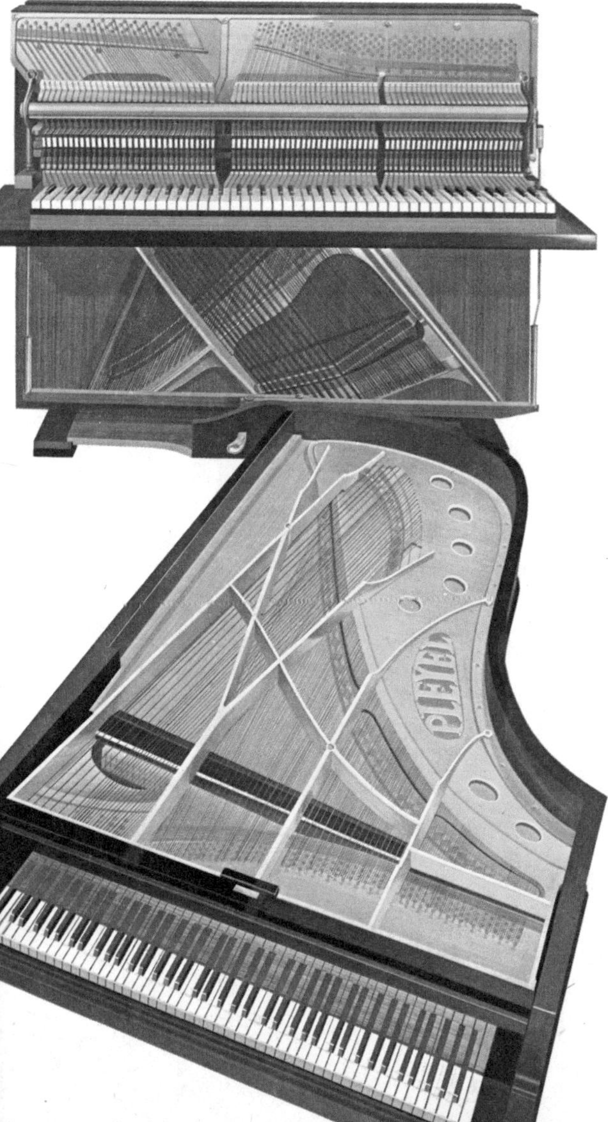

Photosynthesis is the way in which green plants (that is, almost all plants except the fungi and some bacteria) make their own organic food out of relatively simple inorganic chemicals. It is one of the miracles of nature, and it happens as follows. The green colour of plants is caused by a pigment called chlorophyll which is present mainly in the leaves. Chlorophyll is able to trap the energy of sunlight. This energy is then used to drive a series of chemical changes that results in carbon dioxide taken in from the air combining with water to produce sugar. An equation for the overall reaction of photosynthesis looks like this:

$$\underset{\text{carbon dioxide}}{6CO_2} + \underset{\text{water}}{6H_2O} \xrightarrow[\text{of light}]{\text{in the presence}} \underset{\text{glucose}}{C_6H_{12}O_6} + \underset{\text{oxygen}}{6O_2}.$$

Physics is the science which deals with matter and energy, from the nucleus of an atom, studied by nuclear physicists, to stars and galaxies. In physics, everything is divided into matter (such as solids, liquids and gases) and energy (such as light, electricity and heat).

Piano is a keyboard instrument. Its full name is *pianoforte* ('soft-loud'). The piano combines the principles of percussion and strings. Fingers press the keys, causing felt-covered hammers to strike the strings, making them vibrate.

The immediate predecessor of the piano was the harpsichord, in which the strings are plucked. The piano, capable of much greater

An upright *(top)* and a grand piano *(below)*, showing the strings.

variety of tone, was invented in the early 18th century, but not perfected until the second half of the 19th century, when the firm of Steinway became the leading maker. The upright piano, as distinct from the horizontal grand piano of the concert platform, was invented in the early 19th century.

Picasso, Pablo (1881–1973), was a Spanish-born artist, widely recognized as the greatest artist of the 20th century. Few movements in modern art have been unaffected by him.

He settled in Paris in 1904 and his early works were fairly orthodox figure studies. He went through a 'blue' period (when blue was the dominant colour in his paintings) and a 'rose' period. About 1906 he and Braque made the revolutionary change to a type of painting called Cubism, the most important of the new movements in art at that time. Picasso's *Les Demoiselles d'Avignon* (*Girls of Avignon*) of 1907 has been called the most important painting in the history of modern art. In the 1920s he was associated with Surrealism, and produced many works which though technically interesting were very ugly. His painting *Guernica* (1937), protesting against a savage incident in the Spanish Civil War, is probably his best known.

Picasso also produced many works, mainly drawings and etchings, which were humorous – for instance, his playful imitations of the great masters of the past. He was often ready to mock not only art but himself. He was an artist of great power and range, and his work included sculpture, ceramics, graphic illustrations and stage designs.

Pigs include the wild boar, from which the familiar domestic pig was bred. It is found throughout Eurasia, and feeds on almost anything it can root out of the ground using its strong snout. Several other species of wild pigs are found throughout the world. These include the babirusa, a long-legged, nearly hairless creature found on the island of Sulawesi in Indonesia; the warthog, bush pig and red river pig of Africa; and the peccary of South America.

Pike is a highly predatory freshwater fish found throughout the Northern Hemisphere. It lies in wait beneath waterlilies or other vegetation, its long, streamlined body merging well with its surrounding. When another fish, waterbird or small mammal swims past, it darts rapidly from cover and grabs the victim in its huge, powerful jaws. The jaws are armed with many backward-pointing teeth and, once seized, prey can never escape. Pike can grow very large – up to 1.5 m (5 ft).

Monterey pine tree

Pine is the most common species of tree in the Northern Hemisphere. Many pines are extremely hardy, existing in Arctic conditions where a metre or so down the soil is permanently frozen. Pine trees are conifers, bearing their seeds in cones. The leaves are needle-like, and usually borne in clusters along the resinous stems. Pine timber is valued for the manufacture of furniture, toys and other items.

Among the most important species are the Monterey pine, native to California, USA, but now the most common introduced tree in Australia and New Zealand; the Scots pine, the only native British conifer; the lodgepole pine, favoured by the North American Indians for making the supports of their wigwams; and the stone pine of the Mediterranean.

Pinter, Harold (1930–), is an English playwright. His plays had a marked impact on English theatre in the late 1950s and early 1960s. A master of dialogue, Pinter created moods of fear, mistrust and mysterious threat using the simple language of ordinary, often uneducated people. *The Birthday Party* (1957), *The Caretaker* (1960) and *The Homecoming* (1964) are among his most impressive plays. His gift for comedy became more obvious later, and he also became active as a director.

Pioneer is a series of un-manned spacecraft launched by the USA to explore the Solar System and radio findings back to Earth. Early Pioneer craft were aimed at the Moon, but the most famous Pioneer missions (numbers 10 and 11) were sent all the way to Jupiter and Saturn – which Pioneer 11 reached in 1979, seven years after being launched – and produced the first close-up pictures of those giant planets.

Pioneers 10 and 11 will eventually fly out of the Solar System and into interstellar space. Each spacecraft therefore has attached to it a gold-plated plaque which gives brief details of the Solar System, Earth and a drawing of a human being – just in case it is ever found by intelligent beings from another distant planet. *See also* Voyager.

Piranha is the most feared of freshwater fish, although it is quite small – usually between 5 to 20 cm (2 to 8 in) long. Piranha live in South American rivers, and hunt in large shoals, seeking out other fish, as well as unsuspecting deer, cattle and other mammals that wade into the water. Piranhas are armed with razor-sharp teeth, and a shoal of these fish can reduce an animal like a horse to a mere skeleton in minutes, as they attack repeatedly, tearing and swallowing pieces of the victim.

Pissarro, Camille (1830–1903), was a French Impressionist painter. With Monet, he was one of the founders of the group who remained fairly faithful to its original aims, and his kindly character assisted many artists later associated with Impressionism. His most characteristic paintings are of the peaceful countryside, though he also produced many shimmering street scenes in Paris, Le Havre, Rouen and – during a brief visit in 1870–71 – the London suburbs.

Pitcairn Island is in the Pacific Ocean half-way between New Zealand and Panama. Area about 5 sq km (2 sq miles). It is a British possession administered by New Zealand. The island is of volcanic origin. Fruit and vegetables are grown.

Pitcher plant is a carnivorous plant occurring especially in parts of North America and Malaysia. Like other carnivorous plants, pitcher plants can make their own food by photosynthesis, but they can not obtain vital nitrogen from the boggy places in which they live. Therefore, they obtain their nitrogen by catching and eating tiny creatures, such as insects. The leaves of the pitcher plant are shaped like long vases, or pitchers, with a lid partly covering the top. When an insect crawls inside the 'vase', attracted by its colour or a sweet scent, it falls to the bottom. It is then unable to crawl out again because of tiny scales which coat the inside of the pitcher and stick to its feet. Each time it tries to get out, the slippery scales on its feet prevent it from doing so. Eventually the victim falls to the bottom of the pitcher and is dissolved by a watery digestive fluid.

Pitt, William (1759–1806), was a British statesman. The second son of William Pitt, Earl of Chatham, he entered Parliament in 1781. His outstanding abilities soon won him recognition and he became Prime Minister at the age of 24. Pitt reorganized the country's finances, reduced the enormous public debt by his taxation reforms and also introduced changes in the administration of India. He helped to form European coalitions against France during the Revolutionary Wars, brought about the union of England and Ireland in 1800, but resigned in 1801 when George III refused to accept the idea of Catholic Emancipation. Returning to office in 1804, he died in 1806 and was buried in Westminster Abbey.

Pitt, William, 1st Earl of Chatham (1708–1778), was a British statesman. He entered Parliament in 1735 and soon gained a reputation for his oratory and for his refusal to use public office to enrich himself. Pitt was the leading figure in the coalition government of 1757–1761. Through his astute conduct of foreign affairs and his choice of commanders he was largely responsible for Britain's triumph in the Seven Years' War (1756–1763), after a series of brilliant military and naval victories. During his last years he constantly advocated a peaceful settlement with the American colonies.

Pizarro, Francisco (circa 1476–1541), was the Spanish conqueror of Peru. He took part in the expedition under Balboa which discovered the Pacific Ocean in 1513, and subsequently explored the north-west coast of South America. Having received permission from the King of Spain for the venture he set sail in 1530 with 130 men to conquer Peru. The Inca King, Atahualpa, was treacherously murdered by the Spaniards, who gradually brought the whole country under their control. Pizarro was killed in a quarrel with his followers.

Planck, Max Karl Ernst (1858–1947), was a German physicist who studied heat rays. To explain many of the things he found, he put forward the idea that heat rays are made up of tiny packets of energy. These packets are known as quanta.

From this he devised the quantum theory, which states that heat rays, light rays and all other electromagnetic rays are made up of quanta.

The quantum theory is very important. Einstein used it in his work, and Niels Bohr used it to explain the structure of the atom in 1913. Max Planck was awarded a Nobel prize in 1918.

Planet is a large body which goes around and around a star. The Earth is one of the planets in the Solar System. Nine planets orbit the star we call the Sun. They are thought to have been formed at the same time as the Sun, 4600 million years ago. The inner four planets, Mercury, Venus, Earth and Mars, are mainly solid. The next four, Jupiter, Saturn, Uranus and Neptune, are large and mainly gas. The outermost planet, Pluto, is the odd one out. It is quite small and believed to be solid.

Not all stars have planets. Astronomers think that one star in every ten may have planets.

Plankton is the millions of minute plants and animals which float in the surface waters of the sea. The plants are called phytoplankton and the animals are called zooplankton. Phytoplankton are minute algae which make food by photosynthesis. They are food for some of the zooplankton, as well as other creatures that swim or drift in the sea. In fact, all life in the sea depends on phytoplankton directly or indirectly. The zooplankton include the larval forms of animals such as echinoderms, as well as shrimp-like creatures known as krill. Zooplankton is the food for many creatures from herring to some of the mighty whales. *See also* Diatoms.

Plants and animals make up the living world. You might think that it is easy to tell a plant from an animal, for they normally do different things. However, there are some animals which look like plants (anemones, for instance) and there are also some plants which act like animals. For instance, some species of algae can swim or glide about; some flowering plants are carnivorous and eat animals; while some plants can make other sorts of movements if touched – the mimosa quickly shuts its leaves should this happen. So, whilst we can be sure most of the time what is a plant and what is an animal, it is necessary to beware the 'odd plant out'.

Plants differ from animals mainly in the way they make their food. Animals get their food 'ready made' by eating other animals or

A variety of plants growing in a wood.

plants, but green plants must make theirs by photosynthesis. (The exceptions to this are the fungi and a few species of parasitic flowering plants which feed on dead or living organic matter.) Plants also have cellulose cell walls, giving them a rigidity not found in animal cell walls. Many plants also grow throughout their life, whilst most animals do not.

Plants are divided into several major groups. The simplest are the viruses, although they can not be regarded as true plants. Then come the bacteria, followed by the fungi and the lichens. The algae are a large group of non-flowering plants comprising many species. Bryophytes (mosses and liverworts) and pteridophytes (ferns, horsetails and club mosses) come next. Finally there are the seed-bearing plants which include the gynmosperms and the angiosperms. The angiosperms are the dominant plants on Earth today, and include the flowers, shrubs and many well-known trees such as oak, ash, teak, hornbeam, maple, birch and mahogany.

Plasma is a substance made up of electrically charged particles called ions and electrons. One of its more important properties is that it can carry very large electrical currents. If a gas is heated to a very high temperature it forms a plasma. In many stars, such as the Sun, gases are so hot that they become plasma.

The word plasma is also used for part of the blood. Blood plasma is mainly water.

Plastics are substances with very large molecules in the shape of long chains. They are among the most useful substances in the world. Artificial rubber, nylon, polythene and rayon are examples of plastics. When heated, plastics can be made into any shape. Some melt if they are reheated, while other stays hard. *See also* Molecule; Polymer.

Plate tectonics is the theory which explains the movements of the continents of the Earth.

The Earth's crust rests on a layer, called the mantle. This is thought to have a hard surface, divided up into pieces called plates. There are seven main plates which are not the same shape as the continents or the oceans.

The plates move, carrying the Earth's crust with them. Some are moving apart, pushed out by material coming up from inside the Earth. Some slide past each other. Others are pushed together, which can force the crust up to form high mountain chains or down to form deep valleys and troughs. Volcanoes and earthquakes usually occur along the edges of the plates. *See also* Continental drift.

Platinum has the chemical symbol Pt. It is a silver-coloured shiny metal, and supplies of it are very scarce, so it is valuable. It is mined mainly in South Africa, the USSR and Canada.

Jewellery is sometimes made of platinum. Platinum melts only at very high temperatures and reacts with few substances. For these reasons it is used in chemical and electrical equipment. It is an important catalyst.

Plato (circa 427–347 BC), was an Athenian philosopher, who is known as 'father of philosophy'. He is the earliest philosopher whose writings have survived in bulk. He is also the first to discuss thoroughly the questions that have dominated philosophy ever since, for example, how do we obtain knowledge, and is our knowledge reliable? What is the good life? What do we mean by beauty?

He was a great writer, and invented a new and dramatic way of putting over his ideas. This was the dialogue, in which various characters discuss a topic until agreement is reached. The chief character in most of the dialogues is an earlier philosopher, Socrates, who left no written works. Socrates probably thought of some, but not all, of the ideas Plato credits him with. The most famous of the dialogues are the *Republic*, about the ideal state and government, and the *Symposium*, about the nature of love.

Plato addresses pupils in his Academy.

Plato taught his pupils in a grove called the Academy, which has since given its name to many teaching institutions.

Platypus is a strange, primitive mammal which inhabits lakes and rivers in parts of Australia and Tasmania. It looks like a cross between a large mole and a duck! It has short, dense, black fur, but it also has webbed feet, and at the front of its head it has a flattened bill. More unusual is the fact that the platypus lays eggs, rather than giving birth to live young in the way that other mammals do. The platypus grows to a length of about 56 cm (22 in). It hunts mostly in the morning and evening for worms, snails, shrimps and fish.

Pluto is the ninth planet from the Sun. It orbits the Sun in 248 years. Its great dis-

Platypus

tance from the Earth makes it difficult to study and little is known about it. It seems to be very small, possibly smaller than the Moon. It is believed that its surface is covered with frozen methane. For part of its orbit it is nearer to the Sun than Neptune, and some people think that it might once have been a satellite of Neptune.

After the discovery of Neptune, in 1846, many astronomers searched for another planet in the Solar System. Pluto was discovered by Tombaugh in 1930. No other planet has been found since. It is thought that, probably, there are no others.

Plutonium has the chemical symbol Pu. It is a silver-coloured radioactive element, which is not usually found in the Earth. It is made in nuclear reactors by firing neutrons at uranium atoms, which makes some of the uranium change into plutonium.

Like uranium, plutonium can be used in nuclear reactors and atom bombs.

Plutonium stays radioactive for thousands of years. For this and other reasons, it is one of the most poisonous substances in the world. Tiny amounts of plutonium can be dangerous and the large amounts made in nuclear reactors are a serious problem.

Plymouth Brethren is a Christian sect founded in 1828. Its origins were in Dublin, under the leadership of John Darby (1800–1882). Plymouth, England, became their centre in 1831. The Brethren have never been numerous though they have had great influence. They believe in strict interpretation of the Bible and they reject all organized Churches and the priesthood.

Poetry is a form of literature in which the words are carefully arranged, usually according to a certain fixed pattern. A great deal of poetry rhymes, or is written in a standard form (such as ode, sonnet, etc) with a fixed number of lines and syllables per line. However, 'free verse', common in the 20th century but also found in the Bible (notably the Psalms), obeys neither of these rules.

Poison is a substance that harms the health of or kills any living thing. In animals it may be swallowed, breathed in or taken in through the skin. For example, arsenic is a poison if swallowed, and strong acids cause burns if they are spilt on the skin. Known poisons are usually clearly labelled and are kept carefully away from other chemicals. Some substances can make us more healthy if they are taken correctly, but can poison us if taken wrongly or in too large amounts. Other substances are only poisons to certain living things and are quite safe for the rest.

A few animals, such as some snakes, use their natural poison to protect themselves and kill their food.

Poland is a Communist republic in north-east Europe. Capital, Warsaw; area about 313 000 sq km (121 000 sq miles).

History The Polish state was founded in the 10th century AD, becoming an independent kingdom in 1025. During the 15th–16th centuries the country expanded its frontiers so that they stretched from the Black Sea to the Baltic. Under pressure from Russia and Turkey, Poland declined in the 17th century and at the end of the 18th century was divided up between Russia, Prussia and Austria. It became an independent republic in 1918 but was under German occupation during the Second World War. In 1947 it became a Communist state.

Land Most of Poland is gently rolling plains, with mountains in the south. The main rivers are the Vistula and the Oder which, with their tributaries, drain over three-quarters of the country. The climate is generally rather cold, especially in the north-east, where average winter temperatures are well below freezing.

Economy Industrialization has happened rapidly since 1945, making Poland a major steel producer and ship-builder. More than half the population live in the main urban-industrial area. Poland is a major producer of coal and zinc, and other minerals.

Agriculture suffered as a result of the concentration on industry and there were unsuccessful efforts to turn private farms into collectives. Potatoes and sugar beet are the largest crops.

Polarized light is light which is made to vibrate in one direction only. Ordinary light vibrates in all directions. Some substances are able to cut out all the directions except one. These substances are called polarizers. They are used in, for example, some sunglasses and cameras and in many scientific instruments.

Polecat is a long-bodied, agile carnivore related to weasels and stoats. It has short legs and a triangular-shaped head with tiny ears. Polecats reach a length of about 60 cm (24 in). They inhabit woodland and farmland where they hunt a wide variety of rodents, reptiles and birds. They often cause damage on farms, where they find chickens and other domestic fowl easy prey. Polecats can emit a foul smell from their anal glands when cornered. They are wide-ranging animals, with species being found across Eurasia, North Africa and North America. *See also* Ferret.

Pollination is the transfer of pollen from the stamens (the male parts of a plant) to the stigmas (the receptive surfaces of the female parts of the plant). Pollination occurs mainly by insects and the wind. Insects brush pollen attached to their bodies on to the stigmas as they go from flower to flower collecting nectar or some pollen for themselves. The wind blows the pollen from flower to flower. Sometimes other animals such as bats or even

Some examples of how pollination takes place.

birds are used by a plant to help pollination take place.

Pollock, Jackson (1912–1956), was a US painter. He is the most famous member of the school of Abstract Expressionism, or 'action painting'. For Pollock, the act of painting was the most important thing, but the results were often powerful and beautiful.

Pollution is the spoiling of the natural environment. All animals and plants produce waste substances. Much of these can be absorbed by the Earth and are not harmful. However, in many areas, people produce more waste than can be absorbed. This is harmful and causes pollution. Accidents can also cause pollution. For example, oil is carried around the world in large tankers. An accident can spill this oil into the sea. This can kill many animals and plants.

Polo, Marco (circa 1254–1324), was a Venetian traveller. He accompanied his father and uncle on a journey to China in 1271. Marco Polo entered the service of the Mongol Emperor of China, Kublai Kahn, and undertook various missions on his behalf. On his return to Venice he was captured by the Genoans and while in prison wrote an account of his travels, the first description of the Far East by a European.

Polymer is a substance in which the molecules are in long chains. It can be made from a substance, called a monomer which has small molecules, by a process called polymerization.

Ethylene is a monomer. Its molecules can be made to join together into a long chain. It forms the polymer polythene. A substance called styrene can be made into the polymer, polystyrene. This is used to make and insulate buildings. Polymers can also be made from a number of different substances.

Polynesia is the name covering the islands of a section of the central Pacific, stretching from Hawaii in the north to New Zealand in the south and including Easter Island. The Polynesians speak related languages and are thought to be descendants of migrants from Indonesia, south-east Asia and, possibly, South America.

Pop art was a trend in art in the 1950s and 1960s. It can be seen as an attempt to get away from the highbrow character of modern art by concentrating on 'popular' culture – the world of film stars, advertisements, pin-up girls, cheap food, 'hot-rod' cars, etc. But it was not only the subject-matter that was 'popular'. Pop artists frequently made use of 'inartistic' methods, such as photography and cheap printing.

Rather than being a movement of like-minded artists all pursuing the same aims in a similar way, Pop was a tendency, which affected many artists to a limited extent or for a short time. It was therefore an important influence in the development of art.

Pope is the head of the Roman Catholic Church. The pope's authority is assured by the doctrine of infallibility: the official statements of the pope are by definition correct and cannot be questioned by anyone.

The popes claim to have inherited their office from St Peter, regarded as the first bishop of Rome. But the early Christian Church was governed by councils rather than bishops, and the supremacy of the pope was not established until the Middle Ages.

In the 11th century the Eastern Church broke away completely, while in the West a long struggle went on between the pope and ordinary rulers over who should control the Church in their individual countries. Under Innocent III (1198–1216) papal power was at its height; princes and even emperors were forced to obey. The papacy was dangerously weakened by a dispute over the actual person of the pope in 1378–1417. For a brief time there were three men claiming to be pope.

The greatest crisis came with the Protestant Reformation in the 16th century, when Christian Europe became permanently split between Roman Catholics and Protestants, who rejected the pope's authority. Since then the political power of the pope has declined (he is no longer the ruler of a large area of Italy), but his spiritual authority over the world's Catholics is still very strong today.

Pope, Alexander (1688–1744), was an English poet. His work belongs to the Augustan age of English literature, whose characteristics were clarity, order and elegance (as in the Augustan age in ancient Rome, 27 BC – AD 14). His first masterpiece, *The Rape of the Lock* (1714), was a satire in the form of an epic. The *Dunciad* (1728–1743) was written in the same spirit, but Pope owed his fame equally to his translations of Classical authors and his more philosophical poems, such as *An Essay on Man* and *Moral Essays* (1731–1735).

Pop music is a type of non-classical music mainly performed for (and by) young people. It usually consists of songs accompanied by guitars, drums and sometimes other instruments. In this form, pop music dates from the 1950s and the development of rock and roll, which was pioneered by Bill Haley, Elvis Presley and others. It owed much to jazz and folk music.

Pop music was one of the main ingredients of the new 'teenage culture' of the West after the Second World War. Increased leisure, more money and the recording industry all made it possible. Performers like Presley or the Beatles became richer than almost any classical composer and also more famous (according to John Lennon of the Beatles, more famous than Jesus Christ). Pop developed in various ways, some of them rebellious and deliberately anti-social (e.g. punk rock), others reverting to forms closer to the folk music of earlier times.

Porcupine is a large rodent found in parts of Europe, Africa and the Americas. Its most obvious feature is the sharp quills which sprout from the body. These are used in defence, and are modified hairs. When confronted by an enemy, a porcupine first rustles it quills as a warning. If this fails to deter the would-be attacker, the porcupine then rushes backwards into the enemy, impaling it with many painful quills.

Most species of porcupine live solitary lives, snuffling about on the ground for roots and fruit. However, the South American coendou is a porcupine which is particularly well adapted to living in trees.

Porpoise is a small whale, which means it is a mammal and not fish. Like other whales, porpoises have smooth, streamlined, fish-shaped bodies with a powerful horizontal tail, a pair of flippers and, sometimes, a fin on their back. Porpoises hunt for fish such as herring and mackerel, which they eat with their many, pointed teeth. Porpoises are up to 1.5 m (5 ft) long and are very intelligent.

Porpoise

Port is a place where ships can 'park' to load or offload their cargo or passengers and take on new supplies. The earliest ports were in sheltered bays or river mouths, where their location often played a part in the development of major cities – London, New York and Sydney are all built around natural harbours. New York boasts the largest port in the world, with over 1200 km (745 miles) of waterfront; the largest artificial harbour is the Europoort at Rotterdam (in the Netherlands) which can handle over 350 vessels at once.

Portugal is a republic in south-west Europe, sharing the Iberian peninsula with Spain. Capital, Lisbon; area about 92 000 sq km (35 000 sq miles).

History The Greeks founded colonies in the region in the 5th century BC and it later became a Roman province. It was conquered by Visigoths in the 5th century AD and by the Moors in the 8th century. It became an independent kingdom in 1143 and in the 15th century Portuguese navigators opened up trade routes and laid foundations of an overseas empire. The country was ruled by

Spain from 1580 until the Portuguese monarchy was restored in 1640. In 1910 the monarchy was overthrown and a republic proclaimed. A dictatorship was established in 1932, but this was brought to an end in 1974 and a democratic government was set up.

Land and People The land is rugged in the north and east, with plains, hills and lowlands farther south. The climate is mild, and in the Algarve, the chief tourist region in the south, it is almost subtropical. Portugal is rather heavily populated for a basically poor country. Most of the people live in the north-west, and there are few large cities.

Economy This is based on agriculture, despite the need to import some food. Portugal is the leading producer of cork, and other valuable products are wine (including port), olive oil and fish, especially sardines. Mineral resources include coal and tungsten, and hydro-electric power is important for manufacturing. Traditional crafts such as metalwork and pottery are still flourishing.

Portuguese man o'war

Portuguese man-o'-war is often wrongly called a jellyfish. Although related to the jellyfish, it is really a collection of small individual animals, each designed to carry out a particular task. Thus, the purple-coloured float which enables the Portuguese man-o'-war to drift in the warmer oceans of the world is produced by one kind of animal. The trailing tentacles armed with powerful stinging cells are produced by another kind of animal. Yet other kinds digest food such as fish which are caught by the tentacles.

Poseidon, in Greek myth, was the god of the sea. The Romans identified him with a water god called Neptune. Poseidon was the brother of Zeus, but he was not as widely worshipped (the Greeks were not, originally, a seagoing people) and appears much less in myth. In art he was usually pictured as a powerful, mature man, like Zeus but often wilder in appearance and carrying his trident (a three-pronged spear). In the myths, Poseidon is usually a violent and bad-tempered god. His hatred of Odysseus is one of the main themes in Homer's *Odyssey*, and many of the rougher heroes in Greek myths were Poseidon's sons.

Possum, see Phalanger.

Potassium is a silver-coloured metal. It has the chemical symbol K. Potassium is very like sodium, and it reacts easily with substances to form many compounds, the most common of which is potassium chloride. It is found in many rocks and in seawater. Most potassium is obtained from potassium chloride.

Humans need potassium for good health and it is in much of the food we eat. Plants also need potassium, and potassium compounds, such as potash, are used as fertilizers. Potassium compounds are also used to make explosives, medicine and soap.

Poulenc, Francis (1899–1963), was a French composer. He began composing at the age of seven, gaining his first success with *Rapsodie nègre* in 1917. He was one of Les Six ('the Six'), a group of young French composers in the 1920s who shared an interest in Paris street music and often gave concerts together. For Diaghilev he wrote the ballet *Les Biches* (1923), but of all his works his songs are probably the most often heard now.

Power is the rate at which work is done. Horses used to do the work of pulling carts. Two horses are more powerful than one. Two horses can pull a heavier cart or pull a light cart faster than one horse. So, more power can be used to do more work or to do the same work more quickly.

Power is measured in units called watts. An electric fire does the work of heating a room. One bar of an electric fire has a power of about 1000 watts, which is a kilowatt. *See also* Watt, James.

Power station is where electricity is generated. It contains turbines which have large blades like the blades of ships' propellers. The turbine blades are turned, usually by water or steam. The turbine is used to drive a generator and this produces electricity. In many power stations, coal is burnt to heat water into steam; in some the water is heated to steam using nuclear fuel, while others use fast-moving water to turn the turbines. The electricity is carried from the power station to factories, ships and houses, in overhead or underground cables. The cables are usually copper or aluminium wires covered with an insulator, such as plastic or porcelain. *See also* Nuclear reactor; Water power.

Prairie is an area of rolling grasslands. The Argentine pampas, the European steppe and the southern African Veld are examples of prairies, but the name is most often applied to the great central plain of North America. This takes in the southern part of three Canadian provinces (Manitoba, Saskatchewan and Alberta) and a vast area of the USA stretching from the Rocky Mountains to the Great Lakes. In the 19th century, settlers from Europe defeated the Plains Indians and destroyed the huge herds of bison that roamed the prairie. Other characteristic prairie animals survived, including the coyote, or prairie wolf, and the prairie dog (which is actually a rodent). Today the once-open prairie is now largely fenced and given over to the production of wheat, of which the USA has become the world's greatest exporter.

Prairie dog, see Squirrels.

Prawn, *See* Shrimps.

Precambrian is one of the periods of time into which geologists divide the history of the Earth. Precambrian means 'before the Cambrian' and it encompasses all the time from the formation of the Earth's crust about 4500 million years ago to the beginning of the Cambrian era about 570 million years ago.

Precambrian rocks are the oldest on the planet, and some found in Greenland are estimated to have been formed almost 3800 million years ago. *See also* Cambrian.

Prehistoric animal is a term usually used to describe any animal that became extinct before civilized human beings appeared on the Earth. Fossils have enabled us to see not only what some prehistoric animals must have looked like, but also how they evolved from their ancestors, and what sorts of animal they gave rise to.

The earliest prehistoric animals were probably like the simple protozoans that are still living today. However, later prehistoric animals were unlike anything living today. Huge armour-plated fish, giant eel-like whales, sloths that browsed the tops of trees and, of course, the dinosaurs, were just a few of the fascinating animals that once roamed the Earth. *See also* Ammonite; Archaeopteryx; Mammoth; Trilobites.

Prehistoric man is any of the evolutionary stages of human beings before recorded history. The earliest known creature which is recognized as belonging to the family of man is *Australopithecus*, which lived in Africa from about 5 million to 1 million years ago. *Australopithecus* walked on two legs and may have made simple tools. True man, of which the most advanced example was *Homo*

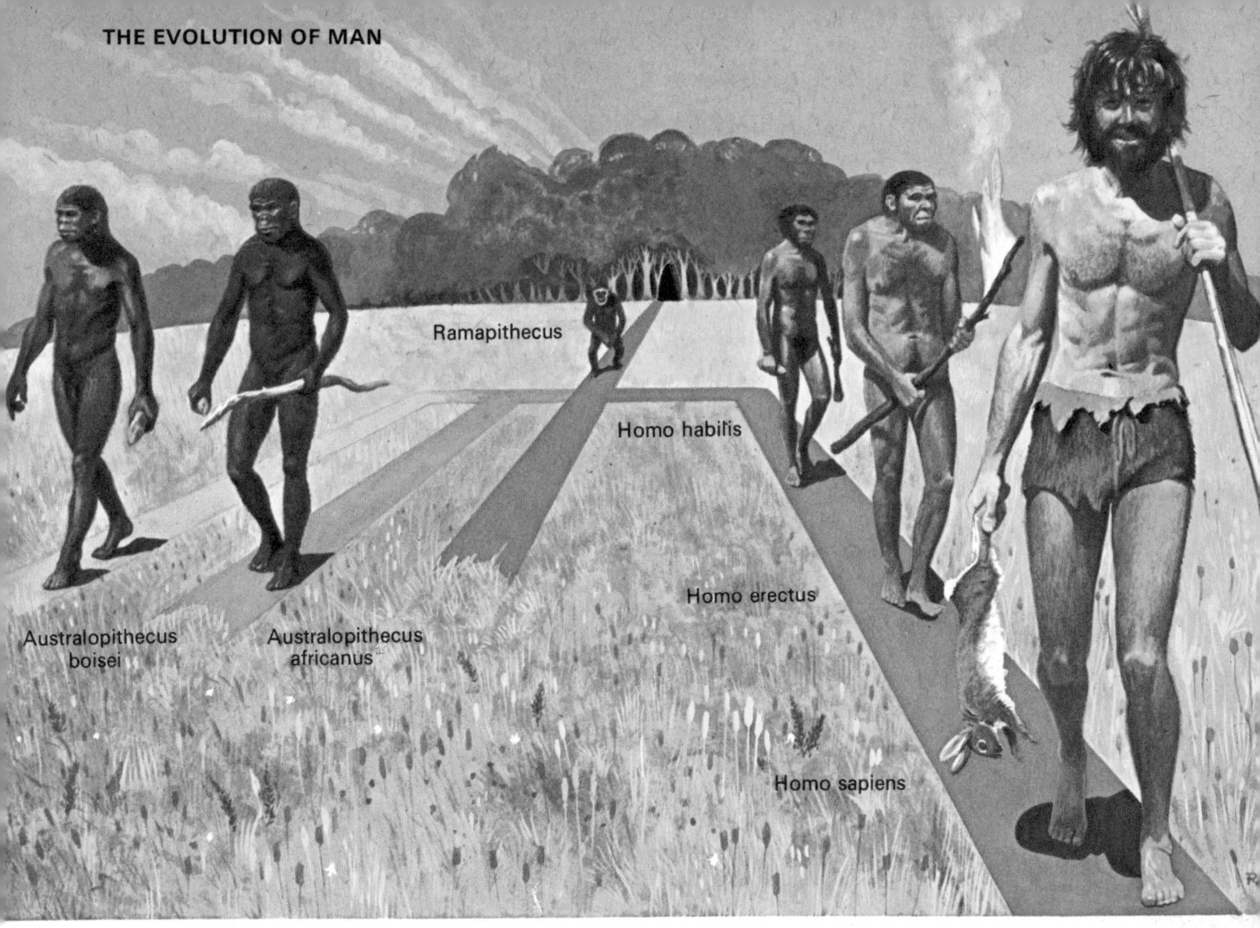

erectus, first appeared about one and a half million years ago. Their mastery of the art of making fire enabled them to survive in the colder parts of the world. Neanderthal man, whose home was in caves, used a variety of stone tools and lived in Europe from about 70 000 to 40 000 years ago. The first modern human beings, known as Cro-Magnon man, moved westwards into Europe about 35 000 years ago and decorated their caves with paintings of animals. The first civilizations probably began with the development of agriculture in the fertile land between the Tigris and the Euphrates about 4000 BC.

Pre-Raphaelites were a group of English artists who formed the 'Pre-Raphaelite Brotherhood' in 1848. Originating as a reaction against the lifeless academic art of the 19th century, it was influenced by the critic John Ruskin's advice to 'return to nature' and by the ideals of artists before Raphael (who was one of the founders of the Classical tradition). Pre-Raphaelite pictures were painted with minutely exact detail and brilliant colour. They helped bring more realism into art generally.

Presbyterianism is a branch of the Christian religion. The Presbyterian Church is governed by elders or presbyters (not bishops), as in the very early Christian Church. There are teacher elders, who are ministers, and ruling elders, laymen, as well as church courts ranging from the local session or presbytery to the national general assembly.

The origin of Presbyterianism was the teaching of the 16th-century reformer, John Calvin. In particular, he influenced John Knox (1505–1572), who made Scotland the strongest Presbyterian country in Europe.

Presley, Elvis (1935–1977), was a US pop singer. In terms of records sold, he was probably the most successful singer so far. Elvis 'the Pelvis' (so named for his antics on stage) started his career in 1953 but his first big success, *Heartbreak Hotel*, came in 1956. His brand of rock and roll, copied by hundreds of others, derived from the blues and country and western music. But his success was largely derived from his moody, magnetic personality. He made many films and earned the approval of the establishment by making no effort to avoid his military service.

Primates are the group of mammals which includes lorises, lemurs, monkeys, apes and human beings. Primates are rather unspecialized creatures – they have not adapted themselves as thoroughly to their environment as, for example, moles have; nor can they fly as bats can. Yet this group of creatures – many of which still live the tree-dwelling existence of their ancestors – are among the most intelligent creatures on Earth. They have large brains, reaching the peak of development in humans. The higher primates (chimpanzees, gorillas and other apes) have the ability to learn to perform quite complicated tasks; chimpanzees are even able to communicate with people by using sign language.

Primates have forward-facing eyes; this enables them to judge distances well, which is essential for creatures that leap from tree to tree. They are also able to grip and manipulate objects much better than any other animals. For a long period the young are carried about, fed and taught how to catch food, and learn the ways of their parents. The smallest primates are the mouse-like tree shrews, while the largest, the gorilla, can grow to a height of 2m (over 6 ft) and weight as much as 225 kg (500 lb).

Printed circuit is an electric circuit forming part of electronic equipment in which the wiring between components, and some components themselves, are printed, or etched on to an insulating board, usually a thin sheet of copper. *See also* Circuit, electric; Electronics; Silicon chip.

Printing makes copies of words and pictures on textile, paper or other surfaces. It is said that the Chinese invented printing about 1200 years ago. Carved wooden blocks were inked and pressed down on material to make a copy. Letters raised in metal are still sometimes used to print words. People or machines, called typesetters, put the letters in the right order. They are then inked and paper is pressed on them. This is called letterpress printing.

The Chinese invented movable type many centuries before it came into use anywhere else.

Grease and water do not mix. This fact is used in another sort of printing, lithography. The text or picture is marked on a flat plate with a grease. Water is put on the plate. A greasy ink will stick to the greasy parts of the plate and not the wet parts. Paper can then be pressed on to the plate to make a print.

Today, much use is made of photographic processes in printing. Also typesetting and printing are often computer-aided and use very fast machines. There are many other methods of printing, such as silk-screen, which are available for special needs.

Prokofiev, Sergei (1891–1953), was a Russian composer. He wrote his first opera at the age of nine, and his best-known is *Love of Three Oranges* (1920), written for the Chicago Opera. He wrote the ballets *Romeo and Juliet* and *Cinderella* and some famous film scores. Besides his symphonies, his symphonic fairy tale *Peter and the Wolf*, for a narrator plus orchestra, is a delightful way of introducing young people to the instruments of the orchestra.

Pronghorn is a North American herbivorous mammal which looks like an antelope. It is an attractive creature, with reddish-brown colouring on the back, neck and legs, and paler fur on the face and chest. Both sexes grow branched horns, which are shed each year. The pronghorn lives in small herds in wild, rocky country. Although it cannot run quite as fast as the cheetah – which can run at speeds of 100 km/h (60 mph) – it can keep up a speed of 90 km/h (56 mph) for much longer distances, and would soon leave a cheetah gasping for breath.

Prose is any written work which cannot be classed as poetry, whether it is a ten-volume philosophical treatise or simply a one-line advertisement.

Protea is South Africa's most famous flowering shrub. There are many different species, some of which grow over 3 m (10 ft) tall, and they flower in spring and summer. Proteas are found all over the Southern Hemisphere, mostly in South Africa, Australia, Madagascar, Malaysia and South America.

Proteins are very important chemical compounds contained by all animals and plants. Probably, life could not exist without proteins. Skin, hair, nails and other parts of the body can not grow without them and they are also needed to mend any parts of the body that are damaged.

Food from animals, such as meat, fish, eggs and milk, contains all the proteins that humans need. Vegetables also contain proteins, and some, such as soyabeans, can provide all the proteins needed by humans in their daily diet. Lack of protein can cause severe illness.

Protestantism is the religion of Western Christians who do not belong to the Roman Catholic Church. The word Protestant was first used in the early years of the Reformation to describe followers of Luther. Today it includes a huge number of different Churches, sects (some of which do not like to be called Protestant) and groups. There are over 250 Protestant bodies in the United States alone.

Basically, Protestants take the Bible as the sole authority in religious matters. But there are a number of other important disagreements with Roman Catholicism. The belief in transubstantiation – that the bread and wine in the Communion service are changed into the body and blood of Jesus – is not held by Protestants. Protestants also believe that all the trappings of religion – the actual churches and their contents, the priests, the ceremony, etc – are less important than their faith.

Proton is one of the two particles in the nucleus of an atom. The other particle is a neutron. They are called subatomic particles. Special equipment, such as a particle accelerator, is used to study these particles.

The proton has about the same mass as the neutron, and has a positive electrical charge. Each element has atoms with a particular number of protons. This is known as the element's atomic number. The nucleus of a hydrogen atom is just one proton with no neutrons, so its atomic number is one. Changing the number of protons in a nucleus changes the atom to one of a different element.

Protozoan is a word meaning first animal, and protozoans probably appeared on Earth before any others. Protozoans are all one-celled animals, although sometimes groups of them join together and move about as colonies. All protozoans are extremely tiny and live in water, often in huge numbers. For instance, 4.5 l (1 gal) of sea water may contain 240 million individual protozoans.

Some protozoans, like *Amoeba*, flow along, engulfing food as they go, and multiply by splitting into two halves. Others move about by beating tiny hairs and 'rowing' themselves along. Many are parasitic, living inside the bodies of other animals.

A few species of protozoan, such as *Euglena*, contain chloroplasts, the structures that trap the energy of sunlight in plants. This makes it very difficult for scientists to decide whether some protozoans are really animals, plants or a little of each.

Proust, Marcel (1871–1922), was a French novelist. He came from a rich and fashionable Paris family, but after 1905 he lived a solitary life, converting his impressions of society into his great work *Remembrance of Things Past*. It was published in eight parts between 1913 and 1927. The subject of the book is the mind of the narrator, Marcel, and the influence on his development of the various incidents and sensations – often insignificant at the time – that he experiences. Proust used memory in a new way, to build up a pattern of experiences and human relationships which work in the novel like themes in a piece of music.

Psychiatry is a branch of medicine, specializing in diagnosis and treatment of illnesses of the mind. Psychiatrists may use drugs, electrical treatment or surgery to lessen the symptoms of mental illnesses and to cure them. Psychoanalysis is also often used. *See also* Freud, Sigmund.

Psychology is the scientific study and measurement of behaviour. It is mainly concerned with the study of humans, although psychologists (people who study psychology) often use other animals to test their theories, or to compare how animals other than humans will react under certain conditions. Psychology is a very new science compared with those such as physics or botany. Because we still know so little of the workings of the mind, much of the work done so far raises as many questions as it answers.

There are several main divisions of psychology. Physiological psychology is concerned mainly with how the brain functions. Cognition looks at how we view the world and how we learn. Psychometry is the study of intelligence and mental ability. Animal psychology is the study of instinct and learning in animals. Motivation looks at why we act the way we do. Social psychology investigates how we interrelate with other social groups and with people at home, at school and at work.

Puccini, Giacomo (1858–1924), was an Italian composer. He came from a long line of church musicians, but he is remembered as the composer of some of the most popular operas ever written, such as *La Bohème* (1896), *Tosca* (1900), *Madame Butterfly* (1904), and *Turandot* (1926). These demonstrate Puccini's marvellous sense of theatre as well as his wonderful melodies.

Puerto Rico is an island commonwealth of the USA in the West Indies. Capital, San Juan; area about 8960 sq km (3460 sq miles). Part of the Spanish American empire, it passed to the USA in 1898 and in 1952 became a USA 'commonwealth', self-governing in internal affairs.

The main island is mountainous, with numerous valleys and a narrow coastal plain. The climate is warm and damp, and hurricanes are frequent. Puerto Ricans are mainly of African and European descent; Spanish is the dominant language and Roman Catholicism is strong.

Agriculture is intensive, with sugar the main export crop, but some food has to be imported. There is a good deal of small-scale industry, but little mining. Tourism is an important source of income.

Puffin is an attractive but rather comical-looking seabird related to the guillemots and razorbills. It is about 30 cm (1 ft) tall and has

black and white plumage. It has short wings, a short tail, and a big, triangular beak marked in the breeding season with red, yellow and black stripes. The puffin nests on cliffs in noisy colonies, and hunts in the sea for fish, often carrying up to half a dozen in its beak at one time. Sadly, chemical pollution of the sea appears to be drastically reducing the numbers of puffins in northern Europe.

Pulsar is a neutron star. This is a very dense star, much denser than a white dwarf. A matchbox full of it would weigh 1000 million tonnes. It is believed that a neutron star is formed when a star explodes or a supernova occurs. A new neutron star spins very fast. As it gets older it spins more slowly. It gives off radio waves in flashes or pulses each time it spins (rather like a lighthouse does). This is why it is known as a pulsar. The first pulsar was discovered in 1967 by astronomers in Cambridge, England. *See also* White dwarf.

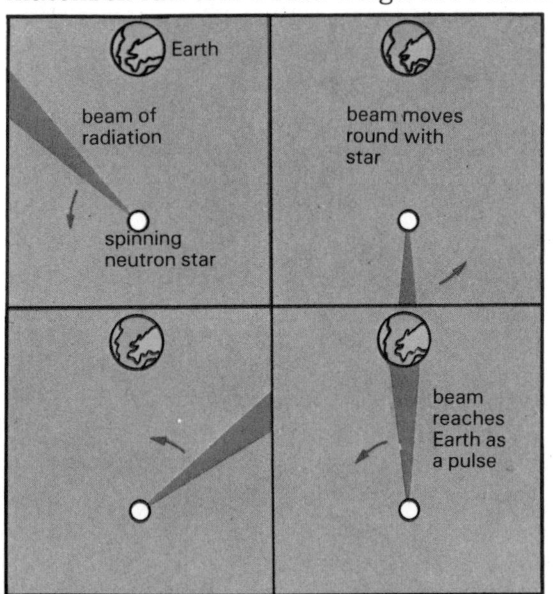

Diagram to show the effect of a pulsar.

Pulse, see Heart.

Puma, or cougar, is a large, carnivorous cat which looks rather like a lioness. It is also called the mountain lion, and is up to 2.3 m (7.5 ft) long including the tail. It lives in the forests, deserts, plains and mountains of the Americas, ranging from Canada in the north to Patagonia in the south, where it hunts deer and other animals.

Pupa, see Chrysalis.

Purcell, Henry (1659–1695), was an English composer. For a time organist of Westminster Abbey, he was the most distinguished English composer before Elgar. Much of his music was written for royal occasions, though perhaps his greatest work was church music and songs (e.g. *Nymphs and Shepherds*). He also wrote one opera, *Dido and Aeneas*. Purcell enjoyed a revival in the 20th century when modern composers like Holst and Britten declared their admiration for him.

Puritanism was a religious revival in England during the late 16th and 17th centuries. The Puritans believed that the Reformation in England had not gone far enough. They objected to the rule of bishops and to the many elements of Catholicism which the Church of England still kept. Their opposition provoked persecution from the government, and many Puritans emigrated to North America to practise their beliefs in freedom.

Others remained at home and played a major part in the conflict which led to the English Civil War. However, the Puritans were themselves divided into Presbyterians and Independents (Congregationalists), as well as many smaller groups. The Restoration of the monarchy in 1660 marked the victory of the Church of England and the end of Puritanism as a political force in England.

Pushkin, Alexander (1799–1837), was a Russian writer. As a young civil servant, he wrote poems in praise of liberty which led to him being exiled from Moscow and later dismissed from his job. He was a magician of words, probably Russia's greatest poet. His most famous works are *Eugene Onegin* (1833), a 'novel in verse' influenced by Byron, and *Boris Godunov* (1831), a play in blank verse. He also wrote history and criticism and collected Russian folktales. He was killed in a duel with one of his wife's admirers.

Pyramids are the great stone monuments built in ancient Egypt to contain the graves of the pharaohs and other important people. Beginning as a square, a pyramid has four sloping, triangular sides which rise to a point. Most were built between about 2800 BC and 2200 BC. No one is certain why the pyramid shape was chosen. The largest is the Great Pyramid at Giza: it was originally more than 146 m (479 ft) high and each wall more than 230 m (755 ft) long. Pyramids were also built in Mexico as the foundations of temples by the Mayas and Aztecs.

Pyrenees are a mountain range on the borders of France and Spain, the highest point being Pico de Aneto at 3404 m (11 168 ft) high. The slopes are steep and there are few passes. Descending rivers are valuable for hydro-electric power and irrigation, especially in Spain. There are marble quarries and forests which are important for timber. The few inhabitants graze sheep and goats, and raise corn in some valleys.

Pythagoras (circa 582–500 BC), was a Greek philosopher and mathematician. He is now best known for his theorem which deals with right-angled triangles. The side of a triangle opposite the right angle is known as the hypotenuse. The theorem states that the square of the hypotenuse is equal to the sum of the squares of the other two sides.

Pythagoras used numbers to explain many things. In music he showed how the pitch of a note depends on the length of a string or pipe. He explained why some notes are in harmony while others sound unpleasant. The followers of his philosophies lived very simple and monk-like lives. *See also* Mathematics.

Pythons are large snakes found in the Eastern Hemisphere. They are not venomous, but kill their prey by constriction, wrapping themselves around the victim until it suffocates. Unlike boas (the equivalents of the python which live in the Western Hemisphere) which give birth to living young, pythons lay eggs. The reticulated python of southeast Asia is the longest python, reaching a length of 10 m (33 ft). However, the royal python of Africa is only 1 m (3 ft) long. A wild royal python rolls up into a ball when frightened, and can even be bowled along in this position, hence its other name of ball python.

Pythons usually feed on warm-blooded animals: rats, mice and pigs are frequently eaten, and even leopards are tackled by the bigger pythons. Many pythons can climb trees, and some prefer to live in or near water.

Left: Asiatic rock python attacking a leopard.

Qatar, State of, is an Arab emirate, forming a peninsula in the Persian Gulf. Capital, Doha; area about 11 000 sq km (4000 sq miles). It was under British protection until it became independent in 1971. It consists of low, sandy hills and desert plains, and is warm even in winter. The economy is based on oil, reserves of which are very large.

Quakers is the popular name for the Society of Friends, a Christian religious organization founded by George Fox (1624–1691). Fox rejected the creeds and ceremonies of all organized Churches, and while respecting the Bible, put the greatest emphasis on the Holy Spirit guiding people from within. The Quakers worship largely in silence; they are pacifists and great supporters of charity and good causes. The beliefs of the early Quakers often brought them into conflict with the authorities. Many emigrated to a colony in Pennsylvania founded in 1681 by the Quaker William Penn.

The name came from the early leaders saying that their followers should tremble in the sight of the Lord.

Quantum means 'a definite amount'. Light, heat and X-rays are forms of energy. All energy may be thought of as small amounts or packets of energy called quanta (the plural of quantum). So, a light ray becomes not a long stream of light, but many tiny quanta. A quantum of light is called a photon.

This way of thinking is known as the quantum theory. It was put forward by Max Planck in 1900, and has been used by other scientists to explain the structure of the atom. *See also* Electromagnetic radiation.

Quark is thought to be a subatomic particle. Atoms are made up of particles called electrons, neutrons and protons. Some scientists believe that these particles are made up of different types of even smaller particles, which are called quarks.

Quartz, the commonest of all minerals, is made of silica. It is found in most kinds of rocks in colourless, often transparent form. There are also coloured varieties including semi-precious stones such as amethyst and cairngorm.

Quartz is extremely hard and will scratch glass. It is the chief constituent of quartzite, sandstone and sand, and has many industrial uses. Quartz crystals are essential components of modern electronic watches.

Quasars, in astronomy, are among the most puzzling objects in the universe. They were thought to be stars: they are bright and some give out radio waves. Then, in 1963 an American astronomer, Maarten Schmidt, found that one of them seemed to be very far away. Such a distant object would have to give out an enormous amount of energy to be observed from Earth. It would have to give out as much energy as many galaxies packed together. Yet it was not very big, and could not be a star. It was called a quasi-stellar object (QSO) or quasar. Quasi-stellar means 'like a star'. Since then many quasars have been studied. Some astronomers think that they may be very young galaxies. The most distant object known in the universe is a quasar. *See also* Pulsar.

Quaternary is the period of the Earth's history that began about 2.5 million years ago and still continues. It is the second major division of the Cenozoic era, following the Tertiary, and is the period during which the human race has existed.

R

Rachmaninov, Sergei (1873–1943), was a Russian composer and pianist. He had a troubled but generally successful career in Russia, where he wrote his famous Piano Concerto No. 2 (1901) as well as his disastrous first symphony, played only once in his lifetime. In 1917 he moved to the United States and began a new career as a concert pianist. He was extremely successful, but had less time for composing.

Rachmaninov was the last of the great Russian masters of the 19th century, in whom a theme of sadness is combined with a marvellous gift for flowing melody.

Racoons are attractive carnivores living in the Americas. There are about seven species of racoon, which are 60 to 120 cm (2 to 4 ft) long. They have greyish fur and, usually, a distinctive 'masked' appearance due to darker fur around the eyes and the front of the face. Although generally found around streams, where they hunt for fish and frogs, they are frequently seen near human dwellings where they scavenge from dustbins and readily take titbits.

Radar is short for Radio Detection And Ranging. It is similar to sonar but uses radio waves instead of sound waves. Radio waves are sent out and are reflected back by any solid object they 'hit'. The farther away the object, the longer will be the time the reflected waves take to return. The shape of the object and its distance away are shown on a screen, similar to a television screen.

Radar was developed in the 1930s and used during the Second World War to detect enemy planes.

Now radar has many uses. It can be used by ships and aircraft to 'see' around them at night or in thick fog. At airports, planes landing and taking off are guided by workers, called flight controllers, using radar.

Radar can also be used to find how fast objects are moving. It is used to check, for example, the speed of cars. *See also* Sonar.

Radiation is rays of particles or waves, travelling from a source. The radiation given off by radioactive substances includes alpha rays, beta rays and gamma rays.

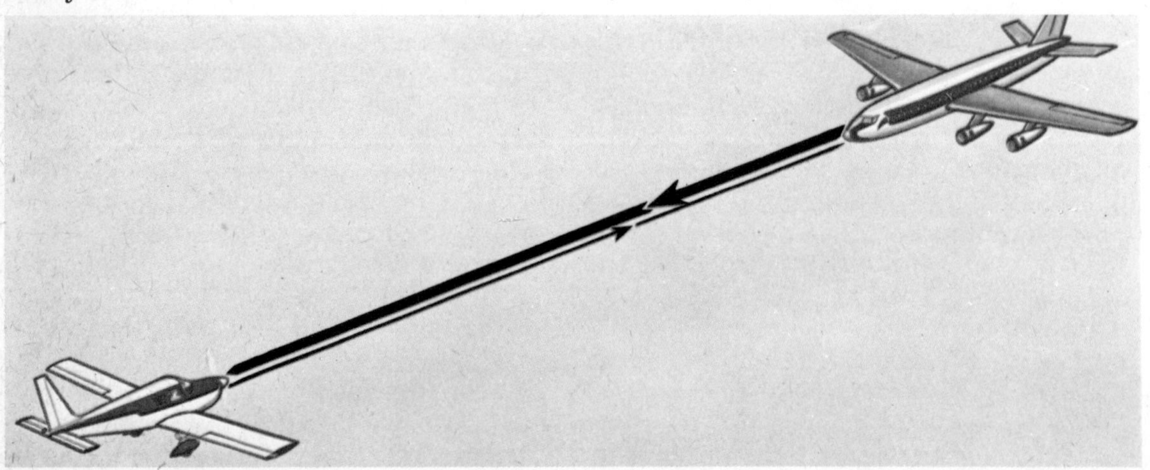

An aircraft can use radar to detect another aircraft nearby.

Light, heat and radio waves are examples of electromagnetic radiation. Other forms of radiation include cosmic rays which reach the Earth from space, and solar radiation which reaches us from the Sun.

Radio uses radio waves to carry sound from one place to another. In radio broadcasting, plays, music or other sounds are turned into electromagnetic waves in a microphone. These are transmitted by an aerial, or a tall mast. They are picked up by another aerial on a receiver. The radio sets in homes are receivers. They change the signal back into sound.

The radio was invented by Guglielmo Marconi, in 1895. The first radios sent messages in morse code. Today, messages are sent all over the world by radio, which is called radiotelegraphy. Soldiers, police, doctors and other groups can keep in touch with each other by radio.

The first radio programmes for entertainment were broadcast from radio stations in the 1920s. Now most countries have a number of radio stations. *See also* Electromagnetic radiation; Radioastronomy.

Radioactivity was discovered in 1896 by a French scientist, Henri Becquerel. He found that a lump of uranium rock was giving off rays. His studies were continued by Marie and Pierre Curie who found that the rock contained the new elements, radium and polonium. These were giving off most of the rays.

Substances which give off radiation naturally are said to be radioactive. Each element has a number of isotopes. Those that give off radioactive radiation are called radioisotopes. There are three sorts of radiation, alpha rays, beta rays and gamma rays. As the radioisotopes give off radiation, their atoms break up, and change into atoms of another substance. This is known as radioactive decay.

The time taken for radioactive decay is measured in half lives. The half life of a radioisotope is the time taken for half of its atoms to break up. Some radioisotopes have half lives of thousands of years, and others

Two examples to show the range of man-made radioactivity; a nuclear explosion and the luminous paint on a watch face. *(Left):* the radioactivity symbol.

have half lives of less than a second.

Radiation from radioactive substances can be harmful. However, radioactive substances also have many valuable uses, in medicine, industry and science.

Radioastronomy is the method by which distant parts of the universe are examined. Energy pours out of objects like the Sun in the form of radio waves, which can be detected over vast distances, well beyond the range of conventional optical telescopes. This detection is done by radio telescopes, which have extracted the most distant objects yet found, the mysterious quasars (small objects which appear to be travelling close to the speed of light and which emit enormous amounts of energy).

Radio astronomy was born from radar, when it was noticed that solar flares interfered with radar reception – radio telescopes are, in fact, very similar to radar receivers and have even been used to send radar waves to Venus, to make crude maps of the planet's invisible surface. The largest single radio telescope in the world is built in a natural 300 m (984 ft) 'bowl' at Arecibo, Puerto Rico, which has the disadvantage that it cannot be steered. Better results have been obtained since the discovery that many radio telescopes all over the world can be linked electronically to work as one huge single telescope. *See also* Radar.

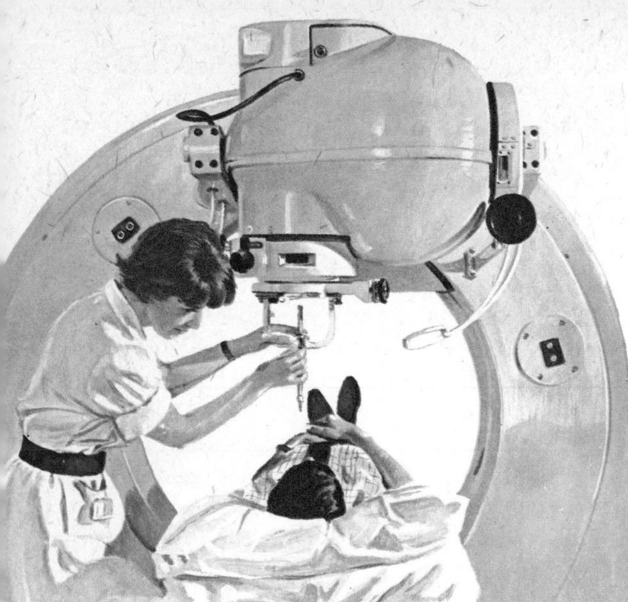

Equipment used in radiotherapy.

Radiography uses X-rays to produce an image of part of a person's body on a fluorescent screen. Bones, teeth, some tissue structure and air spaces all show up. The apparatus includes a camera which records the image for later study.

Radioisotope is an isotope which is radioactive. Every element has isotopes. Carbon has a number of isotopes. One of these, carbon 14, is radioactive. It is called a radioisotope. Our bodies contain a lot of carbon and so we contain a radioisotope. We have such small amounts that it does not harm us.

There are many natural radioisotopes. Thousands of artificial radioisotopes are made in laboratories.

Atoms of radioisotopes, too small to be seen, can be 'looked at' through their radiation. This makes radioisotopes very useful. For example, they are used in hospitals to diagnose illnesses and in factories to check engines for faults. The amount of carbon 14 isotope remaining in fossils can be used to find their age.

The radiation from radioisotopes is used to treat illnesses, such as cancer, and this is called radiotherapy. Radioisotopes can be used to produce electricity. Space probes often contain radioisotope generators.

Radio telescope is an instrument used to receive radio waves from objects in space. There are many different types of radio telescope. All contain aerials (which may resemble television aerials) to pick up the radio waves, and reflectors, which direct radio waves to the aerials. Some of the best known have a large dish-shaped reflector, such as the one at Arecibo in Puerto Rico which has a reflector 300 m (984 ft) across. Others contain a large array of much smaller reflectors and aerials.

Some radio telescopes are fully steerable, allowing any part of the sky to be observed, while others can only view particular parts of the sky.

Radio telescopes are also used to send out radio waves. The time these waves take to travel to, for example, another planet and back again shows how far away the planet is. This is called radar. *See also* Astronomy; Radioastronomy; Telescope.

Radium is a very rare silvery-coloured radioactive metal, which has the chemical symbol Ra. It was discovered by Pierre and Marie Curie during experiments with pitchblende. It is found in very small amounts in many uranium ores, such as pitchblende, and is formed during the radioactive decay of uranium. The radiation from radium is used to treat diseases such as cancer. Radium is also used on the dials of some watches, to make the dials shine.

Rafflesia is the name given to 12 species of stemless plants that grow in Malaysia as parasites on the roots of trees. The most

Rafflesia arnoldiana.

famous species is *Rafflesia arnoldiana*. This has the largest flower known – almost 1 m (39 in) across – and gives off a smell like rotten meat to attract the carrion flies that pollinate it.

Railway is a system of transport using parallel rails which trains travel along. In the first railways, wagons were drawn by horse along wooden tracks, and carried material from mines, probably as early as the 14th century. The first public railway (still for freight only) opened near Croydon, London, in 1803; the first public passenger carrying railway was at Swansea, South Wales, in 1806 – both these were horse-drawn.

Following the invention of steam engines, railways quickly gained in popularity, as it became clear that they could transport people far faster than existing methods. The first true public railway was George Stephenson's Stockton & Darlington, opened in County Durham in 1825 and using steam-powered locomotives.

Railways now operate throughout the world, crossing Asia, America and Australia, and even climbing such formidable mountain ranges as the Andes, the Alps and the Rockies. Steam locomotives are still in use, but most railways favour diesel or electric power.

Rain originates in the water vapour rising from the Earth's waters. This cools to form clouds of water droplets in the atmosphere. As these water droplets merge, they become heavy enough to overcome the upward air currents within the cloud, and fall as rain.

Rainbow is a multicoloured bow or arc, seen in the sky opposite the sun when rain is falling during sunshine. It occurs because the raindrops reflect and refract the sunlight, breaking it up into the colours of the spectrum: red, orange, yellow, green, blue, indigo and violet. Red forms the top band of the main bow. Sometimes a fainter 'secondary rainbow' can be seen (caused by double reflection of the light), and in this the order of the colours is reversed.

Rainforest is a hot, wet forest area in tropical or subtropical regions, notably the Congo basin in Africa and the Amazon basin in South America. It is often-called 'jungle'.

Extreme heat and very heavy rainfall make the rainforests moist, lush places filled with luxuriant evergreen vegetation. Trees festooned with lianas (climbing plants) rise to incredible heights and crowd toward the light to create a green 'roof' that leaves the jungle below in permanent deep shadow.

Ramakrishna (1836–1886), was a Hindu teacher and prophet. He took his name from the two Hindu gods he worshipped. From an early age he experienced religious visions, which later included visions of Allah and Jesus. He concluded that all gods and all religions are basically the same. His per-

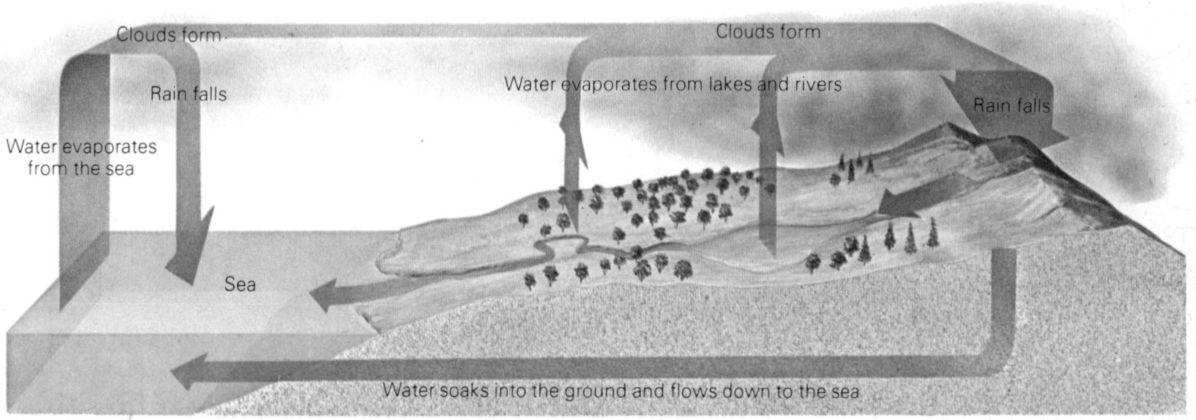
Clouds form
Rain falls
Water evaporates from the sea
Sea
Clouds form
Water evaporates from lakes and rivers
Rain falls
Water soaks into the ground and flows down to the sea

Diagram of the water cycle, showing how rain is formed.

Rameses II

sonal wisdom and saintliness attracted many followers, among them the leaders of a strong revival of Hinduism which took place at the end of the 19th century.

Rambert, Dame Marie (1888–1982), was a Polish-born dancer. In 1913 she was hired by Diaghilev to assist in Nijinsky's choreography of the *Rite of Spring*. She also danced for the Ballet Russe, though not as a soloist. In 1926 she opened a ballet school in London, from which grew the company named after her (the oldest British ballet company with a continuous history). As one of the pioneers of British ballet, she was renowned chiefly as a teacher and director who had a keen eye for spotting talented young choreographers.

Rameses II (died circa 1223 BC), was King of Egypt (circa 1290 BC—1223 BC), of the 19th Dynasty. During the early part of his reign he undertook an inconclusive military campaign against the Hittites, but he is best remembered for his building of splendid monuments, including the temple at Abu Simbel.

Raphael (1483–1520), was an Italian painter of the Renaissance in Rome. His greatest works were produced in the last twelve years of his short life – most of them with the aid of his many assistants. The serene beauty of Raphael's style brought him many followers and influenced great painters down to the 19th century.

Rasputin, Grigori Yefimovich (circa 1870–1916), was a Russian monk. Gaining a reputation as a faith-healer, he became an influential figure at the Russian court because of his apparent ability to cure the haemophiliac Crown Prince Alexis. The Russian nobility, alarmed at the power he wielded over the royal family, and thus the government of the country, had him murdered.

Rattlesnake is a venomous snake found in North America. There are about 20 species, and they get their name from the rattle-like noise they produce. The sound comes from special scales at the end of the tail, which are shaken by the snakes when they are frightened or disturbed. They sometimes grow quite large: the eastern diamond rattlesnake can reach 2.7 m (9 ft) long. Rattlesnakes live in desert, scrub, prairie and woodland, where they hunt lizards, frogs, birds and mammals. They do not lay eggs, but give birth to live young.

Ravel, Maurice (1875–1937), was a French composer. He developed a personal style, including unusual harmonies, which offended many critics. He never held an official post and had few pupils, although his genius was acknowledged (by some people) very early. He was at his best with small-scale works, like the string quartet *Shéhérazade* (1903), one of many compositions which reveal his liking for dance music. Among his large orchestral pieces, the most famous is the ballet, *Daphnis and Chloe* (1912).

Raven is the largest member of the Corvidae, or crow family. It is over 60 cm (2 ft) long and every part of it – plumage, bill and legs – is black. The raven nests on cliffs and in trees in Eurasia and North America, where it feeds on young seabirds and small mammals. It also glides about the skies looking for carrion to eat on the ground below.

Raven

Rayon is a synthetic material. It was once known as artificial silk, and is used to make many things, including clothes, curtains and carpets. Rayon is made from a chemical called cellulose. All plants contain cellulose. Plants such as cotton, and fibres from wood are used to make rayon. They are heated or dissolved in other chemicals to form a thick treacle. This is pushed through small holes to make threads. The threads are spun and woven into rayon material.

Rays are fish, related to the sharks. They have skeletons composed of cartilage instead of bone, and flattened bodies. The small mouth, nostrils and gills are underneath. The pectoral fins are large, and the fish swim by undulations of these fins. In many species the tail is thin and whip-like. Electricity is often produced in the tail and some species also deliver venom from it. All rays lay their eggs in horny capsules with little coils at the ends, which wind around seaweeds so that they do not get washed away. Rays are found throughout the world's oceans.

Razorbill is a black and white seabird related to the puffins and guillemots. It has small wings and webbed feet, and the top half of the beak is curved over like a bird of prey's. Razorbills nest in flocks, and thousands may gather together on cliffs around the North Atlantic and Arctic Oceans.

Reagan, Ronald (1911–), is an American politician. After a successful career as a film actor, he entered politics and was elected Governor of California in 1966, being re-elected in 1970. In 1980 he stood as Republican candidate for the presidency of the USA, and was elected after defeating his Democratic opponent, Jimmy Carter.

Red giant is a large cool star. It is thought that our Sun will one day become a red giant. Hydrogen in the centre of the Sun changes to helium by fusion. This produces the energy, such as light and heat, which we receive from the Sun. When the hydrogen in the centre has all been changed into helium, other reactions will start. These will produce more energy and the Sun will start to swell. As it gets bigger, the outer layers will cool down and it will change from yellow to red in colour. As a red giant, it will be so big that it will swallow up Mercury, Venus and possibly even the Earth. It is thought that the Sun will become a red giant in about 5000 million years time. *See also* White dwarf.

Red Sea is an arm of the Indian Ocean, between Africa and Arabia. Area about 438 000 sq km (169 000 sq miles). It is linked to the Mediterranean by the Suez Canal. It is in one of the hottest regions of the world and no major rivers flow into it so it is rather salty. Rocky islands and reefs make navigation dangerous, but it is a major shipping route thanks to the Canal.

Redshift and blueshift are observed to find if stars and galaxies are moving away from the Earth or towards it. Light is not really white. It is made up of a spectrum of colours from red to blue. These colours have different wavelengths. Red light has a longer wavelength than blue light. The movement of a star changes the wavelength of its light as seen from the Earth. If it is moving away from us, its wavelengths appear to lengthen. They move towards the red end of the spectrum. This is known as redshift. If the star is moving towards us, its wavelengths appear to shorten. They move towards the blue end of the spectrum. This is known as blueshift. Nearly all galaxies show a redshift. This means that they are moving away from us.

Redshift and blueshift are often known as the Doppler effect, after Christian Doppler who described the principle in 1842.

Redwoods are coniferous trees, originally found in Oregon and California, USA, but now planted in many other parts of the world. Some of the redwoods can claim the title of the tallest trees in the world. One Californian coast redwood measures 110 m (362 ft) high.

Refinery is a place used for separating a substance from a mixture. For example, sugar refineries take sugar from sugar beet and cane; metals are taken from their ores in refineries.

Many different methods are used for refining. One of the biggest industries in the world is petroleum refining. Petroleum oil contains many substances. When the petroleum is heated, the different substances boil at different temperatures. In this way different fractions of the petroleum are separated from one another. This is done in large towers called fractionating columns. The petroleum is separated into petrol, paraffin, diesel oil, lubricating oil and other oils. Some of these are used to make more petrol by a process calling cracking. *See also* Petroleum.

Reflection occurs when waves are bounced back from a surface. If you look down into a smooth pond you will see an image of your face in it. This is because some light is turned or reflected back to your eyes by the surface of the pond.

If you make ripples in the water, the image of your face will disappear. Although some light is still being reflected, it bounces off the ripples in many different directions. This means that no image is formed.

Rough and smooth surfaces reflect light. Smooth surfaces, such as mirrors, reflect light in the same direction so that they form an image – a reflection. Sound, radar, heat and all other waves can be reflected. The reflection of sound waves may be heard as an echo.

Reformation was a religious movement in 16th-century Europe which ended religious unity and led to the establishment of Protestant Churches. There had been previous attempts to reform the Roman Catholic Church, but these had failed. However, the revival of learning brought about by the Renaissance made the educated more critical of the teachings of the Church, and many rulers resented the political power of the papacy.

The Reformation really began in Germany in 1517. A monk, Martin Luther, nailed a protest against the sale of indulgences (which offered forgiveness of sins in return for cash payments) on a church door in Wittenberg. Luther's action was condemned by the Pope, but it was decisive in starting the train of events which brought about the Reformation. By the end of the 16th century, Switzerland, Scotland, the Netherlands, Scandinavia, England and many German states had adopted Protestantism.

Refraction is the name given to the bending of light rays when they pass from one substance to another. If you put the end of a pencil in water, the end looks fatter and slightly bent. The pencil has not changed, but it looks different because the light has been 'bent' passing from the air into the water. This is because light travels at different speeds in different substances. Refraction can make objects look bigger or smaller and nearer or further away. Lenses are used in instruments, such as the telescope, to refract light. Refraction can also split light into its many different colours. *See also* Spectrum.

Refrigeration is a process to keep things cool. Meat, vegetables and other foods rot in warm places because bacteria can grow easily there. Refrigerating foodstuffs stops the bacteria growing so easily. Blocks of ice used to be used to preserve food. Now, refrigerators have pipes containing liquids called refrigerants. These pipes carry heat from inside the refrigerator to the outside.

Reindeer of Eurasia is the semi-domesticated form of the North American caribou. Unlike the deer, both sexes bear antlers. The reindeer spends the summer feeding on lichens and grasses on the open tundra, but migrates into the forests during the winter, where it browses on twigs. The caribou may reach a height of 1.5 m (5 ft) at the shoulder, whereas the reindeer is smaller. The reindeer is used for meat, as a pack animal and for its hide.

Relativity is a very important subject in science, particularly to scientists who study the structure of the atom and the universe. Albert Einstein put forward the Theories of Relativity in 1905 and 1916. The following are some of the ideas in his theories.

Reindeer

The speed of an object depends on the speed of the person looking at it, the observer.

Light always travels at the same speed. Nothing can travel faster than light. As an object nears the speed of light, it gets shorter and its mass gets bigger.

Matter and energy are different forms of the same thing. This idea is put into use in nuclear reactors, to change matter into energy, as electricity.

Rembrandt van Rijn (1606–1669), was the greatest artist of the Dutch school in the 17th century. He is one of the greatest

One of Rembrandt's many self-portraits.

painters in all European art. Rembrandt had tremendous range as an artist (his etchings are especially famous), but his greatest gifts, apart from sheer technical ability in the handling of paint, were the power of his imagination and his deep, sympathetic insight into human character. His own self-portraits are among his most moving works, revealing his state of mind more clearly than words could do. He was master of many different subjects – religious and mythological, still-lifes, paintings of ordinary life, landscapes and portraits. He even experimented with the style of India under the Mogul emperors.

Renaissance was the period in European history between the Middle Ages and the modern age. Renaissance means 'rebirth'. It refers to the revival of the ideas, art and learning of the Classical period (ancient Greece and Rome). Equally important were the new ideas and beliefs which developed as a result of this interest and are known under the general name of humanism.

Cultural life in the Middle Ages was dominated by the Christian Church, which taught that human beings are sinful and that the things of this world are to be despised. The humanists, however, like the pre-Christian Greeks and Romans, put the highest value on human beings and their affairs. The result was a remarkable advance in all fields of knowledge – scientific, philosophical and artistic.

The Renaissance began in Italy and was at its peak between 1450 and 1550, when the main centres were first Florence and later Rome. Florence produced a large number of great artists who, inspired by remains from the Roman Empire, started a style that dominated European art for 400 years.

Assisted by the recent invention of printing, Renaissance ideas spread rapidly throughout Europe. Nevertheless, the Renaissance cannot be pinned down to a single century. In literature, it was underway in Italy in the time of Petrarch and Boccaccio (mid-14th century). In architecture the Renaissance had little effect in England (for example) until the 17th century.

Renoir, Pierre Auguste (1841–1919), was a French painter. One of the greatest members of the French school, he was an original member of the Impressionist group, a friend

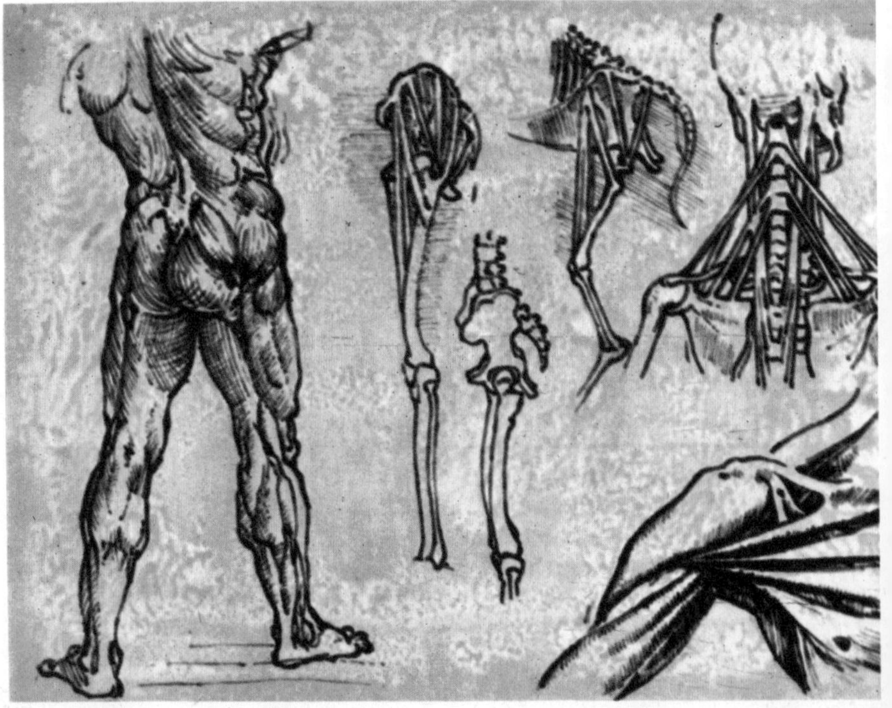

Above: Leonardo da Vinci (1452–1519). He was a great artist of the Renaissance, and was fascinated by, amongst many other things, anatomy. *Right:* some of his anatomical sketches.

of Monet and an exhibitor in the Impressionist exhibitions of the 1870s. Renoir's chief interest was not landscape but the human figure, especially the female figure, and his warm glowing nudes are his most famous pictures.

Until his final period, there is often an interesting conflict in Renoir between his Impressionist loyalties (colour, atmosphere, soft outlines) and his Classical instincts (a harder line, stronger 'modelling' of forms).

Reproduction is the natural process among animals and plants by which new individuals are created, and the species perpetuated. There are two main kinds of reproduction: sexual and asexual.

Asexual, or vegetative reproduction, is the splitting of an animal into two parts of equal size, each of which can become an adult. This is common among one-celled organisms.

Sexual reproduction in its higher forms involves the fusion of an egg cell by a sperm cell. The egg (ovum) is produced by the female and the sperm by the male of each species.

Some animals, such as snails and worms, can produce sperms and eggs simultaneously; others are male at one stage of life and female at another. In parthenogenesis (virgin birth) no sperm is needed; male bees, for example, are produced from unfertilized eggs, although female bees are formed in the normal way. Most animals, unlike human beings, can reproduce only at certain seasons of the year. *See also* Egg; Fertilization; Spore.

Reptiles are a large and ancient group of cold-blooded vertebrates. Some species – for instance, the crocodile – look very similar to the prehistoric reptiles which roamed the earth millions and millions of years ago. Unlike the amphibians, from which the reptiles evolved, reptiles lay shelled eggs. This means that they are less dependent upon water than the amphibians, and do not need to return to it for breeding. However, some species, the sea snake for instance, have chosen to live in water. Reptiles also have protective scaly skins which help them retain their own body fluids.

Painted terrapin

Reptiles are found throughout the warm and temperate regions of the world. There are four main orders, or groups, of reptiles. The tuatara is a primitive lizard-like creature which is found on a few offshore islands near New Zealand. The next order, the lizards and snakes, is the largest group. The third order contains the crocodiles, alligators, caiman and gharials. The last order is made up of the tortoises, turtles and terrapins. *See also* Cold-blooded; Scales.

Resin is a sticky liquid which oozes from plants. In the air it sets into a hard substance, and it dissolves in liquids such as oils. The resins, turpentine and rosin, come from pine trees. Turpentine is used in paints, polishes and medicine. Rosin is used for paints, gums, polishes, varnishes and other things.

Amber is resin from plants which lived millions of years ago. It sometimes contains an insect or other animal which was trapped in the resin when it set. Amber is used for jewellery and ornaments.

Resins are also made from chemicals: polyurethane is an example of a synthetic resin.

Respiration is a complicated process which takes place in animals and plants, resulting in the release of energy. This energy is used to carry out the functions of a living organism, such as muscle movement, cell regeneration and growth.

In most animals, part of respiration

involves breathing – that is, taking oxygen into the body. Fish breathe by means of gills, but when we breathe we use lungs to draw oxygen into our bodies. Plants do not truly breathe, but they take in oxygen by means of tiny holes in their leaves called stomata. Once the oxygen is taken in, it is used by both plants and animals to chemically 'burn' food in the body, releasing energy. The food which is burned is in the form of glucose, and the release of energy is accompanied by the conversion of some of the glucose and oxygen into carbon dioxide and water. The equation for respiration is:

$$\underset{\text{glucose}}{C_6H_{12}O_6} + \underset{\text{oxygen}}{6\ O_2} \rightarrow \underset{\text{carbon dioxide}}{6\ CO_2} + \underset{\text{water}}{6\ H_2O} + \text{energy.}$$

Some simple organisms, such as bacteria and yeasts, respire without using oxygen to break down glucose. This is called *anaerobic* respiration, and the equation for this is:

$$\underset{\text{glucose}}{C_6H_{12}O_6} \rightarrow \underset{\text{ethyl alcohol}}{2C_2H_5OH} + \underset{\text{carbon dioxide}}{2CO_2} + \text{energy.}$$

Yeast is used by brewers because it produces alcohol during its respiration.

Rhea is a flightless South American bird. It is like an ostrich in appearance, with a plump body carried on long, featherless legs, and a long neck. Rheas are the largest birds in the New World, the common rhea standing 1.5 m (5 ft) high.

Rhine is a river in Western Europe. It begins in Switzerland at the junction of the Hinterrhein and Vorderrhein, and flows for 1320 km (820 miles) through West Germany and the Netherlands to the North Sea. The foremost river of Western Europe, flowing through a heavily populated region, the Rhine is an important route for trade. It gives Switzerland an outlet to the sea as barges can be towed as far as Basel. Its valley, in parts, is exceedingly beautiful, and is dotted with ancient castles. Wine is an important product of the Rhine Valley.

Rhinoceros is a bulky, hoofed mammal, whose body is covered in extremely tough skin – so much so that adults have only human beings to fear. Despite their fearsome appearance, rhinoceroses are herbivores, and will only charge if threatened. There are five species of rhinoceros: the Indian, the Javan, the Sumatran, and the white and black rhinoceroses of Africa. All are in danger of extinction, being cruelly hunted for their horns, which are supposed to have magical properties. The 'horns' are in fact really very hard (keratinized) skin.

Rhizome is an underground stem, complete with roots and tiny, scale-like leaves. It lies horizontally in the soil and sprouts new shoots above ground each spring. After the plants have produced seeds or spores, the part of the plant above ground withers. The rest of the plant then exists below ground, using the food reserves stored in the rhizome, until the following spring. Examples of plants which have rhizomes are iris, bracken and couch grass.

Rhodes, Cecil John (1853–1902), was a British colonist and financier. He went to Africa and became a diamond miner, amassing a considerable fortune. In 1881 Rhodes was elected a member of the Cape Parliament representing Kimberley, the site of his diamond mines.

At this time, South Africa was split between areas ruled by Britain and areas ruled by the Boers – descendants of the Dutch settlers. Rhodes's aim was to unite these and bring them into the British Empire.

He helped Britain acquire land in Africa, including the huge area later known as Rhodesia (Zimbabwe). He became Prime Minister of the Cape Colony in 1890 and stayed in office for six years, but was forced to resign when his part in the Jameson Raid was discovered. (The Jameson Raid was an unsuccessful armed raid into the Boer Republic of Transvaal in 1895 led by Sir L S Jameson with the aim of supporting a projected rising of British settlers in Johannesburg.)

Rhône is a river in Switzerland and southern France. It rises in the Swiss Alps and

The young Richard II confronts Wat Tyler and his men during the Peasants' Revolt.

flows west and south for about 810 km (503 miles) to its delta on the Mediterranean. With its chief tributary, the Saône, which joins it at Lyons, it has long been an important communications system between the Mediterranean and northern France.

Rhythm and blues is the style of jazz which developed in US cities out of the older blues of the country regions. The blues, a kind of black lament, followed a strict form of harmony, usually over 12 bars. Rhythm and blues was the main musical inspiration behind the explosion of pop music in the 1960s.

Richard I (1157–1199), was King of England (1189–1199). He came to the throne in succession to his father, Henry II. He was also known as Richard the Lion-Heart. Richard spent most of his reign abroad and neglected his kingdom. He joined the Third Crusade in 1189, and on his return was captured and imprisoned by the Holy Roman Emperor, being released only on the payment of a huge ransom. He died while fighting in France. His expensive wars left England with a heavy burden of taxation.

Richard II (1367–1400), was King of England (1377–1399). He came to the throne in succession to his grandfather Edward III. During his minority his uncle, John of Gaunt, was the effective ruler of the country. Richard showed skill in his dealing with the rebel, Wat Tyler, during the Peasants' Revolt (1381), but his increasingly tyrannical conduct of affairs and his dependence upon favourites made him many enemies. He suppressed one group of rebellious barons, but in 1399 was forced to abdicate and died (possibly murdered) in prison.

Richard III (1452–1485), was King of England (1483–1485). He was the younger brother of Edward IV. On Edward's death he made himself protector of the young Edward V, whom he subsequently declared to be illegitimate. Richard then seized the throne, and Edward V, together with his younger brother, was probably murdered in the Tower of London. Richard succeeded in putting down one rebellion, but was defeated and killed at Bosworth in 1485 by Henry Tudor, the Lancastrian claimant to the throne.

Richelieu, Armand Jean du Plassis de (1585–1642), was a French Cardinal and statesman. When he became chief minister to Louis XIII in 1624, his aim was to make the authority of the crown supreme, and his first task was the suppression of the power of the Huguenots, whom he crushed at La Rochelle in 1629. During the Thirty Years' War he allied France with the Protestant states in order to counteract the influence of the Austrian and Spanish Hapsburgs, and by the time of his death France was becoming dominant in Europe at the expense of Spain. Richelieu was a wealthy patron of the arts and founded the French Academy in 1635.

Rimsky-Korsakov, Nikolai (1844–1908), was a Russian composer. He was a sailor and knew little about composition when he wrote his early works. However, these were good enough to gain him a professorship of composition at St Petersburg (Leningrad). His interest in folk music influenced his own orchestral music, including his operas which, after a period of neglect, have recently come back into favour. Though not of the first rank, his music brilliantly captures the atmosphere of Russia under the last tsars.

Rio Grande is a river in south-west North America. It rises in Colorado and flows south, forming the border between Texas and Mexico, to the Gulf of Mexico. Length about 3034 km (1885 miles). The region is dry and the water level varies. The river carries much silt and has been jokingly described as 'a mile wide, a foot deep, too thin to plough, too thick to drink'. Its changing course has caused past boundary disputes between the USA and Mexico. It has been developed to provide irrigation and power.

RNA, see Nucleic acids.

Robert Bruce (1274–1329), was King of Scotland (1306–1329). He rose in rebellion against Edward I of England and had himself crowned King against Edward's wishes. Forced to go into exile, he gradually recovered his lands. In 1314 he defeated Edward II at the Battle of Bannockburn. This great victory gave Scotland its independence, which was formally acknowledged by England in 1328.

Maximilian Robespierre

Robespierre, Maximilian (1758–1794), was one of the most important people in the French Revolution. A provincial lawyer,he was elected to the Estates General in 1789, and subsequently became the leader of a radical group known as the Jacobins. He supported the overthrow of the more moderate Girondins and insisted on the execution of Louis XVI. When he was elected to the Committee of Public Safety in 1793, a position which gave him supreme power, he established the Reign of Terror. This phase of the Revolution used ruthless, authoritarian methods to resist rebellion and invasion. Robespierre justified these measures with the argument that a revolutionary government must take all steps necessary to defend itself. In 1794 Robespierre was overthrown and guillotined. *See also* French Revolution.

Robin Hood is a character in English legend. He was the leader of a band of outlaws who lived in Sherwood Forest during the 12th century, robbing the rich and giving to the poor. His chief companions were Little John, Will Scarlet, Allan-a-Dale, Friar Tuck and Maid Marian; their great enemy was the sheriff of nearby Nottingham. Robin was loyal to the king, Richard I, but not to the regent, Richard's brother John.

Robot is a complicated machine, which is used to perform tasks. Robots are often controlled by computers. Usually they contain a store of information and instructions which enables them to perform one task or a number of them and to make decisions about how to perform the tasks. Robots are often used to do work which would be dangerous or boring for people.

The word robot comes from a Czechoslovakian word meaning slave.

Rock is the solid material of which the Earth's crust is made. There are three main types of rock: igneous, sedimentary and metamorphic rocks. They have each been formed in different ways.

Hot magma (melted rock) cools when it reaches the Earth's surface to form igneous rock. Most rocks are igneous rocks. They include granite and basalt.

Rock can be worn away by waves, rivers, ice and wind. Pieces of rock, dead animals and plants, are carried away by water and air. They are eventually dropped or deposited and are called sediment. The sediment slowly builds up, and over millions of years it is pushed together to form sedimentary rocks. These include limestone, sandstone and clay. Sedimentary rocks often contain the remains of animals and plants.

Inside the Earth, igneous and sedimentary rocks are pressed down and heated to very

Diagram showing how rocks are formed and shaped.

high temperatures. This forms metamorphic rock, such as slate and marble.

Rocket was the first practical high-speed railway locomotive, built in 1829 by George and Robert Stephenson for the Liverpool & Manchester Railway. *Rocket* featured a new design of boiler, in which water was heated by 25 tubes carrying heat from the fire, and it had an exhaust system which helped draw the hot air through the boiler. Both these features were the basis of all subsequent steam locomotives. *Rocket* could haul a 14 tonne train at almost 50 km/h (31 mph), twice that of rival designs.

Rocky Mountains form a mountain range in North America. They run the length of the USA and Canada near the Pacific coast for about 6500 km (4040 miles), forming a section of the mountain chain that stretches from the southern tip of South America to the western tip of Alaska. The highest point in the Rockies is Mount McKinley in Alaska at 6195 m (20 324 ft) high.

Rococo was a minor style in art which developed from Baroque in the 18th century. Rococo is essentially a decorative style, light and graceful, with elegant curves, and ornament based on shells, flowers and garlands.

Rodents are the most numerous and widespread of all the groups of mammals. There are over 1700 species world-wide, and they range in size from the largest, the capybara of South America which is over 1 m (over 3 ft) long, to the smallest, the harvest mouse, only 6 cm (2.5 in) long. They are herbivorous, often nocturnal animals, whose front teeth are chisel-shaped, enabling them to gnaw through seeds and bark with great ease. It has also enabled many species – rats and mice, for instance – to gnaw through cables, get into food stores and generally be a pest to humans. Rodents of one type or another have succeeded in exploiting almost every type of habitat throughout the world – water, deserts, woodland, jungle, prairie and cities. They can breed very quickly, resulting in huge numbers of them. Some of the most common rodents are rats, mice, porcupines, beavers, squirrels and prairie dogs.

Rodin, Auguste (1840–1917), was a French sculptor, the outstanding sculptor of the modern period. Like Moore, he was not a truly revolutionary artist, though his work sometimes caused fierce arguments. His subject was always the human figure.

Rodin admired the past, especially the Classical tradition and Michelangelo (but also Gothic sculpture), and at the same time pointed the way to the future, some works having an almost abstract quality. In his efforts to get a natural pose, he would tell his models to move about the studio while he captured their movements with quick pencil sketches. *See also* Moore, Henry.

Rolls Royce is the famous company formed by two Englishmen, salesman Charles Rolls (1877–1910) and engineer Frederick Royce (1863–1933). At first they built motor cars, coining the phrase 'best car in the world' for their Silver Ghost model, but the company later moved into aviation and today is one of the world's leading suppliers of jet aircraft engines.

Roman architecture was the style of building in the Roman Empire. Though the Romans learned much from the Greeks, their architecture, unlike Greek, made use of rounded forms (arches, vaults and domes). The column became less important, except as a decoration, because solid walls supported the roof.

The Romans, inferior to the Greeks as artists, were brilliant engineers and technologists, and used manufactured materials like bricks and concrete. They were ready to experiment, and built a greater variety of buildings than the Greeks, including some bridges and aqueducts which are still standing, and their famous roads. Roman houses, or villas, were also large and well built – sometimes with a form of central heating.

The style of architecture in Europe in the early Middle Ages (up to about 1100 in northern Europe) is known as Romanesque ('like Roman'). Its basic feature is the round arch.

Roman Britain is a period of British history from 55 BC to the 5th century AD. The first contacts between Rome and Britain took place in 55 and 54 BC when Julius Caesar brought his legions across the Channel from Gaul (France) and began his invasion. However, the conquest of Britain by the Romans was not begun in earnest until AD 43, when Claudius' army arrived. Eventually most of England and Wales were brought under Roman control, the task being completed by the Emperor Hadrian who built a wall in AD 122 to mark the northern boundary of Roman Britain. The Romans established a network of roads and built towns at London, York, Chester, Bath, Colchester and elsewhere. Roman Britain was a peaceful, settled community, but its civilization came to an end early in the 5th century when the Roman legions began to withdraw, leaving the country undefended against barbarian invasions.

Roman Catholicism is the Christian religious body which acknowledges the pope, under Jesus Christ, as its head. It has a continuous history almost since the death of Christ nearly 2000 years ago, and its world membership today is over 300 million.

At an early date Christianity was divided into the Eastern (Byzantine) and Western (Roman) Churches. In Europe the Roman Church was the only Church. It exercised enormous authority over individuals and governments, and under its leadership Europe was more closely united than it has ever been since. Monasteries were the main centres of civilization outside royal courts.

The Reformation split Western Christians in the 16th century. In England for example it became dangerous to be a Roman Catholic. However, the Roman Church recovered some of its authority during the Counter-Reformation, reforming its own faults and mounting a strong counter-attack against Protestantism.

During the 18th century the Church grew increasingly unpopular, especially in countries like France where it was seen as an obstacle to progress, but another Catholic revival took place in the 19th century. More recently, the Church, like all Churches, has been threatened by the growing desire in Christian society for power and possessions, which was held responsible for a fall in churchgoing, and by Communism, which is opposed to all religions.

Roman Emperors

27 BC – AD 14	Augustus
14–37	Tiberius
37–41	Caligula
41–54	Claudius
54–68	Nero
68–69	Galba
69	Vitellius
69–79	Vespasian
79–81	Titus
81–96	Domitian
96–98	Nerva
98–117	Trajan
117–138	Hadrian
138–161	Antoninus Pius
161–169	Lucius Aurelius Verus

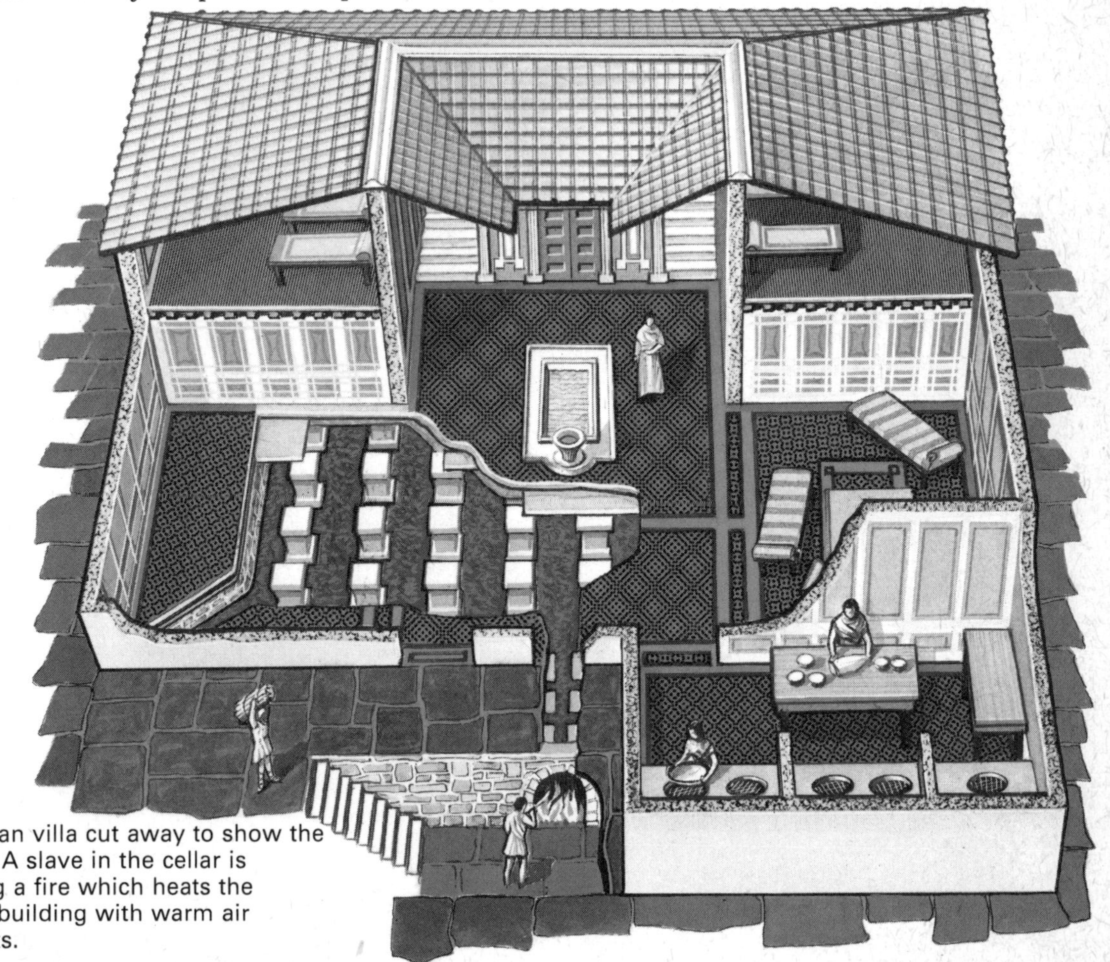

A Roman villa cut away to show the inside. A slave in the cellar is tending a fire which heats the whole building with warm air currents.

169–180	Marcus Aurelius
180–192	Commodus
193	Pertinax
193	Didius Julian
193–211	Septimius Severus
211–217	Caracalla
211–212	Geta
217–218	Macrinus
218–222	Elagabalus
222–235	Alexander Severus
235–238	Maximin
238	Gordian I
238	Gordian II
238	Pupienus
238–244	Gordian III
244–249	Philip
249–251	Decius
251	Hostilian
251–253	Gallus
253	Aemilian
253–259	Valerian
259–268	Gallienus
268–270	Claudius II
270	Quintillus
270–275	Aurelian
275–276	Tacitus
276	Florian
276–282	Probus
282–283	Carus
283–284	Numerian
283–285	Carinus
285–305	Diocletian
286–305	Maximian
305–306	Constantius I
305–311	Galerius
306–307	Severus
306–308	Maximian
306–312	Maxentius
308–313	Maximinus
311–324	Licinius
311–337	Constantine I
337–340	Constantine II
337–361	Constantius II
337–350	Constans
361–363	Julian
363–364	Jovian
364–375	Valentinian I (Emperor in the West)
364–378	Valens (Emperor in the East)
375–383	Gratian (Emperor in the West)
375–392	Valentinian II (Emperor in the West)
379–395	Theodosius
383–388	Maximus (Emperor in the West)
392–394	Eugenius (Emperor in the West)

Caligula, Emperor of Rome from 37 to 41 AD.

Roman Emperors in the West

395–423	Honorius
421	Constantius III
425–455	Valentian III
455	Petronius Maximus
455–456	Avitus
457–461	Majorian
461–465	Libius Severus
467–472	Anthemius
472	Olybrius
473	Glycerius
473–475	Julius Nepos
475–476	Romulus Augustulus

Roman Emperors in the East

395–408	Arcadius
408–450	Theodosius II
450–457	Marcian
457–474	Leo I
473–474	Leo II
474–491	Zeno

Roman Empire was the period in the history of ancient Rome from 27 BC when Octavian became absolute ruler as Augustus, with the title Emperor, until AD 476 when the last Emperor was deposed. As a republic, Rome was already the dominant power in the Mediterranean world and had conquered Gaul and Asia Minor. Augustus pushed Rome's frontiers to the Rhine and the Danube, and created an efficient government which ensured peace and prosperity for the many people under Roman rule.

The Empire reached its greatest extent in the 2nd century AD. In the 3rd century it began to decline, partly as a result of the incursions of barbarian tribes and partly because of a breakdown in administration. In 395 the Empire was divided into two parts. The eastern half became the Byzantine Empire, while the western half eventually collapsed under successive waves of invasions.

Romania is a republic in south-east Europe. Capital, Bucharest; area about 237 000 sq km (92 000 sq miles). Romania emerged from Turkish rule in 1878. During the Second World War it sided with Germany, was conquered by the Soviet Union, and became a communist republic in 1947.

Romania is crossed by the Carpathian mountains which enclose the plateau of Transylvania.

The River Danube flows in the south and east, along most of the boundary with Bulgaria. With its tributaries, it drains most of the country. The population is mixed and includes a large Hungarian-speaking minority.

Cereals and root crops are grown on the plains, and there are large orchards and vineyards. Agriculture is mostly practised on collective farms, and there are few private holdings. Of natural resources, most valuable are the oil and gas reserves. There has been a great increase in industrialization under communist rule. Roads are rather poor, but there is a good railway system.

Rome is the capital of Italy. It is 27 km (17 miles) from the Mediterranean Sea on the River Tiber. Rome was the centre of European civilization in the days of the Roman Empire, and has been an important political and cultural centre for over 1000 years. The Vatican, the headquarters of the Pope, has been there since the Middle Ages. It is an independent state within the city.

Modern Rome is crowded, with a severe traffic problem. It is a major industrial and business centre and a great tourist attraction. It contains many artistic treasures especially of the Classical and Renaissance periods.

Romulus and Remus, in Roman myth, were the twin sons of Mars (Ares). As babies they were set afloat in a basket on the River Tiber, but were rescued by a she-wolf and brought up by a shepherd and his wife. When they grew up they decided to found a city, but when Remus crossed the boundary line into his brother's territory, Romulus killed him. The city Romulus founded was Rome, and he was later worshipped there as a god.

Roosevelt, Franklin Delano (1882–1945), was an American statesman, President of the USA from 1933 to 1945. He was elected President despite being confined to a wheelchair. He took measures to help his country to recover from the world economic depression by stimulating trade, agriculture and industry and providing welfare services for the needy. He introduced Lend-Lease aid to help Britain during the Second World War, and brought the USA into the war after the Japanese attack on Pearl Harbor. The only American President to be re-elected three times, he died just before the end of the war.

Roosevelt, Theodore (1858–1919), was an American statesman, President of the USA from 1901 to 1909. He had become famous during the Spanish-American War of 1898, when he commanded a volunteer cavalry force in Cuba, known as 'the rough riders'. As President he followed an aggressive foreign policy designed to secure North American dominance over South America. In 1903 he obtained control of the Panama Canal Zone. At home he took action to restrict the

Theodore Roosevelt *(left)* and Franklin Roosevelt.

growth of big business organizations. Re-elected President in 1904, he was defeated when he stood for office again in 1912.

Root is the part of a plant which normally grows downwards into the soil, anchoring the plant in position and acting as a means of drawing water and vital minerals into the plant. Some plants produce aerial roots, however, which hang from branches and enter the soil. The root of a dandelion is a long, thick, tapering structure with a few tiny hair-like roots branching from it. This is an example of a tap root. Another sort of root is a fibrous root. Fibrous roots consist of a mass of small roots of even thickness, and are found, for example, in daisies.

Rose family is a large collection of herbs, shrubs, climbers and trees. Some of the more familiar species in the family are blackberry, mountain ash, hawthorn and the beautiful wild and cultivated roses found throughout the world. In addition to these plants, the rose family also includes many of our best-known fruit trees such as the apple, pear, plum, cherry and peach. Wild members of the rose family bear flowers with five petals, but the commercial roses of gardens and parks usually have many more petals.

Rossini, Gioacchino Antonio (1792–1868), was an Italian composer. Once apprenticed to a blacksmith, he wrote his first opera as a student in Bologna. Following success in Milan and Vienna, he became musical director of both opera houses in Naples, where he wrote, among other operas, *The Barber of Seville* (1816). In 1824 he settled in Paris. As director of the Italian Theatre there he wrote several more operas, including *William Tell* (1829). During the next 40 years he only wrote two fine religious works.

Rossini's bubbling, brilliant comic operas (some of them written in a week or two) have kept their appeal to this day.

Rousseau, Jean-Jacques (1712–1778), was a French philosopher and writer. He was one of the most influential thinkers of the age of Enlightenment. *The Social Contract* (1762) explained his doctrine that the highest authority in the state is the 'general will',

Some examples of cultivated roses. *Left to right:*
Ellen Poulsen Rose
hips (fruit of the rose)
Mrs Pierre S Dupont
Rosa Mundi
Masquerade

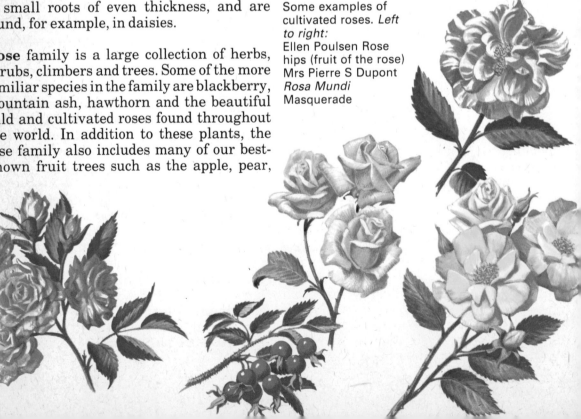

which amounted to an argument for popular democracy. His novel *Emile* (1762) had a powerful influence on educational reform, though the anti-religious views expressed led to a warrant for Rousseau's arrest. His novel *Julie* (1761), with its emphasis on feeling as opposed to reason, foreshadowed Romanticism. His *Confessions*, published in 1782 after his death, is one of the frankest autobiographies ever written.

Royal Ballet is a British ballet company. It gained its present name in 1956 and was previously known as Sadler's Wells. The company originated in the co-operation between Dame Ninette De Valois and Lilian Baylis in 1931 at the Old Vic Theatre. Nearly all the great figures in British ballet have been associated with the company. It gained its great international reputation after the Second World War when it moved into Covent Garden (with a new production of *The Sleeping Beauty*), began to attract international artists like Balanchine, and started regular tours abroad. In recent years it has consisted of two companies – the resident London company and a smaller company which is mostly on tour in the provinces.

Rubber is a springy substance used to make tyres and many other things. Natural rubber is made from a juice, called latex, obtained from rubber trees. Holes are made in the bark of these trees to drain off the latex. Substances are added to the rubber to give it different properties. It is hardened, so that goods can be made from it, by adding sulphur, then heating. This 'curing' of rubber is called vulcanization.

Synthetic rubber is made from petroleum or coal. Most of the rubber used today is synthetic rubber.

Rubber tree, also known as the para or caoutchouc tree, is the main source of the milky sap called latex which is turned into rubber. The rubber tree grows to a height of 18 m (60 ft) along the edges of the River Amazon in the tropical rainforests of South America. In 1876 an Englishman called Henry Wickham collected 70000 seeds of the tree and, evading the Brazilian customs who had placed an embargo on their new-found asset, managed to plant 2700 seeds at Kew, England. The young trees were then sent to Sri Lanka, and from them stemmed the vast rubber tree industry of the Malay Peninsula, Sri Lanka, Burma and India.

A rubber tree and a trunk, showing how latex is extracted by tapping.

Rubens, Peter Paul (1577–1640), was a Flemish painter, the great master of Baroque painting. He was knighted by Charles I of England, and is said to have produced over 3000 paintings (some, like the ceiling of the Banqueting Hall in Whitehall, London, very large), as well as hundreds of drawings. He invented a new technique in oil painting which made possible his powerful light effects, and he created masterpieces in every kind of painting – portraits, religious subjects, peasant life, landscape, etc. He employed an army of assistants but supervised them carefully so that standards of work from his studio remained high. His influence on later painters, such as Delacroix, was enormous.

Ruminants are a group of herbivorous mammals whose diet consists of grass and other plants which must be chewed thoroughly

Cows, which are ruminants, grazing.

before it can be digested. If such animals stood in the open whilst they carefully chewed and digested every mouthful, they would be in danger of becoming a meal for the predators which also roam the places in which they live. Therefore, ruminants quickly eat and swallow great quantities of vegetation. Later, when they are somewhere safe, they pass the food back from their stomachs to their mouths to be chewed properly before again being passed to the stomach. Animals such as cattle, sheep, giraffes and deer are ruminants. You have probably seen cows chewing the cud, as this type of eating is known.

Russia see Union of Soviet Socialist Republics.

Russian Revolution took place in Russia between March and November 1917. A series of defeats had demoralized the Russian army, and many ordinary people were near starvation. The Duma (Parliament) formed a provisional government led by Alexander Kerensky and forced the Tsar to abdicate. However, Kerensky's decision to continue the war made his government unpopular. In November 1917 radical revolutionaries, known as Bolsheviks, led by Lenin and Trotsky, rose in revolt in Petrograd (now Leningrad) against Kerensky. The revolt spread rapidly to other parts of the country, Kerensky resigned and a Communist regime was set up. However, it was only after two years of civil war that the Communists won control of the whole country.

Rutherford, Lord Ernest (1871–1937), pioneered atomic and nuclear physics and made many discoveries including the structure of the atom and the nucleus. He was born in New Zealand, but most of his work was done in Britain and Canada.

Rutherford studied the radiation given off by uranium. He found three sorts of radiation, alpha rays, beta rays and gamma rays. He realized that when a uranium atom gives off radiation it changes into the atom of another element. This is known as transmutation. In 1919, he caused nitrogen to change to oxygen by firing alpha rays at it. This was the first ever artificial transmutation. He was given many awards, including a Nobel Prize in 1908.

Lord Rutherford

Rwanda is a republic in east-central Africa. Capital, Kigali; area about 26 000 sq km (10 000 sq miles). Rwanda gained independence from Belgium in 1962. It is heavily populated and poor. The land is mainly undulating plateau and mountains, with Lake Kiva in the west. The generally high altitude means that the equatorial climate is moderated. Most people are occupied growing enough food for themselves, though cotton, coffee, palm oil and tin ore are exported.

Opposite: left to right:
Ancient Greek merchant ship
The *Challenge* (1851) – an American clipper
Medieval ship *(top)*
Early fighting ship *(bottom)*

Sadat, Anwar (1918–1981), was an Egyptian statesman. He graduated from the Royal Military Academy in Cairo in 1938 and joined the Free Officers Movement to which Gamal Abdul Nasser also belonged. Sadat became President of Egypt on Nasser's death in 1970. In 1973 he launched a war against Israel which did much to restore Egyptian morale. In 1977 he visited Israel, the first Egyptian leader to do so since 1948, and in 1978 was awarded the Nobel Peace Prize jointly with Menachem Begin of Israel. In 1979, he signed a peace treaty with Israel. He was assassinated in 1981 while reviewing a military parade.

Saga is an old Norse word meaning 'story'. The Icelandic Sagas, part history, part legend, are medieval accounts of the early history of Norway and Iceland, written in prose.

Sahara is the largest desert in the world, area about 8000000 sq km (3000000 sq miles). It occupies about one-quarter of Africa, from the Atlantic to the Red Sea and from the Atlas Mountains to the River Niger. Although it is very dry, only certain parts are sandy, others being stony or rocky, and it includes high mountains. The Tibesti Massif in Chad rises to over 3000 m (9840 ft). There are scattered oases and a few nomadic inhabitants.

In the past, the Sahara was less dry. Today, the desert is slowly expanding southward. Discovery of oil and mineral reserves has given the Sahara new importance.

Sailing vessel is a ship powered by the wind, using sails. The earliest sailing ships were reed craft used in Mesopotamia circa 5000 BC, and 2000 years later wooden sailing craft, with square sails hung on wooden masts, were sailing on the River Nile in Egypt. The Egyptians developed sails which could be turned, allowing the boat to steer and to sail in winds which came from the side; they and the Phoenicians used such boats to explore the Mediterranean and much of the coastline of Africa.

The next major development was the triangular sail, invented by the Arabs during the 3rd century AD – this allowed the boat to be sailed as close as 45 degrees to an oncom-

ing wind. By the 15th century, European ships with two or three masts were travelling all over the world, fitted with mixtures of square and triangular sails which made them very versatile.

The fastest and largest sailing vessels were the 19th century clippers (so called because they clipped time off existing journeys) which were over 60 m (197 ft) long and could carry huge amounts of sail to supply power even in the lightest breeze. Fastest of them all was the American *Sovereign of the Seas*, which in 1853 crossed the Atlantic in under 14 days and went from Melbourne (Australia) to London in just 68 days. Speeds of up to 40 km/h (25 mph) were recorded for these clippers, but they were always at the mercy of the wind and could not compete with the reliability of steam ships, even though the early steamers were often much slower.

Saint, in Christianity, is someone who has shown a great love of God during his or her lifetime, and led a very holy life. Today, members of the Roman Catholic Church can be created saints, or canonized, after an investigation into their life. If the findings are approved by the pope, the candidate is beatified, or declared to be among the blessed. Proof of further miracles is needed for full canonization. *See* Paul, Saint, etc. for individual people.

Salamander is an amphibian with a tail, and is related to the newt. It occurs in many parts of the Northern Hemisphere, particularly where there are brooks and streams. Salamanders feed on small invertebrates such as insects and worms; and often have brightly coloured bodies. Most species are quite small – under 15 m (6 in) – but the giant salamander of China grows to 1.5 m (5 ft).

Saliva is the fluid which animals expel, or secrete, into their mouths when they are eating, to help moisten the food. Saliva is secreted from special glands, and usually contains enzymes which help to break the food down whilst it is being chewed.

Salmon are species of fish which spend part of their life in the sea, but swim into rivers to spawn. Like the related trout, salmon have a small fin (called the adipose fin) situated behind their main dorsal fin. Salmon are eagerly sought by fishermen, for they are a tasty food.

Pacific salmon

The Atlantic salmon lives in the North Atlantic Ocean but returns to European and North American fresh waters to breed. To migrate into the rivers of their birth they often have to leap waterfalls when swimming upstream. Eventually they reach the spawning grounds, and after spawning they die.

Salt, often called common salt, is sodium chloride. It is used to flavour and preserve food. Sea water tastes salty because it contains sodium chloride.

Salt is also the name given to substances made from the reaction of an acid with a base. For example, the base, caustic potash, reacts with the acid, hydrochloric acid, to give the salt, potassium chloride. This salt is also found as the mineral sylvine. Most salts that can be made in the laboratory are also found in the Earth.

Salyut is the Soviet orbiting space laboratory, similar to the American Skylab although only one-third as large. There have been seven Salyut craft, the latest of which has remained in orbit for some years and has been visited by dozens of cosmonauts. Salyut is used for long-term experiments in space, including the growing of plants and recycling of air and water. Cosmonauts have spent many months at a time in space, without apparent harmful effects.

Samoa is an island group of Polynesia in the central Pacific. It is divided into two parts, Western Samoa, an independent state since 1962, (capital, Apia), and Eastern Samoa, administered by the USA. The islands are mountainous, with dense forest and fertile lowlands where most of the people live. Farming and fishing are the main occupations.

San Marino is a republic in north-east Italy. Capital, San Marino; area 61 sq km (23 sq miles). Its mountainous position helped to preserve its independence. The people are Italian-speaking and are mostly farmers. One of the main sources of income is the issue of postage stamps.

São Tomé e Principe is a republic in the Gulf of Guinea, about 200 km (124 miles) off the coast of Gabon. Capital, São Tomé; area about 960 sq km (370 sq miles). It consists of four volcanic islands: São Tomé, Principe, Rôlas and Pedra Tinhosas. It is a hot and wet country. (The equator runs through Rôlas.) Most of the people are of Portuguese or African descent, and most live on São Tomé. Exports include cocoa, copra, palm oil and coffee.

Sap is the name given to the fluid contained within a plant. Sap is mainly water, but also contains dissolved food, hormones, minerals and other chemicals. Sap is transported in a series of tubes called xylem and phloem. Xylem is mainly responsible for carrying water and minerals up from the soil to the leaves. The job of the phloem is to transport manufactured food from the leaves to other parts of the plant where it will be used or stored.

Saprophyte is a living organism (animal or plant) which obtains its food from the dead or decaying tissues of another organism, called the host. The tissues of the host are first dissolved by enzymes, and the fluid meal is then taken into the body of the saprophyte. Many fungi are saprophytes, feeding on the dead tissues of trees or on the carcasses of animals.

Sardines are small fish related to the herring, which are found in huge shoals in the shallow coastal waters of southern Africa, parts of Europe and in the Pacific Ocean.

Sartre, Jean-Paul (1905–1980), was a French philospher and writer. His first novel, *Nausea* (1938), expressed his theories of existentialism, which is concerned with the 'dreadful freedom' of individuals to make themselves into what they are entirely on their own responsibility. This was the theme of Sartre's many plays and novels, such as the series called *The Roads to Freedom* (1945–1949). Sartre's philosophy was explained more directly in *Being and Nothingness* (1943).

Satellite is a body which moves around, or orbits, a planet. There are at least 33 satellites in the Solar System. The Earth has one satellite, the Moon. Mars has two satellites, Jupiter has at least 16, Saturn 17, Uranus five and Neptune two.

The Earth also has many artificial satellites. These have been launched into orbit by rocket. Some are communications satellites, some are used by astronomers and other scientists for observing in space and for

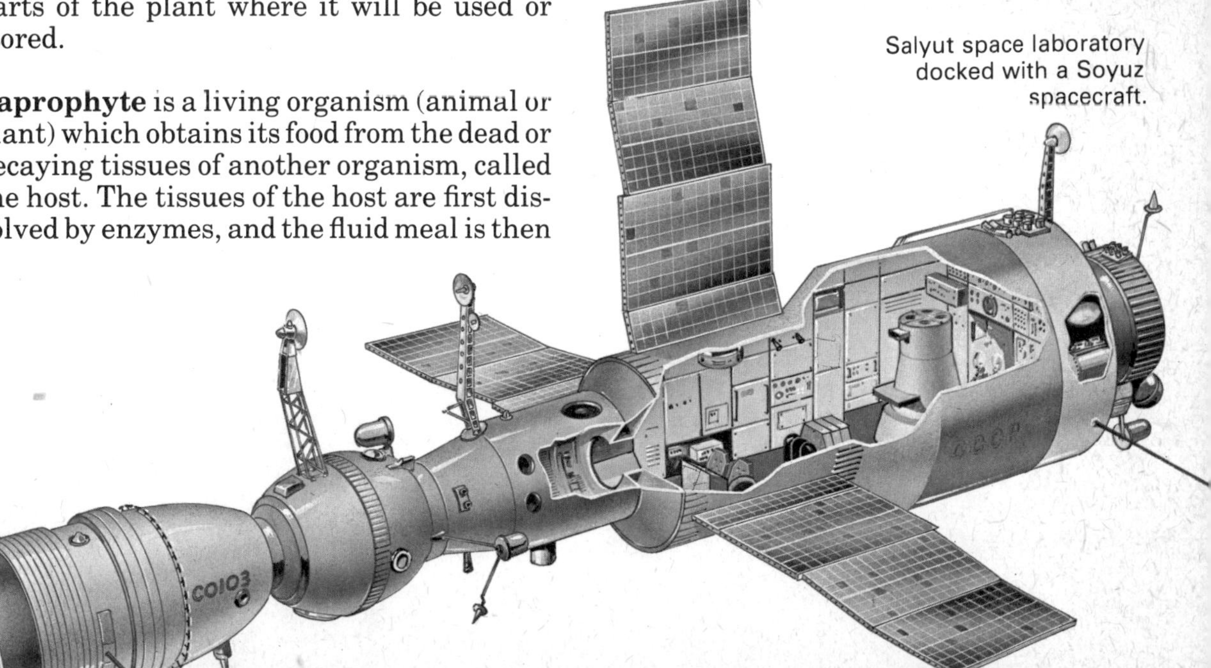

Salyut space laboratory docked with a Soyuz spacecraft.

studying the Earth and its atmosphere from space.

Many signals come from space which do not reach the Earth's surface, for example, many X-rays, gamma rays and cosmic rays cannot get through the Earth's atmosphere. Satellites orbiting above the Earth's atmosphere can monitor these. *See also* Radiation.

Saturn is the sixth planet from the Sun. It travels around it in 29.5 years. It rotates on its axis in just over ten hours, and has a diameter over nine times bigger than the Earth's. A similar planet to Jupiter, it is mainly frozen hydrogen and helium, and its atmosphere includes cloud belts which swirl around the planet. Saturn gives out much more heat than it receives from the Sun.

The farthest planet that can be seen from the Earth without a telescope, Saturn is also the most spectacular. This is because of the three or more bright rings which circle its equator. These rings contain hundreds of small particles.

Saturn has at least 17 satellites. One of these, Titan, is the largest known satellite in the Solar System. It is bigger than Mercury and has an atmosphere.

Saturn rocket is the world's largest and most powerful rocket, used by the Americans to lift the Apollo spacecraft which took men to the Moon. The complete Saturn V rocket stood over 110 m (361 ft) high and weighed

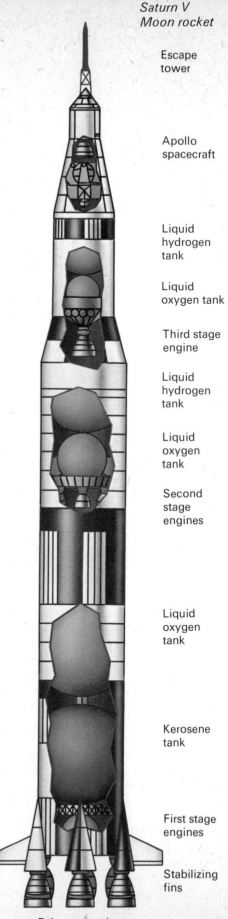

Saturn V Moon rocket

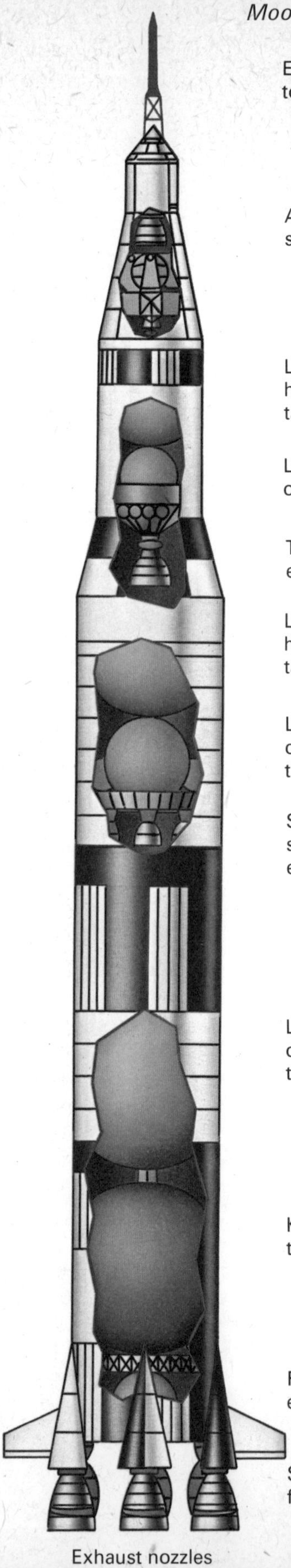

Escape tower
Apollo spacecraft
Liquid hydrogen tank
Liquid oxygen tank
Third stage engine
Liquid hydrogen tank
Liquid oxygen tank
Second stage engines
Liquid oxygen tank
Kerosene tank
First stage engines
Stabilizing fins
Exhaust nozzles

some 3000 tonnes (of this, only the 3.5 m (11.5 ft) high, 5500 kg (12128 lb) command module returned to Earth).

The giant first stage, with its five rocket motors, generated 3400 tonnes of thrust; 95 per cent of its weight was made up of fuel (liquid oxygen and kerosene), which was used up at the rate of 4500 kg (9923 lb) per second. Within three minutes of take-off, Saturn could travel over 100 km (62 miles) and reach a speed of nearly 10000 km/h (6214 mph). The second and third stages were powerful rockets as well, needed to accelerate the heavy Apollo spacecraft to 40000 km/h (24840 mph), the speed at which it could escape Earth's gravity.

Saudi Arabia is an Arab kingdom occupying the major part of the Arabian peninsula. Capital, Riyadh: area about 2400000 sq km (927000 sq miles). It was created by Ibn Saud, a leader of the Wahabi group, who gradually took over the whole region. It was formally proclaimed a kingdom in 1932.

Much of the country is desert, and everywhere it is hot and dry, though often very cold at night. Average rainfall is less than 75 mm (3 ins), except in the mountainous south-west. There are no permanent rivers so irrigation is widely used.

The people are almost all Arab, and there are still many nomadic Bedouin. The largest city is Mecca, the holy city of Islam, which attracts many pilgrims. Many Saudis belong to the strict Wahabi sect.

The country is very rich, for one reason – its large oil reserves. Oil and oil products make up virtually all exports. This modern treasure makes Saudi Arabia a curious mixture of ancient custom and modern culture.

Savannah is an area of tropical grasslands, especially the vast areas in South America and Africa, bordering the equatorial rainforests. The savannahs are lush during the wet season and withered during the harsh, dry season, so the few trees that establish themselves are of the tough palm and cactus type. Large herds of wild animals still roam the African savannah. All the savannahs are suitable for raising great numbers of cattle.

Scales form the protective body covering of fish and reptiles, and are also found on the legs of birds. A scale is a plate of bone – quite thin in fish but extremely thick in reptiles such as crocodiles – embedded in the skin. Apart from giving protection from predators, scales are sometimes coloured for camouflage or to warn enemies that the animal is dangerous. In land animals such as snakes and lizards, they also help to conserve the animal's body fluids by reducing evaporation.

Scales on a fish such as a shark are spiky and rough to the touch, whereas those of a snake are smoother and lie closely against each other. Much can be told from examining scales: apart from giving the identity of the animal, the scales of animals such as fish show yearly rings of growth, and so the age of the fish can be calculated just by looking at its scales.

Scales are also found on the wings of certain insects: the brilliant colours of the wings of butterflies and moths are due to the presence of tiny scales which reflect the light.

Another type of scale is found in the Plant Kingdom, but it has no connection with those found on animals. Plant scales are found on catkins and on the stems of grasses, where they protect the growing plant.

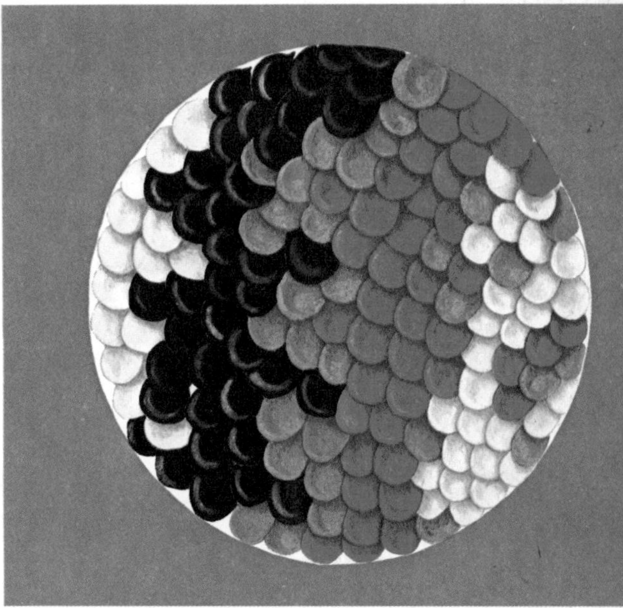

Scales on a butterfly's wing, greatly enlarged.

Scandinavia is a region in north-west Europe. It includes Norway, Sweden and Denmark. Finland and Iceland are sometimes added.

Schmidt, Helmut (1918–), is a West German statesman. He was elected to the German Parliament as a Social Democrat in 1953, later becoming Minister of Defence (1969–1972) and Finance Minister (1972–1974). He became Chancellor of West Germany in 1972, and was a forthright spokesman for west European interests, seeking closer co-operation with France.

Schoenberg, Arnold (1874–1951), was an Austrian-born composer who became a US citizen in 1941. One of the most influential composers in modern music, his early work was in the Wagner tradition. By 1908 he was composing atonal music – music in no particular key, which means that the traditional idea of harmony is abandoned. To most ears, his music sounded discordant and ugly. A great battle began between the opponents and supporters of Schoenberg, and it is still continuing. After a period of silence, in the 1920s Schoenberg introduced the 12-note technique, a method of organizing atonal music: the 12 notes in an octave (7 white, 5 black on piano) were given equal weight; thus there is no 'major' or 'minor' key.

Fleeing the Nazis, Schoenberg left Germany for Los Angeles in 1933. He continued to compose in both the 12-note system and in traditional, tonal style. His opera *Moses and Aaron*, perhaps his greatest work, was unfinshed at his death.

Schubert, Franz (1797–1828), was an Austrian composer. He wrote his first symphony for his school orchestra and an opera at the age of 17, but found his true inspiration as a composer of *lieder* (songs). He wrote over 200 (and once wrote eight in one day). He continued to write other music also and, though his operas were failures, some of his instrumental music (e.g. the 'Trout' Quintet, the 'Unfinished' Symphony) remain among the greatest favourites of concert audiences. His gift for melody has no equal.

Schumann, Robert (1810–1856), was a German composer and critic. He was active in the cause of music generally, encouraging young musicians (including Chopin and Brahms), and discovering Schubert's 'Great' Symphony in C Major in Vienna. As a composer, perhaps his greatest contribution was music for the piano, often played at its first performance by his wife, Clara, who was a brilliant pianist. His songs and chamber music are also of the highest quality, though his larger orchestral works have been less admired.

Scorpion is hard to mistake for any other animal. Its body is usually long and slender with a long 'tail' (really part of the abdomen) ending in a vicious, pointed sting. It also bears claws similar to a crab's. Scorpions are the most ancient group of land-living arthropods, fossils over 400 million years old having been found.

Scorpions live in warm places, from the tropics to southern Europe and the southern USA. They burrow into earth or sand, or live under logs and stones. They catch their food by grabbing insects and other small animals in their powerful claws. When scorpions mate, they often use their claws to grip one another as if holding hands, and they appear to 'dance'. The sting is used in self defence, and the sting of some species can cause death, even to humans.

Scotland is a kingdom in north-west Europe, forming the northern part of the United Kingdom of Great Britain and Northern Ireland. Capital, Edinburgh; area about 79 000 sq km (30 000 sq miles).

History The earliest-known inhabitants in Scotland were the Picts who resisted the invasion of the Romans. Later the Scots migrated from Ireland and by the 11th century the whole country was united under one king. Scotland was in constant conflict with England in the 13th and 14th centuries because of the English kings' claim to overlordship. Scotland became Protestant during the reign of Mary Queen of Scots and in 1603 the crowns of Scotland and England were united. Scotland was made an integral part of Great Britain by the Act of Union of 1707.

Land From north to south, Scotland can be divided into three regions: the Highlands, a mountainous region of glens (valleys), lochs (lakes) and rugged mountains (highest: Ben Nevis, 1343 m; 4406 ft); the central Lowlands, rolling plains and wide river valleys, where most of the population lives; the southern Uplands, with ranges of hills that continue beyond the English border. The west coast is very irregular, with many islands. The climate is relatively mild, wetter in the west, sunnier (though sometimes colder) in the east.

People The Scots regard themselves as Celts, though many of them share Anglo-Saxon ancestry with the English. The national language, Gaelic, is still spoken in a few places in the Highlands and Western Isles. The Scots have a reputation as thrifty, practical people: they played a large part in Britain's colonial and commercial expansion.

Economy Industry is concentrated in the central area, especially in and around Glasgow, one of the biggest centres of traditional heavy industry in Europe. The discovery of oil in the North Sea has recently brought great changes, especially to Aberdeen and other east-coast ports. Scotch whisky, however, is still Scotland's most famous product.

Sheep-rearing is very important in the Highlands and Uplands – Scottish tweed is world-famous – and fishing, though less prosperous today, around the coasts. Farming is very varied: beef cattle, potatoes, cereals and

Some Scottish Highland clans supported the rebellions to try to restore the Stuarts to the British throne. They were brutally defeated at the Battle of Culloden in 1746.

James IV (1473–1513), King of Scotland.

fruit are important in different areas.

The magnificent scenery and sporting opportunities attract many tourists. *See also* United Kingdom; Hebrides; Orkney; Shetland.

Regions of Scotland

Region	*Area* sq km	sq miles
Borders	4671	1803
Central	2631	1016
Dumfries & Galloway	6371	2460
Fife	1305	504
Grampian	8705	3361
Highland	25130	9703
Lothian	1756	678
Strathclyde	13727	5300
Tayside	7665	2959
Island Authority		
Orkney	881	340
Shetland	1427	551
Western Isles	2901	1120

Rulers of Scotland

Malcolm II	1005–1034
Duncan I	1034–1040
Macbeth	1040–1057
Malcolm III	1057–1093
Donalbane	1093–1094
Duncan II	1094
Donalbane (restored)	1095–1097
Edgar	1097–1107
Alexander I	1107–1124
David I	1124–1153
Malcolm IV	1153–1165
William the Lion	1165–1214
Alexander II	1214–1249
Alexander III	1249–1286
Margaret of Norway	1286–1290
Interregnum	1290–1292
John de Baliol	1292–1296
Interregnum	1296–1306
Robert I	1306–1329
David II	1329–1371
Robert II	1371–1390
Robert III	1390–1406
James I	1406–1437
James II	1437–1460
James III	1460–1488
James IV	1488–1513
James V	1513–1542
Mary	1542–1567
James VI	1567–1625

(For rulers after 1625 see United Kingdom)

Scott, Robert Falcon (1868–1912), was a British naval officer and explorer. Having joined the Royal Navy in 1880, he led his first expedition to Antarctica in 1901–1904, when he made a survey of the Ross Sea. In 1911 he set off with a second expedition in the hope of being the first man to reach the South Pole. They arrived at the Pole on 17 January 1912, only to find that a Norwegian expedition had got there first. Scott and his companions died on the return journey.

Sea-anemones are not plants, as some people think, but animals. They are coelenterates, the group of animals which includes the hydra, corals and jellyfish. The body of an anemone is really a hollow bag with a ring of tentacles around the mouth. The tentacles are armed with stinging threads, and these shoot out and capture prey, which is then passed to the mouth in the centre of the tentacles. Although they seem to be fixed in one place, anemones can creep slowly about. Some even climb on to the shells of hermit crabs and share the crabs' food. Anemones are usually found attached to rocks, or burrowing into sand on the seashore and seabed. Those that live on the seashore form themselves into a tight ball so they do not become dry when the tide goes out. *See also* Coelenterates.

Sea anemones

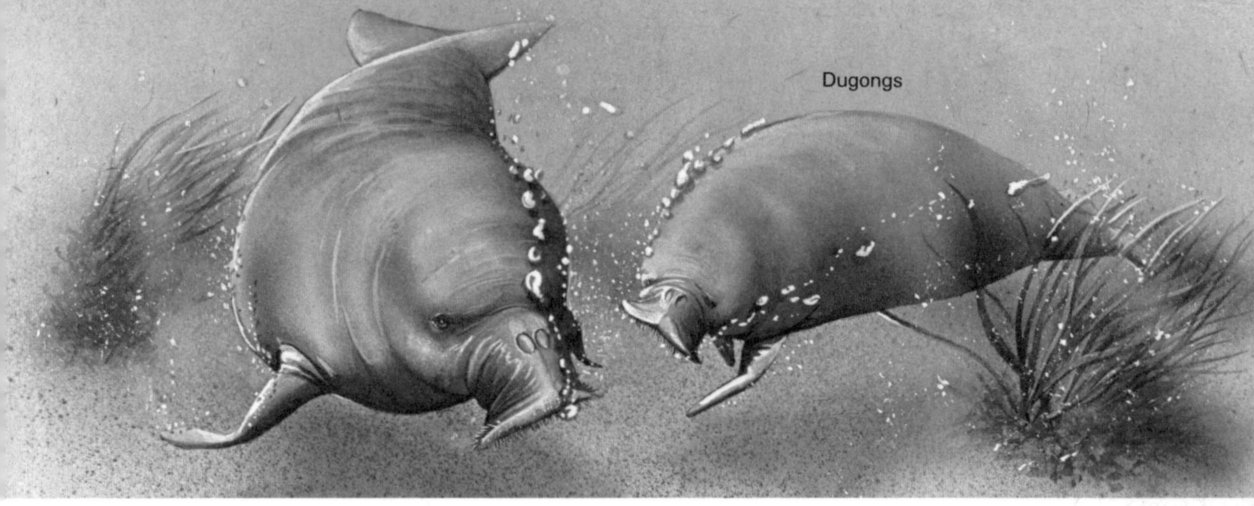
Dugongs

Sea-cow is an aquatic mammal which is found in tropical coastal waters throughout the world. It also ventures into rivers sometimes. Sea-cows are like seals, with powerful, flipper-like fore-limbs, but no hind limbs. Instead, there is a tail which is flattened horizontally like a whale's, and the head has a flattened muzzle. They are placid animals, grazing on vegetation such as seaweed and marine grasses, which they uproot and swallow with little chewing.

There are two kinds of sea-cows. Dugongs live alone or in small groups along the coast of East Africa, Australia, the Philippines and China. They have a notched tail. Manatees live on the coasts and coastal rivers of the southeast USA, parts of South America and western Africa. They live in large groups and have rounded tails.

Sea-cucumbers are not really vegetables at all, but marine animals. They are echinoderms, related to starfish and sea-urchins, and they get their name from their elongated body which looks rather like a cucumber. One end of the body bears a ring of feathery tentacles, and is used to trap small animal and plant remains which the sea-cucumbers find in the mud and sand. Sea-cucumbers move along by means of rows of water-powered tube feet running round the body.

Sea-horses are some of the most unusual fish to be found in the oceans. Their bodies really do resemble the neck and head of a horse, and they even swim along in an upright 'horse-like' position. Sea-horses live in all but the coldest seas, and feed on small animals. They are about 20 cm (8 in) long.

Seal is a marine mammal found throughout the world. It is not as dependent on the sea as the whales or sea-cows, however, and leaves the water to breed, often in huge numbers. Seals are believed to be descended from land-living carnivores. They feed mainly on fish, molluscs, crustaceans and water birds, such as penguins. All seals are superb swimmers, although they are ungainly on land.

There are three families of seals. The true seals have no external ears and are distantly related to the otter. Monk, elephant, common, harp and leopard seals are a few of the more familiar species. Eared seals are related to bears, and include the sea-lions and fur seals. The last family contains the walrus, a huge tusked seal of the Arctic Ocean.

Sea cucumbers

Sea-lion is a seal, related to the fur seal. Both sea lions and fur seals have tiny external ears, unlike other seals. Like the seals, however, the limbs form flippers. The Californian sea-lion is one of the best-known species, for it is often seen performing tricks in circuses. In the wild it feeds on squid and fish, swimming with great skill in the oceans of the Southern Hemisphere.

Sea-slug, see Slug.

Seasons, in temperate countries, are the four periods of the year, spring, summer, autumn and winter. These are based on the cycle of the farming year. Spring is the time of sowing, summer of growing, autumn of harvesting, and in winter the earth lies dormant until the next spring.

Exactly when each season begins will depend on the geographical position and climate of a particular place. In the Northern Hemisphere, spring normally arrives in February or March, and each season lasts about three months. In the Southern Hemisphere the pattern is reversed; spring starts in about September and summer begins around Christmas time.

In the tropics the seasonal pattern is quite different, mainly relating to wet or dry periods of the year. In the Arctic and Antarctic there is virtually no spring or autumn.

Sea-urchins are marine echinoderms in which the body is rounded or globular, and consists of many interlocking chalky plates. The shell-like body is known as a test, and attached to the test are many spines. Sea-urchins use these spines like stilts to climb over rocks and other structures, also using their water-powered tube feet.

Some sea-urchins, the heart urchin for instance, burrow into sand or mud, and a few even burrow into rock or metal using their spines to scrape a way in. The mouth of a sea-urchin is situated at the bottom of the animal, and is used to scrape off seaweeds and to eat dead animals.

Seaweed is the largest and most commonly seen of the group of non-flowering plants called the algae. There are several colours among the seaweeds, red, brown and green. All the seaweeds contain the pigment chlorophyll and make their own food by photosynthesis. However, often the presence of chlorophyll is masked by red or brown pigments so that not all seaweeds appear green.

The brown seaweeds are common plants of rocky shores, where they fix themselves to rocks. Some brown seaweeds – such as the kelps, for instance – are hardly ever exposed to the air, however, for they live in deeper water. The red seaweeds are generally plants of deeper water, but we may see some

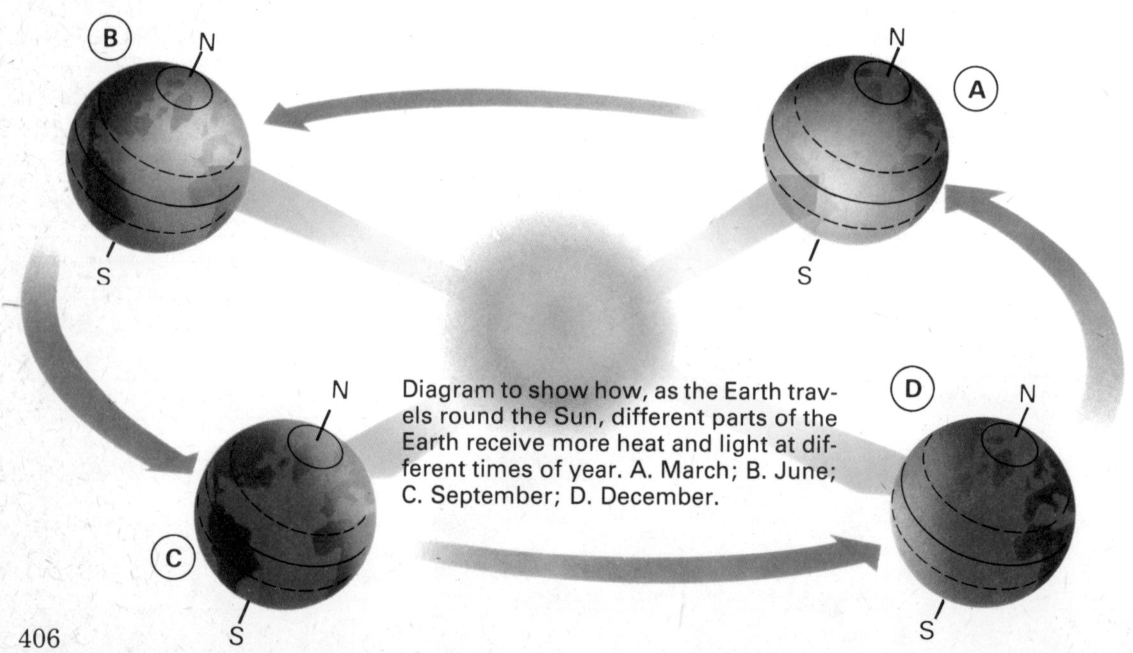

Diagram to show how, as the Earth travels round the Sun, different parts of the Earth receive more heat and light at different times of year. A. March; B. June; C. September; D. December.

Two kinds of seaweed.

species which have been washed up after storms, or those which live in rock pools. Some red seaweeds are very beautiful, looking like the autumn leaves of trees. Others look like pink blobs of paint on the side of rock pools. The green seaweeds are often seen on rocky shores, too. One species looks just like a piece of lettuce, and is, in fact, called the sea lettuce. Some green seaweeds live in fresh water.

The body of a seaweed is called a thallus. Part of the thallus forms a sort of root called a holdfast, from which arises a stem called a stipe. The main parts of a seaweed – which sometimes look like leaves – are called fronds.

Secretary bird is a curious-looking, long-legged bird of prey found in Africa. It gets its name from its appearance, which is reminiscent of an old-fashioned clerk. The secretary bird struts about the bush looking for a lizard, snake or other small animal. When it sees one it darts forward and leaps on its victim, jumping on it again and again until it has literally stamped it to death.

Sedimentary rock is one of the three types of rock making up the Earth's crust (the other two are igneous and metamorphic rocks). As the name suggests, sedimentary rocks were layers of sediment, deposited mainly, although not always, by the sea. Subjected to enormous pressures, the layers of sediment solidified into rock.

Sandstone and clays are examples of sedimentary rocks. Some others have been formed by compression of materials that were originally organic, such as coal (from vegetation) and limestone (mainly from the shells and skeletons of marine creatures).

Seed consists of a minature plant called an embryo, complete with a root, shoot, and one or two leaves, surrounded by a tough, protective coat formed by the wall of the ovule within the ovary. The seed normally comes to lie within the swollen tissues of the ovary, which forms a fruit. The production of seeds enables one individual plant to create many potential offspring – providing the seeds land in a suitable place – thus allowing the species to colonize new ground. It also enables non-perennial species to survive the harshness of winter in the form of seeds, to produce new plants the following spring.

Seed fern was a group of ancient plants which flourished during the Paleozoic era between 550 and 200 million years ago. Seed ferns looked rather like today's ferns with their large, frond-like leaves, but they bore true seeds, instead of scattering spores. Internally, they resembled the gymnosperms. In fact, the seed ferns probably gave rise to the cycads, one of the groups of gymnosperms still living today.

Segovia, Andrés (1893–), is a Spanish guitarist. Besides his brilliant playing, he wrote many pieces for the guitar and inspired other composers to write music for him. More than anyone else, Segovia showed that the guitar has a role in classical music as well as in jazz and pop.

Seismograph is an instrument used for detecting and measuring earthquakes. In a seismograph, a paper tape moves beneath a pen, which is attached to a kind of pendulum. A straight line is drawn on the paper when there are no tremors. If the Earth shakes, the paper shakes too, but the pendulum and pen do not. So peaks appear in the line. The more the Earth shakes, the greater the peaks.

Seismographs may be able to detect earthquakes happening thousands of kilometres (miles) away. Very sensitive seismographs are used in oil prospecting.

Selassie, Haile (1892–1977), was Emperor of Ethiopia (1930–1974). In 1936 he led his people in their resistance to the Italian invasion, and afterwards lived in England until he was restored to his throne in 1941. After the Second World War he was prominent in both the pan-African movement and in international affairs. He was deposed after a military coup in 1974.

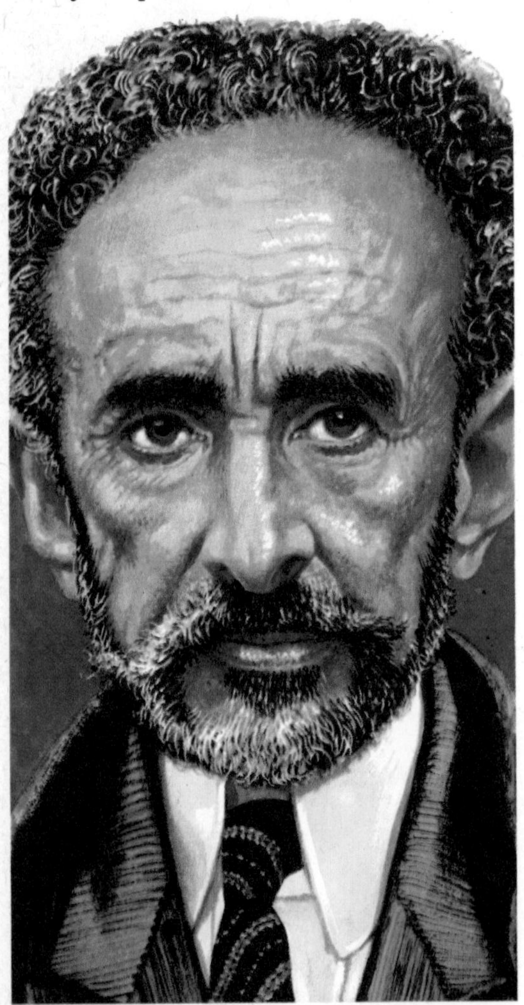

Haile Selassie

Semiconductor is a substance which does not easily conduct electricity when it is pure. When small amounts of other substances are added to it, it will conduct electricity. This is called doping.

Doping can take electrons out of a semiconductor, leaving it positively charged. This is called a positive or a p-type semiconductor. Doping can put more electrons into a semiconductor, making it negatively charged. This is called a negative or n-type semiconductor.

These two types of semiconductor are used to make devices, such as transistors, which are used in electronics.

Silicon and germanium have been the most commonly used semiconductors. *See also* Silicon chip.

Senegal is a republic in West Africa. Capital, Dakar; area about 197 000 sq km (76 000 sq miles). Formerly part of French West Africa, it has been independent since 1960.

The land is generally flat and the soil is mostly rather sandy. Temperatures are high, and there is a long dry season. The Senegalese include a number of different peoples, some of them nomadic. Most of the people are Muslims. Dakar, which is still very French, is the only large city, and most people are simple farmers and herdsmen. There are some mineral resources, and peanuts are exported in large quantities.

September is the ninth month of the year in the modern calendar, and lasts for 30 days. Its name comes from the Latin *septem* meaning 'seventh', because in the ancient Roman calendar it was the seventh month.

Sett is the underground home of a badger. Badgers often dig their setts under steep, tree-lined banks. The sett is a series of tunnels and chambers, often extending for 20 m (65 ft) or more. There are sleeping chambers and nurseries for rearing the young, and fresh bedding in the form of bracken and grass is constantly brought in to replace soiled bedding. Near the entrance to the sett, the badger digs special toilet pits called latrines. These help to ensure that the sett is not soiled. Just after sunset, when all seems quiet and safe, badgers nose warily from the entrance of the sett to begin their night's foraging for food.

Seychelles is an island republic in the Indian Ocean, about 1000 km (620 miles) north-east of Madagascar. Capital, Victoria; area about 400 sq km (150 sq miles). It consists of nearly 100 islands, of which the largest is Mahé. A former French and, later, British colony, the Seychelles became independent in 1976. Farming and fishing are the main occupations. The chief exports, mostly to India, are coconut products, guano (fertilizer from bird droppings) and spices such as cinnamon. The inhabitants are mainly a mixture of French and African descent.

Shag, like the similar-looking cormorant, is a large coastal bird which spends its time hunting for fish. It has a long body and a long, hooked beak. After a fishing expedition shags sit on the rocks with their wings outstretched to dry, for the wings are not waterproofed like those of ducks.

Shaka (or Chaka) (died 1828), was a Zulu chief. He raised a large, efficient army which conquered many neighbouring tribes, and he ruled over the powerful Zulu nation from 1800 until his death, covering all of what is now Natal. He was murdered by his half-brothers, the victim of a conspiracy. One of his brothers, Dingaan (Dingane) (died 1840) succeeded Shaka and was king of the Zulus from 1828 to 1840. He was succeeded by his brother Mpande who was crowned king of Zululand by the Boers.

Shakespeare, William (1564–1616), is generally recognized as the greatest playwright in European literature. He came from Stratford-upon-Avon and joined a company of actors in London about 1586. From about 1591 he began to write plays and poetry: his first plays were the three parts of *Henry VI*. His last play, *The Tempest*, was probably written in 1611, after which he retired to the large house he had bought in Stratford. His collected plays were first published in 1623.

William Shakespeare

Shakespeare's plays fall into three categories: comedies, tragedies and history plays (containing elements of both). Serious dialogue is in blank verse – unrhymed lines of ten syllables – and comic dialogue is in prose.

Since the 17th century Shakespeare's work has been performed more often than any other dramatist's. As Samuel Johnson said, Shakespeare's drama is 'the mirror of life'. The greatest aspect of his genius was his understanding of human nature, and his characters seen as real today as they did when they first appeared on an Elizabethan stage. His command of language has no equal: computer studies tell us he used more words than any comparable writer, but more to the point is the marvellous way he put the words together. Hundreds of his phrases have become common expressions of everyday speech.

Shakespeare's finest plays are probably (critics disagree) the four great tragedies, *Hamlet*, *Othello*, *Macbeth* and *King Lear*. Among the most popular of the others are *A Midsummer Night's Dream*, *The Merchant of Venice*, *As You Like It*, *Twelfth Night* and *The Tempest* (comedies); *Richard II*, *Henry IV* (two parts), *Henry V*, *Richard III* and *Julius Caesar* (histories); *Romeo and Juliet* and *Antony and Cleopatra* (tragic love stories).

Shankar, Ravi (1920–), is an Indian musician. A brilliant player of the sitar (an Indian instrument like a banjo with a very long neck, played by plucking the strings), he had a successful career as music director of Indian radio before he began touring Europe and North America. His recitals created great interest in Indian music generally. He also composed music for films and a concerto for sitar and orchestra.

Shark is a word which to many people conjures up images of man-eating monsters. Although some species, such as the great white shark and the hammerhead shark, are dangerous, the majority of the 200 or so species perform a valuable role in the sea by disposing of sick or dead animals. As well as these scavengers and hunters, there is one species – the basking shark – which eats nothing larger than minute plankton. It is the world's second largest fish, sometimes reaching a length of 14 m (46 ft). The largest shark – which is also the largest fish – is the 15 m- (50 ft-) long whale shark of tropical waters.

Sharks are an extremely ancient group of fish which still retain a skeleton made of cartilage rather than of bone. They have streamlined bodies covered in tiny scales called denticles, which give them a rough feel. The mouth is situated underneath the body and is armed with sharp teeth. These teeth, together with powerful jaws, enable a shark to tear pieces from victims too large to swallow whole.

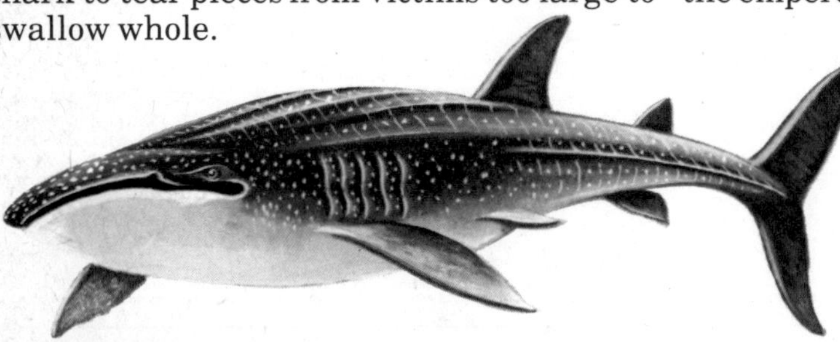

Shaw, George Bernard (1856–1950), was an Irish-born writer, best known for his plays. He arrived in London in 1876, wrote several novels (seldom read now), some excellent music and drama criticism, and became a leading member of the Fabian Society, the socialist society founded in 1883. His career as a dramatist began in 1892 and lasted half a century. Among his most famous plays are *Man and Superman* (1903), *Heartbreak House* (1917), *Saint Joan* (1923), *Arms and the Man* (1906), and *The Doctors' Dilemma* (1911).

Shelley, Percy Bysshe (1792–1822), was an English poet. Of aristocratic background, he became a political revolutionary, and was expelled from Oxford University for writing *The Necessity of Atheism* (1811). He was a friend of Byron and wrote a famous elegy on Keats, *Adonais*. Much of his best work was inspired by his political beliefs, notably the long poem *Prometheus Unbound* (1819). In general, however, his shorter poems, such as *Ode to the West Wind* and *To a Skylark* have proved most popular. Shelley was drowned in a sailing accident at 30.

Shetland is a group of 100 islands only a few of which are inhabited. They lie 100 km (62 miles) north-east of Orkney. Area 1429 sq km (552 sq miles); capital, Lerwick. Shetland is the northernmost administrative region of the British Isles, now a major centre of the North Sea Oil industry with large pipelines and tanker terminals. Other industries include fishing and knitted goods.

Shinto is the ancient religion of Japan. In origin it was a cult of ancestor worship. It encouraged reverence and loyalty towards the emperor and his forebears, as well as personal ancestors. It consisted of a collection of rites and ceremonies, some connected with the seasons and crops. As it has no services and no articles of belief, the Japanese do not consider it a religion at all. The need for an organized faith was filled by Buddhism, still the main religion in Japan.

Shinto was deliberately revived by the government in the 19th century to encourage feelings of extreme patriotism.

Short Take Off and Landing aircraft, see STOL aircraft.

Shostakovich, Dimitri (1906–1975), was a Russian composer, perhaps the greatest since Tchaikovsky. He became world famous at 20 after the performance of his First Symphony. Sympathetic to socialism, he wrote many equally popular works for stage and screen, but in 1936 he was attacked in the Soviet official press. Thereafter he wrote mainly orchestral works (which were less vulnerable to political criticism), such as his popular Fifth Symphony and his wartime Seventh ('Leningrad') Symphony.

Shrew is a tiny, mouse-like mammal with a long, pointed snout. The world's smallest mammal is a shrew. This is the pygmy shrew of North America, which weighs only 3 g (0.1 oz) when adult. Shrews are active, quarrelsome creatures, which spend their lives searching among leaf litter for insects, worms and slugs. They must eat their own weight of food every day in order to survive. They are found all over the world, except in Australasia and the polar regions.

Shrimps are crustaceans, related to the crabs and lobsters. They are found all over the world – floating in the surface waters of the ocean, living at great depths, or hiding away under seaweeds and in rockpools on the seashore. A few species are found in freshwater, too, and grow very large. Shrimps have long, flattened bodies carried on four sets of walking legs. Most species have pincers for seizing tiny animals, and long antennae for feeling their way about. Large species of shrimp are usually called prawns. Shrimps are 5 – 7.5 cm (2 – 3 in) long.

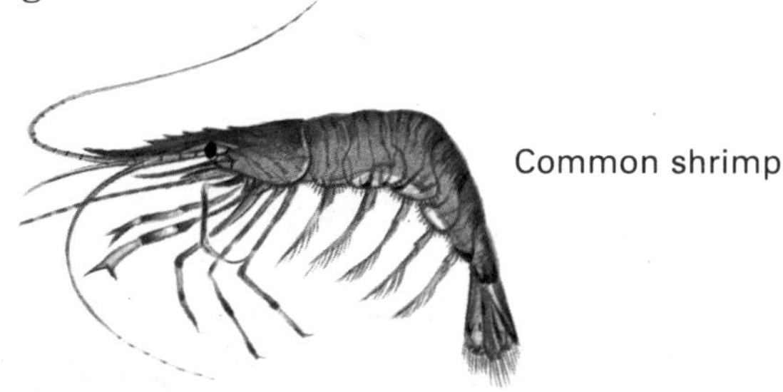

Common shrimp

Shrub is a woody plant which usually has several stems all arising at about ground level. Although some shrubs are exotic tropical plants, many are common plants in temperate parts of the world. Gorse, rhododendron, azalea, gooseberry and laurel are typical shrubs.

Sibelius, Jean (1865–1957), was a Finnish composer, the outstanding figure in Finnish national music. From 1897 the government paid him a grant which enabled him to devote all his time to composing. He responded with *Finlandia* (1899), a tone poem (like a symphony in one movement), which became a kind of national anthemn and remains his most popular work. Otherwise, in Sibelius' large output, the greatest works are his seven symphonies. All are rooted in his feelings for Finland and reflect the spirit and legends of the country. After 1926 Sibelius, for unknown reasons, composed nothing.

Siberia is a region in north-east Asia, making up the Asian part of the Soviet Union. Area about 13 000 000 sq km (5 000 000 sq miles). Russian conquest of Siberia began in the 16th century and was completed in the 19th. Such a vast region naturally contains great variety, but basically Siberia consists of dry plains, drained by great rivers like the Ob, Yenisei and Lena. It has an extreme 'continental' climate with long cold winters, and short hot summers. Central Siberia is forested, but the chief interest economically is the enormous mineral resources, now being rapidly developed. The population is growing fast, but there are still semi-nomadic tribes living as they have for centuries.

Sierra Leone is a republic in West Africa. Capital, Freetown; area about 73 000 sq km (28 000 sq miles). It was the first British settlement in West Africa, in 1787. It became a British colony in 1808 and gained independence in 1961. The countryside ranges from swampy coast and coastal plain to a rugged plateau, with mountains and steep river valleys. Temperatures and rainfall are high. The people are of varied tribal background

and include some descendants of freed American slaves who settled at Freetown in the 18th century. Agriculture is rather poor, but there are considerable minerals, notably diamonds, of high quality.

Sight, see Eyes.

Sikhism is an Indian religion founded by Guru ('Teacher') Nanak (1469–1538). He hoped to reconcile Hindus and Muslims in a new faith, with one god who also represented the various Hindu gods: 'He, the One, is himself Brahma, Vishnu and Siva, and he performs all.'

Beginning purely as members of a religious group, the Sikhs developed into a warlike nation in the late 17th century and became dominant in north-west India. Under Ranjit Singh (1780–1839) they established a Sikh kingdom and they later fought against the British.

Silicon is a non-metallic element which has the chemical symbol Si. After oxygen, it is the most common element in the Earth's crust. Over one quarter of the crust is silicon. It forms many compounds, such as silica and silicates. Silica is the most common mineral.

Silk being taken in caravans of merchants along the Silk Route from China to Asia Minor, around 80 AD.

Sand, quartz and opal are all forms of silica, and it is a common constituent of many rocks.

Silicon is a brown or black solid. It is added in making steel and other alloys. Pure black silicon is a semiconductor.

Silicon chip is made from a tiny slice of silicon. This can be doped – that is, it can have traces of other substances added to it – to form many electronic parts or components. A square silicon chip, with sides only 1 cm (0.5 in) long, can contain a quarter of a million electronic components. These components can form numerous circuits, etched photographically on to the chips.

Silicon chips are relatively inexpensive to manufacture, are generally reliable and consume little power.

The use of the silicon chip has allowed machines to be made much smaller and to perform far more complex operations. It is also called a microchip and its use is called microelectronics ('micro' means very small). Robots, computers, digital watches and calculators all contain microchips. *See also* Semiconductor.

Silk is a soft delicate material. It is made from a fine thread spun by a silkworm, which is the caterpillar of a moth. The caterpillar spins a cocoon in which to change into a moth. The threads of this cocoon are collected then spun and woven to make silk. Silk was first made in China, about 4000 years ago. Nowadays most silk is made in India, Japan and China.

Silurian is a period in the history of the Earth, known from the study of rocks and of the fossil remains found in them (the geological record). It is named after an ancient Welsh tribe, because early investigations of Silurian rocks were carried out in Wales.

The Silurian period is the third major division of the Paleozoic era, following the Ordovician. It began about 430 million years ago and lasted for about 35 million years. It was the era when the first true land plants appeared.

Silver has the chemical symbol Ag. This shiny white metal is quite rare, although not as rare as gold and platinum. It is highly valued and is known as a precious metal.

Silver is a very good conductor of heat and electricity. It can be made into many different shapes, and has been used to make coins, ornaments and jewellery.

Mirrors are often made by coating glass with a silver salt. Some silver salts change colour when light is shone on them. These are used in photography.

Some nuggets of silver over a tonne in weight have been found. Most silver comes from a mineral called argentite. Silver is found with gold in electrum and with mercury in amalgam.

Silverfish are not fish at all, but are small, primitive, wingless insects. They have a silvery body, wider at the head end, and long antennae. The tail end bears three bristle-like structures called cerci. Some species inhabit cool and damp buildings – old houses are a particular favourite – and others prefer warmer places. A few species live out of doors. Silverfish feed on tiny scraps of animal and plant matter.

Singapore, Republic of, is an island republic in south-east Asia, at the tip of the Malay peninsula. Capital, Singapore City; area about 610 sq km (238 sq miles). Singapore has one of the largest harbours in the world, and has long been a great centre of international trade and communications. Singapore was founded in 1919. It was, for a short time, part of Malaysia but withdrew from the Federation in 1965, becoming an independent republic.

The people are of mixed background, but the majority are Chinese. The island is hot and hilly. Farming is intensive, and there are plantations producing crops such as rubber and tobacco for export. Other exports include tin. Ship-building is an important industry.

Sistine Chapel is the pope's chapel in the Vatican, Rome, built for Pope Sixtus IV in 1473–1481. It is famous for the frescoes (paintings) on the walls and vault (ceiling). Michelangelo's *Creation*, perhaps the greatest painting in the world, covers the vault, and his terrifying *Last Judgement* occupies the wall behind the altar. There are also paintings by many other great Renaissance artists, as well as fine tapestries and mosaics.

SI units are a system of metric units. For thousands of years people have measured things, such as the length of a field, or the weight of food. Distances were often measured using part of the body, such as the foot, as a unit. However, people's feet vary in size and are an inexact measurement. So it was agreed that a certain length would be used as a unit. This is called a standard unit. A number of countries have agreed to use the same standard units, which are called the International System of Units, or SI units. SI units include the metre, kilogramme, second, ampere, kelvin, mole and candela.

Siva (or Shiva), a Hindu god, is the third member of the Trimurti (trinity). Brahma is the Creator, Vishnu the Preserver and Siva the Destroyer. He is not, however, a negative god. Destruction also means renewal, and Siva is the god of fertility and creativity. In fact, Siva can be translated 'friendly', and he was the most popular god in many areas, perhaps because it was easy to sympathize with his passions and wild behaviour. He is the lord of the dance, the protector of cattle (sacred animals in Hinduism) and the patron of the arts. Eventually, Siva became associated with the aristocrats and landowners.

Skate are fish with a skeleton composed of cartilage, flattened, diamond-shaped bodies and long tails. Like rays, the eyes of skate are on top of the body, but the mouth is underneath. Skate live in temperate and tropical seas where they feed mainly on crustaceans. The largest skate is the American Pacific big skate, which reaches a length of 2.5 m (8 ft).

Skeleton is the hard framework found in animals, which acts as a support for the body, protects some of the vital organs, and enables the animal to make movements. In vertebrates, the skeleton is made of cartilage or bone and is found inside the body. It is called an endoskeleton. The bones of the vertebrate skeleton store calcium and produce red blood cells. The human skeleton consists of 206 bones. Invertebrates (such as insects and crabs) have an external skeleton, called an exoskeleton, which is made of a substance called chitin.

Skin is the name given to the outer body layer of an animal. Skin varies considerably, depending on the animal, but its purpose is usually to protect the animal, keep its body at the correct temperature, help retain body fluids and enable it to remain concealed or advertise its presence. The skin of fish and reptiles is usually covered with scales, that of birds with feathers (with scales on the legs), and that of mammals with fur. Amphibians, such as frogs and toads, have a skin through which they breathe. Insects have a tough, shell-like skin, rather like a suit of armour.

Skunk is a badger-like mammal, with bold black and white fur and a bushy tail. It is mostly active at night, emerging from its hiding place to feed on birds, mice, nuts and insects. When confronted by an enemy (such as a puma or bobcat) skunks can squirt an evil-smelling liquid over the would-be attacker. This enables them to make their escape. Skunks are found in North, Central and South America.

Skylab is an American space laboratory launched in 1973 and manned for a total of 172 days by teams of three astronauts at a time. Based on the third stage of a Saturn rocket, Skylab was enormous for a spacecraft, 6.7 m (22 ft) in diameter and 14.6 m (48 ft) long. It had a workshop, where maintenance and experiments were carried out, and separate living quarters with ingenious shower and lavatory systems which worked despite the lack of gravity. Because Skylab was badly damaged during launch, the first

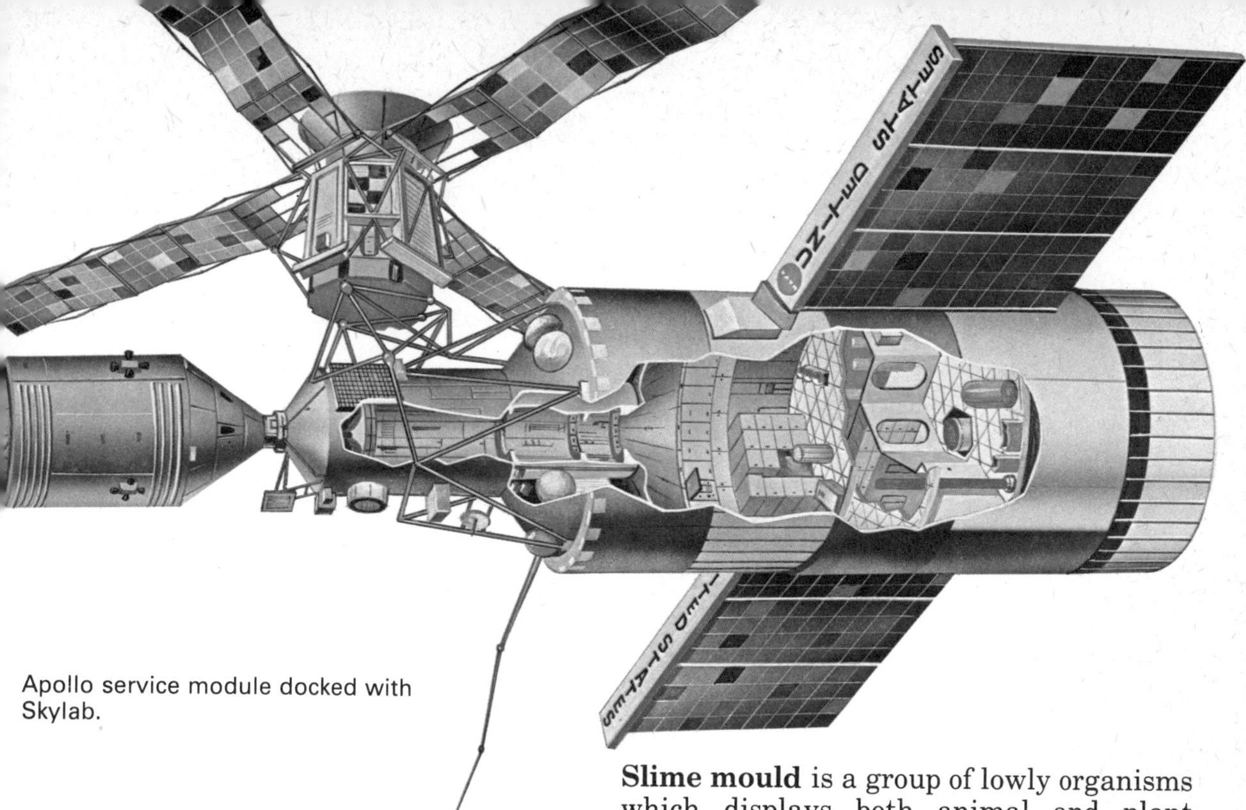

Apollo service module docked with Skylab.

three astronauts had to undertake lengthy repairs outside the craft, which did much to prove that humans could work in space itself. Skylab fell back to Earth in 1979, breaking up in the atmosphere.

Slave trade was the transportation of slaves from Africa for sale in America. It began in the 16th century when the colonists in the New World discovered that the native Indians were not really suitable as slaves. Labour was needed to work on the new sugar, cotton and coffee plantations so great numbers of slaves were brought across the Atlantic from Africa.

The British, Spanish, French, Portuguese and Dutch all took part in the very profitable slave trade. The European slave ships would acquire slaves from African tribal chiefs in exchange for merchandise and then transport them across the Atlantic in dreadful conditions. Opposition to the slave trade grew during the 18th century, and it was made illegal in Britain in 1807, slavery being abolished in 1833. Other countries subsequently followed Britain's example.

Slime mould is a group of lowly organisms which displays both animal and plant characteristics. The body of a slime mould is a mass of jelly-like protoplasm, called a plasmodium. It flows along rather like an Amoeba, and it, too, can feed by flowing around and engulfing small food items. Reproduction is by spores, which release cells that move by beating tiny hairs. When these fuse, they form a new cell which enlarges – sometimes to a metre or more – and forms a new plasmodium.

Sloth is a strange South American mammal. It is a tree-living creature, spending the whole of its life hanging upside down from the branches by its long, hooked claws. Sloths crawl slowly about searching for leaves and buds to eat. In the upside-down world of sloths, even their fur grows the other way up to other mammals so that rain water runs off quickly.

Slug is a mollusc which has lost its shell. Land-living slugs still require a moist environment in which to live, and so are mainly found in damp places or are active at night when the humidity is higher. Land slugs creep along on their muscular foot, probing with their tentacles as they go. One of the pairs of tentacles bears eyes. Most land slugs are herbivorous, but some are carnivorous, feeding on earthworms.

Sea slugs are among the most colourful and beautiful of creatures. They do not have a shell, but their bodies bear tentacles and feathery gills. Some kinds can swim, but most crawl over seaweeds and corals, grazing as they go.

Smuts, Jan Christiaan (1870–1950), was a South African soldier and statesmen. He fought as a guerrilla leader against the British during the Boer War (1899–1902). Afterwards he worked for reconciliation between Britain and the Boers, playing an important part in the establishment of the Union of South Africa in 1910. During the First World War he was a member of the British war cabinet and helped to form the League of Nations. He was Prime Minister of South Africa from 1919 to 1924 and again from 1939, when he brought his country into the Second World War on Britain's side. He was defeated in the 1948 general election by the Afrikaner Nationalist Party.

Snail, see Mollusc.

Snakes first appeared on the Earth about 135 million years ago. They are limbless reptiles whose long bodies are covered in scales, just as those of lizards are. Apart from having no legs, snakes differ from lizards in having no eardrum, and in possessing transparent eyelids, which are always fused together.

Some species of snake are very poisonous. About 35 000 people die from snake bites each year. However, this is usually because they have molested the snake in some way, for most snakes move out of sight at the approach of humans.

Snakes are found in all but the coldest climates, and are most numerous in the tropics. The pythons and boas kill their prey by constriction, but many snakes kill or stun their prey first by biting them with teeth which inject venom into the victim. Snakes always swallow their prey whole, and to do this they have jaws which can separate and stretch wide apart to engulf even a large animal.

Death adder

Snow occurs when water vapour condenses in the atmosphere at a temperature below freezing point, forming ice crystals. These fall as snow. The size of the snowflakes depends on the number of crystals that join together before descending. Whether the crystals actually reach the Earth as snow, or melt into rain, will depend on the temperature at ground level. Often snow can be seen on hills while rain is falling lower down in a valley, where it is warmer.

Soap is used to remove dirt and grease. It is made by boiling fats or oils with alkalis, such as caustic soda (sodium hydroxide) and caustic potash (potassium hydroxide). Oils from plants, such as olive oil and palm oil, are often used.

Soap was made in Mesopotamia about 5000 years ago. The Romans used soap which they made from goats' fat.

When soaps are dissolved in water they loosen dirt and grease.Soaps consist of long-chain molecules, one end of which attaches to grease and the other dissolves in the water so that the grease loosens. However, some water, known as hard water, contains chemicals. Soap mixes with these to form a thin layer, known as scum, on the surface of the water and this collects on the clothes and dishes being washed. *See also* Detergent; Surface tension.

Social insect is one in which the young are fed and cared for by individuals or groups other than their own parents. Social insects include the ants, some species of bees and wasps (there are also many solitary or non-social bees and wasps) and the termites. Although there is much variation in social behaviour depending on the species, a bumble bee colony can be considered as a typical example. The queen (a fertilized female) has the task of laying eggs. These develop into workers (sterile females) whose job is to forage, feed the queen and the new workers which are being hatched, tend to the hive and guard it. Late in the year the queen produces workers which turn into queens. She also produces drones (males). The new queens and drones leave the hive and mate. The drones then die, but the queens hibernate over winter to start a new colony in the following spring.

Honey bees, termites and ants differ in that the colony does not die out at the end of each year. Sometimes, as in the case of termites, a king and queen live together in the nest, and the workers are both males and females.

Socialism, in its modern form, is an idea which developed in the 19th century. During this period of the Industrial Revolution, workers were herded into factories where they were often very badly treated. Socialists proposed that social ownership should replace individual ownership (capitalism). In this way factories and other means of producing wealth could be run for the general good rather than personal profit. Opponents of socialism argue that in practice this will mean everything is run by a dangerously all-powerful state, and that private initiative will be suppressed.

In some countries, social or public ownership (generally called nationalization) has replaced private ownership of the railways, the coal mines and other concerns. However, much industry and agriculture remains in private hands. When both public and private ownership exists in a country, this is described as a mixed economy. A form of socialism exists in the USSR and other communist countries. Many other states call themselves socialist, although the word is often used rather loosely.

Sodium is a soft, grey metal. Its chemical symbol is Na. It is a good conductor of heat, and liquid sodium is used to cool the fuel in some nuclear reactors. Street lights use sodium, which gives out a yellow light.

Sodium forms many compounds. Some of these may be familiar. Sodium chloride is table salt; sodium hydroxide is caustic soda which is used, for example, to clean ovens. It is also used to make soap and rayon. Sodium bicarbonate is baking soda which is used in cooking, to make cakes rise.

Software is a term used by people who deal with computers. Information, and instructions on how to use the information, have to be put into a computer before it can do a job. The information is usually called data, and the instructions are known as a program. Together they are called software.

The software has to be written in a language which the computer understands. There are many different computer languages, which are artificial languages, specially made up for computers. The people who prepare software for a computer are called programers, and they have to learn the computer languages.

Software can be stored in a computer. This store is called the memory.

Solar power is power obtained directly from the Sun. The Sun's rays can be used to heat homes and other buildings. In one system, water is trapped between transparent panes of glass or plastic, sited on the roof, and the heated water is then piped around the building. Similarly, trapped air may be heated and circulated.

A solar furnace

Solar cells contain substances which convert sunlight into electricity. They were first used to provide power in spacecraft and satellites.

Solar System is the Sun and everything which is held by its gravity. It includes nine planets and their satellites, thousands of tiny planets known as asteroids, and numerous comets. All of these travel around the Sun in orbits.

Going out from the Sun the planets are Mercury, Venus, Earth, Mars, Jupiter, Saturn, Uranus, Neptune and, the outermost planet, Pluto. Most of the asteroids' orbits lie in a belt between Mars and Jupiter.

The comets travel throughout the Solar System. Their orbits may go half-way to nearby stars. Some leave the Solar System altogether. Many scientists believe that everything in the Solar System, including the Sun, was formed at about the same time from a cloud of gas and dust.

of solids.

The shape of solids can be changed, although some have to be cut or put under great pressure for this to happen. For example, wood can be cut up to make furniture, and many metals can be hammered into thin sheets.

Most solids are made up of many tiny crystals; and most solids, if heated enough, melt into a liquid, and then boil to a gas.

Solomon Islands are a group of islands of Melanesia, in the west Pacific Ocean. Capital, Honiara; area about 29785 sq km (11500 sq miles). The chief islands are Guadalcanal, Malaita, San Cristobal, New Georgia, Choiseul and Santa Isabel.

The Solomon Islands were first discovered in 1568. The first four became a British protectorate in 1893, the others being added in 1898 and 1899. Full independence was granted in 1978. Coconuts, cocoa and rice are grown and timber is becoming important.

The Solar System:
1. Mercury 2. Venus
3. Earth 4. Mars
5. Asteroids 6. Jupiter
7. Saturn 8. Uranus
9. Neptune 10. Pluto.

Solid is a matter which has a definite shape, without support. Some solids are soft and can be scratched with a fingernail. Others are hard and often make a sound when they are hit. Wood, metal and rock are examples

Solzhenitsyn, Alexander (1918–), is a Russian writer. After the Second World War he was arrested and held in prison camps in Siberia for ten years. That existence was described in his novel *A Day in the Life of*

Ivan Denisovich (1961), published during a brief spell when censorship in the Soviet Union was less strict. His criticism of the Soviet system made him extremely unpopular with the government and he was forced into exile in the West in 1974. His other works include *The First Circle* (1961) and *The Gulag Archipelago* (1974–1978). A man of fierce integrity, Solzhenitsyn also found fault with the evils of Western society.

Somali Democratic Republic, is in East Africa. Capital, Mogadiscio; area about 630 000 sq km (246 000 sq miles).

It was colonized by Muslims from the 7th century AD. From the 1880s it was divided, and part was under British control and part under Italian control. The two parts were joined in 1960 and the republic was founded.

The country is very dry, and much of it is desert. Many of the people are nomadic herdsmen, and agriculture is confined to the south. The main exports are livestock, sugar cane and spices.

Sonar is a system for detecting underwater submarines, developed by the British during the First World War to hunt German U-boats, which were sinking large numbers of Allied ships. It stands for Sound Navigation and Ranging, and it works rather like radar, except that sound pulses are used instead of radio waves. The sound, which is very high-pitched (well beyond the range of human ears) is transmitted and sensitive microphones pick up the echo, measuring the time taken and the direction. Sonar equipment is carried on ships, submarines, helicopters and can be fitted to sonar buoys, which are dropped from aircraft and work remotely, radioing their findings to the aircraft. The main purpose of sonar is military, but peaceful uses include the detection of sunken ships. *See also* Radar.

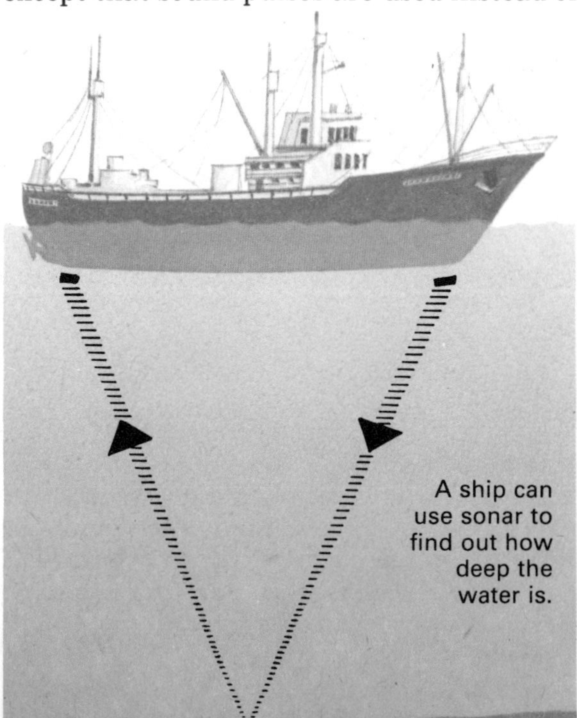
A ship can use sonar to find out how deep the water is.

Sonata is a musical composition, usually in three movements, for one instrument, such as violin, with piano accompaniment. In the 16th century *sonata* meant instrumental music as opposed to *cantata* (sung). Later, music played by a small group of instruments, usually divided into five contrasting sections, was called a sonata. The classical sonata reached its peak with the great Viennese composers, Haydn, Mozart and Beethoven.

Sonnet is a poem of 14 lines, 10 syllables per line (in English), with rhymes according to a fixed scheme. The first great sonnet writer was Petrarch, and it became a popular form in the Renaissance. Shakespeare wrote a long sonnet series. The subject of this type of poem was usually love, but later the range broadened, and the Romantic poets gave the sonnet a new lease of life in the early 19th century.

Sound is the sensation produced in the organs of hearing when soundwaves are caused in the surrounding air. When a guitar string is plucked it moves from side to side, or vibrates. This vibrates the air. These vibrations travel through the air and are heard by the ear as sound. All noises cause vibrations in the air or some other substance. A vacuum does not contain any substance, and sound cannot travel through a vacuum.

A note may sound high or low. This is called the pitch of the note and depends on the frequency of the sound.

Sound travels much more slowly than light. Thunder is the sound of a flash of lightning. Distant lightning is seen a few seconds before the thunder is heard.

Some aircraft can travel faster than sound. They are called supersonic aircraft. *See also* Ultrasonics.

South Africa, Republic of, is the most southerly country in Africa. Capitals, Cape Town (legislative) and Pretoria (administrative); area about 1 220 000 sq km (471 000 sq miles). The Republic of South Africa completely encloses the small independent country of Lesotho.

History Before Europeans arrived in South Africa the land was occupied by Bushmen and Hottentots – peoples of non-Negro physical type, together known as Khoisan. The Bushmen were, and still are, hunters and gatherers. The Hottentots kept cattle and sheep. The Bantu-speaking Negro peoples – the Zulu, the Xhosa, the Tswana, the Sepedi and the Seshoeshoe – were later arrivals.

It was in 1488 that Bartholomeu Dias, a Portuguese navigator, became the first European to reach the Cape of Good Hope, but the first European settlement was not established until the 1650s. Jan van Riebeck, a doctor by training, was commissioned by the Dutch East India Company to establish a colony at Cape Town to supply Dutch ships on their way to and from Asia. By the end of the 18th century there were about 15 000 Europeans, mainly of Dutch origin, settled around the Cape. These settlers spoke a language derived from Dutch, influenced by other European languages, called Afrikaans. The people themselves were known as Boers (farmers) or Afrikaners (Africans).

In 1795, during the Napoleonic Wars, the Cape was captured by the British and, although it was later returned, it was finally formally given to the British in 1814. The Afrikaners naturally resented the arrival of the British. Between 1835 and 1843 about 12 000 Afrikaners left Cape Colony and trekked with their ox wagons into the interior. These people were known as Voortrekkers – advance pioneers.

The Voortrekkers made for two main areas, Natal, south of the Tugela River, and the High Veld, on either side of the Vaal River. But these areas were patrolled by Zulu and Ndebele regiments and conflicts inevitably followed. On December 16th, 1838, the Voortrekkers won a decisive victory over the Zulu at Blood River and many of them then started farms in Natal.

When Natal was annexed by Britain in the 1840s, the Boers moved north again, across the Vaal River. Eventually, in the 1850s, the British acknowledged independent Boer republics in the Transvaal (called the South African Republic) and Orange Free State. Conflict between the British and the Boers continued however, and in 1880 the first Anglo-Boer War broke out over the independence of the South African Republic. The British withdrew after a severe defeat at Majuba in 1881. Problems continued, finally developing into the second Anglo-Boer War in 1899. At first the British suffered a series of defeats but eventually they captured Bloemfontein, Johannesburg and Pretoria, and Kimberley, Ladysmith and Mafeking were relieved after long sieges. Under the leadership of Louis Botha and Jan Christiaan Smuts the Boers continued a guerrilla resistance until peace was made in 1902. In 1910 the Union of South Africa was established, including the provinces of Cape of Good Hope, Natal, Orange Free State and Transvaal.

South Africa fought on Britain's side in both World Wars but in the 1950s its policy of apartheid (separate development for different racial groups) brought condemnation from many countries and controversy over apartheid has continued into the 1980s. South Africa became a republic in 1961, leaving the British Commonwealth. The head of the republic is the State President who is elected for a seven year term.

Provinces and Bantustans South Africa is divided into four provinces: Cape Province, Orange Free State, Natal and Transvaal. Within these provinces, areas (called Bantustans or Homelands) have been set aside for the Bantu-speaking peoples. Some of these regions have now been granted independence: Transkei (the territory of the Xhosa nation) in 1976, Bophuthatswana in 1977, Venda in 1977 and Ciskei in 1981.

Cape Province's capital is Cape Town, which is also the legislative capital of South Africa. It is situated in a beautiful bay on the south-west coast, with Table Mountain in the background. The major ports, apart from Cape Town, are East London and Port Elizabeth. Stellenbosch, lying inland from Cape Town, is the home of the foremost Afrikaans University. Among Cape Province's most important exports are fruit and wine.

Orange Free State is a landlocked province. Its capital is Bloemfontein. There is considerable mineral wealth including gold and uranium in the province. Products include coal, maize, wheat, cattle and sheep.

Natal's capital is Pietermaritzburg but the main industrial centre and port is Durban, which has soap, textile, paper and oil-refining industries and exports a great deal of agricultural produce as well as coal. The Indian Ocean coastline is a holiday area and sugar cane is grown in the warm climate.

Transvaal is the most highly industrialized and populated province. The capital is Pretoria which is also the administrative capital of South Africa. Johannesburg is the largest city however, and is the centre of the Witwatersrand goldmining region. To the south-west of Johannesburg is a major industrial area with huge iron and steel works and coal mines.

Land South Africa consists mainly of vast plateaux, from 200 to 1800 m (220–2000 ft) above sea-level. Their seaward edge is formed by the cliff-like faces of the Great Escarpment. The highest point of the escarpment is the imposing Drakensberg range.

A narrow coastal belt lies between the escarpment and the sea. In the south-west it includes the dry grasslands of the Little Karoo and Great Karoo, which are separated by mountains. Beyond the escarpment is the High Veld, extending northwards into the Transvaal. This immense region has rich mineral resources, prairie-like plains, fertile farmland, and prosperous industry.

Most of the country has a temperate climate. Rainfall is generally light and is sparse in the south-west. Most rain falls in summer. Drought can be a serious problem for farmers; and water conservation is important. Irrigation schemes include the ambitious Orange River Project, which is also important for hydro-electricity.

People Four out of five of South Africa's people belong to Bantu-speaking Negroid groups. The largest groups are the Zulu, the Xhosa, the Tswana, the Sepedi, and the Seshoeshoe. In accordance with the govern-

Piet Retief, the leader of the Voortrekkers, is tricked by Dingaan, the Zulu chieftain. Retief was killed along with 70 of his followers.

ment's policy of separate development, independent homelands have been established for a number of tribal groups, such as Bophuthatswana for the Tswana, and Transkei and Ciskei for the Xhosa.

The next largest population group is that of the whites, the South Africans of European descent. They are divided into two communities, the dominant Afrikaans-speaking people of mainly Dutch descent, and the English-speaking people of mainly British descent.

Two smaller groups in the population are the Coloureds, who are of mixed blood, and the Asians, who are chiefly of Indian descent. The Coloureds live mainly in Cape Province, and the Asians in Natal.

Economy The principal economic activity is manufacturing, followed by mining, and then by agriculture. Manufacturing is concentrated in the Witwatersrand area of the southern Transvaal and around the ports of Cape Town, Port Elizabeth, and Durban. Products include steel, chemicals, textiles, and processed foods.

South Africa is the world's leading source of gold, which is mined chiefly in the Witwatersrand and the Orange Free State. Gem diamonds – seven-tenths of the world's production – are mined in many parts of the country. Other important mineral products are vanadium, antimony, coal and uranium.

Most parts of South Africa have farming activity of one kind or another. It varies from the subsistence farming of many tribal areas to the large-scale commercial production of crops for the home market and export. Among the most important commercial crops are cereals, sugar-cane, and citrus fruits. South Africa's vineyards produce wines of high quality. Cattle are kept for beef and dairy products. Merino sheep and Angora goats graze on the Little and Great Karoos.

Animals and Plants Though their numbers have declined, South Africa still has herds of antelope and zebra, with lions, leopards, cheetahs and other 'big game'. Kruger National Park in The Transvaal, on the border with Mozambique, is a natural zoo, where tourists can see these animals in the wild. It is the largest game reserve in South Africa. South African birds and flowers include many colourful and exotic species.

South America is a continent between the Atlantic and Pacific Oceans. Area about 17 600 000 sq km (6 800 000 sq miles). It is joined to North America by the countries of Central America. There are 13 countries in South America of which only one, French Guiana, is not yet independent.

History The first people to live in South America probably came from Siberia, moving first into North America and then south-

Caracas
Trinidad & Tobago
Panama Canal
VENEZUELA
Orinoco
Georgetown
GUYANA
Paramaribo
Cayenne
SURINAME
FRENCH GUIANA
Bogotá
LLANOS
COLOMBIA
Equator
Quito
ECUADOR
Negro
Amazon
SELVAS
Tocantins
ANDES
Madeira
BRAZIL
Recife
São Francisco
PERU
Lima
BRAZILIAN HIGHLANDS
Brasília
L. Titicaca
La Paz
BOLIVIA
PARAGUAY
Paraná
Rio de Janiero
São Paolo
Tropic of Capricorn
ATACAMA DESERT
GRAN CHACO
Asunción
PACIFIC OCEAN
ARGENTINA
ATLANTIC OCEAN
URUGUAY
Santiago
Buenos Aires
Montevideo
PAMPAS
CHILE
Colorado
Falkland Is. (Br.)
Tierra del Fuego
0
500 miles
0
800 km
Industry
Fishing
Forest
Farming
Barren

wards. Among the most famous of these groups of Indians were the Incas of Peru. The Incas lived in the Andes around their capital city of Cuzco. Their civilization was destroyed by the Spanish who reached Peru in 1532.

Nearly the whole continent was divided between Spain and Portugal in the 16th century, Portugal taking what is now Brazil and Spain the rest. They ruled their colonies for nearly 300 years until the early 19th century, when wars of independence, led by such men as San Martin and Simon Bolivar, freed all Spanish America from Spanish rule. Brazil became an independent empire in 1832 and a republic in 1889. During the 19th century many Europeans emigrated to South America and in the 20th century the South American states have become rapidly industrialized.

Land The Andes Mountains run the entire length of the continent near the Pacific coast. There are several lesser ranges, but otherwise the continent consists largely of plateaux and lowlands. The basin of the Amazon is densely forested. There are deserts in the south-west. Three-quarters of South America lies within the tropics, but the great length from north to south creates a variety of climates.

People Most of the people are of mixed Indian-European descent, though in some countries people are of African descent too. The great majority are Roman Catholics. Spanish is the commonest language, but Portuguese is spoken in Brazil. In the more remote areas, Indian languages are still spoken. South America has about five per cent of the world's population, but the inhabitants are unevenly settled, most living near the coasts or in the tropical highland regions.

Economy Farming and livestock-raising are the chief occupations. Many people are subsistence farmers, growing food for their own needs, but South America also produces large quantities of meat, wool, wheat and coffee. About one-third of the continent is forested, including many valuable hardwoods. Forest clearance is proceeding so fast in some countries that it is giving cause for concern.

Industry and manufacturing are little developed by comparison with Europe or North America. The main industrial regions are around the larger towns, mainly in Argentina, Brazil and Chile. In some regions, the chief means of transport are still the rivers.

South America has large mineral reserves, but they are not used fully. Gold is no longer so common, but some oil has been found, notably in Venezuela, while Bolivian tin is famous. Coal of good quality is scarce, but there is great potential for hydro-electric power.

South Korea, see Korea, South

South Pole is the southernmost tip of the Earth, in Antarctica. The world's record low temperatures have been recorded nearby. The South Pole was first reached by a Norwegian expedition led by Roald Amundsen in December 1911, beating the British expedition of Robert Scott by a few weeks. Only a few people have made the grim journey since.

Soyuz is a series of Russian spacecraft in use since 1967, able to carry three cosmonauts in relative comfort. Soyuz craft were used for record-breaking Soviet spaceflights during which their cosmonauts spent longer in space than ever before. Soyuz craft are now used mostly by cosmonauts travelling to and from the orbiting Salyut space laboratory.

Space is simply the area between the stars, or between the planets of the Solar System. Because 'space' is generally defined as being airless, it starts at about 15000 m (49215 ft) that is, beyond the Earth's atmosphere.

The space taken up by any object is called its volume. *See also* Volume.

Spacelab is a small space station built by the European Space Agency and is designed to fit inside the loading bay of the American Space Shuttle. It does not fly independently, like Skylab, but remains in the Shuttle. It is the first truly European-manned space mis-

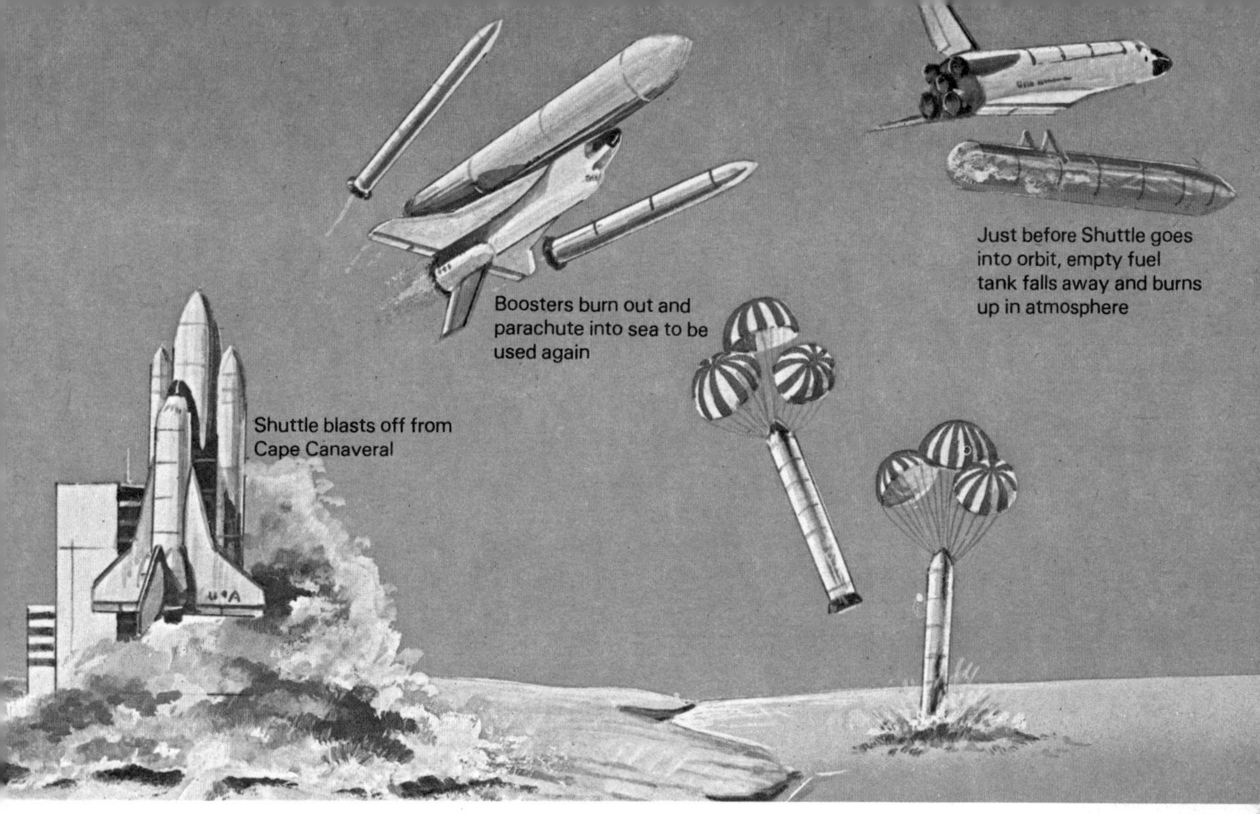

Boosters burn out and parachute into sea to be used again
Just before Shuttle goes into orbit, empty fuel tank falls away and burns up in atmosphere
Shuttle blasts off from Cape Canaveral

How the Space Shuttle goes into orbit.

sion (although a French pilot has flown as a guest cosmonaut in a Soviet capsule).

Space Shuttle is the world's first (and only) re-usable spacecraft. First launched in 1981, it consists of a 37.5 m-(123 ft-)long winged spacecraft, the orbiter, which looks rather like a fat version of an ordinary jet airplane, although its engies are rocket motors which use all their fuel on take-off. The orbiter is attached at launch to a giant fuel tank, which contains the liquid fuel to supply the orbiter engines, and two solid fuel booster rockets. Only the cheap and simple fuel tank is not re-usable: the boosters parachute back to Earth and can be refilled, while the orbiter, after completing is mission in space, glides back to Earth and lands like a conventional aeroplane on a runway. Almost all of the orbiter is given over to cargo space, and the Shuttle will be able to carry several satellites at once and place them in orbit using a remotely-controlled arm which can pick objects out of the cargo area.

The Space Shuttle is the key to America's future in space, as it is expected to cut the cost of placing bulky items into orbit by up to 90 per cent. It will therefore make it possible to assemble permanent space stations.

Spain is a kingdom in south-west Europe, sharing the Iberian peninsula with Portugal. Capital, Madrid; area about 505 000 sq km (195 000 sq miles).
History The country came under Greek, Carthaginian and then Roman control in the 1st millennium (one thousand years) BC. Vandal and Visigothic invasions began in the 5th century AD, but the Visigothic kingdom was overthrown by Muslim invaders in the 7th century. The Muslims ruled the whole of Spain except the north, where small Christian states were formed. Muslim Spain was gradually reconquered by the Christian kingdoms of Castile and Aragon. These were united under one crown in 1479 and the last Muslims were driven out of Granada in 1492.

In the 16th century, under the Hapsburgs, Spain acquired the Netherlands and a vast overseas empire in the New World, but lost many possessions in the War of the Spanish Succession (1701–1714), when most of Europe was plunged into war over several claimants to the Spanish throne. The coun-

Philip II, King of Spain (1566–1598), and the Escorial, a huge monastery which he had built, north of Madrid.

try was under French occupation during the Peninsular War (1808–1813), a phase of the Napoleonic wars. During the 19th century there was conflict between Royalists and Republicans. A republic was eventually established in 1931 but the country was split by civil war during 1936–1939. Francisco Franco won the war and was Spain's dictator until his death in 1975. Democracy was then restored with a constitutional monarchy.

Land and People Spain consists mainly of plateaux fringed by mountains. The highest mountains are the Pyrenees on the French border. The only big lowland area is the plain of Andalusia in the south. The climate is generally mild, though on the Meseta in central and north-west Spain, it is dry and winters are chilly. The average temperature in Madrid is 4.5°C (40°F) in January and 23°C (73°F) in July.

There are considerable regional differences among the people. The Castilians of central Spain regard themselves as the most 'Spanish' and theirs is the official language. In Andalusia Moorish influence is strong, and the Catalonians and Basques of the north-east hardly regard themselves as Spanish at all. Nearly all Spaniards are Roman Catholics.

Economy Though agriculture is the chief occupation, farming is rather backward, largely due to poor soils and low rainfall, though there is extensive irrigation. The old system where there were very small peasant plots or vast estates owned by absentee landlords is disappearing. Livestock, especially sheep, are important on the Meseta. Wine, citrus fruit, olive oil and bananas are major exports.

Fishing is important in some coastal areas, and there are large mineral resources. Mercury has been mined near Almaden for over 2000 years. Manufacturing industry has expanded recently. The main industrial areas are around Barcelona and on the north coast, where there is local coal and hydroelectric power. Tourism is a great money-earner.

Rulers of Spain

United Kingdoms of Castile and Aragon	
Ferdinand II of Aragon and Isabella of Castile	1479–1504
Philip I and Joanna the Mad	1504–1506
Ferdinand V (Ferdinand II of Aragon)	1506–1516
House of Hapsburg	
Charles I (Charles V as Holy Roman Emperor)	1516–1556
Philip II	1556–1598
Philip III	1598–1621
Philip IV	1621–1665
Charles II	1665–1700
House of Bourbon	
Philip V	1700–1724
Louis I	1724
Philip V	1724–1746

Ferdinand VI	1746–1759
Charles III	1759–1788
Charles IV	1788–1808
Ferdinand VII	1808
Joseph Bonaparte (not a Bourbon)	1808–1813
Ferdinand VII (restored)	1814–1833
Isabella II	1833–1868
Interregnum	1868–1869
Francisco Serrano (regent)	1869–1870
Amadeus (King, House of Savoy)	1870–1873
First Republic	1873–1874
House of Bourbon	
Alfonso XII	1874–1885
Alfonso XIII	1886–1931
Presidents of the Republic	
Niceto Alcala Zamora y Torres	1931–1936
Manuel Azana	1936–1939
Head of State	
Francisco Franco	1939–1975
House of Bourbon	
Juan Carlos I	1975–

Spanish Civil War was fought between Nationalists and Republicans in Spain from 1936 to 1939. In July 1936 there was a military revolt, led by General Franco and other army officers, against Spain's Republican government. The rebels (or Nationalists as they were called) quickly occupied large parts of the country, but failed to capture Madrid or Barcelona. The Nationalists, who received help from Germany and Italy, gradually gained more territory, and in 1937 took control of the Basque region of Spain after bombing attacks in which the town of Guernica was destroyed. The war ended with the surrender of Madrid in April 1939.

Sparta was an ancient Greek city in the southern Peloponnese. It originated from Dorian settlements in the 11th century BC. The Spartans gradually increased their territories by conquering Laconia and Messenia during the 9th and 8th centuries BC. During the 6th century Sparta became a warrior state with a ruling class trained for war and physical endurance by a harsh discipline, while the helots (serfs) farmed the land. Sparta's victory over Athens in the Peloponnesian War (404) brought it leadership over the whole of Greece, but its position gradually declined, and Spartan power was shattered by Thebes at the Battle of Leuctra (371 BC).

Species is the smallest unit used in the classification of plants and animals. For instance, the blue whale and the sperm whale are both whales, but they are different species. Throughout the world there are about one million different species of animal, and about half as many different species of plant. Each species has its own characteristic appearance, and its offspring always resemble their parents. Although the blue whale could possibly mate with a sperm whale it would not produce fertile offspring. This is because the genes of one species will not combine properly with the genes of a different species.

Scientists give a species a two-part name, based on either Latin or Ancient Greek. Thus, the fungus known as the fly agaric is called *Amanita muscaria*. *Muscaria* is its specific name and *Amanita* is its generic name. Although there are several sorts of fungus the first part of whose name is *Amanita*, there is only one called *Amanita muscaria*.

Spectroscope is an instrument used to split light into its spectrum. Electricity and heat can make substances give off light. Each element gives off light which has a different spectrum from that given off by any other element. For example, sodium gives off mainly yellow light, while neon gives off mainly red light. An element can be identified from its spectrum.

The spectroscope is used in chemistry to find out which elements are in a substance. Astronomers use it to examine starlight, to find the elements in stars.

Spectrum – light contains many colours called a spectrum of colours. The spectrum of sunlight contains red, orange, yellow, green, blue, indigo and violet light of different wavelengths. Together they look white.

If light is shone through a piece of

specially-shaped glass, called a prism, it is split up into its spectrum. Raindrops split up sunlight into a spectrum which we know as a rainbow. *See also* Spectroscope; Wavelength.

Speed of light is the universal constant, because nothing can travel faster. In the vacuum of outer space, light travels at about 300 000 km (186 000 miles) per second, or 9 460 000 000 000 km (6 000 000 000 000 miles) in one year, this distance therefore being known as one light year. The fastest spacecraft so far built have attained only a tiny fraction of this speed, and the fact that the nearest star to the Solar System is over four light years away means that space travel is likely to be limited to the confines of the Solar System for many centuries. Light takes 1.25 seconds to travel from the Moon, and 8 mins 27 seconds from the Sun. Radio waves and other forms of electromagnetic radiation also travel at the speed of light.

Spiders are among the most familiar of arachnids. They are found in all parts of the world, and live in many different types of habitat – even water. Some species hide away in crevices or burrows waiting to pounce on prey and others spin sticky webs to trap food. There are even species which lasso their victims with strands of silk.

The body of a spider is divided into two parts: the prosoma and the abdomen. Spiders have eight legs, and powerful, biting jaws which can inject venom into their victims. The most dangerous spider is the Australian funnel web spider; its venom can kill a human very quickly. All spiders are predatory, feeding mainly on insects, although the largest ones feed on birds.

The red-back spider of Australia and the katipo of New Zealand are from the same family as the Black Widow, found in North America. The bite of these spiders is dangerous to humans, but proves fatal in only a small percentage of cases.

Spinal cord is the part of the vertebrate nervous system which is located within the backbone. It runs from the brain, through the centre of the bones of the vertebral column and along the whole of the body length. From the spinal cord, nerves run to and from all the muscles and organs, relaying information to the brain and passing the brain's instructions back to the muscles and organs.

Spiny anteater, see Echidnas.

Spiritual is a black American religious folk song. The spiritual probably began in the 18th century as a mixture of old English folk songs, Protestant (especially Wesleyan) hymns, and West African music. It became the music of the black churches in the American South. In the 20th century versions of the spirituals adapted for white audiences

Below: Red-back spider, *Centre:* Black widow spider, *Far right, top:* Bird-eating spider, *Far right, bottom:* Trapdoor spider.

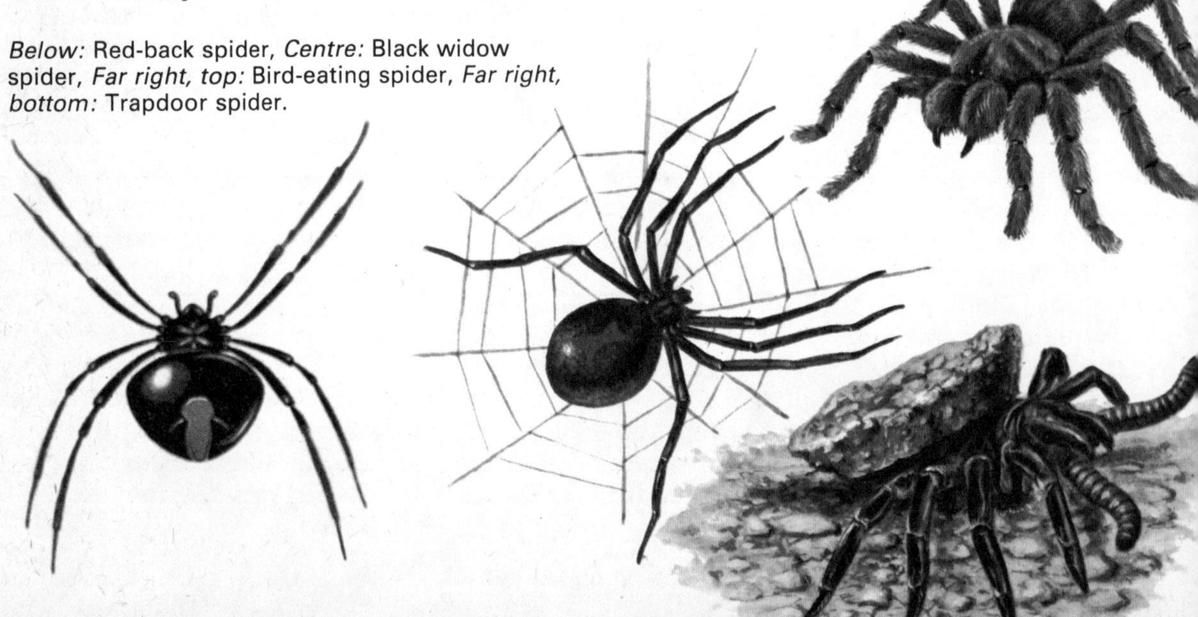

became very popular through the performances of singers like Paul Robeson and Marian Anderson.

Spirogyra is an alga of freshwater ponds and streams. It can be recognized by the fact that each cell possesses a spiral chloroplast containing chlorophyll. Sometimes ponds may become clogged with masses of this green alga. It reproduces by a method known as conjugation. The nucleus of one cell joins with the nucleus of an adjoining cell to form a structure called a zygote, which sinks to the bottom to develop into a new plant.

Sponges are primitive animals consisting of groups of cells joined together by a skeleton composed of a horny substance called spongin. The outer layer of a sponge is muscle-like, and the inner layer is made up of cells called collar cells. These collar cells beat tiny hairs, creating a water current. The body of a sponge is like a vase. The sides of the 'vase' have minute openings through which water and food are drawn in by the beating action of collar cells. Waste leaves the animal through a hole at the top of the 'vase'. Sponges are found mainly in sea water, although some also live in fresh water.

Spore is a reproductive body produced by ferns, mosses, fungi, bacteria and protozoans. Spores are usually tiny, and may be produced in huge numbers. Millions and millions rain down from beneath the cap of a large toadstool. Fern spores are often visible as brown dots on the underside of the fronds. When spores land in a suitable place, they germinate, giving rise to a new generation. Bacteria often form spores in adverse conditions, remaining in this state until more favourable conditions occur.

Springbok is a South African gazelle, *Antidorcas Marsupialis*, which has a habit of springing 3 to 3.5 m (9 to 10 ft) into the air in play or when startled. When springing, the legs are held stiffly and close together, with the head lowered. When the antelope hits the ground it rebounds with effortless ease. It is about 0.8 m (2.5 ft) high at the shoulder.

The Springbok is the national emblem of South Africa. It is a native of the Kalahari Desert, Angola, and South Africa.

Sputnik was the first artificial satellite placed into Earth's orbit. It was launched by the USSR on 4 October 1947. Sputnik 1 weighed only 83.5 kg (184 lb) and did nothing except emit a 'bleeping' radio signal, but it marked the start of the space age. Sputnik 2 weighed 508 kg (1120 lb) and carried a dog, the first living creature to visit space, on 3 November 1957. The name sputnik in Russian means 'travelling companion'. *See also* Satellite; Telstar.

Squid is a mollusc, related to the octopus and cuttlefish. Squid have no external shell, and have a torpedo-shaped body armed with eight short, suckered tentacles and two longer tentacles. They are predatory animals, and can swim well using their large eyes to search for small animals to eat. In turn, squid are a major source of food for seals, whales and some fish. Squid catch their food by grabbing it with the tentacles and pulling it towards the mouth. There are many types of squid in the oceans of the world, some living in shallow water and some in the depths. The giant squid is one of the longest creatures living in the sea. With its tentacles outstretched it can measure 24 m (78 ft) in length.

Squirrel is an attractive-looking rodent found in many parts of the world, such as Europe, America and Asia. The red squirrel of the pine forests of Europe has reddish brown fur and, at certain times of the year, long, hairy ear tufts. It jumps from tree to tree searching for pine cones to eat. The grey squirrel of Europe and North America lives in much the same way, but prefers deciduous woodland. Both species have bushy tails. In southern Asia, and parts of Europe and America, there are flying squirrels. These glide from tree to tree on flaps of skin stretching between their front and back legs. Ground squirrels include the prairie dogs, woodchucks and chipmunks. Seeds form a large part of their diet.

Sri Lanka, formerly Ceylon, is an island republic in south Asia, off the tip of the Indian peninsula. Capital, Colombo; area about 66 000 sq km (25 000 sq miles).
History A Buddhist civilization was established on the island by the 3rd century BC. In 1505 the Portuguese formed settlements in the west and south, which were taken by the Dutch in 1658. Ceded to Britain in 1802, it was made a crown colony in 1833. It achieved independence within the Commonwealth of Nations in 1948, becoming a republic in 1972 and changing its name from Ceylon to Sri Lanka the same year.
Land and People The mountainous centre rises to peaks over 2000 m (6560 ft) with deep valleys creating marvellous scenery. The lowlands are very warm, both summer and winter, and the climate is dominated by the monsoon. The north and east occasionally suffer drought.

The largest group of people are the Sinhalese, but there is a large minority of Tamils. Buddhism is the chief religion, though the Tamils are mostly Hindu. Sri Lanka is a country of villages, and many people are occupied in growing traditional food crops such as rice. Plantations produce tea, rubber and coconuts, which make up most of Sri Lanka's exports. There are some mineral deposits, notably graphite, and manufacturing is growing.

St Christopher (St Kitts) – Nevis is a self-governing state forming part of the Lesser Antilles in the Caribbean. Capital, Basseterre; area about 261 sq km (101 sq miles). It consists of the two islands of St Kitts and Nevis. Great Britain is still responsible for defence and foreign affairs, but it has full internal self-government. The islands are volcanic, but the good climate and fine scenery attract many tourists. The main exports are sugar, cotton, salt and coconuts.

St Helena is an island in the southern Atlantic Ocean. Capital, Jamestown; area about 122 sq km (47 sq miles). It is famous as the island of Napoleon's exile and death (1821). It is a mountainous island and in places, its coast has steep cliffs 300 m (980 ft) high. The people are of mixed European, African and Asian origin. St Helena is a British colony and it administers Ascension Island and the small Tristan da Cunha group of islands.

St Lawrence is a river and seaway in south-east Canada. It consists of the St Lawrence River with a system of canals and locks which permit ocean-going ships to reach the Great Lakes. It also provides hydro-electric power. Created by the combined efforts of the USA and Canada, and completed in its modern form in 1959, it gives, for example, direct access from Chicago, USA, on Lake Michigan, to the Atlantic.

St Lucia is an independent island in the Lesser Antilles, West Indies, in the eastern Caribbean. Capital, Castries; area about 616 sq km (238 sq miles). It was settled by the French in 1650 and ceded to Great Britain in 1814. It gained independence in 1979. Bananas, cocoa and coconut products are the chief products.

St Paul's Cathedral is the seat of the bishop of London. It was built by Wren to replace the old, Gothic St Paul's, destroyed by fire in 1666, and was finished in 1711. It follows the traditional ground plan of a cross, and its great central dome is a famous London landmark. This gives it a slight resemblance to St Peter's, Rome, but St Paul's is the more harmonious building. The west front is divided

into two tiers of columns, and the interior is light and colourful, providing a splendid space for great ceremonial services. *See also* Wren, Sir Christopher.

St Peter's in Rome is the headquarters of the Roman Catholic Church. One of the largest churches in the world, it was begun early in the 16th century. Many of the greatest artists of Renaissance Italy worked on it, including Bramante, Raphael, and Michelangelo, as well as, later, Carlo Maderna and Bernini, who built the *piazza* in front. Inside, it feels like several churches, for the atmosphere varies as you pass from one part of the huge building to another. The Baroque decoration might seem too elaborate in a lesser building.

A museum as well as a church, St Peter's contains famous works of art such as Michelangelo's *Pièta* (the Virgin Mary holding the body of Jesus) and Bernini's extravagant throne of St Peter.

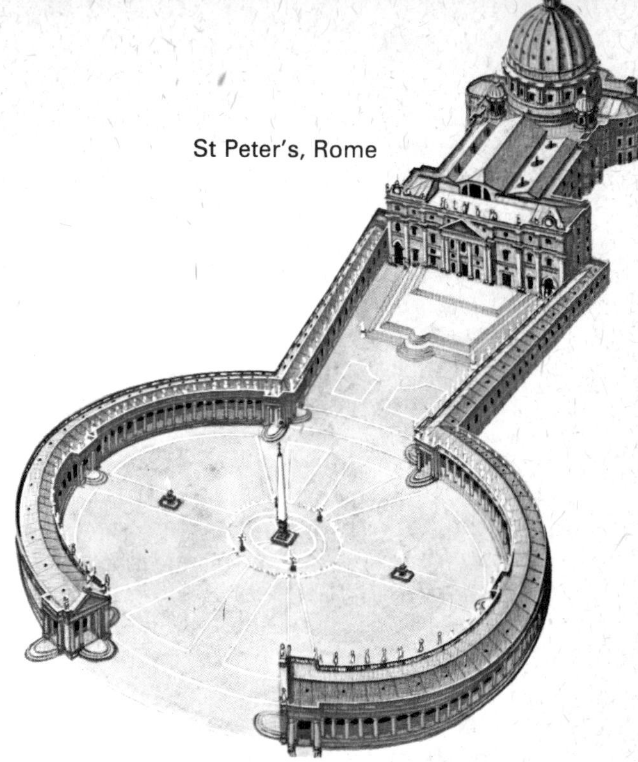

St Peter's, Rome

St Vincent and the Grenadines is an island state of the Windward Islands, West Indies. Capital, Kingstown; area about 389 sq km (150 sq miles). It consists of the island of St Vincent and the Northern Grenadines. First settled by the British in 1762 it gained full independence in 1979.

Stalactites and stalagmites are formed in limestone caves. Limestone is calcium carbonate. Some of this dissolves in the water trickling through the rock. It is left on the ceiling or floor of a cave as the water drips down. After many years, the calcium carbonate builds up to form long shapes which look like icicles. Those that hang from the ceiling are called stalactites. Those that grow from the ground are called stalagmites. Stalactites and stalagmites can join to form a column.

They can grow very large. A stalactite in Spain is 59 m (195 ft) long. The largest stalagmite is in France and is 29 m (96 ft) high.

Stalin, Joseph (1879–1953), was a Soviet Communist statesman. As a youth he entered a theological college, but became involved in political activity and was forced to leave. He joined the Social Democratic Party and when the party split into two groups he joined the Bolsheviks under Lenin. After several periods of imprisonment and exile, he took part in the Russian Revolution, becoming General Secretary of the Central Committee of the Communist Party in 1922. After Lenin's death in 1924 Stalin gradually removed his opponents from positions of power, becoming absolute ruler of the USSR by 1929.

During the 1930s he pushed through a massive programme of industrialization and agricultural collectivization, which caused people great hardship, and at the same time began a purge of those whom he believed opposed him. In the Second World War, when Germany invaded the USSR, he became the supreme military leader of his country, defeated Hitler, and in the post-war years exerted strong Russian influence over the eastern European countries.

Stalingrad, Battle of, was fought between Russian and German forces during the Second World War. In August 1942 German armies began to attack the town of Stalingrad, but the Russians resisted strongly. After several months of fierce fighting the

German forces were surrounded and forced to surrender. The battle marked a major turning point in the war.

Stamen is the male part of a flower. It consists of a stalk called a filament, supporting a pollen sac called an anther. When ripe, the anthers burst and the tiny dust-like pollen grains are ready to be transferred to the stigma of the female flower parts, the carpels, so that fertilization can take place. Some flowers have many stamens, while others have only a small number. There is also variation in the shape of stamens; some have rounded anthers and others have long, thin anthers. Some anthers stand fixed and erect, while others dangle and swivel at the point of attachment to the filament.

Star gives out heat, light and other energy. It produces this energy by fusion. Apart from planets and comets, the bright objects in the sky are stars or groups of stars. Without a telescope, about 2000 stars can be seen in the sky. Many of these have been grouped by astronomers into constellations.

Stars vary in size. Some are only a hundredth of the diameter of our Sun. Others have diameters up to one thousand times greater than the Sun.

They also vary in colour. Cool stars look red while hot stars look blue or white. The Sun is a yellow star which gives out a medium amount of heat. Star distances are measured in light years or parsecs. Our nearest star, after the Sun, is Alpha Centauri, 4.3 light years away.

Starfish are echinoderms (spiny-skinned animals) related to the sea-urchins and sea-lilies. They usually have a body drawn out into five arms. Underneath the arms are the tube feet. These are water-powered, finger-like projections which enable the animal to crawl about. The tube feet can also grip animals whilst the starfish feeds on them. Some starfish have more than five arms, and several species are highly coloured in vivid tones of blue, red or yellow. Starfish occur in most of the world's oceans, but are commonest in warmer regions.

Static electricity is caused by electrical charges which are at rest. The Greeks made ornaments out of a substance called amber. They found that when the amber was rubbed, other lightweight objects would move towards it. You can do the same thing with a plastic comb. If you comb your hair and then hold the comb over small pieces of paper, they will travel towards it and even stick to it. This 'attraction' is caused by electrical charges or static electricity.

Small particles called electrons have an electrical charge. Some substances, like plastic, lose or gain electrons when they are rubbed. This gives them an electrical charge. This charge is very quickly lost. Within a short time after rubbing, your comb will not attract pieces of paper.

The clouds in the sky are charged with static electricity. Lightning and thunder are caused by the clouds' charge being lost, to other clouds or to the Earth.

Steady state is a theory about the universe. Observations by astronomers show that galaxies are moving away from each other. The universe seems to be expanding. According to the Steady state theory, new matter is always being created to fill the space left by this expansion. The new matter moves apart, and forms galaxies which continue to move apart. This means that the universe always looks exactly the same. It has no beginning or end, but is in a steady state.

Many observations suggest that the universe has not always looked the same. Therefore, most astronomers do not agree with this theory. Their theory of how the universe started is the Big Bang theory.

Steam is the gas of water. Water boils or evaporates to steam and steam condenses to water at 100 degrees Centigrade (212 degrees Fahrenheit). Water becomes about 1600 times bigger when it turns to steam. If a kettle is left boiling, the lid will start to shake and may even be blown off by the expanding steam. This power of steam is used in steam engines, which were used in mines and factories and to power trains, ships and other vehicles. Many are still used today.

Steam is also used to drive turbines around. Steam turbines are used to power large ships and to generate current electricity.

Steel is an alloy of iron and carbon. Vast amounts of steel are made each year. Without it, the world would look very different. It is used in buildings, bridges, trains and other sorts of transport. Many of the things we use are made with steel tools and they are held together by steel nuts, bolts and screws.

Iron is found naturally, mixed with many substances, including carbon. All these are taken away from the iron in a refinery. Accurate amounts of carbon are then added to make steel. Other minerals may be added to make special types of steel. Stainless steel contains chromium and nickel. Steel may be hardened by heating it to very high temperatures and then cooling it very quickly. This is known as tempering.

Stem is the part of a vascular plant (in other words, a plant with water-conducting tissues) which bears buds, leaves and reproductive structures, and sometimes branches as well. In woody plants such as trees the stem may be thick, upright and tall, and covered in a protective layer of bark. Despite its great strength, the stem, or trunk, of a tree can sway in the wind to prevent it from breaking. Stems of non-woody plants often wither after the plant has produced flowers. If the plant is perennial, the stem is replaced by a new one in the following spring. The stems of some plants do not appear above ground. Plants such as the iris have a horizontal, underground stem called a rhizome, which is used to store food.

DIAGRAM OF PLANT STEM

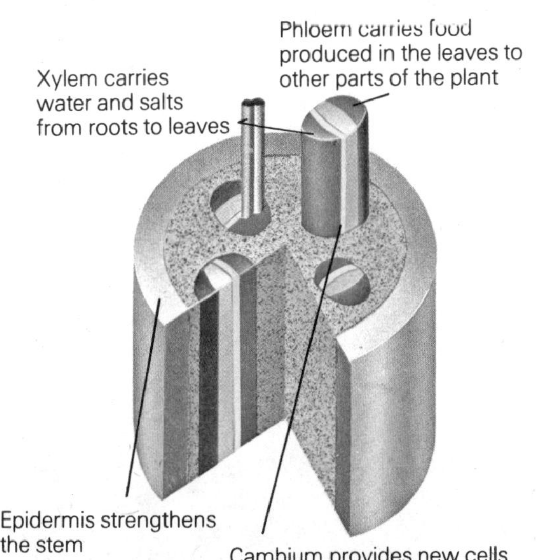
Phloem carries food produced in the leaves to other parts of the plant
Xylem carries water and salts from roots to leaves
Epidermis strengthens the stem
Cambium provides new cells for the xylem and phloem

Stephen (circa 1097–1154), was King of England (1135–1154). He usurped the throne from the daughter of Henry I, Matilda, who subsequently led an army against him. In the civil war that followed, Stephen was captured by Matilda's forces, and she became Queen for a time. Stephen then resumed the throne, but had to recognize Matilda's son as his heir.

George Stephenson's steam locomotive, the *Rocket*.

Stephenson, George (1781–1848), was an English inventor and engineer, and the most important pioneer of the steam-locomotive.

The son of a mechanic, he did not go to school, but he later learned to read and write, and attended evening classes.

Stephenson became the chief mechanic at a coal mine, and built a number of steam engines, running on rails, which were used for hauling coal out of the mines. He built the Stockton to Darlington railway line which opened in 1825. Even more important was the Liverpool to Manchester line which opened in 1830. Stephenson not only built this, but also constructed a locomotive for it – the famous *Rocket*, which defeated all other entrants at a trial race in 1829, reaching a speed of 48 km/h (30 mph).

Steppe is the vast rolling grasslands of Eastern Europe, and central and eastern Asia, stretching as far as Siberia. Most of the steppe area lies within the borders of the USSR. The steppe is flat, treeless and fertile, closely resembling the North American prairies.

The steppe has been of great importance in world history. Its flatness made it easy for nomad conquerors, such as the Mongols, to range from China to Persia and Europe, destroying or taking over old societies and building great empires. New ideas and skills also passed rapidly across the steppe, linking societies remote from one another.

Stevenson, Robert Louis (1850–1894), was a Scottish novelist. His early works recorded his impressions on his many travels, but he became a popular success with his children's adventure, *Treasure Island* (1882), followed by *Kidnapped* (1886). Probably his most famous story is *The Strange Case of Dr Jekyll and Mr Hyde* (1886), an early piece of science fiction. His later novels were mostly written in Samoa, where he settled in search of health.

Stigma is the receptive surface of the carpel (which is the female reproductive organ of flowering plants). It is on the stigma that pollen grains land during pollination. Most flowers produce carpels which have a long narrow portion called the style, and the top of the style is called the stigma.

Stingrays belong to the ray family. Their long, whip-like tail has spines on its upper surface which can deliver a powerful, venomous sting. Stingrays hunt small invertebrates. When not feeding they often lie motionless on the seabed in shallow water. Bathers occasionally stand on the fish and are stung viciously – this sometimes kills them. The largest species lives in the Indo-west Pacific Ocean and grows to a length of over 4 m (13 ft). *See also* Rays.

Stoat is a carnivorous mammal related to the weasel and polecat. In fact, all three animals look very similar. The stoat has a long body and tail, brown above and white on the throat, chest and belly. It has short legs and a small, rat-like face. The stoat is widespread, hunting over mountains, fields, woods and riversides for prey such as rabbits, voles and small birds. It locates its prey with its powerful sense of smell. In winter, the stoat's coat turns white, and the animal is then known as ermine.

Stock Exchange is a place set up for the buying and selling of securities such as stocks, shares and bonds. These are basically documents concerning the ownership of companies or the loans made to them. By issuing securities, companies can raise huge sums of money from the public to finance their operations.

A shareholder owns a percentage – often only a tiny percentage – of the company issuing stocks and shares, and will receive a percentage of any profits the company makes. So, his or her stocks and shares may be valuable and can themselves be bought and sold – the chief business of a stock exchange. Governments also raise money by issuing securi-

Workers at a stock exchange.

ties that are bought and sold on stock exchanges.

The largest stock exchanges in the world are the London Stock Exchange and New York's Wall Street. The London Stock Exchange was set up in 1773. Only recognized professional dealers, called brokers and jobbers, can trade there. Anyone who wants to buy securities must contact a broker, who will in turn contact a jobber on the floor of the Exchange and strike a bargain with them.

STOL aircraft – are Short take off and landing aircraft, specially designed to operate from fields and roads with very little space. STOL aircraft have been made with one, two, three and four engines, are usually propeller driven and generally have wings with special devices to enhance the available lift at low speeds. *See also* VTOL aircraft.

Stomach is a highly muscular sac lying between the oesophagus (windpipe) and the intestine of an animal, where food is stored and where digestion begins. In the stomach, enzymes and acids are mixed with the chewed food to produce a mushy liquid which is then squirted, in bursts, into the intestine where further digestion takes place.

In birds, the last part of the stomach is called the gizzard. The gizzard contains pebbles which help to grind the food up. In ruminants (animals, such as cattle and sheep, which chew the cud) the stomach is divided into four portions. The stomach of the mighty blue whale is big enough to hold several tonnes of krill in it at one time. *See also* Digestion.

Stonehenge is a prehistoric monument on Salisbury Plain, England. It consists of four nearly circular groups of standing stones. The stones of the outer circle are up to 5 m (16 ft) high, 2 m (6 ft) wide and 1 m (3 ft) thick. Some of them were hauled over 161 km (100 miles) from Wales. Building began probably about 2150 BC but the monument was often changed or enlarged and the final phase of building took place about 1250 BC. The finest Bronze Age remains in Europe, it probably had some kind of religious purpose, but no one knows exactly what. It has also been interpreted as a great astronomical clock.

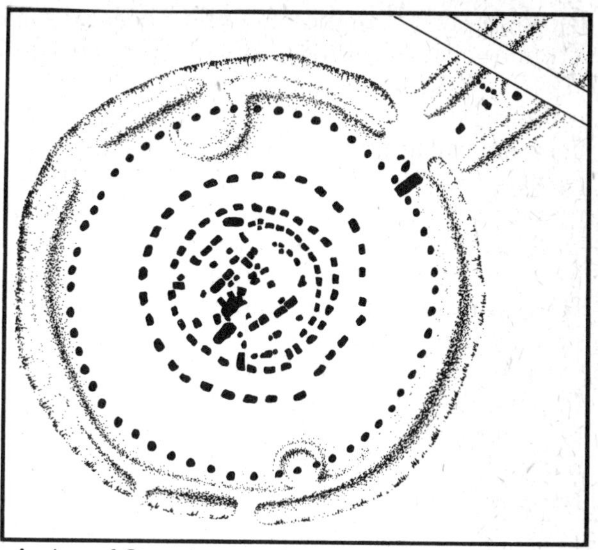

A plan of Stonehenge, showing the rings of stones.

Stork is a large, black and white bird with long legs and a long, thin beak. The 17 species usually inhabit marshy grassland in many parts of the world, where they feed on a variety of small aquatic animals. The ugly-looking marabou stork is a scavenger, feeding on carcasses. The wood stork catches fish by jumping about in the water to disturb them first, and then grabbing the victims with its beak. Storks are strong fliers, and some species undertake long migrations. They have no voice but communicate by clattering their bills.

Strauss is the name of several composers. Johann Strauss, the Younger, (1825–1899), was the most famous member of a Viennese family of composers of waltzes (e.g. *The Blue Danube*). Richard Strauss (1864–1949), a German composer and conductor (not related to the Viennese family), was one of the greatest musicians of his day. He wrote many operas still constantly performed, e.g. *Salome* (1905), *Der Rosenkavalier* (1911). Many of his orchestral pieces, especially his tone poems, are equally popular.

Stravinsky, Igor (1882–1971), was a

Russian-born composer who became a French citizen (1934) and a US citizen (1945). With Schoenberg, he was the most influential composer of the 20th century. He became world-famous with his ballet *The Firebird* (1910). *The Rite of Spring* (1913), probably his most popular work (though it caused a riot when first performed), made him the hero of the avant-garde in music. However, he never fully adopted the atonality of Schoenberg.

In Stravinsky's music, rhythm is of great importance. He was also interested in jazz (e.g. in *The Soldier's Tale*) and wrote several pieces in ragtime. He was extremely versatile, and his work at different periods reflected most of the major developments in music from the 18th to the 20th century.

Strings, in music, are stringed instruments, i.e. instruments in which sound is produced from taut strings of gut or wire. This is done by a bow (violin, viola, cello), by plucking with the fingers (harp, guitar) or a plectrum (guitar). The sound is amplified by a soundbox, usually wooden.

In an orchestra the strings consist of violin, viola, cello and bass (or double bass). They correspond to soprano, alto, tenor and bass in a choir. The harp, which is plucked rather than played with a bow, is often present. Other common stringed instruments are the banjo, guitar – the electric guitar is the dominant instrument in pop music – and the zither. Stringed instruments are also found in non-European music, e.g. the sitar in India and various forms of lyre in the Far East.

Some stringed instruments, like the harp, are ancient. Others developed more recently. The violin, for example, was invented by Andrea Amati of Cremona in the 1550s. The guitar originated about the same time. Historically, both belong the lute family, which can be traced back to about 800 BC and was the most popular instrument in the home in the 16th century.

Sturgeons are large, long-bodied fish found in temperate and Arctic waters. The long, pointed snout is equipped with barbels or feelers with which the fish probe about in the mud for small invertebrates to suck into the toothless mouth. Many species have a series of large, bony plates along the sides of the body, and the tail is shark-like. The eggs, or roe, of some sturgeons are a highly prized food called caviar.

Sudan, The Democratic Republic of The, is in north-east Africa. Capital, Khartoum; area about 2 500 000 sq km (967 500 sq miles). Formerly under Egyptian and then British and French rule, the modern republic was founded in 1956. In area, the Sudan is the largest country in Africa, but much of it is desert, with grassland, forest and mountains in the south. The Nile, whose two major branches join at Khartoum, is very important to it. The people of northern Sudan are basically Arab; southerners are of mixed African descent.

Cotton is the main export crop, followed by peanuts, but irrigation is required and fertile areas are limited. There is much livestock, which provides the main support for nomadic peoples. Among other resources, the Sudan is the world's main supplier of gum arabic.

Suez Canal was built in Egypt to link the Mediterranean with the Red Sea. Designed by a French engineer, Ferdinand de Lesseps,

Ferdinand de Lesseps who designed the Suez Canal.

it was opened in 1869. Great Britain acquired a controlling interest in the Suez Canal Company in 1875, and in 1888 freedom for all ships to pass through the Canal was guaranteed by the Convention of Constantinople. In 1956 the Egyptian government nationalized the Canal, an action which led to an Anglo-French attack upon Egypt. The Canal was closed during the Arab-Israeli war in 1967 and was not reopened until 1975.

Sugar is a group of carbohydrates. It has a sweet taste and dissolves in water.

Green plants make sugar. The white sugar that many people eat is called sucrose, and is made from the roots of a plant called sugar beet and from a tall grass called sugar cane.

Our bodies make all sugars into one, called glucose.

Sulphur is an element with several allotropes. Its chemical symbol is S. When a volcano erupts, one of the substances thrown out is sulphur. Bright yellow crystals and lumps of sulphur can sometimes be seen around volcanoes and hot springs. Sulphur and many of its compounds are found underground and are mined.

Sulphur has many uses. It is used in the manufacture of medicines, gunpowder and dyes. It can be used to kill some of the insects and fungi that attack plants. Rubber is hardened using sulphur. Most sulphur is used to make sulphuric acid.

Sulphur has no smell but some of its compounds have very strong smells. The gas, hydrogen sulphide, smells of rotten eggs. Sulphur dioxide is a poisonous, choking gas. *See also* Allotropy; Volcano.

Sumatra is an island in Indonesia. Area about 524 000 sq km (202 000 sq miles). It was the centre of a Hindu kingdom in the Middle Ages. High mountains, including volcanoes, run parallel with the coast. The island is crossed by the equator, and the plains are flat, wet and hot. The people are mainly of Malay origin.

Sugar, tea and rubber are the main plantation crops, and rice the chief food crop. Coconuts, vegetables and spices are also grown. Domestic animals include water buffalo. The forests provide teak and ebony and the chief mineral product is oil.

Sun is a yellow star and probably was formed 4600 million years ago. Over 100 times wider than the Earth, it is mostly hydrogen. Inside the Sun the hydrogen, in the very hot plasma, changes to helium by fusion. Slowly the amount of helium in the Sun is increasing and the hydrogen is decreasing. The fusion produces huge amounts of energy which radiates throughout the Solar System and beyond. Without this energy there could be no life on Earth. It makes the Earth warm enough for human beings to live on, and provides the light for plants to grow.

Although the Sun is a long way away, it is so bright that it should never be looked at directly or it will damage the eyes. Dark spots, known as sunspots, appear on its surface. The weather on the Earth varies with the number of sunspots. Sometimes bright loops and arches shoot out from the Sun's surface. These are streams of gas and are known as prominences.

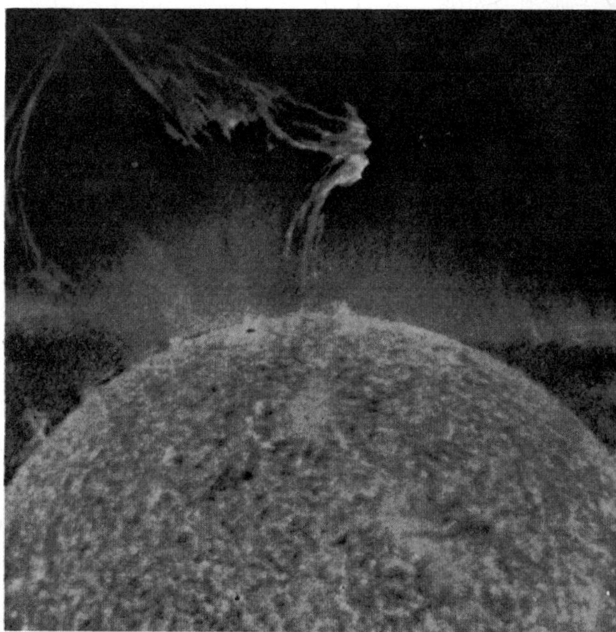

A massive eruption of helium gas stretching 800 000 km (half a million miles) into space from the surface of the Sun. This was photographed through telescopes on Skylab.

Supernova is the explosion of stars. Only stars much larger than the Sun end in a supernova. These stars become brighter and brighter as they reach the end of their life. Eventually they become so hot that a massive explosion occurs. A supernova may be brighter than the millions of other stars in its galaxy put together. It is the most dramatic sight in the universe.

After a supernova, the core of the star may become a neutron star. The rest of the star will slowly spread through space.

A supernova was seen by Japanese and Chinese astronomers in AD 1054. It was so bright that it could be seen during the day. The Crab nebula is the remains of the outer layers of the star that exploded.

Surface tension is the tension that is in the surface of a liquid. Often liquids seem to have a surface 'skin'. If a sewing needle is dropped in a bowl of water it will sink to the bottom. If it is placed very gently, flat in a bowl of water, it will float. It is being held up by the water's 'skin'. This skin effect is caused by the surface tension.

Some insects, such as pondskaters, make use of surface tension. They move quickly over the surface of a pond, feeding on small creatures, without getting wet.

Surface tension causes liquids to form round drops, such as raindrops. It also makes liquids climb up very thin tubes. This is known as capillarity. Water spreads through the soil to plants by capillarity.

Suriname is a republic in north-east South America. Capital, Paramaribo; area about 164 000 sq km (63 000 sq miles). Formerly Dutch Guiana, it became independent from the Netherlands in 1975. From the coastal plain, the land changes to savannah and then highlands. It is very hot and wet, with average rainfall of over 2280 mm (90 in) per year. The population is a great mixture – American Indian, Africa, Asian and European.

The chief export is bauxite (aluminium), and this is very important to the economy. There are plantations as well as small farms, where rice is the main crop.

Surrealism was a movement in art and literature. It grew out of Dada in the 1920s, when the leaders of the movement were the poets André Breton and Paul Eluard. Like the Romantic movement a century earlier, Surrealism emphasized the importance of imagination and individuality. It was opposed to all the new movements in art, and to all middle-class values. Surrealist art was fantastic, often suggesting the irrationality of dreams, but Surrealist artists (e.g. Dali, Ernst, Magritte) worked in quite different styles.

Surrealism had a liberating effect on art in general. Few modern artists have been entirely unaffected by it.

Swallows are small, aerobatic birds which feed on insects. They are found almost throughout the world, where they are often recognizable by their fast flight and their forked tails. There are several species, of which the swallow or barn swallow of Europe and North America, and the red-rumped swallow of Africa are among the most well known. The European swallow migrates from Africa to breed, and builds a mud nest occupied by four to six chicks. They all return to Africa in the autumn.

European swallow

Swaziland (Ngwane) is a kingdom in south-east Africa, mainly surrounded by the republic of South Africa. Capital, Mbabane; area about 17000 sq km (6700 sq miles). Under British sovereignty, the Swazi avoided inclusion in South Africa, and gained full independence in 1968. Many Swazi work in South African mines. Otherwise, agriculture and cattle-raising are the chief occupations, but there are good mineral resources, especially asbestos and iron ore.

Sweden is a kingdom in north-west Europe. Capital, Stockholm; area about 412000 sq km (159000 sq miles).
History During the 1st millennium (one thousand years) AD the country was inhabited by Germanic tribes who formed small kingdoms. By AD 1000 Christianity had been introduced and the country had been unified. In the 12th century Finland was conquered and in 1397 Sweden was united with Denmark and Norway. It broke away in 1523 and during the next 200 years considerably expanded its territories. After being defeated by Russia in The Great Northern War (1700–1721) Sweden lost most of what it had previously gained. In 1814 it acquired Norway, which became independent in 1905. Sweden remained neutral in both World Wars, enjoyed growing prosperity and became notable for the development of its welfare state.
Land Sweden is the largest country in Scandinavia, but is not heavily populated, and most of the people live around Stockholm and Göteborg. Northern Sweden lies beyond the Arctic Circle, and the north and centre are mountainous. South-east of the mountains is a broad plateau, descending to a coastal plain. In the midlands are many hills and lakes, and there are many offshore islands. In general, the climate is milder than might be expected, due to warm westerly winds.
Economy Agriculture is very efficient though restricted to a small area and employing less than one-quarter of the people. Cereals and root crops are grown, but dairying, pigs and chickens are more common. Herds of reindeer are kept in the north.

Coniferous forests cover half the country, making Sweden a leading producer of timber. Annual planting of trees keeps pace with felling. Sweden is short of fuels, but otherwise has rich mineral resources, especially iron ore.

About half the working population are in manufacturing industry. Engineering is outstanding in Sweden, and machines and vehicles are the most valuable exports. Most of the energy for industry comes from hydroelectric power. Transport difficulties have been overcome by efficient railways and modern roads. There is also a large merchant fleet.

Sweet potato, see Yam.

Swift, Jonathan (1667–1745), was an Anglo-Irish satirist. He became dean of St Patrick's, Dublin, in 1713, a reward for his journalistic writings on behalf of the government. Swift wrote a great deal of prose and verse, most of it satirical. He had a gift for clearly developing an argument which leads to a shocking or ironic conclusion. His most famous works of this kind are *The Battle of the Books* (1704) and *A Tale of a Tub* (1704). He will always be remembered for his story *Gulliver's Travels* (1726), which is both a brilliant political satire and an exciting adventure story.

Swifts are the masters of the air. With long, swept-back wings, these birds fly high in the sky, feeding and even mating and sleeping in the air! They feed on insects, snatching them in flight with their large, gaping mouths. A swift's legs are so weak that if it is forced to the ground it can not take off again. They can cling to walls and caves with their feet, however, and this is where they make their nests, glueing straw and grass together with their own saliva. Swifts are up to 23 cm (9 in) long. The fastest animal is the spine-tailed swift of Asia. It can fly at speeds of up to 170 kp/h (102 mph).

Switzerland is a federal republic in west-central Europe. Capital, Bern; area about 41000 sq km (16000 sq miles).
History The earliest known inhabitants

were the Celtic Helvetii, who were conquered by the Romans in the 1st century BC. The region was then overrun by Franks, Alemanni and Burgundians, from the 5th century AD. In the 11th century it came under the Holy Roman Empire, but in 1291 an anti-Hapsburg league was formed, and by the 15th century the country was effectively independent.

In 1798 Napoleon established the short-lived Helvetic Republic, uniting the cantons (states) into a single state. In 1815 the old union of cantons was restored, and Swiss neutrality was guaranteed. After war between cantons, those wanting a more formal confederation won, and the Swiss Confederation was formed in 1848.

Switzerland remained neutral in both World Wars, and became increasingly prosperous after the Second World War.

Land and People Switzerland is extremely mountainous, with the Swiss plateau sandwiched between the lofty Alps in the south (covering more than half the country) and the lower Jura Mountains, which rise along the north western border with France. There are many rivers and lakes. Winters are cold but sunny, summers mild with moderate and even rainfall.

The cantons (states) of Switzerland enjoy considerable independence, and big political decisions are often decided by referendum. The population is concentrated on the Swiss plateau, with about half living in towns. Most Swiss speak a form of German, but 20 per cent (in the west) speak French and six per cent (in the south) Italian, while a small number (south-east) speak Romansch.

Economy Farming is limited by the mountains, so dairying is the main form. Swiss industry is highly advanced. Textiles, machinery, watchmaking and jewellery, and chemicals are among the most valuable manufactures. There is little coal and no oil, but ample hydro-electric power. Despite the mountains, there are good rail and road networks.

Switzerland is an international banking centre, with business concentrated in Zurich and Geneva, and it attracts many tourists, especially in winter.

Sydney Opera House is an arts centre, including concert hall, etc, in the capital of New South Wales, Australia, which was opened in 1973. It was designed by Jøern Utzon as a result of a competition in 1955. It is a group of white, shell-like structures, resembling the sails of the boats in the harbour which surrounds the Opera House on three sides.

Symbiosis (sometimes called mutualism) is the association between two different organisms in which both partners benefit. Sometimes the partnership is such that one can not survive without the other. Lichens are examples of this close dependence. Here, the closely interwoven fungus and algal cells depend on each other for food and shelter. In other instances it is convenient, though not essential, for the two organisms to exist together. For example, certain crabs carry anemones about on their shells. This is beneficial to the crab, which gets protection, and to the anemone, which benefits from scraps of food scattered by the crab and gains a free ride to new feeding grounds. However, each species can exist without the other.

Symphony is a major composition for orchestra, usually in four movements. Traditionally, the form of the first movement of a symphony is the same as a sonata: *exposition*, containing the main theme and lesser theme; *development*, elaboration of the exposition; *recapitulation*, repeat of the exposition in a different form. The basis is relationship between keys.

Like all musical forms, the symphony has changed greatly in the course of time, but in the Classical system of (for example) Haydn and Mozart, the first movement is *allegro* (quick), the second *andante* (slow), the third lively and the fourth *allegro*.

Syria is a republic in south-west Asia, between the Mediterranean and Iraq. Capital, Damascus; area about 186 000 sq km (72 000 sq miles).
History In the 1st millennium (one thousand years) BC Syria formed part of the Egyptian, Persian and, finally, the Roman Empires. Conquered by the Arabs in the 7th century AD, it was ruled by the Ottoman Turks from 1516 to 1917. Largely under French control during 1923–1946, it achieved complete independence as a republic in 1940. From 1958 to 1961 it was linked with Egypt in the United Arab Republic. In the 1970s Syria became involved in the civil war in Lebanon.
Land and Economy The Syrian Desert, with oasis villages and nomads, takes up most of the country, with mountains in the south-west and several fertile valleys. Agriculture is the main activity, cotton the chief export crop. Irrigation is still rather limited, and therefore crop yields are low, though wheat and other produce are exported. Livestock, especially sheep and goats, are important, but there is little profit from the forests, nor from mining or fishing. Syria is thus a poor country, despite its rich cultural heritage. Improvements have been made in recent years with aid from richer Arab nations.

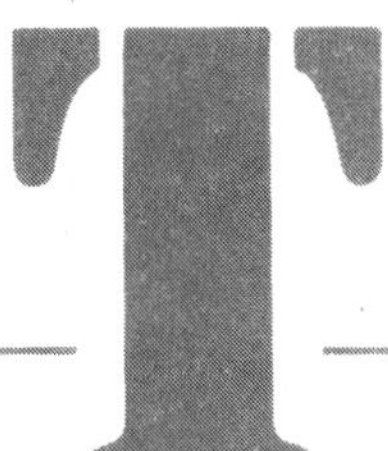

Table Mountain (Tafelberg) is a flat-topped mountain in South Africa, lying to the south of Cape Town and towering above the city.

The highest point, Maclear's Beacon, is 1087 m (3567 ft) high, and the flat top of the mountain is a plateau about 1065 m (3500 ft) high. The mountain forms the northern end of the high and rocky Cape Peninsula.

Tadpole is the aquatic, larval stage of an amphibian, such as a frog or a newt. They develop from eggs, or spawn, laid in the water by the adult female. Tadpoles swim by means of a tail, and feed on animal and plant matter. As they grow, their tails get smaller and they begin to grow legs. Soon the gills disappear, too, and the animal then looks like a miniature version of the adult. It then climbs from the water to begin life on land.

Taiwan (Formosa) is an island republic in the China Sea, traditionally part of China. Capital, Taipei; area about 36 000 sq km (14 000 sq miles). When the Communists gained power in China in 1949, the nationalist government retreated to Taiwan, where it has retained control despite the opposition of the Chinese government.

The island consists of forested highlands and wide plains, with a monsoon climate. Agriculture is very productive, with rice, sugar cane and tropical fruit among the main crops. Fish are also farmed, and there are reserves of coal, natural gas and various minerals.

Industry is highly developed, and certain consumer products, including electronic goods, are widely exported at low prices.

Taj Mahal is one of the most famous buildings in the world, at Agra, India. It was built in 1632–1653 by the Mogul emperor Shah Jahan, as a memorial to his wife, Mumtaz Mahal. It is a white, marble building of beautiful proportions, topped by an onion-shaped

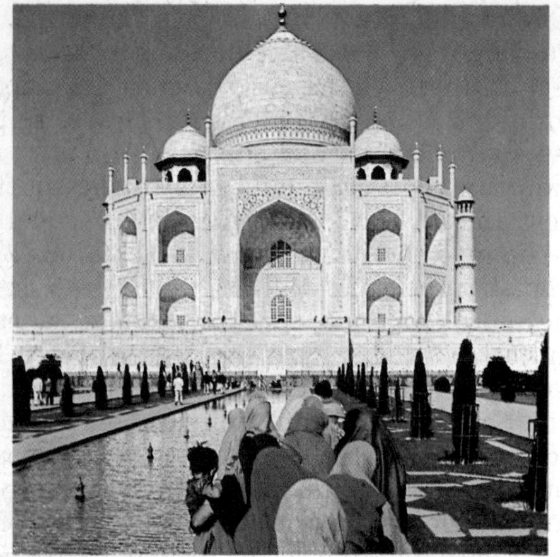

dome and standing on a raised platform amid gardens. The surfaces are decorated with precious stones in rich but delicate abstract patterns.

Talmud is the Jewish law as passed down the generations by word of mouth. It is distinguished from the written law (Torah). The Talmud, a mixture of laws and narrative, was finally compiled in the 3rd and 4th centuries AD in Palestine. A second version, with considerable variations, was recorded in Babylon a little later. *See also* Torah.

Tank is an armoured military vehicle that moves on tracks and is armed with a gun or guns. The first tanks were used in 1916 by the British Army on the Western Front during the First World War. Although its full potential was not immediately realized, the tank revolutionized warfare, since rough ground, barbed wire and machine-gun emplacements (all characteristic of trench warfare) failed to stop it.

The Second World War was, therefore, a conflict of mobile armies. Tanks often played a decisive part – for example, in the German *blitzkrieg* (lightning attack) that defeated France in 1940. The greatest tank battles of the war took place between the British and Germans at El Alamein in North Africa, and the Russians and Germans at Kursk, USSR.

Tanzania, United Republic of, is in East Africa. Capital, Dodoma; area about 945 000 sq km (365 000 sq miles).

Tanzania was created in 1944 by the Union of Tanganyika and Zanzibar. Tanganyika had previously been a British colony and, before that a German one. It became independent in 1961 and united with Zanzibar in 1964.

Beyond the narrow coastal plain is a high, dry plateau, with large lakes in the north, west and south. The average temperature in Dar es Salaam is 25.5°C (77.9°F) and most of the country suffers from shortage of water. The people come from over 100 different groups, but Swahili is a common language. There is a small Asian minority.

The great majority of people are engaged in agriculture or herding, and the government is directing great efforts towards agricultural improvement. The main cash crop is cotton, but Tanzania has a fairly wide range of agricultural exports, though most farmers are poor. Industrial and mineral resources are little developed, though there are diamond and gold mines.

Cross-section of a German A7V tank, used in the First World War.

Taoism is a traditional religion or philosophy of China. It is said to have been founded by Lao-tse in the 7th century BC. As the supposed author of the *Tao Te Ching*, Lao-tse taught that people should strive to reach perfection through patience, simplicity and naturalness. Later, Taoism became associated with the practice of forms of magic, and was organized as a more formal religion.

Taoism borrowed much from Buddhism, including gods, priests, and ceremonies. But it became less popular than Buddhism and less influential than Confucianism, and it had long been in decline before the Communists came to power in China. *See also* Buddhism; Confucianism.

Tapir is a curious-looking mammal like a cross between a rhinoceros and an elephant, for it has a bulky body with hoofed feet, and a head with a small trunk. There are four species of tapir. The Malayan tapir inhabits

the tropical forests of south-east Asia and feeds on shoots and leaves. The other species live in South America, and are also herbivores. One lives in the Amazonian forests, and can dive and swim. The other two species are found on hills and mountains.

Tasman, Abel (circa 1603–1659), was a Dutch navigator. He was sent by the Governor-General of the Dutch East Indies on an expedition during which he discovered Tasmania (called Van Dieman's Land after the name of the Governor-General) and also New Zealand (1643). On a later voyage he explored the northern and western coasts of Australia.

Tasmania is a state of Australia, occupying an island off Victoria. Capital, Hobart; area about 67 800 sq km (26 000 sq miles). It consists mainly of highland plateaux and mountains, with many lakes. A rich wild life includes some animals found nowhere else (e.g. the Tasmanian devil). There are rich mineral resources, a small population, and some magnificent wild country threatened by hydro-electric schemes. *See also* Australia.

Tasmanian devil is a carnivorous marsupial, now confined to the remote parts of Tasmania. It looks like a cross between a small bear and a cat, and grows to a length of 1.2 m (4 ft). A stocky animal, it has dark fur and a large powerful head. It feeds greedily on any animal – live or dead – that it comes across, including livestock, birds, reptiles and small mammals. It is reported that one Tasmanian devil killed 54 chickens, six geese and a cat during two nights of hunting.

Tasmanian wolf, or thylacine, is possibly now extinct. The last definite sighting was many years ago in the remote regions of Tasmania, and the last captive specimen died long ago, too. The Tasmanian wolf was once found across much of Australia and Tasmania, and was the largest of the carnivorous marsupial mammals. It had a red-brown, wolf-like body with a thin tail, and dark stripes running down over the rear parts of the body. Nocturnal, with a well-developed sense of smell, the Tasmanian wolf used to

Tasmanian wolf

hunt kangaroos and wallabies. Settlers' sheep became easier prey, and persecution by farmers was the main reason for its decline.

Taxation is a method of raising money towards the cost of government in which each citizen makes a compulsory contribution (tax). In many modern countries taxation is high, since governments have to finance a wide range of services, such as large armies with sophisticated weapons, a police force, a health service and unemployment benefits.

From the governments' point of view taxation is not only a means of raising revenue (government income). It is also a way of influencing society – (for example, by taxing the wealthy more heavily than the poor and so lessening inequalities). It can also be used to influence the economy – for example, by encouraging or discouraging imports and exports.

One way of classifying taxes is into direct and indirect kinds. Income tax is a direct tax: you pay on the basis of what you earn. Sales tax or value added tax (VAT) is indirect: you pay through buying goods and services, and need not pay at all if you do not choose to buy them.

Tchaikovsky, Pëtr Ilich (1840–1893), was a Russian composer. A teacher and popular conductor, he had a troubled private life but was greatly helped by a rich widow, who supported him financially though they hardly ever met. Tchaikovsky's music has always been extremely popular because it is tuneful, colourful and easily understood. His ballets *Swan Lake* (1876), *The Sleeping Beauty* (1889) and *Nutcracker* (1892) and music drawn from them (e.g. the famous *Nutcracker Suite*), some of his operas (e.g. *Eugene Onegin*, 1879), his symphonic works, piano music and songs are frequently heard today.

Teak is a tall, hardwood tree which grows in Burma, India, Thailand and Indonesia. Although the wood is extremely hard, it is nevertheless light and easy to work, and thus teak is a valuable timber tree. When teak trees are felled they are often still transported to the nearest river or railway by using elephants to push or carry the enormous logs.

Telephone is an instrument used to speak to people over long distances. Each telephone has a mouthpiece into which we speak and an earpiece through which we listen.

The mouthpiece contains a microphone. This changes the spoken word into electrical signals. The electrical signals can be sent through telephone cables or transmitted as radio waves where there are no cables. Radiotelephone waves can be sent to all parts of the Earth, via satellites.

The telephone earpiece is a loudspeaker. This changes the electromagnetic signals back into sound.

The first really usable telephone was invented by Alexander Bell in 1876. Now

An early telephone from 1900 *(top)* and a modern telephone.

many countries have millions of telephones and it is possible to speak to somebody on the other side of the Earth just by dialling the correct number. *See also* Communications satellite.

Teleprinter is a machine used to send and receive typed messages around the world. It is an electric typewriter connected to another typewriter by a cable or by radio. Typing a message on it causes a signal to be sent which types out the same message on the other typewriter. Teleprinters may be connected to many other machines around the world. A message is sent to a particular machine by typing in a code. *See also* Telex.

Telescope is an instrument which allows distant objects to be seen more easily and very distant objects to be detected. It is essential to astronomy. The first telescopes were optical ones. They used lenses to make objects look bigger. They are known as refracting telescopes. The largest refracting telescope is at the Yerkes Observatory in the USA. It has a lens 1 m (40 in) in diameter.

In 1668, Sir Isaac Newton built another sort of optical telescope, which used mirrors to magnify the images of objects. It is known as a reflecting telescope. The largest reflecting telescope is at the Zelenchukskaya Observatory in the USSR. It has a mirror 6 m (20 ft) in diameter, and is powerful enough to see the light from a candle 24 000 km (15 000 miles) away.

There are other telescopes, called radio-telescopes, which detect radio waves sent out by very distant objects.

Television is a system which sends out and receives moving pictures and sound. The first practical television system was invented by John Logie Baird in 1926. The pictures are filmed with a television camera and turned into radio signals. These are sent out, or broadcast, from tall masts called transmitters. Television sets or receivers in homes pick up the signals through an aerial.

There are millions of television receivers in the world. Most of them are used for entertainment. They receive plays, films, sport, news and other programmes. A programme can be seen live all over the world at the same time, transmitted by communications satellites. Television programmes can be recorded as they are being watched.

The first communications satellite. Satellites can be used to transmit television signals.

Closed-circuit television is used in many large factories and shops. Television cameras are placed in each room. Receivers in one room can then be used to see everything happening in the building. *See also* Communications satellite; Video.

Telex is an international communications system, using teleprinters, which are loaned to subscribers by postal authorities. Teleprinters have a keyboard, similar to that of a typewriter, on which messages can be typed. These are telegraphed to other teleprinters, which also act as receivers, printing out the messages which they receive. Telex is a quick, relatively cheap method of sending messages all over the world.

Telstar was the world's first communications satellite, launched by the USA in 1962. It could receive television pictures and relay them 'live' across the Atlantic Ocean. *See also* Satellite; Sputnik.

Temperature is how hot or cold something is. To measure this, a scale divided into degrees is used. The most common temperature scale is the Centigrade scale. This was devised by Anders Celsius in 1742 and is also known as the Celsius scale. A degree Centigrade is often shortened to °C. On this scale, the temperature at which ice turns to water (melting point) is 0 degrees Centigrade, and the temperature at which water turns to steam (boiling point) is 100 degrees Centigrade, at normal air pressure.

The other temperature scale which is often used is the Fahrenheit scale. This was devised by Gabriel Fahrenheit in about 1714. A degree Fahrenheit is often shortened to °F. On this scale, the melting point of ice is 32 degrees Fahrenheit, the boiling point of water is 212 degrees Fahrenheit at normal air pressure.

To change degrees Centigrade to degrees Fahrenheit, multiply by $\frac{9}{5}$ and add 32. To change degrees Fahrenheit to degrees Centigrade, subtract 32 and multiply by $\frac{5}{9}$.

A third scale, the Kelvin scale, is often used in scientific work. The melting point of ice is just over 273 degrees kelvin, and the boiling point of water is just over 373 degrees kelvin at normal air pressure. *See also* Barometer; Thermometer.

Ten Commandments were the laws, engraved in stone, which were given by God to Moses on Mount Sinai during the Exodus (departure) of the Israelites from Egypt. They can be found in *Exodus* 20 and *Deuteronomy* 5 in the Bible, and say: you shall have no gods except Jehovah; make no carved images; do not misuse God's name; keep the sabbath day holy; honour your parents; do not commit murder or adultery; do not steal or tell lies; do not envy your neighbour. *See also* Moses.

Tennyson, Alfred, Lord (1809–1892), was the most popular poet in the Victorian age. As well as his poetic gifts, he represented the beliefs and feelings of his time.

He is best remembered for such popular poems as *The Lady of Shalott* (1833) and *The Charge of the Light Brigade* (1854). His masterpiece, *In Memoriam* (1850), is an elegy inspired by the death of a friend.

Termite is a large social insect which lives in colonies. Although termites look rather like ants, they are more closely related to cockroaches. Most of the inhabitants of the colony, or nest, are workers. The workers do not mate, and their task is to fetch food for the king and queen, and to guard the colony. The queen's task is to lay millions of eggs throughout her life. Some of the mud-built termite nests, such as those found in parts of Australia, may be as high as 8 m (26 ft). *See also* Social insect.

Tern is a seabird related to the gull. It is more attractive than the gull, with a delicate body shape, long wings and a forked tail. Terns are sometimes called sea swallows. They are widely distributed throughout the world, hovering over the sea whilst they grab fish and small invertebrates in their beaks.

Arctic tern and chicks

Terrapin is the name often given to any tortoise or turtle which lives both on land and in water. In fact, terrapins only hunt their food in the water; the rest of their time is spent on the bank. They are found all over the world. Some, like the American painted turtle, have beautiful colours on their body. Another species, the Malayan big-headed turtle, is covered in horny armour like a small dinosaur. The strange American alligator snapper (which is a terrapin, not an alligator) lies on the bottom of a pond with its mouth open, wriggling its tongue like a worm. Any fish that ventures too close gets snapped up by the terrapin.

Thailand is a kingdom in south-east Asia. Capital, Bangkok; area about 514 000 sq km (198 250 sq miles). Thailand, formerly Siam, became a separate state in the 12th century, although it was often overrun by neighbours. It lost territory to European powers, but was never a colony. It became a constitutional monarchy in 1932.

It consists of a large central plain surrounded by mountains (except on the coast), especially in the north and west. The eastern plateau is drained by the Mekong River. The climate is dominated by the monsoon, bringing heavy summer rains. A large part of the country is covered by thick forest.

Most of the people are Thais and there are many distinct groups. There are also large minorities of other races, especially Chinese and Malay. There are no big cities except Bangkok, and most of the people are engaged in agriculture. Rice is the major crop; rubber, timber (teak especially) and tin ore are the main exports. There is a great range of light industry and crafts.

Thames is a river in southern England. Length about 338 km (210 miles). It rises in the Cotswold Hills and flows east, through London, to the North Sea. (Above Oxford it is called the Isis.) The lower Thames is highly industrialized, with docks and factories. A slow-flowing, lowland river, it was once famous for salmon, which have been reintroduced since the polluted lower Thames was cleaned up. Canals link the Thames with the River Severn and the industrial Midlands.

Thatcher, Margaret Hilda (1925–) is a British stateswoman. After graduating from Oxford university she worked as a research chemist then became a barrister. Elected to Parliament in 1959, she was Secretary of State for Education and Science during 1970–1974. In 1975 she was elected leader of the Conservative Party, becoming Britain's first woman Prime Minister when the Conservatives won the general election of 1979. She was re-elected in June 1983.

Theatre is a building designed to house dramatic presentations. The earliest theatres of ancient Greece were open air. Built of stone and semi-circular in shape, these amphitheatres had steeply-tiered seats surrounding a central flat space which was the main performing area.

Medieval mystery plays in England were staged on carts which travelled around the towns and countryside.

Italian architecture produced the proscenium theatre with its picture-frame stage and horseshoe-shaped auditorium.

Elizabethan theatres in England were roughly circular with galleries surrounding the open-air pit. The small stage was raised, with a curtained area behind it used for interior scenes. The most famous of these theatres was the Globe on the south bank of the Thames in London. There were no actresses

The Globe Theatre, London, where Shakespeare acted, and had his plays performed.

– boys played the women's parts – and scenery and costumes were contemporary and minimal.

Nowadays styles of theatres vary enormously. Some theatres still have the traditional proscenium arch. Others are 'in-the-round', where the audience completely surrounds the stage. This is going back to the ancient Greek theatres and arenas. Modern experimental theatre companies often perform in unusual surroundings, such as a portable tent, the back of a lorry or in the street. *See also* Drama.

Thermodynamics looks at the ways in which heat can be made to do work, and can be turned into other forms of energy. It also looks at the ways in which work produces heat.

Heat is used for many sorts of work. It cooks food, heats homes, drives the engines of trains, rockets, and other vehicles. Heat is turned into another form of energy, electricity, in power stations. The electricity then does the work of heating and lighting homes and factories.

Thermometer is an instrument used to measure temperature. The amount of space a substance takes up is called its volume. The volume of most substances gets bigger or expands as the temperature rises. The volume gets smaller as the temperature falls.

The mercury thermometer is a thin glass tube and a glass bulb containing mercury. As the temperature rises, the mercury expands up the tube. When the temperature falls, the mercury contracts down the tube. A temperature scale is marked down the side of the tube. The temperature can be read by looking at the number alongside the surface of the mercury. An alcohol thermometer works in the same way but contains alcohol instead of mercury. There are also many other sorts of thermometers.

Theseus, a hero of Greek legend, was son of Aegeus, king of Athens. In the course of his adventures, Theseus overcame many evil men and monsters, notably the Minotaur in Crete. He told his father that on his return

Centre of a drinking cup (c 500 BC) depicting Theseus and Amphitrite, a nymph of the sea. The goddess Athena stands between them.

he would hoist a white sail, but forgot to do it. Aegeus thought Theseus was dead and committed suicide before his son arrived.

When Theseus tried to rescue Persephone from Hades he was caught and had to be rescued himself. He took part in the battle against the Centaurs and against the Amazons, a race of warlike women whose queen, Hippolyte, he married. He was also one of the Argonauts with Jason.

The Athenians regarded Theseus as the founder of their state. In 472 BC a huge skeleton, found at Scyros where Theseus died, was brought to Athens in the belief that it was the remains of the real Theseus.

Thor, in Norse (Scandinavian) myth, was the god of thunder. He was the most important god after Odin (in some stories more important). The two sometimes appear as rivals, but Thor, though a noble warrior, was a cruder character, even a little stupid occasionally.

Thor's weapon was a hammer which never missed its mark and returned to him after being thrown. There are many legends of Thor the warrior killing giants and monsters – such as the serpent of Midgard. But he was also, with his faithful wife Sif, the protector of married couples and peasants.

Thunder is the very loud rumbling or cracking noises that occur during a thunderstorm.

Thunder is caused by the electrical discharge of a lightning flash, the heat of which makes the air within a thundercloud expand and then contract violently. The resulting noise is produced along the entire length of the lightning flash – that is, at various distances from anybody who is listening to it. The single thunderclap will, therefore, be heard as series of noises.

Light travels very much faster than sound, so the lightning is always seen before the thunder is heard, despite the fact that they occur together. It is possible to calculate how far away the storm is by measuring the time between seeing the flash and hearing the thunder; every five seconds represents about 1.6 km (1 mile).

Thylacine, see Tasmanian wolf.

Tibet is a region of China in central Asia. Capital, Lhasa; area about 1 222 000 sq km (472 000 sq miles). A remote country, it was seldom visited by Europeans until the late 19th century. At an earlier period, it was dominated by China, and in 1950 it became part of China's territory.

Tibet consists of a high plateau bounded by even higher mountains (the Himalayas in the south). The average altitude is 4875 m (15 994 ft), highest in the world. Crops are grown only in river valleys, though livestock, including yaks, sheep and horses are also raised. Barley is the chief grain crop. There has been some economic development under Chinese control, with the building of power stations and roads. There is little mining, however, and the chief products are still traditional Tibetan crafts – metalwork, pottery, wood carvings, medicinal herbs, etc.

Ticks are oval-bodied, eight-legged arthropods which suck the blood of other animals. They seldom grow more than 15 mm (0.7 in) in length. Each species of tick, of which several thousand are to be found throughout the world, is confined to its particular host (the animal on which it feeds).

A tick clings to foliage until an animal passes, and then it 'climbs aboard'. If it is the wrong host, it drops off to try again. If it is the correct host it sinks its mouth parts into the host's skin and gorges itself on blood. A female tick may drink 100 times her own weight of blood over a period of two weeks.

Tick eggs hatch on the ground, and turn into blood-drinking larvae. These in turn become nymphs, which moult to become adults. Ticks are responsible for spreading many diseases.

Tides are the rise and fall of the oceans and seas. The Moon orbits the Earth because it is pulled towards it by the Earth's gravity. The Earth is also pulled by the Moon's gravity. This causes the movement of water on the Earth, known as tides. The Sun also causes tides. Because the Sun is much further away its pull is less than half of that of the Moon. Most places have two tides each day. The second tide is the effect of the Moon's pull on the opposite side of the Earth.

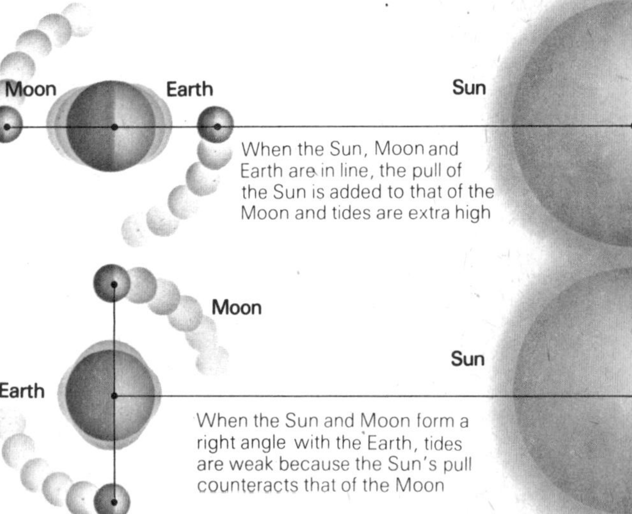

Moon
Earth
Sun
When the Sun, Moon and Earth are in line, the pull of the Sun is added to that of the Moon and tides are extra high
Moon
Sun
Earth
When the Sun and Moon form a right angle with the Earth, tides are weak because the Sun's pull counteracts that of the Moon

When the Sun and Moon are in a line with the Earth, they pull together to give very high tides. These are known as spring tides. When the Sun and Moon are at right angles with the Earth, they pull against each other to give lower tides. These are known as neap tides.

Tiger is the largest of the big cats. This magnificent animal ranges through Asia, Sumatra and Java, but it is in danger of extinction in all of its haunts. It hunts for deer, pigs or antelopes, and is superbly camouflaged by its

tawny fur marked with black vertical stripes. Tigers are usually solitary creatures, only coming together in pairs when mating. Two to four cubs are born, which are taught how to hunt by their mother.

Tigris is a river in south-west Asia. Length 1850 km (1150 miles). It rises in southern Turkey and flows roughly south-east, via Baghdad, to join the Euphrates in Iraq, reaching the Persian Gulf as the Shatt-al-Arab. The river can be navigated, and is used for irrigation. There have been many great archaeological discoveries in its valley, which was the scene of ancient civilizations.

Time is measured by the movement of the Earth. The time it takes for the Earth to spin around on its axis is a day. This is split up into hours, minutes and seconds. The time it takes for the Earth to orbit the Sun is a year. This is split up into months, weeks and days.

Clocks are used to measure time. Sundials and hourglasses are ancient forms of clock. Now we mostly use mechanical, electrical or atomic clocks.

Astronomers use a slightly different measurement of time known as sidereal time. They measure a day by the position of the stars. A sidereal day is four minutes less than an ordinary day.

Tin has the chemical symbol Sn. It is a soft, shiny white metal. It is easy to shape and was one of the first metals to be used by people. Tin is found in the ore, cassiterite, which is tin oxide.

Many metal objects are coated or plated with a thin layer of tin to protect them. Food and drink is often sold in tin cans, which are

steel with a thin coating of tin. Sweets are often wrapped in 'silver' paper. This is lead with a thin layer of tin around it.

Most tin is used to make alloys, such as bronze, pewter and solder. Solder is used to join wires.

Tintoretto, Jacopo (1518–1594), was an Italian painter of the Venetian school. He produced a vast number of paintings, mainly of religious or mythological subjects, as well as portraits. His *Paradise* in the Doge's Palace is said to be the largest work of its kind in the world. He had a wonderful sense of composition and lighting, as well as a brilliant command of colour like many other Venetian artists.

Titan, in Greek myth, was one of the race of creatures who ruled the world before the gods of Olympus. They were the children of Uranus (Heaven) and Gaia (Earth), but rebelled against their parents and made one of themselves, Cronus, the ruler of heaven. The children of Cronus rebelled in turn and, led by Zeus, fought a great war against their father and his fellow Titans. With the aid of the Cyclops, who provided thunder and lightning, Zeus won. He hurled the defeated Titans into Tartarus, a place of darkness below the Earth.

Titanic was the world's largest passenger liner when launched in 1912 – 260 m (853 ft) long and weighing 47 000 tonnes. She was also claimed to be the most luxurious and the safest, with a double-skinned hull and watertight compartments which were said to make the ship unsinkable. On 14 April 1912, during her maiden voyage from Southampton to the USA, *Titanic* struck an iceberg in

the North Atlantic. So confident had her builders been that they had not included enough lifeboats for every passenger. *Titanic* sank in 2 hr 40 min and 1513 people died.

Titanium has the chemical symbol Ti and is a silver-coloured metal. Titanium ores are quite common in the Earth's crust. However, it is very difficult to take the titanium metal out of them. Titanium was obtained for the first time in 1910 and is still expensive.

Titanium corrodes very little and its alloys are much lighter than steel and much stronger than aluminium. For these reasons they are used in ship, aircraft and rocket engines. A Jumbo Jet aircraft contains about four tonnes of titanium alloys. Titanium compounds are used in making paints.

Titian (circa 1487–1576), was an Italian Renaissance painter, the greatest of the Venetian school. In a career of nearly 70 years his style went through several changes. But his genius was universally recognized, especially by the Emperor Charles V and his successor, Philip II of Spain. Many of Titian's greatest works were painted for them. As well as portraits, he also painted luxurious mythological scenes.

Titian developed his own technique of painting, which involved several distinct stages. He sometimes used a finger instead of a brush to work the paint, and his rich colours have great depth. The paintings of his last years are of special interest. His concern with effects of light almost made him an 'impressionist' – three centuries before Impressionism.

Tito (1892–1980), was a Yugoslavian statesman. He was born in Croatia as Josip Broz. He fought with the Red Army during the Russian Civil War, later returning to Yugoslavia where he joined the Communist Party. He fought with the International Brigade in the Spanish Civil War. During the Second World War he organized resistance to the German occupation of Yugoslavia. In 1945 he became head of Yugoslavia's Communist government, but refused to be dominated by the USSR and followed an independent foreign policy.

Tits are small, active birds with large heads and short beaks. There are 65 species distributed throughout the world, apart from South America and Australia. Most species have grey or black plumage, with yellow on the breast and blue on the back. They feed on insects and seeds, constantly moving among the trees, often in flocks, always looking about nervously for danger. Many species build a cup-shaped nest. However, the long-tailed tit builds a ball-like nest, and the penduline tit makes a long, hanging, flask-shaped nest.

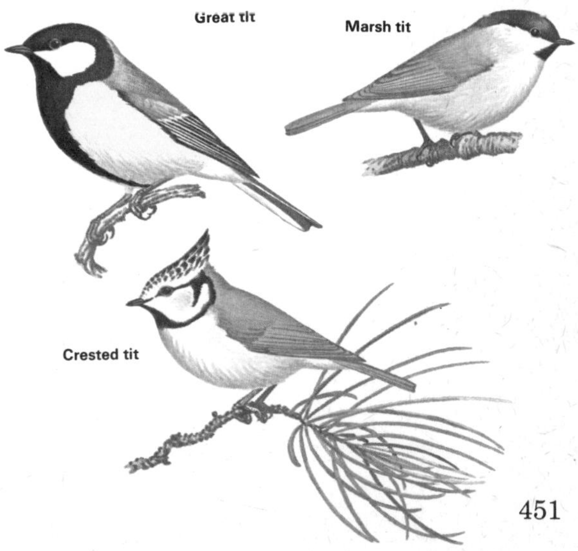

Toads are tailless amphibians, which generally have dry, warty skins. Like the similar and related frogs (normally distinguished by their smooth, moist skins), toads are found in many parts of the world – in woods, forests, grasslands and deserts. They are unable to survive in very cold climates, however, and even those living in some temperate regions must hibernate under a stone or in a bankside hole for the winter.

Normally toads must return to water to lay their eggs, but a few species have reduced even this dependence on water. The male midwife toad carries the eggs about on his legs, and the female clawed toad carries the eggs in tiny pouches on her back. *See also Tadpole.*

Toadstool is the popular name for the fruiting body (the stalk and the spore-bearing cap) of certain types of fungi, such as the red and white fly agaric which appears in the autumn. Usually the word toadstool is used to describe the fruiting bodies of fungi other than mushrooms, or to describe fungi which are poisonous. However, this is a very incorrect way to group fungi, for many so-called mushrooms are inedible, and some so-called toadstools are not poisonous. It is wiser to only eat mushrooms bought in shops for that purpose.

Amethyst toadstool

Tobacco is the common name for plants of the genus *Nicotiana*, and for their cured leaves, smoked in pipes, cigarettes and cigars. Tobacco was used only by the American Indians until the Spaniards brought it to Europe in 1559. It was mainly smoked in pipes until the 19th century, when cigars and cigarettes were introduced. It is now grown in many parts of the world and continues to be widely used despite the danger to health it presents.

Togo is a republic in West Africa. Capital, Lomé; area about 56 785 sq km (21 925 sq miles). It is a narrow strip of land and the second smallest country in Africa. As Togoland it was a German colony, but after the First World War it was mandated to Britain and France. The western part (British) became part of the Gold Coast (now Ghana) and French Togo became the independent republic in 1960. The Ewe people are the largest of Togo's 30 tribes; and most of the people are farmers growing crops at subsistence level. There are plantations including oil and cocoa palms, coffee and cotton.

Tolstoy, Leo (1828–1910), was a Russian writer. A nobleman, he inherited an estate with 330 serfs, studied law at university and served in the army during the Crimean War. Among his many literary works are two of the greatest novels in European literature: *War and Peace* (1864–1866), a long story of Russian life at the time of Napoleon's invasion, and *Anna Karenina* (1875–1877), a contemporary story of marriage and morals. Besides many other novels and plays, he wrote books on education and religion. His last years were saddened by the gap between his high moral ideas and his unhappy family life. He left home secretly in 1910 and died in a lonely railway station ten days later.

Tonga is a kingdom in the south-western Pacific Ocean. Capital, Nuku'alofa; area about 700 sq km (270 sq miles). It consists of about 170 islands and islets. The islands became a self-governing British protectorate in 1900 and became fully independent in 1970. The Tongans mostly work in fishing, or grow coconuts or bananas.

Tooth is a hard, calcified structure in the mouth of most vertebrates, used for chewing food. In humans, teeth also serve as speech organs and improve the appearance. Children grow a temporary set of 20 teeth, which are replaced by a permanent set of 32, of which 28 are usually formed by the age of 15.

The principal parts of a tooth are the hard outer enamel, the less hard dentine beneath it, and the inner pulp, consisting of a mass of tissue, blood-vessels and nerves. The full set of teeth on each side of each jaw, from front to back, is two incisors, one canine, two bicuspids and three molars, the last and smallest of which is known as the wisdom tooth. *See also* Ivory.

Torah is the basic law of Judaism. In fact it is more than 'law': the origin of the word means 'teach', and in a wider sense Torah implies religious instruction and guidance. More exactly, Torah means the first five books of the Bible, sometimes called the Pentateuch, which contain the Law of Moses. *See also* Talmud.

Tornado is a very violent storm consisting of a dark whirling column of air. Like the cyclone and hurricane, it is a form of whirlwind. It is relatively small and short-lived (usually lasting about an hour), but the winds inside it can reach a speed of 300 km (185 mph), destroying any buildings that stand in their path. The tornado mainly occurs in the Mississippi basin, USA where cool, dry air comes into abrupt contact with warm, damp air from the Gulf of Mexico.

Tortoises are an ancient group of reptiles. They are found all over the tropical and subtropical regions of the world, where they inhabit forests and dry, sandy places. Most species are herbivores, pulling up grass and other vegetation with their horny beaks, although a few have been seen scavenging on carrion. The thick shell of a tortoise is really an exoskeleton which protects the body organs. Some species of tortoise are enormous, weighing as much as 200 kg (440 lb). They can also be extremely long-lived; some specimens of the Galapagos tortoise are over 150 years old.

Toscanini, Arturo (1867–1957), was an Italian orchestral conductor. The 20th century produced many great conductors of whom Toscanini is usually regarded as the greatest. He became famous when, as a cellist of 19, he took over a performance of Verdi's *Aïda* at the last moment. He was conductor of La Scala Opera, Milan, of the New York Philharmonic and, from 1937, of the NBC orchestra formed especially for him. He had a reputation as a tyrant but achieved marvellously clear and expressive results, especially in Italian opera. He always conducted from memory – partly because he was too short-sighted to read a score from the music stand.

Toucan is one of the most easily recognizable birds, for it has a huge, rainbow-coloured bill. In some species, the bill may be as long as the bird itself. Fortunately, the bill is very lightweight. Toucans eat fruit and berries, neither of which items seem to demand such a huge bill, so the reason for its great size is a mystery. Toucans occur in the tropical and subtropical forests of Mexico and South America where they live in noisy flocks.

Toulouse-Lautrec, Henri de (1864–1901), was a French artist of aristocratic birth. His legs were stunted by an accident in childhood. He is best known for his pictures of Paris night life – for example, his posters for the Moulin Rouge nightclub.

Tower of London is a group of ancient buildings on the north bank of the Thames at the edge of the City of London. The first part to be built was the White Tower, in 1078, later sections being added in the 12th and 13th centuries. The Tower was, in its time, a royal residence, a state prison (Anne Boleyn, Sir Thomas More and Sir Walter Raleigh were among the famous people imprisoned here) and a mint. It is now a historical museum containing the Crown Jewels and a notable collection of armour.

Trade union is an association of employees, formed to maintain or improve their wages and conditions of work. Trade unions developed because workers had little power to negotiate individually with employers, whose wealth and power enabled them to insist that employees should accept low wages, and to dismiss anyone who stood up for his or her rights. By acting in unity, workers could hope to negotiate more successfully or to use their common funds to finance a strike. In a strike, all the employees refuse to work, and the employer, therefore, loses money and customers – a persuasive form of pressure. However, in recent years it has been argued that trade unions have become too powerful.

Branches of Trade Unions have their own banners.

Trafalgar, Battle of, took place at sea on 21 October 1805 off the south-west coast of Spain. A British fleet commanded by Horatio Nelson decisively defeated a combined Franco-Spanish fleet. The battle ended the threat of a French invasion of England and established British supremacy at sea, although Nelson was mortally wounded.

Tragedy, in drama, is a play ending in the death or ruin of the hero or heroine. However, a tragedy should really be defined more strictly as a play which arouses pity and fear and shows great forces at work, the fate of the central character resulting from some flaw in their otherwise noble character. This was the recipe of the Greek philosopher Aristotle. Greek tragedy followed those rules and so, with minor deviations, did the great tragedians of the Renaissance, notably Shakespeare.

Tragedy fell out of favour in the 18th century. Many modern dramatists from Ibsen onwards have written plays which can be called tragic, though they do not follow the Classical formula for tragedy.

Train is the name given to a railway locomotive *and* its collection of carriages or wagons, not (as is often supposed) the locomotive by itself. There are many famous trains in the world, including Britain's *Flying Scotsman. See also Flying Scotsman*; Locomotive; Monorail; Railway.

Trajan (AD 53–117), was Roman Emperor (AD 98–117). Born in Spain, he had a distinguished military career which brought him to the notice of the Emperor Nerva, who made him his heir. Trajan proved to be an

effective and conscientious ruler. He cut taxes and carried out a large-scale building programme in Rome. He waged a victorious campaign against the Dacians, but was less successful in his attempts to subdue the Parthians. His conquest of Dacia is commemorated by Trajan's Column which can still be seen in Rome.

Trajan's Column is a marble column in Rome, erected in AD 117 to the glory of the Emperor Trajan. The column is covered with a spiral band, about one metre broad, of sculpture in relief (raised against a solid background), picturing the events of Trajan's campaign against the Dacians. Apart from its artistic virtues, it gives a valuable picture of Roman military life and methods of warfare.

Transistor is an electronic component. It is made from substances such as silicon and germanium, called semiconductors.

Transistors have many uses. They can strengthen or amplify signals such as those for radio and television. They can switch signals on or off, and can also make alternating current become direct current in certain cases. In electronics, transistors have largely replaced the large, expensive and fragile thermionic valves that were used.

Transistors are used in radios. In fact, radios are sometimes (wrongly) called transistors. Transistors are also used in televisions and in many other electronic systems, such as computers, digital watches and calculators.

Transpiration is the process by which vascular plants (those with water-conducting systems, such as trees and flowers) lose water, mainly from their leaves. The water passes through tiny holes in the leaves called stomata, which can regulate the degree of water loss. In hot weather more water is lost, and this helps to cool the plant. In addition, transpiration causes a steady flow of water to pass from the soil, through the roots, up the stem of the plant and out to the leaves. This means that the plant obtains a constant supply of water. Plants must have water to help them retain their shape (water helps to keep the cells rigid), to provide a watery solution in which the chemical reactions of their cells can take place, and to bring them vital soil minerals in solution.

Transplant surgery is the transfer of an organ or portion of tissue from one part of the body to another or from one person to another.

Some parts of the body, such as the heart, liver and kidneys, are essential. They are known as vital organs. If they are damaged beyond repair, a person usually dies. Sometimes, a patient can have the damaged organ replaced by a healthy one taken from another person, called a donor.

Everybody has two kidneys, and sometimes one of these is given for use in transplant surgery. Usually, however, donors are people who have been killed in an accident which has not damaged their organs.

Sometimes the patient's body is not able to work with the transplanted organ. This is called rejection.

Transplant surgery is also used to replace the surface of the eyeball, called the cornea, and for other parts of the body.

Trawler is a word commonly used to describe

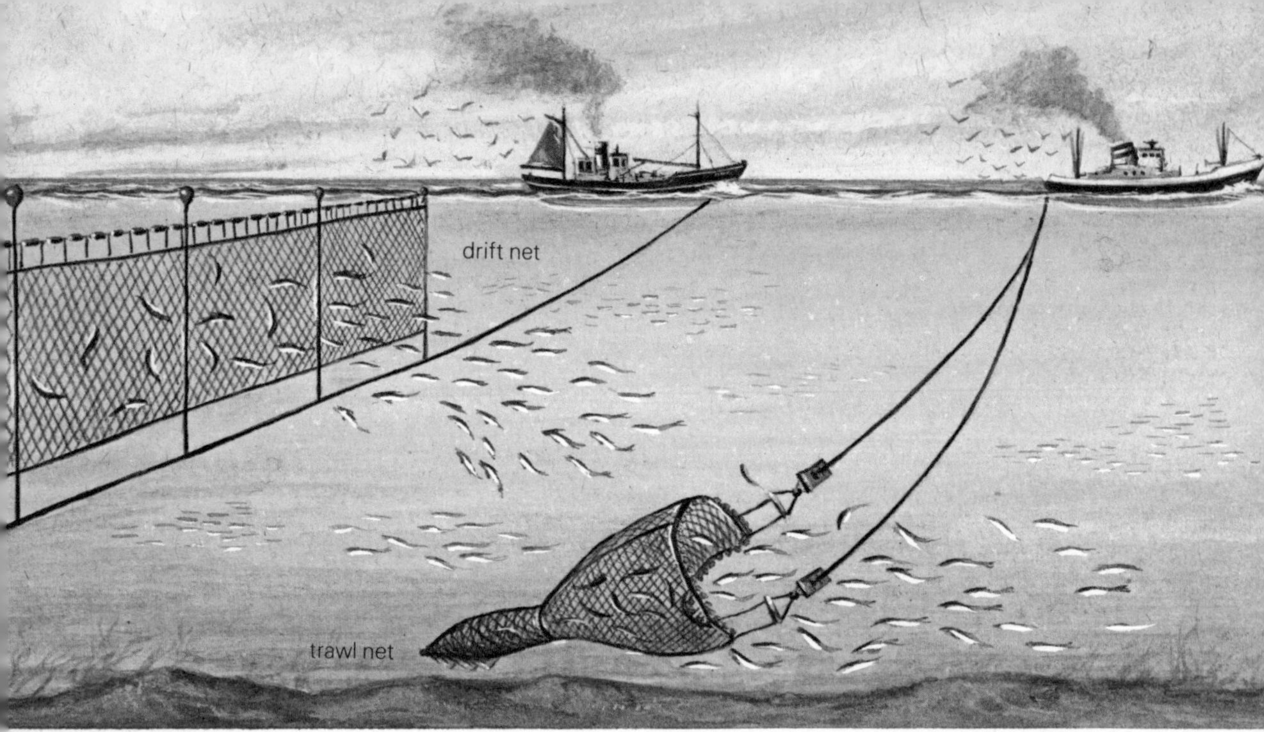

Fishing vessels using a drift net and a trawl net.

any deep-sea fishing vessel, although a trawler is technically a fishing boat which uses a trawl net, similar to a large bag with its mouth held open by a beam, dragged along the sea bottom.

Tree is a large, woody plant, usually producing a single stem, or trunk, and a crown of leaves. There are two main types of tree living today: the coniferous or needle-bearing trees, and the flowering or broadleaved trees. Most coniferous trees are evergreen – retaining leaves all year round. Many broadleaved trees of temperate regions are deciduous, shedding their leaves in autumn and growing new ones in the following spring. Supporting the tree is a huge underground root system. The roots of trees may extend further below ground than the crown extends above ground. The roots not only hold the tree in the soil, but they draw up vital water and minerals.

Some trees are the oldest living things. It is not unknown for oak trees to live for 1000 years. Some trees are also the tallest living things, for example, Californian coast redwood can grow to a height of 110 m (362 ft).

Triassic is a period in the history of the Earth, known from the study of rocks and of the fossil remains found in them (the geological record). It began about 225 million years ago and lasted for about 35 million years.

The Triassic was the first of the three periods of the Mesozoic era, the great age of reptiles. The earliest dinosaurs appeared during this time and the first mammals also appeared in the form of tiny, shrew-like creatures.

Trilobites were a group of marine arthropods. They lived about 400 to 500 million years ago, and were among the most numerous and dominant of the animals living at that time. Some 10 000 species existed, and their sizes ranged from 3 mm to 70 cm (0.1 in to 28 in). They looked rather like round-bodied woodlice and, like woodlice, they could roll up into a ball to protect themselves. Some species swam in the open water and some shuffled along on the seabed.

Trinidad and Tobago is a republic in the West Indies, consisting of two islands off the coast of Venezuela. Capital, Port-of-Spain; area about 5100 sq km (1980 sq miles). Originally a Spanish colony, Trinidad became British in the 19th century. The two islands were united in 1898 and became independent in 1962.

Trinidad is mainly low-lying, with mountains in the north and a very warm climate. The population are a mixture of African, Asian and European. Although most of the people are occupied in agriculture, the most important economic factor today is oil, which provides about 90 per cent of exports.

Triplane is an aircraft having three wings, one above the other, to create additional lift without resorting to very long wings. The system was popular for a while during the First World War, with Fokker (Germany) and Sopwith (England) building successful triplane fighters which were fast and manoeuvrable. However, the system suffered from the same drag problems as the biplane and fell from favour as aircraft speeds rose.

Tropic of Cancer is the northern boundary of the tropics, 23.5° North latitude. The tropics are the area in which the Sun is directly overhead at least once in a year. At the Tropic of Cancer this happens at the summer solstice, 22 June.

Tropic of Capricorn is the southern boundary of the tropics, 23.5° South latitude. At the summer solstice of the Southern Hemisphere, 22 December, the Sun is directly overhead.

Trotsky, Leon (1879–1940), was a Russian Communist leader. He returned to Russia in 1917 after a long period of exile and played a leading part in the revolution that brought the Bolsheviks to power. He later organized the Red Army, which successfully defended the new Communist state. After Lenin's death, Trotsky, who believed in world revolution, clashed with Stalin over future policy. Expelled from the Communist party, he was exiled in 1929 and eventually went to live in Mexico. He was murdered in 1940, probably by an agent of Stalin, but his political views have continued to be influential.

Troy was an ancient city in what is now Turkey. The siege of Troy, which was once thought to be a mythical place, is one of the most famous stories in ancient Greek legend.

The Trojan Horse

The last stages of the war are described in Homer's *Iliad*.

The purpose of the Trojan War was to recover Helen, wife of King Menelaus of Sparta, who had been taken away by Paris, son of King Priam of Troy. The main heroes of the siege were Achilles, Ajax and Odysseus, and the Trojan prince Hector. The Greeks won after ten years by a trick. They built a huge wooden horse in which some of their warriors hid while the rest pretended to sail away. The Trojans took the horse into the city and the Greeks crept out of the horse at night. They opened the city gates, letting in the rest of the Greeks.

The origin of the legend may have been a real Trojan War, probably fought by the Achaeans (Greeks) to gain control of the Dardanelles sea-passage in the 12th century BC.

The site of Troy was rediscovered by a German archaeologist, Heinrich Schliemann, in 1870, but further excavations revealed that several cities had been built one on top of the other over a period of 2000 years, between 3000 and 1100 BC, and between 700 BC and AD 400.

Tsetse fly is a small African fly which looks like the housefly. These flies suck blood from warm-blooded animals, and whilst doing this they transmit to the victim diseases which the flies carry in their own bodies. Tsetse flies spread the human disease known as sleeping sickness, and the disease of cattle called nagana. Because of tsetse flies, many fertile parts of Africa are uninhabited by people or their animals.

Tundra is the name for the treeless plains that occupy much of the land above the Arctic Circle. The temperature is below freezing point much of the year and the subsoil (just below the surface) is usually permanently frozen.

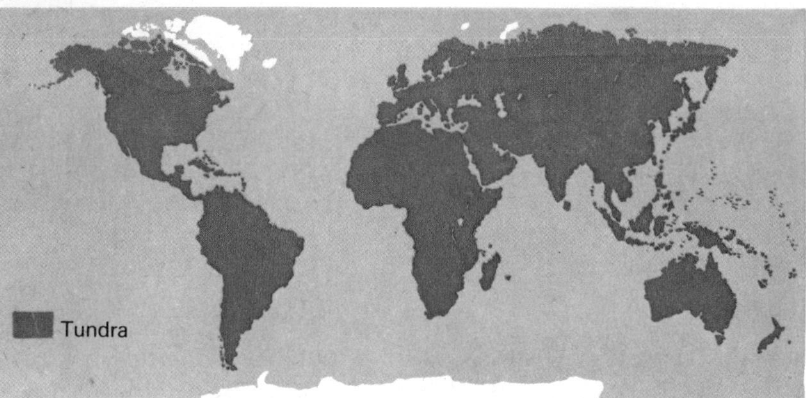

Left: A map showing the tundra regions of the world.

Tungsten was once called wolfram, so its chemical symbol is W. It is found in the ores wolframite and scheelite.

This white metal is very hard but it breaks easily. It changes to a liquid at a higher temperature than any other metal, at over 3300 degrees Centigrade (6000 degrees Fahrenheit). It is used to make the wire filaments in electric light bulbs. It is also added to metals to make alloys with special properties. Tungsten steel can be used at high temperatures. Tungsten carbide is used at the cutting tips of high-speed drills and for making dies to draw wires.

Tunisia is a republic in north-west Africa. Capital, Tunis; area about 164 000 sq km (63 000 sq miles).

Below: Bayazid II, sultan of the Ottoman Empire, the region of present-day Turkey, is defeated and captured at Ankara in 1402. This gave Byzantium a short respite from the attacks of the Turks who finally succeeded in capturing Constantinople, the centre of the Byzantine Empire, in 1453.

History The coast of North Africa was colonized by Phoenicians who founded Carthage in Tunisia in the 9th century BC. The area then became part of the Roman Empire, and later a Muslim state. In the mid-16th century Tunisia became part of the Ottoman Empire. It fell under French rule in 1881, but eventually became independent in 1956, and a republic was formed.

Land and People The Atlas Mountains extend from Morocco, through Algeria, to northern Tunisia. The south of the country is dry, but less so near the coast. There are forests and fertile valleys in the northern highlands, desert in the south. At Tunis the average temperature in January, the coldest month, is 13°C (55.4°F). In July the average is 27°C (80.6°F). Northern Tunisia is densely populated and the people are mainly Arab. There are Berber villages in the less hospitable south.

Economy Agriculture employs more than half the people, and though good land is scarce, a great variety of crops are grown, including flowers for perfume. There are large flocks of sheep and goats. Industry is little developed, but phosphate, iron, lead and other minerals are produced. Handicrafts, especially carpets, textiles and pottery, are important and tourism is growing.

Turkey is a bird found in Central and North America. It is fat and heavy, with a featherless head and neck. A characteristic flap of skin beneath the chin, called the wattle, is used in display. Turkeys spend much of their time scratching about for insects, seeds and fruit on the floor of their forest homes. The domestic turkey was bred from the common turkey, which is found from Canada to Mexico. The other wild turkey is the ocellated turkey of Mexico and northern Central America.

Turkey is a republic partly in south-east Europe and partly in south-west Asia. Capital, Ankara; area about 779 000 sq km (300 000 sq miles).

History In the 11th century the Seljuk Turks, who originated in Central Asia, established an empire in Anatolia. This empire later collapsed when the Mongols invaded in the 12th century, but another small state was founded in the region by Ottoman Turks. They gradually extended their boundaries at the expense of the Byzantines and in 1453 captured Constantinople, bringing about the downfall of the Byzantine Empire. The Ottoman Empire expanded into south-western Europe and its rulers also brought Egypt, Syria and Mesopotamia under their control. The Empire began to decline in the 16th century and finally collapsed in 1918. Then in 1922 Turkey became a republic. There was much political unrest in the 1960s and 1970s, and

relations with Greece became strained over the question of Cyprus.

Land and People The narrow straits between the Aegean and the Black Sea, recently bridged, separate the small portion of European Turkey from Anatolia (Asian Turkey). Most of Anatolia is a broad plateau with coastal mountains. The total coastline is over 6500 km (4000 miles). Near the coasts, the climate is Mediterranean. In central Anatolia it is dryer and more extreme.

The Turks once ruled a large empire. They are Muslims, but in many ways Turkey is more similar to the West than other Islamic states.

Economy Agriculture is the main occupation. A high proportion of land is used for grazing, especially sheep and goats. Wheat is the leading crop, but tobacco and cotton are grown for export. Turkey has large coal reserves as well as other minerals, notably chrome. Industry has developed fast since the First World War, largely under government control. However, some traditional Turkish products, such as hand-knotted carpets, have declined.

Turks and Caicos Islands, The, are a British colony in the West Indies. Capital, Grand Turk; area about 430 sq km (192 sq miles). They became a separate colony in 1973 after being associated with the colonies of the Bahamas and Jamaica. The colony consists of more than 30 islands and islets, only six inhabited, and the chief exports are salt, sponges and shellfish.

Turner, Joseph Mallord William (1775–1851), was an English landscape painter. Unlike Constable, he travelled widely, noting in his sketchbook the effects of changing light and weather, and he was not drawn to a particular type of scenery. His later pictures like *Rain, Steam and Speed* and *Norham Castle, Sunrise* which contain very little outline or form, were the forerunners of future developments such as Impressionism.

Turtle, in some countries, is the name used to describe all the members of the order Chelonia to which turtles, terrapins and tortoises belong. Thus, an animal which might be described as a tortoise in one part of the world is confusingly called a turtle in another.

Marine turtle

However, to many people turtles are thought of only as marine chelonians. They usually possess the bony shell characteristic of their land-dwelling relatives, but their legs are flattened to enable them to swim through the seas. Marine turtles occur in many of the world's temperate and tropical oceans, where they feed on fish and other animals. They must lay their eggs on land, however, and drag themselves up the beach at night to deposit them in the sand. The tiny creatures which hatch from the egg have to undertake the hazardous journey back to the sea, many being eaten by predators before they reach the ocean. Even there, they may still fall prey to fish.

Tutankhamen (died circa 1340 BC), was an Egyptian Pharaoh of the 18th Dynasty. He came to the throne when he was about 12 years of age, dying some six years later. During his short reign he moved the capital of Egypt from Akhetaton back to Thebes and restored the god Amon to prominence. The discovery of his tomb in the Valley of the Kings in 1922 revealed much about the life and art of ancient Egypt.

The ante-chamber of Tutankhamen's tomb, as it was discovered in 1922.

Tuvalu is an island state of Micronesia in the west Pacific Ocean. Capital, Funafuti; area about 24 sq km (9 sq miles). Formerly the Ellice Islands, Tuvalu was a British protectorate until independence was granted in 1978. Coconut palms are the main crop, but fruit and vegetables are also grown.

Twain, Mark (1835–1910), was a US writer whose real name was Samuel Clemens. He worked on Mississippi steamboats, which gave him some of his best material, and as a journalist and humorous lecturer. From about 1872 he was a full-time writer. His most successful books – *The Adventures of Tom Sawyer* (1876), *Life on the Mississippi* (1883), *The Adventures of Huckleberry Finn* (1884) and *Pudd'nhead Wilson* (1894) – were based on frontier life on the Mississippi in his youth. He attacked the morals of society in *The Gilded Age* (1873).

Uganda is a republic in East Africa. Capital, Kampala; area about 237 000 sq km (91 000 sq miles).
History Before Europeans discovered it in the mid-19th century, Uganda was a collection of small kingdoms. It became a British protectorate in 1894, and achieved independence in 1962.
Land and People Uganda consists largely of grassy or wooded plateau, bordered by mountains which are over 3000 m (9840 ft) high in the Ruwenzori, to the west. The Equator runs through Uganda, but the high altitude keeps temperatures reasonably moderate. There are many races and tribes in Uganda. Swahili is a fairly common language. Chris-

tianity is the chief religion, but there is a large Muslim minority.
Economy The drier regions are occupied by herdsmen. Elsewhere, food crops are grown, as well as cotton, coffee, tea and other export crops. Mining is limited, copper being the most valuable mineral, but manufacturing has expanded since the Nile has been harnessed, as it leaves Lake Victoria to provide hydro-electric power.

Ultrasonics are sounds whose frequencies are too high for people to hear. Some animals can hear ultrasound. Bats squeak in ultrasound and they use the echo from these noises to locate solid objects in their path. In a similar way humans can use ultrasonics to find submarines and other underwater objects.

Ultrasonic sound can pass safely through the human body. It is used in medicine, for example, to look at an unborn baby in its mother's womb.

It has many uses in industry, for example, to look for cracks and other flaws in metals, and it is used for cutting, welding and cleaning. *See also* Sonar.

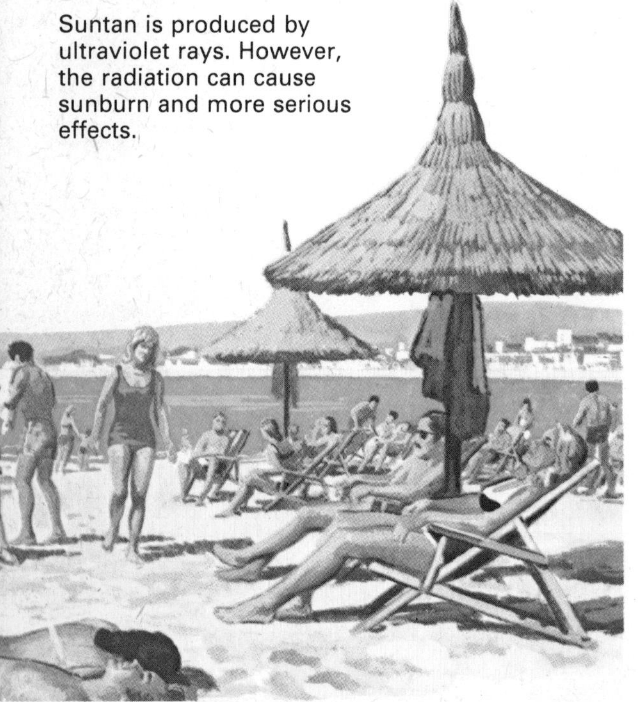
Suntan is produced by ultraviolet rays. However, the radiation can cause sunburn and more serious effects.

Ultraviolet radiations are electromagnetic rays which are like light rays, but are not visible to the human eye. The Earth receives ultraviolet rays from the Sun. Too many ultraviolet rays can burn and kill. A layer of the Earth's atmosphere, called the ozone layer, stops too many coming through. The few that do come through help to form vitamin D in the body and also cause suntans.

Ultraviolet rays make some substances shine. This is called fluorescence. These rays can be used to look at tiny amounts of fluorescent material, too small to be seen otherwise. *See also* Electromagnetic radiation.

Underground railway is a railway system running beneath the ground in order to save space; it is therefore found in many of the world's largest and most crowded cities. The first-built and most extensive underground railway is in London, where the system covers almost 400 km (248 miles) with 273 stations. Although the very first underground trains were hauled by steam locomotives, all such railways now use electric power because this does not produce any fumes and allows the tunnels to be made smaller.

UNESCO stands for the United Nations Educational, Scientific and Cultural Organization, which was founded in 1945 and has its headquarters in Paris. Its aim is to promote peace by improving the standard of education throughout the world, and to bring nations together in cultural and scientific projects. It also gives aid to developing countries.

Ungulate is the name given to a hoofed grazing mammal. Ungulates include horses, deer, antelopes, cattle, camels, rhinoceroses, tapirs, giraffes, pigs and hippopotamuses. *See also* Ruminants.

Unidentified flying objects, or UFOs, are objects which are seen in the sky that cannot be explained. They are also known as flying saucers because they sometimes appear to look like a spinning disc. Many UFOs have later been found to be the planet Venus,

Red Square in Moscow, the capital of the USSR.

which is often very bright. Others are shown to be aircraft, city lights, satellites, weather balloons and other known objects, although there are a small number which have not yet been identified. Some people think that they may be spacecraft from another planet, but there are no facts to prove this. *See also* Extraterrestial life.

Union of Soviet Socialist Republics, (USSR), known as the Soviet Union, is the largest state in the world, stretching from nothern Europe to the Pacific, from the Arctic Ocean to Iran and China. It is partly in Europe, partly in Asia. Capital, Moscow; area about 22402000 sq km (8650000 sq miles). It is also often called Russia, but Russia is really the largest republic of the USSR. The USSR is divided into 15 Soviet Socialist Republics.

Republics of USSR

Republic	*Area (sq km)*	*Area (sq miles)*
Armenia	29800	11500
Azerbaijan	86600	33400
Belorussia	207600	80150
Estonia	45100	17400
Georgia	69700	26900
Kazakhstan	2717300	1049150
Kirgizia	198500	76600
Latvia	63700	24600
Lithuania	65200	25200
Moldavia	33700	13000
Russian Soviet Federated Socialist Republic	17075000	6592700
Tadzhikistan	143100	55200
Turkmenistan	488100	188000
Ukraine	603700	233100
Uzbekistan	447400	172700

History Russia was settled by Slavs during the 1st millennium (one thousand years) AD. During the 10th century Scandinavians established a number of principalities, notably at Kiev and Novgorod. The whole region was occupied by Mongols and Tartars from about 1240, but in the 14th century the princes of Moscow began to expel the Tartars and to subdue rival princes. In the 15th century Russia became a unified country under Ivan the Great. In the 16th century, Ivan, the Terrible, crowned himself Tsar (Caesar) of all the Russia's.

The Romanov dynasty was founded in 1613 and during the next 100 years, Russia expanded westwards, becoming an important European power. During the 19th century it remained an economically backward country, which was inefficiently ruled by the tsars, and discontent among the people led to the unsuccessful revolution of 1905.

In 1917 the Tsar, Nicholas II, was overthrown and later that year a Communist regime was established. In 1922 the country became the Union of Soviet Socialist Republics (USSR) and in the following years, under Stalin, was rapidly industrialized. After the Second World War the USSR became one of the two great powers (the other being the USA), both through its military strength and through its science and technology.

Land About half the country is huge lowland plain, stretching from the Baltic to the Yenisei River and crossed by the Ural Mountains. There are mountains and plateaux farther east, while in the north the land is open to the Arctic Ocean. Much of European Russia is rolling plains, with occasional hilly ridges. There are higher mountains in the south, especially the Caucasus range. The Soviet Union contains several of the world's largest lakes and rivers. Its coastline is not long when compared to total area, and much of it is icebound.

The climate is generally 'continental', with extreme temperatures, especially in the east. The coldest place in the Northern Hemisphere is in northern Siberia. The only region with a really mild climate is the Crimea, on the Black Sea. Rainfall is generally rather low.

People The Soviet Union is a land of many nations. There are over 150 distinct racial or national groups. About three-quarters of the people are Slavs, including the Russians who make up about half the total population, the Ukrainians and Belorussians. The next largest group (over 20 million) are descendants of Turkic tribes of central Asia who are mostly Muslims. The Slav peoples are Christians (Eastern Orthodox) by tradition. The Russian language is spoken by a majority, but not all the people. The population is unevenly distributed. Large regions have very few people, and more than half the population live in southern European Russia. A large and growing proportion live in cities. Social services are highly developed. Great advances have been made under communist rule, especially in education. The Communist Party is all-powerful and government is highly centralized, despite the great size of the country.

Economy The economy is based on common ownerships. In practice, this means ownership by the state. Government control of the economy has had mixed results. In industry especially, enormous achievements have been made, and the Soviet Union has a greater industrial output than any country except the USA. Nearly half the total labour

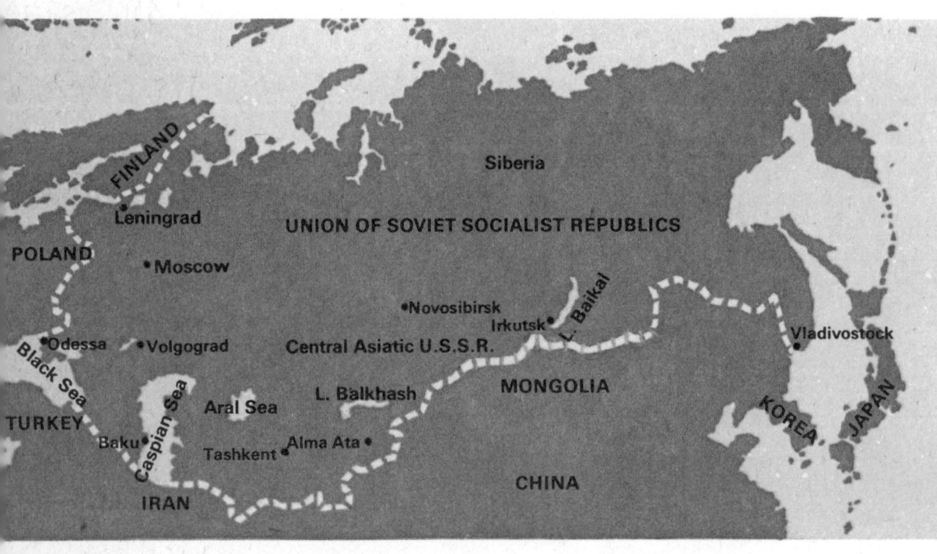

force are women. Agriculture is organized through state farms or collectives, though peasants are allowed private plots. Good farming land is limited, although there are very fertile areas in the south and west, but drought or early frost are widespread hazards. Much land has been ploughed for the first time in recent years, but the Soviet Union still has to import some basic foods (e.g. wheat). After wheat, rye and barley, potatoes are the largest food crop. Cotton and other fibres are also grown on a large scale, especially in the Asian part.

Nearly one-third of the country is forested, mainly by coniferous varieties, giving plenty of timber and other wood products. Most coastal waters have good fishing. Sturgeon, which provide caviare, are caught off the Volga River.

The greatest strength of the Soviet economy, however, is its large amount of mineral resources. Coal and oil provide fuel, and the country has large reserves of almost every mineral from iron to diamonds. Hydro-electric and nuclear power also provide energy. There is an enormous, efficient rail network, but good roads are less common.

The Soviet Union's trade is mainly with other eastern European countries which are associated with it in COMECON (equivalent to the EEC in Western Europe).

Far left: A map of the USSR, showing neighbouring countries. *Below:* Norilsk, a large, modern town in Siberia.

Rulers of Russia

House of Rurik	
Ivan III the Great	1462–1505
Basil III	1505–1533
Ivan IV the Terrible	1533–1584
Fyodor I	1584–1598
Boris Godunov	1598–1605
Fyodor II	1605
Dimitri	1605–1606
Interregnum	1606–1613
House of Romanov	
Michael Romanov	1613–1645
Alexis	1645–1676
Fyodor III	1676–1682
Ivan V and Peter the Great	1682–1689
Peter the Great	1689–1725
Catherine I	1725–1727
Peter II	1727–1730
Anna	1730–1740
Ivan VI	1740–1741
Elizabeth	1741–1762
Peter III	1762
Catherine II	1762–1796
Paul I	1796–1801
Alexander I	1801–1825
Nicholas I	1825–1855
Alexander II	1855–1881
Alexander III	1881–1894
Nicholas II	1894–1917

United Arab Emirates is a federation of seven small states in the south-east of the Arabian peninsula, in the Persian Gulf. Federal capital, Abu Dhabi: area about 92 000 sq km (32 000 sq miles). Formerly the Trucial States, so called because they had truces with Britain, they were under British domination until the present federation was founded in 1971.

The Emirates are mainly desert, with agriculture confined to oases. Fishing, including pearl fishing, and herding are traditional occupations, but the main economic factor today is the oil production of three of the states; Dubai, Abu Dhabi and Sharjah.

United Kingdom of Great Britain and Northern Ireland consists of Great Britain and the north-eastern corner of Ireland – that is the kingdoms of England and Scotland, the principality of Wales and the province of Ulster. It also includes many small offshore islands (like the Isle of Wight), but not the Isle of Man or the Channel Islands which are dependencies of the Crown. Area about 244013 sq km (94214 sq miles); capital, London.

History For history prior to 17th century see individual countries. In 1603 the crowns of Scotland and England were united. (The realms were formally united in 1707.) In the 17th century conflict between king and Parliament led to the Civil War, and the establishment of a republic. The Glorious Revolution of 1688 and the Bill of Rights (1689) made Parliament finally supreme. During the 18th century a cabinet system of government became firmly established. In the 19th century more and more people were given the right to vote.

In the 1700s, the United Kingdom was the birthplace of the Industrial Revolution – the change from an agricultural to an industrial economy. It became history's most prosperous nation, 'the workshop of the world'. By the 1900s, it was also the centre of the world's greatest empire, which included about one-fifth of the earth's land surface and a quarter of its people. Since the middle of the 20th century, however, nearly all of its overseas territories have become independent. Many of them still retain a link of friendship as the Commonwealth of Nations.

Ireland became part of the United Kingdom in 1801 and broke away as the Irish Free State in 1922. (The Republic of Ireland was established in 1949.)

Britain took part in the First World War and suffered from the general trade depression of the 1930s. After the Second World War Britain joined NATO and EEC, but experienced a gradual economic decline, largely due to increased competition from other trading nations.

Rulers of the United Kingdom

Stuart	
James I	1603–1625
Charles I	1625–1649
Commonwealth	1649–1660
Charles II	1660–1685
James II	1685–1688
William III & Mary	1689–1702
Anne	1702–1714

Busy London docks in the later part of the 17th century.

Hanover	
George I	1714–1727
George II	1727–1760
George III	1760–1820
George IV	1820–1830
William IV	1830–1837
Victoria	1837–1901
Saxe-Coburg	
Edward VII	1901–1910
Windsor	
George V	1910–1936
Edward VIII	1936
George VI	1936–1952
Elizabeth II	1952–

Prime Ministers of the United Kingdom

Sir Robert Walpole	1721–1742
Earl of Wilmington	1742–1743
Henry Pelham	1743–1754
Duke of Newcastle	1754–1756
Duke of Devonshire	1756–1757
Duke of Newcastle	1757–1762
Earl of Bute	1762–1763
George Grenville	1763–1765
Marquis of Rockingham	1765–1766
Earl of Chatham	1766–1767
Duke of Grafton	1767–1770
Lord North	1770–1782
Marquis of Rockingham	1782
Earl of Shelbourne	1782–1783
Duke of Portland	1783
William Pitt	1783–1801
Henry Addington	1801–1804
William Pitt	1804–1806
Lord Grenville	1806–1807
Duke of Portland	1807–1809
Spencer Perceval	1809–1812
Earl of Liverpool	1812–1827
George Canning	1827
Viscount Goderich	1827–1828
Duke of Wellington	1828–1830
Earl Gray	1830–1834
Viscount Melbourne	1834
Sir Robert Peel	1834–1835
Viscount Melbourne	1835–1841
Sir Robert Peel	1841–1846
Lord John Russell	1846–1852
Earl of Derby	1852
Earl of Aberdeen	1852–1855
Viscount Palmerston	1855–1858
Earl of Derby	1858–1859
Viscount Palmerston	1859–1865
Earl Russell	1865–1866
Earl of Derby	1866–1868
Benjamin Disraeli	1868
William Gladstone	1868–1874
Benjamin Disraeli	1874–1880
William Gladstone	1880–1885
Marquis of Salisbury	1885–1886
William Gladstone	1886
Marquis of Salisbury	1886–1892
William Gladstone	1892–1894
Earl of Rosebery	1894–1895
Marquis of Salisbury	1895–1902
Arthur Balfour	1902–1905
Sir Henry Campbell-Bannerman	1905–1908
Herbert Asquith	1908–1916
David Lloyd George	1916–1922
Andrew Bonar Law	1922–1923
Stanley Baldwin	1923–1924
Ramsay MacDonald	1924
Stanley Baldwin	1924–1929
Ramsey MacDonald	1929–1935
Stanley Baldwin	1935–1937
Neville Chamberlain	1937–1940
Winston Churchill	1940–1945
Clement Atlee	1945–1951
Winston Churchill	1951–1955
Sir Anthony Eden	1955–1957
Harold Macmillan	1957–1963
Sir Alec Douglas-Home	1963–1964
Harold Wilson	1964–1970
Edward Heath	1970–1974
Harold Wilson	1974–1976
James Callaghan	1976–1979
Margaret Thatcher	1979–

Land Geographically the islands of Great Britain and Ireland have two similar main features: the mountains and highlands of the north and west, and the lowlands of the south-east.

Altogether the UK has an extraordinary variety of scenery for so small an area. The most mountainous parts are the Highlands of Scotland (roughly the northern half) and North Wales. Northern England is also hilly, dominated by the Pennines, with the scenic Lake District in the north-west. The rest of England is mainly rolling plains, with broad river valleys and low hills. The hills are higher in Wales and south-west England, where there is also extensive moorland.

Among smaller but unusual regions are the low-lying fens and broads of eastern England.

The very centre of Britain is little more than 100 km (62 miles) from the sea, and the long coast, plus numerous rivers, have been important in making a great trading nation.

The mild and rainy climate is strongly influenced by the North Atlantic Drift, a warm current in the North Atlantic Ocean. Weather changes are frequent, because of the development of anticyclones and depressions. The Pennines and the Scottish mountains are the coldest parts of the country: with the Cumbrian Mountains, they are also the wettest.

People The United Kingdom is one of Europe's most densely populated countries. More than 70 per cent of its people live in cities and towns. The majority of them are descended from various groups of invaders and settlers who made their homes in the British Isles between the 3000s BC and the AD 1100s – including early Mediterranean peoples, Romans, Angles, Saxons, Jutes, Norsemen and Normans. In the second half of the 1900s, the country's population acquired a multi-racial character by the addition of about two million citizens of Asian, African, and West Indian origin.

Economy The United Kingdom has petroleum (in the North Sea), coal, natural gas, and iron deposits, but is otherwise relatively poor in natural resources. More than three-quarters of the land area is put to farming use, either for grazing or for cultivation. The farms are among the most highly mechanized and efficient in the world. The most extensive arable lands are in eastern England, where crops include wheat, vegetables, and sugar-beet. Scotland is known for its beef cattle, and dairy farming is common in all parts of the country.

British industries are varied, and many of them used imported raw materials. Among those for which the United Kingdom has traditionally had a high reputation are the manufacture of textiles, steel, industrial tools and machinery, aircraft, road vehicles, rolling stock, armaments, glass, ceramics, and paper. Shipbuilding and petrochemical industries are also of major importance.

See also England; Scotland; Wales; Northern Ireland.

United Nations is an international organization of countries whose purpose is to maintain world peace and security and to encourage co-operation among its members. It was founded in 1945 in succession to the League of Nations, and its charter was signed by 51 nations. Now almost all the countries of the world belong to the United Nations, which has its headquarters in New York, and they meet every year in the General Assembly. Problems affecting world peace are dealt with by the Security Council, and other important UN bodies are the Food and Agriculture Organization (FAO) and the United Nations Educational, Scientific and Cultural Organization (UNESCO).

The UN Assembly.

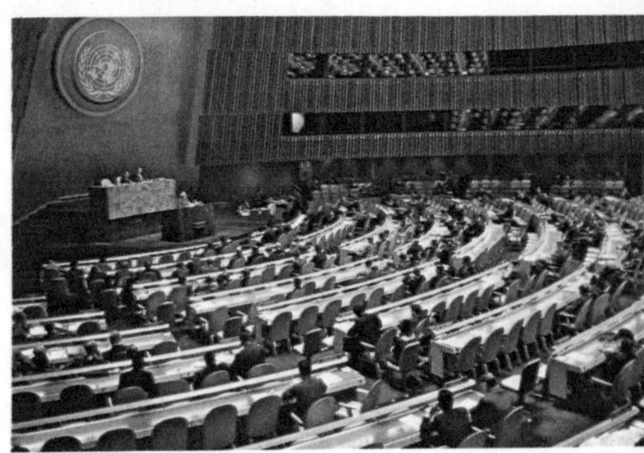

United States of America (USA), is a federal republic in North America. Capital, Washington, DC (District of Columbia); area about 9 363 000 sq km (3 615 000 sq miles). It consists of fifty states, including Alaska and Hawaii. The states have a degree of internal self-government.

History When European settlers reached the continent of North America in the 15th and 16th century, they found tribes of people they called Indians who had come from Siberia through Alaska more than 20 000 years before.

The first Spanish settlements were made in Florida in 1565 and the first English ones in Virginia in 1607. The 13 colonies which

State	*State Capital*	*Area sq km*	*sq miles*
Alabama	Montgomery	133 700	51 600
Alaska	Juneau	1 518 800	586 400
Arizona	Phoenix	295 000	114 000
Arkansas	Little Rock	137 500	53 000
California	Sacramento	411 000	158 700
Colorado	Denver	270 000	104 000
Connecticut	Hartford	13 000	5 000
Delaware	Dover	5 300	2 000
Florida	Tallahassee	151 700	58 600
Georgia	Atlanta	152 500	58 900
Hawaii	Honolulu	16 700	6 400
Idaho	Boise	216 400	83 600
Illinois	Springfield	146 100	56 000
Indiana	Indianapolis	94 000	36 300
Iowa	Des Moines	145 800	56 300
Kansas	Topeka	213 100	82 000
Kentucky	Frankfort	104 600	40 400
Louisiana	Baton Rouge	125 700	48 500
Maine	Augusta	86 000	33 200
Maryland	Annapolis	27 400	10 600
Massachusetts	Boston	21 400	8 200
Michigan	Lansing	150 800	58 200
Minnesota	St Paul	217 700	84 000
Mississippi	Jackson	123 600	47 700
Missouri	Jefferson City	180 500	69 700
Montana	Helena	381 000	147 100
Nebraska	Lincoln	200 000	77 200
Nevada	Carson City	286 300	110 500
New Hampshire	Concord	24 000	9 000
New Jersey	Trenton	20 300	7800
New Mexico	Santa Fe	315 000	121 700
New York	Albany	128 400	49 600
North Carolina	Raleigh	136 500	52 700
North Dakota	Bismarck	183 000	70 670
Ohio	Columbus	106 800	41 200
Oklahoma	Oklahoma City	181 100	69 900
Oregon	Salem	251 200	97 000
Pennsylvania	Harrisburg	117 400	45 300
Rhode Island	Providence	3100	1200
South Carolina	Columbia	80 400	31 000
South Dakota	Pierre	199 600	77 000
Tennessee	Nashville	109 400	42 200
Texas	Austin	692 400	267 300
Utah	Salt Lake City	219 900	84 900
Vermont	Montpelier	24 900	9600
Virginia	Richmond	105 700	40 800
Washington	Olympia	176 600	68 200
West Virginia	Charleston	62 600	24 200
Wisconsin	Madison	145 400	56 200
Wyoming	Cheyenne	253 600	97 900

General Andrew Jackson, president of the USA (1829–1837). He had become the national hero of the 1812–14 war against the British.

were established along the Atlantic seaboard came to resent British rule and finally declared their independence in 1776. In the 19th century the United States gained new territory from France (Louisiana Purchase, 1803) and from Mexico. The Civil War (1861–1865) resulted in victory for the North and the abolition of slavery. In the later 19th century there was a rapid economic expansion, a great increase in European immigration, and more territorial gains.

By the early 20th century the United States had become the world's leading industrial power. It took part in the First World War from 1917 and in the Second World War played a leading part in the defeat of the Axis powers and in the establishment of the United Nations. During the postwar years the United States was involved in wars in Korea and Vietnam and was the dominant Western power in relations with the USSR and its allies.

At home the United States had to deal with such problems as racial integration, the depletion of natural resources and inflation.

Land The continental USA has two mountain ranges parallel with the Atlantic and Pacific oceans: the Appalachians in the east and the higher Rocky Mountains in the west. Between the two are vast central lowlands, drained by the Mississippi and its tributaries, and including the prairies of the Mid West. In the north, on the Canadian border, are the Great Lakes. There are great differences between – and within – the main regions, with desert in the south-west, forests in the north, and large swamps in the south-east.

The climate varies enormously too. Florida is tropical, but North Dakota in winter is often colder than the Arctic. It is generally drier in the west, and on both coasts the influence of the ocean moderates summer heat and winter cold.

People The present inhabitants are mainly of European descent; a large minority are of African origin, descendants of the slaves who worked the Southern plantations. The Indians, the original inhabitants, now form only a tiny minority. English is the official language, though Spanish is widely spoken in certain areas. A majority of Americans belong to Christian Churches.

Americans have one of the highest standards of living in the world, but there are nevertheless great variations. Welfare and social services vary from state to state, and there is considerable poverty in some parts. More than 75 per cent of the people live in towns and cities, the north-east and west coast being the most densely-populated regions. Some western states, such as Nevada and Wyoming, are very thinly populated.

American society can be divided into a number of regions, each with its own charac-

teristics, although divisions are becoming less obvious. The biggest division is still between North (industrial, prosperous) and South (rural, less prosperous). The traditional dominance of the north-east in business, politics and culture is increasingly rivalled by California in the west. The heartland of the USA is the Mid West, which is mainly farming country but with many large industrial cities. There are probably more millionaires in Texas, where there is much oil and ranching, than any other state.

Economy The USA is the land of 'free enterprise' meaning that most businesses, property, etc are privately owned. However, there are in fact some large enterprises, such as the Post Office, run by the federal government, and government departments play a large part in controlling the economy indirectly.

The USA is the largest manufacturing nation in the world. Industry is chiefly concentrated in the north-east, though there has been growing development elsewhere in recent years. California has also become a major manufacturing state since the Second World War.

Agriculture employs less than 10 per cent of the people, but output is enormous, and huge quantities of food are exported. The Mid West, with its endless fields of wheat, has been called 'the breadbasket of the world', but all types of farming and livestock-raising are practised on a large scale in different regions.

Manufacturing depends largely on the country's rich mineral resources. Most oil and gas come from the central south-west and Alaska, while coal comes from the Pennsylvania region. There are large supplies of important minerals such as aluminium and copper and some uranium and gold.

Despite the rich natural resources of the country, oil must still be imported from the

Middle East and timber products, like paper, from Canada. Other imports are mainly food products such as coffee, and certain metals.

Transportation, whether oil pipeline, road or airline, is very highly developed.

Presidents of the USA.

George Washington	1789–1797
John Adams	1797–1801
Thomas Jefferson	1801–1809
James Madison	1809–1817
James Monroe	1817–1825
John Quincy Adams	1825–1829
Andrew Jackson	1829–1837
Martin Van Buren	1837–1841
William H Harrison	1841
John Tyler	1841–1845
James K Polk	1845–1849
Zachary Taylor	1849–1850
Millard Fillmore	1850–1853
Franklin Pierce	1853–1857
James Buchanan	1857–1861
Abraham Lincoln	1861–1865
Andrew Johnson	1865–1869
Ulysses S Grant	1869–1877
Rutherford B Hayes	1877–1881
James A Garfield	1881
Chester A Arthur	1881–1885
Grover Cleveland	1885–1889
Benjamin Harrison	1889–1893
Grover Cleveland	1893–1897
William McKinley	1897–1901
Theodore Roosevelt	1901–1909
William H Taft	1909–1913
Woodrow Wilson	1913–1921
Warren Gamaliel Harding	1921–1923
Calvin Coolidge	1923–1929
Herbert C Hoover	1929–1933
Franklin D Roosevelt	1933–1945
Harry S Truman	1945–1953
Dwight D Eisenhower	1953–1961
John F Kennedy	1961–1963
Lyndon B Johnson	1963–1969
Richard M Nixon	1969–1974
Gerald R Ford	1974–1977
James Earl Carter	1977–1981
Ronald Reagan	1981–

Universe is everything there is. The Earth, Solar System, galaxies and beyond are all part of the universe.

Until the 16th century, the Sun and planets were believed to move around the Earth. The stars that were visible seemed to be on a dome or sphere around the Earth. This sphere and everything inside it was the universe, and the Earth was the centre of the universe. Then, in 1543, Nicolaus Copernicus, a Polish astronomer, suggested that the Sun was the centre of the universe, and that the Earth orbited it. This forced astronomers to look at the sky differently.

Since then the telescope has shown that there is a vastly greater universe. The Earth is known to be the third planet from the Sun, a medium-sized star lying two-thirds of the way from the centre of our Galaxy. Our Galaxy is one of countless galaxies all moving away from each other. Ideas about the universe are studied in cosmology.

Upper Volta is a republic in West Africa. Capital, Ouagadougou; area about 274 000 sq km (105 790 sq miles). It became a separate colony in 1919 from the colony of Upper Senegal and Niger. It became independent in 1960.

Upper Volta is a landlocked country, mostly flat plateau crossed by several rivers. Most of the people are occupied in farming. Animal products are the main export, but cotton, groundnuts and sesame seeds are also exported.

Urals are a mountain range in USSR, usually regarded as the boundary between Europe and Asia. They stretch for about 2500 km (1550 miles) north to south, and the highest peak is Mount Narodnaya at 1894 m (6214 ft) high. The central region of the Urals is industrially important because of the vast mineral resources.

Uranium has the chemical symbol U. It is a silver-coloured radioactive element and has many yellow-coloured ores, such as pitchblende. Although uranium ores are not common, they can be found easily by the radiation given off by uranium.

Atoms of uranium are heavier than the atoms of any other natural element. The atoms of one of the isotopes of uranium can split in half. This produces enormous amounts of energy. Uranium has been used to make atom bombs and to generate electricity in nuclear reactors. Plutonium is made from uranium.

Uranus is the seventh planet from the Sun. It orbits the Sun in 84 years. Its diameter is nearly four times bigger than the Earth's. The planet looks green because its atmosphere contains methane as well as other gases, and it is mainly rock, ice and frozen hydrogen.

One very unusual thing about Uranus is that it is tilted on its side. This means that its poles receive more sunlight than its equator. In all other planets, including the Earth, the equator is hotter and brighter than the poles. Like Saturn, Uranus has rings of small particles around it. These rings are much thinner than Saturn's and are not bright. There may be up to nine of them. They were discovered when Uranus passed in front of a star in 1977.

Uranus has at least five satellites. The planet was discovered in 1781 by Sir William Herschel.

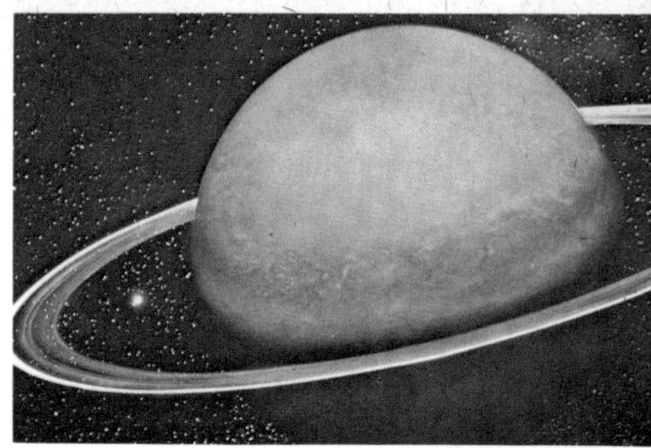

An artist's impression of the rings of Uranus.

Uruguay is a republic in central South America. Capital Montevideo; area about 187 000 sq km (72 000 sq miles). In colonial times it was disputed between Spain and Portugal. The Spaniards won, and when Spanish rule ended in 1814 Uruguay was temporarily part of Brazil. It has been independent since 1828.

Uruguay is mainly pampas with low hills in the north. The climate is temperate, though rather hot in summer. It is the most densely populated country in South America, and a high proportion of people are of European descent.

Stock-raising is the basis of the economy, with large sheep and cattle ranches, and wool and meat are the chief exports. Mining and manufacturing, mainly in the Montevideo area, are less important.

USA, see United States of America

USSR, see Union of Soviet Socialist Republics

V1 and V2 were weapons developed by the Germans during the final stages of the Second World War. V1 (Vergeltungswaffe Ein, or Vengeance Weapon One) was a simple jet-propelled bomb with wings, which had a limited range and very poor accuracy. V2, however, was a formidable 14 m-(46 ft-)long rocket which carried 900 kg (1985 lb) of high explosive at 5000 km/h (3105 mph). It landed without warning, and the Allied forces had nothing to combat it, halting its use only by destroying the factories and launch sites. V2 was the first modern rocket and the man who built it, Wernher von Braun, played a major role in the American space programme after the Second World War. Captured V2s were also used to start both Russian and American space exploration before each nation developed its own launch systems.

Vaccine is a substance which is introduced into the body in order to help it build up a resistance or immunity to a particular disease. A vaccine is really a minute amount of the very disease which it is intended to protect against. Very small quantities of the disease cause the body to set up its own defence (called an antibody) against the disease. Then, should the body ever come into contact with larger quantities of the disease, it is able to fight and defeat the disease before it causes the body any harm.

Vacuum is a completely empty space. An 'empty' room still contains air. Even the 'empty' space between stars contains tiny amounts of gas. A perfect vacuum does not exist, but near-vacuums can be made. As much as possible of the air is pumped out of a container, which is then sealed.

Containers surrounded by a near-vacuum layer are used to keep food and other things warm or cool. They are called vacuum flasks.

Valhalla, in Germanic and Norse (Scandinavian) myth, was the great golden hall in Asgard which was the home of brave warriors killed in battle. It had 540 doors, each one wide enough for 800 warriors to march through in line abreast. Every day the heroes engaged in fierce battles for sport, and their wounds were miraculously healed.

Valkyries, in Germanic and Norse (Scandinavian) myth, were beautiful young women, attendants of Odin. They decided who should win a battle, who should die, and who should be admitted to Valhalla. They sometimes took part in the battle themselves, and some had mortal husbands or lovers. They were pictured either as helmeted goddesses carrying flaming spears, or as girls in swans' feathers flying through the air.

Stories of the Valkyries in the *Nibelungenlied*, a medieval German epic, were used by Richard Wagner in his operas called *The Ring of the Nibelung*.

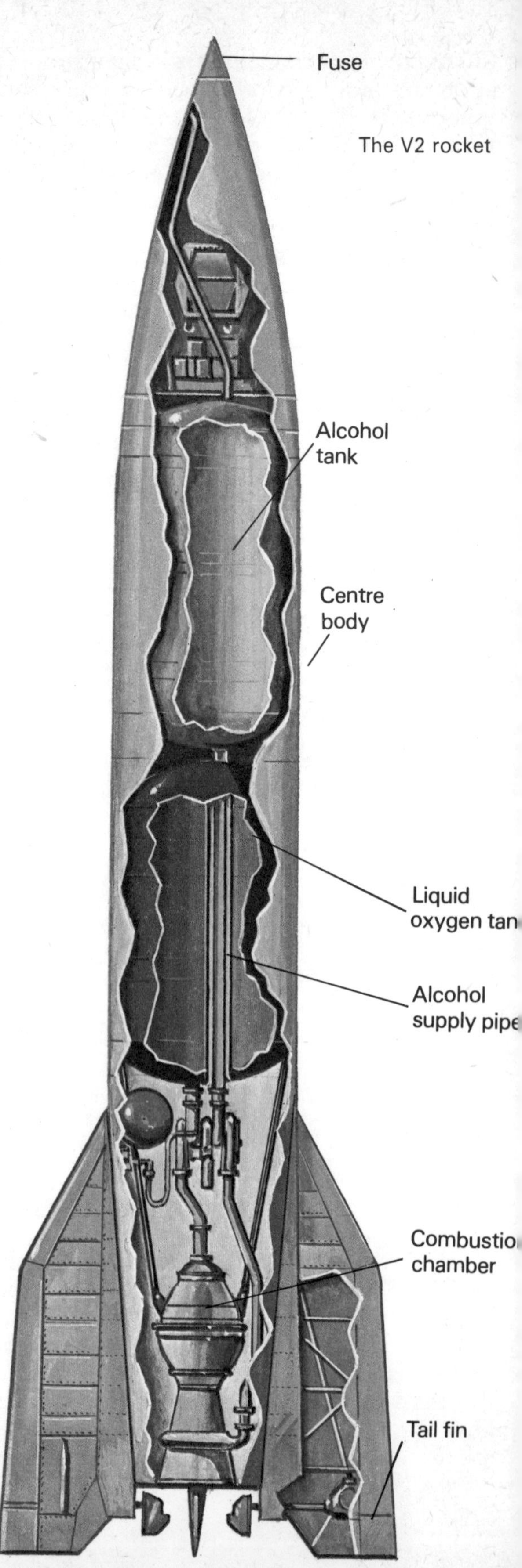

The V2 rocket

Vampire is an imaginary blood-sucking monster that appears in many folk-tales, especially in Eastern Europe. Vampires were believed to be men and women who had been buried but continued to exist by sucking the blood of sleeping people; if the victims eventually died, they too became vampires. Vampires were creatures of the night, compelled to return to their grave or coffin by daybreak. They could be identified by the fact that their bodies cast no shadows and created no reflections in a mirror. Various charms (a crucifix, a string of garlic, and others) would protect sleepers from their attentions. They could only be killed by a stake thrust through their heart or by the destruction of their daytime resting place.

In modern times, it was Bram Stoker's novel *Dracula* (1897) that made vampirism a popular subject for horror stories, and interest in it has been kept up by the many Dracula films made for the cinema and television.

Van Dyck, Sir Anthony (1599–1641), was a Flemish painter. He was a pupil, and later the rival, of Rubens in Antwerp, though a very different artist. Van Dyck is best known for his portraits, especially of the royal family in England. He was employed by Charles I from 1632 until his early death, just before the English Civil War, and he painted noble and dignified portraits of him.

Van Eyck, Jan (circa 1390–1441), was a Dutch painter. He is one of the great figures from the period when the Gothic art of the Middle Ages was being affected by the approach of the Renaissance, and he is considered the founder of Flemish painting. He and his brother Hubert were pioneers in the new technique of painting in oils, on which Van Eyck's brilliant colours largely depended. He was a marvellous portraitist, who also had an idea of perspective (the illusion of depth) far in advance of contemporary Italian artists.

Van Gogh, Vincent (1853–1890), was a Dutch painter, though he left Holland for France in 1886. He is usually classed as a Post-Impressionist, and it was largely the influence of Impressionism that lay behind his riotously colourful paintings of the countryside around Arles, where he lived from 1888.

Vanuatu is an island republic about 805 km (500 miles) west of Fiji in the Pacific Ocean. Capital, Vila; area about 14 760 sq km (5700 sq miles). Formerly the Condominium of the New Hebrides, the group of islands became an independent republic in 1980. Crops grown include copra, cocoa and coffee.

Vatican City State is an independent state in Rome, Italy, headquarters of the Pope and the Catholic Church. Area about 44 hectares (109 acres). It was established by the Lateran Treaty of 1929, and is the smallest independent state in the world.

Vegetable is any herbaceous plant whose seeds, fruits, roots, stems, leaves or flowers are used as food by people. However, some plants which fall within this wide-ranging definition are grouped separately because of common features. For example, the cereals form a separate group because they are all members of the Graminae, and provide food in the form of seed, or grain. Vegetables are usually cultivated as crops, and careful breeding has produced those plants with the most useful characteristics, such as hardiness, disease resistance, flavour, and high yield.

Among the most common vegetables are

Above: the Pisani Palace in Venice.
Left: some different vegetables.

members of the Brassicae, the cabbage family. From the original wild cabbage we now have Brussels sprouts (we eat the buds), cauliflower (we eat the flowers), cabbage (we eat the leaves) and kohl rabi (we eat the stems). Other important vegetables include the potato (we eat the swollen stem), the carrot (we eat the swollen root), and members of the family Leguminosae such as beans and peas (we eat the seeds and their seed cases, or pods).

Vein is a blood vessel which carries blood from the tissues back to the heart. All veins except the pulmonary vein carry deoxygenated blood. (The pulmonary vein carries oxygenated blood from the lungs.) Veins have thinner walls and larger cavities than arteries.

A vein is also the name given to the thin, supporting tubes found in an insect's wing, as well as to the groups of water- and food-conducting tissues found in plants.

Velasquez, Diego (1599–1600), was a Spanish painter. His early works recorded peasant life, but he is best known as a court artist, particularly for his group portraits in which his sad and sympathetic awareness of ordinary human nature is evident.

Veld is the grassy open country of southern Africa. The word means 'field' in Afrikaans, the language of the Dutch (Boer) settlers who arrived in the region early in the 19th century.

Velocity measures speed in a particular direction. How fast something is moving is called its speed. Suppose a motorcar is travelling north at 50 km/h (30 mph). Its velocity northwards is 50 km/h (30 mph). Its velocity to the west is zero, because it is not moving west at all. Another motor car may be travelling west at 50 km/h (30 mph). This car has no velocity northwards but has a velocity of 50 km/h (30 mph) to the west. Both cars have a speed of 50 km/h (30 mph).

Venezuela is a republic in northern South America. Capital, Caracas; area about 912 000 sq km (352 000 sq miles). After 300 years of Spanish rule, Venezuela became part of independent Greater Columbia, but separated in 1830.

The mountain and valley country near the coast gives way to the plains of the Orinoco River. The southern half is again mountainous. The climate is warm at all seasons, and there are large areas of tropical forest.

Most of the people are of mixed Indian,

Spanish and African origin; a minority of pure Spanish descent tend to be dominant. The population has grown rapidly in the past 40 years, and most people live in the northern region. There is a huge difference between rich and poor.

Venezuela is rich in minerals, especially oil, iron ore, gold and diamonds. Oil from the Lake Maracaibo region is by far the most valuable export. Cattle-raising is now less important than it was, and the chief agricultural export is coffee. There has been large industrial development since the 1940s, based on money obtained from oil, and there are valuable timber resources.

Venice is a city and a former state in north-east Italy. The home of many great Italian artists and architects, the city itself is a work of art. It is built in a lagoon on a number of islands separated by canals, which act as streets do in an ordinary city. Among the many buildings of special interest are the Doge's Palace, St Mark's church and the Bridge of Sighs.

In the early Middle Ages several neighbouring towns came together to form a union headed by an elected magistrate, the doge. Venice soon became a great sea power, with a large navy and a supreme position in the valuable Mediterranean trade. In particular, Venice controlled trade between Europe and the Middle East. Venetian merchants also travelled overland to India and China. Colonies were founded in Crete, Cyprus and Greece, and the Venetian republic's territory expanded in Italy and along the Dalmatian coast (Yugoslavia).

The extraordinary prosperity of Venice was threatened in the 15th century, first by the Turks, and then by the Portuguese discovery of a sea route to India and the East.

Early in the 16th century Venice lost a large part of her mainland territory, and the struggle with the Turks continued until the 18th century. By that time Venice was a power of little importance, but she remained independent until Napoleon conquered northern Italy in 1797. From 1815 until 1866 (after the foundation of the kingdom of Italy), Venice was part of the Austrian empire.

Venus is the second planet from the Sun. It travels around it in 225 days, and rotates on its axis in about 243 Earth days. It is the closest planet to Earth. Sometimes it is the brightest object in the sky. However, its surface cannot be seen from Earth because it is covered with thick cloud. The series of Venera space missions, which landed on Venus, and the spacecraft Mariner 10 found out much about the planet.

Venus is similar in size and structure to Earth. Its surface has volcanoes, mountains, craters and a long crack like the Rift Valley in Africa. The surface temperature is thought to be about 480 degrees Centigrade (896 degree Fahrenheit), hotter than Mercury. The dense atmosphere is mainly of carbon dioxide and the clouds are made of sulphuric acid. No life, such as we know it, can exist there.

Venus fly trap lives in the boggy, nitrogen-lacking areas of the southern USA, and is one of the most unusual of the carnivorous, or meat-eating, plants. Like other carnivorous plants, the Venus fly trap can make most of its own food by photosynthesis, but it cannot obtain vital nitrogen from the soil.

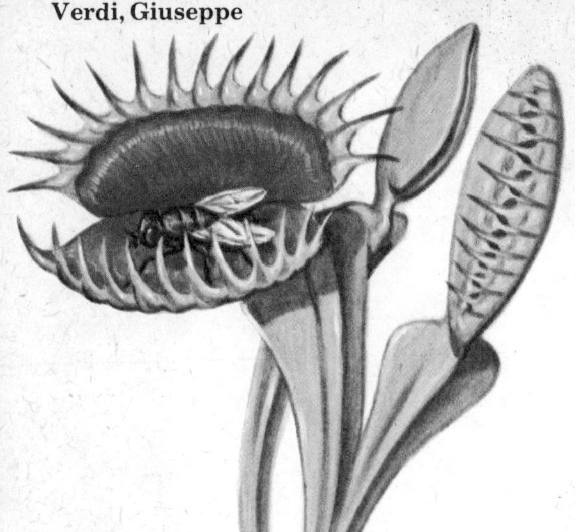

Therefore, it obtains it in the form of tiny animals which it catches and digests. It does this in a remarkable way. The outer ends of the leaves of the Venus fly trap are divided into hinged halves, each half lined with stiff hairs. When an insect touches one of the hairs or lands on the leaf, having been attracted by its bright colour, the two halves of the leaf snap shut, the stiff hairs now acting like the bars of a cage. For the helpless victim there is no escape, and its fate is to be dissolved and digested by the plant.

Verdi, Giuseppe (1813–1901), was an Italian composer. An innkeeper's son, he had no musical background and was rejected by the Milan Conservatory of music. His first opera was *Oberto* (1839). He almost gave up composing in 1840 after the death of his wife and children, but *Nabucco* (1842), his first great success in Italy, set him on his way. *Rigoletto* (1851), followed by *Il Trovatore* and *La Traviata* (1853) established his reputation. *Aïda* (1871), *Otello* (1887) and the comic opera *Falstaff* (1893) were also huge successes. Verdi was no revolutionary in music and the quality of his works varies, but he was one of the greatest of all opera composers.

Versailles was a royal palace, near Paris. It was built for that grandest of monarchs, Louis XIV, by Louis le Vau and Jules Hardouin-Mansart in the late 17th century. The vast formal gardens were planned by André le Nôtre. It was the most magnificent building, or citadel, ever seen, and rulers all over Europe were inspired to build grand palaces in imitation, though none were on the scale of Versailles.

Versailles contains a chapel, opera house and a vast and glittering Hall of Mirrors, as well as the lavish royal apartments. There is a magnificent collection of French art and furniture and a couple of smaller palaces in the park. It is still standing, and remains a symbol of the splendour of France.

Vertebrate is an animal with a backbone. Vertebrates form a division of the phylum Chordata, and include the fish, amphibians, reptiles, birds and mammals. It is among the vertebrates that the most complex, advanced and intelligent animals are to be found, and the group includes human beings. All vertebrates have a skull enclosing a brain, and a skeleton of cartilage or bone. Despite the size and importance of the vertebrates, they only comprise about five per cent of the whole Animal Kingdom.

Vertical Take Off and Landing aircraft, see VTOL aircraft.

Victoria (1819–1901), was Queen of Great Britain and Ireland (1837–1901) and Empress of India (1877–1901). The only child of George III's fourth son, the Duke of Kent, she ascended the throne on the death of her uncle, William IV. She took an active interest in her country's government and, after her marriage to Prince Albert of Saxe-Coburg and Gotha in 1840, relied greatly on his advice. After Albert's death she went into seclusion, which made her unpopular for a while, but was later persuaded to return to public life. She reigned during a period of increasing power and prosperity, and at the time of her death was recognized as the symbol both of a new concept of British monarchy and of the many achievements of her country in her lifetime.

Queen Victoria and Prince Albert attend the Great Exhibition of 1851 at the Crystal Palace.

Video is a system which records moving pictures and sound as magnetic patterns on a special tape. It was first used in 1956, in the USA. The pictures can come through either a television aerial or a video camera. Cinematographic film has to be processed before it can be seen. Pictures recorded on video tape can be seen on an ordinary television screen right away without being processed. Making copies of a video tape is easier and less costly than with film. *See also* Television.

Vietnam is a republic in south-east Asia. Capital, Hanoi; area about 300 000 sq km (127 400 sq miles). Formerly under French rule from 1884 Vietnam was divided in two in 1954, but the communist regime of North Vietnam never accepted the division and began to invade South Vietnam. The South received support from the USA against communist guerrillas, and in 1964 a full-scale war began. The US forces were unsuccessful and withdrew, 1972–1973, whereupon the country was reunited under the communist government in Hanoi.

Vietnam is a long, narrow country, only 50 km (31 miles) wide in parts. A rugged, largely forested mountain chain runs the length of it, but the deltas of the Red and Mekong rivers are very fertile and support a large population. Rice is the main crop; fish provide most protein.

Vietnam War was fought between communist North Vietnam and South Vietnam, supported by the USA. It lasted from 1957 to 1975. In the late 1950s Communist guerrilla forces from North Vietnam began to invade South Vietnam. The USA came to the assistance of South Vietnam in 1964, and by the late 1960s nearly 500 000 US soldiers were involved in the war, fighting both guerrillas and North Vietnamese army units. After the USA withdrew its troops in 1973, North Vietnam launched a strong offensive and overran the whole country. By 1976 the whole country was unified under a Communist government.

Vikings were Scandinavian seafarers and warriors. From about AD 800 they began raiding the coasts of Europe and Britain. They established settlements in England (eventually founding an Anglo-Danish dynasty), in Normandy, Iceland and Green-

A re-construction of the Sutton Hoo ship, in which a Viking king was buried. The ship was discovered by archaeologists in Suffolk, England. Among the treasures found inside was this king's helmet.

land, and, using their longships, are believed to have reached the coast of North America about AD 1000. Sailing eastwards they settled in Russia, creating the first Russian state, and they travelled as far south as Constantinople.

Virgil (70–19 BC), was a Latin poet. With Homer, he was the greatest poet of the Classical era, and has been regarded as a leading figure of literature in its noblest form. Born on a farm, he admired the rural life, and his *Georgics* (37–30 BC) is devoted to the praise of agricultural pursuits. His greatest work, written in the last 12 years of his life, is an epic, the *Aeneid*, which records the travels of the Trojan hero Aeneas who becomes the founder of the Roman race.

Virgin Islands are in the West Indies, east of Puerto Rico. The southern group (68) of these numerous but very small islands, including St Thomas and St Croix, were formerly Danish but have been governed by the USA since 1917. Capital, Charlotte Amalie; area about 340 sq km (130 sq miles). The northern group (36) form a British colony, and include the islands of Tortola and Virgin Gorda. Capital, Road Town; area about 130 sq km (59 sq miles). The British Virgin Islands were first settled by the Dutch but were taken over by English planters in 1666.

The chief products of the islands are sugar, rum, fruit and cattle, and the chief industry is tourism.

Virus is a microscopically small particle which seems to be on the border between living and non-living matter. It can be dried and then dissolved again just like certain chemicals, yet it is able to reproduce itself. Viruses cannot exist on their own; instead, they must invade a plant or animal cell. Once inside, the virus instructs the cell to produce more viruses which are released by rupture of the host cell wall. At the same time this causes disease to the infected animal or plant. Viruses are responsible for a large number of diseases in both plants and animals, such as tobacco mosaic in plants, and the common cold and smallpox in animals.

Vishnu, a Hindu god, is the second member of the Trimurti (trinity). Vishnu is the Preserver, the sustainer or 'saviour'. Whenever his enemies arise to threaten the peace of the world, Vishnu appears in order to prevent them. He is recognized in a number of avatars or incarnations, including those of Rama and Krishna which are especially important among modern worshippers. As Krishna he became associated especially with workers and peasants. His ninth incarnation is Buddha, which represents the Hindu characteristic of easily embracing other religions, and his tenth and last is Kalki, 'Judge of the Last Day', which is yet to come.

Vitamins are organic chemical compounds, essential in small quantities for life processes to occur. Vitamins usually just allow certain chemical changes to occur; they do not have food value themselves. A lack of any essential vitamin eventually causes illness and even death. Plants can manufacture their own vitamins, but animals must obtain theirs from food. Wild animals often eat the body organs (such as the liver) of their prey first, as these contain vital vitamins. One of the reasons a balanced diet is necessary is because certain vitamins are only present in particular foods. To obtain the full range of vitamins needed it is necessary to eat meat, fruit, dairy products and vegetables.

Vivaldi, Antonio (1678–1741), was an Italian composer. A priest and violin teacher, Vivaldi published his first composition in 1705. From 1710 he began to compose operas which, together with instrumental works like the famous *Four Seasons* concerto, brought him an international reputation.

Vivisection is the practice of performing experiments on living animals that involve surgical or other cutting operations. Most countries now have laws putting some limits on vivisection, but whether they are strict enough is a matter of fierce debate. People who defend vivisection say that it is important as a means of gaining scientific knowledge and testing drugs that may benefit (or harm) humanity. Anti-vivisectionists question our right to inflict suffering on other creatures. They also argue that the majority of experiments are unnecessary, and that the minority could be replaced by other experimental procedures which do not involve cruelty.

Vocal cords are folds of mucous membrane lying in the larynx (part of the throat) of vertebrates. Vibration of the cords as air is passed over them causes sounds to be created, giving animals a 'voice'. Muscles attached to the vocal cords can alter the tension of the cords and so vary the sound which is produced.

Volcano is a hole or crack through which molten rock, called magma, from inside the Earth pours out on to the Earth's surface. When magma forces its way to the surface, this is called a volcanic eruption. When the magma reaches the surface it is known as lava.

Sometimes the lava spreads out over a very wide area before cooling, and forms a large rock plateau. The lava can also form huge, cone-shaped mountains of rock, which are also called volcanoes.

Volcanoes which no longer erupt are said to be extinct. These which have not erupted for many years but are not extinct are called dormant. The rest are known as active volcanoes. There are over 500 active volcanoes on the Earth, some of which are under water.

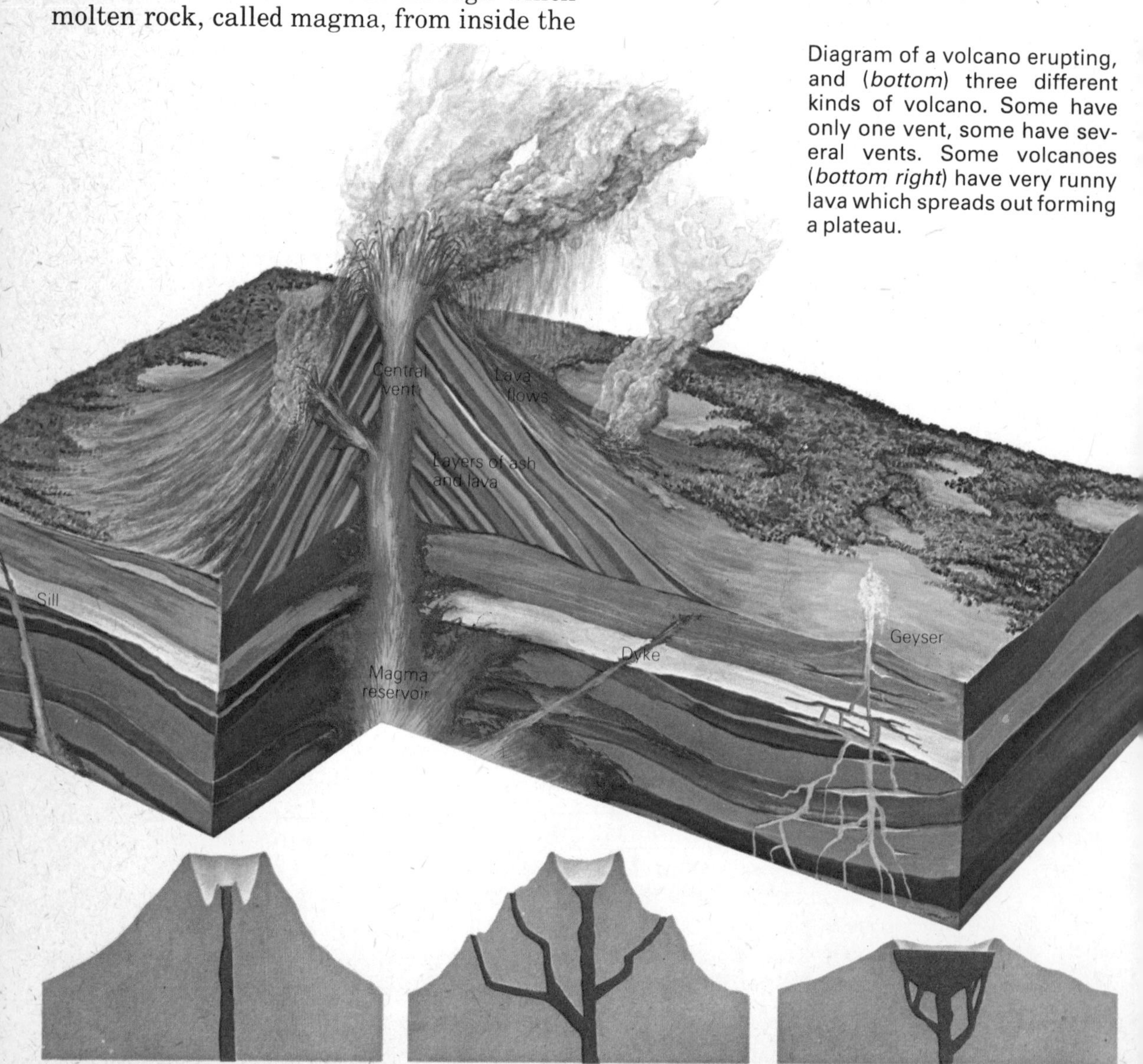

Diagram of a volcano erupting, and (*bottom*) three different kinds of volcano. Some have only one vent, some have several vents. Some volcanoes (*bottom right*) have very runny lava which spreads out forming a plateau.

Some volcanoes erupt with a huge explosion, shooting lava, ash, dust and gas into the air. The biggest explosion was the eruption of Krakatoa in Indonesia in 1883. Rocks were thrown 48 km (30 miles) into the air and the dust eventually spread right around the Earth. Tidal waves from the explosion killed 36 000 people.

The highest volcano in the world is Aconcagua in the Andes. It is 6960 m (22 834 ft) high and is extinct.

Vole is a small but heavily built rodent, which can be distinguished from a rat by its short muzzle and small ears, eyes and tail. They are up to 18 cm (7 in) long. The European field vole, the water vole, and the American meadow vole are some of the more common species. Voles tend to hide away in banksides and among vegetation by day, venturing forth at night to feed on seeds, bark and small animals. The water vole (sometimes incorrectly called the water rat) is a strong swimmer and also feeds on frogs and fish. Voles are the prey of animals such as owls.

Bank vole

Voltaire (1694–1778), was a French writer whose real name was François-Marie Arouet. The greatest figure among the *philosophes* ('intellectuals') of the age of Enlightenment, he wrote a great deal of prose and poetry. Today his most popular work is *Candide* (1759), a witty adventure story which is also a commentary on society. In his own day Voltaire's poetry, history and philosophical writings were more famous.

Volume is the amount of space an object takes up. The volume of a solid object is sometimes found by measuring it and using mathematics. For example, the volume of a brick is its length multiplied by its width and by its height. Volumes of solids can also be found by putting them in a full bowl of water and collecting the water that flows over. The water collected has the same volume as the solid object. The volume of a liquid can be measured by pouring it into a container marked with a scale. In the home, measuring jugs are used for this.

Voortrekker, see South Africa.

Vostok was a series of early Russian staffed spacecraft. On 12 April 1961 Vostok 1 carried Yuri Gagarin into space. He was the first man to travel in space. Vostok 6 (the last of the series) carried the first woman into space, when Valentina Tereshkova was launched on 16 June 1963. Vostok craft (all single seaters) were also the first staffed craft to rendezvous in space, when the Russians twice placed pairs of capsules in orbit and had them manoeuvre to within 5 km (3 miles) of each other. *See also* Gagarin, Yuri.

Voyager is a sophisticated unmanned spacecraft whose job is to examine the planets of Jupiter, Saturn and Uranus. Two Voyagers were launched from the USA in 1977. They passed Jupiter in 1979, sending back detailed colour pictures and other information about the planet and its many moons; Saturn was passed in 1980 and 1981, when the cameras captured the first close-up pictures of the famous rings; one of the craft will encounter Uranus, a planet about which very little is known. Both craft will eventually pass out of the Solar System, and they have been equipped with a message for any alien beings who might find them in centuries to come. Unlike the simple plaques affixed to the Pioneer craft, however, Voyager contains a special record disc, which (if played correctly) produces human speech, music, and a mass of photographic and scientific information about Earth.

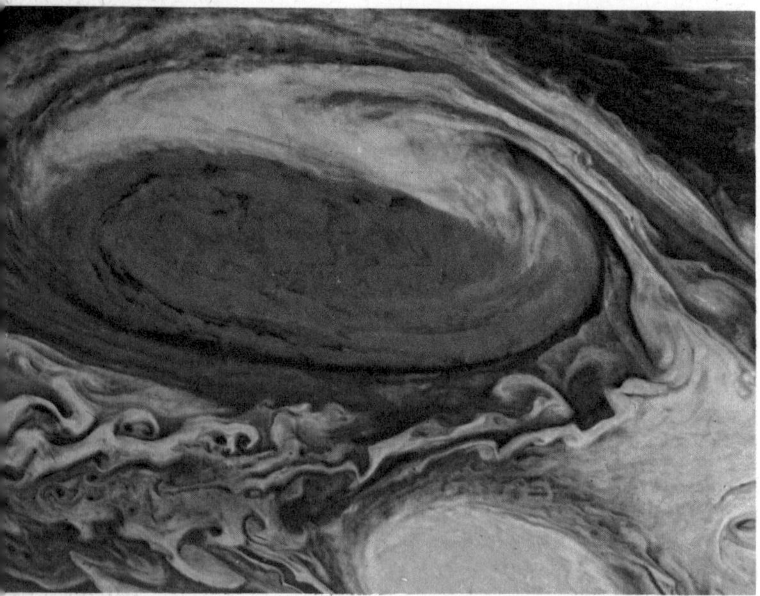

Close up of the red spot in Jupiter's clouds, taken by Voyager 1.

VTOL aircraft are Vertical take off and landing aircraft, a term which should include helicopters but is usually applied only to winged aeroplanes which can take off and land vertically. Only two such aircraft are in service, the British Harrier 'jump-jet' and a Russian design, both fighters. The Harrier uses a single jet engine with an exhaust under each wing. The exhaust nozzles can be swivelled through 100 degrees, to point directly downwards or even slightly forward, so that Harriers can hover or fly backwards. The Russian jet is less versatile, having separate engines pointing downwards to supply lift. *See also* STOL aircraft.

Vultures are birds of prey which, instead of catching their own food, swoop down to feed

VULTURES – THEIR HIERARCHY OF FEEDING

White-backed vultures feed on the flesh of the carcass

Lappet-faced vulture tears the carcass with its bill

White-backed vulture returns with white-headed vulture

Egyptian vultures pick the bones when the carcass is almost clean

on dead animals. The New World vultures (those from the American continents) include the condor, a huge South American bird. The true vultures are Old World birds (those from the Eastern hemisphere), and are placed in a different family. Most vultures have naked heads and necks. This is because they feed by probing deep inside the carcass with their hooked beaks, and feathers would soon become matted and useless. Vultures often soar aloft on their huge wings, keeping a watchful eye for food below. If they spot a dead animal, they may have to wait until other animals, such as hyenas, have had their fill before they can eat their share. *See also* Condors.

Wagner, Richard (1813–1883), was a German composer. One of the most important figures in the history of Western music, his influence on opera was enormous. In his 'music dramas', as he liked to call them, the orchestra became as important as the singers, and as a composer, he made tremendous demands on both. The subject of his operas was Germanic myth. His most popular operas are the *Ring* cycle (*Das Rheingold*, *Die Walküre*, *Siegfried* and *Gotterdämerung*, 1854–1874), *Tannhäuser* (1844), *Tristan und Isolde* (1859), *Die Meistersinger von Nürnberg* (1867) and *Parsifal* (1882).

Wales is a principality within the United Kingdom of Great Britain and Northern Ireland. Capital, Cardiff; area about 21 000 sq km (8100 sq miles).

History The country was settled by Celts in prehistoric times, and came under Roman rule during the 1st century AD. It resisted the Anglo-Saxon invasions, but was conquered by Edward I of England in 1284, becoming a principality. There were several rebellions against English rule but Wales was finally united with England in 1536.

Land and People Most of Wales is mountainous. The highest peaks are in Snowdonia, in the north where Snowdon, the highest mountain in England and Wales is 1085 m (3560 ft) high. The only large lowland areas are the southern plains, where most of the population and industry are concentrated, the Lleyn peninsula and the island of Anglesey, off the north-west coast. Central Wales, where the soil is poor with many bogs, has few people.

Economy The large, rich coalfields of South Wales support a number of large mining and industrial towns, containing about two-thirds of the total population. South Wales was once the largest coal-exporting region in the world, but it has been seriously affected by the economic recession of the 1970s and the 1980s. The steel industry has also diminished. In recent years many new industries have been introduced, but unemployment is still high.

Agriculture plays an important part in the economy though, due to the nature of the soils and climate, dairying and sheep-raising are more important than crop-raising. *See also* United Kingdom.

Counties of Wales

County	*Area* *sq km*	*sq miles*
Clwyd	2426	937
Dyfed	5765	2226
Gwent	1376	531
Gwynedd	3866	1493
Mid-Glamorgan	1019	393
Powys	5077	1960
South Glamorgan	416	161
West Glamorgan	816	315

Wallaby is a kangaroo-like marsupial found in Australia and New Guinea. It usually rests alone by day, sheltering from the sun by lying under a tree or large rock. It becomes active at night.

Rock wallabies are extremely agile, leaping around on rocky crags with ease. Other wallabies live in swamps, scrubland or woodland.

Walnut was originally a tree of eastern Europe and parts of Asia, but it has long been grown in southern and western Europe, as well as North America. There are also varieties grown in China and Japan. The fruit of the walnut is encased in a hard, protective shell and has long been prized for its taste. The nuts also provided oil for cooking and burning, and the husks were used for dyeing. The timber of the tree proved to be excellent for gun stocks and furniture.

Walpole, Sir Robert (1676–1745), was a British statesman. In 1721 he became First Lord of the Treasury and Chancellor of the Exchequer. As such he was effectively head of the government. He did much to increase national prosperity in order to strengthen the Hanoverian dynasty. He helped to establish the responsibility of the cabinet to Parliament, and did his best to avoid getting Britain involved in foreign wars. However, he was forced into conflict with Spain in 1739, and resigned two years later.

Walrus is a large seal which has huge tusks formed from the upper canine teeth. The tusks may reach a length of 70 cm (28 in), and are used for digging shellfish out of the seabed. Walruses live in herds consisting of cows, calves and young bulls. Outside the breeding season, the old bulls live in separate groups. A walrus may weigh up to a tonne.

Warm-blooded animals are those which can keep their bodies at a constant temperature, whatever the temperature of their environment. Birds and mammals are warm-blooded. This means that they are able to remain active for longer periods, and to live in colder places, than cold-blooded animals such as reptiles, since they do not require the environment to warm them up. Birds maintain their body temperature by means of feathers. Mammals use hair to retain and lose body heat in the same way. Blood vessels in the skin can control how much heat is lost from the blood, and this also keeps the body temperature level.

Wars

Name	*Date*	*Description*
Peloponnesian War	431–404 BC	Sparta and allies defeated Delian League led by Athens.
Punic Wars	264–146 BC	Rome eventually defeated and destroyed Carthage.
Crusades	1096–1291	Attempt by Christian countries to recover Jerusalem and the Holy Land.
Hundred Years' War	1337–1453	After acquiring much French land English finally defeated by French.
Wars of the Roses	1455–1485	Struggle between Houses of York and Lancaster for English crown.
Peasants' War	1524–1526	Unsuccessful attempt by German peasants to abolish serfdom.
Thirty Years' War	1618–1648	Caused by rivalry between Catholic and Protestant princes in Germany.
English Civil War	1642–1652	Struggle for power between king and Parliament.

Great Northern War	1700–1721	Caused by rivalry between Russia and Sweden for control of Baltic.
War of the Spanish Succession	1701–1713	Ended with crushing of French supremacy in Europe.
War of the Austrian Succession	1740–1748	Several European countries involved in conflict over succession to Emperor Charles VI.
Seven Years' War	1756–1763	War fought in Europe, India and North America. As a result Britain became a leading colonial power.
War of American Independence	1775–1783	The 13 North American colonies won their independence from Britain.
French Revolutionary and Napoleonic Wars	1792–1815	Revolutionary and later Napoleonic France fought various coalitions of European powers.
War of 1812	1812–1815	Inconclusive war between Britain and the USA.
Mexican-American War	1846–1848	Caused by American annexation of Texas. Mexico ceded California and New Mexico to the USA.
Crimean War	1853–1856	Britain, France, Turkey and Sardinia fought Russia in order to check Russian expansion in the Balkans.
American Civil War	1861–1865	Fought between Northern states and Confederacy, with North finally victorious.
Seven Weeks' War	1866	Prussian victory over Austria.
Franco-Prussian War	1870–1871	Prussian victory over France, leading to unification of Germany.
Spanish-American War	1898	Spain forced to cede Philippines and Puerto Rico to the USA.
Boer War	1899–1902	British victory over the Boer Republics.
Russo-Japanese War	1904–1905	Victory over Russia gave Japan control of Manchuria and Korea.
First World War	1914–1918	Fought between the Allies (France, Britain, Italy, Russia, USA, etc) and the Central Powers (Germany, Austria-Hungary, Bulgaria and Turkey).
Sino-Japanese War	1931–1945	Japanese occupation of Manchuria and attempts to invade other regions of China.
Abyssinian War	1935–1936	Italian invasion of Abyssinia (Ethiopia).
Spanish Civil War	1936–1939	Overthrow of Republican government by Fascist forces.
Second World War	1939–1945	Fought between the Allies (Britain, France, USSR, USA, etc) and Axis powers (Germany, Italy, Japan, etc).
Korean War	1950–1953	Fought between United Nations forces and North Korea supported by China.
Arab-Israeli Wars	1947–1948, 1956, 1963 and 1967	Fought between Israel and neighbouring Arab states.
Vietnamese War	1957–1975	Fought between North Vietnam and South Vietnam supported by the USA.

Warship is any seagoing vessel used for fighting, ranging in size from small river patrol boats, through frigates and destroyers, to the giant battleships and aircraft carriers which are the flagships of major modern navies.

Even the earliest ships were used by armed raiders or invasion forces, but specially-built warships were first used in large naval battles in the Mediterranean during the 1st century BC. By the 16th century, cannon were carried both in warships and merchant vessels, and the man o'war was developed to carry as many guns as possible in rows along the ship's side.

The development of iron ships and the introduction of steam engines transformed the warship, which soon became an armour-plated dreadnought carrying massive guns. The largest battleships ever built were two Japanese vessels sunk during the Second World War – each was 263 m (863 ft) long and 39 m (128 ft) wide – but even larger than these is the American nuclear powered aircraft carrier *Enterprise*, which is 336 m (1102 ft) long and 78 m (256 ft) wide, yet can travel at over 64 km/h (40 mph).

Courageous, a British cruiser converted to an aircraft carrier. Warships were converted before aircraft carriers started to be designed and built.

Modern warships often rely on powerful aircraft or guided missiles for their firepower, rather than simple guns. The most powerful warships of all are nuclear-powered submarines, which carry long-range missiles with nuclear warheads capable of devastating entire nations.

Wars of the Roses (1455–1485) were the struggle between the House of Lancaster (whose emblem was a red rose) and the House of York (whose emblem was a white rose) for the English throne. It began when Richard, Duke of York, claimed the throne of the Lancastrian king, Henry VI, whose grandfather, Henry IV, had been a usurper. A number of battles followed, with first one side and then the other gaining the upper hand. Eventually the Duke of York's son, Edward, secured the throne as Edward IV. After the death in the Tower of London of his son, Edward V, Richard III became King (1483), but was killed at Bosworth by the Lancastrian Henry Tudor. As Henry VII he united the two Houses by marrying Edward IV's daughter.

Warthog is an ugly-looking pig, inhabiting the open woodland and savannah of Africa. It gets its name from its warty face, which also bears two upward pointing tusks. When a warthog runs, perhaps after being disturbed whilst taking a mud bath, it holds its tail erect like a happy dog. Warthogs snuffle about for grass, berries and the occasional meal of carrion. They are about 76 cm (2.5 ft) at the shoulder.

Washington, George (1732–1799), was an American statesman and soldier. A landowner from Virginia, he began his military career in the French and Indian War. As a member of the Virginian House of Burgesses, he was a strong opponent of British colonial rule. When the American War of Independence broke out he was given command of the Continental Army (1775) against the British. He won victories which led to the British

George Washington, as first president of the USA, receives a copy of the constitution.

surrender at Yorktown in 1781 and American independence in 1783. He presided over the council which created the constitution of the USA. Unanimously elected his country's first President, he took office in 1789 and was re-elected in 1792.

Wasp is an insect related to bees and ants. Many wasps can be distinguished by their bodies which usually bear slender wings and have a narrow 'waist' between the thorax and the abdomen. Like their relatives the bees, female wasps bear a formidable sting. Also like bees, some species of wasp live socially in nests, while others are solitary, laying their eggs in banks or holes in the ground or parasitically on other animals. Wasps are found in many temperate and tropical parts of the world. *See also* Social insect.

Water is a colourless liquid. It is a chemical compound of hydrogen (H) and oxygen (O), and its formula H_2O. As a solid it is called ice, and as a gas, it is called steam. It is the most important liquid in the world. Over 70 per cent of the Earth is covered with water. Animals and plants contain a lot of water, and over two-thirds of the human body is water. After about four days without water to drink a human will die.

Most water is in the oceans. When this water is warmed it evaporates. It then rises and cools to form clouds made of water droplets. These droplets may then fall as rain or snow. Much of the water on the land finds its way into rivers and flows back into the oceans. This movement of water from and into the oceans is known as the water cycle.

Many industries use large amounts of water. Some industries dump their waste into rivers and seas, which can cause water pollution.

Apparently pure water can contain tiny animals and plants, and many chemicals. In many countries, water is cleaned and sterilized to remove these, before it is drunk.

Water power uses the energy that flowing water produces. For over 2000 years, water has been used to turn wheels. It was also used to drive pumps, saws and other machines. In some countries waterwheels are still used – to grind corn, for example.

Water is also used to turn the turbines which make electricity. The power produced is called hydro-electric power, and utilizes the water from natural waterfalls or from dams across rivers. The largest power station in the world is a hydro-electric one in the USSR.

The tides move the water in the seas and oceans, and the energy from this can be used to make electricity. The first tidal power station was built off Brittany, France, in 1966. Today many people are also looking at ways to use the energy of the waves in the seas and oceans. This is called wave power.

Waterloo, Battle of, was the final battle of the Napoleonic Wars. It took place near the village of Waterloo, a few miles south of Brussels, on 18 June 1815. The French army under Napoleon attacked an Anglo-Dutch army led by the Duke of Wellington before it could join forces with its Prussian ally. Wellington's army stood firm against repeated French onslaughts, and the arrival of the Prussian army later in the day ensured Napoleon's defeat.

Watt, James (1736–1819), was a Scottish inventor who made steam transport possible.

While working at Glasgow University he was given a model of a Newcomen steam engine to repair. He found many improvements that could be made and his version became more popular than the Newcomen engine, in Britain. It was used to pump water out of mines. After Watt had invented a mechanism which allowed his engine to turn a wheel around, it was used with machinery of all kinds. He also invented a governor, which controlled the steam supply in the engine and so controlled the speed of the engine. He designed a steam train, and his inventions were used to develop steam transport. He also made important contributions to other areas of science. The unit of power, the watt, is named in his honour.

Wattle tree, see Acacia.

Wave is caused in the sea by the wind blowing. The surface of the sea moves up and down as the waves travel into the shore.

Sound, light, radio and other sorts of energy are also said to travel in waves. The distance between the top of one wave and the top of the next is called the wavelength. The number of waves that travel past a point in one second is called the frequency.

Wavelength and frequency are related. A wave with a high frequency has a short wavelength. A wave with a low frequency has a long wavelength. *See also* Electromagnetic radiation.

Wavelength is the distance between the top of one wave and the top of the next one. The waves may be those in the sea, or sound waves, or electromagnetic waves. Wavelength is measured in metres. Light has wavelengths of less than a millionth of a metre. (Wavelengths of light are often measured in angstroms; one metre equals ten thousand million angstroms.) Radio wavelengths may be up to 1000 m (3280 ft) long.

In sound waves, long wavelengths are heard as low or deep sounds, and short wavelengths are heard as high sounds. *See also* Wave.

Weasel is a small, sinuous-bodied carnivore related to the stoat, which it closely resembles. The long body is carried on short legs and the small, triangular head bears short ears. The stoat ranges across Eurasia. It is active by day as well as by night, investigating any likely spot for prey, and then pouncing when in range. From three to eight young are born in spring, and are cared for by the parents until they are about fully grown.

Weaverbird is a small, seed-eating bird related to the sparrow, found throughout Africa. They get their name from their nests, which they make by weaving together grass and other plant material. The nests are suspended from branches and look like long pouches. Sociable weaverbirds build their nests tightly together so that from a distance the tree looks as though it is covered in thatch.

Stages of the building of a village weaver bird's nest. It uses palm fibres and first builds a ring (1), then enlarges it step by step (2) into an egg chamber (3). Then it constructs an antechamber (4) and finally an entrance to the nest (5).

Weevil is a beetle found all over the world. Its head is pulled out into a long, pointed snout. The feelers or antennae are often on the snout. Weevils use the mouthparts on the end of their snouts to bore into wood or seeds, and some species do enormous damage to fruit and stored grain. Some weevils also use their mouthparts to bore holes into which they lay their eggs.

Wellington, Arthur Wellesley, 1st Duke of (1769–1852), was a British soldier and statesman. He entered the army in 1787 and first saw active service in India. In 1808 he took command of the British forces in the Iberian Peninsula and eventually drove the French armies out of Spain in 1814. He was in command of the German, Dutch and British forces which defeated Napoleon at Waterloo in the following year. From 1818 he served in various Tory governments, becoming Prime Minister in 1828. His opposition to parliamentary reform made him unpopular and led him to resign in 1830, although he later served as Foreign Secretary.

Western Isles, see Hebrides.

Western Samoa is a sovereign state in the Southern Pacific Ocean. Capital, Apia; area about 2830 sq km (1093 sq miles). It consists of several islands and islets, four of them inhabited. It became independent in 1962 after being a trusteeship of the United Nations since 1946. The main products are coconuts, cocoa, taro (a herb grown for its root) and bananas.

West Germany, see Germany, Federal Republic of

West Indies is a chain of islands extending in a 4000 km (2500 mile) arc between North and South America. The West Indies enclose the Caribbean Sea – to the north lies the Gulf of Mexico and to the east the Atlantic Ocean. They can be divided into two main groups: the Greater Antilles (including Cuba, the Dominican Republic and Haiti, Jamaica, and Puerto Rico) and the Lesser Antilles (including Barbados and Grenada).

The West Indies got their name because when Christopher Columbus reached the islands in 1492 he thought he had sailed right around the world to India. Most West Indians are now of African descent – brought by force to the islands to work as slaves for European plantation owners – but there are also many people of mixed origin.

The West Indies are noted for their warm climate and for their ample, often seasonal, rainfall. Sugar and bananas are important exports and other cash crops (grown to be sold abroad) include coffee and cocoa. Cuba also grows tobacco. Some of the islands have mineral resources. There is nickel and iron ore in Cuba, bauxite (the ore from which aluminium is made) in Jamaica and Haiti, and oil in Trinidad.

Tourism is important on many of the islands and all of them produce maize and other foodstuffs for local consumption. Many people still live off the land. *See also* entries on individual countries.

Westminster Abbey is the coronation church of English monarchs, in London. Although in a sense the English national church, the design is French in character, and there is a resemblance to Reims cathedral, the coronation church of the French kings. Besides the tombs of famous people, Westminster Abbey contains some marvellous works of art, and the famous chapel of Henry VII represents the dramatic final flourish of the Gothic style in England. Originally founded in 960, the present building was begun in the 14th century, but much added to or altered later. The famous towers actually belong to the 18th century.

Whales, despite their fish-like appearance, are warm-blooded mammals. Their whole life is spent in the water, and their bodies are adapted for this way of life, being streamlined and almost hairless. The forelimbs form flippers, while the hind limbs have been lost completely. Whales swim by means of a massive horizontal tail which propels them through the water, often on non-stop migrations of thousands of kilometres (miles). To keep warm when swimming in freezing polar seas, whales have a thick layer of fat beneath their skin, called blubber.

There are two kinds of whales. Baleen whales, such as the mighty blue whale and the right whale, have no teeth. Instead, their gums are fringed with long, bristle-like structures called baleen. A baleen whale cruises among the masses of tiny shrimp-like creatures which abound in most waters, and gulps in great mouthfuls of them. Water is strained out through the sides of the baleen, but the food is trapped and swallowed.

Blue whale

The second group of whales is the toothed whales. These include the killer whale, sperm whale, porpoises and dolphins. Killer whales hunt other whales and seals, sometimes roaming in packs. Sperm whales feed on fish and squid, and may dive to great depths for up to an hour whilst they search for food. Porpoises and dolphins are among the most intelligent of mammals, and there are many instances of these animals coming to the rescue of drowning sailors. Dolphins are a favourite at many of the larger ocean aquaria.

Wheat is a cereal which is very widely grown. Its grain is ground to make flour, used in bread, cakes, pastry, pasta etc. Wheat has been cultivated in the Middle East since 7000 BC, and may be identified by its seed-head which is about 8 to 12 cm (3 to 5 in) long.

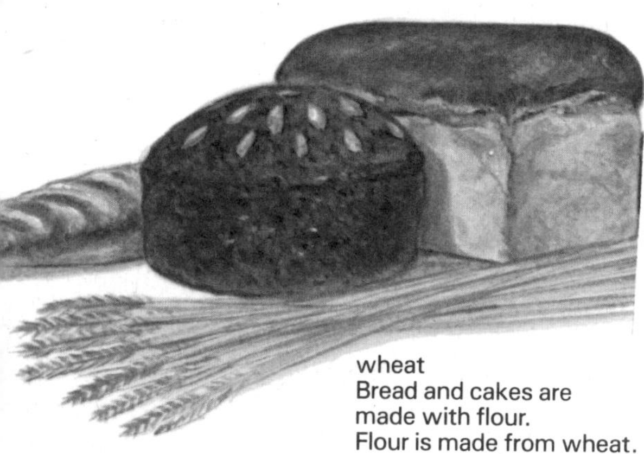

wheat
Bread and cakes are made with flour.
Flour is made from wheat.

Wheel was invented over 5000 years ago. Food and other goods could be moved much more easily using wheels. Later, turning wheels were used when making pots and jugs. They were also used to spin threads which could be woven into clothes. Wheels turned by water were used to water the land and grind corn.

Notched wheels, called gear wheels, are used to move machine parts. They are also used to change the speed at which machines move.

Today, wheels are used for many forms of transport, and in clocks, engines and other machines. *See also* Motion.

White dwarf is a very dense small star. It is so dense that a matchbox full of it would weigh ten tonnes. The first white dwarf was discovered in 1862, and is known as Sirius B. It is thought that a white dwarf comes from a red giant. A red giant has a hot dense core and cooler outer layers of gas. It slowly loses the outer layer of gas and becomes a planetary nebula. The hot core of the red giant becomes a white dwarf. It no longer produces any energy and slowly cools.

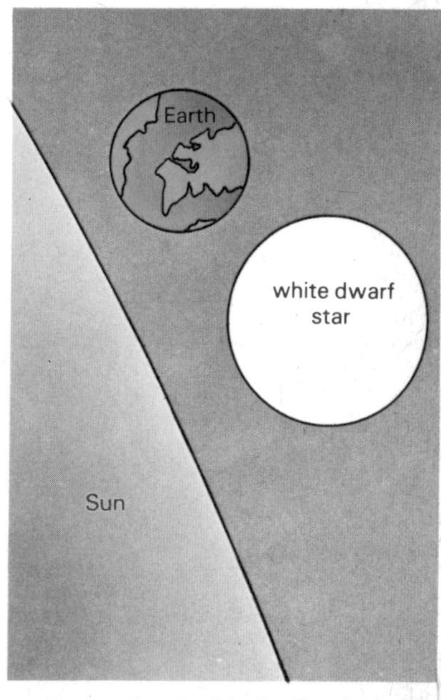

White dwarf compared with the Earth and a segment of the Sun.

White House is the official residence of the President of the USA, situated in Washington, D.C. It is a large, two-storey building, painted white, which was designed by James Hoban in 1792 and finished in 1800. During the British invasion in 1814 it was burned down, then rebuilt with porticoes in 1820.

White, Patrick (1912–), is an Australian novelist. Though set in Australia, his novels, like *Voss* (1957), *The Solid Mandalla* (1966) and *The Vivisector* (1970), are about universal things, not limited by place or time. Joyce was an early influence on White, whose novels are not always easy to read. In 1973 he was the first Australian to win the Nobel prize for literature.

Wild boar is found mainly in Asia, although it also occurs in Europe. The wild boar is similar in appearance to some domestic pigs except that it is slimmer, and is covered in dark, coarse fur. It has strong tusks with which it can defend itself, although it usually relies on its ability to run quickly through the woods to escape enemies. The wild boar is omnivorous, rooting about on the ground for food with its sensitive snout.

Wildebeest, see Gnus.

Wilhelm II (1859–1941), was Emperor of Germany (1888–1918). He was the grandson of Queen Victoria. Soon after coming to the throne he dismissed Otto von Bismarck as Chancellor, and he ruled autocratically, strongly opposing any extension of parliamentary power. Abroad he pursued an aggressive nationalistic policy, and supported colonial expansion. His actions alarmed other countries, and he bore considerable responsibility for the outbreak of the First World War. He abdicated in 1918 and died in exile in the Netherlands.

William I, the Conqueror (circa 1027–1087), was the first Norman King of England (1066–1087). He inherited the dukedom of Normandy from his father in 1035. On the death of King Edward the Confessor in 1066 he invaded England, claiming that Edward had promised him the English throne. He defeated the English near Hastings in October 1066 and was crowned King of England on Christmas Day. William gradually extended his control over the whole country, replaced English nobles and churchmen with Norman ones and established the feudal system in England.

William II (circa 1056–1100), was King of England (1087–1100). He came to the throne in succession to his father, William the Conqueror, and was known as Rufus. He spent much of his reign at war with his brother Robert, Duke of Normandy. In England he was a firm ruler who antagonized both the barons and the Church by his methods. He was killed by an arrow while out hunting.

William III (1650–1702) and Mary (1662–1694), were jointly King and Queen of England, Scotland and Ireland. As Prince of Orange, William led the resistance to the aggressive policies of Louis XIV of France. In 1688 the opponents of his father-in-law, James II, invited him to invade England. In 1689, after James II had fled, he and his wife Mary were together offered the throne. They ruled jointly until her death. In 1690 William defeated James at the Battle of the Boyne, and they devoted the rest of their reign to curbing the ambitions of Louis XIV.

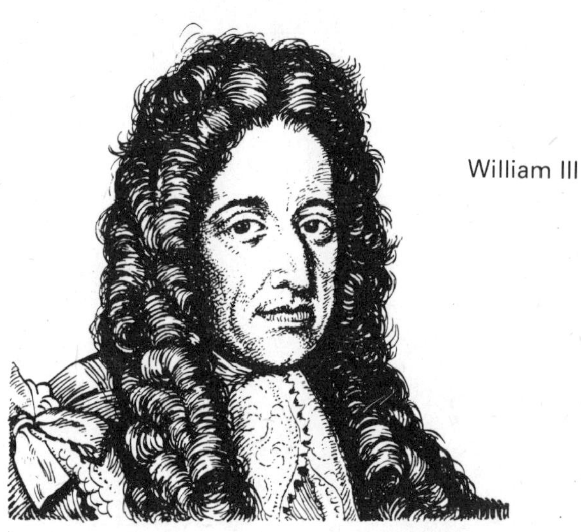

William III

William IV (1765–1837), was King of Great Britain and Ireland (1830–1837). He came to the throne in succession to his brother, George IV. During his reign the crisis over the Reform Bill arose, and he had to agree to create new peers in order that the Bill could be passed through the House of Lords (1832). Since his two children had died in infancy, on his death he was succeeded by his niece Victoria.

Willows grow throughout the cool regions of the Northern Hemisphere, usually preferring damp situations such as by river banks. The weeping willow is a beautiful tree whose thin branches droop as the tree grows, producing a green cascade of leaves. It is thought that the weeping willow originated in China.

The cricket bat willow is grown for its

wood which is used, as the name suggests, to make cricket bats. The common osier is a species often pollarded, and then cut to provide stems for basket weaving.

Wilson, Thomas Woodrow (1856–1924), was an American statesman, and President of the USA (1913–1921). Although he tried to keep his country out of the First World War, he was compelled to declare war on Germany in 1917 because of that country's policy of all-out submarine warfare. At the Peace Conference (1919–1920) he was largely responsible for setting up the League of Nations. In 1920 he was awarded the Nobel Peace Prize.

Wind is a mainly horizontal current of air above the Earth's surface, moving at various speeds up to those of hurricanes. Winds are generally described by the direction from which they blow – for example, a west wind blows from, not to, the west. Winds that are known by a particular name include the mistral (southern France), the föhn (Alps) and the sirocco (Mediterranean). *See also* Hurricane.

Wind instruments are musical instruments in which the sound is produced by the player blowing into the mouthpiece or through a reed. They fall into two groups, woodwind and brass, according to the material they were originally made of. (Nowadays, woodwinds are not always made of wood, nor brass instruments of brass.)

In an orchestra, the main woodwinds are: piccolo, flute, oboe, cor anglais, clarinet and bassoon. The brass are: trumpet, horn, trombone and tuba. There are of course many wind instruments besides these, ranging from the mouth organ or harmonica and the recorder (an important instrument in the Middle Ages) to the family of saxophones, an instrument invented by Adolphe Sax in the mid 19th century.

Windmills use the energy of the wind, to do work. They have sails which are turned around by the wind. Windmills were first built in Persia in the 7th century AD. They have been used, for example, to grind corn, to saw wood and to pump water. Windmills are still used in many parts of the world for these purposes, and to water crops and to drain water off land, and to make electricity.

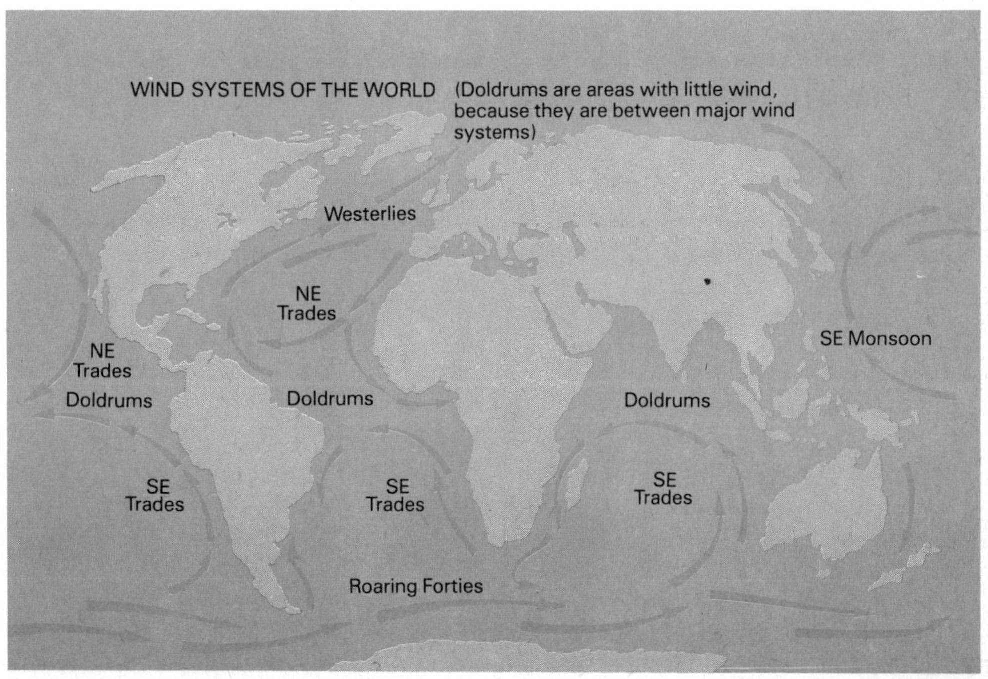

Wine is an alcoholic drink, usually made from the fermented juice of grapes. It comes in many varieties: red, white, rosé, sweet, dry, sparkling and still. The distinctive character of the different varieties depends on the species of grape, where they are grown and the method of cultivation. Wine can also be made from other substances, such as fruit or plants.

Winkles are small molluscs found on rocky shores in temperate parts of the world. They closely resemble snails, for they move about on a muscular foot and can withdraw into their spiral shell whenever they are exposed to dry air. At low tide, winkles can be found sheltering under seaweeds or in crevices or rock pools. When the tide comes in, however, they creep about, grazing on seaweeds and rasping pieces off using their horny tongues.

Wolf is possibly the ancestor of the domestic dog. Once widespread throughout the Northern Hemisphere, it is now confined to the remote parts of Europe, although it is still fairly common over much of Asia and North America. An adult is about 1.2 m (4 ft) long, shaggy coated with a bushy tail and powerful jaws. The wolf hunts by day, using its sense of smell to locate prey. Hunting in packs, wolves will run tirelessly after prey until it is cornered or exhausted. Then they attack as a group.

Wolf

Wolfe, James (1727–1759), was a British soldier. Entering the army in 1742, he saw action in the War of the Austrian Succession and in the Jacobite Rebellion of 1745. During the Seven Years' War he was sent to Canada and took part in the siege of Louisbourg. In 1759 he was given command of an expedition against Quebec. His victory over the French at the Plains of Abraham ensured British supremacy in Canada, but he was killed in the battle.

James Wolfe

Wolsey, Thomas (circa 1475–1530), was an English statesman and Cardinal. Of humble origins, he entered the service of Henry VIII in 1509, having first been Chaplain to his father, Henry VII. He became Archbishop of York in 1514 and Lord Chancellor and Cardinal in 1515 and effectively ruled England in the King's name. He amassed great personal wealth and built Hampton Court Palace. However, when he failed to persuade the Pope to let Henry VIII divorce Catherine of Aragon, he was arrested on a charge of treason, but died before he could be brought to trial.

Wolverine, or glutton, is a bear-like animal which lives in forests near the Arctic circle. It is not a bear, in fact, but the largest member of the weasel family, reaching a length of 1.2 m (4 ft). It certainly deserves its name of glutton, for it is a ferocious and greedy hunter, roaming at night for any animal it can find to eat. It will also pick fights with any other animal eating a meal – even much larger adversaries – and try to gobble down their food.

Wombat is a marsupial mammal related to the koala. Wombats are chunky, bear-like animals which spend most of their lives burrowing into the ground. They live in parts of Australia and Tasmania where they feed on

Above: common wombat.
Right: hairy-nosed wombat.

bark, roots and leaves, gnawing away at tough plant material with their rabbit-like front teeth. Wombats produce one offspring each year.

Wood is the hard, fibrous material found in perennial plants such as trees and shrubs. It forms the bulk of the tissues found beneath the bark. Wood is composed of masses of tiny tubes called xylem, which transport water from the soil to the leaves. As the tree or shrub grows, so more xylem is produced, making the plant wider. Eventually the xylem in the centre of the trunk or stem becomes crushed and no longer carries water. It is then called heartwood. The xylem which is still conducting water, and that which is added to the outside of the plant, is called sapwood.

Wood is extremely valuable to us for fuel and for timber. Hardwood is wood obtained from broadleaved or flowering trees, such as oak or mahogany. Softwood is wood which comes from coniferous trees, such as pine.

The word wood is also used to describe a small group of growing trees which, together with the other plants and animals associated with them, form a habitat. *See also* Forest.

Wood, Sir Henry (1869–1944), was an English orchestral conductor. He is remembered chiefly as the first conductor (and virtual creator) of the annual Promenade concerts ('the Proms') in London, from 1895 until his death. He was an influential figure in other ways, raising the standards of orchestral playing and introducing many unknown composers to British audiences.

Woodchuck is a North American rodent related to the squirrel. It grows to a length of 60 cm (2 ft) and can defend itself fiercely if cornered. The woodchuck inhabits woodland and grassland, where it likes to burrow at the first sign of approaching danger. It feeds on grasses and similar plants, and often becomes a pest by eating crops too.

Woodcock are ground-dwelling wading birds of Europe and North America. The plumage – black and brown, resembling fallen leaves – enables them to remain hidden on the woodland floor. Woodcock hunt by day among marshy ground for insects and other small creatures, probing about in the mud with their long, sensitive bills. The eyes of a woodcock are situated on the side of the head and so it can see behind as well as in front. At the first sign of danger the bird rises steeply away on its short wings.

Woodpeckers are usually handsome, brightly coloured birds up to about 40 cm (16 ins) in length. There are over 200 species distributed throughout most of the world except for Australasia. Woodpeckers are superbly adapted for clinging to tree trunks whilst they search for insects among the bark and foliage. They have claws which can grip well, and specially strengthened tail feathers which act as a prop to help hold the bird in position. Many species hammer at the bark of trees with their pointed beaks in order to chip pieces away to reach insects. They then lick the insects out of crevices with their long tongues. The nest is usually a hole in a tree, again chipped out with the beak.

Wool is the coat covering some animals, including sheep. It was the first fibre to be spun and woven into material. Wool is a warm fibre and keeps its shape well. It may be fine and smooth or rough and coarse.

Most smooth sheeps' wool comes from Australia, New Zealand and USSR. It is used to make serge, tweed and gaberdine clothes, and blankets. India produces most coarse sheeps' wool, and this is used mostly to make carpets.

The covering of goats and other animals is also called wool. Angora, Mohair and cashmere wools are made from the coats of goats. The llama and alpaca, relatives of the camel, have long fine coats which are used to make wool, too.

Woolf, Virginia (1882–1941), was an English novelist. She came from a literary family, was a leader of the Bloomsbury Group of intellectuals and, with her husband Leonard, founded the distinguished Hogarth Press (1917). A deeply serious, experimental novelist, her reputation stands high among literary critics. In novels such as *Jacob's Room* (1922), *Mrs Dalloway* (1925), *To the Lighthouse* (1927) and *The Waves* (1931), she moved away from traditional story-telling in an effort to capture the essence of mind and feeling. Besides novels she wrote critical essays.

Wordsworth, William (1770–1850), was an English poet, the greatest of the Romantic poets of the early 19th century. Though he soon abandoned his youthful enthusiasm for political revolution, and his atheism, he kept his love of nature and, after 1799, settled permanently in the Lake District, where he was born. He sought the deepest and purest feelings in human personality and believed they should be expressed in natural speech.

Lyrical Ballads (1798), published with Coleridge, caused a sensation by its simple language and choice of subjects. The *Poems* (1807) was perhaps his richest work. Thereafter, Wordsworth's poetry tended to decline, though his reputation grew. The *Prelude*, which contains some of his finest work, was written mainly before 1805 though not published until 1850.

World War, First (1914–1918), was fought between the Allies (Great Britain, France, Russia, Serbia, Montenegro, Japan and, later, Italy, Romania, Greece and the USA) and the Central Powers (Germany, Austria-Hungary, Bulgaria and the Ottoman Empire). Relations between France and Germany had remained tense since the Franco-Prussian War of 1870. Russia's desire for

influence in the Balkans was resented by Austria-Hungary, and Germany under William II had ambitions to become a world power. The declaration of war by Austria-Hungary on Serbia led to a general conflict. There followed several years of bitter fighting in Belgium and France, Russia, Italy, the Balkans and the Middle East. When Russia collapsed, the Germans were able to bring more troops from their eastern front to western Europe, but the intervention of the USA on the Allied side proved decisive, and the Central Powers were forced to surrender.

World War, Second (1939–1945), was fought between the Allied Powers (Great Britain, France and, later, the USSR and USA) and the Axis Powers (Germany, Italy and Japan). It began on 1 September 1939 when Nazi Germany invaded Poland. Britain and France had promised to help Poland if it should be attacked and therefore declared war on Germany. The Germans rapidly overran Poland and in 1940 occupied Norway, Denmark, the Low Countries and France. Italy entered the war on Germany's

The Battle of Britain, 1940.

side in 1940, and in 1941 the Germans launched their invasion of Russia. Japan's attack on Pearl Harbor in December 1941 brought the USA into the war, which now became a world-wide conflict. The war in Europe ended with Germany's surrender in May 1945. Later the same year, after the dropping of atomic bombs on Hiroshima and Nagasaki, the Japanese surrendered.

Worm is a name given to many types of animal, all very different to each other. The simplest types of worms are the flatworms. These are generally leaf-like creatures living in ditches and other watery places. The flatworms also include the parasitic liver flukes and tapeworms.

The roundworms are also common animals – in fact, the world's most numerous animal is a type of roundworm. Some species of roundworm are parasitic, causing many diseases in plants and animals. Others are non-parasitic, living in the soil.

In the sea and on the seashore live many other kinds of worm, for instance ribbon worms, which are long, thin creatures that often feed on other animals.

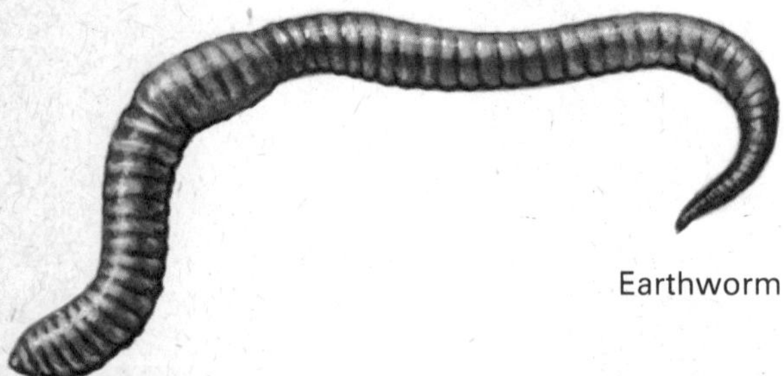

Earthworm

The best-known group of worms, however, is the annelid worms. They get their name from the way their bodies are arranged in segments. Annelids include the blood-sucking leeches, the burrowing earthworms of gardens and meadows, and the bristleworms. Most bristleworms live on the seashore where some species burrow in the mud and filter small food particles, and others are fierce hunters of small creatures.

Wren, Sir Christopher (1632–1723), was England's greatest architect. An able scientist, he was professor of astronomy at Oxford, where he designed the Sheldonian Theatre, before becoming surveyor of royal buildings.

Sir Christopher Wren and St Paul's Cathedral.

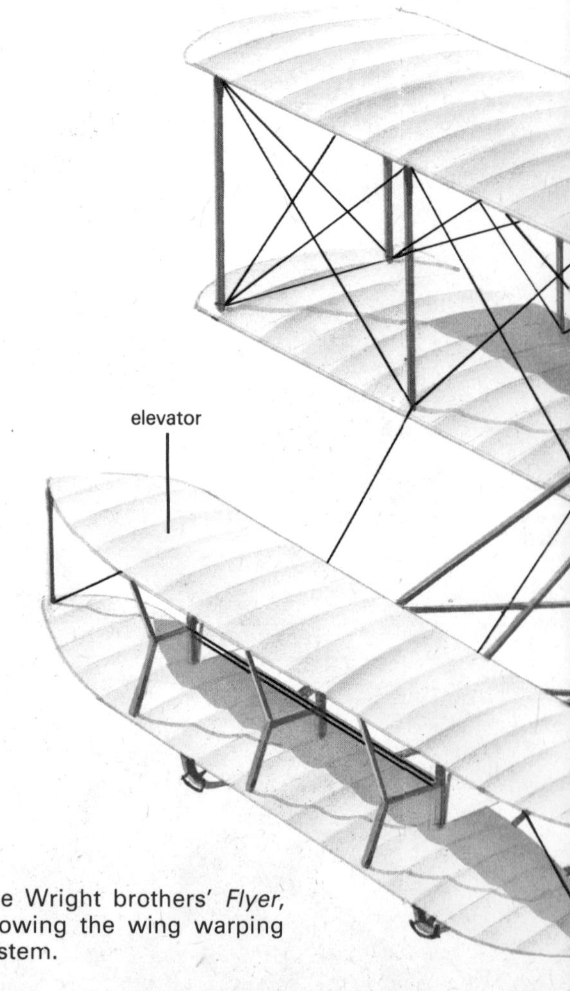

The Wright brothers' *Flyer*, showing the wing warping system.

The Fire of London (1666) gave him his great chance, and though his ambitious plans for redesigning the city were blocked, he built at least 50 churches and – his most famous achievement – St Paul's Cathedral. Wren's style was in the Classical tradition, but he was also influenced by French Baroque. His church architecture (including St Paul's) represented a sharp break with English tradition, which could only have been accomplished by a man with great – and justified – confidence in his own abilities.

Wright brothers, Wilbur (1867–1912) and Orville, (1871–1948), were the first people to fly a controlled heavier-than-air machine. They were American bicycle manufacturers who became interested in flight and carried out many experiments with kites, gliders and powered models. On 17 December 1903 their *Flyer 1*, powered by a 12 hp petrol engine of their own design, took to the air and flew 260 m (853 ft) at Kitty Hawk, North Carolina. Within two years, *Flyer* was able to travel 39 km (24 miles) in 36 mins. Their aircraft was controlled by pulling wires which 'warped' each fabric-covered wing, altering its lift and turning the aircraft.

Wright, Frank Lloyd (1869–1959), was the greatest American architect of his age. He first gained a reputation as a designer of houses which showed great respect for place, building materials, purpose, etc. This was not always true of larger projects, like the astounding Guggenheim Museum in New York. His 'prairie houses' looked like part of the landscape. He was also very inventive, using decorative concrete blocks when bricks were scarce. Always new and exciting, he belonged to no international style or movement.

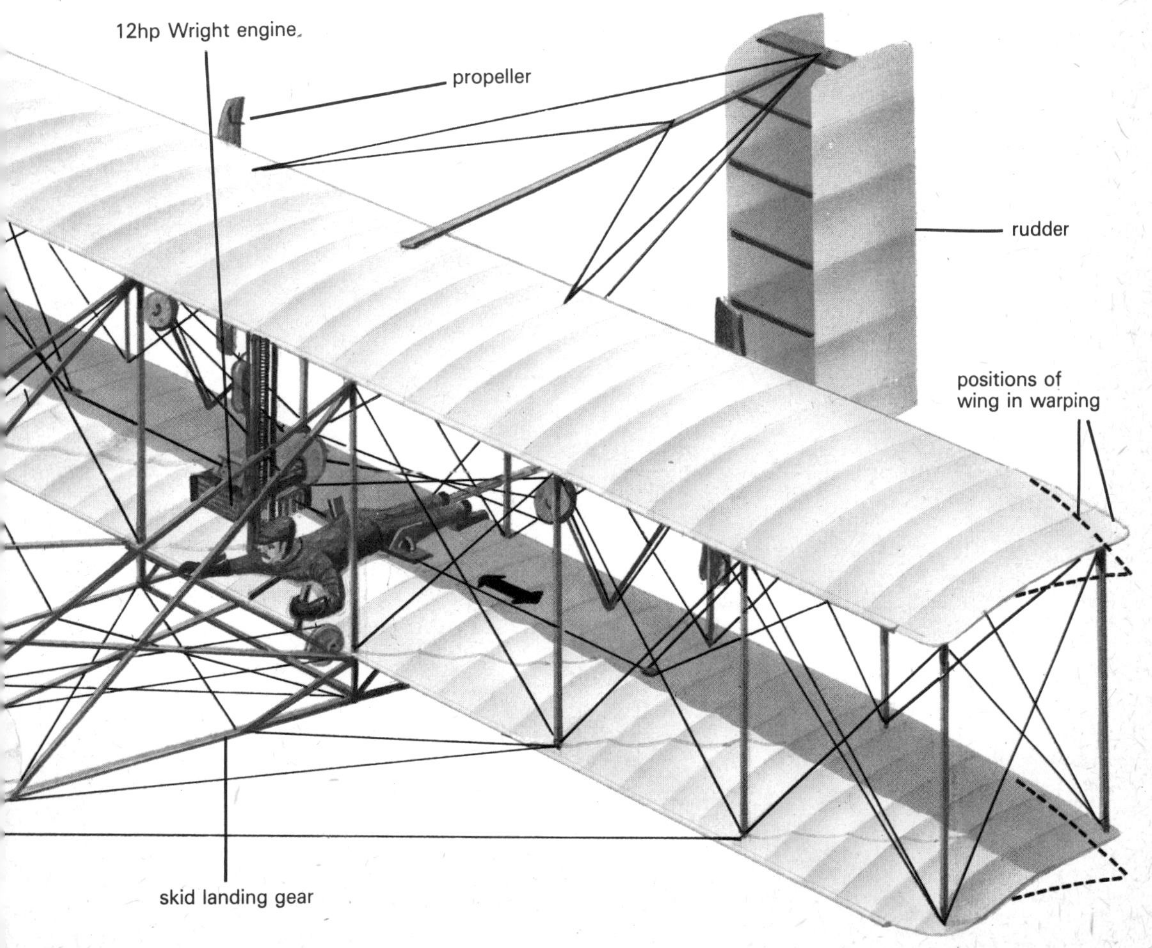

Xavier, Saint Francis (1506–52), was a Spanish missionary. He was one of the original members of the religious order known as the Jesuits, who produced many great missionaries, and he is known as 'the Apostle to the Indies'. After some years in India, he brought Christianity to Japan in 1549. Before he was forced to leave in 1550, he gained many converts, and he was travelling to China when he died.

Xerxes (died 465 BC), King of Persia (486–465 BC), came to the throne in succession to his father Darius the Great. After suppressing a rebellion in Egypt he invaded Greece and defeated the Spartans at Thermopylae in 480 BC. However, the destruction of his fleet at Salamis the same year and his defeat by allied Greek forces at Plataea in 479 forced him to withdraw. He was subsequently assassinated.

Xhosa is a cluster of related tribes living in the Transkei district of Cape Province, South Africa. They were granted self-government in 1963. The Xhosa form part of the Cape, or Southern, Nguni group of Bantu-speaking tribes, all of whom speak dialects of Xhosa. They are agriculturalists, keeping some cattle.

X-rays are a form of electromagnetic radiation. They have a much shorter wavelength than light. Light cannot go through our bodies but X-rays can. They are used in medicine to look at bones and organs, and to treat some diseases. Too many X-rays will harm us.

X-rays were discovered in 1895 by Wilhelm Röntgen. He was experimenting with a tube, similar to the television tube of today. The tube gave off invisible rays which turned a photographic plate black. When he put his hand between the tube and a photographic plate, he found he had pictures of the bones of his hand.

Persepolis, a new city built by Darius, Xerxes's father.

X-rays are used in industry, for example, to examine metal parts for flaws and cracks; and in art, to examine old paintings. Crystals are studied using X-rays, and this is known as X-ray crystallography. *See also* Radiography; Wavelength.

X-ray source is an object which gives out X-rays. Astronomers look for X-ray sources in space. Objects in space give out many different sorts of radiation. For thousands of years astronomers have looked at one sort of radiation, light. Much more recently, they have looked at longer wavelength radiation, radio waves. This is radioastronomy. Now they also look at shorter wavelength radiation, such as X-rays. X-ray telescopes orbit the Earth in satellites.

Very hot gases give out X-rays. X-ray sources include exploded stars called supernovae, and pulsars. One X-ray source, Cygnus X-1, may have a Black Hole.

Yak is a large, shaggy coated member of the cattle family which lives in the cold regions of Tibet. It has long horns which spread out sideways from its head, sometimes to a length of over 1 m (3 ft). Apart from the huge humped back, its body shape is like a cow's. The yak feeds on the sparse grasses which grow in the region, and is often domesticated for use as a beast of burden and for milk.

Yam is the swollen, tuber-like root of a climbing plant which is grown for food in many of the warmer parts of the world. The root contains mainly starch. In some parts of the world the yam is known as the sweet potato.

Yeast is a widely distributed, single-celled fungus. Yeasts reproduce by budding – one cell grows a tiny replica of itself which then becomes free and develops into a full-sized cell. They are vital plants in the brewing and baking industries. In brewing, yeasts can turn sugar into alcohol. In baking they produce carbon dioxide, which causes the dough to rise.

Yeats, William Butler (1865–1939), was an Irish poet, born in Dublin. He reacted against the harsh materialism of Victorian culture and turned towards Irish myth and folklore, major themes of his early works. From 1899 to 1909 he was busy building up the Abbey Theatre, the Irish national theatre in Dublin, for which he wrote many plays (notably *Cathleen ni Houlihan*, 1902). His poetry grew more severe, less Romantic, and most of his best work was written in his last 20 years, during which his reputation as one of the finest poets in English literature was established. Major works of W. B. Yeats' last period are *The Wild Swans at Coole* (1919), *The Tower* (1928) and *The Winding Stair* (1933).

Yemen is a region in south-west Arabia, divided between the Yemen Arab Republic (capital, Sana'a; area about 195 000 sq km (73 300 sq miles) in the north and the People's Democratic Republic of Yemen (capital Aden; area about 287 700 sq km (11 000 sq miles) in the south. South Yemen was formerly the British colony of Aden and became independent in 1967.

The region is hot and dry, merging into desert in the interior. There are many fertile valleys and oases, and irrigation is used all over the region. Cotton is grown for export, and there is oil-refining in South Yemen. Cattle-raising and fishing are important activities, but there are few mineral resources and little industrial development.

Yew is often seen as a neatly clipped hedge or shrub, but if left to grow naturally it will develop into a 12 m (40 ft) high tree. The yew is an evergreen tree with needle-like leaves. The leaves, seeds and branches are all poisonous. Yews do not produce cones, but instead produce a bright red, jelly-like cup called an aril, in which the seeds develop.

Yew timber is used for wood veneers, fences and gate posts. Once, it was highly prized for making longbows. Yews used to be planted in English graveyards as a pagan symbol of immortality, and many can still be seen in these places.

Yolk is the food store in animal eggs, which the developing embryo feeds upon. It consists of protein and fats. In chicken eggs, yolk is the yellow part we see when we break an egg. The yolk is not always enclosed within the egg shell, however. In fish such as trout, the tiny hatched fish swim at first with yolk sacs suspended beneath their throats.

Inside a turkey's egg at 23 days, showing how the embryo feeds off the yolk.

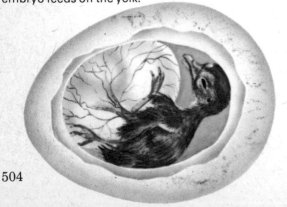

Yugoslavia is a federal republic in south-east Europe, on the Adriatic Sea. Capital, Belgrade; area about 256 000 sq km (98 800 sq miles).

History In 1882, Siberia became a kingdom after gaining independence from the Ottoman Empire. Serbia and Austria quarrelled and the Austrian archduke, Franz Ferdinand, was murdered in 1914, bringing about the First World War. After the war, the Austrian territories of Croatia, Slovenia, Bosnia and Hercegovina were united with Serbia to form the kingdom of the Serbs, Croats and Slovenes. Montenegro also joined. In 1929 a dictatorship was established and the name of the country was changed to Yugoslavia. During the Second World War, the country was occupied by the Germans. By the end of the war a resistance leader, Josip Broz, called Tito, was the dominant leader, and became head of a communist republic in 1945.

Land and People Yugoslavia is largely mountainous, except for the Danube plains in the north. The Adriatic coast is spectacular, attracting many tourists. In general, the climate is hot in summer but cold in winter. Besides the Serbs, Croats and Slovenes, there are several other large minorities of people such as Macedonians, Montenegrins and Albanians. There are three official languages, but some people speak none of them. Religious background is equally mixed.

Economy The economy is organized mainly on a communal system. There is, for instance, an interesting form of power-sharing which allows workers to influence the way their factory is run. Agriculture is still the largest occupation, mainly in the north and in river valleys, and there are many private holdings. Yugoslavia produces cereals and root-crops and plums, from which plum brandy is made. Mineral resources are small but very varied and there is some oil and natural gas, as well as ample hydro-electric potential. Manufacturing has increased rapidly since 1945, mainly in the north-west.

Z

Zaire is a republic in Central Africa. Capital, Kinshasa; area about 2345400 sq km (895300 sq miles).
History The region was explored by Henry Morton Stanley in the 1870s. The Congo Free State, which was ruled personally by King Leopold of the Belgians, was established in 1885. It was annexed to Belgium as the Belgian Congo in 1908. In 1960 it became an independent republic, later changing its name to Zaire.
Land and People This huge country consists mainly of the basin of the great Zaire River, ringed by mountains. The land is mostly rather low, except for the Katanga plateau. The north is covered in dense forest, and the south is mainly savannah. Temperatures throughout are high. There are several national parks to protect the rich wild life.

The people are a mixture of races, and include Pygmies in the forests. At least 200 languages or dialects are spoken in Zaire. The majority of people are poor farmers.
Economy Agriculture is generally poor, but Zaire has great mineral resources. It is the world's largest producer of industrial diamonds and cobalt, a major source of many other minerals, and Katanga is rich in copper. Some plantation crops, such as rubber, coffee, tea, cotton and peanuts are exported. Communications are very difficult in the dense forest, and the Zaire River is still the main transportation route, but it is interrupted by rapids.

Zambezi is a river in south-east Africa. It rises in north-west Zambia and flows south and east to the Indian Ocean in Mozambique. Length about 3540 km (2200 miles). The Victoria Falls on the Zambezi are the largest in the world (maximum drop 108 m/355 ft; width over 1700 m/5580 ft). The Kariba and Cabora Bassa dams provide valuable power and irrigation for Zambia and Zimbabwe, but the river, like most African rivers, is of limited use for transportation.

Zambia is a republic in south-central Africa. Capital, Lusaka; area about 753000 sq km (290600 sq miles).
History It was formerly the British colony of Northern Rhodesia, administered by the British South Africa Company from 1889–1923. It became independent under President Kaunda in 1963.
Land and People Zambia is a landlocked country, mainly plateau over 1000 m (3280 ft) above sea level, with mountains in the north-east. The altitude moderates the tropical climate, but rainfall is low in the south and, despite several large rivers, water supply is a major problem. The people come from several different groups. The Tonga live in the south, and another large group, the Bemba, live in the north-east. Most people speak one of the six Bantu languages, but there are over 60 dialects. English is spoken by many people.
Economy Most people live in villages and are poor farmers and herdsmen, but Zambia has many mineral resources, especially copper which is much the most valuable export. Efforts are being made to develop other minerals and agriculture. There is abundant woodland and teak is a minor export.

Zebra is a large, hoofed mammal related to the horse. It is easily recognized by its attractive black and white striped body. All three species of zebra live in Africa. The mountain zebra is the smallest of the species, and prefers rocky terrain in southern Africa. The common zebra and Grevy's zebra live on the plains. Zebras form large grazing herds usu-

Zebras grazing

ally led by an old stallion, and are constantly on the lookout for their greatest enemy, the lion.

Zeppelin was the name given to German airships during the years before the Second World War, named after Graf Ferdinand von Zeppelin (1838–1917), the German count who was responsible for developing the hydrogen-filled airship during its pioneer days. A Zeppelin was usually cigar-shaped, and any balloon or airship of that general shape is sometimes still called a Zeppelin.

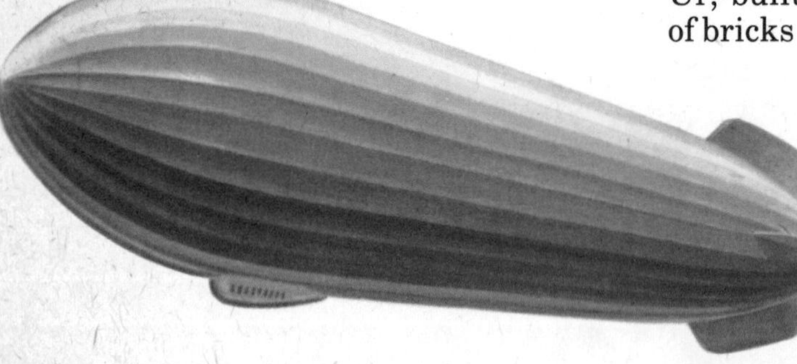

Left: The Graf Zeppelin, which made a record flight around the world in 1929.

Zeus, in Greek myth, was the father of the gods, who became identified with the Roman Jupiter. After the victory over the Titans, Zeus and his brothers divided the universe between them, Hades taking the Underworld, Poseidon the Sea and Zeus the Earth. His wife is Hera, and among their children are Ares and Hephaestus. Zeus, however, had countless love affairs (fiercely resented by Hera) and a great many other children, including several lesser gods and goddesses and many of the mythical Greek heroes.

Like all the ancient gods, Zeus had many human characteristics. When he lost his temper he hurled his thunderbolt, causing thunder and lightning, and he was pictured as a powerful, bearded man, often attended by an eagle. He was worshipped widely, and carried great authority.

Ziggurat is a temple tower of a kind built in ancient Assyria and Babylon. A ziggurat resembles a pyramid except that it rises in stages, not in a continuous line. Ramps lead from one stage to the next and there is a shrine or altar at the top. The ziggurats of Ur, built before 2000 BC, were constructed of bricks over hard clay, and faced with tiles.

Zimbabwe is a republic in south-central Africa. Capital, Harare, area about 390 000 sq km (151 000 sq miles).
History As Southern Rhodesia, it was administered by the British South Africa Company from 1889–1923. It became a self-governing colony in 1923. In 1965 it declared itself independent. After a guerrilla war, elections took place in 1980 and a majority black government was established. The country was renamed Zimbabwe after some stone ruins which may be the remains of an ancient Afri-

can civilization. Salisbury was renamed Harare in 1982.

Land and People Zimbabwe is mostly high veldt – undulating savannah. The east is more mountainous and forested, and the valleys of the Zambezi and Limpopo Rivers cut through the country. There are many wild animals and game reserves.

The two main groups of people are Shona and Ndebele (Matabele). There is still a large white minority, of mainly British origin, and English is widely spoken.

Economy Zimbabwe is suffering from the recent political upheavals, but has great potential in agriculture and mining. Plantation crops such as tobacco are exported, and there are large mineral reserves including chrome, lithium, iron, coal and gold. A hydro-electric scheme on the Zambezi river provides most of the country's power.

Zinc is a soft, blue-white metal. It has the chemical symbol Zn. It is found in the ore sphalerite. Lead and zinc ores are often found and mined together.

Iron and steel are sometimes coated with zinc to stop them rusting. This is called galvanizing.

Zinc is used to make the cases of dry batteries for torches, radios and other equipment. It is mixed with other metals to make many alloys, such as brass, which is an alloy of copper and zinc. Some types of zip fastener are made from another zinc alloy.

Zinc salts are used in paints and medicines; zinc carbonate is also called calamine and is used in calamine lotion.

Zoroastrianism is a Persian (Iranian) religion which survives today among the Parsis (Parsees) of India. It was founded by the Prophet Zarathustra (Zoroaster) who lived about the 6th century BC, and it was an important influence throughout the history of the Persian empire.

According to Zarathustra, there are twin spirits in the universe which are good and evil, and life is a constant battle between them. Zoroastrianism has four basic rules for the believer: they should be aware of the One God, Ahura Mazda, at every moment of their life and should act as if under his immediate guidance; they should be generous and charitable; they should be obedient; they should till the soil themselves.

A Zulu warrior from the uMbonambi which fought against the British in 1879.

Zulus are a Bantu people of Natal, South Africa. In the early 19th century, under the leadership of Shaka, they conquered the surrounding tribes and created the powerful Zulu nation, which was based upon efficiently organized army regiments. The Zulus came into conflict with both British and Boers. They were eventually defeated by the British who annexed their country and made it part of South Africa. In 1972 the South African government created a Zulu homeland. *See also* Shaka.

Countries of the world and their capitals

Australasia

For map of Australia, New Zealand and surrounding islands, see page 50.

Country	Capital
Australia	Canberra
Fiji	Suva
French Polynesia	Papeete
Kiribati	Tarawa
Nauru	Nauru
New Zealand	Wellington
Cook Islands	Avarua
Niue	Alofi
Ross Dependency	—
Papua New Guinea	Port Moresby
Samoa	
Eastern	Pago Pago
Western	Apia
Solomon Islands	Honiara
Tonga, etc.	Nuku'alofa
Tuvalu	Funajuti
Vanuatu	Vila

Africa

For map of Africa, see page 13.

Country	Capital
Algeria	Algiers
Angola	Luanda
Benin	Porto Novo
Botswana	Gaborone
Burundi	Bujumbura
Cameroon	Yaoundé
Cape Verde Islands	Praia
Central African Rep.	Bangui
Chad	Ndjaména
Congo	Brazzaville
Djibouti	Djibouti
Egypt	Cairo
Equatorial Guinea	Malabo
Ethiopia	Addis Ababa
Gabon	Libreville
Gambia	Banjul
Ghana	Accra
Guinea	Conakry
Guinea Bissau	Bissau
Ivory Coast	Abidjan
Kenya	Nairobi
Lesotho	Maseru
Liberia	Monrovia
Libya	Tripoli
Madagascar	Antananarivo
Malawi	Lilongwe
Mali	Bamako
Mauritania	Nouakchott
Mauritius	Port Louis
Morocco	Rabat
Mozambique	Maputo
Niger	Niamey
Nigeria	Lagos
Rwanda	Kigali
St Helena	Jamestown
Ascension Is.	Georgetown
Tristan da Cunha	Edinburgh
São Tomé e Principe	São Tomé
Sénégal	Dakar
Seychelles	Victoria
Sierra Leone	Freetown
Somali Democratic Republic	Mogadiscio
South Africa	Pretoria Cape Town
S.W. Africa (Namibia)	Windhoek
Sudan	Khartoum
Swaziland	Mbabane
Tanzania	Dodoma
Togo	Lomé
Tunisia	Tunis
Uganda	Kampala
Upper Volta	Ouagadougou
Zaïre	Kinshasa
Zambia	Lusaka
Zimbabwe	Harare

Asia

For map of Asia, see page 40.

Country	Capital
Afghanistan	Kabul
Bahrain	Manama
Bangladesh	Dacca
Bhutan	Thimpu
Brunei	Bandam Seri Begawan
Burma	Rangoon
China	Peking
Hong Kong	Victoria
India	New Delhi
Indonesia	Jakarta
Iran	Tehran
Iraq	Baghdad
Israel	Jerusalem
Japan	Tokyo
Jordan	Amman
Kampuchea	Phnom Penh
Korea	
North	Pyongyang
South	Seoul
Kuwait	Kuwait
Laos	Vientiane
Lebanon	Beirut
Malaysia	Kuala Lumpur
Maldives	Malé

Mongolia (Outer)	Ulan Bator
Nepal	Katmandu
Oman	Muscat
Pakistan	Islamabad
Philippines	Manila
Qatar	Doha
Saudi Arabia	Riyadh
Singapore	Singapore
Sri Lanka	Colombo
Syria	Damascus
Thailand	Bangkok
* Turkey	Ankara
United Arab Emirates	—
* USSR	Moscow
Vietnam	Hanoi
Yemen	Sana'a
Yemen PDR	Aden

** Turkey and the USSR are partly in Asia and partly in Europe.*

Europe

For a map of Europe, see page 176.

Country	Capital
Albania	Tirana
Andorra	Andorra La Vella
Austria	Vienna
Belgium	Brussels
Bulgaria	Sofia
Cyprus	Nicosia
Czechoslovakia	Prague
Denmark	Copenhagen
Finland	Helsinki
France	Paris
Germany	
West	Bonn
East	E. Berlin
Gibraltar	Gibraltar
Greece	Athens
Hungary	Budapest
Iceland	Reykjavik
Irish Republic	Dublin
Italy	Rome
Liechtenstein	Vaduz
Luxembourg	Luxembourg
Malta	Valetta
Monaco	Monaco
Netherlands	Amsterdam
Norway	Oslo
Poland	Warsaw
Portugal	Lisbon
Romania	Bucharest
San Marino	San Marino
Spain	Madrid
Sweden	Stockholm
Switzerland	Berne
* Turkey	Ankara
United Kingdom of Great Britain and Northern Ireland	London
* USSR	Moscow
Yugoslavia	Belgrade

** Turkey and the USSR are partly in Europe and partly in Asia.*

North America
including central America and the West Indies

For map of North and Central America, see page 331.

Country	Capital
Anguilla	—
Antigua and Barbuda	St John's
Bahamas	Nassau
Barbados	Bridgetown
Belize	Belmopan
Bermuda	Hamilton
Canada	Ottawa
Cayman islands	George Town
Costa Rica	San José
Cuba	Havana
Dominica	Roseau
Dominican Rep.	Santo Domingo
El Salvador	San Salvador
Grenada	St. George's
Guadeloupe	Point à Pitre
Guatemala	Guatemala
Haiti	Port-au-Prince
Honduras	Tegucigalpa
Jamaica	Kingston
Martinique	Fort-de-France
Mexico	Mexico City
Monserrat	Plymouth
Nicaragua	Managua
Panama	Panama City
St Kitts-Nevis	Basseterre
St Lucia	Castries
St Vincent	Kingstown
Trinidad and Tobago	Port-of-Spain
Turks and Caicos Is.	Grand Turk
USA	Washington, D.C.
Virgin Islands:	
British	Road Town
US	Charlotte Amalie

South America

For a map of South America, see page 423.

Country	Capital
Argentina	Buenos Aires
Bolivia	La Paz
Brazil	Brasilia
Chile	Santiago
Colombia	Bogotá
Ecuador	Quito
French Guiana	Cayenne
Guyana	Georgetown
Paraguay	Asuncion
Peru	Lima
Suriname	Paramaribo
Uruguay	Montevideo
Venezuela	Caracas

ARCTIC

Arctic Ocean

EUROPE

NORTH AMERICA

Mediterra

Atlantic Ocean

AFRIC

Caribbean Sea

Pacific Ocean

SOUTH AMERICA

Southern Ocean

ANTARCTIC